3302454204

C000185286

Bombers Over Sand and Snow

Bombers Over Sand and Snow

205 Group RAF in World War II

Alun Granfield

Pen & Sword
AVIATION

First published in Great Britain in 2011 by
Pen and Sword Aviation
An imprint of
Pen and Sword Books Ltd
47 Church Street
Barnsley
South Yorkshire
S70 2AS

ISBN 978 1 84884 528 2

Printed and bound by CPI UK

Pen and Sword Books Ltd incorporates the imprints of Pen and Sword
Aviation, Pen and Sword Maritime, Pen and Sword Military, Wharncliffe
Local History, Pen and Sword Select, Pen and Sword Military Classics and
Leo Cooper.

For a complete list of Pen and Sword titles please contact
PEN AND SWORD BOOKS LIMITED
47 Church Street, Barnsley, South Yorkshire, S70 2AS, England
E-mail: enquiries@pen-and-sword.co.uk
Website: www.pen-and-sword.co.uk

Contents

Acknowledgements

Winston Brent of Freeworld Publications for permission to quote from *The Men Who Went to Warsaw* by Lawrence Isemonger. Anette Fuhrmeister, Rights Manager of the The History Press for permission to quote from *Beam Bombers* by Michael Cumming. Christopher Tordoff of Crécy Publishers for permission to quote from *Wellington Wings, an RAF Intelligence Officer in the Western Desert* by F.R. Chappell. John Davies of Grub Street Publishers for permission to quote from *Lie in the Dark and Listen* by Ken Rees, and *Malta: The Hurricane Years and Malta: The Spitfire Year* by Christopher Shores, Brian Cull and Nicola Malizia. David Westwood of MLRS Books for permission to quote from the various Air Historical Branch narratives used in the book (printed under MoD licence by MLRS Books; Crown Copyright Reserved). Judy Noakes of the National Archives for help with the copyright issues and licensing of extracts and photographs from: *RAF Middle East, the official story of air operations, Feb. 1942 – Jan. 1943; History of the Second World War, The Mediterranean and Middle East*, I.S.O. Playfair, C.J.C. Molony, F.C. Flynn; and *Royal Air Force 1939–1945*, Dennis Richards and Hilary St George Saunders. Tim Padfield of the National Archives for his advice on the use of quotations from Crown copyright operational record books. Simon Parry of Air Research Publications for permission to quote from *It's Dicey Flying Wimpys Around Italian Skies* by Maurice G. Lihou. Yvonne Oliver of the Imperial War Museum for her help and advice in obtaining the necessary licences for the use of their photographs. Peter Jackson and Barbara Walker for permission to use photographs from their collections. David Clark's family for allowing me access to his log book and photographs. Alun Jones for allowing me to use his material on his uncle Sergeant James Jones.

Special mention also needs to be made of David Gunby, author of *Sweeping the Skies, a History of 40 Squadron Royal Flying Corps and Royal Air Force* and *Bomber Losses in the Middle East and Mediterranean* (with Pelham Temple). David has not only given me permission to quote at length from his work, but has also read and commented on this book.

I have tried to contact everybody whose work has been quoted from in this book, but have not always received a reply to my enquiries. I thank them for their part in my research, and hope that I have done justice to their work.

Alun Granfield

Preface

Among the many justifications for writing military histories are that the story is 'little known' or 'forgotten' and/or that the author, through diligent and original research, has discovered some new and startling facts. It certainly can be argued that the story of the force of 'strategic' night bombers operating in the Mediterranean and the Middle East has been somewhat eclipsed by that of Bomber Command in the UK. This is not surprising, as Bomber Command was always about ten times bigger than No. 205 Group, and played a much more significant and controversial role in the Second World War. However, the night bombers in the Mediterranean and the Middle East operated under much more difficult conditions on the ground, and played an important part in some of the crucial land battles in North Africa and Italy. Although aspects of their story have been told by others, it is believed that this book is the first comprehensive history of the Group. It certainly does not claim to reveal new and startling facts, but simply tells the story of No. 205 Group and its antecedents in the time between June 1940 and May 1945. It is, I hope, a story worth telling.

My interest in the Group came about almost by accident. About ten years ago I started to build a database of Bomber Command operations based on *The Bomber Command War Diaries* by Martin Middlebrook and Chris Everitt and the volumes of Bomber Command losses compiled by W.R. Chorley. This eventually led to many visits to the National Archives at Kew, and to the Operational Record Books of the groups and squadrons. Friends came to know of my interests, and one mentioned that a good friend of his had been an air gunner in Wellingtons in Bomber Command and would I like to see his log book. It eventually arrived, along with a combat report, a newspaper clipping, and a photograph of an aircrew standing in front of a Vickers Wellington bomber.

The log book had belonged to Flight Sergeant David Clark, and it turned out that he had flown, not with Bomber Command, but No. 150 Squadron of No. 205 Group in Italy. David was from Tiers Cross, near Haverfordwest in Pembrokeshire, South West Wales, and the newspaper clipping told of 'shaky dos' flying over snow-covered mountains in Yugoslavia, 'not knowing whether the damaged and battered 'plane could maintain the height necessary to clear them'. The combat report told of a fight with a Ju 88 during a raid on the port of Piombino in Northern Italy on the night of 10/11 April 1944. David fired at the enemy aircraft, and it was last seen with 'small bursts of fire coming from the cockpit and port engine'.

I had already read *Wellington Wings* by F.R. Chappell, so knew something about No. 205 Group, and now my visits to Kew became focussed on the records of the Group and its antecedents. Another database began to grow, and an intention to turn it all into a book one day. Some time later another casual conversation led me to the nephew of someone who had served on Wellingtons in North Africa with No. 148 Squadron. Sergeant James Jones was the navigator in Wellington AD637, which had been shot down over Benghazi on 13/14 November 1942, and the crew are commemorated on the Alamein memorial. The nephew, Alun Jones, had carried out a huge amount of research into his uncle's death, and gave me a massive file containing photographs, letters, and official documents.

This book, then, is dedicated to David Clark and James Jones, and to all the men who flew the bombers by night and day over North Africa and Italy during the Second World War. It is based mainly on the records kept at the National Archives, and a full list of those consulted is contained in the references. Good use was also made of the various official histories of the RAF and the USAAF in the Second World War, of the campaigns in the Mediterranean and the Middle East, and of the Air Historical Branch narratives of the Middle East Campaigns. There are also a few books written about aspects of the bomber operations by those who took part, and by those who have an interest in some of the squadrons belonging to the Group.

The book contains many operational statistics, all compiled from my own databases and based on my own research. As always with these things, it is sometimes difficult to be sure about exactly how many aircraft took off on an operation. The squadron ORBs have two forms covering operations, Forms 540 and 541, and sometimes the two disagree. Where summary statistics are given, either in the squadron ORBs or Group ORB, they sometimes disagree with the data drawn from the individual operations. All the statistics in this book, therefore, are the best that I can arrive at based on my own research.

CHAPTER ONE

Introduction

Beside the main road from Bucharest to Ploieşti, some twenty-five kilometres north of the capital, by Tincăbeşti village, is a small, carefully maintained graveyard. This is the Commonwealth War Graves Commission Cemetery containing the dead of two World Wars. In this peaceful place lie the graves of 83 Commonwealth servicemen who lost their lives in Romania in World War 2. Of these 80 are aircrew of the RAF, RAF(VR), RAAF, RCAF, RNZAF and SAAF who died between May and August 1944.[1]

These young men (most were in their early twenties and two were only eighteen years of age) all flew with No. 205 Group, Royal Air Force, and died on active service in the skies over Romania. Many more equally young men lost their lives while serving with the Group, and their graves are scattered in cemeteries in most of the countries that fringe the Mediterranean shore and beyond. Others have no known grave, and are commemorated on the war memorials at El Alamein and Malta. The Battle Honours, reproduced in Appendix I, state that the Group provided the only mobile force of heavy night bombers in the Mediterranean theatre in the Second World War. It operated mainly from bases in Egypt, Libya, Tunisia and Italy, with occasional excursions to Malta, Greece and Iraq, attacking tactical and strategic targets according to the demands of the wider war in the theatre.

The force was relatively small compared with the numbers of aircraft available to Bomber Command in the European theatre, and it carried on using the venerable Vickers Wellington long after this aircraft had been relegated to the training role in the United Kingdom. Like their UK-based counterparts the night bombers were intended to operate in a strategic role, bombing targets away from the immediate battlefront. However, as we shall see, the demands of the war in the Middle East and Mediterranean soon diverted the bombers from their strategic role and saw them operating much closer to the front line in support of the hard-pressed ground forces.

When Italy declared war on 10 June 1940 there was only a single squadron in Egypt capable of operating in the night-bomber role. This was No. 216 (Bomber Transport) Squadron flying the obsolescent (if not obsolete) Bristol Bombay. The first Wellingtons arrived in the Middle East in September 1940, and by the end of the year there were three Wellington squadrons based in Egypt and one at Malta. At first the bombers operated under the direct control of RAF Headquarters Middle East and RAF Headquarters Malta. Soon, however, the bombers in Egypt were organized into a wing (No. 257 Wing), and later into a group (No. 205 Group). The Group continued to control the operations of most of the British and Commonwealth heavy bomber squadrons in the theatre until the end of the war.

There can be no argument that the activities of No. 205 Group were on a much smaller scale than those of RAF Bomber Command, and its losses, while not insignificant, were also much smaller. For example, in November 1941 Bomber Command had 427 heavy bombers available with crews. In Egypt, as the important *Crusader* offensive got underway in the Western Desert, the seven Wellington squadrons could put up a maximum of about fifty aircraft to attack enemy positions and supply lines. A year later, when General Montgomery launched the Eighth Army into the Battle of El Alamein, the largest operation by No. 205 Group involved only ninety-five sorties by the Wellingtons. In order to reach this number some of the bombers had to return to re-arm and refuel, and go out a second time. In England, Bomber Command had over 400 four-engined heavy bombers, including about 170 Lancasters, available with crews. During 1943 Bomber Command launched 66,649 sorties and lost 3,154 aircraft (a loss rate of 4.7 per cent), while No. 205 Group launched 12,965 sorties and lost 237 aircraft (a loss rate of 1.8 per cent).

While it was much more dangerous flying heavy bombers over German territory, it seems that most aircrew in the Middle East and Mediterranean were glad when their tours were over and they could return to the UK. Despite the hazards, there were some advantages to be gained from operating from home soil. The squadrons of Bomber Command based in Lincolnshire or Yorkshire operated from permanent bases, with hangars to shelter their maintenance crews and tarmac runways from which to launch their aircraft. A pub was never far away, and family and friends just a short journey away. The bomber squadrons in North Africa usually operated from Advanced Landing Grounds (ALGs) scraped out of the bare desert, with only a few tents for shelter. In Italy, they did have more or less permanent bases, but they still lived in tents (if they were lucky), often surrounded by a sea of mud. There were no pubs, often no beer, and the only contact with their families were the eagerly awaited letters from home. Also, the squadrons in England did not have Rommel continually knocking on their door. Thus, the operations of the night bombers in the Middle East and Mediterranean were often governed by the general progress of the war in the theatre. The ebb and flow of the land battles not only determined the activities of the night bombers, but also determined their location. This book tells their story.

*   *   *

The Middle East Command of the RAF had existed almost as long as the military use of aircraft. Headquarters, RFC Middle East was set up in Cairo in 1915 to control the air war over the Mediterranean and Red Seas and the countries on their shores. When the new independent RAF came into being on 1 April 1918 it had to battle hard to retain its independence, and developments in the Middle East were to provide it with a new *raison d'être*. A financially strapped Britain had been left with several new and expensive colonial obligations in the form of League of Nations mandates to govern Palestine, Transjordan and Iraq. A few aircraft had been effective in putting down a minor rebellion in British Somaliland in 1919–20, and this gave rise to the idea of *Air Control*. The Chief of the Air Staff, Sir Hugh Trenchard, proposed that the RAF be given full responsibility for conducting military operations in Britain's most troublesome new mandate – the former Ottoman province of Mesopotamia. He promised that the RAF could police the mandate with a few squadrons of aircraft and some armoured cars, supported by a few British and locally recruited troops, at a fraction of the cost of a large army garrison.

The argument proved irresistible in Whitehall, so in October 1922 Air Marshal John Salmond took command and assumed military responsibility for Iraq. The Air Control doctrine worked remarkably well, and throughout the 1920s and 1930s the RAF was able to quell minor rebellions and deal with tribal banditry by swiftly punishing the culprits from the air. Policing by means of air power became popular in other colonies as well. Bombing raids largely replaced the army's traditional punitive expeditions against troublesome tribes on India's Northwest Frontier, and the British also used air power on numerous occasions in Aden to deal with trouble in the interior. Thus there was always a relatively strong air force presence in the Middle East, although the aircraft were often obsolete by European standards.

When the Second World War started the defence of the Middle East became crucial to Britain's prosecution of the war. The security of the Suez Canal was the first concern, and the region from Egypt to the head of the Persian Gulf had gained in importance with the growth of aviation. It had become an essential link in the air route to India and beyond. The Anglo-Iranian oilfield at the eastern end of this area was still the principal source of British-owned oil, and the pipelines from the new Kirkuk field in northern Iraq crossed the area to emerge at the Mediterranean ports of Haifa in Palestine and Tripoli in Syria. As long as the French were in the war on Britain's side then the defence of the Western Mediterranean was assured. When France was defeated in June 1940, only the Royal Navy was left to defend the sea. A small army protected the land border with the Italian colony of Libya, and the RAF was there to command the sky.

However, at the outbreak of war in September 1939 there were only five permanent RAF Stations in Egypt, at Aboukir, Ismailia, Abu Suier, Heliopolis and Helwan. There were also various landing grounds in the Western Desert as far west as Mersa Matruh and south to Luxor and Wadi Halfa. Mersa Matruh was a good civil airfield, with some permanent technical accommodation. Outside Egypt there were three airfields in Palestine, two in Iraq, two in Malta, one in the Sudan, two at Aden and one in Kenya, none of which could accommodate more than one squadron. With the exception of one airfield in Egypt and another in Palestine that had proper runways, all were unsuitable for the operation of modern bombers and fighters. When war broke out work was started immediately on six new stations near the Suez Canal, each designed to take two heavy bomber squadrons. In Palestine the construction of a new two-bomber station at Aqir (near Lydda) had begun in July 1939. However, temporary landing grounds could be made almost anywhere in the desert, and little work was necessary apart from the clearance of scrub. In most places the natural ground also provided a satisfactory foundation for permanent runways. The comparatively quick process of laying mix-in-place bitumen runways created airfields that stood up satisfactorily to intense operations throughout the whole campaign.

As the official history points out, the fighting in the Mediterranean and Middle East went on for five years. For nearly two years this was the only theatre with a land front on which Allied and German troops were in contact. It goes on to say:

> So it was mainly here that the techniques of land warfare were kept constantly up-to-date, the intimate tactical co-operation of land and air forces evolved and perfected, and the conduct of large and intricate landing

11

operations put to the practical test. Thus the Mediterranean and Middle East was the workshop in which the weapon of invasion was forged and the trial ground on which it was proved; it was here that the highest commanders learned their business of handling it. [2]

This was particularly true of the RAF. On 13 May 1940 Air Chief Marshal Sir Arthur Longmore relieved Sir William Mitchell as Air Officer Commanding-in-Chief, Middle East. He was put in command of all British air forces in Egypt, the Sudan, Palestine and Transjordan. Aden, Iraq and Malta dealt directly with the Air Ministry concerning administration, but Longmore had authority to draw on or interchange their resources as necessary. In 1940 the 'resources' available to Longmore were scanty even by Britain's standards of military preparation at the time. He had twenty-nine squadrons with around three hundred first-line aircraft. Almost half of these were based in Egypt, mainly of the more up-to-date types, while older aircraft were relegated to subordinate theatres. Few of the machines were really modern, and the nine of the fourteen bomber squadrons that were armed with Blenheims mostly had to make do with the older Mk Is. The rest of Longmore's bombers were an odd assortment, including biplane Valentias, obsolete Wellesleys and the obsolescent Bombays. There were even some Ju 86s of the South African Air Force. The first genuinely long-range 'heavy' bomber, the Vickers Wellington, arrived with No. 70 Squadron in the late summer of 1940.[3]

What partly saved the day in the battle for the Mediterranean was the quality of the air commanders on the ground. Longmore and Air Commodore Raymond Collishaw, the Commander of No. 202 Group, worked wonders with their meagre resources in the early days. Then the greatest airman of the Second World War arrived in the Middle East in 1940 in the form of Air Marshal (Acting) Arthur Tedder. He had as his tactical air commander another great leader in Air Vice Marshal (Acting) Arthur Coningham. Between them, they revolutionized the use of British air forces in Army cooperation, and created the doctrine by which the tactical air forces later operated in Europe.

However, in order to be able to fight the air war in the Middle East the aircraft would need airfields within range of the key 'strategic' targets in Libya and beyond. As Philip Guedalla, in his excellent contemporary account of air power in the Middle East, puts it:

> ...aerodromes are the first requisite of any exercise of air power. There is nothing so immobile as a grounded aircraft. Until it can refuel, it is militarily non-existent; and unless this takes place within range of its objective, it is as harmless as a gnat...This seemed to point to something in the nature of a new direction for military operations, since the possession of aerodromes was now recognisable as a fact of primary importance...It was evidently time for some revision of the doctrine that the enemy's armed forces constitute the main, if not the sole, objective of all military operations...Napoleon, the high-priest of modern warfare, had admitted that 'war is an affair of positions'; and now positions, in the form of aerodromes, were evidently of supreme importance...and...land operations might resolve themselves into a war for aerodromes.[4]

Never was this fact more true than in the deserts of North Africa. It was around 300 miles from Alexandria to Tobruk, 540 miles to Benghazi, and 850 miles to Tripoli.

The RAF would need landing grounds near the frontier between Egypt and Libya. The hard, flat surfaces in this area made the actual construction of landing grounds an easy matter, but to be of any use they would have to be stocked with fuel and other essential requirements. These ALGs would also be in range of enemy aircraft and vulnerable to advances by enemy land forces. Everything would have been all right if the front lines in the desert war had been relatively static. As we know, however, the battlefront moved forwards and backwards many times, and the aircraft had to move in harmony with the land battle. It was not until the bombers were established at Foggia in Italy in January 1944 that they could settle down to a proper strategic bombing offensive.

*   *   *

As we have said, the operating conditions for the RAF personnel in the Western Desert were very different from those experienced by their compatriots in England. Although the bomber squadrons did have permanent bases around Cairo, these were usually too far away from their targets, and they had to operate from the ALGs in the desert. Here they lived nomadically, on airfields without tarmac runways, hangars or buildings. The landing ground was nothing more than a large space of desert, scraped smooth and hard, and large square marquees called EPIP (European Personnel Indian Pattern) housed the messes and operations control rooms. Around them were rows of ridge tents as sleeping quarters for officers and men, and the rest of the show was on wheels. The office of the commanding officer was a caravan trailer, signals operated from special vehicles with portable aerial masts, workshops were built into lorries, and the cookhouse was often a trailer with a field kitchen dumped alongside. In an emergency, and there were many in the Western Desert, the whole camp could be bundled into trucks and be on the road within an hour or so.

In summer it was extremely hot by day, with millions of flies, but in the evening and early morning it was perfect. By night it was a paradise, silent and splendid underneath a dome of stars and an almost day-bright moon. Unfortunately, the latter often gave enemy aircraft clear targets to aim at, but it also helped the Wellingtons to aim their bombs accurately at Benghazi and Tripoli. In winter the days were usually bright, but the nights were bitterly cold. Sometimes torrential rains turned landing grounds into sticky swamps, bogging down aircraft and vehicles. However, the chief torment of the desert was the fine, gritty sand that got into everything – eyes and ears, food and drink, engines and weapons. When the dust was whipped up by a storm, especially the *Khamsin* of the spring, a hot wind from the south with the strength to rip down a tent, it was hell on earth. The dust storms had the density of a London fog in which every particle was grit, turning day into half-night, and reducing visibility to a few feet.

The desert was no place for a formal uniform. In summer the men wore khaki shorts, a light cotton shirt and an RAF cap. In winter it was battledress augmented by every sweater and jersey the wearers could lay their hands on. The Irving flying jacket was worn in the air *and* on the ground in winter. Nevertheless, the desert was a healthy place, except for desert sores – small cuts that became infected when sand filtered into them. There was almost no sickness, and life was simple and sleep usually plentiful. There was nearly always enough water for a cup of chlorinated tea, and the food was adequate – just! The bomber crews in the Middle East and

13

Mediterranean also flew in a much more healthy environment, in that they rarely met the co-ordinated flak and night fighter defences that became commonplace over the skies of Germany.

Things did not improve much when the squadrons got to Italy. The official history of the RAF in the Second World War describes the area surrounding Foggia as 'a bleak plain', in the middle of which was 'the dusty town of Foggia, of which the general appearance had not been improved by the frequent air attacks made upon it'. Much of the country around Foggia was flat and fen-like, with mountains in the distance to the left (the Apennines) and to the right (Monte Gargano). The main problem was the rain, which came down by the bucketful and turned the airfields and camps into quagmires. In the winter the snow fell and the mud froze, and in the summer the mud turned to a fine dust that got into everything.

Another problem for the RAF in the Middle East and Mediterranean was aircraft maintenance and serviceability. Spares were always in short supply and there was very little local industry capable of making up the shortages. Ground crews often had to work minor miracles to keep the aircraft in the air. Many arguments would ensue between Longmore and Tedder in Egypt and Churchill in the UK about the quantity of aircraft available for operations in the Middle East. Churchill seemed to regard all aircraft dispatched to the Middle East as capable of immediate action against the enemy. In reality, of course, they often needed extensive modification, and many were unserviceable through lack of spares. Thus, although it can be argued that more Wellingtons should have been sent to the Middle East in 1940 and 1941, it must be borne in mind that the constraints imposed by a lack of airfields and problems of serviceability would have to have been tackled first. Spares were not so much of a problem in Italy, but most maintenance had to be done in the open, in the wind and rain.

*   *   *

The island of Malta will play a not insignificant role in the first half of this book, and it is worth commenting on the vital part that it was to play in Mediterranean strategy. The night bombers were to operate frequently from the airfield at Luqa on Malta, and always did so under the most difficult conditions. The importance of Malta was due mainly to its geographical position, for its excellent harbour lay more or less midway between Gibraltar and Port Said – the western and eastern entrances to the Mediterranean. It was the headquarters of the Mediterranean Fleet in peace, and its dock and repair facilities, reserves and resources had been built up at great cost over many years. Its airfields acted as a stepping stone on the air route and as a centre for air reconnaissance over the central Mediterranean.

Unfortunately, Malta was very vulnerable to attack by the Italian Metropolitan Air Force, and its air defence was extremely difficult. The island is less than half the size of the Isle of Man, and all its most important objectives were crowded together in the area around the harbour. They were easy targets for strong air forces working from well-established bases only half an hour's flight away. Its radar facilities only gave limited cover, and the defending fighters would be severely handicapped. The few airfields on the island would not permit the use of more than a handful of squadrons, and it would be difficult to add more in the limited space available. The number of anti-aircraft guns and searchlights was small in 1939, and had not grown very much by the time that Italy went to war.

The only air establishments on Malta before the war were the seaplane base at Kalafrana, some engineering workshops, and two small grassed airfields. One of the airfields was used mainly by the Fleet Air Arm, and the other by Italian civil air lines. Work on a third airfield was begun in October 1939, and completed with four runways by May 1940. When aircraft began to operate from Malta in June 1940, the workshop facilities were poor, and had to cope with a bewildering array of different types. These included various flying boats, Swordfish, Walrus, Magisters, Queen Bees, Gladiators, Hurricanes, Hudsons, Glenn Martins, Wellingtons, Blenheims and Fulmars. However, in spite of all the difficulties, they were able to keep aircraft flying by means of improvisation, and by manufacturing spare parts from whatever materials could be obtained locally.

*   *   *

Given the prevailing doctrine in the RAF at the time it was inevitable that the bombing of strategic targets would become a feature of RAF operations in the Middle East as soon as war came to the area, and given the early experiences of Bomber Command it was also inevitable that these operations would have to be carried out by night. The use of bombers in a strategic role had become a feature of air operations in the First World War, and it was to this aspect of air power that some military thinkers directed their energies after the war came to an end. The Italian General Giulio Douhet envisaged a war that would still be nasty and brutish (in some ways even more nasty and brutish than the First World War), but it would at least be short. Douhet also believed that the mere possession of large air forces could act as a deterrent to war. The power of the bomber to wreak havoc on the civilian population would create such a pressure to avoid war in democratic nations that their leaders would never again be allowed to use warfare as a means of solving diplomatic problems. Such a theory of warfare was appealing to those who wished to restrict expenditure on the military in the depressed economic conditions that pertained in the 1920s and 1930s.

The limited experience of strategic bombing in the First World War given by the Zeppelin and Gotha raids on Britain and by the Allied air forces late in the war provided conflicting evidence about its efficacy. Nevertheless, the desire to avoid another war at almost any cost and a desire to avoid the stalemate of the trenches should another war occur, provided support for the theorists of air power such as Douhet, General 'Billy' Mitchell in the USA, and Trenchard in the UK. That civilians would suffer and die in such a campaign was well recognized by Trenchard, when he circulated a memorandum in May 1928 that clearly stated that 'in future wars air attacks would be ... carried out against most vital centres of communication, and munition centres, *no matter where they were situated*' (my italics). The original intention of Trenchard and the RAF was that the strategic bombing offensive would be carried out mainly by day, with formations of aircraft battling their way through enemy skies to drop their loads on his factories, ports, and railways. Night bombers would also be used to conduct a 'round-the-clock' offensive, but it was recognized that night bombing would be less accurate and therefore less effective.

However, the ability of formations of day bombers to defend themselves was put into question on 14 December 1939 when forty-two aircraft, the biggest operation of the war to date, were dispatched on an anti-shipping operation. Twelve Wellingtons found a convoy in the Schillig Roads, north of Wilhelmshaven,

15

but were engaged by flak and fighters and five out of the twelve were shot down. An even greater disaster overtook a force of twenty-four Wellingtons dispatched to attack shipping off Wilhelmshaven on 18 December. The aircraft reached the target area in perfect weather conditions, but were detected seventy miles out to sea by an experimental *Freya* radar station on the island of Wangerooge. A ground controller directed a large force of German fighters onto the bombers and twelve were shot down. The force included six Wellingtons of No. 37 Squadron (which was to serve with distinction in the Middle East and the Mediterranean between December 1940 and May 1945) and only one returned to its base at Feltwell. Bomber Command was forced to re-think its strategy, and, in future, the strategic bombers would mainly be forced to attack by night.

There were few 'strategic' targets in the Western Desert, Cyrenaica and Tripolitania, with no industrial targets to attack and little in the way of a communications infrastructure. It was not until the bombers got to Italy at the very end of 1943 that they could begin to play their part in the strategic bombing offensive. Also, the RAF in the Middle East did not have the luxury of operating behind the secure barrier of the English Channel. It was always acutely aware that the enemy was breathing down its neck. Its landing grounds were often in the front line (and occasionally even *behind* the lines), and the airmen, the soldiers and the sailors could clearly see that they were all in it together, fighting a common enemy. Inevitably, support for the Army and the Royal Navy had first call on the meagre resources available to Longmore and Tedder, and strategic bombing a low priority. As we shall see, the demands of the war in the Middle East and Mediterranean soon diverted the bombers from their 'strategic' role and saw them operating much closer to the front line. Nevertheless, the majority of the enemy's supplies came by sea, and there were ports to be bombed. There were also enemy airfields that could benefit from the attentions of night bombers, and supply dumps and camps to be attacked. And so, for practical rather than doctrinal reasons, a force of long-range 'heavy' bombers[5] was employed by the RAF in the Middle East and Mediterranean theatre during the Second World War. That force was No. 205 Group.

NOTES

1. From *Through Darkness to Light*, by Patrick Macdonald, page 9. This is an excellent account of the operations by No. 205 Group over Romania.
2. From the British official histories of the Second World War, *The Mediterranean and Middle East*, by Major General ISO Playfair, Volume I, page xxv. The seven volumes of this work have been used extensively in the preparation of this book, and in future will be referred to as TMAME.
3. The very first Wellingtons in the Middle East had arrived with No. 1 GR Unit at Ismailia at the end of May 1940. These were DWI (mine-sweeping) Wellingtons, and on the eve of the outbreak of war three of the aircraft carried out a sweep of the harbour at Alexandria and the Great Pass. Ken Delve's book *Vickers Armstrongs Wellington* provides good coverage of all the Wellington types.
4. Philip Guedalla, *Middle East 1940–1942: A Study in Air Power*, 1944, pp. 63–4.
5. The force mainly operated with the Vickers Wellington, which was designated as a heavy bomber in 1940, but would be re-classified as a medium bomber as the war progressed. No. 216 Squadron used the Bristol Bombay between June 1940 and January 1941, and this aircraft could not really be described as a bomber at all.

CHAPTER TWO

The Early Operations Against the Italians – June 1940 to March 1941

At 1645 hours on Monday 10 June 1940 the Italian Minister for Foreign Affairs informed the British Ambassador in Rome that at one minute past midnight the King of Italy would consider himself to be at war with the United Kingdom and France. Air Commodore Raymond Collishaw, Commanding Officer of No. 202 Group, was waiting in his underground operations room near Maaten Bagush, some 185 miles west of Cairo. Nine minutes after midnight he received the message from Air Chief Marshal Arthur Longmore that Italy had declared war. At dawn on Tuesday 11 June, six Blenheims took off on an armed reconnaissance of targets in Libya, and were followed two hours after first light by eight Blenheims that attacked El Adem, the main Italian air base in Cyrenaica. The bombers found the enemy completely unprepared for the commencement of hostilities, and no opposition was encountered from their fighters. However, the ground defences soon came into action, and one of the Blenheims was hit and crashed in flames into the sea off Tobruk. Another crash-landed at Sidi Barrani and burst into flames, and a third force-landed but was repairable.

No. 202 Group only had four bomber squadrons, three equipped solely with Blenheim Mk Is and the fourth with a mixture of Mk Is and a few Mk IVs. These would have to carry the main weight of the bombing offensive in the first stages of the war in the Middle East, and Collishaw could not afford the kind of losses experienced on this first attack. Nevertheless, the Blenheims kept up the pressure, and one attack on Tobruk on the night of 12/13 June hit the elderly cruiser *San Giorgio*, which caught fire and was beached on a sandbank. It remained half-submerged in the harbour as a stationary flak ship, and would prove a nuisance for the night bombers for many months to come.

At this time there was only one night-bomber unit in the Middle East, No. 216 (Bomber Transport) Squadron, based at Heliopolis on the eastern outskirts of Cairo. It was equipped with Vickers-Armstrong Valentias and Bristol Bombays, and was more used to ferrying troops and supplies around the Middle East. The biplane Valentia was a development of the Vickers Victoria, re-engined with the more powerful Bristol Pegasus engine. It flew for the first time in 1934, and although obsolete by 1940, it was still capable of doing good service in the transport/troop carrying role. The Valentia could be fitted with underwing racks for 2,200 lb of bombs, and did conduct a few bombing operations in November and December 1940. The Bombay was a high wing twin-engined monoplane with a fixed undercarriage, and was a sturdy and competent aircraft. Its normal bomb load was eight 250-lb bombs, carried on external under-fuselage racks. It could also carry smaller (usually 20-lb) bombs and incendiaries in the cabin, to be dropped by hand through the side door, and was armed with two hydraulically operated single-gun turrets in the nose and tail. The first Bombays were delivered to the RAF in April 1939, but the aircraft was hardly capable of carrying out a proper bombing role at the outbreak of the war in the Middle East.

When the Italians declared war the Bombays were immediately dispersed around the airfield at Heliopolis and hurriedly given black undersides ('paint, dope, and all things black were used'¹), and all personnel were confined to camp. On the evening of 11 June 1940 ten aircraft, each fully loaded with eight 250-lb bombs, flew from Heliopolis to an ALG at El Daba to await instructions for a raid on Tobruk. This was just about a 'maximum effort' for No. 216 Squadron, as it only had fifteen aircraft serviceable at the time. It was necessary to move the aircraft forward to the ALG because it was approximately 400 miles from Heliopolis to Tobruk, and this was well outside the range of a Bombay with a full fuel and bomb load. In the event the raid was cancelled at the last minute due to worries about bombing non-military targets. Nine of the Bombays returned to Heliopolis on the following day, leaving behind one that had been badly damaged when a Blenheim of No. 211 Squadron taxied into it.

Tobruk was a name that would become famous as the campaigns in the desert proceeded, and was strategically important for several reasons. It had a deep, natural and well protected harbour, and had been heavily fortified by the Italians. There were a number of escarpments and cliffs to the south, providing substantial physical barriers to any advance on the port from that direction, and it was also on a peninsula, allowing it to be defended by a minimal number of troops. Numerous heavy anti-aircraft batteries were situated on the peninsula and on the cliffs to the south. At the outbreak of war reconnaissance had shown the harbour to be full of ships, and large naval oil reserves were stored along the waterfront and in underground tanks east of the town. Various military and air force headquarters and barracks were known to be located in the town, and there were many aircraft based on the landing grounds nearby. Most of the supplies for the Italian forward positions on the Libya/Egypt border came through Tobruk, and it was the obvious target for the night bombers.

The first operation by No. 216 Squadron eventually took place on the night of 14/15 June. A single Bombay took off from Heliopolis at 1435 hours on Friday 14 June and landed at Mersa Matruh at 1640 hours. It then took off for Tobruk at 2025 hours to bomb 'petrol dumps and port', but found the target obscured by haze. The aircraft dropped eight 250-lb bombs from 10,000 feet, but no results could be seen. It landed again at Mersa Matruh at 0140 hours on 15 June, and later returned to Heliopolis. The enemy was evidently surprised by the night attack, and there was no flak or fighter opposition. However, when the attack was repeated on the following night the enemy was prepared, and heavy and accurate flak was encountered. The Squadron went back to Tobruk twelve times by the end of August 1940, flying twenty-seven sorties and dropping in the region of twenty-four tons of bombs on the port. Other targets attacked at this time included the major airfields at El Gubbi and El Adem, the port facilities at Derna and Bardia, and the flying-boat base at Bomba.

The attacks on Tobruk tended to follow a similar pattern. The Bombays would spend a long time in the target area, making a number of bombing runs and

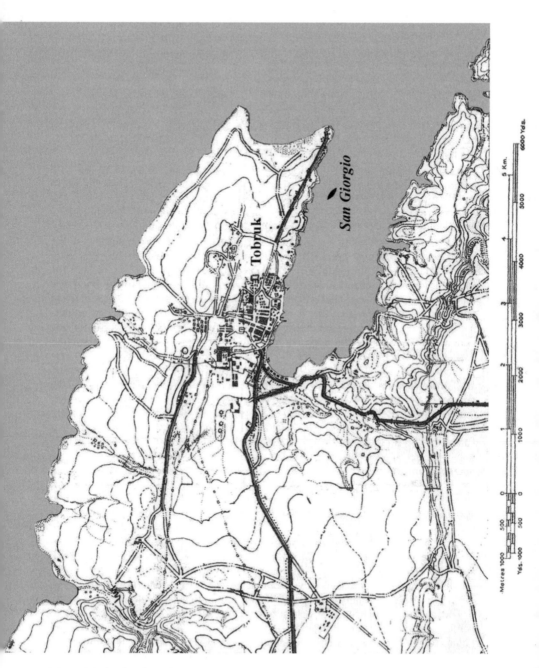

Map of Tobruk taken from an Italian map dated 1936 and used by Advance HQ Western Desert Force during its attack in January 1941.

dropping a few bombs or incendiaries at a time. Sometimes the Bombays tried to surprise the defences by approaching high over the sea, cutting their engines, and gliding silently over the target. Heavy flak and 'flaming onions' (light AA fire with incendiary ammunition) were often encountered over the target area, but this was mostly inaccurate, and few of the slow-moving aircraft were hit. Night fighters were almost non existent at this time. The Squadron suffered its first loss on the night of 20/21 June, when Bombay L5850 failed to return from an attack on the airfield at El Gubbi. It was last seen over the target, and four of the crew are buried in the Knightsbridge War Cemetery at Acroma and one was taken prisoner by the Italians.

For most of July the Tobruk area remained the focal point for the bombers, with shipping in the harbour and the wharves, stores and oil tanks along the north foreshore the main targets. The Bombays generally operated via Fuka, where the squadron kept a small party of about ten men to refuel the bombers and control the night flying. On 13/14 July six Bombays carried out the biggest single raid to date, with the first aircraft taking off from Fuka at 1920 hours and the remainder leaving at intervals up to 2120 hours. All of the attackers met with much searchlight activity over the target, and the usual heavy but inaccurate flak. In order to mislead the enemy gunners the ground controllers sent fake radio messages to the Bombays, telling them to make low-level attacks, and the ruse seems to have had the desired effect as some pilots saw the barrage bursting well below them. Other fake messages gave the impression that fighter escorts were operating, and the Italians joined in by sending false instructions to the Bombays to bomb in a particular manner and at a prescribed height.

On the next night another six Bombays attacked the naval oil tanks at Tobruk, and all crews reported that their bombs burst in the target area. Unfortunately, the aircraft encountered low cloud and heavy ground mist over the Western Desert, and two failed to return. One ran out of fuel and force-landed in fog on the south-west corner of Lake Mariut (a landlocked sea south of Alexandria). The aircraft was shot at by Egyptian forces after landing and the crew were all taken prisoner, but they were quickly released once it was realized that they were RAF personnel. The other aircraft flew into the escarpment forty kilometres south of Mersa Matruh, and was completely burned out. Three of the crew died in the crash, and the two survivors were badly burned. It was obvious that some sort of RDF navigation system was needed for the desert landing grounds to help the aircraft find their way home. The headlights of motor vehicles were used as guiding beacons, but these were visible to the enemy and often bombed. As a result of the two losses Headquarters Middle East confined further night attacks to sections of three aircraft on 15/16 and 16/17 July, but one of the Bombays in the first raid was shot down by a night fighter. The body of one of the crew was washed up near Sollum on 18 July and the remainder are commemorated on the Alamein Memorial.

During August the focus of operations for No. 216 Squadron moved briefly to Somaliland and Ethiopia, mainly in its transport role. On the third of the month Italian forces had invaded British Somaliland, and on 10 August a Bombay left Helwan for Aden carrying Major-General A.R. Godwin-Austen, who was to take command of British forces in the area. Unfortunately, he was a bit too late. On 11 August the Italians launched an attack on the Tug Argan pass, the key approach to Berbera, and the outnumbered British and South African troops were forced to yield the pass after a four-day battle. The Italians occupied Berbera on 19 August, and on the following day all British troops began to withdraw from British Somaliland.

While this was going on No. 216 Squadron made a small contribution to the battle on the night of 14/15 August when a Bombay involved in passenger duties to Aden also carried out a raid on Italian installations at Diredawa (Ethiopia). It was unable to reach its objective due to an electrical storm, but the aircraft bombed Zeila (British Somaliland) as an alternative on its way back to Aden. The aircraft in question had, in fact, left Heliopolis at 1245 hours on 12 August, and flown via Summit to Aden. After the attack, and after some passenger-carrying activities ferrying personnel of No. 223 Squadron between Aden and Summit, it eventually returned to Heliopolis at 1340 hours on 25 August. All in a fortnight's work for an aircraft of No. 216 Squadron! Otherwise, the Squadron was involved in a few attacks on Tobruk, with just four sorties carried out during the moonlight period as a retaliatory measure each time the Italians bombed Alexandria.

*   *   *

It was obvious that the few and ageing Bombays of No. 216 Squadron could not sustain a proper night-bombing campaign in the Middle East. More and better aircraft were needed, and in September 1940 plans were made to replace the Valentias of No. 70 Squadron with Vickers-Armstrong Wellingtons. The Wellington IC was an excellent aircraft. Powered by two Bristol Pegasus XVIII engines, it had a maximum speed of 235 mph, a ceiling of 18,000 feet, and a range of 1,200 miles, with a maximum bomb load of 4,500 lb. The aircraft carried two 0.303-inch machine guns in each of its nose and tail turrets, and a further two machine guns in beam positions.

When Italy declared war No. 70 Squadron was based at Helwan, but quickly moved to Heliopolis alongside No. 216 Squadron. It carried on operating in its transport role until the Wellingtons arrived, and the first reached the Middle East at 1330 hours on 1 September, via Malta. Their journey had begun on 30 August 1940, when six Wellingtons ICs supplied by No. 3 Group Bomber Command flew to Malta on the first stage of their move to the Middle East. The flight of six Wellingtons had assembled at Stradishall, but as the aircraft were heavily loaded (including overload petrol tanks) the longer runway at Newmarket was used for the take-off. Five of the crews had been sent to the UK from Egypt for conversion to the new machines and the sixth was provided by No. 3 Group and was led by Squadron Leader R.J. Wells. Despite encountering searchlights and slight flak over Northern France, all landed safely at Malta on the next morning, with time in the air varying between nine hours ten minutes and ten hours twenty-five minutes. The six aircraft then left for Heliopolis early the next morning, but one turned back with engine trouble shortly after take-off. This was repaired, and it later resumed the flight.

No. 70 Squadron moved to Kabrit on 9 September, and continued to receive Wellingtons throughout September and into October. Three more left Stradishall on 22 September but one crashed on landing at Malta, and another three left on the 26th of the month and arrived at Kabrit on 30 September. Bad weather had been experienced during the first stages of the flight from the UK, and one of the aircraft had been forced to jettison most of its heavy freight in order to eke out its petrol to reach Malta. Another was delayed at Malta due to ignition trouble, but all eventually reached Kabrit. Finally, another five left Stradishall on 26 October, and all arrived safely at Malta and eventually went on to Kabrit. By this time the Squadron had become operational, carrying out its first mission on the night of 18/19 September when five aircraft attacked targets in the Dodecanese Islands. Two of the Wellingtons bombed hangars, barracks and slipways in Porto-Lago Bay on Leros, another two attacked hangars and buildings on the airfield at Maritza on Rhodes, and the fifth Wellington attacked dispersed aircraft and petrol stores at Calato on Rhodes. Flak of all types was encountered, but it was reported to be erratic and all the aircraft returned safely.

*   *   *

The Wellingtons had arrived just in time, as the Italians were on the move at last. On 13 September five divisions crossed into Egypt from Libya in the first major offensive of the war in North Africa. It all began with a spectacular artillery barrage on an unoccupied camp at Musaid and on the deserted airfield and barracks at Sollum. When the dust cleared the enemy lorries and light tanks were revealed drawn up in long columns as if on parade, awaiting the order to advance. British troops did not seriously contest the frontier, contenting themselves with harassing operations, and withdrew to their first major defence positions around Mersa Matruh, 120 miles to the east. However, the Italians only advanced fifty miles to Sidi Barrani, and then halted and established a series of fortified camps. During this time the Bombays of No. 216 Squadron only flew a few operations over the Western Desert, using Fuka Satellite as an Advanced Landing Ground. Nine aircraft attacked the airfield at Benina on 16/17 September, where much damage was caused, confirmed by photographs taken on the following day. On 17/18 September a single Bombay carried out a reconnaissance of the Derna–Tobruk–Bardia area, and on two nights (18/19 and 20/21) six aircraft bombed military encampments and motor transport at Derna, Tobruk, Bardia, Capuzzo, Sollum and Sidi Barrani for continuous periods of four hours. Two Bombays also attacked the Italian forward positions around Sidi Barrani on 19/20 September, but no enemy movements were observed.

With the Italians sitting tight in their fortified positions around Sidi Barrani the Bombays and Wellingtons concentrated most of their efforts on attacking lines of communication. There was evidence that German mechanized forces were moving southwards through Italy, and it became increasing important to direct as much of the bomber effort as possible towards Benghazi. Optimistic views existed in Whitehall about the results that could be obtained by the small bomber force in Egypt, and the Chiefs of Staff signalled Longmore:

> If Benghazi could be made unusable any plans for large scale Axis Advance against Egypt would be seriously delayed, if not entirely dislocated.[2]

Thus, Benghazi became a regular target for the Bombays for the next two months and a Wellington target for the next two years. With the existing resources the scale of attack was limited to a maximum of three Bombays and three Wellingtons each night. From 19 September to the end of November, Benghazi was attacked on fifteen occasions and forty-two sorties despatched. Tobruk was bombed seven times, with fifteen sorties despatched. So it can be seen that the number of aircraft operating on any particular night was small, and many attacks were made by single aircraft and had a nuisance value rather than doing any great damage to the enemy. However, the bombers kept the defences of Benghazi and Tobruk awake at night, and obviously helped to disrupt the already strained supply position for the Italians at Sidi Barrani.

The supply difficulties were exacerbated by the lavish conditions under which the Italian forces existed, or at least those under which their officers existed. An insight into the situation is provided by the war correspondent Alexander Clifford, who accompanied Wavell's forces in the Allied offensive in December. At one of the first Italian camps to be taken (Nibeiwa) he found:

> ...stores of foodstuffs infinitely more varied and succulent than our own: great tins of ham, huge Parmesan cheeses, long blue packets of spaghetti, seven-pound pots of tomato extract, green vegetables and delicious fruits in tins, jams and quince jelly, tongues and tunny fish in olive oil. There were great vats of exceedingly good wines. There were barrels of brandy. Oil and vinegar stood on mess-tent tables in artistic porcelain vases. Crockery and cutlery were of the finest.[3]

Other targets for the Wellingtons were to be found in the Dodecanese Islands. Leros and Rhodes had been attacked on 18/19 September, and further attacks were made on the airfields on Rhodes on 17/18 and 18/19 October. The main object of these raids was to discourage enemy bombers from continuing their increasingly frequent operations against Palestine and Alexandria. However, the attacks did not completely deter the *Regia Aeronautica* from bombing Alexandria and Haifa, which suffered considerable damage on 21 September, and Cyprus was also attacked at this time.

Then on 28 October Italian forces invaded Greece from Albania, and additional targets for the night bombers presented themselves. Six aircraft from No. 70 Squadron flew from Kabrit to Eleusis (near Athens) on 6 November, and from there made a daylight attack on the harbour and airfield at Valona (Albania) on the following day. Clouds obscured the outward journey but cleared over the target, where they were engaged by enemy fighters. One Wellington exploded in mid air, another went down in flames, and two more were severely damaged. The remainder dropped their bombs, claiming hits on aircraft and ships, and one Fiat CR 42 and one Breda 65 were believed to have been shot down. On the return journey two of the Wellingtons fired on a formation of Cant Z 506Bs, and thought that they had brought one of them down.

No. 216 Squadron only carried out one bombing operation during the month of November, being mainly occupied with transport operations. However, it was a particularly interesting one in that it involved a Valentia (K3605), which bombed enemy concentrations at Sidi Barrani on the night of 10/11 November. The aircraft operated via Maaten Bagush, and it seems to have been the first and only time that a Valentia was used on a bombing operation in the Western Desert. The attack was declared to be 'successful as no AA or fighters were encountered' and eighty 20-lb bombs were dropped, but results were not observed. This venerable (and vulnerable) biplane flew at about 100 miles per hour, and would have been an easy target for the Sopwith Camels that No. 70 Squadron flew in the First World War, let alone the CR 42s of the *Regia Aeronautica*. There were no external bomb racks fitted on the Valentia, and so all bombs had to be dropped by hand through the cargo door. This aircraft was destroyed on the ground by enemy fighters at Maaten Bagush on 12 November.

Bombing operations were again carried out on 11/12 and 12/13 November by No. 70 Squadron in support of the Greeks fighting in Albania. Six Wellingtons operated from Tatoi, and four of them attacked the dock area and jetties at Durazzo. Bombs were seen to burst across the jetty in the middle of the harbour, but no results were observed. The other two Wellingtons bombed ammunition dumps and troop concentrations at Valona. One of the Wellingtons that bombed Durazzo had a petrol pipe shot away during the raid, and could not take part in the second attack. On 12/13 November one Wellington successfully attacked an oil refinery at Bari in Italy, and returned safely to base. Another two set off for Durazzo again, but only one reached the target due to bad weather conditions. A petrol fire was started that lasted for over twenty-four hours and was visible for a hundred miles. Finally, two more Wellingtons were despatched to Valona, where one bombed concentrations of motor transport, but visibility was poor and definite results could not be observed. The second aircraft took off late, and returned before reaching the target as it would have been over it in daylight. These small scale and difficult operations can have done little to aid the Greeks, but were the best that the few night bombers could do under the circumstances.

During November there was little sign of any further offensive intent by the Italians, and plans were underway in Egypt for the first British offensive in the Western Desert. On the eighty-eight nights between the Italian invasion of Egypt and the start of the British offensive, the night bombers operated on thirty-eight nights and flew 215 sorties. The Bombays of No. 216 Squadron launched sixty-five sorties, and the squadron also sent out the single Valentia on 10/11 November. The newly arrived Wellingtons in Egypt despatched ninety-eight sorties, eighty-one by No. 70 Squadron and seventeen by Nos 37 and 38 Squadrons (see below). The Wellingtons on Malta (see also below) contributed another fifty-one sorties. Ports received 139 of the sorties (65 per cent of the total effort), with Benghazi and Tobruk attracting most of the attention of the bombers in Egypt, with those on Malta favouring Naples and Bari. Some 23 per cent of the sorties were directed at airfields in Libya and the Dodecanese, and 11 per cent involved attacks on military targets during the Italian invasion.

*   *   *

Reinforcements were desperately needed by the RAF in the Middle East if any offensive against the Italians was to succeed, and this posed many problems for the overstrained Home establishment. Any such reinforcement would inevitably mean a corresponding reduction in the Metropolitan Air Force, and both Fighter and Bomber Commands in the UK were themselves under strength. If additional air units were sent to the Middle East then there would be a fairly long period when they would be out of action and of no use to anyone. The difficult route through Malta could be used for sending aircraft reinforcements to existing units, although the loss of the landing grounds at Sidi Barrani made this route even more difficult. If additional squadrons were to be sent out to the Middle East they would need a full establishment of ground crews and vehicles, and these either had to take the long sea route around the Cape of Good Hope or risk the journey through the Mediterranean.

It was decided to take the risky option and send two squadrons of Wellingtons from the UK while the Royal Navy still had ascendancy in the Mediterranean. On 4 November No. 38 Squadron at Marham was ordered to prepare for departure for overseas, and on the following day No. 37 Squadron at Feltwell also received orders to 'pack up and move overseas to reinforce the Middle East Command'. All personnel were recalled from leave, and instructions given as to the amount of kit to be carried by airmen and flying personnel. Both Nos 37 and No. 38 Squadrons were very experienced, having operated with Bomber Command from the very first days of the war. No. 37 Squadron had carried out 91 operations, flown 661 sorties and lost 16 aircraft, while No. 38 Squadron had carried out 94 operations, flown 654 sorties and lost 9 aircraft.

Six aircraft of No. 37 Squadron left Feltwell on 8 November en route to Malta, but one returned soon after take-off due to trouble with the fabric on the main plane. The other five arrived safely on Malta, although one was attacked in the vicinity of Pantellaria and two members of the crew wounded. The departure of the rest of the air party of No. 37 Squadron was delayed due to adverse weather conditions on the route to Malta, but another seven eventually left the UK on the night of 12/13 November and the last three on 19 November. All arrived safely at Malta. The aircraft of No. 38 Squadron started their move on 22 November, and while on the island one of the aircraft of A Flight was hit by incendiary bullets and destroyed during an attack on Luqa by six CR.42s from the 23° *Gruppo*. The remainder flew on to Ismailia on 24 and 25 November. At this time a detachment of Wellingtons was being built up on the island (the 'Luqa Wellington Detachment' – see below), and some of the aircraft of No. 37 Squadron operated with the detachment while in transit to Egypt. Four attacked Taranto on 13/14 November, along with six others from the island. Two then left Malta on 14 November and two more on the 15th, proceeding to Heliopolis and Kabrit respectively, and five more went on to Kabrit on the afternoon of 20 November.

The sea parties for the two squadrons both began their move from the UK on 12 November. The party from No. 38 Squadron boarded a train at Downham Market railway station, with the Marham Station Band playing them off. On the same day the sea party of No. 37 Squadron left by train from Lakenheath railway station, and at 2000 hours they joined up with No. 38 Squadron at March, Cambridgeshire. The train stopped at Doncaster for thirty minutes for tea and cakes, and reached the George V Dock at Glasgow at 1130 hours on 13 November. Both sea parties embarked on HMT *Franconia*, along with other RAF and Army units, and the ship left Glasgow at 1230 hours on 14 November. It moved down the Clyde and anchored in the Gareloch before joining its convoy at 0630 hours on 15 November. The convoy consisted of three other merchant ships, the cruisers HMS *Manchester* and HMS *Southampton*, the aircraft carrier HMS *Furious*, and fourteen destroyers. A Sunderland patrolled overhead as the convoy passed north of Ireland into the Atlantic, and some of the warships left the convoy to sweep for a German raider. Officers and senior NCOs of both squadrons were detailed as aircraft spotters on the bridge during the voyage, as the convoy moved through the Atlantic in a heavy swell and 'blowing over half a gale'. No. 38 Squadron ORB (Operations Record Book) reported:

...men's quarters not too good and this was the cause of a great deal of sickness on board. However, no complaints about food, which was excellent.

The convoy continued on through rough seas, with a report that an enemy submarine had been sighted nearby on the night of 18/19 November. On the 20th there was a day of fine weather, warm and sunny, and the men played 'deck tennis for the first time'. The African coast was sighted at 1100 hours on the 21st, and the Straits of Gibraltar were passed at 1500 hours. The *Franconia* tied up at Gibraltar at 1800 hours, but no one was allowed ashore for reasons of secrecy. Only two hundred men were allowed on deck at the same time, and no one was allowed on the port side of the ship facing the Spanish Coast. No. 38 Squadron ORB records that the *Franconia* was 'beginning to smell' by 22 November, and on 23 November that the smell was 'getting worse'. An air raid alarm created something of a diversion when one enemy aircraft approached the harbour through cloud cover, but it was fired at by the guns of the warships and those on the Mole and was driven off.

In the very early morning of 25 November the personnel of both squadrons transferred from the *Franconia* to two cruisers for a fast run across the Mediterranean to Alexandria. Those of No. 37 Squadron boarded HMS *Manchester* and those of No. 38 Squadron boarded HMS *Southampton*. The cruisers sailed at 0700 hours, packed to the gunwales with the sea parties from the two squadrons, other RAF personnel, and 'also a few of the khaki gents' – about 900 men in all on each ship. No one was allowed on deck until the cruisers were out of sight of Gibraltar. They joined up with HMS *Renown*, *Ark Royal*, sixteen destroyers, HMS *Sheffield*, and a light cruiser. Little did the airmen realize that they would experience a full-blown sea battle on the way to Egypt!

On the night of 17 November the passage of a convoy to Malta had been disrupted by an Italian naval force and forced to return to Gibraltar. It was eventually sent out again with much more support, and this included HMS *Manchester* and HMS *Southampton* with the airmen on board. The convoy was spotted by the Italians, who set sail towards it, and the British sent their forces north to intercept them before they could come anywhere near the cargo ships. At 1145 hours on 27 November the British were informed that the Italians were only fifty miles away and closing for battle. The two forces were fairly even, although the Italian ships had better range and heavier fire, and met off Cape Spartivento, Sardinia. The ORB of No. 37 Squadron tells the story:

> At noon 'Action Stations' were sounded as enemy ships had been sighted in two forces, one consisted of two battleships, three cruisers and a screen of destroyers, and the other of three cruisers and several destroyers. In an attempt to cut off the latter force from its base the cruisers *Manchester*, *Southampton*, *Sheffield*, *Newcastle* and *Berwick* went into action with HMS *Manchester* leading. They were supported by two capital ships, the *Renown* and *Ramilles*. At 1220 hours the enemy opened fire with a salvo which straddled the *Manchester*. The cruiser replied a minute later at extreme range and continued firing for an hour and a half. The enemy were soon in retreat covered by a smoke screen and at 1330 hours when it was clear that they could not be intercepted and the *Manchester* was in range of the Italian capital

ships the action was broken off and a further attack was made from HMS *Ark Royal* by aircraft.

Although HMS Manchester had been at one time [under] the fire of seven Italians and although she was straddled by fourteen salvoes she suffered no damage. One of her shells registered a hit on one of the Italians '8' (sic) Cruisers which was later seen on fire and disabled. During the engagement an officer of the Squadron (F/O Yates) was shut up in the 'Y' turret disposing of empty cordite cases and two airmen volunteered to take the place of two ratings whose fingers had been damaged handing ammunition from the magazines to the guns. At 1630 hours the AA guns of HMS *Manchester* were active during an attack made by 15 Italian aircraft on HMS *Ark Royal*. During the attack officers of the Squadron were spotting on the bridge.

The ORB of No. 38 Squadron adds that HMS *Southampton* increased speed to approximately thirty knots and opened fire at 1220 hours. She fired 839 rounds from her 6-inch guns, and although straddled nine times, suffered no hits. *Southampton* hit one Italian cruiser, which was seen to be on fire. At 0800 hours on 30 November HMS *Southampton* reached Alexandria, followed at 1000 hours by HMS *Manchester*, and all personnel were disembarked. They proceeded to Fayid in a special train, arriving at 2330 hours. Due to the lateness of the hour they were supplied with a hot meal and slept on the train. At 0600 hours on 1 December they detrained and marched into Fayid, their equipment being brought up in lorries.

All serviceable aircraft of No. 37 Squadron moved from Kabrit to Fayid on 30 November, while at Ismailia No. 38 Squadron's aircraft were being serviced and fitted with tropical installations. Meanwhile, the two Squadrons spent most of their time at Fayid getting organized, laying telephone wires, erecting tents etc. The Commissariat facilities were reported to be very bad, with most of the food coming out of tins. Quite a number of men of No. 38 Squadron went down with stomach trouble, and tent inspections revealed that they were not taking enough care in keeping themselves and their personal surroundings clean. The following day the men were paraded and given a lecture about personal hygiene and cleaning up their living quarters. To add to the problems, there had been much difficulty in locating the Squadrons' equipment, which came on the *New Zealand Star*, and although some of it was found at Alexandria, a great deal went missing. Three units had come out to the Middle East, No. 73 (Fighter) Squadron and Nos 37 and 38 (Bomber) Squadrons, and the stores and equipment of all three had been marked identically without anything to show to which Squadron any particular case or box belonged. It was estimated that it would take at least three weeks to sort them out.

Headquarters RAF Middle East was anxious to get the new aircraft operating as soon as possible, and two aircraft of No. 37 Squadron were ordered to proceed to the Western Desert on 6/7 December. However, severe dust storms in the area caused the cancellation of the operation, and the aircraft returned to base during the afternoon. Then orders were received that a maximum effort would be required from both squadrons for 8/9 December, the target was the Benina airfields and the squadrons would operate in cooperation with Nos 70 (Wellington) and 113 (Blenheim) Squadrons. Seven aircraft from No. 37 Squadron operated via LG 09 (Bir Koraiyim, near Daba) and six from No. 38 Squadron operated via LG 60 (near Maaten Bagush and 'believed to be a dried up lake with a very hard surface'). They flew out to sea, flying in formation, and then turned towards Benghazi, keeping about fifty to sixty miles off the coast. As it became dark they broke formation, and proceeded independently to Benina. Bombs and incendiaries fell among buildings and aircraft on the ground at both airfields, and the aircraft also machine-gunned the landing grounds from low level. Widespread fires and explosions were seen among buildings, dispersed aircraft, and what was believed to be a fuel dump. There were now three Wellingtons squadrons operational in the Middle East, and a fourth had formed in Malta.

* * *

The movement of Wellingtons to the Middle East via Malta had begun on 30 August 1940 (see above), and seventeen had found their way to No. 70 Squadron by 26 October. Two more left the UK a few minutes after midnight on 29 October, and these aircraft were destined to stay in Malta and begin the formation of what was at first known as the 'Luqa Wellington Detachment'. The original intention was that the detachment would consist of 'reinforcing aircraft' – i.e., those en route to the Middle East to re-equip/reinforce the squadrons already there, but it eventually acquired a life of its own as No. 148 Squadron. The two that arrived on 30 October were followed by another six Wellingtons of No. 115 Squadron, which left Marham on 30 October under the command of Squadron Leader P.S. Foss. Patrick Foss has told how he heard about his new posting after a hospital visit to one of his crews, which had been hit by flak over the Ruhr and staggered back to Norfolk and crashed near the coast:

> When we got back to Marham, after midnight, the sentry on the gate directed me urgently to the Station Operations Room. There the new Station Commander was hard at work organizing a special operation in the Mediterranean. I had been selected to lead it. I was to take off for Malta in just sixteen hours time with six Wellingtons from Marham's two squadrons and six from Mildenhall's two squadrons. We were to attack a highly secret target in Italy and then return…in about ten days.[4]

The people at Marham knew little about the facilities at Malta, and packed in as much gear as the aircraft would carry – and a little bit more – Squadron Leader Foss took his portable typewriter! The Wellingtons at Marham had about 6,000 feet of grass for their take-off, and they needed all of it, just clearing the boundary fence and climbing steadily for more than 100 miles before they reached their cruising altitude. One of the Wellingtons returned due to wireless failure and bad weather conditions, and another hit a barrage balloon cable at Langley (near the site of the present Heathrow airport). It crashed and burned out on the railway station at Iver, killing all the crew. The other four were fired on by flak when they crossed the French coast at Le Havre, and as daylight broke they were near Sardinia, heading for Cap Bon in Tunisia. They gave the island of Pantellaria a wide berth, as Italian fighters were believed to be stationed there, and also kept well clear of Sicily. They arrived safely at Luqa between 0730 and 0830 hours.

The 'special operation in the Mediterranean' came about due to a change in Air Ministry policy, communicated to the Commander in Chief of RAF Bomber Command in a memo dated 28 October and accompanied by a detailed set of instructions. The memo stated that:

28

Owing to critical situation resulting from invasion of Greece by ITALY it has been decided immediately to undertake retaliatory bombing of ROME and NAPLES from MALTA. A/c and crews for this purpose are to be found from your command.[5]

The memo went on to outline the requirements, which included at least six aircraft with experienced crews, and at least one squadron leader and one flight lieutenant. The first target was to be Naples, with the central railway station as the aiming point, and the second attack was to be on Rome. Attacks were to be sustained against both objectives 'until each aircraft has completed 4 repeat 4 sorties or operational or maintenance factors prevent continuance'. The surviving Wellingtons would then go on to the Middle East. Another memo from the Air Ministry followed on 29 October changing the plan significantly in that 'attacks on objectives in ROME shall not repeat NOT be carried out until specific orders are received from AM'. Subsequent attacks could be made on the naval bases at Taranto and Brindisi, and on Sicily. It went on to say that:

It is now [the] intention to make these operations by reinforcing aircraft a regular feature whenever opportunity occurs during the next 2 or 3 months so long as operational and maintenance factors permit. A contingent of about 75 WELLINGTON maintenance personnel is to be despatched immediately by Bomber Command in HM Ship with additional stores and technical equipment and should reach MALTA in about 8 days.

It was planned that around two hundred heavy bomber sorties would be flown from Malta during November, December and January (see Table 1 below). Instructions were also given to the AOC Malta that the Squadron Leader and a nucleus of experienced flying personnel should remain permanently at Malta to 'assist in organizing, leading and controlling operations of subsequent reinforcing a/c under your direction'. It is clear from Squadron Leader Foss' account that nobody had told him that he was to be on Malta 'permanently', and Air Vice-Marshal Samuel Maynard (AOC Malta) seemed not to know what the Wellingtons were doing there – although he did seem to know that Rome was out as a target and that the first attack should be made on Naples.

So, six Wellingtons had arrived at Malta by 31 October. The station commander at Luqa, Wing Commander R. Carter Jonas, was somewhat concerned about the variety of aircraft he was expected to operate, and commented that the station 'might be described as a kind of 'aerial liquorish allsorts'.[6] Despite his misgivings 'the impossible was achieved' and the bombers were prepared for their first bombing raid on Naples on the night of 31 October/1 November. Patrick Foss tells us that this was only made possible by shanghaiing 'anyone, Air Force, Navy, Army or civilian, who could be persuaded to help lift bombs, arm guns, refuel or service aircraft'. Wing Commander Jonas' account continues:

Naturally, being the first occasion that heavy bombers had ever operated from the island, it was regarded as something of a special operation; and as I walked along the road...towards the big wooden hut where the flying crews were assembled, I saw by the cars outside that both the Governor (Dobbie) and the AOC (Maynard) had already arrived. I listened to the commanding officer (Sgn Ldr P. S. Foss) who was to lead the raid, 'briefing' the pilots,

> navigators, wireless operators and air-gunners who stood in an irregular semi-circle around him ... I was surprised to see how young most of them looked ... an hour later I stood by the control tower in the darkness, watching the looming black shapes of the bombers roaring past me down the runway. Watching the long orange flames from the exhausts, climbing away down the valley. Watching the red dot of light on the rudders, until they too had disappeared among the stars.

Foss had been worried about the ability of his crews to find the blacked-out island in the dark, so he decided to take off around midnight in order to be back over Malta at dawn. All six got off and five of them bombed Naples between 0300 and 0345 hours. The sixth failed to find the target area and returned to Luqa with its bombs. The other five also returned safely, and reported that Naples was poorly blacked-out at first, and that light and heavy flak was intense but inaccurate. Next morning a Maryland took some excellent photographs that showed several oil tanks severely damaged. The report to the Air Ministry from Malta stated that wireless silence was 'unbroken by our a/c therefore good possibility MALTA unsuspected as base for the raid'. The report on the raid caused Norman Bottomley, SASO at the Air Ministry to send a note to Portal (then C-in-C Bomber Command) stating that this was 'extremely good work and reflects great credit on all concerned'. Portal responded with a message to AOC No. 3 Group and HQ Mediterranean passing on his congratulations.

Wing Commander Jonas at Malta sounded a note of caution, however. He knew that the airfield at Luqa was 'by no means large enough for the operation of heavy-laden bombers'. Also, the rarefied air over the island, which is found in all hot places, provided another difficulty for the pilots of the Wellingtons. Watching the take-offs on that first night had been a nerve-racking experience, as the bombers took an age to unstick themselves from the runway and lift into the air. One hit a tar sprayer with its wheels as it just cleared the wall at the end of the runway. Squadron Leader Foss comments that the one long runway at Luqa was only 900 yards in length, with a grass overrun of about 400 yards, and at its end stood a 20-foot tall memorial chapel. His aircraft barely cleared it on take-off, and a watcher estimated that the clearance was about six feet. In the warm air the aircraft needed a longer run than in the UK, and crews were tempted to pull their Wellingtons off too quickly, which could make them sink back to collide with the chapel. The short-term solution was to lighten the load carried by the bombers, thus reducing their already limited effectiveness. The longer-term solution was to demolish the chapel and lengthen the runway.

The solution was to come too late for a number of brave men when the second operation was launched on the night of 3/4 November. Six Wellingtons prepared for take-off, and Wing Commander Jonas again takes up the story:

> ...as the first bomber thundered past me I remarked to the doctor who was standing beside me, that as far as the weather was concerned it might be considered an ideal night for the trip. And then number two roared towards us, materialized itself momentarily into a shapeless form, and was gone. Half blinded with dust and grit from the slipstream, we watched the little red tail light climbing up amongst the stars and heard the strange echo from the engines as the aircraft swept over the steep valley beyond the aerodrome.

And then terrifying in its inevitability and steadiness, we watched the red dot of light sinking, sinking towards the ground. What could have happened? There was no answer ... instead the pulsating beat of the distant motors ceased abruptly and a burst of livid red flame like a Guy Fawkes bonfire, appeared across the valley. The Wellington crashed and was burning, with a full load of petrol and bombs aboard.

Despite the mishap, number three was already on its way, and number four soon followed. It climbed slowly across the valley and commenced its turn gently to the right. Then the red tail light again began to sink towards the ground, and soon another horrifying silence was followed by flames and explosions as the bombs went up. Squadron Leader Foss, who took charge of the operation from the ground, immediately abandoned the mission. The first aircraft to crash had flown into a hill almost parallel with the ground and had broken up against the stone walls lining the tiny fields on top of the hill. Amazingly, all survived bar the second pilot, who died later in hospital. Sergeant Lewin received the George Cross for his brave efforts to save the life of his second pilot, going back into the burning aircraft and pulling him clear just before the bombs exploded.

The second crashed aircraft came down on the roof of a big house, and the front part of the fuselage containing all but one of the crew broke off and fell into a quarry and caught fire. A Maltese policeman thought he saw a crewman trying to escape and had himself lowered into the quarry, where he pulled out one of the crew. For this he was awarded the British Empire Medal. However, three of the crew in the front section were killed and the rescued man died later in hospital. Foss tells us that the rear gunner was found the next morning 'asleep...inside the wrecked fuselage and apparently not aware of what had happened'. Certainly, the rear gunner (Sergeant D. Palmer) survived the crash, and was probably unconscious rather than asleep in his turret! Of the four aircraft that set off for Naples, three found and bombed the vicinity of the railway station, but the fourth was unable to locate the target and returned with its bombs.

We know very little about the subsequent operations by the four survivors, supplemented by the 'reinforcing aircraft' of No. 37 Squadron en route to the Middle East (see above) over the next three weeks or so. The AHB Narrative, *The Middle East Campaigns, Volume XI: Malta* (Appendix VIII) tells us that following the two attacks on Naples the Wellingtons went to Brindisi on 5/6, 7/8 and 28/29 November (thirteen sorties), to Naples again on 9/10 November (five sorties), to Taranto on 13/14 (ten sorties – see below) and again on 22/23 November (one sortie), and to Bari on 16/17 (see below), 19/20, and 22/23 November (nineteen sorties). We also know that seventeen aircraft had been delivered to the Luqa Wellington Detachment by the end of November 1940. The AHB Narrative *The Middle East Campaigns, Volume I* states that:

> The detachment at Malta continued to operate against ports used by the enemy for supplying troops in Albania, particularly Bari and Brindisi. Naples was considered as a secondary target only and the reason why Naples and Taranto received so much attention was that bad weather frequently prevented operations over the east coast of Italy. Naples was raided four times from Malta between the beginning of November and the 9th December. On each occasion the main targets were oil refineries and the railway

junction...Taranto was raided on 13th November and Catania, which was used for flying aircraft to Libya, and Augusta were also successfully raided as alternative targets. The weather in fact prevented the major effort being directed to support the Greek campaign.[7]

Four aircraft from No. 37 Squadron attacked the Italian Navy base at Taranto on 13/14 November, part of a larger force of 'ten Wellingtons from Malta' mentioned in the official history of the war in the Mediterranean and Middle East.[8] It states that the aircraft 'attacked the inner harbour and naval oil tanks' at Taranto, causing further fires and explosions. The attack was made in cooperation with the Royal Navy, and in spite of intense AA opposition hits were obtained in the target area. On the night of 16/17 November the Wellingtons on Malta attacked Bari on the Italian east coast, and one from No. 37 Squadron failed to return. The crew were originally buried in a communal grave at a monastery in Yugoslavia, and after the war were re-interred in Belgrade War Cemetery. This suggests that the aircraft missed the target area and flew on towards Yugoslavia, eventually running out of fuel.

The clearest account of the early operation of the Wellingtons from Malta is that found in the Malta Operational Intelligence Summary for the period 11 October 1940 to 10 February 1941.[9] It states that a lack of senior officers and NCOs in the detachment soon became apparent, and it had no identity and lacked *esprit de corps* due to its *ad hoc* nature. The solution was the formation of No. 148 Squadron, and from 1 December 1940 we have the new Squadron ORB to guide us. The official date of formation of the new unit was 14 December, and on that day the following signal was received at Luqa:

> Personal from AOC to OC Luqa, for 148 Squadron....You have been born and also reached years of discretion at the same time. Your prenatal activities indicate a healthy child. Good luck to you all and may 148 Squadron and its association with Malta prove of ever increasing benefit to the Empire.

The first operation mentioned in the ORB took place on 2/3 December when ten Wellingtons were detailed to attack oil and railway targets at Naples, with port facilities at Messina as a target of last resort. The raid 'was split up into two parties, 37 Squadron taking off early and Wellington detachment later'. It seems that the new unit was using some Wellingtons that had formerly belonged to No. 37 Squadron, although the first formation to take off is shown simply as 'A' Flight on Form 541. Of the ten aircraft operating, one returned after twenty minutes due to the pilot becoming ill, and another returned early due to a fault in the bomb gear that caused all the bombs to jettison while testing the switches outbound. Eight bombed the target, but the attack 'was of little success due to bad weather'. Three or four aircraft located the target through gaps in the cloud and started several fires, and one also dropped incendiaries on the airfield at Catania, setting fire to one aircraft dispersed on the landing ground.

On 7/8 December 1940 the new Squadron carried out its second operation when eleven aircraft took off to attack the airfield at Castel Benito, south of Tripoli. One Flight, led by Squadron Leader Foss, was scheduled first to attack Mellaha airfield east of Tripoli as a diversion. Another five aircraft were to attack Castel Benito singly at intervals of a quarter of an hour. Foss crossed the North African coast in daylight, but missed the airfield at Mellaha and thus was the first to arrive over Castel Benito:

> At that moment I spotted Castel Benito coming up, and on the airfield a remarkable sight – line upon line of three engined bombers, drawn up as though for inspection. My guess was that there were at least two hundred...It was evident that I was the first Wellington crew on the scene...and told the pilot to turn to the right and drop the bombs along the length of the target. This he did. Then I caught sight of the Italian bi-plane fighter climbing fast just ahead of us. I told MacDougall to turn against the fighter's turn...Just as MacDougall rolled over to dive, the fighter made his first attack.[10]

The Wellington dived towards the ground, going so low that clouds of dust blew up from the desert, putting off the Italian pilot, who seemed to be scared of hitting the ground. A number of bursts from the CR.42 did hit the Wellington, and Foss' rear gunner returned fire until he was wounded in the ankle. With white smoke pouring out of one wing (probably from a damaged self-sealing tank) and black smoke from the other, the Wellington limped home to Luqa. The aircraft got down safely but burst a tyre on landing and swung round on the grass near the boundary, coming to a stop without further damage. Two more aircraft landed safely, but then the next Wellington down, which had also been shot up by a fighter, couldn't get its undercarriage down due to damaged hydraulics. It belly-landed in the middle of the flare path, blocking the runway, and Squadron Leader Foss rushed around to find men and lorries to haul it away. There was a twenty-minute delay before the fifth aircraft landed, followed closely by the other six. One of these landed without flaps, overran the tarmac, and got bogged down while turning off to taxi. The operation was reported to be a great success, with two hangars hit and one of them destroyed by fire. Administrative buildings, barracks and a petrol dump were also hit, and about sixteen aircraft damaged by fire or machine gun attacks.

The Wellingtons on Malta played an important part, not only in damaging Italian aircraft on airfields out of range of bombers from Egypt, but also in hindering the establishment of the *Luftwaffe* in Sicily. No. 148 Squadron carried out a further six operations during the month of December, one directed at the port facilities at Valona in Albania, two at naval vessels in the harbour at Naples, and two at the Castel Benito airfield. The sixth attack, on the night of 30/31 December, was on Naples and Taranto, the object of which was to drive the Italian Fleet out to sea. Both raids were successful, with all bombs being dropped in the target areas, although the AA opposition at Taranto was said to have increased considerably. Attacks on Naples and the Sicilian ports of Messina and Palermo continued in February, as well as further attacks on the Sicilian airfields. The latter were particularly important during the period when HMS *Illustrious* was in the Grand Harbour for repairs and under continuous attack between 11 and 23 January.

The Malta Operational Intelligence Summary for the period gives a table of No. 148 Squadron's operations (including those carried out by the Luqa Detachment), and further details of operations to the end of February are given in AHB Narrative, *The Middle East Campaigns*, Volume I (see Table 1).

Table 1 Summary of operations carried out by the Wellington bombers on Malta between 31t October 1940 and 28 February 1941[11]

Target	No of attacks	No of sorties	Types and weight of bombs dropped in lbs		
			GP	SAP	Incends
Catania Airfield	9	41	134,250	–	14,860
Tripoli Harbour	6	46	135,000	35,900	9,800
Castel Benito Airfield	4	38	87,980	–	16,520
Bari Harbour	3	18	27,500	–	3,590
Brindisi Harbour	3	13	16,750	5,000	1,680
Taranto Harbour	3	16	23,000	13,750	2,400
Augusta Harbour	1	1	2,000	–	–
Comiso Airfield	5	7	15,750	–	6,720
Crotonne Chemical Works	2	2	1,750	2,750	240
Palermo Harbour	2	3	2,500	5,250	–
Capodichino Airfield	1	3	6,750	–	720
Mellaha Airfield	1	2	1,000	–	480
Messina Harbour	1	7	9,000	9,000	480
Syracuse Harbour	1	1	2,500	–	960
Torre Annunziata Arsenal	1	1	–	2,750	–
Naples Harbour	3	21	5,000	36,250	1,360
Naples Oil Refinery	5	10	21,500	–	6,160
Naples Railway Station	4	9	19,250	–	1,200
Valona (Albania)	1	4	9,000	–	960
TOTALS	56	243	520,480	110,650	68,130

During this period the Wellington Detachment/No. 148 Squadron had seven men killed, eleven wounded and nineteen missing in action. Six Wellingtons had been lost on operations (four due to enemy action and two in accidents), and three destroyed on the ground.

At first, life on Malta was fairly pleasant for the men of No. 148 Squadron, and the ORB reports that the crews were able to take time off to go roller skating at Sliema when bad weather prevented operations – an occurrence that was not infrequent. The traditional Christmas festivities took place, with the officers serving dinner to the airmen and the sergeants invited into the officers' mess for a party. The Armourers' block won the prize for the best decorated barracks. The island only had to contend with a few bombing raids by the *Regia Aeronautica* at this time, and these were rarely pressed home with any determination. The Wellingtons could therefore operate with little interference, but more difficult times lay just around the corner. The first *Luftwaffe* attack on the harbour came on 16 January 1941, and on Luqa on 18 January. Four hangars were hit, and two were badly damaged. One aeroplane was destroyed by fire, and all were damaged by shell splinters. One bomb dropped near the wireless section, destroying part of the building and killing two members of the ground crew sheltering in a surface trench.

From now on the story for No. 148 Squadron was one of dodging air raids, filling in bomb craters, and trying to keep as many aircraft as possible operational. The Squadron retaliated by bombing German airfields on Sicily, but never had enough aircraft to make a difference. It only managed thirty-one sorties in five operations in February, and then was almost wiped out on 25 February. On this day Luqa was dive-bombed by Ju 87s and Ju 88s at 1300 hours, the attack lasting for approximately fifty minutes. Six of the Squadron's Wellingtons were burnt out, one was a write-off, and four were declared unserviceable for periods varying from three weeks to three months. The fighting force was thus reduced to two aircraft. Two pens were destroyed, although damage to buildings was slight and there were no casualties. The Squadron ORB comments 'A sad day for the Squadron', but it could be proud of its record in its first period on Malta.

No. 148 Squadron did not carry out any operations in the month of March. The Squadron ORB tells a story of aircraft and airmen being shifted around, mainly towards the Middle East, but with some Wellingtons going back to Malta from Egypt. Aircraft were also arriving from the UK, and some remained on the island for a while, although most were quickly moved on to Egypt. It was clear that Wellington operations from Malta were at an end for the moment, and on 9 March a signal was received from HQ Mediterranean that stated: 'All Wellington aircraft, except 2 for Flying Practice to be flown to Kabrit direct.' On 13 March another signal was received from HQ Middle East:

> Aircraft of No. 148 Squadron will operate from Cyrenaica and will move forthwith. Malta will be used as advanced Landing Ground for re-fuelling and maintenance. Sufficient personnel to be left behind to perform these duties.

On 23 March seven officers and seventy-nine airmen left for Egypt, embarking on HMS *Bonaventure* and leaving the Grand Harbour at 1800 hours. They arrived at Alexandria on 25 March and proceeded by train to Kabrit, which they were to share with No. 70 Squadron. It was described as 'a very pleasant camp, and a rest for everyone after Luqa'. The Squadron was desperately short of everything it needed to become operational, and did not operate again until 13 April. We will catch up with its career in the next chapter.

*   *   *

In the early morning of 9 December Wavell launched the first British offensive of the desert war, Operation *Compass*, carried out by the 31,000 strong Western Desert Force under the command of General Richard O'Connor. The tank group began its march forward at dusk on 8 December, while a Bombay flew overhead to drown the noise of their engines. As the operation got underway three Bombays of No. 216 Squadron bombed defended camps in the Sidi Barrani and Sollum areas, and on the same night twenty Wellingtons from Nos 37 and 38 Squadrons attacked the main Italian airfields at Benina. Air Chief Marshal Longmore considered that the attacks greatly reduced the scale of the attack that the *Regia Aeronautica* was able to make at the beginning of the offensive. The Italian forces in Egypt were outflanked and cut off at Sidi Barrani, and two thousand prisoners were taken in the first hours of the fighting. Sidi Barrani fell on 11 December, and the British forces were at the Halfaya Pass by nightfall.

Then, as the Army advanced into Cyrenaica, so did the targets for the Bombays and Wellingtons move further away from their bases in Egypt. During the next three weeks the night bombers first attacked targets at Sollum and on the Sollum–Bardia road, and then the focus shifted at various times to Bardia, El Adem, Tobruk, Derna, Benina, Berka, Benghazi, Tmimi and Gazala. O'Connor had taken Sollum by the 16th of the month, and was pressing on into Libya. Bardia was also surrounded and besieged by mid-December. On 19 December Mussolini requested German assistance in Cyrenaica, asking for a Panzer Division, *Luftwaffe* units, and logistical support. These would arrive soon, and everything would change in the desert war.

On 20 December 1940 an important administrative change occurred for the heavy bombers in the Middle East. No. 257 (Heavy Bomber) Wing was formed at Shallufa, and Group Captain Lachlan Loudoun MacLean was appointed as its Commanding Officer. MacLean was an interesting character. In 1935 he got into trouble while commanding the Air Fighting Development Establishment for criticizing Air Ministry plans regarding the development of the new monoplane fighters. This, together with his outspoken attitude to some of his Commanding Officer's actions, resulted in him being placed under close arrest. Following the consequent Court of Inquiry, his CO (Joubert de la Ferté) was posted to India and MacLean was posted to No. 3 Group, and later took early retirement. However, political events intervened, and he was recalled to service from 25 August 1939 until 2 August 1944. The function of the new wing was: 'to administer and operate the following Stations and Heavy Bomber Squadrons: SHALLUFA, KABRIT, Nos. 37, 38, 70 and, on re-equipment, No. 216 Squadron.' The Wing would come under the direct control of Headquarters, RAF Middle East. As it turned out, No. 216 Squadron did not receive Wellington bombers and reverted to a purely transport role from January 1941, and thereafter disappears from our story.

Meanwhile, elements of five Italian divisions were locked up in Bardia and prepared to make a fight of it. The Bombays and Wellingtons, often accompanied by the Blenheims of No. 202 Group, bombed the enemy positions and the town eleven times between 12 December 1940 and 2 January 1941, flying some fifty-five sorties against this target. During the week 16 to 22 December over a third of all bomber sorties was directed on the fortress, on troop concentrations in the vicinity, and on supply dumps in the wadi north-west of the town. The biggest raid was on 15/16 December, when thirteen Wellingtons and two Bombays joined two squadrons of Blenheims and a detachment of the Fleet Air Arm, making a total force of thirty-six aircraft. What was described as 'Unusually large concentrations of aircraft' were reported on the airfields near Benghazi, at Benina and Berka, and these were attacked successfully on 17/18 and 19/20 December.

Bardia eventually fell on 4 January, and the next objective for the troops was Tobruk. This, too, was heavily bombed by the Wellingtons on nine occasions over the next two weeks, but on 12 January the Wellington effort available to AOC No. 202 Group was reduced to six aircraft per night, as the remainder were now required to assist the Greek campaign. On 20/21 January eight bombers carried out a sustained attack on Tobruk between 0300 and 0600 hours to cover the assembly of tanks, and at dawn British and Australian units broke through the defences. The war correspondent Alexander Clifford was on board one of the aircraft of No. 38

Squadron, captained by Pilot Officer Slade, and gives an account of his experiences in his book *Three Against Rommel*:

The night before...I went with the pilots of a Wellington squadron to a sandy, fly-haunted shack beside a remote desert airfield [Fuka Satellite]... As darkness fell every one trooped in for a noisy, boisterous meal of stew, potatoes, and onions.

Afterwards, for the few intervening hours, we dozed on straw mattresses. Then, booted, helmeted, and very warmly overalled, we walked out to the dimly silhouetted plane...In a matter of minutes we had climbed aboard, roared down the winking flare-path, and lifted gently into the night. I stood with my head in the little glass bubble which stuck out above the top of the machine, and watched the desert sink away into a misty blur...A dim white streak was the coastline, and the sea beyond it looked like another desert.

As the plane droned on into Libya I fell asleep. Then someone was shaking me awake and yelling 'Tobruk'. I fumbled my way forward and peered out of the plane's transparent nose to see earth and sky slashed with flame. Groups of big yellow flashes were bombs landing. Clusters of incendiaries wove crazy patterns of dazzling white flame athwart the landscape. A parachute flare hung like a great orange star burning steadily above Tobruk Bay.

To my unaccustomed eyes the ack-ack barrage seemed stupendous. String after string of red tracer shells spurted up like ruby necklaces. Ack-ack shells bursting splashed the sky with sudden stars and left little balls of smoke hanging aimlessly about. It was our turn to go in...I clambered back through the plane's darkened belly, past the bomb aimer lying flat on his stomach, and over the racks of sleek yellow bombs waiting to be released. Clumsily I eased myself into the rear gunner's turret – and another, bigger bubble, half filled with intricate gun mechanism. That was my grand-stand seat.

Through my earphones I heard the bomb-aimer's steady monologue: 'Bomb-doors open...left...left...steady...right...steady...' then a pause, and then sharply, 'Bombs gone.' I swivelled my turret round, manœuvring to see the bombs land. I had almost given them up when the earth below erupted into five flaming volcanoes.

Stuff was coming up all round us. The sky seemed filled with coloured tracers, and the heavy ack-ack guns were firing for all they were worth. By now the whole Tobruk area was picked out in dazzling lights as cluster after cluster of incendiaries sprang into flame. The pilot called me up on the 'intercomm'. 'We're going in again', he said. 'Tell me if anything bursts close behind us.'

Back we turned and plunged again into the fantastic blaze of bursting shells. Another flare was burning, and Tobruk's bay and promontory showed up like a gigantic thumb sticking out into the dark sea. We made straight for the target, but showers of tracers met us and barred the way. The pilot swerved aside and tried from another angle. Again I heard 'Bombs gone,' and this time I saw flame belch straight across the road junction at which we were aiming.

Two blinding flashes on my left made me rock in my seat. 'Ack-ack shells close behind,' I reported to the pilot, and for a couple of seconds we swerved and twisted, eluding the gunners. Then we jockeyed into position for the third run. This took us through the thickest barrage. The Italian cruiser *San Giorgio*, half sunk in the harbour, was pumping up stream after stream of tracers…Right in the middle of the barrage our bombs fell, and a flare with them. This time the result was spectacular. A large, barn-like building flashed into orange flame, and its roof soared gently upward, then fell back in fragments.

Those were our last bombs. But we still had some leaflets to drop – why I don't know, for the Italians were going to be given no time to read them…Then we made for home…While dawn was just glimmering in the east we met a squadron of Blenheims on their way to continue the raid. Then we circled down to our airfields again, to a good hot breakfast of fried bread and bacon.[12]

The town fell on the next day and Wavell's troops now headed for Benghazi, and the Wellingtons' attentions were also directed at its port and to the airfields between Tobruk and Benghazi. Benghazi was attacked repeatedly throughout January, and then RAF reconnaissance aircraft reported on 4 February that the Italians were beginning to evacuate the town and starting to withdraw towards El Agheila. The 7th Armoured Division was ordered to cross the desert to try to cut them off, and this action culminated in the final battle of Wavell's campaign at Beda Fomm.

By 12 February it was all over, and the Allied forces took up positions at El Agheila and there they stayed for the moment. Two weeks later their forward elements were skirmishing with reconnaissance units of the German 5th Light Division. With the possession of airfields around Benghazi it became possible to operate the Wellingtons via Benina, and also from El Adem and Gambut near Tobruk. Thus Tripoli came within their range, and attacks on the Libyan capital began on 24 February and continued until the end of March. The AHB Narrative *The Middle East Campaigns* comments that:

The outstanding success of the bomber force was that it succeeded in preventing the Italians from using…ports between the frontier and Benghazi, thus compelling them to use the roads which became increasingly strenuous and dangerous. On the experience of the campaign, it seemed that the destruction of warehouses produced the best return for aerial bombing. Material damage otherwise was generally small in comparison with later years and the destruction of aircraft when well dispersed was better achieved by gunfire or by small bombs. On the other hand the moral effect of sustained bombing from the air even with such a small force was great.

There seems to be little doubt that the 'moral effect of sustained bombing' on the Italians was not inconsiderable, but the Germans would prove to be tougher nuts to crack.

At the end of March 1941 a new phase in the war in the Mediterranean and the Middle East began. General Rommel had arrived at Tripoli on 12 February, and the first units of the *Deutsches Afrikakorps* (DAK)[13] were close behind him. The 5th Light Division, the first unit of the DAK to arrive in Libya, occupied an excellent defensive position in the salt marshes at Mugtaa, twenty miles west of El Agheila. Its reconnaissance unit, a strong and partly armoured force, had already had a few brushes with patrolling British units. On 24 March this unit, suitably reinforced, moved forwards to attack the fort and landing ground at El Agheila, along with its much needed water supply. It easily drove off the few British and Australian troops there, and then sat down to wait further instructions from General Rommel. These arrived on 30 March, ordering an advance on Mersa Brega, a further twenty miles along the coast. At Mersa Brega were elements of the 2nd Armoured Division's Support Group holding a front of eight miles, with the 3rd Armoured Brigade about five miles to the north-east. Both these formations were under strength and ill-equipped to deal with the onslaught that was about to hit them. The war in the desert was about to be transformed.

In the 105 days/nights between the start of Wavell's offensive and the first attacks by Rommel's forces at El Agheila, the night bombers operated on 73 nights and flew 638 sorties. The Bombays and Valentias of No. 216 Squadron only managed 20 sorties before withdrawing from the action early in January. The Wellington squadrons in Egypt despatched 412 sorties, No. 148 Squadron on Malta another 166 sorties, and the Greek diversions (see below) accounted for an extra 40 sorties. A total of 14 aircraft were lost on these operations. Airfields received 44 per cent of the sorties, with landing grounds in Libya and the Dodecanese attacked from Egypt, and those on Sicily raided from Malta. Some 41 per cent of the sorties went to port facilities and ships in harbour, with most going to Benghazi and Tobruk until these ports fell into British hands, and Tripoli coming under attack later as the Army advanced into Cyrenaica. The bombers on Malta attacked both Naples and Tripoli four times. Battlefield targets received 90 sorties (14 per cent of the effort) during Wavell's offensive, with most going to the Italian positions at Bardia.

*   *   *

Following the Italian invasion of Greece from Albania in October the RAF, including the night bombers, had become increasingly involved in operations in support of the Greeks. A detachment of Wellingtons of No. 70 Squadron, operating from Eleusis near Athens, made their first attacks from Greece on 7 November (see above). The Squadron flew a number of further operations from Eleusis and Tatoi, attacking Valona, Tirana and Durazzo (all in Albania) and Bari and Brindisi (in Italy).

This first detachment was back at Kabrit by 24 November, but another detachment of four Wellingtons from No. 70 Squadron left for Greece on 14 December for temporary operations under British Air Forces (BAF) Greece. Operating from Menidi airfield near Athens, they carried out attacks on the docks at Durazzo on 15/16 December and on the railway station and oil tanks at Brindisi on 19/20 December. A large concentration of shipping was seen in the harbour at Durazzo, and a large fire was started and a big explosion observed. Fires were also started at Brindisi, where the flak was intense. One aircraft was struck in the port engine and lost its propeller, and it returned to its base at an average height of 1,000 feet, having jettisoned all moveable equipment. The detachment returned to Kabrit on 23 December.

The next detachment of night bombers went to Greece on 11 February 1941, when No. 37 Squadron was ordered to send six aircraft to Greece to operate from Menidi. The aircraft left Shallufa on the 12th, and a maintenance party and a number of armourers and signallers were ferried to Greece in two Bombays. The aircraft operated on the same night against targets at Durazzo and Tirana, hitting

39

buildings and causing fires and explosions at Durazzo, and bombing dispersed aircraft and hangars at Tirana. On 15/16 February three aircraft attacked the airfield at Brindisi, where a seaplane hangar was set on fire and three aircraft destroyed on the ground. One of the Wellingtons was shot down by flak, with three crew members dead and two taken prisoner. On 17 February five aircraft flew from Menidi to Paramythia, a small airfield nearer the Albanian border, in order to operate with a full bomb load. However, operations were cancelled due to bad weather and the aircraft returned to Menidi on the following day through heavy rain and low cloud.

On 20 February two aircraft of No. 37 Squadron 'were detailed for the unfamiliar role of operating by daylight in close proximity to the front lines', to drop supplies to Greek troops fighting in the mountains in Albania. They were to operate in company with a Ju 52 of the Greek Air Force, and with an escort of fifteen Gladiators. The Wellingtons again operated via Paramythia, and after following the river valleys northwards they reached Kelcyre in Albania without incident. Continuing to a point between Balli and Corovode, they dropped three tons of supplies to the Greek troops. Many enemy fighter patrols were engaged by the Gladiators during the operation, and four were claimed as shot down. The Wellingtons left Paramythia for Menidi the following morning, but the undercarriage of one of the aircraft collapsed as it was taking off from the water-logged airfield and it was damaged beyond repair. The detachment left Greece and returned to Shallufa on 22 February, the ground party flying back in Bombays.

As March began plans for a raid on the Romanian oil industry were mooted, calling for an attack by two squadrons operating from airfields in the Athens area and using Guida and Sedes in the Salonika region as emergency landing grounds. Long-range fuel tanks holding 120 gallons would have to be carried by the aircraft, thus reducing the bomb load from 2,500 lb to 1,250 lb. Long-range tanks were fitted to aircraft of No. 37 Squadron on 4 March, and these were flight tested over the next two days. The sea party left Shallufa on 6 March and embarked on the cruiser HMS *Orion*, arriving at Piraeus on the 8th. On 7 March seven aircraft of No. 37 Squadron left Shallufa in two flights and flew to Menidi, but as one of them was preparing to land it was sent around again as an aircraft of the Greek Air Force was already taking off. While making the second circuit one of the propellers flew off, and the Wellington crashed into a wood at Kyphyssia. Five of the crew and passengers were killed instantly and one died later in hospital. After all this trouble the plans for the attack on the Romanian oil industry were shelved due to Greek sensitivities about the German response, and the Wellingtons attacked targets in Albania and the Dodecanese instead.

They carried out their first operation on 8 March, when four aircraft attacked harbour installations at Durazzo. Hits were observed on the quayside and harbour buildings, and three good fires were burning steadily as the last aircraft left the target area, still visible at Valona on the return journey. On 10 March six aircraft set off to attack the airfield at Calatos–Lindos with two of them also detailed to carry out a reconnaissance of Maritza afterwards. Bombs were seen to fall amongst airfield buildings and hangars at Calatos–Lindos, and several large fires and explosions were reported. Flak was more intense than usual, and at least four searchlights were in operation. On 12 March six aircraft were despatched to attack the airfields on Rhodes, and two of them were to carry out a reconnaissance of

Scarpanto en route. The first aircraft over Scarpanto dropped a stick of bombs on what was believed to be the airfield, but the second aircraft reported explosions near a village some miles to the north-west. Both these aircraft then went on to bomb Kattavia on Rhodes, two bombed Maritza, and the other two went to Calatos–Lindos.

On 15 March eight aircraft operating from Paramythia attacked the airfield and military and government buildings at Tirana, but the airfield appeared to be water-logged and the incendiaries refused to burn. A large white building in Tirana was set on fire, and some fires and explosions were reported on the airfield. One Wellington was shot down in flames by enemy fighters, with three crew members killed and three taken prisoner, and two other aircraft were badly damaged by flak. On 17 March the bombers were detailed to attack Durazzo and Tirana, again operating from Paramythia, but encountered very bad weather, with considerable cumulus cloud at varying heights, hailstorms, and severe icing conditions. The aircraft sent to Tirana failed to locate its target and joined in the attack on Durazzo instead, where bombs were dropped in the vicinity of the power station, along the quayside, and among warehouses. The detachment returned to Egypt shortly afterwards, with the sea reaching Alexandria on 22 March and the aircraft returning to Shallufa on 23 March.

*   *   *

In the 286 days/nights between 11 June 1940 and 23 March 1941 one or other of the night bomber squadrons was in operation on 129 of them, flew 890 sorties against the enemy, and lost 26 aircraft. Almost all the operations had been flown during the hours of darkness, although a handful had taken place by day. The numbers of aircraft involved in each operation had necessarily been small, with only one squadron (No. 216) operating until September, and only two squadrons (Nos 216 and 70) and the few Wellingtons at Luqa operating until December. On nineteen nights only single aircraft operated, and on another twenty-one nights only two or three aircraft operated. On only four occasions did more than twenty aircraft take off, and the largest number despatched during the period was twenty-two aircraft.

The Middle East was a much safer place to operate than in the skies over Europe at this time. Total losses due to enemy action was only twenty-six, or 2.9 per cent, with seventy-seven aircrew dead, seven seriously injured, and twelve captured. Four of the aircraft losses were due to accidents on take-off, and nine crashed on the return trip (six on landing), although in some of these cases the aircraft had been damaged by enemy action. Only five were definitely lost following attacks by fighters, and only three definitely lost after being hit by flak. Almost half the sorties (48 per cent) were directed at port facilities and ships in harbour, with Benghazi and Tobruk receiving the lion's share. Some 38 per cent went to airfields, mostly in Cyrenaica, and 13 per cent to military targets, which included enemy camps, supply dumps, barracks, and motor vehicles. However, the pattern of operations clearly showed that when the Army was in action (during the Italian invasion of Egypt and Wavell's offensive) the night bombers would be there to support it. They might be few in number, but were always on call.

An entry in the No. 38 Squadron ORB on 12 March reports some interesting modifications in the field under the heading 'GADGETS'. Pilots were complaining that their windscreens iced up on operations, and in order to try to cure this problem a pipe was taken from the carburettor de-icing pump to the windscreen. This allowed the pilot to deliver de-icing fluid to the engine, the windscreen, or both. The Engineering Officer went on a test flight to note the spread of the liquid under the action of the airflow, and after a few minor adjustments one of the Squadron's Wellingtons went on operations and reported excellent results. Up to one and a half inches of ice was cleared in thirty seconds. The modification was afterwards adapted for all Wellingtons.

Another modification concerned navigation lights, which were sunk in the wing tips and not visible from the cockpit. The pilots often forgot to switch them off when making their attacks, and this was obviously a bonus for enemy flak in the target area. The Engineering Officer fitted a simple reflector of tinned mild steel, which reflected the light of the lamps into the cockpit, and this proved to be a great success.

The third modification came about due to the inaccuracy of the petrol gauges. Aircraft were making forced landings through an apparent lack of petrol when there was as much as 100 gallons still in the tanks. The Engineering Officer's solution was a reserve tank of known capacity to be turned on after remaining fuel had been exhausted, giving the pilot a fixed period of time in the air. It was decided to use the nacelle tanks in this way, each having fifty-eight gallons and therefore giving one and a half hours flying time after being turned on. These tanks could not normally be turned on in the air, so a simple attachment was devised leading into the fuselage. The modification was suggested to HQ No. 3 Group in the UK and to the makers, who adopted the system with some improvements.

NOTES

1. See *Bomber Squadrons of the RAF*, Philip Moyes, page 211.
2. Air Historical Branch Narrative, *The Middle East Campaigns*, Volume I, page 63.
3. Alexander Clifford, *Three Against Rommel*, page 42.
4. From *Climbing Turns* by Patrick Foss, page 98. There is no mention of the six aircraft from Mildenhall in No. 3 Group's ORB or elsewhere.
5. See National Archives references AIR 2/7397 and AIR 14/830 – *Operations against Italy from Malta*.
6. *Malta: The Hurricane Years*, by Shores, Cull and Malizia, has a good account of the first days of the Wellington operations, see pages 76–80. Much of the story of these first operations from the island is taken from this source.
7. Air Historical Branch Narrative, *The Middle East Campaigns*, Volume I, page 74.
8. TMAME, Vol. I, page 237.
9. National Archives, AIR 24/908.
10. Foss, *Climbing Turns*, pages 108–111.
11. Taken from ORB of Headquarters (Unit) RAF Mediterranean for June 1940 to August 1942, National Archives reference AIR 24/908, and AHB Narrative, *The Middle East Campaigns*, Volume I, Appendix XXI.
12. Alexander Clifford, *Three Against Rommel*, pages 51–4. The Squadron ORB tells us that he flew in Wellington T2706, taking off at 0220 hours and landing again at 0615 hours.
13. The initial German commitment in North Africa was known as the *Deutsches Afrikakorps*, abbreviated as DAK. Italian units in the theatre were eventually incorporated into a larger German command structure, known variously as *Panzergruppe Afrika* (August 1941 – January 1942), *Panzerarmee Afrika* (January 1942 – October 1942), *Deutsch-Italienische Panzerarmee* (October 1942 – February 1943), and *Heeresgruppe Afrika* (February 1943 – May 1943).

CHAPTER THREE

Enter Rommel – April to October 1941

On 22 March 1941 elements of the 5 Light Division of the DAK in the forward areas in Tripolitania began to adopt a more aggressive stance, clashing with patrolling British units. On the 24 March this unit attacked the fort and landing ground at El Agheila, and drove off the troops stationed there, and a few days later a major advance on Mersa Brega began. When Rommel decided to attack there was little that Wavell could do to block his progress. Many of his troops had been sent to Greece, and those that were left were at the end of long and tenuous supply lines. The single armoured brigade of the 2 Armoured Division in the forward area was scattered, disorganized and short of petrol. Its support group suffered heavy casualties in the early fighting, and was forced to withdraw. The German offensive succeeded with an ease that surprised Rommel, and this encouraged him, although he needed little encouragement, to push on with his limited forces. It was clear to Wavell and the local commander, General Neame, that they didn't have the men or material to withstand the German advance. The Armoured Division was forced to withdraw on 3 April, thus uncovering Benghazi, and General Neame had no choice other than to implement the demolition plan and abandon the town.

When Rommel's offensive got underway the four Squadrons of No. 257 Wing[1] were scattered far and wide across the Middle East. No. 37 Squadron had only just got back from Greece, its aircraft arriving at Shallufa on the afternoon of 23 March and the sea party disembarking at Alexandria on the following day. On 3 April they would be off to Greece again, and would play no part in operations in the Western Desert for almost two weeks. No. 38 Squadron was based at Gambut, and flying most of its operations from Benina near Benghazi. This put it right in the front line, with Rommel soon to be just a few miles away. No. 70 Squadron had a detachment at El Adem, near Tobruk, and was also flying most of its operations from Benina. Both Nos 38 and 70 Squadrons would soon be scrambling backwards towards the Canal Zone. No. 148 Squadron had been forced to abandon Malta in March and was moving to Bu-Amud, near Tobruk, but was not yet operational in the Middle East. At the end of March and during the first few days of April Nos 38 and 70 Squadrons were sometimes able to carry out operations over Tripolitania, but most of the Wellingtons were elsewhere or non-operational. Thus, the enemy build-up was able to proceed largely unmolested by the night bombers.

The few armoured units continued to retreat, desperately short of petrol, and as their fuel ran out the better tanks were filled up from the worse until only a handful remained. The Germans, too, were tired and short of petrol, but Rommel drove them on ruthlessly. By 7 April they had cut across Cyrenaica and reached the main coastal road near Derna, and had an unexpected bonus on the outskirts of the town when they stumbled upon a car containing Generals Neame and O'Connor. The latter was, of course, the man who had driven the Italians out of Cyrenaica just two months previously, and now two of the top generals in the Middle East were 'in the bag'. By the night of 7 April elements of the 9 Australian Division were fifteen miles west of Tobruk holding a defensive position astride the main coast road, and a small force was at El Adem, watching the approaches from the south. Other units under General Gambier-Parry were bottled up in Mechili, and most were captured along with their general. Tobruk was invested by 11 April, and by the middle of April Rommel's forces were established in strong positions based on the Halfaya Pass, Sollum, Bardia and Fort Capuzzo. The Allied forces were on the general line Buq Buq–Sofafi, about twenty miles west of Sidi Barrani and more or less back where they had started at the beginning of Operation *Compass*.

When all this started No. 38 Squadron was at Gambut Main Landing Ground, about thirty miles east of Tobruk, and two of its aircraft were out trying to find Tripoli through a thick ground haze. Its ORB reflects the general uncertainty at the time. Rumours were already 'going round as to position of German ground forces and the possibility of evacuation', and on 4 April they could 'see a lot of traffic moving up to the front'. On the next day instructions were issued for the demolition of buildings, petrol and bomb stocks in case this should become necessary. An Evacuation Committee was set up after dinner on 6 April, and orders were received that the Squadron was to give up Gambut to No. 55 (Blenheim) Squadron and 'packing began feverishly'. In the meantime, the weather worsened until 'a terrific sandstorm was blowing up from the South'. The weather cleared by 0700 hours on 7 April, by which time 'the first convoy of vehicles was well on its way to SIDI AZEIZ and No. 55 Squadron were arriving to take up residence'. The latter were to stay at Gambut for only two days before they too were on their way back towards Egypt.

Sidi Azeiz is about thirty miles east of Gambut by air, but by road it is more than forty-five miles along a difficult track. Due to a shortage of vehicles three journeys had to be made before all personnel and equipment was evacuated. All the petrol and a few bombs were left for the incoming squadron, but the Royal Engineers were busy exploding dumps of Italian bombs as the last vehicles left, with 'each explosion rattling windows fiercely'. As they moved eastwards, convoy after convoy of Army personnel and supplies passed them on the road, rushing to the West. The last load finally arrived at Sidi Azeiz by 1830 hours on 8 April, with everyone feeling quite satisfied but very tired, but no sooner had the Squadron personnel started to take breath than orders were received to move again. They were to go on to Sollum, which was 'a matter of one and a half hour's drive'. The lorries and trailers got underway again, but some kit and equipment had to be abandoned. All vehicles were at Sollum by 2300 hours, and the men had just been fed and were getting down to sleep when yet more orders arrived to move on to Fuka Satellite, about 110 miles to the East.

The ORB contains the following 'appreciation from a Squadron Member', describing the scramble back to Fuka:

On 11th March 1941 aircraft of the Squadron proceeded to Great Gambut in enemy occupied territory. Certain maintenance personnel travelled by air and the remainder of the ground staff by road, this move was carried out without incident. The aerodrome surface and size presented no difficulties for our aircraft. Accommodation was limited – consisting of three large corrugated iron huts, one of which was used for the airmen's dining hall. Officers and NCOs were accommodated in wood huts and tents.

The maintenance personnel in spite of considerable inconvenience caused by severe sandstorms, continued to maintain the high standard of serviceability for which our Squadron has such an exceptionally good record. All inspections, with the exception of majors, were carried out at GAMBUT.

Not withstanding the difficulties encountered in operating large twin-engined bomber aircraft so far away from their base (600 miles) all operational commitments were met without the loss of a single aircraft during the period of five weeks in the desert…

Instructions for the immediate withdrawal from GAMBUT were issued by the officer commanding No. 257 Wing at 2130 hours on 6th April 1941 on which night eight of our aircraft were operating.[2]

The withdrawal was seriously hampered by a severe sandstorm which raged all night – so severe was this storm that the lamps of the flare path were blown away. Among the incidents of the night were the number of personnel who were lost in the storm and the transport which found itself running over and among fused Italian bombs.

It is significant that the withdrawal to SIDI AZEIZ was carried out without a hitch in spite of the sandstorm and the arrival of two Blenheim Squadrons with over 100 MT.

SIDI AZEIZ was reached the same day and ten aircraft were prepared for immediate operations.[3]

An advance convoy was sent off at 1330 hours on the 8 April to establish a base at FUKA satellite where it was proposed that maintenance of aircraft should be carried out. The convoy stopped at SOLLUM in order to give maintenance crews a rest but after a brief stop of approximately 2 hours the detachment left for FUKA, leaving 6 airmen behind to look after kit and equipment with instructions to proceed of their own accord if transport was not sent within three days or if orders were given them by HP officers who were present at SOLLUM. These airmen were however returned to FUKA on the 11th April. During their brief stay at SOLLUM the airmen attempted to make serviceable two or three discarded motor cycles for emergency withdrawal if necessary.

The convoy arrived in FUKA at 1400 hours and was immediately despatched to base Shallufa, where the whole Squadron had returned. Aircraft arrived in the evening 9.4.41.

The incident that occurred at Fuka was the attempted take off of the Aircraft with brakes resulting in its tipping on its nose and bending both airscrew blade tips and collapsing the tail wheel fork. Despite the damaged condition of the Aircraft it was immediately flown to base and was operationally serviceable in 24 hours. The total casualties during these fine works were five airmen. Two of whom died and three who received injuries as the result of accidents.

The general health of the personnel was excellent and the Espirit de Corps of the Squadron and its high efficiency was clearly marked during this strenuous period. Finally great praise is due to the fine work put in by the maintenance staff at base.

After arrival in Fuka some of the convoy were ordered to continue home while others had to return to Sollum to pick up men and supplies and bring what they could. This was done though again some equipment had to be left behind. When these were back again at Fuka most of the equipment and all the remainder of the transport had to be left on this aerodrome as a forward striking aerodrome in charge of 257 Wing and 70 Squadron who were then arriving.

The remainder of the personnel with their kit they had left had to be taken back to Shallufa in two lorries that were nearly unserviceable. The last lorries arrived in Shallufa at 11 a.m. on 12.4.41…

While at Fuka a message was received from an unknown source which asked for a flare path to be laid ready between midnight and dawn. It was known that the telephone lines were tapped and there was a very distinct possibility that the colours of the day were known. The flare path was prepared and also our three machine guns were in a lorry. If a plane then wanted permission to land the machine guns were to be rushed up behind the chance light so as to cover the airfield and landing strip in case of emergency.

A similar story can be found in the ORB of No. 70 Squadron. On the night of 31 March/1 April the Squadron was at El Adem, and sent one Wellington to bomb Tripoli. It continued to operate from El Adem until the night of 5/6 April, and, increasingly, the targets were enemy motor transport on the roads heading east across Cyrenaica. On 5/6 the ORB reports: 'Convoy [of] 14 heavy vehicles seen on road 60 miles S.W. EL ADEM and reported to TOBRUK.' During the period 6 April to 10 April the detachment from El Adem was on the move all the time, evacuating its personnel from each base as it moved back. On 6 April they moved to Sidi Azeiz, about seventy miles to the east, with each aircraft doing a double trip in order to get away as many men and as much equipment as possible. The next day a further retirement was made to Capuzzo, about ten miles west of Sollum, and again a double trip was done by each aircraft. On 8 April the detachment moved back to Fuka Main, and after a two-day stay the machines were brought back to Kabrit. On the night of 10/11 April two Wellingtons from Kabrit bombed the airfield at Derna and the Derna–Tobruk road, and on the next night two Wellingtons bombed Msus and Gazala. Tripoli was now many hundreds of miles away, and the enemy was at the Egyptian frontier once again.

Meanwhile, No. 148 Squadron was at Kabrit, having just got back from Malta in an extremely disorganized state and desperately short of men and aircraft. The ORB reports that '62 bodies of all trades' arrived on 2 April, and another forty arrived on the next day. At the end of March they had been ordered forward to Bu Amud, ten miles east of Tobruk, and an advance party left Kabrit on 30 March and the rest of the road party on 3 April. The story in the Squadron ORB is very confused during this period, reflecting conditions on the ground. By 6 April it seems that eight aircraft had been sent on to Bu Amud, but 'no signal received as yet of safe arrival'. However, there were already indications that the detachment 'had moved to rearward 'drome', and on 7 April information was received that '148 Detachment located Fuka Main'. Headquarters Middle East could not confirm the new location, but on the 8th 'definite information' was received that the detachment was now at Fuka. As a sign of things to come, the ORB also reported that three Wellingtons were 'on stand by for a special "Show the Flag" flight over IRAQ', but the operation was subsequently cancelled.

When Axis forces cut the Tobruk–El Adem road there was no longer any base in the desert from which Tripoli could be attacked, and as an emergency measure six Wellingtons were ordered to Malta. The task fell to No. 148 Squadron, and on 9 April it received orders that it was to send a detachment of three aircraft back to Malta. It was having great difficulty getting any aircraft serviceable at the time, as practically all its experienced ground crews were at Fuka. Three Wellingtons were got ready and left for LG 29 (Amiriya) en route to Malta, but one ran out of fuel and ditched, and all the crew were lost. Three more Wellingtons left for Malta on 12 April and another three over the next few days, and we will pick up the story of these aircraft later in this chapter. Meanwhile, a few of No. 148 Squadron's aircraft remained in Egypt and carried out a small number sorties against targets in Cyrenaica, operating via Fuka.

All this confusion was mirrored everywhere, and headquarters units could not keep up with events. The three squadrons (Nos 38, 70 and 148) were under the immediate control of No. 257 Wing Advanced HQ, which had been established at Great Gambut. This, in turn, was under the operational control of HQ Cyrenaica, 'with whom communication had hitherto been difficult, if not non-existent'. At 2030 hours on 6 April the Wing Advanced HQ received orders that Nos 38, 70 and 148 Squadrons were to move back to the Fuka area, with Advanced Landing Grounds at Sidi Azeiz and Capuzzo North. In the absence of any alternative means of communication, the Wing SASO and the Acting Senior Intelligence Officer (Pilot Officer Lord Kinross) drove throughout the night to transmit the new orders to the squadrons. They had great difficulty in locating the airfields in the darkness and with 'a disconcerting lack of landmarks', but they succeeded in rousing No. 148 Squadron before dawn and No. 70 Squadron shortly afterwards.

At the same time No. 257 Wing Advanced HQ was itself on the move from Great Gambut to Sidi Azeiz, and spent an uneventful night in the open on 7/8 April. When they got to Sidi Azeiz the morning was spent digging an operations room out of the sand and roofing it with relics from a nearby Italian hut. The builders were obviously not up to the job, because the roof promptly fell on the head of the SASO – 'who escaped apparent injury'! Soon afterwards, instructions were received by telephone from HQ Cyrenaica to move the Wing Advanced HQ and the Advanced Landing Ground parties back to Fuka. The departure of the final party was hastened by the sight of a series of red lights floating in the sky some miles to the west of the landing ground. The enemy was close at hand.

During the first two weeks in April the squadrons in the Western Desert managed to fly only forty-eight sorties. Between 1 and 6 April they attacked Tripoli on four occasions (eighteen sorties), but the Libyan port was soon to be well out of their range. Enemy columns on the roads between El Agheila and Mersa Brega were also attacked at this time, as well as the airfield at Calatos on Rhodes. By the end of the fortnight the aircraft were operating from Fuka, and on 13/14 April four aircraft of No. 38 Squadron attacked the airfields at El Adem and Gambut. On the same night a single Wellington of No. 70 Squadron bombed the El Adem road and machine-gunned the airfield, camp and transport. On the following night four aircraft of No. 70 Squadron attacked the airfields at Derna, El Adem and Menastir.

By the middle of April, Benghazi had once again become a primary target for the night bombers. The enemy was experiencing considerable difficulties in getting supplies up to the front line due to a shortage of motor transport for the long haul to the frontier area, and was using Benghazi as a major staging point. He was landing most of his supplies at the port, carrying them by train to Benina, and then distributing them to the forward area by transport aircraft. In the last two weeks in April Benghazi was attacked on ten nights and some thirty-six sorties despatched against shipping and dock facilities. This effort was insufficient to deny the enemy the use of the port, and he was able to get enough material through to support his existing force in Cyrenaica. However, it seems to have done enough to prevent him from building up his strength for a further advance into Egypt. The bulk of the attacks on enemy airfields was concentrated against Derna, and the advance landing ground at Gazala and El Adem also received some attention. The night bombers also continued their attacks on motor transport between Benghazi and the forward area.

Rommel's thrust towards Egypt eventually fizzled out during the third week in April. His supply problems increased, and he failed to take Tobruk in the two attacks launched between 13 and 17 April. The Axis forces settled down in strong defensive positions between Sollum and Fort Capuzzo, and the next few months Wavell mounted two abortive attempts to seize the initiative, Operations *Brevity* and *Battleaxe*. The latter was a major offensive against the Axis positions at Halfaya, Sollum and Capuzzo, launched between 15 and 17 of June. Wavell knew that his command was still largely untrained in the kind of operations they would have to perform in a major offensive against strong enemy positions, but as usual Churchill was nagging him to attack. The result was that after three days of fighting the Allied and Axis forces were all back on their start positions. Tobruk was unrelieved, and its garrison would have to fight a brave and skilful battle for almost another six months.

Attacks against enemy landing grounds as part of the build up for *Battleaxe* began on the night of 6/7 June, when four Wellingtons made a successful attack on Derna. Three further raids (ten sorties) were made on this target up to 15 June, and two attacks (eight sorties) on the landing ground at Gazala. Sometimes eager crews would machine gun the airfields from low level on the way home from Benghazi, and motor transport was also attacked whenever targets presented themselves. On the night of 17/18 June two Wellingtons of No. 70 Squadron gave support to the forward troops by attacking motor transport at Bardia, while others attacked Benghazi and the airfields at Derna and Gazala. The fighting now died down until the launch of *Crusader* in November. From 17 June to 18 November 1941 nothing much happened in the Western Desert except for the relentless battering on the door at Tobruk by the Axis forces. In July, General Wavell was relieved of his command and replaced by General Sir Claude Auchinleck, who set about rebuilding his forces ready for the next Allied offensive.

In the eighty-six days/nights between the first moves in Rommel's offensive on 24 March to the end of *Battleaxe* on 17 June, the four Wellington squadrons in Egypt operated on 77 nights, flew 601 sorties and lost 17 aircraft. The targets were fairly evenly split between airfields (272 sorties, 45 per cent of the total effort) and ports and shipping in harbour (267 sorties, 44 per cent). As March came to an end, and up to 6 April, the target was Tripoli, but as the Axis forces advanced and the bombers were forced back into Egypt, Benghazi once again became the main target.

The airfields in Cyrenaica, which were quickly occupied by Rommel's forces, at Benina, Berka, Martuba, Gazala and El Adem, also came under attack at various times. As the debacles in Greece and Crete unfolded then airfields in the Dodecanese, on Sicily, and on Crete itself, became the focus of attention (see next section). There were very few battle area operations, mainly due to the fact that it was often difficult to know where the front line was.

*　　　*　　　*

As the flight into Egypt gathered momentum, some of the Wellingtons were ordered to Greece to help the Greek and Allied forces in their battle with the invading Germans. They would not be there for long. The official history of the war in the Mediterranean and the Middle East describes the campaign on the mainland of Greece as 'from start to finish a withdrawal'.' The Germans invaded Greece on 6 April, before the Allied forces were able to set up a blocking position in the north. The rapid defeat of the southern Yugoslav Army meant that their left flank had already been turned, and two major withdrawals followed. By 21 April the decision was taken to evacuate the British and Commonwealth forces from Greece, and the only real success of the operation was the fact that of the 58,000 service personnel transported to Greece, some 55,000 were got out again.

No. 37 Squadron was ordered to move to Greece on 2 April, and thirteen aircraft flew from Shallufa to Menidi over the next few of days. On 6/7 April six aircraft took off to attack the railway junction and marshalling yards at Sofia in Bulgaria in order to disrupt the transport of German supplies to the front line in Salonika. The operation was carried out in excellent weather, and the aircraft had no difficulty in locating the target. Fires and explosions were reported in the yards, and one aircraft went in low and machine gunned searchlights and flak concentrations. Another strafed transport in the Struma Valley. One of the Wellingtons was hit by flak that wounded the front gunner, and he subsequently died of his wounds. After a couple of days of poor weather the Wellingtons went out again on 10 April to attack German transport concentrations near Veles and Prilep in Yugoslavia, but they ran into unfavourable weather north of Salonika, with heavy cloud and poor visibility. One strafed a long convoy of motor vehicles near Kilkis village, which broke up and scattered, and another machine gunned enemy transport on a road near Salonika.

Ten aircraft and crews of No. 38 Squadron left Shallufa for Eleusis on 11 April, while the remainder of their aircraft stayed in Egypt to continue to harass the enemy. That night four Wellingtons of No. 37 Squadron attacked the airfield at Calatos on Rhodes and then flew on to Egypt as bad weather was forecast for their return to the Athens area. The aircraft of No. 38 Squadron carried out their first operation on the night of 13/14 April, when six aircraft of No. 37 and eight of No. 38 Squadron set off to attack the marshalling yards east of the main railway station at Sofia. They encountered accurate heavy and light flak, and between a dozen and twenty searchlights were operating. One aircraft that carried out a reconnaissance of the Struma valley reported many motorized columns moving south through the night. On the night of 15/16 April No. 38 Squadron attacked a bridge over the River Vardar at Veles, and No. 37 Squadron carried out harassing attacks against German convoys and troop concentrations in the Florina–Ptolemais–Kozane Valley areas.

After just fifty-three sorties in six operations both Squadrons received orders to return to their bases in Egypt on 17 April, and the aircraft were back home before their ground crews and equipment had even arrived in Greece. The sea party had sailed from Alexandria on 15 April on board HMS *Dumana*, and after an eventful voyage had anchored in Suda Bay in Crete. She was still there on 20 April, when she was ordered to return to Egypt, and on the following day she joined a convoy of twenty-six vessels heading for Alexandria. At 1100 hours, and without any warning, machine gun fire and exploding bombs were heard. It transpired that an attack had been made by two enemy aircraft, and further air attacks followed, but the convoy reached Alexandria on 24 April and the sea party disembarked. They were back in Shallufa by 0400 hours on 25 April after a dangerous and wasted ten days for all concerned.

Following the Greek interlude, almost all the efforts of the night bombers up to the end of April and during the first few days of May were directed at targets in Cyrenaica. Benghazi was attacked twelve times, and targets at El Adem, Derna, Berka, Gazala, Capuzzo and Benina were also visited. However, as it became clear that the Germans were preparing for an assault on Crete, attention moved to the airfields on Rhodes and in Greece, where a big build-up of enemy transport and military aircraft was apparent. The first attacks on Calatos–Lindos, Kattavia and Maritza on Rhodes were made on 12 May by five Wellingtons. Hassania and Menidi airfields in Greece were attacked on 13/14 and 14/15 May, some of the Wellingtons bombing those same airfields on which they had been based just a few weeks before. Topali, Menidi, Hassania and Eleusis in Greece were all attacked over the next few days, but following the German airborne attack on Crete on 20 May, the bombers were soon called upon to attack the airfields on Crete itself. Maleme was bombed on 23/24 May, and Retimo on 24/25 May. Attacks on targets on Crete, and on Scarpanto and Kattavia continued until the last night of the evacuation from Crete on 31 May/1 June. In all, 159 sorties were flown by the night bombers during the brief campaigns in Greece and Crete, and six aircraft were lost.

During June and the early part of July, the Wellingtons continued to attack airfields in Greece, Rhodes, and Crete, in the expectation that the Germans might try to employ the same tactics that had been so successful on Crete in an attack on Cyprus. By this time British, Commonwealth and Free French forces were involved in operations in Syria, and these could have been seriously hampered by a large scale intervention by the *Luftwaffe*. However, the German parachute troops had suffered unacceptable casualties in the battle for Crete, and there was no enthusiasm for another airborne operation. Also, *Luftwaffe* units were being moved away from the Mediterranean in preparation for the attack on Russia. Thus, by mid-June all of the night bombers could go back to the old familiar targets at Benghazi, Derna, Bardia, and elsewhere in Libya.

*   *   *

At the end of the First World War the League of Nations granted the area that now comprises modern Iraq to the United Kingdom as a mandate, and a treaty signed in 1930 required the Iraqis to allow the free passage of British forces through the country. There were no British troops left in Iraq after 1937, but the RAF retained bases at Shaibah near Basra and at Habbaniyah on the Euphrates. Iraq was thus not only a major supplier of oil for the Allied war effort, but also an important part of the land and air bridges between Egypt and India. At the outbreak of war the pro-

British uncle of the four-year-old King Faisal II, was regent, but the real power lay in the hands of four prominent Army and Air Force officers known as 'The Golden Square', and in the person of Sayyad Rashid Ali al-Gillani. During the 1930s Rashid Ali had been strongly influenced by the Mufti of Jerusalem, who had been exiled from Palestine for his nationalist and anti-Jewish activities. When Rashid Ali was appointed prime minister of Iraq in 1940, he strengthened his links with Italy and Germany, and furthered his nationalist goals by refusing to allow British troops to cross through Iraq.

Britain responded with economic sanctions, and the British victories in North Africa dulled support for Rashid Ali's government. On 31 January 1941 he resigned as prime minister under pressure from the Regent, but seized power again two months later. On 16 April the British Ambassador informed him that the British intended to land troops at Basra, bound for Palestine, and the first troops from India arrived on 17 April. Rashid Ali was obviously concerned about the build-up of British and Commonwealth forces at Basra, and was himself militarily weak without German aid. He therefore decided to bring matters to a head by sending an Iraqi force to invest the RAF base at Habbaniyah at the end of April. Churchill immediately ordered Wavell to send troops to break the siege, and then to go on from there to occupy Baghdad.

RAF Habbaniyah was hopelessly situated for defensive purposes, overlooked as it was by a steep escarpment and wide plateau that entirely dominated the base. At 0430 hours on 30 April the garrison awoke to discover that the escarpment was occupied by a large number of troops, artillery, and armoured vehicles. The RAF in the Middle East acted quickly, and on the night of 30 April/1 May nine aircraft of No. 70 Squadron left for Shaibah. One of the aircraft forced landed thirty miles west of Habbaniyah due to engine failure, and had to be abandoned. Three of its passengers were slightly injured, but all were subsequently rescued and brought to Shaibah. On 2 May the eight surviving aircraft attacked the Iraqi troop concentrations on the escarpment south of Habbinayah as dawn was breaking. The attack was carried out in conjunction with the Audaxes, Gordons, Gladiators and Oxfords of the flying training school at RAF Habbaniyah. Squadron Leader Tony Dudgeon was leading one of the Habbaniyah formations, and recalled the confusion of those first few hours:

> As the daylight got stronger we could see that the air above the plateau was like the front of a wasp's nest on a sunny morning. The ten Wellingtons were there from Basrah [sic] making a total of forty-nine aircraft of five different types and speeds, clustering and jockeying over an area not much bigger than a minor golf course. It was a hairy experience. In my Oxford I would peer down into the dusk, trying to distinguish a juicy target like a gun-emplacement – and an Audax would swoop past at some crazy angle. Or a Wellington would sail majestically across my bows, giving me heart failure and leaving my machine bucketing about in its slipstream. Luckily, no one hit anybody else, but there were some very close shaves indeed.[4]

The Wellingtons caused severe damage to motor transport, and two gun positions were silenced by direct hits. All the aircraft were hit by rifle fire; one was badly damaged and the observer was hit in the leg and died of his wounds a few days later. One Wellington was forced to land at Habbaniyah, and was eventually destroyed by enemy gunfire.

Reinforcements were soon on their way. Ten aircraft of No. 37 Squadron left for Shaibah on 2 May, and four operated in the late afternoon. Hits were reported on gun positions, transport in the gullies, 'armoured lorries' and a group of tanks. The only opposition from the ground was rifle and some machine gun fire. Earlier in the day No. 70 Squadron had again hit enemy positions on the escarpment, concentrating on artillery positions. Two of the guns were silenced, and the aircraft then dived down and machine gunned the troop positions. The aircraft were intercepted by 'two Northrop and two Gladiator fighters', which made half-hearted attacks but broke away after twenty minutes. One of the Wellingtons sustained damage to its port wing from ground fire, and had to land at Habbaniyah. Repairs were carried out with shells bursting all around, and the aircraft was later escorted clear of the field of operations by two Gladiators.

Attacks on enemy positions on the escarpment and near the Fallujah Bridge continued over the next few days. The Wellingtons also maintained a security patrol above the enemy lines, dropping bombs at intervals and generally making a nuisance of themselves by machine-gunning transport and troops on the ground. On 4/5 May a Wellington of No. 37 Squadron took off to create a further nuisance over Habbaniyah, but shortly after leaving the ground it fell back, struck a barbed wire fence at the boundary of the airfield, and burst into flames. Four members of the crew escaped with slight burns, and another, although seriously injured, succeeded in kicking a hole in the side of the fuselage large enough to crawl through. One member of the crew was still trapped in the aircraft when some of the bombs exploded, but three of the crew 'displaying great courage and resourcefulness' managed to get him out through the rear turret, still alive but severely burned. A few seconds later another violent explosion occurred. Both of the injured men later died of their wounds.

Then, in the early hours of 6 May, a single aircraft of No. 37 Squadron left Shaibah to carry out another security patrol over enemy positions at Habbaniyah, and reported that 'no opposition was encountered and no activity seen'. At dawn it was found that the Iraqis had gone away, abandoning large quantities of arms and equipment. A small force covering the bridge at Fallujah was quickly driven off, and that afternoon a column moving up from Fallujah was destroyed by aircraft from Habbinaya. The siege was over, but the Wellingtons still had work to do. As well as attacking the enemy positions at Habbaniyah, the aircraft of Nos 37 and 70 Squadrons had also been attacking the Iraqi Air Force. The main target was the airfield at El Raschid (Hinaidi) near Baghdad, which was attacked successfully at dawn on 4 May and during the night of 4/5 May. One Wellington was attacked by enemy fighters, and a two-seater biplane was shot down and another damaged. One aircraft did not return from the second operation, and was later located on the ground twenty miles south of Baghdad, but there was no sign of the crew (however, see below for their story). Dame Freya Stark was a prisoner in the besieged British Embassy in Baghdad at the time, and described with elation her first sight of a bombing raid against the city:

> About 4 a.m. in faintest beginning of light, five of our bombers came over to plaster Rashid camp and machine-gun the airfield – wild and ineffectual popping of Iraq firearms. A very beautiful sight – a great Wellington, slowly

sailing along at about 1,000 feet, up the river from south to north, very dark against the green sky and the sleeping houses. The dull sound of bombs, dull but clear: the AA very sharp and crackling … The raid lasted about three hours.[5]

These first attacks on the airfield cost the Iraqi Air Force some twenty-nine aircraft. The Wellingtons also dropped leaflets over Baghdad, assuring the population that Britain's fight was with the usurper government, and not with the people of Iraq. Further attacks were carried out on the airfields at El Raschid and al-Washash (Baghdad Airport), and on 8 May the aircraft of No. 37 Squadron attacked the airfields at Sharnaban and Ba'quba, where the surviving aircraft of the Iraqi Air Force were believed to have been dispersed. The two Wellington squadrons had a day off on 9 May to rest and recuperate, and then the next day they were off again. Six aircraft flew to Habbaniyah to refuel and bomb up in preparation for an attack on military barracks at Mosul and Kirkuk, but found that the facilities at Habbaniyah were 'so meagre that eventually only four were able to operate' against Mosul.

On 10 May four aircraft from No. 70 Squadron bombed the airfield at Qaraghan, the last operation by the Squadron in Iraq, and on 12 May the surviving five aircraft returned from Shaibah to Kabrit (one that was found to be unserviceable was left at Shaibah). No. 37 Squadron carried out one more attack on 11 May, on El Raschid, and on the next day their eight aircraft flew from Shaibah to Shallufa via Palestine. In all, the Wellingtons had carried out seventy-seven sorties in Iraq, and there is no doubt that the Wellingtons had played a significant part in suppressing the Iraqi insurrection. As Dame Stark's comments suggest, the mere sight of the big bombers provided a great boost to morale at Habbaniyah and elsewhere. The *Luftwaffe* only managed to get five Heinkel 111s to Iraq, and these were all quickly destroyed or disabled in subsequent air operations. Without the sort of facilities afforded by the RAF bases at Shaibah and Habbaniyah, it was enormously difficult to maintain large aircraft in the country, and the token intervention by the *Luftwaffe* could never account to much.

The No. 37 Squadron ORB gives an interesting account of the experiences of P/O Rush and his crew after their forced landing in Iraq on 4 May (see above):

After the attack on RASCHID we scattered leaflets over BAGHDAD and then carried out a recce of the airport. We set course for base, flying at about 2,000 feet, and must have passed in range of a battery of 20-mm guns firing green tracer which we failed to see. There was a good deal of noise as if we were flying through a barrage, and I suspected that there might have been a Gladiator behind us, so made a steep left turn. We saw the Gladiator, but he was a long way off. I put the nose down, and we followed the river. By RASCHID aerodrome we went down very low, then climbed to 1,500 feet. At this point, the rear gunner reported his turret u/s, and shortly afterwards the front gunner did the same. The 2nd Pilot and Wireless Operator pumped three gallons of oil into each engine, but the starboard engine began to run very rough; gradually the boost and the revs dropped off, and I put her into coarse pitch and closed the throttle. We gradually lost height using one engine. I tried the starboard again, but there was no response. The boost gauge was steady at 'C'. When we ran out of height and air speed we made a forced landing in a green field, after hitting the ground three times with the middle of the fuselage before coming to rest. The bomb beams and doors were ripped off, but there was otherwise little damage done. All the crew got out unhurt, and we collected the 'K' guns and six pans of ammunition, the axe and the Verey pistol and all available cartridges.

Some local tribesmen were watching, and seemed very pleased that we were down. There was a fair-sized sailing boat on the river which we made for, in the hope of sailing down the river to a plain that was marked on the map. But to reach it we had to pass the tribesmen, some of whom were wearing white and some black headgear and robes. We tried to make them understand what we wanted, but failed. They took the money we offered them but that was all. As we walked along with them they seemed friendly enough, and presently we reached their encampment. There they motioned us to sit down by their tents, but we argued, and I tried to get two of them, apparently headmen, to understand about the blood chit[6] and the money. However, they couldn't read, and my efforts were in vain. Meanwhile, the other tribesmen were removing the guns from the rest of the crew; an argument followed, bitumen sticks and so on were produced and a general scuffle ensued. I went forward, and was cracked on the head and knocked out for a short time. When I came round again, I saw Sergt Cambell still struggling; he managed to get up and was cracked across the back. We told him to sit down and be quiet, whereupon Sergt Howard received another blow for his pains. We were then robbed of everything we had – two of us our shoes even. Luckily all our rings and watches came off easily, otherwise we might have lost our fingers and hands with them.

Then a fellow on horseback arrived; he was something to do with the army. He told us to get up and we were marched off towards some troops who were arriving to take us over. They were friendly but obviously disappointed that we had already been robbed. We were taken across the river to a small fort on the north bank. After being questioned, our head wounds were bandaged; much telephoning followed; we were blindfolded and driven in a car to somewhere near BAGHDAD. On the way Sergt Campbell had started spitting bright red blood, and must have had a broken rib in his lung; they asked my permission to take him to hospital, which I said they had better do as soon as possible.

Then we were blindfolded again, and taken in a car around the streets, presumably of BAGHDAD. There was much cheering, and the officer next to me stood up and waved something. We ended up at the Ministry of Defence, where more questioning followed. Amongst other things I was asked who bombed the Isolation Hospital at RASCHID at 0830 hours that morning – later the medical people told me that a nurse and a doctor had been killed. Our wounds were properly cleansed and bandaged, and we were given an anti-tetanus injection. Some tea was brought, and we were informed that we would be treated in accordance with international law. One man took us to his house, (blindfolded) and treated us very well, giving us tea, oranges and a sour milk drink apologizing for the absence of spirits. I was told that I should receive the same food as the sergeants in my crew, only 'better cooked'. Then we went back to the Ministry of Defence, and were put in two rooms at the back, with a service hatch in the wall between them. Fresh Japanese clothing and shoes were given us.

P/O Rush and his crew remained in Baghdad for ten days, during which they were joined by other prisoners of war. Then they were moved to Kirkuk and later to Service Station K1, further prisoners being added to their number at both places. When the armistice was signed they were sent to Baghdad in an unguarded train, visited the British Embassy, and were taken to Habbaniyah in a Vickers Valentia. From there, a Bombay took them to Heliopolis, where they were collected by one of No. 37 Squadron's aircraft. Meanwhile, Sergeant Douglas Campbell had died of his wounds in hospital, and was buried in the Baghdad (North Gate) War Cemetery.

Trouble was also brewing elsewhere in the Middle East. Syria had been mandated to France by the League of Nations after the First World War, and the period of the Mandate had been marked by increasing nationalist sentiment, civil disorder and a number of brutally repressed revolts. With the fall of France in 1940, Syria came under the control of the Vichy Government, and more and more Germans arrived in the country. The Vichy French rulers were, if anything, more virulently anti-British and pro-German than Rashid Ali, and this was of deep concern to the British. General de Gaulle and his Free French emissaries in the Middle East were optimistic about bringing Syria round to the Allied cause, but there was little evidence to support their belief. Turkey was also worried about the arrival of Germans in Syria, and in May 1941 it moved troops towards the Syrian frontier. What was not known by either Turkey or the British was that the Germans had decided to withdraw from Syria in order to give the British and Free French no pretext for moving into the country. It would fall into their hands once Operation *Barbarossa*, the invasion of the Soviet Union, was complete anyway. Nevertheless, Britain decided to occupy Syria, and on 8 June 1941 British and Free French forces crossed the border. The fighting only lasted five weeks, but the Vichy French fought well and with great bitterness at the use of their own countrymen against them. As the battle progressed, many of the Free French forces showed less and less inclination to fight, and it was largely left to the British and Commonwealth troops to finish the job.

The bombers of No. 257 Wing did not get involved in the Syrian campaign until 29 June, and over the next week flew a mere twenty-eight sorties in six operations against the harbour and shipping at Beirut. The object was to disrupt the flow of reinforcements and supplies that the Vichy Government tried to get through the Eastern Mediterranean from Salonika. The final operation against Beirut took place on 4 July when four aircraft hit the harbour area, causing large explosions and fires. One of the Wellingtons was hit several times by flak, and was only brought back to base with difficulty. The attentions of the bombers then shifted to the airfield and railway targets at Aleppo in order to interrupt the movement of troops in northern Syria. The attacks started on the night of 5/6 July and ended on 10/11 July, and between those dates the four Wellington squadrons despatched some twenty-four sorties. The defences at Aleppo got stronger as the raids continued, and the heavy flak was particularly accurate. One aircraft of No. 148 Squadron failed to return on 6/7 July, and was eventually found sixty-seven miles east of Ismailia on the Palestine Road, completely burnt out. The rear gunner was injured and the rest of the crew killed. On 7/8 July one of the aircraft of No. 70 Squadron was attacked by night fighters, and claimed to have shot two down (one confirmed and one unconfirmed) and damaged another. The Wellingtons flew fifty-four sorties against targets in Syria before hostilities ended on 11 July, much to the relief of both sides, and now Britain could turn all its attentions to the Germans in the Western Desert.

*   *   *

Following the end of the *Battleaxe* operation there was little or no fighting on the ground until *Crusader* began in November 1941. The lull was only once seriously interrupted, when Rommel launched a probing attack on 14 September to test the Eighth Army's strength above the escarpment. However, the night bombers had plenty of things to occupy them. On most nights the name 'Benghazi' appeared somewhere on the flight board for the squadrons in Egypt. Whether it was shipping, the harbour area, or the nearby airfields at Benina and Berka, the bombers kept on going back to this target. It became known to the bomber crews as the 'mail run', and was commemorated in the famous song of No. 70 Squadron, *The Mail Run Melody* sung to the tune of *Clementine*:

> Down the flights each bloody morning
> Sitting waiting for a clue,
> Same old notice on the flight board,
> Maximum effort – guess where to.

Chorus: Seventy Squadron, Seventy Squadron,
Though we say it with a sigh,
We must do the bloody mail run,
Every night until we die.

> Out we go on to dispersal,
> To complete our Night Flying Test,
> Rumour says we're going Northwards,
> But we know we're going West.

Chorus: Seventy Squadron, Seventy Squadron, etc.

> Take off from the Western Desert
> Fuka, 60 or 09 (Sixty or Oh-nine),[7]
> Same old Wimpey, same old aircrew,
> Same old target, same old time.

Chorus: Seventy Squadron, Seventy Squadron, etc.

> 'Have you lost us, Navigator?
> Come up here and have a look;
> Someone's shot our starboard wing off!'
> 'We're all right then, that's Tobruk.'[8]

Chorus: Seventy Squadron, Seventy Squadron, etc.

> Fifteen Wimpys on the target,
> Two forced landed in the drink,
> Another couple crashed on landing,
> Bloody Hell, it makes you think.

Chorus: Seventy Squadron, Seventy Squadron, etc.

> Snooping round the Western Desert,
> With the gravy running low,
> How I wish I could see Fuka,
> Through the dust storm down below.

Chorus: Seventy Squadron, Seventy Squadron, etc.

> Trying to get your forty raids in,
> Thirty-nine, now don't get hit,
> If you don't, you go to Blighty,
> If you do (Well, never mind!)

Chorus: Seventy Squadron, Seventy Squadron, etc.

> Oh, to be in Piccadilly,
> Selling matches by the score,
> Then I shouldn't have to do that
> Ruddy Mail Run any more.

Chorus: Seventy Squadron, Seventy Squadron, etc.

A different view of the 'mail run' is given by Ken Rees, who was posted to No. 38 Squadron in August 1941:

> Any initial joy was soon stifled after sitting in the mess and listening to the crews talking about their ops. Most of the trips then were against Benghazi, mainly because at that time there was not much else around to bomb. They called this 'the mail run'. You took off, bombed Benghazi, then landed at a desert landing strip where you refuelled from four-gallon drums, then returned to base. Ho-hum. The trips were generally uneventful, except for heavy flak over the target.[9]

This, of course, was the view of a man who had flown twenty operations over Germany before volunteering to come out to the Middle East to avoid being taken off ops and transferred to an Operational Training Unit! Whatever the difficulties of the night bombers in the Middle East, and there were many, they were nothing compared with those experienced by the squadrons of Bomber Command. Rees was relieved when he heard that he was to join the No. 38 Squadron detachment in Malta, where he eventually managed to get a transfer to his old squadron, No. 40, which had just come out to the Mediterranean. We shall hear from him again later in the chapter.

As we have said before, Benghazi was the biggest port near to the Axis front lines, although still over three hundred miles away as the crow flies and a great deal further by the poor roads around the Cyrenaica coastline. With Tobruk in the hands of the British and Commonwealth forces, it was really the only source of supply for Rommel's troops at this time. There was Tripoli, of course, but this was many more miles away and linked to Cyrenaica by a single road. Most of the supplies that got into Tripoli thus had to be moved forward by sea anyway, and their ultimate destination would have to be Benghazi. There were limited port facilities at Derna, but it was the damage and disruption caused at Benghazi that would have the greatest effect on the fighting efficiency of Rommel's troops. And so it was to Benghazi that the bombers had to go, night after night.

The harbour at Benghazi contained a number of key features that were to become frequently mentioned in the Operations Record Books of the squadrons of No. 257 Wing (and later No. 205 Group). It was bounded by the Giuliana Mole and Outer Moles. The Cathedral Mole jutted out between these two, creating what was effectively an 'inner' and 'outer' harbour, and in the area between the Cathedral Mole and the Outer Mole were moored a number of hulks that acted as jetties. The most famous of these was known as 'George', and the others were 'Johnny', 'Harry', 'Ink' and 'Beer'. Two other Moles within the main harbour were the Central Mole and 'Molo d'Italia'. Many of the main targets in the harbour area, such as the Custom House, railway sidings and workshops, the Governorate, seaplane station, barracks, W/T station, telephone exchange and the Fondugh (Funduq) Palace were located at the bases of the three main Moles, and on the Giuliana Point. An oil pipeline ran from the tip of the Giuliana Mole to a storage and pumping tanker moored offshore.

On 15/16 July the aircraft of No. 257 Wing carried out their first mine-laying operation (known as 'gardening') at the entrance to Benghazi harbour. The weather conditions were perfect, with good visibility and no cloud, but, unfortunately, the predicted winds were incorrect. This meant that some of No. 38 Squadron's aircraft were over the target nearly half an hour too soon, and one of them 'stooging round above the target saw a lot of light tracer firing out to sea 15 minutes before zero'. The early attacker was one of the four minelayers, and he was forced to fly directly into the face of the light flak and machine-gun fire coming from the moles. Nevertheless, he let his mines go in the correct position, flying low and slow across the harbour, and flew out from the target zone at sea level. During the first part of his dive his aircraft had been hit by a 40-mm shell, which exploded in the starboard wing causing a large hole. His air gunners were busy all this time, firing 800 rounds apiece at the gun positions and searchlights. Three of the aircraft of No. 38 Squadron planted six mines (codenamed 'cucumbers') in the harbour mouth, but a fourth minelayer failed to return, and the last message received from them was that they would bale out over Tobruk if they couldn't reach Sidi Barrani. It was subsequently learned that all the crew were prisoners of war. Eleven other aircraft from Nos 37, 38 and 70 Squadrons created a diversion over Benghazi, spending between forty minutes and an hour over the target dropping bombs and incendiaries to distract the defences.

On 10/11 August the aircraft of No. 257 Wing carried out the largest single bombing raid launched to date by the night bombers. Thirty-six aircraft attacked 'targets of military importance within the town of Benghazi, and around the docks and railway sidings, workshops and barracks'. Huge fires were started in many districts, and the last aircraft over the target could see the fires from many miles away. Bombs were seen to fall near the Governorate, the Custom House, the telephone exchange, north of the Cathedral Mole, and in the area of the railway sidings. Many results were not seen due to the intensity of the flak and the need to take evasive action. The aircraft were fired on by 'guns of all calibres, three flakships were active, and from five to eight searchlights were in operation'.

As the No. 70 Squadron song tells us, the Wellingtons operated from Advanced Landing Grounds at or near Fuka, which was around 480 miles from Benghazi as the aeroplane flies. This allowed for some margin of error by the navigators, but not a lot. Very often the bombers had to turn back due to engine trouble or other technical problems, and most looked for good targets of opportunity on the way home. The harbours and stores at Derna and Bardia came in for quite a bit of attention anyway, frequently appearing on the flight boards as targets in their own right. Derna was a small port used for schooner traffic, with a variety of supply dumps, repair shops and military barracks in the general area. Bardia was also a small port used by small craft from Crete and Greece, with reserves of petrol and ammunition in the vicinity. The other targets for the Wellingtons were the landing grounds from which the *Luftwaffe* and *Regia Aeronautica* were operating. As well as those near Benghazi, at Benina and Berka, the airfields at Barce, Derna, Martuba, Tmimi, Gazala, El Adem, and Gambut were all bombed on many occasions.

On the 127 days/nights between 18 June and 13 October the Wellingtons in Egypt operated on 103 nights, flew 1,068 sorties, and lost 15 aircraft. The bulk of the effort from Egypt was carried by Nos 70 (331 sorties), 37 (299 sorties), and 148 (255 sorties) Squadrons. No. 38 Squadron only contributed 121 sorties from Egypt, spending a long time on Malta during this period (see below). The four squadrons were joined by the newly formed No. 108 Squadron in August (see also below), but this unit was only able to launch 62 sorties during this time. As we have seen, the main task of the bombers in Egypt was to disrupt enemy supply lines by attacking ports and ships in harbour. A total of 870 sorties (81 per cent of the effort) were so directed, with Benghazi the main target, and with Derna, Barce and Bardia also receiving some attention. Another 187 sorties (18 per cent) went to airfields, with those in Greece, Crete, and the Dodecanese receiving the most attention.

*   *   *

On 1 August 1941 the fifth heavy bomber squadron in the Middle East, No. 108 Squadron, was formed at Kabrit, equipped with Wellington ICs from 'one of the older squadrons'. In fact, the new Squadron seems to have acquired a motley collection of aircraft from various sources. On 20 September the ORB of No. 148 Squadron stated that thirteen of its old Wellington ICs were transferred to No. 108 Squadron, and the latter was none too happy about getting the hand-me-downs. On 15 October its ORB comments that the 'folly of equipping newly formed Squadrons with old aircraft has now become apparent'. Out of the eighteen Wellingtons on its charge, one required a complete fabric recovering, two required both engines changed due to heavy oil consumption, three were unserviceable for operational flying and six were on 240-hour inspections. This left 'six aircraft only for operational flying'.

It was intended to form the new Squadron gradually, commencing with one flight and the Squadron HQ and adding a second later. Squadron Leader B.J. McGinn was posted from No. 204 Group Advanced Headquarters to assume temporary command. Over the next few weeks the Squadron was involved in recruiting personnel and setting up the necessary support organizations. The 'personnel' included twelve Italian prisoners of war, who helped to dig out the positions for tents etc. A few aircraft also started to arrive, and by the end of August the ORB proclaimed 'No. 108 Squadron Camp at Kabrit now completely self-contained.' Their first operation was launched on 2/3 September, against Derna. On 12 September the Squadron moved from Kabrit to Fayid, but it seems that RAF

Fayid was totally unprepared for its reception. The ORB tells us that 'innumerable difficulties' were experienced, the officer's accommodation was 'inadequate' and that for the airmen was 'appalling'! Altogether an unhappy start for No. 108 Squadron, but the circumstances were not untypical in the under-privileged and under-resourced Middle East.

The reason why No. 148 Squadron was stripped of its old aircraft was that it was being re-equipped with the Merlin-engined Wellington Mark II. On 3 September its ORB reports that 'One Wellington II (Merlin) collected by S/Ldr Wells DFC, ex Shallufa – gave an exhibition over aerodrome showing how slow Wellington ICs are.' On 18 September the ORB states that the Squadron started to receive its Wellington IIs, but the new aircraft were not to prove a great success in desert conditions[10] and squadrons were later glad to have their Mark ICs back. However, the Mark IIs could carry the new 4,000-lb bombs that began to arrive in the Middle East in October, and the first of the big bombs was used in an attack on Naples from Malta on the night of 16/17 October (see next chapter).

*   *   *

When we last visited Malta we saw No. 148 Squadron being forced to abandon the island due to the *Luftwaffe* attacks. However, the short-lived success of Wavell's offensive meant that the Wellingtons could operate briefly from bases near Benghazi, and this put the main Axis supply port of Tripoli within their range. Thus, the loss of Malta as a base for the night bombers was not a great problem until Rommel's first offensive drove the bombers from their advanced bases. Now targets in Tripolitania were once more out of their range, and the port of Tripoli was now a secure supply base from which stores could be moved forward by land and sea. The Commanders-in-Chief in Egypt asked the Chiefs of Staff in the UK to consider sending a squadron of heavy bombers with sufficient range and hitting power to bomb Tripoli effectively from Egypt. However, the Chief of the Air Staff considered that it was useless to send non-tropicalized Stirlings or Manchesters 'barely through major teething troubles, and without spares, ground equipment or maintenance personnel'. Instead, he suggested that the risks involved in operating from Malta should be accepted, and the first unit to return was, appropriately, a detachment of No. 148 Squadron. On 9 April the Wing SASO was called to HQ Middle East, where he was instructed to send three aircraft to Malta, but one failed to arrive and it was presumed to have run out of fuel and ditched. Others followed over the next few days, and operations against Tripoli commenced almost immediately.

We know little about the operations of this small detachment from No. 148 Squadron, except that they appear to have flown thirty-four sorties on seven nights between 13/14 and 24/25 April.[11] In every case the target was Tripoli, and on 21 April the bombers acted 'as a precursor to a naval bombardment'. The Squadron ORB goes on to say 'this is considered a good effort considering there were no losses for the fortnights work'. Considerable damage was believed to have been caused to ships in the harbour, and the *Romaena* (149 tons) was sunk during a Wellington and Swordfish raid on 17 April. Six of the aircraft arrived back at Kabrit on 26/27, with three detained at Malta with serviceability problems. The reason for their departure was that it had been decided to station detachments of Blenheim IVs from No. 2 Group Bomber Command on Malta as these could provide a more flexible day striking force for anti-shipping and coastal operations. There were then no proper Wellington operations from Malta in May, but the Luqa ORB mentions that on 8 May 1941 four Wellingtons arrived from Gibraltar and three of them attacked Tripoli on 10 May as a diversion for Swordfish that were laying mines off the harbour. One aircraft of No. 148 Squadron also operated here, and this must have been one of those left at Luqa 'with serviceability problems'.

On 25 June six aircraft of No. 148 Squadron were again ordered to proceed to Malta to continue the bombing offensive against Tripoli, and four of them operated against the port on the night of 26/27 June. The detachment continued to operate from Malta until 20 July, when they returned to Egypt to make way for the Beaufighters of Nos 252 and 272 Squadrons. Details on the Wellington operations during this period are again rather sketchy, but No. 148 Squadron ORB has an entry on 10 August 1941 that states that the 'Squadron's effort at Malta during period 25 June to 20 July was 102 sorties, weight of bombs dropped 327,500 lbs.' The bombers mainly attacked Tripoli, and the available records from the Squadron and Luqa ORBs suggest that at least 60 per cent of the sorties were directed at this target. They also went to Naples on at least two occasions, and to Sicily (Messina and Palermo) on another two nights. The operations obviously took their toll, and a message was received from Malta on 14 July requesting 'immediate relief for detachment as all crews are tired'. On 22 July four aircraft returned to Kabrit and three more aircraft arrived on the following day, all carrying ground crew as passengers.

The next unit to go to Malta for what would turn out to be a long period was No. 38 Squadron. Nine aircraft were ordered to Malta on 5 August, and they carried out their first operation on the night of 7/8 August when six attacked Tripoli. The aircraft were over the target from 0155 to 0350 hours, dropping their bombs in sticks at intervals throughout the two hours. The normally very effective smokescreen was not as good as usual, possibly due to wind – it took twenty minutes to start and never covered the target properly. Nearly all the bombs fell in a concentrated area just west of the Spanish Mole, and at least two fires were started. Although there were no spectacular explosions, there is no doubt that the concentration and length of attack must have caused considerable disruption for the inhabitants. One aircraft was over the target for nearly an hour, and its pilot reported that there was hardly a pause in events, with bombs exploding and AA guns firing throughout. The defences did not open up until the first bombs had exploded, and both flak and searchlights were ineffective.

A pattern was quickly established, with Tripoli becoming as much of a 'mail run' as Benghazi for the Wellingtons of No. 38 Squadron. They went to Tripoli on nineteen occasions between 7/8 August and 5/6 September, flying 161 sorties. The pattern of attacks rarely varied, and neither did the reported results. The main target areas were the Spanish Quay and the Karamanli Mole, which bounded the harbour on the west and east sides respectively. The north-west area of the town came in for a great deal of attention, as the densely packed buildings west of the harbour offered a tempting target. The railway lines and station to the west and south of the town were also frequently attacked, as these served the port area and also went eastwards towards Tagiura. The power station, the Palazzo del Governatore, the Castello, the seaplane base, the municipal offices, and the post office, most of which were on or near the foreshore between the Lungomare Conte

Volpi and the Corso Vittorio Emanuele III, were all popular targets for the Wellingtons. On the way home the Wellingtons also couldn't resist using up their machine gun ammunition on any motor convoys proceeding to and from the port.

A particularly successful attack by fifteen Wellingtons took place on 29/30 August. The first aircraft to arrive at the target took the defences completely by surprise, and lights were still burning in the town. It dropped all its bombs in one stick in a dive attack that set two motor vessels fire and caused an explosion in one of them. Half an hour later a fire accompanied by explosions was started in the area south-west of the Castello. Other fires were started at the base of the Karamanli Mole, most probably from petrol tanks, as they gave off clouds of black smoke. One aircraft started a large fire, visible for 100 miles, in the area of the Petrolibia Depot. Three of the Wellingtons involved were Merlin-engined Mark IIs, each carrying 5,000 lb of bombs. One of the bombers was hit by light flak, but returned and landed safely despite a burst tyre. An aircraft attacking Tripoli on the next night reported that fires were still burning east of the harbour and near the Castello, and the two ships were smouldering in the harbour. Shores and Cull tell us that during a raid on Tripoli on the night of 31 August/1 September the 6,630-ton steamer *Riva* was sunk.

The Wellingtons from Malta also made two attacks on Catania in Sicily. On 14/15 August four Wellingtons made two sorties each against shipping in the harbour, where several hits were reported on the Central Mole but it was too dark to see the results from the first attack. In the second attack all the aircraft found the target in very clear moonlight, and most of the bombs burst on the main mole, damaging stores and the railway line. The next night nine Wellingtons went back to Catania, attacking in two waves. The first hit the town area north of the base of the Central Mole, and very few bombs were wasted. The second wave attacked the target just before dawn, dropping their bombs and incendiaries just north of the port railway station near the base of the Central Mole. Several hits were made on stores on the Mole itself, and possibly to shipping alongside. Two moderate fires were burning for some time afterwards, and one huge fire and intermittent explosions probably came from oil tanks and was still visible sixty to seventy miles away.

The Wellingtons went back to Sicily on the night of 7/8 September, when nine aircraft attacked shipping and the dock area at Palermo, the aircraft leaving in three waves at two-hour intervals. The smoke screen was in operation by the time the first aircraft arrived over the target, and the results were difficult to see. Two bursts were seen on the small jetty just to the north of the three main Moles, and one of the aircraft that found the northern dock clear of smoke saw its bombs burst on the main sheds and near the dry dock, causing a series of moderate explosions. They went back to targets in Sicily on the next four nights, bombing harbour installations at Palermo on two occasions, and ferries, landing stages and the power station at Messina on two nights. The usual fires and explosions were reported, although few results were actually observed. On 12 September seven aircraft attacked a convoy north-west of Tripoli, which they found steaming in line ahead and being circled by destroyers. No opposition was encountered until the attack began, and then the destroyers opened fire with light flak along the water, clearly expecting an attack by torpedo-carrying aircraft. The convoy dispersed and the destroyers started laying a smoke screen, but the attack was claimed to be successful, with four ships hit and fires started on two of them. On the next night one of the aircraft attacking

62

shipping alongside the Spanish Quay at Tripoli reported a large ship aground thirty to forty miles west of the port, blazing furiously. It was presumed to be one of the vessels hit during the previous night's attack.

The Wellingtons were despatched to Tripoli again on 14/15 September, with eight aircraft ordered to bomb the Spanish Quay to create a diversion, while two more laid mines in the harbour. Weather conditions were very bad, with low cloud and rain storms hampering visibility, and the first two aircraft failed to find the target after a thorough search. The weather improved slightly towards the end of the raid, but a combination of low cloud and the smoke screen still made the attack difficult. Bombs were dropped on the Quay, causing a large explosion, and the two mine-laying aircraft dropped their mines either in the centre of the harbour or near the harbour entrance. The exercise was repeated on the next night when five aircraft attacked Tripoli to cause a diversion while two Wellingtons and a few Swordfish aircraft laid mines in the harbour. The minelayers were back on 17/18 September when three aircraft caused a diversion while another two laid mines.

Operations against targets at Tripoli and Palermo continued through to the end of September, sometimes creating diversions for mine-laying by their own aircraft or by Swordfish of the Fleet Air Arm. On 22/23 September three aircraft were ordered to attack a 24,000-ton liner believed to be in the neighbourhood of Kuriat Island (in the Kouriate group, about twelve miles from the coast of Tunisia). The aircraft attacked two ships, but neither was thought to be the liner. Then, after a break of three nights, nine Wellingtons of No. 38 Squadron and two aircraft of the Special Duty Flight[12] were despatched to attack a convoy reported to be in the South Ionian Sea. The two SDF Wellingtons failed to locate the convoy, and the Squadron aircraft were no more successful. Eight of the aircraft returned to Luqa with their bombs, but the ninth went on. It had started to go home when it was overtaken by another Wellington, and thinking that this aircraft might have located the convoy, it turned around again and followed the course from which the second aircraft had come. The pilot continued on the same course for about forty minutes, but saw no ships and eventually struck the coast near Benghazi. Searchlights began to try to catch the Wellington in their beams, so the captain released all his bombs in one salvo over the harbour and set off for home once more. He returned to base with only 20 gallons of petrol left in his tanks.

Shipping and harbour installations continued to be the main targets for the Wellingtons of No. 38 Squadron, then on 10/11 October six aircraft and two of the SDF aircraft were despatched to attack a convoy sighted earlier in the day. At 2220 hours the convoy was located by the SDF aircraft and its location reported to the other aircraft. They found the convoy scattered and partly obscured by low cloud, with one vessel seen to be stopped and with a destroyer circling it. Three attacked the stationary ship, and each obtained one hit and one of them also machine-gunned the vessel. Other ships in the convoy were attacked, but only one was hit and no explosions or fires reported.

Ken Rees arrived in Malta in early October, flying a new Wellington from Shallufa. His experience illustrates very nicely that flying is a dangerous profession, even if nobody is shooting at you. He had just passed the point of no return when:

> ...in the dark ahead I could make out a line of huge clouds, cumulonimbus clouds, tall cloud-formations made partly of ice-crystals, characteristic of

thundery conditions. Not nice. There was no way around them…I was going to have to fly right through them. We were flying at around 5,000 feet, and as we entered the thick cloud I don't think I have ever experienced anything – not flak, tracer-fire, nothing – like the next ten minutes in all my years of flying. Outside the aircraft it was pitch black, and I could hear hailstones banging at the cloth fabric of our bomber, while abrupt shifts in pressure kept tossing us about as if by a large cat's paw. With the co-pilot's help I had literally to fight the controls…My arms ached as we both continued to struggle with the controls, and … suddenly we appeared to have been spat out into a relatively blue sky. I looked at the altimeter: 10,000 feet. Incredible. Even though I had put the Wimpy's nose down, the terrific up-currents … had lifted us right up about 5,000 feet, and a Wellington weighs…about 30,000 pounds.[13]

Rees comments on conditions for aircrew on the island when he arrived. The officers were in wooden huts on the airfield, as were the NCO aircrew at first. As the air raids increased in October the latter were moved to what had been the Poor House and Leper Hospital, owned by an order of nuns and fifteen minutes' walk from the airfield along the Valletta road. These were large, barn-like buildings, cold, damp and uncomfortable, and the food was extremely poor. Ken Rees comments that 'More than anything else daily life in Malta prepared me for Stalag Luft III.'

His first operation was to Naples (probably on 16/17 October – see next chapter), and the large amount of flak over the target surprised him. These were more like Northern European conditions and the gunners were probably German – although Italian artillerymen were also pretty good. He missed Malta on the way back, another hazard of operations from this small island, but eventually managed to find it again. After only three operations he was told that No. 38 Squadron was going back to Egypt, to be replaced by his old squadron, No. 40 from Alconbury (see also next chapter). Rees quickly wangled a transfer, and was to spend the next three months operating from Malta with his old unit.

*   *   *

Before we move on, it is worth taking a quick look at three operations launched against the Corinth Canal in Greece in August and September 1941, the first time that this target appears in the Middle East itinerary. A co-ordinated attempt was made by all the squadrons of No. 257 Wing to deny the enemy the use of the Canal by causing landslides to block it, and by laying mines at its eastern entrance. On 8 August a major operation was launched, with thirty-seven aircraft from four squadrons operating in what was the largest operation by the Wing to date. Ten aircraft of No. 37 Squadron and five of No. 38 Squadron were detailed to drop their bombs as near as possible to the edge of the Canal at a point 3,000 yards from its eastern end. Results were described as 'not spectacular, as all that could be seen was either a gout of earth or a flash from a bomb'. One of the Wellingtons of No. 37 Squadron ran out of petrol due to high fuel consumption caused by the bomb doors not completely closing, and came down in the sea. Their dinghy was spotted by a Maryland, but no surface vessel was available to pick them up. Eventually, they managed to reach the shore at El Daba by their own efforts after being adrift for over fourteen hours.

During the operation six aircraft of No. 148 Squadron were detailed to lay mines in the Canal, and five others to act as decoys to draw AA fire. The minelayers laid eight mines, dropping them from fifty feet, and one was hit in the front turret, badly injuring the front gunner. Most of the other minelayers also suffered some damage from the intense flak over the target. One of the aircraft brought one mine back due to a failure of the electrical release mechanism, and another jettisoned a mine due to damage sustained by the aircraft and casualties to the crew incurred on its first run. A sixth aircraft jettisoned both its mines due to petrol shortage. The Squadron ORB reports that 'All flying crews returned with their tails up and thought it was grand fun'! Reconnaissance after the bombing led to the conclusion that, overall, a fairly good job had been done, and later reports suggested that the Canal would be closed for about one month.

While all this was going on eleven aircraft of No. 70 Squadron attacked a variety of targets in support of the operations. Two were detailed to bomb targets at the centre of the Canal, but one of these was forced to return to base due to a failure of his petrol gauges. On the way back the starboard engine cut, compelling him to land in the desert. The other attacked the entrance to the Corinth Canal, where bursts followed by clouds of dust were observed. Six aircraft attacked targets at Isthmia as a cover for the mine-laying, and also machine-gunned enemy flak positions. One building was set on fire, followed by explosions and much smoke. One attacked Crete, dropping its bombs on the beaches near Pyrgos on the south coast without visible effect, and two attacked the airfield at Eleusis, where bursts were observed on a runway and buildings west of the landing ground, followed by explosions and fires.

On 13 August the aircraft carried out another 'maximum effort' attack on the banks of the Corinth Canal. Ten aircraft of No. 37 Squadron, six of No. 38 Squadron, and eight of No. 70 Squadron participated, two carrying 1,000-lb bombs, and the remainder a mixture of 500-lb and 250-lb bombs. One did not reach the Canal as the starboard engine began to splutter north of Crete, and he jettisoned his bombs into the sea. Four dropped one 250-lb bomb each on the airfield at Heraklion as they passed over it, but no results were observed. Nine of the aircraft bombed in the target area, where bombs were seen to hit the banks of the canal and cause at least one collapse. One aircraft reported 'that the canal was completely blocked', but most results were not observed. Ten aircraft of No. 148 Squadron, some carrying mines as before, were also 'detailed for operations against Corinth Canal as part of the combined Wing effort', but no other comment is made in the Squadron ORB.

A few weeks later, on 8 September, seven aircraft of No. 37 Squadron, ten of No. 70 Squadron, and nine of No. 148 Squadron were again ordered to attack the Corinth Canal. Although most of the bombs were reported to have fallen in the Canal and on the banks, few positive results were observed. Considerable clouds of dust were seen, and one large fire was observed 300 yards north of the canal. One aircraft noted that the bank had slipped into the Canal for 200 yards, blocking half the width. The reports of the crews returning from all these attacks gave every indication that the desired results had been obtained, but later evidence showed that the Canal was never closed by these raids.

*   *   *

In the 213 days/nights between 24 March and 13 October 1941 the night bombers operated on a total of 192 of those nights and launched 2,361 sorties. There were only four squadrons operating until August, when No. 108 Squadron was reformed in Egypt and joined the fray. It only contributed one sortie in August, and did not get into its stride until October. However, the average number of sorties per squadron did not increase greatly until the build-up and support for the *Crusader* battles commenced late in October (see next chapter). Attacks on ports and ships in harbour took up 69 per cent of the effort, with Benghazi the main target in this respect – about half of the total effort was directed at the port. At various times Tripoli also came in for close attention, and a few sorties were despatched to ports in Italy and Greece. Airfields were the next significant target type, involving 22 per cent of the sorties despatched.

On 21 May No. 38 Squadron ORB records that they received a postagram from No. 257 Wing, giving a copy of a signal from the AOC in C, RAF Headquarters Middle East, reading:

> Please tell all personnel of your Squadron how deeply I admire the magnificent effort they have made during the last three weeks operations. They have operated under difficult and novel conditions, sometimes far from their normal bases and facilities, and once again have unshrinkingly upheld our Service tradition of being able to tackle any emergency. We are passing through a critical phase of the war and it may well be that the blows struck by your Squadrons may prove to have a vital effect on the course of the war. For the past I can only say you have done grand work. For the future I wish you good hunting.

On 8/9 October an American war correspondent (Harold Denny) was on board an aircraft piloted by Pilot Officer I.D.M. Lawson, and the No. 148 Squadron ORB comments that the correspondent wrote in the *New York Times* that: 'My airplane's captain was the typical well-bred young English and public school and University man, member of a family of famous English airplane manufacturers.' The ORB sees fit to add three exclamation marks after Pilot Officer Lawson's name!!!

NOTES

1. The Wing took operational control of No. 148 Squadron on 29 March 1941.
2. Five aircraft were attacking Tripoli and another three went to airfields on Rhodes. The latter three were diverted to Mersa Matruh due to the sandstorm. However, it had subsided somewhat as the five aircraft from Tripoli came in, and they landed safely between 0700 and 0750 hours, despite the chaos that reigned around them.
3. They did not operate, but were instead directed to retire to Shallufa via Fuka satellite.
4. Robert Lyman, *First Victory*, page 76.
5. From *Dust in the Lion's Paw*, Freya Stark, page 91. It is assumed that she was commenting on the dawn raid on 4 May.
6. A blood chit is a note carried by military personnel, usually aircrew, with a message aimed at civilians that asks them to help the crew member if they are shot down. It also usually carries the promise of a monetary reward if they do so.
7. These were all Advanced Landing Grounds used at various times by most of the Wellington squadrons.
8. The garrison at Tobruk was naturally quick on the trigger during the siege of April to December 1941, particularly at night.

9. Ken Rees, *Lie In the Dark and Listen*, page 58. Rees eventually returned to Bomber Command in the UK and was shot down in October 1942. He was in Stalag Luft III (Sagan) at the time of the 'Great Escape' and was one of the men who dug the tunnels, but he didn't get out himself.

10. See Appendix III for further details of the various Wellington types used by the squadrons of No. 257 Wing/No. 205 Group.

11. The Squadron ORB records that 'as far as can be ascertained' approximately forty sorties were carried out by the Squadron during its detachment to Malta, but the author can only find thirty-four in the Luqa ORB.

12. The Special Duties Flight (SDF) was a small formation of ASV-radar equipped Wellingtons that were sent to Malta in September 1941 to increase the effectiveness of the anti-shipping operations.

13. *Lie in the Dark and Listen*, page 59.

CHAPTER FOUR

Operation *Crusader* – November 1941 to May 1942

As the month of October came to an end there was a major change in the administration of the heavy bomber squadrons in the Middle East. On 31 October 1941 the Operational Record Book for No. 257 (Heavy Bomber) Wing suddenly comes to an end, and the next page for 1 November (Page No. 126) is headed No. 205 (Heavy Bomber) Group. There is nothing else to mark the beginnings of the Group in the ORB, but this was a significant date in the history of the night bombers in the Middle East and Mediterranean theatre. The ORB for RAF Middle East tells us that the Group was formed in place of No. 257 (Heavy Bomber) Wing with effect from 23 October at RAF Station Shallufa. The new Group remained under the control of Group Captain (later Air Commodore) L.L. MacLean, and it would control the five Wellington squadrons in Egypt:

Nos 37 and 38 Squadrons at Shallufa

No. 70 Squadron at Kabrit

Nos 108 and 148 Squadrons at Fayid

No. 38 Squadron had just ended a long stint on Malta, and its aircraft only began to move back to Shallufa on 25 October. Its place on Malta was taken by a unit new to the Mediterranean theatre, No. 104 Squadron, and for a few days the two units operated together. The advance party from No. 104 Squadron had left Driffield on 14 October in a Wellington Mk II and flown to Stanton Harcourt under the command of the redoubtable Squadron Leader H.M. 'Dinghy' Young.[1] On the following day another twelve aircraft moved to Stanton Harcourt and three to Portreath, and should have left for Malta on the 16th, but adverse weather reports delayed their departure. Eventually, six left on the following night and arrived safely at Malta, and a seventh aircraft followed from Portreath. These were all Wellington Mk IIs, capable of carrying 4,000-lb 'blockbuster' bombs, and all flew direct to Malta without needing to break the journey at Gibraltar. They didn't have long to settle in. Six operated on 19/20 October against Tripoli, along with eleven aircraft of No. 38 Squadron.

After No. 38 Squadron moved back to Egypt, No. 104 Squadron carried on alone for a few days, but further reinforcements were already arriving. On 23 October 1941 No. 3 Group ORB reported that it had been decided that No. 40 Squadron 'should be posted abroad for temporary duty in the Middle East'. The Squadron was not in good shape at this time, having just lost six crews in three operations, and only had eight trained crews and two freshmen on its strength. No further operations were flown after 16 October, and six new crews arrived to bring the operational strength up to sixteen. The decision was taken for the Squadron to fly direct to Malta, as No. 104 Squadron had done, with each aircraft taking as much equipment and as many ground personnel as possible. The first flight of eight aircraft left Alconbury on the night of 23/24 October, but one of them failed to arrive and was found to have run out of fuel and ditched north of Sicily. Six aircrew and three passengers died; there was only one survivor, washed ashore unconscious on the coast of Sicily.

The next flight was scheduled for take-off on the night of 25/26 October, this time routed via Gibraltar and taking off from Hampstead Norris – a small OTU field. The first two aircraft got off, but both the heavily laden Wellingtons were damaged by hitting the hedgerows and small trees at the end of the take-off run. The third crashed after taking off and burned out – all ten occupants were killed. It was clear that fully loaded Wellington ICs could not operate safely from Hampstead Norris, and the departure of the remaining aircraft was cancelled. They eventually left via Portreath, and while at Portreath Squadron Leader Bill Craigen got a signal from the Air Ministry to go into Redruth and pick up all the Sanatogen nerve tonic that he could lay his hands on for the Governor of Malta! Six of the nine aircraft that had arrived in Malta operated on the night of 29/30 October, against the marshalling yards at Tripoli.

The headquarters of the new No. 205 Group in Egypt was thrown straight away into the build up for Operation *Crusader*, the planning for which had been underway for some time. The Air Plan for *Crusader* fell into four phases:[2]

1. A 'softening up' period of approximately thirty days (D-35 to D-6 inclusive), commencing on 14 October.

2. A period of about six days (D-5 to D-day, 13 November to 18 November) during which the Army was to concentrate and move forwards.

3. A period of approximately five days (D+1 to D+5, 19 to 28 November) was then allowed to cover the battle between the opposing armoured forces and the relief of Tobruk.

4. A subsequent unpredetermined period (D+6 onwards) covering the enemy's retreat.

The Plan emphasized the importance of disrupting the enemy's supplies, and the central roles of Benghazi and Tripoli in the supply system. Thus, as far as the night bombers were concerned, nothing would change very much once the Air Plan for *Crusader* was put into effect. Their job was always to do all they could to help win the war in North Africa, and there were very few ways in which they could affect the outcome of the fighting on the ground. Their main contribution was to disrupt the enemy's supply system, and the best way that they could do this was by bombing the ports at which the supplies were landed. Their main secondary task was to bomb airfields to try to disrupt the activities of the Axis air forces, and occasionally they might be able to assist the ground forces by bombing enemy concentrations in the desert. Whatever might be happening on the ground, it was to the ports and airfields that the bombers would have to go. As we shall see, the *Crusader* battle did not go according to plan, and Phase Three, in fact, lasted until 16 December. However, this mattered little to the night bombers, which simply went about their business of bombing ports and airfields.

Thus, the night bombers in Egypt kept on going back to Benghazi, which was the 'railhead' for the enemy forces in Cyrenaica. Supplies of food, ammunition and petrol were shipped by fast convoy from Italy to Tripoli and then transferred by coastal shipping to Benghazi, although in some instances road convoys made the journey directly to the forward areas. Derna was sometimes used as a staging post between Benghazi and the front line, and the forward delivery points for stores were situated along the road between Gazala and Tobruk. On the night when the 'softening up' was supposed to begin, the Wellingtons in Egypt were all grounded due to a severe dust storm that blew up over the Western Desert. Then on 15/16 October seventeen aircraft went to Benghazi, bombing the Giuliana district, the Moles, and the railway sidings. Between this date and the end of the month the Wellingtons in Egypt flew sixty-four sorties to Benghazi, but most of the attacks were by small numbers of aircraft and mainly intended to have a nuisance value.

Although the Wellington effort resulted in further damage to the port facilities and virtually stopped off-loading at night, the attempt to hit ships in the harbour proved most difficult. On 4 November Tedder reported:

> The relatively small ships which go into Benghazi are poor targets – though we know the heavies got one petrol and one ammunition ship (the gap in the outer mole which the latter blew up must be a nuisance now when winds are fresh). Ships come in at dawn and lie outside at night, and as far as possible material is…cleared from the wharves during daylight.[3]

It was originally intended that the bomber forces should be conserved for a maximum effort for three nights around D-Day itself (17/18 to 19/20 November), but Tedder felt that this was too risky as this was a moonless period and there was a chance that the weather would deteriorate.[4] It was therefore decided that the Wellingtons should operate at maximum effort from the night of 5/6 November, still concentrating on shipping and the port facilities at Benghazi and Tripoli. On this night twenty-seven aircraft went to Benghazi and started large petrol fires on the Giuliana Mole, but other results were unobserved due to intense searchlight activity. On the next night the target for twenty aircraft was Derna, where bombs fell in the vicinity of the post office and one explosion was so severe that it lifted the aircraft. Some of the aircraft attacked MT (Military Transport) and workshops on the landing ground at Derna, where fires were started among buildings and dispersed vehicles. During the three nights 13/14 to 15/16 November the Wellington effort was continued against the enemy's supply organization, attacking storage dumps at Berka and Bardia, stores and MT workshops at Derna, and the harbour installations at Benghazi. The Wellingtons in Egypt also attacked the airfields at Berka, Derna, Benina and Martuba, although the weather was often poor and hampered both the scale and the success of the effort against these targets. As the date for the start of *Crusader* drew near, the airfields close to the Axis front line at Martuba, Gazala, Tmimi and El Adem were also attacked.

In all, the Wellingtons in Egypt launched 428 sorties between 14 October and 18 November, 329 of which went to the ports and almost all of these went to Benghazi. Another ninety-three sorties were directed at the airfields. Two firsts occurred during this period. No. 148 Squadron had been re-equipped with Merlin-engined Wellington Mk IIs from September 1941, and could now carry the 4,000-lb bombs that began to arrive in the Middle East in October. No. 38 Squadron on Malta, also equipped with some Mk IIs, had already used the big bombs in an attack on Naples on the night of 16/17 October (see below), and now it was to be Benghazi's turn. Three 'special' aircraft of No. 148 Squadron took 'these bombs 12 ft long and 3 ft across' to the port on 7/8 November. Of the three 'specials', one was forced to jettison its bomb into the sea, one bombed Bardia as an alternative, and one did not return and was found to have force-landed in the desert. Not an auspicious start.

On the following day two Fortresses of No. 90 Squadron bombed Benghazi in the first bombing operation by these aircraft in the Middle East. The Squadron had tried to use the Fortress I by day from the UK, but this early version of the aircraft was not well suited to daylight operations over Europe and a detachment of four aircraft was then sent to try its luck in the Middle East. The AHB Narrative *The Middle East Campaigns* states that 'steps were taken to press into service the small force of Flying Fortresses as soon as possible' to supplement the daylight bombing effort, but their performance was 'disappointing'.[5] Three of them were prepared for their first operation on the night of 7/8 November, but only with great difficulty. The bombing up took twelve hours, and one developed engine trouble due to an internal leak in a petrol tank and was unable to take part in the attack. The other two took off for Benghazi, and were over the target between 1245 and 1310 hours. Some of the bombs had to be 'kicked off over Soluch owing to the bomb release being frozen', and one of the aircraft ran out of fuel on the way home and forced-landed west of Fort Maddelena. The captain of the aircraft that got back to base reported that the flying performance was much inferior to that expected. The rate of climb was poor and the engines over-heated, and it appeared that the warm conditions over the desert affected performance. Another inauspicious start.

The crew of the missing aircraft was eventually discovered by Marylands of No. 12 Squadron SAAF, which dropped supplies and water, and later led a Lysander of No. 208 Squadron to the scene. It picked up the Fortress's captain, and a ground column brought back the remainder of the crew after destroying any instruments that had escaped damage when the crew set fire to the aircraft. It was learned that shortage of petrol had caused the forced landing, and the aircraft that had returned was also found to have virtually no fuel left in its tanks. The Squadron flew two or three more sorties with their Fortresses, the last one coming on 19 November when a single aircraft bombed Derna through 10/10th cloud. They relinquished them soon afterwards and the aircraft and crews were reallocated to No. 220 Squadron. This unit continued to operate them in a maritime reconnaissance role in the theatre until 9 March 1943.

The bombers on Malta also played their part during the early phases of the Air Plan for *Crusader*, their main targets being the ports at the western and southern ends of the enemy's supply lines – Naples and Tripoli. There were no operations on 14/15 or 15/16 October, and No. 38 Squadron's involvement in the 'softening up' began on the next night with an attack by sixteen aircraft on Naples. This attack was noteworthy in that three 4,000-lb bombs were dropped for the first time in the Mediterranean theatre. The first two aircraft started fires that led the others to the port, and when the last Wellingtons arrived over the target it was well alight. Bombs fell on the Valiana Torpedo Factory, which was reported to be almost completely destroyed by fire. Other bombs hit the Royal Arsenal, railway lines and engine sheds, the IMAM airframe factory and other factory buildings in and around the main target area. On the next night three aircraft attacked the airfields at Trapani (Sicily) and Elmas (Sardinia). At Trapani, bombs were seen to fall among buildings at the end of the runway, starting a steady fire visible for forty-five miles, and at Elmas bombs fell on the runways, barracks and in the dispersal area. Results at both targets were difficult to observe due to the fact that a high proportion delayed action bombs were dropped.

No. 104 Squadron operated for the first time on 19/20 October when six aircraft went to Tripoli, along with eleven aircraft of No. 38 Squadron. Bombs fell across the Custom House, in the native quarter and on warehouses, with fires started and one large explosion reported. Another seven aircraft arrived from the UK on 20 October, and thirteen operated against Naples with eleven of No. 38 Squadron on the night of 21/22 October. One of the Squadron's Wellingtons crashed on landing, resulting in the death of the front gunner, and the captain and three other crew members were taken to hospital, one severely injured. Six of the nine aircraft of No. 40 Squadron that had now arrived in Malta operated on the night of 29/30 October, against the marshalling yards at Tripoli.

On 31 October four aircraft of No. 104 Squadron were ordered to attack a convoy located by the SDF, and their efforts proved very successful. The convoy was sighted at 2330 hours, comprising two merchant ships and a destroyer. Six hits were obtained on the stern of a large ship, which was practically brought to a stop, issuing clouds of white and black smoke from its stern. Their efforts earned the following signal from AOC Mediterranean Command:

> For Wing Commander Beare, 104 Squadron. Will you please congratulate the crews for me, who were engaged on bombing the convoy last night. It is not an easy job to find the convoy, quite apart from hitting it. They managed to do both. Well done. A first class performance.

Between 14 October and the end of the month the Wellingtons on Malta flew fifty-six sorties to Naples, fifty-eight to Tripoli, six to Palermo on Sicily, and seven to the airfields at Trapani (Sicily) and Elmas (Sardinia). They launched another 155 sorties between 1 and 18 November, with Naples attacked on seven occasions during this period, and a few sorties going to Tripoli. On 8/9 November seventeen aircraft attacked Naples, but clouds obscured the target area and prevented observation of results in many cases. In another attack on 11/12 November an aircraft of No. 40 Squadron was shot down by two MC.200s that were scrambled over the Bay of Naples. Many of these attacks on Naples and Tripoli were by small numbers of aircraft, and were designed to have a nuisance value rather than to cause much damage in the target areas. The Wellingtons also turned their attentions to Brindisi, the most important port in the Southern Adriatic and from which the enemy was sending convoys direct to Benghazi. A major attack that was delivered on the night of 7/8 November by twenty-one Wellingtons was described as 'highly successful', with hits registered on the marshalling yards, railway station, tracks, sea-plane factory and barracks.

In spite of bad weather over North Africa the Malta-based bombers also exerted pressure on the enemy's rear air bases in Tripolitania. The main effort was directed against Castel Benito, which was attacked on two nights by a total of thirty-nine Wellingtons. In the attack on 2/3 November a considerable number of aircraft were seen dispersed around the airfield. Many were destroyed and fires were started in hangars and administrative buildings. The aircraft of No. 40 Squadron went in at low level after bombing and strafed aircraft and buildings, and Sergeant C.A. Armstrong won an immediate DFM for the attack. One Wellington failed to return, and is believed to have been shot down by Italian night fighters. Three nights later ten Wellingtons of No. 104 Squadron attacked the airfields at Mellaha and Castel Benito, and one of the aircraft machine-gunned barracks about eight miles west of Tripoli on the way to the target.

*   *   *

At dawn on 18 November three British Armoured Brigades crossed the frontier into Cyrenaica in torrential rain and dust storms, which effectively covered their initial advance. They moved to a central position near Gabr Saleh to await an anticipated counter-attack by the German Panzer Divisions. However, Rommel believed that the move was just a reconnaissance in force, and remained focussed on launching another attack on Tobruk. Thus, the Germans did not react as expected, and as the official history puts it, the British 'were in the odd position of possessing the initiative, and, because the enemy did not act, of being uncertain how to use it.'[6] Some confused and indecisive fighting between the armoured forces of both sides followed over the next two of days, the most significant result of which was that elements of the 7th Armoured Division occupied the airfield at Sidi Rezegh. This threatened the Axis positions around Tobruk, and Rommel ordered the whole DAK to attack the troops holding the airfield.

The three days of fighting at Sidi Rezegh were the fiercest yet seen in the desert. The battle for the airfield and escarpment was one of confusion, rapid changes in the situation, and of smoke, dust and noise. Tanks of both sides made sudden appearances, first from one direction and then from another. Ground was won, lost and won again. Four Victoria Crosses were won, and Brigadier J.C. 'Jock' Campbell of the 7th Armoured Division Support Group became a desert legend. Generally, the Germans had the better of the fighting, and by 23 November the Eighth Army was just about hanging on and its commander, General Cunningham, was reaching the end of his tether.

The third phase of the Air Plan for *Crusader* had only allowed five days (D+1 to D+5, 19 to 23 November) for the land battle, which it was hoped would include the defeat of the Axis armour and the relief of Tobruk. As attacks against the port installations at Benghazi would have little immediate influence once the land battle was joined, it was decided, initially, that the night bombers should concentrate on supply dumps near Benghazi and Derna. However, as the AHB Narrative remarks, 'a dump in the middle of the desert is as bad a target as it is possible to choose' for a night attack,[7] and the bombers were therefore directed to attack airfields instead. Forty-five aircraft from Egypt were despatched to Derna and Bardia on 19/20 November, but the weather was bad and few results were observed. One of the aircraft from No. 38 Squadron crashed at El-Imayid and blew up, killing all of the crew. Another was abandoned after getting lost on the return trip, and all made successful parachute descents. At dawn they gathered around their burning aircraft, which had crashed nearby, and then started to walk north, thinking that they were not far from the coast. They were eventually rescued at 1100 hours on 22 November by a patrol from the Egyptian Army.

In a change of routine for the Malta bombers, three aircraft were detailed to attack supply dumps at Benghazi on 19/20 November. Another five carried out nuisance raids on Naples, four went to Brindisi, and one went to Messina. A large fire in the vicinity of the railway junction at Naples was still visible thirty-five miles away, and hits on the oil storage tanks at Brindisi caused a series of explosions and columns of dense black smoke that were visible for 200 miles on the bombers' return journey. On the next night thirty-four aircraft from Egypt attacked the landing grounds at Gazala and roads nearby. Eight aircraft also left Luqa to carry out further nuisance raids on Brindisi and Naples, but the weather was poor and most attacked the alternative target at Messina. One aircraft reported starting a big fire in the target area, but few results were observed due to an effective smokescreen.

On 21/22 November sixteen aircraft from Malta attacked a convoy, but no actual hits were obtained due to a smokescreen laid by the escorting destroyers. However, the convoy scattered during the attack, which would have slowed them down somewhat. Meanwhile, the Wellingtons kept up their attacks on the airfields while the fighting at Sidi Rezegh and Tobruk was at its height. On 22/23 November nine aircraft from Egypt attacked Benina, bombing dispersal areas and hangars and a large concentration of tents and troops half a mile north of the airfield. Six aircraft from Malta attacked the nearby Berka Satellite landing ground. On 23/24 November five aircraft from Luqa attacked the airfield at Castel Benito, where excellent results were claimed. Twelve aircraft from Egypt attacked the airfields at Benina and Berka, causing 'a terrific explosion followed by a large billowing red fire' at Benina, and small fires and explosions at Berka.

Thus, the time originally allowed for the third phase of the Air Plan for *Crusader* came to an end with the Axis armour undefeated and Tobruk unrelieved. On 24 November Rommel launched the so-called 'dash to the wire' – a counter-attack over the Egyptian frontier into the British rear areas designed to relieve the pressure on his beleaguered forces in front of Tobruk. Cunningham was now near panic, and asked permission to pull back, but Auchinleck insisted that he stand his ground. He soon relieved him of his command and replaced him with General Ritchie. By late afternoon Rommel had reached the frontier, with the whole Afrika Korps strung out behind him for over forty miles. His audacious move failed as the panzers outran their supplies and ran into increasing resistance, and he had no recourse other than to call off the escapade after spending three days on the frontier. The fourth phase of the Air Plan had envisaged that by now the enemy would be defeated and in retreat, but the fighting south-east of Tobruk and at Sidi Rezegh, El Duda and Belhamed continued with unabated ferocity. On 27 November the New Zealand Division briefly linked up with the Tobruk garrison, but Rommel came back on the scene and drove them from Sidi Rezegh and severed the link.

Meanwhile, the night bombers in Egypt paid their ritual visits to Benghazi. On 24/25 November fourteen Wellingtons attacked the port, and a 'highly successful raid was made'. Bombs fell at the base of the Cathedral Mole and on warehouses in the harbour, but effective searchlight activity prevented observation of most results. The bombers also attacked the harbours at Bardia and Derna, with the port and landing ground at Derna receiving particular attention. The enemy were flying fuel from Eleusis to Derna, and submarines were also bringing in aviation fuel to the port. The Wellingtons attacked Derna on the night of 26/27, but 'no outstanding results' were claimed. On the following night fifteen aircraft attacked the landing ground, and started many fires among dispersed aircraft and tents. On 27/28 November twenty aircraft from Malta carried out an extremely successful attack on the Royal Arsenal at Naples. Several hits were obtained on the torpedo factory, airframe works, oil tanks, railway station and marshalling yards. Terrific explosions were caused, and fires were visible fifty miles away. Smoke from three burning oil storage tanks reached a height of 3,000 feet. One of the Wellingtons had an encounter with two enemy fighters and ditched on approaching Luqa, but the crew were all picked up the next morning by the Kalafrana rescue service.

Further attacks on Benghazi were made on 29/30 November and 1/2 December, but the target was obscured by cloud, and searchlights and flak were particularly effective. Between 24 November and 1 December the Wellingtons in Egypt and on Malta flew 160 sorties to Benghazi in six major attacks, making it extremely difficult to move anything through the port at night. The bomb loads included an increasing number of 1,000-lb and 4,000-lb bombs, and the targets attacked included the moles, harbour installations, railway sidings and shipping. One Wellington failed to return from these operations and another crashed on landing, but these were insignificant casualties considering the intensity of the anti-aircraft fire and the 'tenacious searchlights'.

In early December the Wellingtons in Egypt began to attack troop concentrations and motor transport near El Adem and on the El Adem–Acroma–Gazala road. The landing grounds at Derna, El Adem, Benina and El Magrun were also attacked. On 3/4 December Wellingtons and Fleet Air Arm Albacores from Egypt were directed against enemy positions and MT as a preliminary to an imminent ground offensive on the El Adem area. Twenty-four aircraft attacked between 2005 and 2255 hours, and direct hits were claimed on hangar buildings and among vehicles concentrated nearby. In the second attack nine aircraft bombed and machine-gunned tents and transport between 0326 and 0440 hours. Advanced HQ Western Desert commented that:

> Our troops had a grandstand view of the whole bombardment. They were much impressed. The moral support was as great as the material damage.

From 3 December to the night of the 8/9th the Wellington squadrons carried out 101 sorties in direct support of the troops on the ground, mainly bombing the enemy's 'vulnerable tail of transport and supply' along the El Adem–Acroma–Gazala road. A few Wellingtons extended their activities to Derna, and even as far as Benghazi. By now the *Afrika Korps* was only a skeleton of its former self, and Rommel finally acknowledged that he would have to withdraw. Tobruk was relieved on 10 December, and by December 12 Rommel had retreated to a defensive position at Gazala.

Attacks on Benghazi were also carried out by the two Squadrons on Malta on three nights in December, on the 10/11th, 13/14th and 14/15th, by a total of twenty-six aircraft. The attack on 13/14 December by eight aircraft of No. 40 Squadron was a minelaying mission, and Bruce Holloway stated that:

> ... our spirits dropped, especially when we found out it was a special job of minelaying in the harbour. This had never been attempted before and it was a dangerous job. The idea being for four machines to approach the harbour at 500 feet and drop their mines while another four flew low over the target and draw the searchlights and ack-ack fire.[8]

The Tripoli area, including the airfields at Castel Benito and Misurata, was bombed on nine nights, on one occasion as a diversion for another minelaying operation. On 5/6 and 6/7 December a total of thirty Wellingtons went to Naples, bombing the arsenal, torpedo factory, marshalling yards, and docks. One of the aircraft of No. 40 Squadron was shot down by an Italian fighter over the city after a long running battle. The pilot and one crew member baled out, but the other four were killed. Another, piloted by Flight Lieutenant S. Storey, was also attacked by a night fighter, but drove it off and returned safely to base. He had already been credited with shooting down four enemy aircraft in the Battle of France when flying Blenheims, and was later awarded the DFC. On 11/12 December six aircraft were despatched to attack shipping in the harbour at Patras in Greece, but two returned without dropping their bombs due to 10/10 cloud over the target area. Black smoke was reported drifting from a ship north of the quay, and another vessel was also bombed without results being observed.

On 7 December 1941 No. 148 Squadron ORB records an incident that says a great deal about the strain of operating the Wellingtons in the Middle East at this time. Flight Lieutenant Culley was placed under close arrest for disobeying an order given by Wing Commander Rainsford. It seems that the Flight Lieutenant was not currently 'crewed up', but entered himself as rear gunner in an aircraft operating on the night of 7/8 December. When the officer commanding 'A' Flight, Flight Lieutenant Baird, asked him his reasons for doing this, Culley said that he wanted to operate and thought that he would detail himself. Flight Lieutenant Baird tried to explain to him that this could not be done, but Culley 'became very truculent' and Baird told him that he would have to be reported to the CO The latter interviewed Culley, and 'told him that he was resting him from operational flying with effect from today'. The CO also congratulated him on his work with the Squadron.

Culley said that he did not wish to return to England, and wanted to continue on operations. The CO 'was very tolerant, but when Culley became truculent he was dismissed'. The Flight Lieutenant then walked out to the aircraft at about midnight and sat in the turret. The Adjutant spoke to him and told him to return to the Mess, but Culley refused and said that he was operating tonight and until the aircraft went off he was going to sit in his turret. The Adjutant, 'fearing that Culley was suffering mental stress', notified the CO, who went out to the aircraft and ordered Culley to get out of the turret. Culley then became 'very argumentative and refused to do so', and was eventually placed under close arrest and taken to his room under escort. On 9 December poor Culley proceeded to HQ Middle East to attend a medical board, and there is no further mention of him in the Squadron ORB. However, there are many reports of sickness and of men being 'operationally tired' at this time, and this was probably as much due to the difficult conditions under which they had to operate as to the actual operations themselves.

*   *   *

On the first day of Operation *Crusader*, as the armour crossed the frontier and moved deep into the German positions, two Wellingtons flew overhead, low and slow, to and fro over the enemy lines. They were part of a detachment from No. 109 Squadron, popularly known as 'Winston's Wellingtons', and their task was to try to jam radio communications on the 28 to 34 megacyles wave band used by the enemy armoured columns. Exactly who came up with the idea (code-named Operation *Jostle*) is not known, and whether Winston Churchill played any major role in the Wellingtons' deployment is doubtful, but it was the sort of operation that would have delighted the fertile imagination of the Prime Minister. Certainly, there were those in the Air Ministry who believed that the jamming of the radio communications was possible, and that it would therefore seriously disorganize the activities of the panzers. These Wellingtons would eventually form the basis of a new unit, No. 162 Squadron, which would operate in the Middle East and Mediterranean theatre until September 1944.

The history of No. 109 Squadron is an interesting one. Prior to and during the Battle of Britain it was discovered that the Germans were using radio beams to guide their bombers to their targets in Britain. In order to identify the frequencies and directions of these beams a unit was set up in October 1940 called the Wireless Intelligence Development Unit, and on 10 December it was re-designated as No. 109 Squadron, based at Boscombe Down in Wiltshire. Under the control of No. 80 (Signals) Wing, the Squadron carried out a variety of tasks, including the location of new enemy radio beams and bombing the sources of known beams. It was also involved in the development of various other radio countermeasures, and of the *Oboe* blind bombing equipment. In the late autumn of 1941 it was given its new role in the Middle East theatre, jamming the communications between the enemy armoured columns. The wide open spaces over which the columns operated ruled out ground jamming, so the use of aircraft was proposed for this purpose. No. 80 Wing was given just two weeks to produce the necessary aircraft and get them and their crews out to the Middle East.

This was a totally new kind of operation for the Squadron, and new equipment would have to be built and installed and the crews trained in its use. The radio equipment would consist of standard RAF sets converted by the Marconi-Ekco company with assistance from the Telecommunications Research Establishment:

> With the use of a *Hoover* motor it was eventually found possible to convert a general purpose transmitter to emit musical jamming tones over 28–34 MCS wavebands; the power came from an ASV alternator specially fitted into the aircraft.[9]

The transmitters went under the name 'Jostle', which subsequently became the code name covering all such jamming activities in Bomber Command. Six new Wellingtons were procured for the Squadron, suitably modified to provide peak performance under tropical conditions. The Squadron also had to design, make and fit a special aerial, and to decide where all the jamming equipment would be installed in the aircraft. The aerial was said to be 'akin to a section of an old iron bedstead', made of three-inch brass tube, some seven foot in length, and let down in flight through a hole made in the bottom of the fuselage.

The first three Wellingtons were prepared within eight days, and the first crew formed solely from No. 109 Squadron personnel. The other two crews were made up of personnel drafted in from Bomber Command, and the three aircraft left Harwell on 15 October 1941. Another three aircraft, also crewed from Bomber Command, were similarly fitted out, and all six aircraft were in place in the Middle East and ready to operate by the end of October. Known as No. 109 Squadron Detachment, Middle East, the whole party was under the command of Squadron

Leader W.B.S. Simpson from No. 80 Wing. The delayed start of the *Crusader* operation provided a useful breathing space for the crews to become more familiar with their equipment and their new operating environment over the Western Desert. On 14 November three of the Wellingtons moved to LG 75, about thirty miles south of Sidi Barrani, followed two days later by the other three aircraft. The hope was that the aircraft would be able to jam all German inter-tank signals between armoured units over a range of about twenty to thirty miles. The Wellingtons would have to fly by day over or near the battle area, and this was clearly going to be a very dangerous occupation. It had been recognized that fighter escort might be needed for these operations, but there was a lot for the few fighters in the Middle East to do at the time, and escorts were rarely available in the right place at the right time.

There was a promising start when the first two sorties took place over the Sidi Omar area on 20 November, with the jammers operating for two-and-a-half hours. Prisoners taken at the time reported that their efforts had caused a breakdown of tank-to-tank communications. The Squadron put up four sorties the next day, carrying out eight hours of jamming in the Fort Capuzzo area, but it also experienced its first casualty. One of the Wellingtons failed to return, and was probably shot down by MC.202 fighters. It contained Lieutenant Colonel R.P.G. Denman, the top War Office specialist in radio countermeasures. Another was badly damaged in a running battle with three Macchi 200 fighters that left its rear turret useless and the wireless operator wounded. The damage was so extensive that the aircraft was unable to take part in any further operations.

Thus, after just two days of operations over the Western Desert the detachment was down to only four aircraft. Things soon got worse when in a further series of long sorties over the El Adem area one Wellington was posted missing and another was damaged in combat with as many as nine Macchi 200s. Despite the attacks, the pilot continued with his mission for a further hour. An enemy air attack on one of No. 109 Squadron's landing grounds created further problems when another two Wellingtons were badly damaged by bombs. Nevertheless, the remaining two aircraft kept up the jamming operations. In the end, Operation *Jostle* spanned a five-week period from 18 November to Christmas Eve, and a total of twenty-two sorties were flown. The surviving aircraft were released by the Eighth Army on 23 December 1941, but continued to operate from Kabrit on special wireless investigation flights under the control of No. 205 Group. In January 1942 the flight became the 'Signals Squadron', and was eventually given the numberplate of No. 162 Squadron. It was involved mainly in radio calibration and radio counter measures activities, identifying enemy radar and radio installations and then jamming them. The Squadron's aircraft often figured in 205 Group ORB, carrying out various 'special' reconnaissance operations. During the emergency in June and July 1942 it carried out many normal bombing missions, and, in fact, routinely carried bombs on most of its radio intelligence operations as well.

*   *   *

The fourth phase of the Air Plan for *Crusader* – the pursuit of a defeated enemy – had been projected to begin on D+6 (23 November) but did not start in earnest until 17 December. The main battle (including the enemy's stand at Gazala) had lasted a little over three weeks longer than originally anticipated. The AHB Narrative *The*

Middle East Campaigns, Volume II, divides air operations during the period of the retreat into three distinct sections covering the pursuit (17 to 26 December), the delaying action at Agedabia (26 December to 6 January), and the stand at El Agheila (7 to 20 January).

The last attacks on Benghazi during the pursuit took place between 17/18 and 19/20 December. On the morning of 17 December HQ Middle East informed No. 205 Group that a convoy was expected to enter Benghazi harbour the following morning, and requested that a mining operation be carried out. However, due to heavy rain both of the forward landing grounds (LG 09 and LG 60) were unserviceable, and it was impossible to move aircraft up from the Canal Zone. The only aircraft available were twelve from No. 70 Squadron, briefed to attack Benina and stranded at LG 60 by bad weather on the previous night. It was arranged, therefore, that they should deliver their attack on Benina first and then fly on to Benghazi and simulate a mining attack by dropping empty petrol or tar barrels into the harbour! On the following night five aircraft from No. 148 Squadron successfully planted real mines in the harbour, and a diversion laid on by other aircraft was so successful that no opposition was encountered. It was only after the minelayers had completed their task that the searchlights swung out to sea, but by now the predominantly Italian defenders of Benghazi might well have had other things on their minds. The port was in the hands of the Eighth Army again by Christmas Day 1941, and Alexander Clifford was there to see what the bombers had done:

> Now it was a ruin … Every window was shattered and every door barred. The roadway see-sawed up and down over half-mended bomb craters, and palm trees and lamp standards lay uprooted or drooped drunkenly. Every house was ripped and scarred with shrapnel. Iron shop-shutters were torn and twisted by blast. The fair white walls were blackened by fire … There was that same stench and dirt and desolation that you always get in a town which has come straight out of the firing line…
>
> Outside on the water-front … [the] whole roadway all round consisted of filled-in bomb craters. Again and again the Italians had had to renew the railway lines which ran alongside the harbour … From the water itself funnels and masts and hulls were jutting grotesquely. The top of a big dredger was sticking up from the very middle of the harbour. This had been Rommel's chief supply port and the RAF's chief target. Only the Cathedral, which was right in the middle of the target area, seemed to have been spared a serious direct hit. It looked like either astoundingly accurate bombing or else a miracle.[10]

Twenty-three sorties were directed at Benina between 17 and 20 December. Twelve aircraft of No. 70 Squadron made the final attack on 19/20 December, and lost two aircraft in the process. Alexander Clifford also went to have a look at Benina:

> They told us Benina beat all records for airfield cemeteries…So we drove out to see it and counted the 117 wrecked planes round its vast, water-sodden expanse. Many stood quite whole and perfect save where wandering Bedouin had broken in and stolen the neat black cases containing the pilot's emergency rations. Some of the workshops looked as though the mechanics

had just gone away to lunch, and the big stores of pale-blue high octane aviation spirit were untouched.[11]

Berka was bombed on the night of 18/19 December by seven Wellingtons, and on 21/22 December the target for twenty-one Wellingtons was the landing ground at El Magrun, which was being used by the enemy to provide air support for his ground forces retiring to the Agedabia area. Unfortunately, bad visibility hindered the attack, and most of the aircraft were unable to locate the target accurately. A similar result was achieved in an attack on the landing grounds at El Agheila and Marble Arch by twenty Wellingtons on 23/24 December. After 22 December, attention shifted to the El Agheila area, as the bombers started to attack the enemy columns retreating to their new defensive positions. The Wellingtons of No. 205 Group in Egypt carried out an attack on MT on the Agedabia–Sirte road on the night of 24/25 December, but in general the direct support targets then available were 'not worth the effort'. Thus, apart from the few attacks on airfields, the entry 'Operations cancelled' appeared regularly in the Group ORB – appearing five times in the eight nights between 20/21 and 28/29 December.

With the front line now near the Tripolitanian border and the ports in Cyrenaica lost, Tripoli became a critical source of supplies for Rommel's forces. On 18/19 December four Wellingtons from Malta laid four mines just outside the harbour entrance at Tripoli and two just inside. Another three aircraft created a successful diversion by bombing the town. However, enemy air attacks often disrupted operations from Malta at this time. On 19 December, while the Wellingtons of No. 40 Squadron were waiting to take off, an intruder – probably from I/NJG 2 – strafed Luqa. One aircraft was hit, and all the crew were casualties. The navigator, Pilot Officer John Tipton, recalled that 'the explosion of the aircraft and its bomb load damaged all (the other) aircraft waiting to take off that night'. Two were destroyed, and other aircraft were damaged. In another raid on Luqa on 26 December, six aircraft were destroyed on the ground and three damaged. Then on 29 December Malta saw the heaviest day of action since the return of the *Luftwaffe* to Sicily. Luqa was attacked by twelve Bf 109s and bombers, and fifteen aircraft were destroyed. No. 40 Squadron had three aircraft burnt out and others damaged. Fires broke out in an area where several bombed up Wellingtons were dispersed, and where the bomb dump was situated. One of the bombers caught fire, and Flight Sergeant A.J.M. MacDonald – in charge of the Luqa Fire Section – successfully put out the fire with a portable fire hydrant, thus saving two other Wellingtons from destruction. He was later awarded the BEM for this and other actions during the air raids on Luqa.

Despite the attentions of the *Luftwaffe*, the Malta Wellingtons kept on flying. They continually attacked the harbour installations and shipping at Tripoli, flying thirty-four effective sorties between the nights 23/24 and 26/27 December. Also, as the enemy's air forces had to withdraw from their Cyrenaican bases, the main Tripolitanian airfield at Castel Benito became of increased importance and was attacked on 21/22 and on the evening of 22 December.

Between 26 December 1941 and 6 January 1942 the enemy fought a delaying action at Agedabia while defensive positions were being prepared in the marshes around El Agheila. The Wellington squadrons in Egypt operated on eight nights during this period, and on six of those nights they operated under instructions from advanced Air HQ Western Desert. The targets were supplies and road transport in the enemy's immediate rear, but weather conditions were often poor and greatly hindered the attacks. Also, the rapid advance of the Allied forces meant that the Group's targets were west of El Agheila and its main bases east of Cairo – on the Suez Canal at Shallufa, Fayid and Kabrit. All of their operations were being carried out from Advanced Landing Grounds much further forward. The landing grounds between Daba and Maaten Bagush were some 300 miles from the Canal Zone, and many operations were launched from El Adem near Tobruk, another 300 miles forward. As we shall see, problems with communications and fuel supplies at the forward bases often hampered operations as *Crusader* came to an end.

At the end of December and into January the Wellingtons squadrons of No. 205 Group were given the job of trying to neutralize the enemy's submarine base at Salamis, Greece. Attacks at two-squadron strength were attempted on the nights 28/29 and 30/31 December, but both failed due to terrible weather conditions. On the first attack there was 9/10 to 10/10 cloud and icing conditions, and most of the aircraft bombed alternative targets or abandoned the operation. A similar result was obtained in the second attack, although a few did claim to have bombed at Salamis. On 31 December/1 January, thirteen aircraft were detailed to attack Salamis, but only one located the target area. Three attacked alternative targets, four jettisoned their bombs, and five returned to base with their bombs. On 3/4 January three aircraft bombed Salamis, and bursts were observed near the torpedo school, submarine base, munitions factories, and ordnance works. Five other aircraft abandoned the operation for various reasons. The main alternative targets bombed at this time were the oil storage facilities Piraeus and the airfields on Crete (Maleme, Kastelli Pediada and Heraklion), but bombs were also dropped at Suda Bay, Cape Sideron, and Laurium, and this dispersion of effort meant that no serious damage was caused at any of these locations.

While the Axis forces held their position at Agedabia, it became known that they were using improvised off-loading facilities at various points along the coast west of Agheila. Reconnaissance aircraft reported the presence of six small ships off Ras El Ali (north of Marble Arch), and about 100 lorries waiting at the jetty. On the night of 31 December/1 January, six aircraft bombed Ras El Ali, and on the following night five aircraft attacked MT concentrations reported near Marble Arch. On 2/3 January four aircraft attacked MT on the Ras Lanuf – Marble Arch road and also machine-gunned targets on the ground. For the following two nights the Wellingtons attacked shipping at Beurat El Hsun (halfway between El Agheila and Tripoli), claiming a near miss on one ship and bursts on roads, the jetty, and buildings in the target area. However, the AHB Narrative comments that:

> The night bomber effort against the supply points and road transport in the immediate rear of the battle area…only sufficed to achieve a small measure of interference with the enemy's off-loading and road transportation.[12]

Even relatively 'safe' operations held their dangers. On 7/8 January a Wellington from No. 37 Squadron, piloted by Squadron Leader Alexander, took off from El Adem to carry out an aerial reconnaissance of the airfield at Capuzzo to determine its suitability as a forward base for Wellington aircraft. The airfield was just a few miles south of enemy positions at Sollum and the Halfaya Pass, but Squadron Leader Alexander had previously carried out a special mission to the area and had been well briefed on the disposition of enemy troops. He had been told that they were located along the escarpment near the coast, and after carrying out his task from 300 feet, he turned south and climbed to normal flying height. When he was about seven miles from the coast, and ostensibly well clear of the enemy positions, he suddenly came under fire from the ground. He immediately took violent evasive action, and shortly afterwards felt a lack of elevator control. He assumed that the control rods had been shot away, and therefore decided to try to make a forced landing using the tail actuating gear for fore and aft control. The Wellington hit the ground at about 100 miles an hour, and the second pilot sustained a broken leg and the wireless operator a bruised rib. The rest of the crew and six passengers were uninjured, and shortly afterwards all were picked up by an Army patrol, although not before they had come under fire from enemy artillery. One of the passengers was Lewis G. Merritt, who subsequently became a brigadier general in the United States Marine Corps.

As the New Year dawned, the only Axis outposts left in Cyrenaica were the garrisons at Bardia, Sollum, and the Halfaya Pass. These were now over 350 miles behind their own front line as the crow flies, and much further away by the long road around the Cyrenaica coastline. They could not last long, and Bardia fell on 2 January 1942 and Sollum and Halfaya on 17 January. The only contribution that the Wellingtons made to their fall was an abortive attempt to persuade the garrison at Halfaya to surrender by dropping a forged message from Rommel.[13]

Bad weather constantly interfered with the night bomber's operations during the enemy's stand at Agedabia and the subsequent retreat to El Agheila, but there were also problems with delays in signal traffic between the bomber Wings and Advanced Air Headquarters Western Desert. Thus, the former were often receiving orders too late for operations to be carried out, and the latter were unable to assess the results of those operations that did take place. The Wellington operations were at times hindered by changes from distant targets (such as Tripoli) to near ones (such as El Agheila), and on 15 January the CO of No. 37 Squadron reported to the AOC No. 205 Group:

> It is a regrettable fact, but a true one, that the amount of engine hours and general effort recently expended by the squadron is not in proportion to the results achieved. It does not seem to have been realized that a Heavy/Medium Bomber Squadron can only operate efficiently if reasonable warning of targets is given. As an extreme example, a change from a distant to a near target may involve the draining of 400 gallons of petrol from each aircraft, the removal of a long-range tank, the removal of a bomb load and the substitution of another with different fusing, consisting perhaps 16 bombs to each aircraft. The chaos produced by a last minute change, when perhaps 17 aircraft are involved, has to be seen to be believed.

Another problem was the need to conserve fuel in the forward area. On 9 January the AOC, HQ Western Desert had informed the SASO, HQ, RAF Middle East that the petrol situation was improving at El Adem and that ten Wellingtons could be refuelled there each night. The arrangement was for the AOC, Western Desert to inform No. 205 Group each day of the amount of petrol available, but on occasion conflicting messages were passed to the Group and operations suffered as a result. All these difficulties limited the operations of No. 205 Group during the lull at El Agheila (7 to 21 January) to only twenty-one effective sorties.

The two Wellington squadrons on Malta also had their problems. At the beginning of January they had been reduced to a handful of aircraft due to the German bombing. In December 1941 *Luftflotte* 2 was transferred from the Russian front, and German aircraft reappeared in strength in the skies over Malta. The bombing was devastating. The airfields were torn up time and time again, many aircraft were destroyed on the ground, and just after Christmas the Poor House was hit. On 2 January No. 104 Squadron was ordered to get out and move to the Middle East. That night six aircraft left Luqa at 0200 hours and all had arrived safely at Kabrit by 0900 hours on 3 January. They left behind two Wellington Mk IIs capable of carrying 4,000-lb bombs, and these were soon in action with No. 40 Squadron. In its first operation in the New Year this unit had only been able to despatch a single aircraft on a nuisance raid to Tripoli, but its ground crews were working desperately hard to repair the many damaged Wellingtons by cannibalizing wrecks and achieving miracles of improvisation. On 2/3 January the Squadron managed to put up six aircraft on nuisance raids to Naples and Tripoli, including the two Mk IIs from No. 104 Squadron. One of No. 40 Squadron's navigators, Pilot Officer John Tipton, explained the purpose of the nuisance raids:

> The Tripoli raids were against shipping which had arrived in the harbour and were often combined with a run up the coastal road to look for convoys. Other port attacks were similar except that the task at Naples and Brindisi were 'nuisance raids'. The purpose was mainly to fatigue workers and damage morale and so a single aircraft stayed over the port for two hours, the alert being maintained through the night. The purpose could be achieved by keeping the AA guns firing and when they paused a single bomb among the harbour shipping would start them up again. With luck some useful damage could be done.[14]

Earlier in the day Sergeant Tony Armstrong's crew had been doing their Daily Inspections when a formation of Ju 88s arrived over Luqa, and they watched helplessly as two sticks of bombs hit the neighbouring aircraft and set it on fire. On the same night Hal Far and Luqa were subjected to yet another raid. The Ju 88s would come in on a shallow dive and drop a single bomb, and then fly out to sea to return for another attack until their bomb loads were exhausted, keeping this up throughout the night. Five Wellingtons were still out on nuisance raids to Naples and Tripoli, but others under repair at their dispersals were hit and burnt out. Hundreds of *Sprengbombe Dickwandig* ('butterfly') anti-personnel bombs littered the runways, and all hands were needed to clear them and to fill in the bomb craters before the Wellingtons returned. The destruction continued the next day when bombers and strafing Bf 109s destroyed another two of the Squadron's aircraft, and two Whitleys of No. 138 Squadron were also burnt out. These had been on detachment to drop agents and supplies to Yugoslavia, and had been stranded at Luqa for almost two months awaiting repairs.

Reconnaissance aircraft had reported a concentration of transports and bombers at Castelvetrano in Sicily, and that night five Wellingtons attacked the airfield. Four of them were then refuelled and rearmed, and went out again to the same target. The attacks were a great success, with twelve enemy aircraft destroyed and forty-two damaged, 500 drums of aviation fuel went up in flames, and vehicles and buildings were damaged. Fires were still visible when the aircraft were well into their return journey. One of the former aircraft of No. 104 Squadron that took part in this attack dropped its 4,000-lb bomb just east of the runway, and a 'terrific explosion resulted throwing up debris and dust'. The Wellingtons reported that the single runway at Castelvetrano stood out 'like a large white strip', and the aircraft 'were greeted with very active anti-aircraft gunfire.' Squadron Leader Bill Craigen did a glide approach down a great column of black smoke from burning aircraft on the ground, and as he came out of the smoke and over the fire in the centre of the airfield he was 'lit up like daylight so things began to get quite exciting.' He could see people leaning out of barrack block windows firing at him with rifles and pistols. One of the aircraft from this second wave was brought down by flak.

The storms that had raged over Sicily since the end of December now struck Malta, and forced the cancellation of all but one small raid during the following week. Three aircraft attacked shipping in the harbour at Tripoli on 6/7 January, but no tangible results of the bombing were observed. The target was an Italian convoy that had got through to Tripoli on the previous day, carrying fifty-four urgently needed tanks for Rommel. Despite atrocious weather, the Wellingtons went back to Tripoli on six consecutive nights between 11 and 16 January, flying seventeen sorties in a series of nuisance raids. Pilot Officer McCrorie carried out his crew's second such sortie on successive nights on 15/16 January, flying through continuous electrical storms with the temperature dropping to minus fifteen degrees. There was 10/10 cloud down to 4,000 feet, and then more cloud and rain down to 1,000 feet. Despite these terrible conditions the Wellington remained over the target area for two and a half hours, and the AOC Malta personally congratulated the crew on their return.

The Wellingtons on Malta now turned their attentions to Sicily, sending eight aircraft to the airfield at Catania on 18/19 January. The object was to bomb continuously throughout the night to disrupt an anticipated German bomber attack on a supply convoy from Alexandria. The first aircraft arrived over Catania soon after dusk, and the last got there just before dawn, each making three bombing runs. Pilot Officer McCrorie got to the airfield just as landing lights were switched on to enable two Ju 88s to land. He followed them in and was able to drop a stick of bombs along the runway from east to west as they were landing. A violent red explosion was seen, and the crew believed that one of the Junkers had run into the exploding bombs. A night fighter of 4/NJG 2 followed a Wellington back to Malta and manoeuvred into a favourable position, only to find that his guns wouldn't fire. He tried again, stalking another bomber into Luqa, but this time his luck ran out and he was shot down by the airfield defences. Two aircraft went back to Sicily on 21/22 January, carrying out further nuisance raids over various airfields.

The middle of January 1942 found the Eighth Army and the Axis forces in loose contact in the difficult country near the bend of the Gulf of Sirte. There, Rommel defied all further attempts by the Eighth Army to advance. The Allied troops were by now exhausted and at the end of a very long and tenuous supply line, whereas Rommel was only 500 miles from his main supply base at Tripoli. The Eighth Army required some 1,400 tons of supplies a day, but was only receiving in the region of 1,150 tons, and it was impossible to build up a reserve that would enable the advance to continue. The bombers of No. 205 Group had added to the problem by leaving the harbour at Benghazi strewn with wrecks and with many holes in the Outer Mole, making the task of reconstruction very difficult. However, the general failure to disrupt the flow of supplies to Rommel through Tripoli was to have a serious impact on the war in North Africa in the very near future. Not only were the Axis forces able to withdraw to the safety of the position at El Agheila, but their strength was growing day by day.

*   *   *

On the morning of Sunday December 7 1941 the Japanese attacked Pearl Harbor on Hawaii, and on 11 December America declared war on Germany and Italy. The British and Commonwealth forces fighting in the Middle East now had a powerful ally, but it would be some time before American forces appeared in the theatre. However, the United States had been supplying Britain with aircraft for some time, and we have already seen that Flying Fortresses had made a brief appearance in the bomber role. However, it was to be the Consolidated B-24 Liberator[15] that made the greater impact with the RAF in the Middle East. On 24 November, while the operations in support of *Crusader* were going on, Wing Commander Wells of No. 108 Squadron visited Group HQ and was informed by Air Commodore MacLean that his squadron was going to be re-equipped with Liberators. The first one turned up with an American crew on 29 November, and the Americans would remain with the Squadron for training purposes. What should have been the first aircraft to arrive had crashed 200 miles south-west of Khartoum and was a complete write-off, and it was arranged that all serviceable parts would be salvaged and sent on to the Squadron.

The arrival of these first four-engined heavy bombers in the Middle East was not without problems, as they were arriving without tail turrets and without 'guns of any description'. A representative of the Armaments Branch ME Command visited the Squadron on 30 November and reported that there were no turrets in the Middle East capable of being put into the Liberators. The arrival of the new aircraft also created some administrative problems in that the Base Personnel Office still regarded No. 108 as a Wellington Squadron, and 'will not play by giving us an increased number of technical personnel'. It was expected that 'their attitude will probably change in the course of a few days'. However, a lack of 'publications and information regarding Liberator aircraft is going to make a considerable amount of work for the Squadron personnel'.

On 4 December a ferry Liberator arrived bringing various technical experts to the Middle East Command. The first aircraft was made serviceable and a training programme commenced. Two more Liberators arrived on 9 and 10 December, and by the 12th the Squadron reported that conversion to Liberators was 'proceeding very satisfactorily, solo flying having already been undertaken by W/Cdr Wells DFC and S/Ldr Vare'. A fourth Liberator arrived on 13 December, but when bombing practice commenced on the Shallufa Bombing Range using the American Sperry bomb sight, results did not prove very satisfactory. This was put down to a failure 'to determine wind velocity at various heights'. Nevertheless, some pilots had adapted themselves very rapidly to the new aircraft, and had gone solo after only five hours' dual flying. On 19 December the Squadron ORB records that 'A' Flight was still operating with Wellingtons, but operations would cease when the next Liberator arrived as this had been allotted to the Flight for conversion purposes. The aircrews of 'B' Flight were 'progressing rapidly with the conversion programme and will very soon be capable of carrying out operational flying with

85

the Liberators'. However, it was expected that the Squadron would not operate with Liberators for some time, 'as the armament problem has presented new difficulties'. Adequate provisions for gun turrets had still not been made, and new modifications were needed.

On 11/12 January one Liberator of No. 108 Squadron took part in an attack on Tripoli in what was the first operational flight for these new aircraft in the Middle East. This was more in the nature of a test flight for the purpose of getting accurate petrol consumption figures. The aircraft took off from LG 09 at 2340 hours, but encountered a strong head wind that slowed the outward journey. No problems were experienced on the way to the target, but the bombing was marred by three hang-ups due to electrical failures. A total of twelve 500-lb bombs were dropped, and the return trip was uneventful. The aircraft had flown a total of 2,240 miles and had spent ten hours and twenty-five minutes in the air by the time it landed again at Fayid.

One of the Squadron's Liberators took part in an even longer and more significant series of flights. On 18 January it left Fayid for Singapore carrying spares for No. 84 (Blenheim) Squadron, which was moving to the Far East. It was expected that the trip would be accomplished in three stages, the first being from Fayid to Karachi, and this would be the first time that an RAF machine had flown non-stop from Egypt to India. It returned to Fayid on 25 January, having made two stops on the outward journey – at Karachi and Bangalore – before landing at Palembang. No difficulties were experienced, although incorrect information in relation to W/T frequencies and call signs were given to the wireless operator at Karachi, and there seemed to be something of a lack of inter-Command co-operation. The Liberator left Palembang at 2350 hours on 22 January, stopping en route at Madras and Bangalore, Karachi and Habbaniyah. The aircraft completed 18,000 miles in seven days, with a total flying time of 57.5 hours and an average ground speed of 210 mph.

*   *   *

Meanwhile, Rommel was being reinforced with more tanks and men. The two convoys that had arrived at Tripoli in late December and early January had brought with them fifty-four tanks and crews, other badly needed reinforcements, and some 2,000 tons of aviation fuel. This had transformed Rommel's position, and he soon began to look eastwards again. The expectation of the senior Allied commanders was that it would be almost impossible for him to take the offensive for a long time, but, unfortunately, they once again underestimated the recuperative powers of the German formations under his command. On 12 January Rommel's senior intelligence officer, Major F.W. von Mellenthin, predicted that for a short while the Axis forces would actually be slightly stronger than the forces immediately opposed to them. The head of his Operations Section, Colonel Westphal, then suggested a spoiling attack in the Agedabia area. Rommel did not jump at the idea, but finally warmed to it. In the early morning of 21 January he set off towards Cyrenaica again, advancing in three columns, but with only three days' rations in hand and fewer than a hundred tanks.

In the first few weeks of January it was still hoped that the Eighth Army's advance into Tripolitania could still go ahead, and plans were made to move the bomber squadrons forward. The first to be ordered forward was No. 37 Squadron, first of all to LG 75 (about twenty miles south of Sidi Barrani), and then to Benina (near Benghazi). The advance party actually set off en route to Benina via LG 75 on 19 January, and had got as far as Derna by 1200 hours on the 24th. Shortly after leaving Derna three lorries broke down and had to be left behind for repairs, and a little later the officer in charge of the party (Flight Lieutenant Draper) received a recall signal from No. 231 Wing instructing him to go back to LG 76 immediately. Meanwhile, the main party had left Shallufa on 24 January, got to LG 75 on the 26th, and reached LG 76 on the 27th. For a few days it looked as though the Squadron would settle at LG 76, but by now the enemy were near Gazala and a further retreat to LG 09 near Daba was ordered.

The enemy's advance had begun soon after 0800 hours on 21 January, and the weak Allied forces fell back, inflicting as much damage as they could as they retreated. Rommel had reached Agedabia by 1100 hours on the 22nd, and a few hours later captured the airfield at Antelat. The advance continued on the next day, and although Rommel's superiors ordered him to end the 'spoiling attack', he replied that he meant to attack for as long as he could and only orders direct from Hitler would stop him. By 25 January he was at Msus, where he was forced to pause because his fuel was running out, and also because he needed time to consider what to do next. In the end, he decided to go for Benghazi, across the notoriously difficult country to the south east. The Eighth Army was forced to retreat fast, and by 28 January Benghazi was back in enemy hands and the 'mail run' would soon be on again for No. 205 Group. The retreat continued until a line was stabilized between Gazala and Bir Hacheim around 6 February 1942. The Eighth Army was now back to the very same place where, only seven weeks before, Rommel had broken away and retreated to Agedabia and then El Agheila. A long lull now followed in the Western Desert as both sides took stock of the situation and built up their forces ready for the next round.

At the end of January the Wellington squadrons of No. 205 Group had a total strength of 105 aircraft, with seventy-nine serviceable or serviceable within three days, and No. 108 Squadron also had four serviceable Liberators. Between 25 January, when the seriousness of the situation in Cyrenaica became obvious, and 6 February the squadrons of No. 205 Group flew ten operations and 176 sorties against enemy concentrations and motor transport, mainly between El Aghelia and Agedabia. Six of these sorties were flown by the Liberators of No. 108 Squadron. On 25/26 January forty aircraft attacked MT columns immediately behind the enemy's advanced units, with the main weight of the attacks falling on the Agedabia bottleneck. The attacks continued on the following night, but results were obscured by cloud. On 27/28 January adverse weather conditions whittled down the effective effort, but two attacks were carried out on supply columns on the El Aghelia–Agedabia road. The weather continued to be a hindrance over the next few days, but the attacks on the road continued and spread to include those in the more immediate rear of the battle area, on the Benghazi–Benina–Barce road.

No. 40 Squadron on Malta added another thirty-three sorties against motor transport between Tripoli and Buerat, which was ferrying supplies forwards to the rapidly advancing front line. Their orders were to bomb anything of importance on the road, and then to go down and machine-gun the convoys. This was a task always approached with relish, and crew members often vied with each other to have a go on the guns. The Wellingtons also carried out anti-shipping sweeps off the North African coast, and attacks on transport depots at Tripoli. The problem always was to try to find enough aircraft to launch a worthwhile attack. During January more than fifty aircraft of all types had been destroyed on the ground, and to try to reduce the losses large blast-proof pens were constructed at Luqa. To house a Wellington required no fewer than 60,000 four-gallon petrol cans filled with earth or limestone rubble, and it was estimated that it took 200 men working eighteen hours to produce one such structure! Hard work on the starvation rations on Malta.

Conditions for the aircrew were equally rough, of course. The 'Poor House' had been bad enough, but now with the constant air attacks making things worst, the NCO aircrew were moved to the Naxxar Palace, forty-five minutes' drive from Luqa. They found the place to be filthy, with nowhere to put their clothes except on the floor, and the beds so close together that there was no room to stand between them. The food ran out at breakfast, and then they were ordered to clean the place up and to make room for *more* men to move in. They refused until conditions improved, but got an unsympathetic reception from the officers in charge – who were, of course, much more comfortably billeted elsewhere. The resentment was intensified by a comparison with conditions on the cruiser HMS *Penelope*, which some of the men had experienced recently. Here, they had had hot rolls and butter, roast beef, roast potatoes and cabbage, and peaches and jelly for dessert. At Naxxar, lunch consisted of pieces of corned beef and/or the ubiquitous and awful M&V (Maconochie's Meat and Vegetable Stew). Conditions did improve slightly before the Squadron moved to Egypt, but not by very much.

Between 21 and 24 January the bombers on Malta were also busy attacking Tripoli, mainly in 'nuisance raids', operating in very small numbers, and probably doing little damage. Hits were claimed on a naval vessel at the Karamanli Mole, and on a flak ship in the harbour, both of which were reported burning throughout the night. Pilot Officer McCrorie was in action again on 22/23 January – he was chased by a night fighter, but managed to shake it off during a 300 mph dive. He then found that another (or possibly the same aircraft) had followed him home to Luqa, but the airfield guns kept it at bay and allowed him to land safely. On 22/23 January eight aircraft from No. 205 Group bombed Buerat El Hsun again, where bursts were observed among buildings at the base of the jetty, and one bombed motor transport at Sirte. Aircraft from Malta also attacked motor vehicles on the road between Tripoli and Buerat El Hsun on 29/30 January, and at least sixteen lorries claimed destroyed. On 5/6 February Benghazi was back on the schedule for the bombers in Egypt, when fourteen aircraft were ordered to carry out diversionary attacks on the docks and the airfield at Berka while other aircraft carried out 'gardening' operations in the approaches to the harbour. Benghazi had been in British hands for little more than a month, but now the need to prevent the enemy's free use of the port became even more vital than in earlier times.

Another convoy had been sent through to Tripoli on 23 January, when the Malta strike force was down to fewer than thirty aircraft of all types – Swordfish, Albacores, Blenheims and Wellingtons. Nevertheless, a plan was hurriedly devised whereby attacks would be made on the convoy by naval units from the island, and by Fleet Air Arm and RAF aircraft from Malta and Egypt. Five Wellingtons of No. 38 Squadron formed part of the strike force from Egypt, and one was to have carried torpedoes in the first attack of this kind by the Squadron. Unfortunately, the naval units ran into a minefield, losing a cruiser and a destroyer in the process, and turned back. The torpedo-bombers from Malta had better luck, with a Beaufort of No. 39 Squadron disabling the Italian liner *Victoria* in the afternoon, later to be finished off by Albacores of No. 826 Squadron from Berka. The eight Wellingtons of No. 40 Squadron, with Squadron Leader Steel acting as illuminator, were guided to the area of the convoy by a shadowing ASV Wellington, and commenced their attack just before 2130 hours. Flares were dropped from 8,000 feet to give a maximum period of illumination, but few ships were seen. Hits were somewhat optimistically claimed on a merchantman and a cruiser, but none of the ships actually sustained any damage from the bombing attacks. All but one of the ships got through to Tripoli, and the Eighth Army would pay dearly for the inability to prevent these supplies from reaching their destination.

*   *   *

The lull in the Desert began on 7 February, when the Eighth Army stabilized its defensive line between Gazala and Bir Hacheim, and ended when Rommel struck again on 26 May. During these 113 days there was almost no military activity on the ground, although the air forces were still fighting hard in the skies over the Western Desert, over Malta, and over the Mediterranean itself. The loss of the airfields in Western Cyrenaica had two important consequences. First of all, it made it more difficult to get convoys through to Malta, and it was only from Malta that the sea-traffic from Italy to North Africa could be attacked to good purpose. The battle for Malta had to be won, and would be more easily won if Rommel was pushed back again into Tripolitania. Secondly, Tripoli was again a safe port for the Germans, out of range of the bombers now far away in Egypt.

Operating conditions at Luqa were still very bad and getting worse. Large numbers of soldiers joined the airmen and the Maltese civilian workers in filling in craters, building and repairing the protective pens, and extending the dispersal areas. For six weeks everywhere on the island had been under heavy attack, with an average of twelve air raid warnings a day. Nowhere was safe. On 5 February Luqa was strafed and bombed while the Wellington crews were doing their Daily Inspections, and night intruders were bombing the runway as the aircraft took off for Tripoli. To complete an eventful night, a raid was in progress when the aircraft returned, and they had to wait off the coast until it was over. However, No. 40 Squadron would not have to endure the battering for much longer.

On 6/7 February seven Wellingtons attacked the airfields near Sirte, and then carried out three attacks (nineteen sorties) on Tripoli between the 7/8th and 12/13th of the month. The defensive barrage was now noticeably heavier than when the Squadron had made its first attacks on the town in November 1941, yet they had only lost one aircraft in thirty-one raids to the Tripoli area – and that during the very first attack on 2/3 November. As well as the attacks on Tripoli the Squadron also sent crews on nuisance raids to airfields in Sicily as part of the cover for a convoy on its way to Malta. On 14/15 February the Squadron flew its last-but-one Malta operation when fifteen crews attacked the Sicilian airfields in two waves. In the first wave two aircraft bombed Gerbini and six Catania, while in the second seven were despatched to Comiso. The last aircraft in the second wave left at 0355 hours, and its crew twice had to run for cover during an air raid while they waited to take off. Two and a half hours later they landed again in yet another raid.

Rumours had been circulating for some time that the Squadron was to leave for the Middle East, which disappointed many of the men as they had hoped that they would be going back to the UK. In the afternoon of 14 February the Squadron personnel were paraded in the garden of the Naxxar Palace for a talk by Air Vice-Marshal Lloyd, who told them that their job in Malta was finished, and thanked them for their efforts. The exodus of the Squadron's aircraft began on 15 February, when four aircraft got away. Bad weather then prevented further departures until the 19th, and the last five got away two nights later. During this time a single Wellington had made a final operation to Tripoli, as part of a diversion for a minelaying operation on 16/17 February. Many of the ground crew remained on Malta, the intention being to try to repair the many unserviceable Wellingtons littering Luqa. This proved a vain hope, as most of the aircraft were destroyed in further raids, but the ground crew did not rejoin the Squadron until June.

The defensive line now occupied by the Eighth Army ran inland for about thirty-five miles from Gazala, where the coastal road passed through a narrow gap that could be easily blocked. The Army suffered from many problems at this time. Its tanks were greatly inferior to those of the Afrika Korps, and it was also deficient in leadership and training. Any new offensive in the Western Desert could not begin until more and better tanks were available, and until the troops were better trained. The Commanders-in-Chief in Egypt communicated their intentions in a telegram to the Chiefs of Staff in London on 7 February, and this set off a debate between London and Cairo that went on until May. The question was when could General Auchinleck start an offensive in the Western Desert, with Churchill and the Chiefs of Staff pushing for an early start and the Commanders-in-Chief arguing for a delay until Auchinleck had the tanks he needed to give him a reasonable chance of success.

A long and tedious argument between London and Cairo about tanks filled most of the lull in the Desert, and there were also disagreements about the establishment of German and Italian armoured formations. Although Rommel had his own problems, the neutralization of Malta meant that supplies were getting through to him with little hindrance. Churchill, however, continued to nag, and when Auchinleck refused to come to London for a 'consultation', the Prime Minister asked Sir Stafford Cripps, the Lord Privy Seal, to break his forthcoming journey to India to review the situation in the Middle East. Cripps agreed with Auchinleck that the British and Commonwealth forces were not strong enough for an offensive to be started before mid-May. On 10 May the Prime Minister brought matters to a head with a telegram stating that Auchinleck should fight in May if possible, and at the latest in early June to help the passage of a dark-period convoy to Malta. This telegram, in fact, gave Auchinleck the choice between complying or resigning, and he chose compliance but with reservations.

During the lull the RAF spent the time reorganizing and preparing for the next active phase on land, while continuing to harass the enemy as much as possible. The bulk of the night-bombing effort was carried out by Nos 37 and 70 Squadrons, with some support from Nos 104, 108 and 148 Squadrons. Increasingly, No. 38 Squadron was occupied in its new maritime role, and No. 40 Squadron had temporarily disappeared from the order of battle. The first operation by the Liberators of No. 108 Squadron had taken place on 11 January 1942, but for now the relatively small number of Wellingtons would have to soldier on alone. The enemy had quickly re-opened the harbour at Benghazi, and would soon begin to use it to the fullest extent to avoid the long haul by road from Tripoli. Many of the operations against the port at this time involved the mining of the approaches to the harbour, covered by diversionary bombing attacks. The first took place on 5/6 February (see above), and further 'gardening' and bombing attacks took place on 7/8, 14/15, 16/17 and 24/25 February, and these attacks were the prelude to a sustained air offensive against Benghazi.

During the lull (7 February to 26 May) the Wellingtons in Egypt flew 1,597 sorties, and most of these (998 sorties – 62.5 per cent) were directed at shipping and dock installations at Benghazi. The surrounding airfields at Berka and Benina also received some 200 sorties, either directly or as alternatives. Many of the attacks were 'gardening' (minelaying) operations in the approaches to the harbour, and many of the bombing operations were diversions for the gardening. The official history, commenting on part of this period, states that:

> …in three months the total day and night bomber sorties against the port and its surroundings, including the laying of mines of the harbour entrance, amounted to 741, or an average of 8 sorties every 24 hours. Some of the attacks were heavy; for example on 8th May twenty-eight aircraft bombed the port and ships in the offing.

However, it goes on to say that:

> …judging from the enemy's statements of cargo unloaded, the interruption was not so serious as was hoped. The capacity of the port steadily rose, though without these attacks it would presumably have risen even faster.[16]

No. 38 Squadron ORB tells the stories of two of their aircraft lost at this time. One failed to return from a minelaying operation on 24/25 February. On reaching the Giuliana Mole the aircraft was hit by flak, and the mines were immediately dropped. The pilot, Pilot Officer Knowles, brought the aircraft clear of the barrage by means of a very skilful bit of flying, and climbed and set course for home. He then revealed that he had been hit in the leg, and the second pilot took over. The only instruments in working order were the ASI, the altimeter and the compass, and the aircraft flew for two hours, slightly north of track, hoping to reach Mersa Matruh. The ASI then suddenly gave out, conditions were very bumpy, and it was a hopeless task to try to keep the aircraft on an even keel. Realizing this, Pilot Officer Knowles took over again, and gave the order to bale out. Sergeant White, the front gunner, baled out first, followed by Sergeant Hammett, the second pilot, and Sergeant Docherty, the wireless operator. Sergeants Hammett and White met in the morning, and together they searched for the aircraft without success. They decided to walk back, and were picked up by an Army convoy late in the morning and eventually arrived back at Shallufa on the morning of 2 March . News was later received that an Army Padre had been taken to the scene of the crash by an Arab, where he found the body of Pilot Officer Eric Knowles lying outside the aircraft and the remains of two other bodies (Sergeant K.W. Bevan and Sergeant A.R.B. Durie) inside. He buried them all at the crash site, but the graves were lost and all three are commemorated on the Alamein Memorial.

The second Wellington (captained by Wing Commander J.H. Chaplin) was lost during an operation by torpedo-carrying aircraft on 9/10 March, shot down by two

Bf 109s on his own side of the lines. It was on its way to the Advanced Landing Ground at Bu-Amud (LG 147) with two torpedoes on board, and had been routed via Fort Maddalena and ordered to fly low. Just after crossing the escarpment he saw numerous Army vehicles, moving at high speed and likely to shoot at any aircraft that approached them. Thus, expecting to be fired on, he fired the colours of the day, and was almost immediately hit by a burst of machine-gun fire. At first, he believed that the firing was coming from the vehicles on the ground, but then the rear gunner reported that they were being attacked by two enemy fighters. Being loaded with two torpedoes and a full load of petrol, it was difficult for the aircraft to manoeuvre out of danger, and by now a fire had broken out midships. The Wing Commander put the Wellington down on some flat ground, but it soon began to disintegrate as it bounced over the rough terrain. When it eventually skidded to a halt it was found that the navigator and second pilot were dead, probably killed in the attack. The other four crew members got out of the wreck, the torpedo fitter having received bullet wounds in the leg and buttocks, and crawled away from the aircraft. The Wellington was now well ablaze, and being strafed by the two fighters. The survivors were picked up by officers of the 4th Indian Division and taken to their camp, where the torpedo fitter was put in hospital and the Wing Commander treated for minor injuries.

As well as operations over the desert, twelve attacks were directed at ports in Greece and Crete, involving five Liberator and 109 Wellington sorties. The main targets were at Salamis, Menidi, Piraeus, Leros, Heraklion, and Portolago Bay. Eight operations (forty-eight Wellington sorties) were directed at shipping at sea, twelve by the torpedo-carrying Wellingtons of No. 38 Squadron. These were usually an unprofitable exercise for the night bombers, and the torpedo-bombers did little better. Thirty-two operations launched against airfields, involving one Liberator and 353 Wellington sorties. In Libya the main targets were at Berka, Benina, Martuba and Derna, and in Greece and Crete the targets were at Tymbaki, Calatos-Lindos, Maritza, Heraklion and Kastelli Pediada. Photographs taken by day and night suggested that there had been considerable destruction, but German reports disclosed less positive results. A feature of many of the night attacks at this time was the successful use of FAA Albacores as 'pathfinders' for the Wellingtons. Only five operations, involving two Liberator and thirty-three Wellington sorties, were directed at ground targets during the lull. For example, on the night of 13/14 March eight aircraft of No. 70 Squadron were ordered to attack an Italian motorized division about six miles north-east of Mechili. The target area was illuminated by the Albacores, and its exact position was further indicated by the Army, which put out a flare path eight miles to the east of it. However, all the vehicles were well dispersed and camouflaged, and no definite results were reported.

*   *   *

As we have seen, conditions on Malta were very bad throughout the period covered by this chapter. On 26 February Air Marshal Drummond (Deputy AOC Middle East and acting as AOC while Tedder recovered from an attack of influenza) signalled the Chief of the Air Staff in London:

Malta is now an expensive liability. In last three weeks enemy action has destroyed 16 aircraft in the air and also 16 on the ground and damaged a further 28. These figures do not include 12 missing from delivery flights, of which several destroyed by enemy action. Damaged aircraft must all be regarded as serious owing to long time taken to repair them with constant air raids in progress.[17]

He went on to say that Malta's Wellington strength had been reduced to fourteen aircraft, of which two were torpedo carriers. Nevertheless, the Wellingtons would continue to operate from the island. No. 40 Squadron was replaced in Malta by a detachment of No. 37 Squadron, which was placed under orders to move to Luqa on 12 February, and the first six aircraft eventually left on the 21st of the month. Almost immediately, five of them were damaged by shrapnel, and on 23 February the '37 detachment could muster but one solitary Wellington to aid the FAA's attack on Tripoli'. Thick haze and a smokescreen over the target made it impossible to find any shipping, and so the Wellington bombed the harbour installations instead. Seven more Wellingtons flew to LG 09 en route to Malta on 22 February, where one landed heavily, breaking the main spar and damaging the tail wheel. Bad weather prevented the other six going on to Malta, but they got off on the night of the 24th and landed at Luqa early the next morning. On 24/25 February three aircraft went back to Tripoli, where they found a very effective smokescreen covering the target area, and although all three bombed on estimated position, no results were observed.

The detachment stayed on Malta until 16 March, by which time it had just about been wiped out by the incessant bombing attacks on the island. During this time it had flown sixty-five sorties in thirteen operations, eleven of which went to Tripoli, either bombing (forty-two sorties) or minelaying (five sorties). One operation was carried out against shipping in the harbour at Palermo on 2/3 March, and one to the airfield at Catania on 16/17 March. On 8/9 March five aircraft were prepared to take off for Tripoli, and just after midnight one commenced its take-off run. When it was two-thirds down the runway and almost airborne it collided with another Wellington that had moved on to the runway without receiving a 'green'. Both caught fire and their mines exploded, killing five crew members and injuring six others. The wireless operator of the first aircraft was blown to pieces, and no trace of his body was found. Operations were cancelled for the night. In all, the Squadron lost three aircraft in accidents, but nine had been destroyed on the ground and others badly damaged by enemy attacks, and on 18 March the detachment only had one serviceable aircraft left.

The *Luftwaffe* was concentrating its air attacks on Malta's airfields, and the few defending Spitfires and Hurricanes could make little impact on the attackers. A convoy sent through in March came in for close attention, but two ships got through to the Grand Harbour. A third (HMS *Breconshire*) was hit and disabled, and eventually sunk on 27 March. Since April 1941 the *Breconshire* had made seven trips to Malta, and had never had to turn back. Even after she sank she performed one last service when hundreds of tons of fuel oil were pumped from her hull. The two ships that got through to the Grand Harbour were both hit while they were being unloaded, and one had to be scuttled lest her cargo of ammunition should explode. Only about a quarter of their supplies were eventually unloaded. By mid-April most of the Spitfires that had arrived in March had been destroyed, and the number of serviceable fighters dwindled until there were only six available. By the middle of March there were 335 enemy fighters and bombers in Sicily, almost the same number as there had been a year before, and the enemy hoped that Malta could be so badly hurt from the air that it would no longer be a serious nuisance. The invasion of Malta was under consideration, and in January 1942 the Italians had began to train for an attack by sea and air. For now, however, it was the air attacks that would constitute the greatest threat, and Malta would be brought to the brink of defeat in April and May 1942.

The next unit of No. 205 Group to enter the cauldron was No. 148 Squadron. On 21 April eight aircraft landed at dawn, but two were destroyed in an air raid almost immediately. Five managed to operate that night, bombing the airfield at Comiso on Sicily. The intention was to carry out two sorties per aircraft, but enemy attacks interfered with bombing-up and only one sortie was carried out. Weather over the target was very bad, and the raid was not completely effective due to poor visibility and low cloud. The Squadron managed seven sorties by the four serviceable aircraft on the next night, and then launched the final operation in this brief detachment on the night of 23/24 April. Two more aircraft had been flown to Malta, but further damage was done to aircraft on the ground and the detachment only had five aircraft available for operations. Between them they managed nine sorties, but two of the Wellingtons were shot down, another was badly damaged by flak, and others received minor damage. One of the lost aircraft was piloted by Flight Lieutenant A.R.H. Hayter, who was captured and later took part in the 'Great Escape'. He was murdered by the *Gestapo* on 6 April 1944, and is buried in Poznan Old Garrison Cemetery. The two remaining aircraft from the detachment flew back to the Middle East on 26 April.

Forty-seven Spitfires were flown off the US carrier *Wasp* on 20 April, but heavy attacks by the *Luftwaffe* followed almost immediately. By the 23rd seventeen had been destroyed on the ground and twenty-nine damaged. On 15 April the Commanders-in-Chief in the Middle East asked the Chiefs of Staff to send out a strong force of heavy bombers from the UK to smash the airfields in Sicily, and also to attack Tripoli and the Italian ports. The request was refused, and as the official history comments:

> As Germany was now being heavily attacked from the United Kingdom, this naturally raises the whole issue of the strategic allocation of British bombers, which is outside the scope of this book.

'Bomber' Harris had got his way again, fighting his own private war, and Portal once again failed to rein in his unruly subordinate. In the end, all that could be done was to fly in another big batch of Spitfires, and more anti-aircraft ammunition would be brought in by fast minelayer and possibly by submarine. With this slight relief Malta must hold out until mid-June. A lot would depend on the success of Auchinleck's offensive in the Western Desert, planned for late May/early June. If he could take the airfields at Martuba and around Benghazi then the chances of getting a convoy through would be greater. Fortunately, after 28 April there was a sudden falling off of German activity, and this marked the end of Malta's worse period. As we have stated elsewhere, the defence of Malta only made sense as long as the island had an *offensive* capability – as a base from which submarines and bombers (particularly torpedo-bombers) could attack enemy shipping. However, in the first five months of 1942 the offensive capabilities of the island were almost completely destroyed, and the few Wellingtons able to operate from Luqa could do little to damage the Axis supply lines. The last of the night bombers left Malta on 11 June, as the new crisis in the Western Desert gathered force, and would not return until November 1942.

*   *   *

The period between the opening of the first phase of the Air Plan for *Crusader* (14 October 1941) and the end of the lull in the desert (25 May 1942) lasted for 224 days/nights. During this time the night bomber squadrons in Egypt operated on 186 nights and despatched 3,124 sorties (including the RCM activities of No. 109/162 Squadron), an average of about seventeen sorties per night. The bulk of the effort in Egypt was carried by Nos 37, 38, 70, 108 and 148 Squadrons. The Liberators of No. 108 Squadron managed thirty-six sorties as they worked through their teething troubles. During the period Nos 40 and 104 Squadrons returned to Egypt from Malta, but the former only carried out one operation while kicking its heels at Shallufa before temporary disbandment on or about 24 March 1942. Only two sorties by the Fortresses of No. 90 Squadron are mentioned in the Group ORB, but a few more seem to have been carried out before the unit gave up its aircraft. Ports and ships in harbour comprised the most common category of target attacked from Egypt (1,670 sorties, 54 per cent of the total), with airfields next (777 sorties, 25 per cent) and direct support operations in the battle area taking up another 379 sorties (12 per cent).

The Wellington squadrons on Malta operated on ninety-nine of the 224 nights between 14 October 1941 and 25 May 1942 and despatched 865 sorties, an average of only about nine sorties per night. This, of course, was a reflection of the difficulties experienced by the units trying to operate out of Luqa, many of which were only there for a very short time and lost most or all of their aircraft in the process. Not surprisingly, the records kept by the units on Malta were sometimes very sketchy indeed, and difficult to interpret. Once again, ports and ships in harbour comprised the most common category (608 sorties, 70 per cent), with airfields taking up another 189 sorties (22 per cent).

NOTES

1. Henry Melvin Young would later become famous as a member of No. 617 'Dambusters' Squadron, and was shot down by flak as he crossed the Dutch coast on the way back from dams raid on 16/17 May 1943. Young and all his crew were killed, and are buried in the Bergen General Cemetery. He earned his nickname from the number of times he had ditched in the sea on operations from the UK.
2. AHB Narrative, *The Middle East Campaigns*, Volume II, page 86.
3. AHB Narrative, *The Middle East Campaigns*, Volume II, page 105.
4. On the eve of the battle (17 November) the worst storm of the year broke out over the desert, and the ambitious bombing programme arranged for that night had to be called off, so Tedder was right.
5. AHB Narrative, *The Middle East Campaigns*, Volume II, page 106.
6. TMAME, Volume III, page 39.
7. AHB Narrative, *The Middle East Campaigns*, Volume II, page 124.
8. Gunby, Sweeping the Skies, page 182. In fact, No. 38 Squadron had already carried out two mine-laying operations at Benghazi.

9. See Michael Cumming's book on the *Beam Bombers'* for a good account of the activities of No. 109 Squadron.
10. Alexander Clifford, *Three Against Rommel*, pages 203–204.
11. Alexander Clifford, *Three Against Rommel*, page 204.
12. AHB Narrative, *The Middle East Campaigns*, Volume II, page 252.
13. According to the AHB Narrative *The Middle East Campaigns*, Volume II, page 279, on the night of 29/30 December a Wellington of No. 37 Squadron approached Halfaya from the sea to simulate the arrival of a German bomber from Crete. A container was dropped purporting to carry a message from Rommel authorising the Commander of the garrison to surrender, but he was not deceived.
14. Shores, Cull and Malizia, *Malta: the Spitfire Year*, page 30.
15. This aircraft was usually known as the B-24 in USAAF circles and as the Liberator in the RAF, but we will refer to them all as 'Liberators' to prevent confusion. Likewise, the Flying Fortress was usually called a B-17 by the USAAF, but here they will all be referred to as 'Fortresses'.
16. TMAME, pages 209–210.
17. AHB Narrative, *The Middle East Campaigns*, Volume III, page 68.

CHAPTER FIVE

Crisis and Recovery in the Desert – May to November 1942

We left the Eighth Army holding a defensive line running inland for about thirty-five miles between Gazala and Bir Hacheim. There had been little activity on the ground since about 6 February, as both sides took breath and prepared for the next round. On 26 May the dispositions of the night bombers was as follows:

1. No. 37 Squadron was at LG 09 (Bir Koraiyim), between Fuka and El Daba and about 250 miles from Gazala.

2. No. 38 Squadron was at Shallufa in the Canal Zone, and operating from various ALGs in the desert.

3. No. 40 Squadron had recently been reformed at Abu Suier, but was not yet operational.

4. No. 70 Squadron was at LG 104 (Qotafiyah II), about five miles west of El Daba and also about 250 miles from Gazala.

5. No. 104 Squadron was at LG 106, about fifteen miles west of El Alamein and about 260 miles from Gazala, and had a detachment of ten aircraft operating from Malta.

6. The Wellingtons of No. 108 Squadron were at LG 105 (El Daba), and its Liberators were at Fayid on the Great Bitter Lake. The latter carried out their last bombing operation to Taranto on 11 June, and thereafter were involved only in 'special operations'.

7. No. 148 Squadron was at LG 106, alongside No. 104 Squadron.

The Wellingtons of No. 162 Squadron were at Bilbeis carrying out their radio countermeasures operations over the desert and the Mediterranean. Although never part of No. 205 Group, it would soon be called up to operate under Group control as a night bomber squadron.

Almost as soon as the Eighth Army had stabilized its position at Gazala the Prime Minister and Chiefs of Staff in London were pressing for an early resumption of the offensive in the desert. The original date for the completion of preparations for an Allied offensive was 15 May, but this was postponed to 1 June. As part of the build up for the projected offensive the night bombers were ordered to attack the landing grounds in the Martuba area, immediately behind the Axis front line. Ninety-five sorties were despatched to these airfields between 21/22 and 25/26 May by Nos 37, 70, 108 and 148 Squadrons. However, by the middle of the month it had become clear that the enemy were likely to strike first, and this is what happened.

On the night of 26/27 May, as the Axis offensive got underway, the focus of attention for the night bombers was still the Benghazi area. Six aircraft of No. 38 Squadron successfully laid mines in an area south of Benghazi, and one machine-gunned vehicles on the Benghazi–El Agheila road and dispersed aircraft at El Magrun. Two more aircraft of No. 38 Squadron attacked a convoy north-west of Benghazi. One aimed its torpedo at a large vessel, which was later reported to be on fire and beached thirty miles north of Benghazi. The other aircraft located the convoy, but the smokescreen made an attack impossible. In a third operation during the night fourteen Wellingtons from Nos 70 and 108 Squadrons bombed dispersed aircraft at Martuba, starting several fires. Their attentions would soon move elsewhere.

On the afternoon of 26 May elements of the DAK under General Crüwell began to move towards the British positions between Gazala and Sidi Muftah, and paused for the night some fifteen miles south of Bir Hacheim. The advance around the 'box' at Bir Hacheim was resumed at sunrise on the 27, and by 0930 hours about 250 German tanks were being engaged by the British 1 and 7 Armoured Divisions. The German armour overcame the British resistance, and swung north towards El Adem. However, the first phase of the battle ended in failure for the Axis forces as British ground and air attacks on the line of communications south of Bir Hacheim began to take effect. By 28 May Rommel's supply situation was critical, his losses not insignificant, and his forces scattered. He was trapped in a region that became known as 'the Cauldron', and was forced to attack *westwards* through the Allied minefield to clear his supply lines. The fighting in the Cauldron continued until the end of May, but Rommel was able to consolidate his position and prepare for another assault.

At the time Chappell was based at LG 106 with the two squadrons of No. 236 Wing (Nos 104 and 148 Squadrons), fifteen miles west of El Alamein and about 260 miles east of Gazala, and he recorded in his diary that various clues had indicated that a 'push' was imminent. He had seen Crusader tanks going up on their trailers, a very large convoy of fifty ambulances, and another convoy of armoured cars and scout cars, all moving westwards towards the front. Then, on 27 May the Group HQ ordered a change of target and bomb load for the Wellingtons – Rommel had struck first! At first the enemy's movements caused little concern in Allied ranks. Auchinleck was happy to accept battle in positions of his own choosing, and the early reports suggested that his forces were winning. The Wellingtons carried on with their attacks on the enemy landing grounds, and on 27/28 May Tmimi, very close to the battle front, was the target for twenty-one aircraft. Six more were prevented from operating by an accident at LG 09. A Wellington had just begun its take-off run when the port tyre burst, and it developed a violent swing to the left. Before the captain could shut the throttles the nose of the aircraft began to skid along the ground, the starboard undercarriage collapsed, and the starboard engine bursts into flames. As soon as the aircraft came to a halt the crew quickly abandoned ship and none was injured, but all further flying was cancelled.

Twenty-six Wellingtons took off to attack the landing grounds at Martuba on the night of 28/29 May, and most bombed their targets successfully. Then it was back to Tmimi on 29/30 May, which was bombed by twenty-one aircraft, starting several fires on the south side of the landing ground. Two aircraft failed to return, but news came in later that both crews were safe. One had lost an engine over the target area, and belly-landed behind enemy lines five kilometres north of Bir Hacheim. After walking for two days the crew was found by a Free French patrol that had been cut off from their main force during the fighting in the Cauldron. The patrol broke through the lines the next night, and the crew eventually returned to base. The other belly-landed after an engine caught fire south of Sidi Barrani, and was destroyed by the crew. They then walked back to the frontier wire at El Beida, and signalled a passing Bombay. This returned later and dropped a message and water bottles, and the crew were soon picked up by a lorry and returned to their unit.

The attacks on the airfields continued on 30/31 May, when twenty-one Wellingtons went to Derna and Martuba, and another twenty-three aircraft went back to the same targets on the next night. One of the aircraft of No. 148 Squadron was attacked and crippled by a night fighter near Derna, and caught fire. It was crash-landed by Flying Officer W. Astell and Pilot Officer A.W. Dodds after the other four crew members had baled out. Astell and Dodds made their way to the front line, which Astell crossed successfully on the night of 5 June, but Dodds was captured. Another crew member, Sergeant F. Mackintosh, also evaded capture, but the other three who baled out all became prisoners of war. Meanwhile, No. 38 Squadron had been continuing its torpedo and minelaying operations. On 28/29 May six torpedo-carrying aircraft went looking for ships to attack, but five of them failed to locate any targets and returned to base. The sixth saw an attacked some ships, but no hits were claimed. Then on 29/30 May and 31 May/1 June a total of eight aircraft successfully planted mines off Benghazi, and also bombed the Benghazi area without observing any definite results.

The battle on the ground now died down for a couple of days while Rommel recuperated and the Allies dithered and dallied. The Eighth Army had the advantage in everything except leadership, whereas the Axis forces had Rommel. Although the Allied troops fought well, and the 'middle management' led by example in difficult conditions, their top leaders bickered, hesitated, and simply failed to understand what was happening around them. Their efforts at this stage were beginning to show clear signs of a failure of command, and the official history states that:

> The British system of command was too complicated to deal with the unexpected, and was no match for the strong personal control of the enemy Commander. This caused an unfair burden to be laid on the divisional commanders and resulted in many fine troops being thrown away.[1]

The focus of the fighting between 2 and 10 June was the 'box' at Bir Hacheim, defended by Free French forces and a British counter-attack at 'Knightsbridge'. The counter-attack failed, and eventually the brave defence of the French came to an end and they were forced to withdraw.

As Rommel consolidated his position in the first few days of June the Wellingtons again devoted most of their attention to the airfields. Between 1 and 6 June they flew 105 sorties to the landing grounds at Derna, Tmimi, and Martuba, but the weather was often poor and the attacks did little to interfere with the activities of the *Luftwaffe* or the Axis ground forces. The Wellington squadrons at their Advanced Landing Grounds often came under attack from enemy bombers at this time, and on 31 May Chappell records that they had a 'hot time for a while from two or three enemy bombers'. Flares fell right over the camp at LG 106, and incendiaries and anti-personnel bombs were dropped around the dispersals, fortunately doing no damage. On 6 June a Red Alert was called in the middle of a briefing for an attack on an enemy fighter landing ground (Martuba No. 3) by No. 104 Squadron. Four bombers managed to get off in spite of the bombs and flares falling in the vicinity, but those on the ground spent some anxious moments in a slit trench ('a hole dug for a latrine!') while anti-personnel bombs dropped all around.

The Wellingtons continued to do their best to disrupt Rommel's supply route through Benghazi by minelaying and bombing operations in the harbour and torpedo attacks on convoys approaching the port. On 2/3 June two aircraft of No. 38 Squadron successfully planted four mines off Benghazi, and on 5/6 June another five also mined the Benghazi area, but brought back their bomb loads as no suitable targets were seen. One machine-gunned a ship in the target area, and silenced one of its guns. On 3/4 June seven Wellingtons from No. 38 Squadron were detailed to attack a convoy north-west of Benghazi, but no sighting report had been received from the ASV aircraft by the time that the Wellingtons had to turn for home. Five of the aircraft returned with their torpedoes, but two decided to carry on searching and eventually saw some flares in the distance. Some of the returning aircraft had spotted the convoy on their way back to base and illuminated it just in case other aircraft might be able to launch an attack. One of the Wellingtons launched two torpedoes at a large merchant vessel, and a hit was claimed on the stern of the ship. The other carried out a determined attack, but no definite hit was claimed. Two torpedo-carrying aircraft went out again on the next night, but no ships were seen. On 7/8 June twenty-one aircraft bombed the harbour at Benghazi, but low cloud and haze made it difficult to see any results. One aircraft of No. 148 Squadron was unable to maintain height after an engine cut due to high oil temperature, and the aircraft eventually force-landed in the desert. The crew took the emergency rations from the dinghy and walked east for two days before attracting the attention of a Baltimore. They were later picked up in a weak condition by two other aircraft of No. 148 Squadron.

The night bombers in Egypt now turned their attentions to targets in Crete and Greece as part of the air operations during the preparations for the *Vigorous* convoy to be sent from Alexandria to Malta (see also below). The landing ground at Heraklion was attacked by twenty-six aircraft on 9/10 June, and twenty-one bombed Kastelli Pediada on the following night. One aircraft of No. 108 Squadron failed to return from Kastelli Pediada, and was believed to have been hit by flak over Maleme and to have ditched in the sea off the coast of Crete. All the crew were lost.

Back in the desert, the Allied armoured formations launched a major attack on the panzers, and, in a series of actions between 11 and 13 June, they were effectively destroyed. At the conclusion of the tank battles the British armour in the Acroma area was reduced to some fifty tanks, while the enemy was believed to possess at least twice that number. Moreover, the panzer divisions were in possession of the battlefield and able to recover and repair their damaged tanks, whereas the damaged British tanks were lost for good. Rommel had won his battle, and the Allies were in retreat past Tobruk. Early on 18 June Rommel invested Tobruk, and attacked it on 20 June. On the following day he took the town, and some 32,000 soldiers were taken prisoner. The fourth and final phase of the Gazala Battle had come to an end.

While this fighting was going on the Wellingtons attacked a variety of targets. On 11/12 June oil installations at Piraeus were bombed by seventeen aircraft, but few results were observed. The bombers were back over Benghazi on 12/13 June, minelaying and bombing shipping in the harbour. One Wellington of No. 104 Squadron was coned by searchlights and hit by flak; it crashed into the sea two kilometres south-west of Benghazi harbour and all the crew were killed. On 14/15 June three aircraft from No. 38 Squadron successfully planted six mines at Benghazi while seventeen Wellingtons carried out a diversionary attack on shipping in the harbour. One of the aircraft of No. 108 Squadron force-landed 64 km south-east of Bir Hacheim, and all the crew were captured. The target was Benghazi again on 18/19 June, when five aircraft mined the harbour while seventeen others flew a diversion over the town and harbour, and on 19/20 sixteen aircraft bombed shipping in the harbour. The remainder of the effort of 194 sorties between 11 and 21 June was directed at the airfields at Derna, Berka, Siret el Chreiba, Tmimi, and Gazala. However, nothing could halt the onward flow of *Panzerarmee Afrika*. In an attack on the Gazala landing grounds on 21/22 June one of the aircraft of No. 148 Squadron captained by Wing Commander D.A. Kerr was hit by flak, and exploded. One crew member woke up on the ground about eight kilometres east of Benghazi with his open parachute beside him, but the rest were all killed.

As the Eighth Army retreated, it was originally planned that the next position to be held would be at Mersa Matruh, but the enemy would give the Allies no time to prepare the defences. Rommel's forces had begun to cross the frontier on 23 June, and by the 25th had captured the Halfaya Pass, Sollum and Sidi Barrani. At this stage in the battle Auchinleck took personal command of the Eighth Army, but could not stop the rot. Mersa Matruh was evacuated by the end of June, after heavy fighting, and the Eighth Army took up its final defensive positions at El Alamein. Rommel battered at the door for a few days, but could not break in.

Following the fall of Tobruk, No. 205 Group was called upon to produce a maximum operational effort every night for an indefinite period to try to stem the advance of the *Panzerarmee*. On 22/23 thirty-eight aircraft were despatched to Tmimi, where bursts were seen to straddle several aircraft, starting many fires followed by explosions. On the next night forty-five Wellingtons were despatched to attack the landing grounds at Gazala, where fires and explosions were observed at many points, including among dispersed aircraft. Things really got going on 24/25 June, and No. 205 Group ORB commented that the night's operation 'heralded the commencement of our intensified effort'. Seventy Wellingtons and nineteen Liberators took off for Benghazi, and carried out a very successful attack. One Wellington of No. 37 Squadron failed to return, and another from No. 40 Squadron ran out of fuel on the return flight, with both engines cutting out simultaneously. The aircraft flew into the ground nineteen kilometres south of LG 115 and caught fire, and four of the crew quickly got out. The captain was dazed and had a black eye, the 2nd pilot was badly hurt, the navigator was bruised and dazed, and the wireless operator (Sergeant Price) was cool and unhurt. The rear gunner was stuck in the aircraft, but Sergeant Price got him out by using the butt of his revolver to widen the gap between the turret and the airframe. Unfortunately, there was no hope of getting the front gunner out. The navigator and Sergeant Price walked north and were spotted by SAAF personnel, who rescued the three others. Another aircraft also had a difficult night. It was hit by flak over the target area and suffered a hydraulic failure, and it staggered back towards base at 100 mph with bomb doors, undercarriage and flaps down. It just made it to a landing ground, where it was 'set down without further damage'.

On 25/26 June the Wellingtons launched ninety-six sorties in the biggest ever operation by No. 205 Group to date. It was also the start of a new development in tactical bombing in the desert war – the direct participation of the night bombers in the land battle. For some time the Albacores of the Fleet Air Arm had assisted the bombers in their attacks on the enemy airfields, flying low and slow to identify the targets and illuminating them with flares. Now the Albacores and Wellingtons became adept at finding and attacking concentrations of troops and vehicles in the desert. Added to the efforts of the light bomber squadrons by day, the night attacks meant that there was now a 'round the clock' assault on the enemy. It gave him no respite by day or night, interfered with his sleep, and forced him to disperse his armour and MT by night and day. The Wellingtons made attacks on enemy concentrations in the battle area every night throughout the remainder of the withdrawal to the El Alamein position, flying a total of 373 sorties to such targets between 25/26 June and the end of the month.

On 25/26 June the bombers attacked enemy columns between Mersa Matruh and Sidi Barrani. The No. 70 Squadron ORB states that the 'operation...made the aircrews feel they were really assisting directly in the War'. Three aircraft were lost, a small cost for such a major operation. One of the Wellingtons of No. 37 Squadron was attacked by a fighter and set on fire, and the crew were ordered to prepare to bale out. One crew member misheard the order and jumped – no trace of him was ever found. The others stayed with the aircraft, which was belly-landed in the desert. The crew walked towards the British lines and was picked up after three hours by an Army patrol. An aircraft of No. 70 Squadron was also attacked by a night fighter and the rear gunner fatally wounded. Small fires were started in the aircraft, which the navigator managed to extinguish, but the aircraft was badly damaged and made a belly-landing off the flare path on return so as not to impede the landing of other aircraft. During the flight back the wounded wireless operator continued to send out messages, and the navigator dressed wounds, gave injections, and generally tended to the injured crew members. The Squadron ORB comments that this was 'a case where initiative and good crew drill were instrumental in bringing the aircraft back to its LG'. One of the aircraft of No. 148 Squadron crashed in a forced landing south-east of Fuka railway station following engine failure, but all the crew were safe.

Forty-one Wellingtons were despatched on 26/27 June, carrying out their attacks from low altitudes. However, the enemy seemed to have learnt a lesson from the previous night, and his convoys were much better dispersed. Three aircraft were lost. One of No. 40 Squadron was shot down by a night fighter and crashed near Halfaya railway station. One of No. 70 Squadron was also attacked by a fighter, and an engine was set on fire. Four members of the crew successfully abandoned the aircraft, which then dived into the ground. The bombs exploded, scattering wreckage over a wide area, and no trace could be found of the other two crew members. The four survivors walked towards Allied lines, and sighted a truck that took them to Fuka. One of the Wellingtons of No. 108 Squadron was attacked by a Ju 88, and abandoned after catching fire. Many of the crew consisted of 'tour expired' personnel who had volunteered to return to operations due to the crisis at the front. The wireless operator, Sergeant O. Ackerman, returned to base on 5 July. He and the front gunner (Sergeant J. Brookes) had both baled out from the stricken aircraft. They were picked up by a forward unit of the 7th Armoured Division. Sergeant Brookes had hurt his foot on landing, and was later admitted to hospital. It was believed that the rear gunner had been killed in the crash, but nothing was known about the others.

The Wellington squadrons operated from their desert landing grounds until the last possible day – withdrawing behind the Delta to the Canal Zone bases in some cases only hours before enemy tanks arrived. As the front crumbled all the squadrons in Egypt were under intense pressure as the enemy bombing became more troublesome. On the 24/25 June Nos 104 and 148 Squadrons received the most hectic bombing so far when enemy aircraft attacked them from 2230 to 2315 hours and again at 0130 hours – bombing and strafing unopposed. They set some petrol on fire in the dispersal area and destroyed the Wing 'ops' tent. On the next night the enemy attacked again, dropping flares as the aircraft landed from the first sortie. Sticks of bombs fell across the landing ground, and one bomb made a direct hit on one of the Wellingtons about to take off for the second sortie. It was set on fire and its bomb load went up in a series of tremendous blasts. During the night and early morning of 26 June Nos 37 and 70 Squadron got ready to evacuate LG 09, and by 0700 hours all tents were struck and all serviceable equipment packed and loaded to move at a moment's notice. The road convoy left for LG 224 at 1000 hours, and the remainder of the ground and air personnel were ferried to the new base by Wellingtons. The evacuation was completed by 1300 hours, and the road convoy arrived at LG 224 at approximately 0800 hours on 27 June. Despite the move both Squadrons operated on 26/27 June and 27/28 June. Nos 104 and 148 Squadrons evacuated LG 106 on 27 June after operating double-sorties against the battle area on the night of 25/26 June, and were in operation from Kabrit by 27/28 June.

In the evacuation back to the Canal Zone the maintenance crews usually travelled in the Wellingtons with the aircrews, and Chappell records that in the evacuation flurry at LG106 two Wellingtons – one taking off and one taxying – met head on. Both were write offs, but of the twenty-six men on the two aircraft, only one was injured. As Chappell set off down the road to Alamein it was crowded with vehicles going both ways, and his convoy passed the 9th Australian Division going up to occupy the Alamein defences at the northern end. The Australians looked fit and cheerful, which was most encouraging in the circumstances. Another happy sight was that of Hurricanes and Spitfires patrolling low overhead to prevent enemy bombing attacks. On 29 and 30 June Nos 104, 108 and 148 Squadrons were carrying out intensive operations from Kabrit, with the three Squadrons all operating at maximum serviceability because of the extremely serious position in the desert. Every aircraft was sent to the battle area, usually on double sorties. Aircrews were literally taken off the boat to participate in operations, and some did not come back. The crews were tired, the aircraft were tired, and so were the maintenance personnel, but they all carried on.

On 27/28 June fifty-nine Wellingtons and ten Liberators were despatched to attack enemy headquarters, landing grounds and vehicles in the battle area, and on the next night around eighty aircraft took off to attack similar targets. Sixty-four Wellingtons were detailed to repeat the attacks on 29/30 June, but one crashed on take-off because the flaps were prematurely raised, and it blew up. One had an engine cut on take-off, and decided to jettison its bombs. These had already been fused, contrary to instructions, and they blew up. The Wellington was only at around 600 feet and the explosions caused the aircraft to dive into the Great Bitter Lake. Five crew members were killed.

The Liberators of No. 159 Squadron and the Liberators and Fortresses of the USAAF (see below) also conducted a 'mini-offensive' against the ports between 9/10 June and the end of the month, flying five sorties to Taranto, thirty-four to Benghazi, and forty-nine to Tobruk. On 25/26 June three Liberators of No. 159 Squadron and four of the USAAF 'flew a diversion for a RAF Albacore attack on two merchant vessels at Tobruk'. This was the first operation against the port since it fell on 21 June, and the last time it had been attacked was on 20 January 1941 during Wavell's offensive against the Italians.

In the thirty-six days between 26 May and the end of June the night bombers of No. 205 Group in Egypt flew 1,305 sorties, often under difficult circumstances and with their Advanced Landing Grounds under attack from enemy bombers until they were forced to withdraw to the Canal Zone towards the end of June. The main effort was carried by Nos 37 (254 sorties), 70 (225 sorties) and 148 (228 sorties) Squadrons, with significant contributions by Nos 104 (143 sorties) and 108 (168 sorties) Squadrons. The RAF Liberators contributed sixty-eight sorties, and the aircraft of the USAAF added another fifty-six sorties. The attacks on airfields accounted for 549 sorties (42 per cent of the total effort), and the attacks on targets in the battle area towards the end of June accounted for another 373 sorties (29 per cent). The continuing assault on ports, ships in harbour and ships at sea involved 364 sorties (28 per cent).

*   *   *

Although Bomber Command in the UK was reluctant to release four-engined bombers for the Middle East, reinforcements did arrive in June. The first two units to join the fight were Nos 159 and 160 Squadrons, both equipped with Liberators, and both intended for operations from India. The early records of the two Squadrons are incomplete, but we do know that the air echelon of No. 159 Squadron arrived at Fayid from the UK on 7 June, en route to India, and were detained by Tedder due to the crisis in the desert. The air echelon of No. 160 Squadron arrived four days later, and was also grabbed by Tedder and effectively absorbed into 159 Squadron. Five of its aircraft were used almost immediately to provide long-range air cover for the west-bound convoy to Malta (see below). While operating from Egypt the two units were known as Nos 159 and 160 Squadrons (Middle East Detachments). In June they flew a total of 63 Sorties, often in conjunction with the B-24s of the Halverson Detachment (see also below) and mainly to Benghazi and Tobruk.

However, the big news on the heavy bomber front during this period was that the Yanks had arrived! Just as Rommel's offensive reached its most threatening stage, a force of American heavy bombers landed at Fayid in Egypt. The Halverson Detachment (code-named HALPRO), commanded by Colonel Harry A. Halverson, was a carefully chosen task force of aircraft and crews originally trained in the greatest secrecy for bombing operations against Japan from bases in China. It comprised 231 officers and men, with a complement of twenty-three Liberators (B-24D) long-range heavy bombers, and had been assembled at Fort Meyers, Florida. The original intention was that they should fly halfway round the world to the province of Chekiang on the Chinese coast, which would have brought them within range of the Japanese mainland. However, by the time the force was ready to leave the USA it had become clear that it could not be supported in China, and permission was granted instead for a surprise raid on the Ploesti oil refineries in Romania.

The force took off from the USA in the early dawn on the morning of 20 May 1942, and all twenty-three aircraft completed the hazardous journey across the Atlantic, across the swamps and jungles of the Gold Coast, then over the dry, hot highlands of the Sudan. They eventually landed at Fayid in the Nile Delta, and were presented with an existing RAF plan for an attack on Ploesti that involved approaching the target over the Aegean, rendezvousing near the target at daybreak, and returning by the same route. However, Halverson preferred an exit route that took them over neutral Turkey, to land at Habbinayah in Iraq. Late in the evening of Thursday 11 June thirteen B-24s took off singly from Fayid, but one was forced to turn back to Egypt when frozen fuel transfer lines cut power to three engines. The remaining aircraft reached Ploesti at dawn, and bombed what was believed to be the Astra Romana refinery through and below an overcast at about 10,000 feet. Only four of the returning aircraft made Habbinayah, three landed at other fields in Iraq, two landed in Syria, and four were interned in Turkey. Though damage to the target was negligible, the raid was significant because it was the first AAF combat mission in the European-African-Middle East Theatre in the Second World War, the first attack on a 'strategic' target, and the first strike at a target that later became famous in the annals of USAAF operations.

Despite Halverson's best efforts to move his unit to China, HALPRO was detained in the Middle East, where it joined the Liberators of No. 159/160 Squadron of the RAF as the only Allied four-engined bomber unit in the theatre. The decision to keep Halverson in the Middle East was partly brought about by the intervention of Colonel Bonner Fellers, the Army military attaché at the US embassy in Cairo, acting as observer with British forces in the Middle East. He had cabled the US War Department stating that all possible effort must be directed towards staging heavy bombers into the Mediterranean for the purpose of attacking Axis supply lines. So, following the attack on Ploesti, the detachment was handed over to Tedder to aid in the attack on enemy shipping and ports in the Mediterranean, operating under the control of No. 205 Group. Even before the Ploesti mission had taken place Tedder had put in a request that the Halverson Detachment help in fighting through a convoy to hard-pressed Malta. After some hesitation the US War Department approved the request on 10 June.

Thus, on Monday 15 June seven Liberators of the HALPRO detachment, along with two RAF Liberators of No. 159 Squadron, carried out an attack on the Italian fleet that was sailing to intercept the *Vigorous* Convoy (see below). The attack took place midway between Malta and Crete on the morning of 15 June, and a possible hit was claimed on a cruiser, a hit and near misses on the battleship *Littorio*. The Americans also claimed at the time that the *Vittoria Veneto* had been heavily damaged, with direct hits abaft of the funnels causing fires and smoke. According to the official history the one bomb hit on the *Littorio* 'did not seriously inconvenience her', and it was later confirmed that little or no damage was done to any of the ships in this attack. Later in the month the Liberators joined in on the attacks on Benghazi and Tobruk, bombing shipping and harbour installations.

In July the Halifaxes of Nos 10 and 76 detachments arrived in the Middle East, and their story is even more confused and complicated than that of the Liberators. Sixteen Halifaxes each from Nos 10 and 76 Squadrons Bomber Command were detached to Egypt at the beginning of July, but brought with them little in the way of ground personnel to service their aircraft. A temporary solution to the problem was achieved by attaching the ground elements of two other squadrons (Nos 227 and 454) who were without aircraft – and thus the linked squadrons 10/227 and 76/454 were set up. This arrangement continued until 7 September, when all the Halifaxes were formed into No. 462 Squadron. By July the fighters and medium bombers Desert Air Force had been pressed back into the lap of the Egypt-based night bomber squadrons, and there were not enough airfields to go around. Thus the heavy bombers (the Liberators and Halifaxes) were forced to move to Palestine (Aqir and St Jean), and the Wellingtons to Shallufa, Kabrit and Abu Suier in the Canal Zone. In Palestine the aircraft of No. 159 Squadron were being serviced by personnel of Nos 458 and then 454 RAAF Squadrons, and then in September the No 159 Squadron element continued on to India, and the Liberators left in the Middle East adopted the identity of No 160 Squadron.

During July the American heavy bombers were reinforced with a few Fortresses from India. Major General Lewis H. Brereton, Commander of the 10 Air Force, had been ordered on 23 June to gather every heavy bomber he could muster and proceed to Egypt on temporary duty. Two days later he left India with 225 men and nine clapped-out Fortresses of the 9 Bombardment Squadron – described in the official history as 'near cripples' – and arrived at Cairo on 28 June. He was immediately placed in command of US Army, Middle East Air Forces (USAMEAF), which comprised the Halverson Detachment, the 9th Bombardment Squadron, and the other personnel that Brereton brought from India. When Rommel advanced into Egypt the Fortresses were moved to Lydda in Palestine, but the HALPRO Liberators stayed at Fayid until 16 July.

The inclusion of the USAAF Liberators in the Middle East Command was granted on the understanding that these aircraft should not be employed in 'local operations, nor in a manner unsuited to their characteristics'. In other words, they should be used in daylight bombing operations against strategic targets. The Chief of the Air Staff in London advocated a similar policy for the RAF Liberators, and for the Halifaxes that had arrived in the theatre. He had obtained the release of these aircraft from Harris' Bomber Command and from the task of bombing Germany with some difficulty. It was seen as an experiment in strategic mobility, switching heavy bomber units from one theatre to another according to the needs of the moment, and not as a permanent transfer. Tedder assured him that the heavy bombers would only be used against the enemy's supply routes to Tripoli and Cyrenaica by attacks on ports and shipping, but the crisis in the desert meant that all available forces would be needed to stem the German advance.

Air Marshal Harris was also concerned about what he saw as another continuous drain on his resources – the fact that all pilots for the medium and heavy bombers had to be sent out from the UK as there were no OTUs (Operational Training Units) for these types in the Middle East. In March 1942 he signalled Tedder that he believed that many trained bomber crews in the Middle East were either misemployed in ground jobs or 'kicking their heels in units'. With typical Harris hyperbole he stated that the situation was so serious as a result of a shortage of trained aircrews in Bomber Command that 'we either alter this hopeless state of affairs and at once, or we perish.' Tedder responded by stating that Harris' information was 'fantastically incorrect', and he appealed to the CAS to put a stop to the 'poison tongues...active at home spreading half-baked stories'. Harris raised the matter again in August, and the Air Council sent the Deputy Director of Postings to the Middle East to check on the facts of the situation. Once again, Harris was proved to be completely wrong, and there was no evidence that aircrew were being wasted.

*   *   *

The key to the whole strategic situation in the Mediterranean was Malta, and if the air and naval forces on the island were to be effective in threatening Rommel's supply lines then they too had to be supplied. By April 1942 the situation on the island was very serious, and unless rearmed and revictualled, it could not be expected to hold out for much longer. Operations to capture Malta had been prepared by both the Italians (Operation *C.3*) and the Germans (Operation *Hercules*), and might soon be put into effect. With enemy air forces based on Sicily and Sardinia, and now holding the bases in Cyrenaica as well, it was extremely difficult to get a convoy to the island from the east or the west.

Nevertheless, at the height of the battles at Gazala, two convoys were sent to Malta, one west-bound from Alexandria (Operation *Vigorous*) and one east-bound from Gibraltar (Operation *Harpoon*). Attacks on both convoys from the air were certain, and interception of one or both by the Italian Fleet was possible and even probable. The task of the RAF, therefore, was to provide the maximum fighter cover for the convoys, and to attack the Axis air forces at their bases and the Italian Fleet in harbour and at sea. The ten aircraft of No. 104 Squadron, which had been sent to Malta on 23 May, were detailed to attack the Axis air force bases and the Italian Fleet in harbour. The attacks began in the last week in May, when the Wellingtons operated against Taranto, Messina, and the Sicilian and Sardinian airfields. They would stay on Malta until 11 June, flying eighty-three sorties in fourteen operations and losing three aircraft in the process.

The aircraft of No. 104 Squadron went to Catania on 28/29 and 29/30 May, where bombs were seen to burst on the main runway and amongst buildings. One of the Wellingtons lost an engine over enemy territory, and the crew jettisoned everything they could to maintain height on the return trip to Luqa. They managed to get back, but the aircraft crashed and burst into flames on its approach. Three died in the crash and the second pilot died later in hospital.

Two of the Malta Wellingtons went to Messina on 30/31 May, where a 4,000-lb bomb was seen to burst near oil tanks, but other results were unobserved due to the smokescreen. Seven went back on the following night, bombing the harbour and airfield. The commercial oil tanks were believed to have been hit, as repeated explosions and huge fires with black smoke visible for forty miles were caused. One of the aircraft had engine trouble and ditched five kilometres off Malta on return, but the crew were rescued by an ASR launch from Kalafrana. Another had engine failure on its approach to Luqa, but its distress signals were not seen and permission to land was not given. The pilot attempted to go around again, but lost height and landed across the flare path, colliding with two parked aircraft. The targets for No. 104 Squadron between 1/2 June and 10/11 June were the airfield at Catania (twelve sorties in two attacks), shipping in the port of Taranto (twenty-three sorties in three attacks), Cagliari (twelve sorties in two attacks), Naples (one attack of six sorties) and the submarine base at Augusta (one attack of three sorties).

In June, No. 38 Squadron, now operating in its new torpedo-bomber role, flew twenty-one sorties from Malta. An attack on the Italian fleet on the 15/16th as part of the *Vigorous* operation resulted in a hit on the battleship *Littorio*, which put her out of action for more than two months. Further attacks on enemy convoys were carried out between 26/27 June and 3/4 July. On 26 July four aircraft carried out a torpedo strike against shipping off Tobruk, and this was the last operation carried out by the Squadron under the control of No. 205 Group. On 28 July a postagram was received from HQ No. 205 Group informing No. 38 Squadron that with effect from that date the Squadron was transferred to the operational and administrative control of No. 201 (Naval Cooperation) Group. From now on they would operate almost solely on mining and torpedo bombing operations.

Meanwhile, the Liberators of Nos. 108 and 159 Squadrons took advantage of their long range to attack Taranto on three nights between 9/10 and 13/14 June, but only five sorties were despatched and again few results were observed. As stated above, seven Liberators of the HALPRO Detachment attacked Italian Naval Units on 15 June, and believed at the time that the *Vittoria Veneto* had been heavily damaged. However, little or no damage was done to the ships in this attack.

In addition, Wellingtons from Egypt attacked the Axis airfields in Crete in the second week of June, and a special attack on the bomber bases at Derna and Siret el Chreiba on the night of 13/14 June, immediately before the west-bound convoy was due to pass through 'Bomb Alley' between Crete and Cyrenaica. Eight aircraft bombed the target area, but no results were seen. The No. 148 Squadron ORB states that this was 'Another unsatisfactory op' – none of the aircraft saw any aircraft on the ground, let alone hit any. Fog started formed after the first aircraft landed, but four more got down with visibility down to 100 feet. One failed on its first attempt to land, and tried to go round again. After it raised its flaps it crashed into the airfield, caught fire and burnt out. All the crew were shaken but safe. A sad postscript to this incident occurred two days later when one of the crew of this aircraft (Sergeant R.G. Gravell) was 'put up as unfit for further operations' – partly as a result of the crash.

The *Vigorous* convoy set off from Alexandria on the afternoon of 13 June, but air attacks and fear of interception by units of the Italian Fleet that had left Taranto caused it to turn back, and on 15 June it abandoned its task and returned to port. The convoy from Gibraltar, *Harpoon*, battled through to Malta, although it lost four merchant vessels, a cruiser and two destroyers. Nevertheless, the two merchant vessels that got through ensured the survival of the island for the time being, until another convoy could be sent through from Gibraltar during August (Operation *Pedestal*).

*   *   *

The two sides slugged it out on the El Alamein position for the whole of July, with neither able to gain a decisive advantage. Auchinleck was able to stop Rommel, but not to defeat him. The fighting at El Alamein during the month was almost continuous, often very heavy, and much of it is difficult to follow. Offensive and counter offensive were launched with bewildering complexity, and little advantage was gained by either side. The enemy also failed to take advantage of the proximity of his forward air bases to hit sensitive spots in the British back areas. The pursuit to El Alamein had made the Advanced Landing Grounds at El Daba available to the *Luftwaffe*, and these were only ninety miles from Alexandria, 185 miles from Cairo, and less than 250 miles away from the Delta and the Canal Zone. Yet, apart from fairly large raids from 3 to 7 July and again between 25 and 30, the enemy showed little inclination to use his bombers to attack these areas.

At last light on 1 July the enemy succeeded in capturing the important position at Deir el Shein, opening a gap in the Alamein line and making possible a typical Rommel operation in which he could cut the coast road just south of El Alamein and then make a sweep towards the south. During the night eighty-two Wellingtons and the Blenheims of No. 14 Squadron[2] continued the attacks in the battle area that had begun on the night of 25/26 June, the primary focus being on the coast road area to the west of El Alamein. They also bombed enemy concentrations to the south-west of El Alamein in the Deir el Shein sector, and the landing grounds at El Daba and Fuka. Some of the flares dropped by the Albacores were too high for efficient bombing, and enemy vehicles were reported to be 'well dispersed and not seen in any great numbers'. Nevertheless, the attacks were generally successful, and the bombers left behind a trail of fires, exploding ammunition trucks and bomb-blasted lorries. Two aircraft failed to return after a very large explosion followed by falling burning debris was seen in the sky, and it was thought that they had collided over the target area.

These operations in support of the troops on the ground were quite different in character from other 'ops'. They had to be improvised to cope with the quickly changing military situation, and in the main they were directed against tanks, transport concentrations or columns, ammunition dumps etc. They were, in effect, 'seek and destroy' operations, as this was a mobile war with few static targets. They could be protracted and were carried out at low levels in the light of flares from the Albacores. Sometimes there was little opposition in the form of flak, but the target area was a night fighter's paradise, with the bombers themselves lit by the flares and showing up against the illumined surface of the desert. Although dangerous, the battle area operations were popular with the crews because they knew that they were assisting directly in the ground fighting. The combination of target illumination by FAA Albacores and attacks by the Wellingtons often caught concentrations of vehicles in leaguer and interfered seriously with the work of maintenance. However, the AHB Narrative *The Middle East Campaigns* makes the point that the use of the term 'concentration' is misleading in the context of the battle area attacks:

> The impression obtained by the use of the word in this context is of a vast car park presenting a wonderful target for air bombardment. The term is, however, merely relative and aerial photographs taken at the time give very much the impression of coarse grains of sand scattered loosely over a plate. These reports of concentrations of as many as three thousand MT vehicles

which were observed in assembly areas to the rear of the front-line troops and tank formations certainly presented targets, but often comparatively unproductive ones, especially for night bombing, each vehicle being perhaps fifty to one hundred yards from its neighbour and, in the aggregate, possibly covering several square miles of open, more or less featureless desert.[3]

Such 'concentrations' were often ignored by the night bombers in favour of attacks along the coast road, where the enemy transport was restricted by the narrow, winding road and congestion often built up. The thirty miles of road between Gazala and El Alamein were the last stages in the essential pipeline for supplies and reinforcements for the Panzer Army. The desert railway, stretching back through Matruh for nearly 350 miles as far west as the port of Tobruk, also ran along the coast, and the main series of enemy landing grounds at El Daba and Fuka were close to the road and railway. Often, in a single night raid attacks would be launched on convoys and dumps along the road, on trains along the track, and any spare bombs could be unloaded on dispersed aircraft and tented camps around the landing grounds.

On 2 July, following the success at Deir el Shein, German radio announced that El Alamein had been taken and the Eighth Army was again in full retreat. The announcement was premature, and although Rommel attacked again in the afternoon of 2 July, covered by severe dust storms and overcast that hampered the activities of the RAF, he was running out of men, machines and supplies. During the night eighty-seven Wellingtons and fourteen Albacores went to the battle area again, and generally the operation was considered by the crews to be 'most successful'. One of the aircraft of No. 37 Squadron caused a huge explosion, followed by a red glare covering the whole area and clouds of black smoke reaching to 5,000 feet. The aircraft was very badly rocked, the bomb aimer's Perspex shattered, and the starboard engine began to give trouble. The pilot immediately set course for home, but the starboard propeller fell off near Wadi Natrun and the engine caught fire. The captain ordered the crew to bale out and four landed safely, but two bodies were recovered later from the crash site. Another aircraft from No. 37 Squadron was shot down by a night fighter twenty-four kilometres west of El Daba, and one crew member was captured and the rest killed. One Wellington of No. 104 Squadron was hit by flak and lost an engine, and eventually crash-landed in the desert. The crew walked east for three days before being captured just short of the Allied lines.

On 3 July there were only two engagements between the opposing land forces, but in them Rommel staked all that was left of his Army's strength – and lost. The ceaseless attacks by the RAF during the day strangled his lines of communication, and the attacks continued throughout the night. Seventy-two Wellingtons, seven Albacores, five Blenheims and two USAAF Fortresses attacked railway installations and motor transport concentrations in the Ghazal, El Daba and Fuka areas, and hits were claimed on dumps, MT and an ammunition train. The loss of ammunition was to have serious repercussions, as on the following day the Afrika Korps War Diary recorded that batteries were reduced to ten rounds per gun. The two Fortresses were carrying out the first operation by the 9th Bombardment Squadron, recently arrived in the Middle East. Twelve aircraft of No. 40 Squadron were given a specific mission to bomb the tank repair depot east of Mersa Matruh, but the majority appeared to have missed the primary target. One of the aircraft was hit by flak on the bombing run, and went down in flames.

On 4 July 1942 Rommel informed the General Staff of the *Wehrmacht* that he must temporarily suspend further attacks and go over to the defensive for approximately two weeks in order to bring up men and supplies. An enemy attack in the afternoon failed so completely that a large group of the exhausted German infantry decided to give up the fight and surrender. They were immediately fired on by their own artillery, and many were killed. In the evening there were signs of a general withdrawal of the enemy tanks and infantry westwards along the Ruweisat Ridge. That night the final battle area attack before the first phase of the fighting at El Alamein died down was carried by eighty-four Wellingtons. They attacked a variety of targets in the northern coastal area, mainly in the vicinity of El Daba and Ghazal. A violent explosion was followed by a fire with flames up to 1,500 feet at El Daba, and a direct hit on an ammunition train west of Ghazal caused another enormous explosion with smoke up to 4,000 feet. Thus ended what the AHB Narrative, *The Middle East Campaigns*, calls the First Phase of the El Alamein battles. Targets in the battle area continued to be attacked by the night bombers throughout the month of July, but the most intensive phase was over. There was now a gradual switch to strategic targets again, bombing shipping in the ports of Tobruk and Mersa Matruh.

There was, of course, much more fighting in July. On 10 July Rommel commenced a full-scale offensive in the central sector, which was brought to a halt by the combined efforts of the 5 New Zealand Brigade and the 7 Armoured Brigade. On the same day Auchinleck launched an attack on the XXX Corps front with the limited objective of capturing Tel el Eisa, catching the enemy of guard and securing a useful salient in the north. Auchinleck then tried twice to break through the enemy's centre – on the Ruweisat ridge between 14 and 16 July, and again on this ridge and at El Mreir on 21 and 22 July – but both were repulsed with heavy loss. After a short pause XXX Corps again attacked near Tel el Eisa and the Miteira Ridge, but this, too, was unsuccessful, and Auchinleck then decided that he must make a long pause to rest, reorganize, and re-train his battered army. The main night-bombing effort for the rest of July was directed at Tobruk in an attempt to starve the Axis forces of fuel and ammunition.

When Rommel's offensive ground to a halt at El Alamein in July he was faced with dilemma. He could either retreat back to the Egyptian frontier and await the outcome of Operation *Hercules* against Malta to clear his supply lines and build up his forces, or he could stand on the El Alamein line. He chose the latter, and would soon pay for this error with a major defeat. The increase in the offensive capacity of Malta meant that shipping movements on the western route from Italy to Tripoli and Benghazi had to be temporarily suspended, and so he was now largely dependent on the supplies that could come through Tobruk. Even if the supplies got to Tobruk and were not destroyed at the port by the night bombers, there was then that precarious 350 miles of road and railway between the port and El Alamein. On 11 July the Chief of the Air Staff in London signalled Tedder, rather pointlessly impressing on him the 'vital importance of denying the ports of Benghazi and Tobruk to the enemy'. Tedder's reply was short and sharp, pointing out that he was well aware of the importance of the ports, and that the scale of effort of his Wellingtons had 'been far beyond any sustained by home Wellington squadrons'.

It was not surprising, therefore, that Tobruk appeared on the ops board on twenty-nine nights during July, and a total of 1,299 sorties were despatched to attack shipping and harbour installations. Another fifty-eight minelaying sorties were carried out on the entrance to the harbour, and a few attacks were also carried out on a convoy approaching the port from Italy. Most of these attacks were carried out by the Wellingtons of Nos 37, 38, 70, 104, 108, 148 and 162 Squadrons, but the RAF Liberators and Halifaxes and the USAAF Liberators and Fortresses also contributed to the effort. Thirty-six aircraft were lost (thirty-three Wellingtons, one Liberator and two Halifaxes). 17 July was marked by a new enterprise – the first *daylight* raid by the heavy bombers on Tobruk. A force of thirteen RAF and USAAF Liberators approached the port from the sea and attacked it successfully without suffering any loss.

Although the Squadron and Group ORBs are full of positive comments on the operations against Tobruk, an analysis of photographs made at the end of July suggested that very few ships were actually destroyed in the attacks. The AHB Narrative states that 'the sum total of the expenditure of effort against Tobruk…appear to have given most disappointing results[4]', but also acknowledges that damage to installations on the shore must have caused many problems for the enemy. The final analysis concludes that the night attacks achieved largely a negative effect by deterring the enemy from using the port to anything like its full capacity. Shipping had to be routed further to the west, to Benghazi, and it also compelled the enemy to extend the hopelessly uneconomic use of aircraft and submarines to get supplies through to Rommel.

Benghazi was now a long way away from the bomber bases in the Canal Zone and in Palestine, and only the Liberators could reach the port with an economic bomb load. Only seventy-seven sorties were despatched to the port, and a few also went to the subsidiary ports at Bardia, Sollum and Mersa Matruh. The attacks by USAAF Liberators and Fortresses on Tobruk and Benghazi were supplemented by attacks on shipping in the Mediterranean en route to North Africa, and at Suda Bay and Pylos Bay in Greece. The total number of heavy bombers available was only .twenty-eight (nineteen Liberators and nine Fortresses), of which seven and three respectively were operationally fit on 19 July. On 20 July the aircraft were organized as the 1st Provisional Group under Halverson's command. However, reinforcements were on the way, as the 98th Bombardment Group was assigned to USAMEAF on 23 July, and its Liberators would start arriving in the Middle East on 25 July, when the air echelon of the 344th Squadron flew into Ramat David in Palestine. By 7 August the complete Group had arrived, with two squadrons each at Ramat David and St Jean d'Acre. Their first mission (by the 344th Squadron) was on 1 August, when seven of their aircraft attacked a tank repair depot and port facilities at Mersa Metruh. The Americans also began to take their heavy bombers to Navarino Bay in the Peloponnese and to Suda Bay off northern Crete, assembly points for convoys, and to places as distant as the Corinth Canal.

On the night of 11/12 July a single Halifax took off to attack shipping at Tobruk, and the two linked squadrons (10/227 and 76/454) would increasingly add their weight to the night-bombing effort. They flew eighty-one sorties during this period, all against Tobruk. They were joined by the Liberators of Nos 159/160

Squadrons, which flew 124 sorties during the period in question, to Benghazi, to Tobruk, to the battle area, to Suda Bay, and to Navarino. The harassing effect of 'round the clock' bombing was noted with growing frequency in the enemy's diaries, and Rommel himself referred to it as the main feature of the violent and bloody battles of July. On 21 July Rommel had made a long and depressing report to OKH – a report of the failure of his plans. He was down to 30 per cent of his effective strength, and the losses in experienced men were particularly serious, as the replacements were found to be only partly trained.

*   *   *

Rommel's situation at this time was made worse by the partial recovery of Malta as an offensive base. The *Pedestal* convoy delivered just enough supplies to keep the island alive and kicking, especially the precious cargo of the tanker *Ohio*, which struggled into the harbour on the morning of 15 August. Now there were fewer enemy bombers available to attack the island, and there were enough fighters to go out to meet the enemy attacks over the sea. The 10th Submarine Flotilla returned to Malta towards the end of July, and the submarines soon made their presence felt again. By 29 August only about 1,500 tons of supplies had arrived at Tobruk, but Rommel still resolved to attack at El Alamein at the end of August. The serious loss of ships caused by the resurgence of Malta meant that more use had to be made of the air route from Crete, from where around 500 transport aircraft were being used to carry men and supplies to Egypt and Libya. Small numbers of Wellingtons and Liberators of No. 205 Group attacked the airfields in Crete, where they doubtless caused some disorganization and damage, but their main target was always Tobruk.

On 13 August General Bernard Law Montgomery took command of the Eighth Army, and immediately stamped his own brand of authority on the situation. He was determined to attack Rommel as soon as he felt able, but was not going to rush things. At this time Rommel was far from fit, and had long been suffering from a stomach complaint, aggravated by the mental and physical strain of the past few weeks and by the climate. On 22 August he asked for a substitute to be sent out in time for the coming offensive, but later decided that he felt well enough to command the operation and would then have to take a long rest in Germany. It is therefore not surprising that the old fire and enthusiasm was lacking in what became known as the Battle of Alam el Halfa.

During month of August the bombers of No. 205 Group, supported by the Liberators and Fortresses of the USAAF, flew 1,920 sorties. The major part of the effort was carried by the Wellington Squadrons (1,493 sorties), with the Halifaxes contributing 155 sorties, the RAF Liberators 76 sorties, and the USAAF Liberators and Fortresses another 196 sorties. Of these, 1,336 sorties (70 per cent) were directed against ports, 359 (19 per cent) against targets in the battle area, and 158 (8 per cent) against airfields. Tobruk was attacked on twenty-eight nights (1,298 sorties), and the bombers also attacked Bardia, Sollum and Mersa Matruh to try to prevent coastal vessels and barges bringing in small amounts of supplies. Tripoli was a long way behind the front line in Egypt, and had almost completely dropped out of use as a supply port. Only the biggest Axis ships were using Benghazi, and, anyway, only the few Liberators and Halifaxes could reach it now. The raids on Tobruk usually encountered fierce opposition from flak and searchlights, as powerful

113

defences had been assembled around Rommel's chief supply port. Gunby tells of a raid recalled by Flying Officer Eric Laithwaite of No. 40 Squadron, who was acting as bomb aimer:

> Target coming nicely down the parallel wires of the bombsight. Then just at release point, all the searchlights in Tobruk got us. And the flak. The smell of the cordite was strong. The bombs went – I did not think in the circumstances that I would get a medal for asking for a second run. Never had I experienced evasive action such as that performed by Squadron Leader Booth. The rudder bar was clanking behind my head as I tried to resecure the bombsight which came off the spigot, tried to operate the camera, tried to recover my parachute and harness, both of which came undone. All in the blinding light of the searchlights and the exploding of the ack-ack shells.[5]

Attacks on Tobruk were usually made at a height of about 8,000 feet, and from 5 August a 'New Plan' was put into operation. This was really the method that had been employed by Bomber Command for some time, and involved 'blitz' attacks. The bombers attacked at specific times so as to prevent the defences concentrating on single aircraft over the target, and special aircraft were detailed as illuminators. In North Africa the flak and searchlights were concentrated at a few key points, and the night fighters lacked a sophisticated ground controlled radar system to direct them onto the bombers. The crews were thus able to relax more than their counterparts over Europe, and there were many other benefits for the bomber crews, recalled by Sergeant Stan Brew of No. 40 Squadron and again reported by Gunby:

> The Tobruk runs were about eight and a half hours, the trip each way a little like the Arabian Nights, moonlight, stars, the gleaming Med. We would listen to the BBC on the way home and often had a sing-song if the tunes were known – good spirits all round, and a super crew.[6]

No. 40 Squadron had been at Shallufa since June, and this was a well-equipped permanent RAF station. Servicing was carried out in hangars, and the men were accommodated in comfortable huts and looked after by cheerful Italian prisoners. It then moved to Kabrit on the Great Bitter Lake in August, where the men had to live in tents and fend for themselves. The move had been initiated by Wing Commander Ridgeway, who anticipated that the Squadron would soon be on the move from the Delta bases and back to living rough in the desert. There were compensations, however, in that the camp was only yards from the lake, and some of the men found an abandoned twelve-foot sailing dinghy and were soon enjoying sailing on the lake. Others took to the water in improvised canoes from scraps of wood and doped aircraft fabric. The snag with Kabrit was the bed bugs, and a solution was found by placing the bed legs in tins filled with paraffin. Otherwise, the beds were regularly slung into the lake to 'sweeten' them.

Battle area attacks by the night bombers started again on 21/22 August, as the build up for the Battle of Alam Halfa began. Seventeen aircraft were despatched and a concentration of small tents was located and attacked, but the enemy had dispersed his transport and tanks very well and good targets were difficult to find. One crew saw and bombed about twenty tanks moving north, and another bombed a concentration of vehicles. On the next night forty-one Wellingtons were out over the battle area, and many direct hits were claimed on vehicles and tanks. No. 148 Squadron ORB reports that the crews were glad of a change of target, as Tobruk had been hit fifteen times so far this month. The attacks continued on every night until 4/5 September, with the Albacores doing their usual good job of illuminating the target areas. GHQ *Panzerarmee Afrika* later reported that the continual heavy air attacks by day and night caused many casualties to men and much damage to equipment, and affected the morale of both Italian and German troops.

*   *   *

Rommel's last attempt to break the Alamein Line, the Battle of Alam Halfa, began on 30 August. His plan was simple and bold. A very strong striking force from the 15 and 21 Panzer Divisions would move eastwards around the left flank of the Eighth Army, and then wheel to the left. This would bring it into a long line facing north and it was then scheduled to attack the rear of the Eighth Army at 0600 hours on 31 August. This meant that the panzers had seven hours in which to travel thirty miles over entirely unreconnoitred ground, which was known to be mined but the extent of the minefields was unknown. This was wildly optimistic, and, anyway, Ultra[7] had told Montgomery that Rommel was coming. He knew that the blow would fall on the 13 Corps sector, and the key to the position was the Alam el Halfa ridge. Montgomery had made his dispositions accordingly. The ridge was strongly fortified, held by the 44 Division and the tanks and anti-tank guns of the 22 Armoured Brigade.

At last light on 30 August the final concentrations of the Axis forces were seen by a single reconnaissance aircraft of No. 208 Squadron, and by 0100 hours on 31 August the flare-dropping Albacores had arrived on the scene, closely followed by a force of Wellingtons. By the time that the enemy's striking force had reached the first minefield it was under attack by twenty Wellingtons from Nos 37, 70 and 104 Squadrons, which bombed and machine-gunned 'well scattered MT'. No. 70 Squadron ORB reported that 'Jerry's long-awaited drive for Alex and the Delta' had started, and their Wellingtons attacked targets in the battle area between 0104 and 0246 hours. One of their aircraft failed to return, but two days later the crew turned up at base 'none the worse'. It had been attacked by night fighters and set on fire, but the pilot made a successful belly-landing within our own lines and the crew were picked up by the Household Cavalry. Two aircraft of No. 104 Squadron, searching for targets of opportunity in the battle area, located and bombed a tented camp, which turned out to be the DAK Headquarters:

> ...the Commanding General and several officers were wounded by a serious direct hit at Corps Battle Headquarters. General Nehring, slightly wounded, is seeking the main dressing station. Lt von Burgdorff and Civilian Specialist Schmidt have been seriously wounded. They succumbed later to their injuries. Until further notice the Chief of the General Staff, Staff Colonel Bayerlein, will take over the command of the Corps.[8]

To add to the misfortunes Major General von Bismarck, the Commanding Officer of the 21st Panzer Division, was killed at the head of his troops. As the panzers tried to advance they were strongly harassed by elements of the 7th Motor and 4th Light Armoured Brigades and attacked from the air. They made desperately slow progress, and Rommel arrived at 0800 hours to assess the situation. His first inclination was to call a halt, but after discussion with Bayerlein decided to have a go at capturing the Alam el Halfa ridge. The attack was due to go in at noon, but the DAK had difficulty forming up due to a dust-storm and got off to a late and ragged start.

The tanks of the 21st Panzer Division ran onto the anti-tank screen set up by the 22nd Armoured Brigade and the 44th Divisional Artillery, and received a hot reception. The 15th Panzer Division threatened to get round the Brigade's left flank, but darkness was falling and ammunition and fuel was running low, and von Vaerst called the attack off. On 31 August the following message was received by all squadrons from AOC-in-C Middle East:

> The Battle of Egypt has begun. This is a vital battle perhaps the most vital battle of the war. The Commander in Chief of the Army has called upon our troops to stand fast and destroy the enemy at all costs. It is for us to support the Army to the utmost limit of our ability. During the last battle [First El Alamein] your effort in the air and on the ground, in the squadrons and in the workshops were magnificent and decisive, so once again I confidently call on every officer and man whatever his job to put forth a supreme effort. Every one of us must do his utmost and more than his utmost. In the last battle the enemy was stopped when he thought victory was certain. This time he can and must be finally crushed.

During the night of 31 August/1 September the Wellingtons of Nos 40, 108 and 148 Squadrons again attacked targets in the battle area, many carrying out two sorties. The area in which the enemy lay was brilliantly lit up by flares from the ubiquitous Albacores, and tremendous havoc was caused among the concentrations of vehicles. The first attacks were made by twenty-eight aircraft between 2057 and 2340 hours, and the second attacks by twenty aircraft went in between 0040 and 0315 hours. No. 148 Squadron ORB states that the crews all had been impressed with the 'vital urgency of tonight's operation and the need for accurate bombing'. They found the target well illuminated, and many direct hits and fires were claimed by all the crews. All the aircraft from the first sortie returned safely, and were hurriedly prepared for the second attack. One was unable to take off due to a damaged engine cowling, but fourteen were in the air again forty-five minutes after landing. Fires were still burning from the first attack, and many more started. No. 148 Squadron was justifiably proud of its efforts on this night, stating that the operation 'will go down in the Squadron's records as the most successful since the Squadron formed.' On the same night twenty-six Wellingtons from Nos 37, 40, 70 and 104 Squadrons and sixteen B-25s of the 12th USAAF Medium Bomber Group also attacked the enemy landing grounds around Fuka and El Daba.

The night of continuous bombing left a pall of smoke from countless petrol fires and burning vehicles. The *Panzerarmee Afrika* War Diary recorded that not only was the damage very great, but officers and men were badly shaken and their fighting capacity considerably reduced by the enforced dispersal, lack of sleep, and the strain of waiting for the next bomb. Their diary reports that:

> ...about 8 parachute flares were dropped over the defence area shortly before 2130 hours, followed immediately by 6–10 bombs, most of which fell among 33rd Reconnaissance Unit (baggage) transport, setting a full tanker lorry on fire...After the fuel tanker lorry was set on fire, the first enemy aircraft

formation was reinforced by a second wave which also dropped flares immediately, so that for a time the defence area was lit up as bright as day...Attempts to move the vehicles out of the effective area of the flares failed, as any movement, even by individual soldiers, was immediately prevented by a low-level bombing attack. All the aircraft dropped their bombs singly on identified targets – practically no sticks were dropped...[9]

Major-General Verney, in his book *The Desert Rats*, also describes the scene:

The 22nd Armoured Brigade...were in positions south of the Alam Halfa Ridge and the enemy reached them in the evening of the 31st August. The German attacks were repelled and as night came the RAF bombers, who had not been able to act previously on account of the great clouds of dust, began to hammer the enemy. Major H. Woods of the KRRC described the scene: At 12:30 a.m. our bombers...found his whole strength had moved eastwards and located him with flares in the valley below us. It was one of the most awe-inspiring sights I shall ever see, I think, – there were seldom less than 20 flares in the air at any one time and the whole valley with its mass of the Afrika Korps stationary was lit up like a huge orange fairyland. All the time, red-orange, white-green tracer was darting hither and thither like 100 mph coloured fairies. The huge flash of the bombs, which included two of 4,000 lbs, also inspired the whole thoroughly warlike scene, with little figures silhouetted against their vehicles as they tried to find cover from our bombs. The bombers were so accurate that they bombed right up to the minefield beyond which, 2,000 yards away, was another of our companies.[10]

Early on 1 September units of the 15th Panzer Division launched another attack on the 22nd Armoured Brigade but were held, and by the afternoon they were fast running out of fuel. Rommel was unable to get any more fuel forward, and was forced to go over to the defensive where he stood – and the area where he was standing was due for another heavy attack by the night bombers. Sixty-four Wellingtons of Nos 37, 40, 70, 104, 108 and 148 Squadrons and twenty-six Albacores attacked in two waves between 2230 hours and 0555 hours. Forty-one Wellingtons started the attack, led by the Albacores, and good fires were started over a wide area. One huge explosion rocked aircraft at 4,000 feet, and this developed into 'a hearty fire which exploded and blazed until the last aircraft left the target area at 0555 hours'. Although the ground crews at LG 224 were 'distracted from their work by a stray Ju 88 which dropped a stick of bombs', they managed to get eight aircraft of Nos 37 and 70 off on a second sortie. The second wave consisted in all of twenty-three aircraft, and these attacked between 0250 and 0555 hours. They started many small fires, and four larger ones that were burning well when they left for home. One of the aircraft of No. 104 Squadron returned with the starboard engine feathered, and the port engine then cut on approach to LG 237. It stalled and crashed on landing, but all the crew were safe.

On 2 September the main enemy armoured formations were still massed to the south of 22nd Armoured Brigade positions on the Alam el Halfa Ridge, and there they remained throughout most of the day. But the battle was lost, and at 1230 hours the Panzer Divisions were ordered to withdraw. That night the bombing in the battle area reached a peak of destructiveness. A total of seventy-six Wellington and eight Albacore sorties were flown between 2330 and 0500 hours, a bomb was dropped on the enemy at an average of one every forty seconds, and the weight of bombs dropped totalled 112 tons. The DAK War Diary estimated the number of aircraft operating on this night as about 300, and the number of bombs dropped as about 2,400, which is a reflection of the general effect of these night raids on the morale of the enemy. Two ammunition trucks or dumps were seen to explode, and over twenty fires were counted after the attack. Some were definitely petrol fires, and many 'explosions of pyrotechnics' were reported. The No. 70 Squadron ORB states that this attack 'was the most successful of all the Battle Area nights', and the Army 'admitted that this night's bombing marked the turning point of the Battle'. One aircraft of No. 40 Squadron blew up on landing at LG 237 as two bombs that had hung-up fell off and exploded under the aircraft. Four crew members died and two were injured.

On 3 September it was reported that the enemy was withdrawing to the south and south-west, and elements of the 7 Armoured Division followed up cautiously with its armoured cars, suspecting that the retreat might be a ruse to entice the Allied armour into battle. During the night sixty-two Wellingtons and nine Albacores were once again sent to attack tanks and MT concentrations in the battle area. The attacks were made between 0030 and 0500 hours, but the enemy had improved his dispersal and targets were more difficult to find. However, many fires were claimed among motor transport, some of which were still burning when the last aircraft turned for home. One of the aircraft of No. 148 Squadron crashed into high ground near LG 224 on return, with one crew member killed and three more injured. An even more important attack was carried out on 3/4 September by the former members of No. 205 Group, No. 38 Squadron now operating with No. 201 (Naval Cooperation) Group. Six torpedo Wellingtons and two bombers sank two tankers on their way to Tobruk, and this meant that while the Battle of Alam el Halfa was in progress, four out of five ships carrying urgently needed supplies to the Panzer Army were sunk or so damaged that their cargoes were effectively lost.

On 4 September the weather closed in, with severe dust-storms that limited air operations during the day. Rommel was intent on keeping his forces as intact as possible as he withdrew, and was able to do so with little interference. The battle area operations by the Wellingtons also tailed off, and during the night only twenty-one Wellingtons attacked scattered motor transport between 2056 and 2250 hours. One of the aircraft of No. 148 Squadron burst a tyre on take-off, but the captain decided to carry on with the operation and made a successful landing in soft sand on return. On the following night no bombing operations were carried out in the battle area, the Wellingtons turning once again to Tobruk. The Battle of Alam el Halfa was over, and the final lull in the desert now took place as Montgomery got ready to launch his own offensive. The battle had put an end to the Axis' hopes of reaching the Delta, and increased the morale and confidence of the Eighth Army. For the rest of September, following the Alam Halfa peak, bombing operations continued at a high level, but below that of the maximum efforts and furious pace of June, July and August. On 23 September Rommel left the desert on medical leave, and handed over command of *Panzerarmee Afrika* to von Thoma.

Between the night of 5/6 September and the end of the month almost all the sorties carried out by the Wellingtons were directed at Tobruk. The Group despatched 766 sorties in twenty-two attacks on the port and lost twenty-six aircraft in the process – a reflection of the strong AA defences erected around the harbour. One of the losses was BB462 of No. 70 Squadron, caught by searchlights and hit by flak on 8/9 September.[11] The tail gunner was Sergeant Trevor Bowyer; he tells how the starboard engine stopped, and the aircraft gradually lost height. The captain, Flying Officer R.C. Elliott, nursed the stricken aircraft back towards friendly territory, but it was a losing battle. Although the starboard engine started up again, it later died, and the Wellington came down in the Qattara Depression behind enemy lines. The crew began the long walk home, and after two days in the desert they heard the sound of vehicle engines coming closer. Were they friend or foe? Eventually, three armoured vehicles came into view, and an English voice called out to them. They had been found by a patrol of the 11th Lancers. Another crew had qualified for the Late Arrivals Club, the unofficial and prestigious club of 492 airmen who had returned from behind enemy lines during the North African campaign.

The night before[12] Trevor Bowyer's aircraft was lost his very good friend Dennis Bebbington had also failed to return from an attack on Tobruk. He and the rest of his crew were still missing when Trevor got back to base, and it was only after a month had elapsed and many adventures encountered that his friend turned up again. His Wellington (Z8976) had also been caught by searchlights and hit by flak, eventually coming down 350 miles behind enemy lines. After walking as far as Sidi Barrani, and with the rear gunner Flight Sergeant Croisiau suffering terribly with his feet, they came upon some Italian trucks. They decided to try to capture one of the vehicles, and after dark four of them crept up to the first truck. Flight Sergeant Croisiau grappled with the driver, but lost his revolver in the process. In the fire-fight that followed Croisiau was captured, and Dennis Bebbington was surrounded by Italian soldiers. However, in the darkness they failed to realize that he was a British airman, and he joined them in a search for his comrades! He met up again with the rest of the crew after twenty-four hours on his own in the desert, and with the help of friendly Arabs their journey homewards continued. They were eventually picked up by a South African patrol, and returned to base thirty days after they had come down in the desert.

On the night of 13/14 September the bombers of No. 205 Group carried out a series of attacks on the defences at Tobruk in order to create a diversion for a raid on the port (Operation *Agreement*). A force of Special Service troops was to penetrate the Tobruk perimeter at dusk and seize an inlet east of the harbour. Here, it would be reinforced by troops carried from Alexandria in MTBs, and the combined forces would then work their way westwards, capturing coastal defence and flak batteries on the way. A third force of Royal Marines would land from destroyers north of Tobruk town, capture the guns on the north side of the harbour, and enter the town. After causing general mayhem in the port some of the force would be withdrawn by sea and others would proceed westwards by land to cause further destruction. The concept was a bold one, and both Tedder and Montgomery had serious reservations about the whole operation.

A total of 103 aircraft took part in the attack, including sixteen Liberators and five Fortresses of the USAAF. Several large fires were started on the peninsula and a number of exceptionally large explosions reported. A particularly violent explosion was seen near the naval fuel tanks, followed by two big fires. A 4,000-lb bomb dropped on the western encampment area was claimed to have 'created

119

more debris than ever before seen by the crews'. Gun positions were heavily attacked, and it was 'significant that whereas twenty-four guns were firing effectively during the first hours of the operation, they diminished and became erratic as the attack developed'. The last aircraft to leave the target area reported that not more than three guns were still firing intermittently.

Four of the Wellingtons failed to return. The crew of one was captured, but several of them attempted to escape and three were killed in a skirmish with a patrol on the Sidi Barrani–Sollum road on 18 September. Another made a forced-landing on the return journey, and the crew started walking back. On the way they met a member of No. 148 Squadron (whose aircraft had crashed in the desert on 19/20 September). Gradually, the crew members started to drop out with exhaustion, and only two made it back to Allied lines. A third Wellington lost an engine over the target and eventually force-landed in the desert behind enemy lines. The crew evaded capture until 20 September, but eventually became prisoners of war. The fourth Wellington sent a message that it was returning with engine trouble, but force-landed and all the crew were captured. One died later when the ship in which he was being transferred to Italy was torpedoed.

Also, on 13/14 September twenty Liberators of No. 159 Squadron and the 1st Provisional Bombardment Group attacked Benghazi between 2045 and 0001 hours as part of Operation *Bigamy*. The object of the operation was similar to that of Operation *Agreement*, the temporary capture of Benghazi to carry out major demolitions in the port, but only a land force was involved. Results of the bombing were obscured by 10/10 cloud, and only bursts were seen in the target area. Operation *Bigamy* was abandoned after a preliminary attack by the land force found the defences on the alert. Operation *Agreement* was a disaster, as the naval force was discovered after only a few men were put ashore, and two destroyers and the light cruiser HMS *Coventry* were sunk. The land force withdrew without penetrating the Tobruk defences. Tedder and Montgomery were right to have reservations about these harebrained and unnecessary 'special operations'.

In September the bombers flew 1,286 sorties, which was considerably fewer than the effort during the crisis months of June, July and August. Of these, 978 sorties were by the Wellingtons of Nos 37, 40, 70, 104, 108, 148 and 162 Squadrons. The Halifaxes of No. 10/76/462 Squadron contributed 118 sorties, and the Liberators of No. 159/160 Squadron launched another 88 sorties. Some 23 sorties were flown by the Wellingtons of the Special Operations Flight, 11 to the Balkans, 10 to Greece, and 2 to Crete. The USAAF units operating in the Middle East managed 79 sorties, with a few B-25 operations now being mentioned in the Group ORB. Of these, 871 were bombing operations directed against ports, with another 31 minelaying sorties and 21 directed at ships at sea. Thus, a total of 923 sorties (72 per cent of the effort) was involved in the attempt to strangle Rommel's supply lines. Of the rest, 231 (18 per cent) went to targets in the battle area during the Battle of Alam el Halfa, and 103 (8 per cent) to the airfields.

*   *   *

The 'special relationship' between the Albacores of the Fleet Air Arm and the Wellingtons of No. 205 Group in June 1942 was suddenly endangered after the end of the Battle of Alam el Halfa when the Admiralty announced its intention to withdraw the Albacore squadrons and to replace them with twelve Swordfish aircraft. On 9 September Tedder wrote to the Chief of the Air Staff in London arguing that 'the technique which has evolved between the Albacores and the Wellingtons has been most effective', and 'is one of the most potent factors in land warfare which has emerged as a result of our experience':

> The point is that the Albacore flies slowly, and the pilot can put his head out and get clear vision, and in consequence, can amble about the countryside looking for targets with the help of the moon, and/or flares, until he finds something appetising on which to direct the Wellingtons.

Another problem was the steady decline in the Wellington strength in the Middle East. In July the number of serviceable aircraft had been approximately 130, but by October it was down to about eighty. Although there were six Wellington bomber squadrons in the theatre, the Wellington strength was only equal to that of four squadrons. When the Battle of El Alamein opened in October the Wellingtons of No. 205 Group and the heavy bomber units in Egypt were organized thus:

- No. 231 Wing (Nos 37 and 70 Squadrons) was based at Abu Suier, near the Suez Canal, equipped with Wellington ICs.

- No. 236 Wing (Nos 108 and 148 Squadrons) was based at LG 237 (Kilo 40 or Gebel Hamzi), about 25 miles west of Cairo, also equipped with Wellington ICs.

- No. 238 Wing (Nos 40 and 104 Squadrons) was based at Kabrit, on the Suez Canal, equipped with Wellington ICs and Wellington IIs.

- The Liberators of No. 160 Squadron came under the operational control of No. 242 Wing at Aqir, Palestine, and the Halifaxes of No. 462 Squadron came under the control of No. 245 Wing at Fayid, on the Suez Canal.

The month of October began with a stand down for Wellington squadrons, which the No. 70 Squadron ORB called a 'strange interlude' and which the ORB of No. 108 Squadron puts down to adverse weather conditions – 'electrical storms are very frequent just now in the target areas.' However, the Liberators of No. 160 Squadron were active on 1/2 October, eight of them attacking a convoy sailing between Crete and the North African coast and claiming a few near misses. The Wellingtons did not operate until the night of 5/6 October, when Tobruk was the target for forty Wellingtons and eight Halifaxes. The bombers went back to Tobruk on nine nights between 6/7 and 20/21 October, with a total of 352 sorties sent to bomb shipping and dock installations or to lay mines in the harbour. On 11/12 October twelve aircraft successfully laid mines outside the harbour, and twenty-nine bombers and two flare droppers not only succeeded in drawing away attention from the minelayers, but also carried out a highly satisfactory raid on gun positions, stores, and landing craft on the southern shore of the harbour. What was described as the largest fire ever seen at Tobruk was started in the stores area north-west of El Gubbi Landing Ground, another good fire was seen in the docks area, and other smaller fires were also reported.

Eight Liberators went out after a large Motor Vessel with five destroyers in convoy south-west of Crete on 6/7 October, but two abandoned the task and two failed to locate the target. The remaining aircraft attacked the convoy at 1845 hours, but only near misses were claimed. On the following night seven Halifaxes of No.

462 Squadron set out to attack a tanker that had been sighted in Suda Bay, with two Wellingtons of No. 162 Squadron acting as illuminators. Two returned early, a third was late and jettisoned its load, and the other four failed to locate the tanker and bombed the jetty area without visible results. On 11/12 October eight Liberators were despatched to attack a convoy sighted off Crete, but one returned early and the remainder were unable to locate the target. Two attacked secondary targets – oil installations at Suda Bay and a flare path at Heraklion – but no results were seen apart from the bomb bursts. One of the aircraft was attacked by a night fighter, and its hydraulic tank was holed. Two engines failed on approach to Aqir, and the pilot was unable to go round again. He put the aircraft down, but it swung and the undercarriage collapsed. The crew were all safe, but the aircraft was damaged beyond repair. On 16/17 October ten Liberators of No. 160 Squadron were despatched to attack shipping at Benghazi, but four abandoned their task and the remainder did not reach the target due to cloud and icing conditions and bombed Mersa Matruh instead.

Before looking at the events in North Africa in the build up to the Battle of El Alamein in detail, it is worth a brief consideration of what was happening on Malta at this time. By the end of September the threat of invasion had receded, and the island had partly recovered from the severe bombing of the previous April. Her submarines and aircraft were again causing loss and damage to the enemy's shipping. In October seventeen ships carrying 44 per cent of the supplies to the *Panzerarmee* were sunk, and on 19 October General Stumme reported that there was only enough fuel in North Africa for about eleven days at current rates of consumption and enough ammunition for roughly nine days' fighting. Then came news that the tanker *Panuco*, due at Tobruk on 20 October with 1,650 tons of petrol, had been hit by a Wellington of No. 69 Squadron from Malta and forced to put in at Taranto.

Malta was still desperately short of food, however, and of fuel for its aeroplanes. The fast minesweepers *Welshman* and *Manxman* were able to bring in some supplies, and submarines continued to carry in aviation spirit and such special foodstuffs as their limited stowage permitted. On 11 October the enemy's bombing of Malta was once more stepped up, although it was not comparable with the peak reached in the previous April. This was a response to the increasing losses of shipping – a consequence of the decision to abandon the plan to capture Malta in favour of advancing into Egypt – and involved the move of aircraft to the airfields on Sicily. The new blitz, however, was soon defeated. Raids were usually met and broken up over the sea north of the island. At first formations of as many as eighty Ju 88s were escorted by about twice that number of fighters, but by October 15 as few as fourteen bombers were being escorted by nearly 100 fighters. By the 18th of the month the enemy gave up using his Ju 88s altogether, and relied upon Bf 109 fighter-bombers, which could do little damage.

By 19 October the blitz had patently failed and heavy attacks had come to an end. Although the number of sorties during the nine-day battle was close to 2,400, the total weight of bombs dropped on the island was only 440 tons. The German records show that nine fighters and thirty-five bombers were lost, and Italian losses were probably similar. The main target had been Luqa airfield, but none of the Malta airfields had ever been put out of action for more than half an hour, and strikes against Axis shipping were carried out every night except one. On 20

November the *Stoneage* convoy reached Malta, the day that the Eighth Army entered Benghazi (see below), and on 5 December the *Portcullis* convoy arrived. The siege was effectively at an end, and from now on ships could move with relative safely between Egypt and Malta.

As the Eighth Army prepared to attack at El Alamein the RAF set out to subdue the enemy's fighters in the forward area, which were mainly based around El Daba and Fuka. The German dive-bombers were based at Sidi Haneish, and a substantial Italian bomber force was at Mersa Matruh. The *Luftwaffe* had begun to move units from Sicily and Crete to the Desert, but the October 'blitz' on Malta had disrupted the process and the losses sustained had made things more difficult for the German Air Force. Attacks on enemy airfields by No. 205 Group began on the night of 9/10 October, when forty-six Wellingtons carried out a very successful attack on Landing Grounds 17 and 18 at Fuka. The target area was well illuminated by Albacores, and crews reported seeing up to twenty aircraft on the ground, believed to be He 111s and/or Ju 88s. Direct hits were seen on two of these, a third blew up, and a fourth was set on fire. Four large and a dozen smaller fires were started on and between the Landing Grounds, and a number of violent explosions reported.

On 21/22 October the target for the Wellingtons was LG 16 (Fuka Satellite), where up to fifty enemy aircraft were seen on the ground. Very good illumination was provided by the Albacores, and many bursts were seen among dispersed aircraft and on blast shelters. A number of fires were started 'with pyrotechnics exploding from them', and clouds of black smoke. One Wellington attacked LG 18 (Fuka South) and claimed a direct hit on buildings, and some of the aircraft also machine-gunned dispersed aircraft, MT and tents at Bagush. The crew of one of the attacking aircraft stated that some of the enemy aircraft on LG 16 were 'huge' and 'much larger than Ju 52s'. There were some FW 200 'Condors' in the theatre at this time, and some may have been used to fly supplies into North Africa. One of the Wellingtons of No. 70 Squadron failed to return. Finally, on 22/23 October, the night before the guns opened fire at El Alamein, thirty-eight bombers were despatched to attack two of the Landing Grounds near El Daba. The targets were LG 104 (Qotafiyah II) and LG 20 (Qotafiyah I), where bombs fell among dispersed aircraft on both landing grounds. One of the Wellingtons of No. 108 Squadron claimed to have destroyed a single-engined fighter, which was last seen diving towards the sea with smoke pouring from it.

Meanwhile, the long-range four-engined bombers were attacking targets further afield, not always with great success. On 10/11 October six Halifaxes of No. 462 Squadron, with three Wellingtons of No. 162 Squadron acting as illuminators, set out to attack dispersed aircraft at Maleme and Tymbaki on Crete. One of the illuminators returned early with engine trouble, another failed to locate the target area, and the third arrived an hour late after engine trouble prior to take-off. None of the Halifaxes located the primary target at Maleme, and three jettisoned their bombs and returned to base. Two bombed at Tymbaki, and two good fires with explosions were started. The sixth Halifax was struck in the nose by flak, and two crew members were wounded. All electrical services in the forward fuselage were severed, and both outboard engines were put out of action. The damage to the aircraft made it impossible to jettison all the bombs, but the aircraft eventually made a successful forced landing thirty miles east of Mansura. For his courage in continuing to fulfil his duties despite severe injuries, the navigator, Flight

Lieutenant F. T. Collins, was awarded an immediate DFC. On 22/23 October four Halifaxes and eight Liberators went to Maleme again, and all of them saw their bombs bursting on the airfield. Some half dozen fires were seen, including one very large red one, and there was black smoke up to up to 4,000 feet. The Halifax crews reported that they 'were fired on from every part of Crete'. One of the Halifaxes ditched with engine trouble twenty kilometres north of Crete; the dinghy failed to inflate, and only one crew member survived.

*　　*　　*

At 2140 hours on 23 October 1942 more than a thousand guns opened fire on the Axis positions at El Alamein as the Eighth Army's XXX Corps began its drive on the northern end of the battle line. By 4 November Rommel's forces were in full retreat, and although the Allied pursuit was hesitant and badly handled, there would be no coming back this time. From the night of 23/24 October the main effort of the night bombers switched to the battle area, and they were briefed 'to destroy by bombing gun positions and other defences...and to cause the maximum amount of irritation and loss of sleep'. Chappell was aware that the 'business is about to begin!' and he watched the crews of No. 104 Squadron off from the cliffs at Kabrit – 'as always it was a stirring sight.' Sixty-six Wellingtons and twelve Albacores went out on the first night of the battle, and throughout the night they attacked enemy gun positions, motor transport concentrations, and other targets in the northern and southern sectors of the battle area. Some of the aircraft of Nos 104, 108 and 148 Squadrons carried out double sorties, and the attacks lasted from 2200 to 0145 hours. Five Wellingtons of No. 162 Squadron also operated, jamming enemy tank R/T in the battle area between midnight and 0545 hours on 24 October.

One large and three medium fires were started in the northern sector of the battlefront, and a terrific explosion that rocked the aircraft at 6,000 feet indicated that a gun emplacement and/or an ammunition dump was hit. One heavy and two light guns were silenced, and a large concentration of stores and vehicles was shot up on the coast road. More vehicles and possibly some tanks were located in the southern sector, but these were fairly well dispersed. Several direct hits and near misses were reported, and one large fire was started, which lasted for forty-five minutes. Two light AA guns were hit, and exploding ammunition seen. At 0400 hours returning aircraft reported that 'our guns' were in action throughout the entire front, from the sea to the Qattara Depression.

The aircraft again attacked targets in the battle area between 2200 and 0500 hours on 24/25 October, with the aircraft of Nos 37 and 70 Squadrons carrying out double sorties. Altogether, seventy-one sorties were despatched, and over 135 tons of bombs were dropped. The aircraft found the target area to be well illuminated by the Albacores, and the bombing was mainly directed against elements of the 15th Panzer Division on or near the Sidi Abd el Rahman track. The operation was declared to be 'fairly good and results...satisfactory', although a slight haze over the target area made observation of results difficult. One direct hit on a vehicle was claimed, and numerous bursts seen amongst others. A very large fire was started south of Sidi Abd el Rahman, with a trail of black smoke stretching for three miles towards the sea. Around another eleven fires were started, two of which developed into big fires and one gave off explosions. Three moving convoys of MT were straddled with bombs.

On 25 October Montgomery switched the attack to the north, and the following order of the day was received from the AOC-in-C:

For the defence of Egypt I called for a supreme effort. You gave and gave magnificently. We now pass to the offensive. Once again it is for each one of us, wherever our duty calls us, to do our utmost and more. Our duty is clear, to help our comrades in the Army in their battle and relentlessly to smash the enemy in the air, on land and at sea. With the inspiration of a great cause and cold determination to destroy an evil power we now have our great opportunity to strike a decisive blow to end this war. On with the job.

The ORB for No. 148 Squadron reported that tour - expired crews were put back on operations, aircraft on 240-hour inspections and other damaged Wellingtons were returned to service, and a high sortie rate could be expected during the battle period. The Liberators of No. 160 Squadron carried out a search for a convoy in the North of Derna during the day, but no shipping was seen. During the night seven Wellingtons of No. 70 Squadron attacked the Stuka base at Sidi Haneish South between 2320 and 2342 hours, where two fires were started. However, the main operation on 25/26 October was another big attack in the battle area, with double sorties put up by Nos 40 and 104 Squadrons and sixty-four sorties flown altogether. The aircraft attacked targets between 2200 and 0330 hours, bombing well dispersed vehicles and possibly tanks as well. Direct hits and many near misses were claimed, with one big exploding fire and several smaller ones started. The DAK Battle Headquarters was repeatedly raided, and its war diary remarked upon the incessant bombing attacks.

On 26 October Montgomery took stock, realizing that the first stage of the battle (Operation *Lightfoot*) had not achieved all that had been hoped of it. He began re-grouping his divisions for the final breakout, creating a reserve in order to restore the impetus to his attack. On 27 October a counter-attack by the 21st Panzer Division attempting to push the Eighth Army back into the German minefields failed, costing them fifty tanks and leaving Rommel with just eighty-one operational tanks. The Wellingtons of No. 205 Group played a significant part in breaking up the attack (see below). Further attacks by the Australians in the coastal bulge on 28/29 October and, again, two nights later achieved considerable success, and Montgomery was also creating a new striking force by milking the southern front. This would be used to deliver what he hoped would be the knockout blow – Operation *Supercharge*, which got underway on 2 November.

The battle area attacks carried out on the next six nights involved fewer aircraft as the night bomber squadrons and the Eighth Army took breath and prepared for the next major effort. In all, 144 sorties were despatched, bombing tanks and MT, although the enemy was dispersing his vehicles well by now and good targets were difficult to find. The briefing to the Wellingtons on the night of 26/27 October was 'to destroy by bombing the concentration of enemy troops and vehicles in the Battle Area, and to prevent the enemy concentrating still further'. Only twenty-six Wellingtons and six Albacores were available, augmented by five Wellingtons of No. 162 Squadron, which carried out their routine jamming operations and also bombed targets in the battle area. Good targets were illuminated by the Albacores, and four direct hits were claimed, as well as near misses among and close to vehicles. Five medium fires were started, and one large one with black smoke and

125

bursts of green and white smoke. Two aircraft also strafed vehicles in the area. No. 148 Squadron ORB records that 'great havoc' was caused amongst badly dispersed vehicles, and many fires were observed and flying debris filled the air. Enemy documents later revealed that the results were even more effective than those claimed at the time, and had more bombers been available then the attack that fell on the 21st Panzer Division might have had a more decisive effect on the battle.

Four further attacks by small numbers of Wellingtons (fifty-four sorties) were also carried out on Landing Grounds 13 and 14 (Maaten Bagush) where new concentrations of enemy aircraft were reported. The heaviest single attack was carried out on 30/31 October when eighteen Wellingtons raided LG 14, where reconnaissance had shown that the enemy had landed a considerable force of fighter reinforcements. Unfortunately, the flares were scattered and the results disappointing. The four-engined bombers focused their attentions on Maleme airfield at this time, with the Halifaxes of No. 462 Squadron flying twenty-two sorties and the Liberators of No. 160 Squadron flying twenty-four sorties to Crete. The critical state of Rommel's fuel supply had caused the Germans to fly petrol in from Crete, and the bombers took their toll of the Ju 52s detailed for the task. The Liberators reported about twenty aircraft at Maleme on 27 October, and claimed at least eight good fires with black smoke. Some of the fires were visible thirty miles south of the Island. One of the Liberators was shot down near the target area, and all eight crew members are buried in Suda Bay War Cemetery.

The Official History, commenting on the part played by the air forces during the period between *Lightfoot* and *Supercharge*, states that there is plenty of evidence of the cumulative effect on both Germans and Italians of the persistent round-the-clock bombing to which they had been subjected for some time. While bombing by day or by night causes few casualties among men crouching in narrow trenches or among vehicles and guns sunk in pits, during the dog-fight phase of the battle, 25 to 31 October, there was much movement of troops behind the enemy's front, and the air forces found good targets among men and vehicles on the move. It states that:

> The night-bombing attacks made by the skilful and experienced team of Wellingtons and flare-dropping Albacores never wanted for targets among the leaguers and transport concentrations and the various activities that went on by night in what may be called the front of the back area.[13]

The most important respect in which Operation *Supercharge* differed from Operation *Lightfoot* was in the employment of the night bomber force in a massive 'softening-up' operation lasting seven hours. Due to the weakness of the night bomber force it was only possible to maintain the heavy scale of attack by a system of double sorties. A total of ninety-three Wellington sorties were flown against targets in the battle area on the night of 1/2 November, supported by fourteen Albacores. The weight of bombs dropped totalled 184 tons, representing approximately 26 tons of high-explosive hitting the enemy every hour. It was the most concentrated bombing seen up to that time in the Middle East. The first attacks were south of Sidi Abd el Rahman, at Tel el Aqqaqir, and then around Ghazal station. Not a great deal of transport was seen in the early attacks, although small fires were started in the Rahman area. There was 'an abundance of targets' at Ghazal, and many direct hits claimed. Some extremely heavy explosions were caused, and around thirty big fires were started. As a result of an attack on the Afrika Korps Advanced Battle Headquarters about midnight, all telephone communications broke down.

Montgomery's offensive opened with a powerful barrage at 0105 hours on 2 November, and achieved early success. An armoured car regiment of the Royal Dragoons broke through south of Tel el Aqqaqir, and spent the day doing mischief before halting for the night south of El Daba. That night, Eighth Army requested that 'the maximum bomber effort' should be maintained on the enemy positions in the north. A total of eighty-seven Wellington sorties were flown against targets in the battle area between 2115 and 0500 hours, with the Albacores adding another eleven. The first attacks were east and west of Ghazal station, and many good targets were found with the help of some excellent illumination by the Albacores. Large numbers of fires and explosions and direct hits on vehicles were reported. A considerable number of vehicles were seen between the road and the coast as the attacks came to an end, but most of the aircraft had dropped their bombs by then. One of the aircraft of No. 70 Squadron developed engine trouble on its return trip, and the pilot was forced to crash-land sixty-four kilometres north of Wadi Natrun. The crew walked for ten hours before being spotted by an RAAF Wellington, which landed and picked them up. On the same night nine Halifaxes and seven Liberators attacked the airfield at Maleme, and one very large fire was started west of the landing ground and smaller fires were reported south-west of and on the landing ground.

By 3 November, Rommel was down to about thirty-five tanks, and was bombed throughout the day by the Western Desert Air Force. After conferring with von Thoma, he decided to withdraw to a new position at Fuka during the afternoon. Hitler, as usual, ordered him to stand and fight, but he, nevertheless, carried out a partial withdrawal of some of his forces. All available Wellingtons and Albacores attacked the retreating enemy columns on the coast road in the Fuka–El Daba area between 1845 and 0440 hours on the night of 3/4 November, despatching 114 Wellington sorties and another twenty-one by the Albacores. This was a record number of sorties on a given area, a total of 187 tons of bombs was dropped, and the duration of the attacks also broke all previous records. In particular, the aircraft attacked a mass of vehicles between El Daba and the coast, and later in the night concentrated on the point where the main road climbed the escarpment at Fuka.

Excellent results were claimed by the returning crews, with many direct hits on vehicles and fires and explosions reported. So many fires were seen that it seemed to some of the crews that the enemy was setting fire to his own supply dumps. The Group ORB states that this 'was undoubtedly a most successful operation and a most useful contribution to the War in the Desert as a whole'. Only three aircraft were lost, which was a small cost for such a success. One Wellington of No. 148 Squadron crashed on take-off, and exploded on impact with the ground. Two of the dead crew had only arrived on the Squadron that morning; and the pilot was on his first operation as captain and was blown clear and sustained head injuries. One of No. 162 Squadron lost height as the undercarriage was retracted on take-off, and the propellers struck the ground. The aircraft crashed and burst into flames, and three of its bombs then exploded. There was only one survivor. One of No. 108 Squadron force-landed in the battle area after an engine cut, but the crew were uninjured.

During the morning of 4 November the Afrika Korps reported that their front had been broken in several places, and in the afternoon the Korps commander, General von Thoma, was taken prisoner. As Rommel continued his withdrawal elements of the Italian 20th Motorized Corps was caught and destroyed, and the Axis forces were down to about twelve tanks. More than ten thousand Axis prisoners were captured, including nine generals. It was the last day of the Battle of El Alamein. On the night of 4/5 November the retreating forces near Fuka and Galal and along the El Daba road were again subjected to a non-stop bombardment from 1905 to 0315 hours, with seventy-four sorties despatched. Good results were claimed by most of the bombers, with many direct hits, fires and explosions. The aircraft carrying out second sorties reported that 'from between 0100 and 0200 hours onwards El Daba was a sheet of flame, there being so many fires that they merged into one huge mass', and No. 70 Squadron ORB records that many 'sitting targets were found with the help of the illumination by the Albacores'. On the same night nine Halifaxes and seven Liberators again attacked Maleme, but most results were unobserved and only one short-lived fire was started.

On the night of 5/6 November the Fuka–Sidi Haneish area was reported to be packed with enemy vehicles, and was hit by over ninety sorties between 2056 and 0444 hours. The bombers dropped 150 tons of bombs, and for the first time the Halifaxes of No. 462 Squadron joined in the attacks. Although targets were not as closely packed as on the previous nights good results were again reported, with many direct hits and over thirty fires started. The nine Albacores that illuminated the target area reported that many fires were already burning when they arrived, and were probably due to the enemy burning stores as they retreated. One of the Halifaxes had a hung-up bomb fall off on landing, and was destroyed by fire. The night bombers kept up the pressure on the retreating Germans on the next night, when the Mersa Matruh–Sidi Barrani area came under attack. It was bombed by over fifty aircraft between 0105 and 0415 hours, but the weather was poor, with electrical storms and heavy rain en route and cloud in the target area, and the Albacores were not available for flare-dropping. Excellent targets in the Mersa Matruh area were missed, and the best targets were found at Buq Buq, on the Sollum zig-zag, and the junction of the coast road and the Halfaya Pass.

The Sollum–Halfaya Pass area was attacked again on 7/8 November by more than fifty aircraft, but the enemy had retreated so fast that the target area was now well out of the range of the Albacores, and the illumination by the Wellingtons themselves was not completely successful. It was also unfortunate that the briefing did not specifically mention that a special effort should be made to blow up the pass itself, as the two Wellingtons of No. 104 Squadron that carried 4,000-lb bombs would have been very suitable for the task of 'road-busting'. As soon as the enemy had cleared the pass he blew a huge crater that caused the Eighth Army a very considerable delay, and the Wellingtons might have done the job much earlier and trapped Rommel's force instead. Forty-seven Wellingtons and five Halifaxes attacked the Sollum–Halfaya Pass area again on 8/9 November, but once more no instructions were given to block the pass. A total of seventy-five tons of bombs were dropped in under five hours, and between forty-five and fifty fires started. During the night of 9/10 November the *Deutsch-Italienische Panzerarmee* (as it had become in October 1942) finally left Egypt, and No. 205 Group hastened their departure with attacks in the Capuzzo–Sollum–Halfaya Pass area. Fifty-one Wellingtons and four

Halifaxes attacked the area between 2345 and 0430 hours, where very good targets were found and many bombs were seen to burst amongst them, starting several fires. One large explosion was seen, which 'flung MT into the air' and the No. 70 Squadron ORB comments that the aircraft 'had quite a good party'. By the early morning the whole of the Afrika Korps had crossed the frontier into Cyrenaica, and the battle for Egypt was over.

*   *   *

In the 168 days/nights between 26 May, when Rommel struck at Gazala, and 9 November, when the last Axis forces were driven out of Egypt, night bombers went out on 164 of them. The Wellingtons of No. 205 Group and the few units of four-engined bombers now operating with the Group flew 7,128 sorties and lost 151 aircraft. The Wellingtons of No. 162 Squadron, as well as carrying out their RCM duties, also contributed another 229 bombing sorties and lost two aircraft. Almost half of all the sorties (4,304) were directed at ports and shipping, and another 2,703 (31 per cent) were involved in ground support operations in the battle area.

NOTES

1. TMAME, Volume III, page 235.
2. During the crisis period at the end of June and in July the Blenheims of No. 14 Squadron operated at night alongside the Wellington squadrons.
3. AHB Narrative, *The Middle East Campaigns*, Vol. IV, page 20.
4. AHB Narrative, *The Middle East Campaigns*, Volume IV, page 143.
5. Gunby, *Sweeping the Skies*, page 209.
6. Gunby, *Sweeping the Skies*, page 209.
7. Ultra was the designation used for signals intelligence obtained by 'breaking' high-level encrypted enemy communications. Much of the German cipher traffic was encrypted on the Enigma machine, hence the term 'Ultra' has often been used almost synonymously with 'Enigma decrypts'. However, Ultra also encompassed decrypts of the machines used by the German High Command, and other Italian and Japanese ciphers and codes.
8. AHB Narrative, *The Middle East Campaigns*, Volume IV, page 168 (quoting the DAK War Diary).
9. AHB Narrative, *The Middle East Campaigns*, Volume VI, page 177 (quoting the *Panzer Armee Afrika* War Diary).
10. Quoted in Chappell, *Wellington Wings*, page 89.
11. Its story is told in Kenneth Ballantyne's book *Another Dawn Another Dusk*.
12. I have followed Kenny Ballantyne's account here, although Gunby (*Bomber Losses in the Middle East and Mediterranean*) has Bebbington's aircraft lost on 6/7 September and Bowyer's aircraft down on 7/8 September.
13. TMAME, Volume IV, page 63.

CHAPTER SIX

Torch and Tunisia – November 1942 to March 1943

This chapter covers the period from the end of the Battle of El Alamein to the end of the battles on the Mareth line. It opens with the Axis forces in retreat, scuttling through the Halfaya Pass and out of Egypt. It ends with the Eighth Army advancing to meet with the First Army in Tunisia. As Rommel brought his exhausted troops out of Egypt and into Libya, British and American forces were landing on the Atlantic coast of Morocco and at a number of beaches on either side of Oran and Algiers inside the Mediterranean. Operation *Torch* had begun, and the war in North Africa had entered a new and very different phase. It meant that American ground forces were involved in the battle against Germany for the first time, and it also meant that that there were now two fronts in the Mediterranean theatre. It is worth, therefore, spending a little time considering the implications of increased American involvement and of the need for the Air Forces to operate over two widely separated fronts.

In the Middle East the USAAF heavy bombers of the 98th and 376th Bombardment Groups began to move from Palestine into Egypt on 8 November, and on 12 November US Army Middle East Air Force (USAMEAF) was dissolved and replaced by HQ Ninth Air Force. General Brereton took command of the Ninth Air Force, and IX Bomber Command was to be commanded by Brigadier General Patrick Timberlake with its HQ at Ismailia. The operations of the American heavy bombers had long disappeared from the ORB of No. 205 Group, the last one being reported on 19/20 September 1942 when fifteen Liberators of the 98th Bombardment Group had attacked shipping in Navarino Bay. However, they continued to operate in a similar fashion to the four-engined bombers of the RAF, mainly attacking shipping at sea and the harbours at Benghazi and Tobruk.

In the Northwest African theatre the only air units operating in the early stages of *Torch* were fighter squadrons flown from Gibraltar into Tafaraoui airfield in Algeria. On 9 November Major General James H. Doolittle, Commanding General of the Twelfth USAAF, arrived in Algeria from Gibraltar, followed by the HQ Twelfth Air Force from the UK. Other fighter and reconnaissance units moved into the theatre over the next few days, and the first medium bombers (B-26s) arrived at St Leu on 10 November. On 13 November the Headquarters of the 97th Bombardment Group and the 340th Bombardment Squadron arrived at Maison Blanche in Algeria with their Fortresses. The first heavy bomber operation in the theatre came on 16 November, when six Fortresses of the 97th Bombardment Group left Maison Blanche to bomb Sidi Ahmed Airfield at Bizerte. The 97th had flown the first US heavy bomber mission from the UK on 17 August 1942, and now became the first Twelfth Air Force heavy bombardment group to fly a combat mission in Northwest Africa.

No. 205 Group was also moving and changing. Early in November it was ordered to move some Wellingtons back to Malta as part of the air support for *Torch*. On 5 November 1942 a detachment of six aircraft of No. 104 Squadron was sent to the island so that it could attack targets in Tunisia. On the following day four aircraft of No. 40 Squadron joined them at Luqa, and further aircraft from both Squadrons were despatched to Malta throughout the month. The ground echelons of the two Squadrons were at Kabrit at the beginning of the month, and were progressively moved forwards during November. By the middle of the month they had got to LG 104 (a few miles west of El Daba), but while these moves were going on both were being gradually stripped of their aircraft and aircrews for duty in Malta. By the end of November almost all their aircraft were at Luqa, and all operations were being conducted from there. The twenty-two Wellingtons in Malta were increased to thirty-four on 8 December when a detachment of twelve Wellingtons of No. 148 Squadron arrived. The two squadrons of No. 231 Wing (Nos 37 and 70 Squadrons) moved from Abu Suier (near Ismailia) to LG 224 (about ten miles west of Cairo) on 6 November, then to LG 106 (fifteen miles west of El Alamein) by the 13th, and finally to LG 140 (fifteen miles west of Bardia) by the end of the month. A detachment was soon operating from Benina, near Benghazi, and the two squadrons had moved there by 20 January. One of the squadrons of No. 236 Wing (No. 148 Squadron) was also moved forwards, from LG 237 (twenty miles west of Cairo) to LG 106 on 12 November, and on the following day to LG 09 (five miles west of El Daba).

As well as the loss of the two squadrons to Malta, No. 205 Group also lost two units through disbandment. On 24 November 1942 No. 108 Squadron learned that it was to be broken up, and its aircraft and crews given to Nos 37, 70 and 148 Squadrons. For the moment the Squadron would move back to LG 237 and take control of the Special Operations (Liberator) Flight. The Squadron ORB records that this was 'a sudden blow to all personnel of this unit'. It went on to say that: 'Nevertheless, we take great pride in recording that 108 Squadron played a major part in the defence of Egypt and even more so in the attack and disillusion (sic) of the German and Italian forces in North Africa.' Since August 1941 the Squadron had flown 1,775 sorties, and lost twenty-eight aircraft on operations and another fourteen in accidents or on the ground. Seventy-four airmen were killed, twenty-three wounded, and forty-three were captured and became prisoners of war. The Special Operations Flight was disbanded on 25 December 1942, bringing a temporary end to the Squadron as a whole. It was reformed on 1 March 1943 from a nucleus provided by No 89 Squadron at Shandur in Egypt, and would operate over Egypt and Libya as a night fighter unit equipped with Beaufighters.

The Group was soon to lose another unit. On 1 December No. 148 Squadron moved to Bir el Beheira No. 2, near Gambut, and on the 8th the detachment of twelve Wellingtons was sent to Malta (see above). A week later the Squadron was disbanded and its crews and aircraft absorbed by the other Wellington units on the island and in Libya. In the Operational Record for No. 148 Squadron from December 1940 to December 1942 given in the Squadron ORB on disbandment it is stated that the unit flew 2,862 sorties involving 17,644 operational hours, and dropped 6,539,040 lb of bombs on the enemy. All these operations were not carried out without loss, and 206 personnel were reported missing or killed and 106 aircraft were either destroyed or missing. Of these, sixty-eight were lost on operations, and thirty-eight destroyed in accidents or on the ground due to enemy action. The Squadron won seventy-nine honours, comprising one George Cross, one OBE, one BEM, twenty-nine DFCs., thirty-eight DFMs and nine Mentions in Despatches. The Squadron ORB ends with the following:

> Thus it will be seen from the foregoing, that 148 Squadron have left a noteworthy record behind them. All Officers and ORs deserve the greatest praise for the conditions in which they have worked and their never ceasing devotion to duty. If 148 Squadron should rise again, it will be founded on the traditions and sure foundations which have left their mark during the two years the squadron have operated.

The Squadron would rise again. On 14 March 1943, it reformed at Gambut in the 'Special Duties' role, equipped with Halifaxes and Liberators. It would now be responsible for supplying Partisan groups throughout the Balkans and as far afield as Poland, as well as undertaking bombing missions when not otherwise occupied. At the end of the war the Squadron re-equipped with standard bomber Liberators, moving back to Egypt in November 1945, where it was again disbanded on 15 January 1946.

The four-engined bombers also suffered disruption during this period. The Liberators of No. 160 Squadron moved from Aqir in Palestine to Shandur on the Great Bitter Lakes on 8 November, and some of the aircraft began moving to India – which had been its intended original destination. Those left in the Middle East continued to carry out operations from Shandur until 15 January 1943, when the Squadron was amalgamated with elements of No. 147 Squadron to form No. 178 Squadron. The Halifaxes of No. 462 Squadron moved to LG 237 on 14 November, with a detachment operating from LG 09. On 27 November the Halifaxes came under the operational and administrative control of No. 236 Wing instead of No. 245 Wing, and moved to LG 167 for two weeks. It only carried out one operation from there, on 2/3 December, and then, on 10 December it was ordered to move back to LG 237. On arrival it became temporarily non-operational, and tour-expired aircrews were returned to the UK. The aircraft were retained at LG 237 pending the arrival of fresh crews from England, and carried out their next operation on 31 January/1 February 1943.

On 13 November the Headquarters of No. 205 Group moved from Ismailia to a site near Burg El Arab, between Alexandria and El Alamein, and on 18 November it moved again to a site near Quotafiya, in the El Daba area west of El Alamein. Then on 28 November it moved to Menastir Landing Ground, about eight miles west of Bardia, and had thus crossed the border into Libya once again. In the middle of December the Air Officer Commanding the Group decided that Squadrons, Wing and Group Headquarters should move forward to Benina. This would make it easier to operate against the Tripoli area, as desired by the Advanced Headquarters, Western Desert. However, this move was not allowed by the latter headquarters, and the Group HQ remained at Menastir until January, when it followed Nos 37 and 70 Squadrons to the Magrun area. The Group ORB makes it abundantly clear that much confusion reigned at this time, with operations scheduled and then called off, moves ordered and then cancelled, and advance parties sent out and then recalled. The Group was trying to serve two masters – Headquarters, RAF Middle East and Advanced Headquarters, Western Desert. On

20 December the ORB comments that an enemy force that had been cut off at Mathatin and then had succeeded in breaking out, might have been successfully attacked if the Group had been allowed to move forward earlier. On 22 December 1942 Air Commodore A.P. Ritchie left No. 205 Group for an appointment in England, and was succeeded by Air Commodore O.R. Gayford.

In December 1942 the Air Ministry managed to prise two Wellington squadrons out of the grasp of Harris and Bomber Command and despatch them to Algeria to support the fighting in Northwest Africa. The two units chosen were Nos 142 and 150 Squadrons of No. 1 Group, based respectively at Waltham (Grimsby) and Kirmington. During December both Squadrons were stood down from operations and prepared for movement to North Africa. In the early days of the month tropicalised Wellington IIIs started to arrive at their bases, and twenty-six were then flown to an advanced base at Portreath in Cornwall to prepare for the long flight to their new homes. The air party of No. 142 Squadron, led by Wing Commander T.W. Bamford, left Portreath for Gibraltar between 18 and 20 December, and most went straight on to Blida after refuelling. One crashed on take-off at Portreath, and another burst a tyre on take-off at Gibraltar and crashed on landing at Blida. We have less information about the movements of the air party of No. 150 Squadron, under the command of Wing Commander J.D. Kirwan, but all were at Blida by 21 December. Meanwhile, the sea parties of both Squadrons left Plymouth aboard the cruiser/cinelayer HMS *Adventure* on 12 December, and arrived at Gibraltar on 20 December after a stormy but uneventful journey. They went on to Algiers aboard HMS *Totland*, arriving safely after a brush with submarines on the way, and were reunited with their aircrews at Blida by 25 December. No. 330 Wing was formed in North Africa on 9 December to take control of the two squadrons. Conditions in Algeria in December of 1942 were terrible, with lots of rain and few airfields capable of operating heavy bombers. Blida and Maison Blanche had tarmac runways, but both also had plenty of mud and were invariably congested. Nevertheless, the two squadrons performed their first operation on 28/29 December when seven aircraft took off from Maison Blanche to attack the docks at Bizerte.

The two Wellingtons squadrons at Blida generally operated in support of the Allied armies in Tunisia and against targets in that country. The Wellingtons of Nos 37 and 70 Squadrons operated for the whole of the period from bases in Libya and generally in support of the Eighth Army's operations in Libya and southern Tunisia. The two Squadrons in Libya were later joined by the Wellingtons of Nos 40 and 104 Squadrons and by the Halifaxes of No. 462 Squadron, which returned to No. 205 Group control towards the end of January. The five squadrons then operated in concert as a Group until the end of the fighting in North Africa. Meanwhile, the few Liberators of No. 160/178 Squadron remained at Shandur in Egypt under the operational control of 9th USAAF Bomber Command, bombing a wide variety of targets at an equally wide variety of locations. With all the changes going on, and even with the reinforcements provided by Nos 142 and 150 Squadrons, the night bombers carried out relatively few operations between the end of the first week in November 1942 and the end of March 1943, compared with the huge effort expended during the crisis in the desert. They were operating from three widely separated base areas (Malta, Algeria and Libya) and over two widely separated battle areas, and were frequently on the move throughout the period.

*　　*　　*

As stated above, early in November No. 205 Group was ordered to move Wellingtons to Malta as part of the air support for *Torch*, and on 5 November a detachment of six aircraft of No. 104 Squadron were sent to the island. On the following day they were joined by four aircraft of No. 40 Squadron, and further aircraft from both squadrons were despatched to Malta throughout the month. By the end of November almost all their aircraft were at Luqa, and the twenty-two Wellingtons were increased to thirty-four on 8 December when a detachment of twelve Wellingtons of No. 148 Squadron arrived and were absorbed by Nos 40 and 104 Squadrons.

The Wellingtons on Malta began their operations in support of *Torch* on 7/8 November, when seven Wellingtons left Luqa to attack the airfields at Decimomannu and Elmas in Sardinia, from which enemy aircraft might interfere with the landings at Algiers. It was not a happy beginning, as one crashed into high ground just after take-off and all the crew were killed. Due to haze and poor visibility, two of the Wellingtons jettisoned their bombs and one brought its bombs back to base, and the three other aircraft could only locate Cagliari town, which they bombed without observing any results. The Wellingtons went back to Decimomannu and Elmas on the next three nights, launching twenty-one sorties and achieving generally good results. However, it is unlikely that these attacks did much to interfere with enemy air operations from Sardinia, and they can have had no more than a nuisance value. On 10/11 November the starboard engine of one of the aircraft of No. 40 Squadron seized on the return journey, and the Wellington was eventually ditched south of Gozo. It floated for ninety seconds and then sank, but the crew took to their dinghy and were later rescued by fishermen.

The Allied landings met with little organized resistance from the Vichy French forces, and by 9 November US troops were advancing on both sides of Oran. However, on the same day reports came in that about forty German aircraft had landed at El Aouina airfield near Tunis that morning, and these carried German paratroops who immediately secured the airfields around Tunis and Bizerte. On the next day photographic reconnaissance of El Aouina showed about a hundred German aircraft of various types dispersed around the airfield. The Germans had a strong force of transport aircraft available, and began to ferry in troops at an average of around 750 a day. Things were soon to get much more difficult for the Allies in Northwest Africa. The Wellingtons on Malta launched their first attack on El Aouina on the night of 11/12 November, when five aircraft were despatched from Luqa. Extremely bad weather conditions forced three of them to jettison their bombs and return to base, one attacked the estimated position of the airfield starting a small fire, and the fifth aircraft attacked gun positions in the vicinity of Tunis town. The Wellingtons attacked El Aouina with more success on four nights between 12/13 and 18/19 November, but only fifty-one sorties were despatched and extremely bad weather often hampered the operations.

The Axis build-up in the Tunis bridgehead thus proceeded with little interference from the Wellingtons on Malta or from the US Twelfth Air Force. General Nehring, who had taken command of the Axis forces in Tunisia, was already pushing out battle-groups to oppose any advance from Algeria, and the first clash on the ground came on 17 November. Units of the British First Army were moving eastwards into Tunisia, and bumped into German forces heading for Tabarka.

On the night of 19/20 November seventeen Wellingtons were despatched to the airfields at Catania, Gerbini, and Comiso on Sicily. Thirteen located and bombed the airfields, with bursts reported across the runways and dispersal areas, starting several fires. One of the Wellingtons of No. 104 Squadron was shot down over Catania, and all the crew killed. The airfield at Sidi Ahmed at Bizerte was attacked by eight Wellingtons on 20/21 November and again by six aircraft on 21/22 November. Bursts were seen on the runway and among dispersed aircraft, starting a few fires. Also on 21/22 November two Wellingtons, one carrying a 4,000-lb bomb, attacked the airfield at Trapani on Sicily. The next attack on a Sicilian airfield was by twelve Wellingtons on Gerbini on 26/27 November, where a large fire was started in the north-west corner of the landing ground. One of the aircraft of No. 104 Squadron crashed into the sea on the return journey, and five were captured and one killed. The last attack on the Sicilian airfields during this period was by thirteen aircraft on Trapani on 30 November/1 December. Otherwise, towards the end of November the ports of Bizerte and Tunis became the main targets for the bombers from Malta, with eighty-six sorties launched on seven nights between 22 and 30 November. Low cloud and rainstorms often made conditions particularly difficult, and some of the aircraft brought their bombs back rather than risk bombing the towns instead of the docks themselves.

Chappell, the intelligence officer with No. 104 Squadron, was disappointed that he was not allowed to go to Malta, as there was a resident intelligence section at Luqa. However, he was later called up to join the Squadron, and left Egypt on 12 November. On the way out he flew over the El Alamein battlefield, and saw the old defence lines, bomb and shell craters, and many vehicle wrecks lying about. Almost immediately after his arrival at Luqa he went down with 'Malta Dog' – intense diarrhoea and sickness – but was soon working in the station intelligence office. Heavy rain caused the cancellation of operations on 15/16 and 16/17 November, but a visit to the cinema and a few bars and many drinks with the Wing Commander (D.T. Saville) and Squadron Leader (Leggate) passed the time satisfactorily. During the drinks session they met up with two English girls married to civilians on the island, and learned about the food situation – they were living on one tin of bully beef and one tin of sardines a fortnight and getting by mainly on the bread ration. Like most civilians they carried nasty blotches on their arms and legs, a sign of their malnutrition.

Food was still very short in Malta during the winter of 1942 and old Malta hands knew what to expect, but the new boys of No. 40 Squadron did not, and one recalled his first meal on the island: 'a plate of fatty bacon rind running in liquid and fat.' He went on:

> Everyone of us pushed it away and ate the small pieces of bread supplied with it. On the next table we noticed several lads who had been loitering, volunteer to eat it. These were regulars at Malta. On questioning them why, we were told in no uncertain terms that 'You bloody well will eat it in two or three days' time.' It was certainly true. The food was terrible. I've never been so hungry in my life.[1]

On 20 November, while completing the summaries for the previous night's operations to Catania, Gerbini and Comiso ('to give indirect support for a convoy nearing Malta from Alexandria'), Chappell became aware of 'an unusual bustle of life and excitement outside and in the harbour area – the convoy has arrived!' This was the *Stoneage* convoy, and all four ships arrived unharmed and would do much to ease the situation on the island. On 5 December another convoy (*Portcullis*) arrived, and the siege was now over. On 20 November Chappell flew back to Egypt with Wing Commander Saville to arrange for more aircraft and the No. 238 Wing HQ to fly out to Malta. They flew out 'in a discarded Wellington with two worn out engines' that 'had been condemned as 'ropey' and unsuitable for operations…owing to excessive oil consumption'. Ginn[2] described it as 'an incredibly scruffy Wimpy IC ex 40 Squadron', which was 'still in a pen and hadn't been touched for a fortnight'. The dilapidated state of the aircraft did not deter the imperturbable Wing Commander, and after a not-uneventful flight they landed safely at LG 106 (Sidi Abd El Rahman, twenty-five miles west of El Alamein). On the next day they moved on to LG 237 (forty kilometres from Cairo), where the 'flies are ghastly'! Saville was able to persuade HQ that the rest of No. 40 Squadron should go to Malta, and at midnight on 24 November nine Wellingtons left, each carrying four ground crew. They were accompanied by another two aircraft of No. 104 Squadron, and all arrived at Luqa just after daybreak.

No. 40 Squadron began operating in strength from Luqa on 27 November, but a combination of battle damage and engine and equipment faults made things difficult for the ground crews. As in the desert, conditions were harsh and facilities primitive, and it was remarkable that a high serviceability rate was able to be maintained on the rapidly ageing Wellington ICs. The Axis supply ports were fiercely defended, and although the searchlights and flak rarely brought down an aircraft, they made bombing difficult and hampered the observation of results. Night fighters were only rarely encountered, but a more serious hazard was the weather, which was often extremely violent. Mechanical failure also continued to be a hazard, due to the difficult conditions on the ground and the age of the aircraft. The Wellington IC had been superseded by the Mk III in Bomber Command early in 1942, and the first squadrons in 205 Group were now slowly being re-equipped with the newer aircraft.

Early in December the enemy counter-attacked successfully, securing Bizerte and Tunis and establishing weak defensive positions about thirty miles to the West. The Allies prepared to renew their advance, but worsening weather caused first postponement and then cancellation by the end of the year. On 12 December Chappell noted that 'in Tunisia the First Army seems to be enduring a nasty hammering from the *Luftwaffe*', but there was little that the Allied air forces could do about it at the time. After the attempt to reach Tunis and Bizerte failed in December 1942, it was the enemy's turn to launch a major counter-attack code-named *Eilbote*. This opened on 18 January, and ruined any hopes of a quick Allied victory in Tunisia.

The middle of December saw a marked increase in the weight and scope of Allied air attacks in Tunisia. The ports and airfields of Tunis and Bizerte continued to be the principal objectives, and were being bombed round the clock. The scale of attack on targets on the east coast of Tunisia was also increasing, just as Rommel was withdrawing from El Agheila. In all, the bombers from Malta flew 372 sorties on 24 nights in December, almost all of which (335 – 88 per cent) went to Bizerte,

Tunis, Sousse, and Sfax, with six aircraft lost. Of the sorties despatched, almost a fifth were abortive for one reason or another, mainly because of the poor weather that attended most of the operations. Although the number of losses was relatively small, they were all deeply felt by the small, close-knit detachment at Malta. One of the Wellingtons of No. 104 Squadron (captained by Flight Lieutenant Charles Dallas) failed to return from an attack on Tunis and La Goulette on 17/18 December, and Chappell states that they were 'one of our best crews and really good chaps'. Three aircraft were sent out from Malta to search for them, but no dinghy was sighted. It transpired that Flight Lieutenant Dallas was a prisoner of war, but the rest of his crew were killed. There were night fighters on the prowl that night, and another of the Squadron's aircraft was shot up and the wireless operator wounded. Yet another came back dripping petrol from two big holes in the wing, the gunner wounded, and the hydraulics and the turret unserviceable.

A tragedy occurred on 17 December when a Halifax of No. 138 Squadron on a ferry flight back to the UK was forced to return to Luqa with engine problems. It crashed while trying to land, and all seventeen men on board were killed. Most were 'tour-expired' aircrew on their way back to England for a rest, and one of them was Flight Lieutenant Len Vaughan of No. 40 Squadron. He was 'a tail gunner of great experience and a real character in the mess', and had survived a hundred operations only to die in this tragic accident. There were other non-operational hazards at Luqa as well. On 18 December there was an air raid that destroyed seven Wellingtons and damaged three others. A Wellington of No. 104 Squadron was bombed up and preparing to take off when the crew received a signal advising them that '30 plus bandits have been picked up on the radar screen, on course for Tunisia – if a change of course takes place in the direction of Malta you will be signalled immediately.' Just afterwards they got another signal stating 'bandits heading for Malta', and at the same time the bombs started falling. The crew ran for the nearest cover, ending up in a disused quarry about 100 yards away, and one of them broke his collarbone as he dived for shelter.

The Wellingtons on Malta continued attacking Sousse and Tunis until 12/13 January, and also carried out a few attacks on Tripoli in support of the Eighth Army's operations between 12 and 17 January. On 17 January one of the aircraft of No. 104 Squadron was on the run up to the target at Tripoli when it was suddenly illuminated by searchlights, accompanied by a barrage of accurate heavy flak. The run up was completed and the bombs dropped in the target area, after which severe evasive action was taken. This resulted in large strips of fabric being torn from the fuselage, which seriously affected the flying qualities of the aircraft. It suddenly rolled onto its port side in a steep dive, still held by searchlights, and it was only with the greatest difficulty that the Captain was able to straighten up and pull out of the dive at about 500 feet. Severe vibration resulting from the damage to the fuselage made it difficult to control the aircraft, and it was also found that two bombs had hung up and couldn't be dislodged. Nevertheless, the Captain (Flying Officer 'Ham' Fuller) brought the aircraft home and landed safely. When the extent of the damage was examined the pilot remarked 'It did feel a bit chilly on the way back; now I know where the draught was coming from.'

The Wellingtons on Malta began to return to Egypt on 17 January when five aircraft of No. 40 Squadron left to rejoin the rear echelon at LG 237, carrying thirty-two aircrew and twenty ground personnel. Another would follow on the next day, flown by Wing Commander Morton and carrying six ground personnel. On 21 January No. 104 Squadron left Malta and returned to LG 237 in the Middle East. No further operations were carried out by the Squadron to the end of the month as it was being re-equipped prior to a further move. No. 40 Squadron had also moved from Malta by this date, its last aircraft leaving on 20 January. The following signal was received from AHQ Malta:

> AOC sends farewell message to No. 238 Wing and wishes to thank them also 40 and 104 Squadrons for their very fine bombing effort during the past two and a half months. Malta is proud to have had the Wellington Bomber Squadrons join their team and hopes to have them back again later in the year. Meanwhile we all wish you the best of luck.

In December 1942 No. 238 Wing lost both of its squadron commanders. Wing Commander Donald Teale Saville relinquished command of No. 104 Squadron on 19 December 1942, and Wing Commander Dick Ridgway stood down from No. 40 Squadron on the following day. Wing Commander Saville had taken over his squadron on 4 August 1942 and Wing Commander Ridgway his on 30 April. They had had months of intensive operations, usually taking part in those that were the most difficult and dangerous. Wing Commander Saville had earned the reputation of being a supremely confident and fearless man, alert and daring, but also understanding and humane. Off duty, he had a remarkable ability to relax, as many of the tales told by Chappell attest, and a splendid sense of humour. Wing Commander Saville returned to the UK and assumed the command of No. 218 (Gold Coast) Bomber Squadron on 28 March 1943, flying Stirlings. He was shot down over Hamburg on 25 July, and is buried in the Hamburg Cemetery. Wing Commander Ridgway was a relaxed, good-humoured and sociable man, who gave high priority to fostering squadron spirit, and made all his men, from cooks to pilots, feel part of every raid. He had been getting the 'shakes' in the air for several days, and put it down to flu. However, the doctor had other ideas, and told him that it was exhaustion. Sir Keith Park (AOC Malta) knew all about the fatigue that comes from constant operations under difficult conditions, and told Ridgway that he was to be rested immediately. He survived the war to be guest of honour at a dinner held by No. 40 Squadron in the Officers' Mess at Bassingbourn on 10 March 1950.

*   *   *

As we saw in the previous chapter, the last elements of the *Deutsch-Italienische Panzerarmee* left Egypt during the night of 9/10 November, hastened on their way by an attack by fifty-five aircraft in the Capuzzo–Sollum–Halfaya Pass area. On the next night the primary target was Tobruk and thirty-four Wellingtons and five Halifaxes were despatched, but one Wellington crashed on take-off, killing all on board except for the tail gunner. Most of the aircraft bombed the jetties at Tobruk as ordered, but the flak and searchlights were reported to be 'worse than ever' and many of the bombers could not see any results due to the need to take evasive action. Some of the aircraft bombed enemy vehicles on the Tobruk–Gazala road, but the operation was spoiled by poor visibility. One of the Wellingtons crashed near Fuka due to the failure of both engines on the return trip, but all the crew escaped unhurt and made their way back to base. One of the Halifaxes failed to return, and on 15 November the Observer (Flight Lieutenant J. Watts) returned to Fayid. Apparently, the aircraft was hit by flak immediately after bombing the target, and caught fire. It lost height and the mid-gunner, flight engineer and wireless operator baled out. The observer, after adjusting the captain's harness, jumped himself. He swam some four miles to the shore, and was eventually discovered by our troops and brought back to base.

On 11/12 November the attacks on retreating enemy columns continued, this time on the Gazala–Tobruk road, and forty-one Wellingtons and three Halifaxes were despatched. The weather was good at first, but deteriorated after midnight. The bombers found some poorly dispersed MT at the bottleneck near Gazala, and direct hits on the road and on vehicles were reported. Tobruk was reported to be 'ablaze with as many as 100 fires, Axis forces burning up their stores etc'. The starboard engine of one of the Wellingtons caught fire on the return flight and had to be shut down. It crash-landed and all the crew were brought back to base by the Army. On the following night the targets were in the Derna–Cirene area, and thirty Wellingtons and four Halifaxes were despatched. However, the targets on the ground were now getting scarce, and Derna appeared to be deserted, with a very large fire burning near the Mole. A single Wellington of No. 104 Squadron carried out the last mission by the unit in the Western Desert for some time, as the rest of its aircraft were now in Malta. One of the Wellingtons crashed in the desert on return, and another crashed on landing and was completely burnt out. One of the Wellingtons of No. 148 Squadron had engine trouble and was abandoned near Derna. Three of the crew evaded capture, but two were picked up by the enemy. Both were interrogated by the Germans, but one of them managed to escape by knocking out his guard.

The Eighth Army swept into and past Tobruk for the third and last time on 13 November, and Alexander Clifford tells us that the port:

...presented the strange illusion of still having the shape of a town when seen from a distance. But inside it was quite perceptibly more destroyed, for British bombers had been over it on a hundred consecutive nights. Miraculously, the church spire still stood. And outside the town was a food dump where the ground was puddled redly with wine, and the Arabs were carting away their bi-annual quota of loot. They probably felt that this much is due to them from the Armies that have turned their fields into battlefields.[3]

The team set up by Solly Zuckerman to investigate the effects of air attacks in North Africa was also an eye-witness to the damage caused at Tobruk:

Tobruk had been bombed in a much more concentrated way, and from the point of view of damage to shipping, and to the timely destruction of one tanker in particular, our air operations there had been far more significant to the outcome of the war in the desert. The damage to Tobruk had also been far more extensive than in any comparable area of England. Every house showed some signs of damage, and about half had been damaged beyond repair.[4]

Due to the movement of the squadrons to Malta, and to the inevitable disruption caused by the moves forward in the desert, operations by the squadrons in the Middle East were carried on at a much reduced level. Benghazi was back on the agenda on 13/14 November when twenty-four Wellingtons took off from LG 106, followed by six Liberators of No. 160 Squadron operating from Shandur. One of the Wellingtons failed to return, and this was AD637, the aircraft of Sergeant James Jones, which was shot down over Benghazi, and the crew are commemorated on the El Alamein memorial. Another lost its propeller on the return trip and was belly-landed between Fuka and El Daba. The crew eventually found an abandoned Italian lorry and drove it to LG 106, which they reached at 1900 hours on 14 November. Eight Liberators went back to Benghazi on 14/15 November, reporting one enormous explosion near the base of the Cathedral Mole and a fire that was visible sixty miles away. On 20 November the British entered Benghazi for the third and last time, and on the night of 23/24 November the enemy finally withdrew into the El Agheila position. The meagre supplies that were still coming through to the *Deutsch-Italienische Panzerarmee* were now being landed at Tripoli, and on 21 November ten Liberators flew to LG 139 (Gambut Main) and during the night eight of them bombed Tripoli harbour. No shipping was seen due to the smokescreen, but four fires were claimed in the target area. The Liberators attacked Tripoli again on 24/25 and 28/29 November, with bursts seen south of the Spanish Mole, at the base of the Karamanli Mole, and near the power station.

The increasingly small numbers of Wellingtons did not operate again until 23/24 November when fourteen Wellingtons attacked Kastelli Pediada airfield on Crete, where three good fires were started south-east of the runway and three elsewhere in the target area. One aircraft of No. 37 Squadron failed to return, and was believed to have been shot down following a combat with a night fighter. On the same night six Halifaxes and eighteen Wellingtons attacked the airfield at Heraklion. Cloud hampered observation of results, but at least four good fires were started. The attention of the Wellingtons was then directed at the Marble Arch Landing Ground (thirty miles west of El Agheila), which enemy aircraft were using for attacks on the Eighth Army. On 25/26 November twenty-eight aircraft were despatched, and they reported that a number of aircraft were seen dispersed on the airfield and 'quite a lot of motor transport on the road'. A number of fires were started, one being fairly large and visible for some distance. This was the last bombing operation carried out by No. 108 Squadron. Seventeen Wellingtons attacked the Marble Arch Landing Ground again on 27/28 November, but the weather was poor and searchlights and rain and cloud obscured the results.

At first, the operations in December carried on much as they ended in November, with the Liberators going to Tripoli and the Wellingtons attacking airfields. Between 1 and 7 December No. 160 Squadron flew nineteen sorties on three nights to Tripoli, but the weather was consistently poor and few positive results were claimed. On the night of 2/3 December seventeen Wellingtons and eight Halifaxes dropped forty-five tons of bombs on the airfield at Heraklion, where a large force of enemy aircraft had been reported. There was a considerable amount of cloud over the target, and no results were observed. This was the last bombing operation by No. 148 Squadron after their long stint in Malta and in the Desert, and also the last by the Halifaxes of No. 462 Squadron for some time. On the following night the Group could only put up twelve aircraft for an attack on Marble Arch Landing Ground, but due to adverse weather conditions none of them could find the target area and seven attacked targets of opportunity instead.

On 5 December a signal was received from Advanced Air HQ Western Desert that all available Wellingtons (which was a pathetically small number at this time) were to be bombed up and on stand-by to attack Army targets. The proposed operations were cancelled on 5/6 and 6/7 December, and then on 7 December, a signal was received from Headquarters RAF Middle East ordering that twelve more Wellingtons were to go to Malta. No. 148 Squadron had exactly twelve serviceable aircraft at the time, and these were briefed to go. They took off safely at 1700 hours, but one crashed on landing at Malta with four men killed and seven 'dangerously injured'. The Group ORB comments that 'Thus the Group became depleted by yet one more squadron.' Soon after the Wellingtons left for Malta a further signal was received instructing that sixteen Wellingtons were to be sent to Algiers on 8 December. The Group ORB states that 'This meant that the Group was being almost entirely denuded of all its serviceable aircraft with the exception of the Halifaxes of 462 Squadron and...two aircraft of 148 Squadron and speculation as to our future was rife.' Preparations for the despatch of these aircraft (ten from No. 37 Squadron and six from No. 70 Squadron) continued through 8 December, but the following day another signal was received cancelling the move. The few aircraft of No. 205 Group did not operate again until 15 December, and the AHB Narrative comments:

> Further diversions to Malta left the Group...with no more than 10 serviceable aircraft available for operations. This was a most unhappy period for the Group which had made such a valuable contribution to the victory in the Middle East. Policy was changed constantly, squadrons were broken up and personnel posted with, so it seemed, but little thought of the effect on morale of the teams which had accomplished such fine work together.[5]

The Group ORB records that on 13 December 'the 8th Army commenced their advance against the enemy's defence positions at AGHEILA, but finding resistance there was very weak had little difficulty in breaking through'. Montgomery had brought forward the date of the attack, as there was clear evidence that the enemy was pulling out. A flanking move by the New Zealand Division had been spotted by Rommel's reconnaissance aircraft, and he had ordered a further withdrawal west of the El Mugtaa narrows. The Allied advance was slowed down by the great numbers of mines and booby traps that had been cleverly laid on the roads and verges, and by a pugnacious rearguard action fought by the Italian *Ariete* Division. El Agheila was entered by the 7th Armoured Division on 15 December, and on the same day the New Zealanders were south of Marble Arch, thirty miles west of El Mugtaa. The 6th New Zealand Brigade struggled towards the main coast road across difficult country, and by dawn on the 16th they were near the road and could hear enemy traffic moving steadily westwards. Rommel had slipped through the forces sent to block his retreat once again. By January 1943 he had retreated to a new position at Buerat, short of men, short of tanks, short of fuel, and short of time, but still dangerous.

The night bombers also came under attack as the Eighth Army made its move on El Agheila. At about midday on 13 December an enemy aircraft, believed to have been a Ju 88, dropped ten bombs on LG 140. Two direct hits or very near misses were scored on two Wellingtons that were bombed and fuelled in readiness for an attack that night, and another was set on fire and burned out. A fourth Wellington was severely damaged by bomb splinters and blast. Several pilots played a risky but brave part in taxiing aircraft away from the danger areas while bombs were still exploding. No personnel were injured, and No. 37 Squadron ORB reports that the entire Squadron turned out after lunch and cleared the runways of wreckage. The bombers did manage to get in a few attacks at this time. The No. 70 Squadron ORB comments that on 15/16 December, after 'a long and somewhat puzzling period of inactivity, only partly caused by cancellation, the Squadron gladly resumed work'. Twenty-two bombers set off to attack enemy aircraft on Castel Benito and Tamet airfields. Cloud made precise location of the target very difficult at Tamet, although four aircraft bombed the immediate vicinity of the target and four claimed to have bombed the airfield itself. Only one small fire was reported. The mission to Castel Benito was cancelled when the aircraft were in the air, but they carried on anyway. The weather was very poor en route, but the aircraft 'came out into bright moonlight over the target'. Many dispersed aircraft were seen, and bursts, explosions, fires and clouds of smoke were reported. Twelve aircraft went to Tamet again on 16/17 December, where the weather was 'not very favourable', but two fires were started, one being very large with heavy black smoke rising to 3,000 feet.

The bombers were given battlefield targets on 18/19 and 19/20 December, attacking enemy motor transport retreating along the coast road towards Buerat-el-Hsun. Weather conditions were perfect on both nights, with no cloud and excellent visibility. The first attack by sixteen aircraft found practically no transport at first, but bombs were dropped on the road and buildings and several direct hits obtained. Later aircraft had considerable success, however, with a fairly large number of vehicles identified and half a dozen fires started. Opposition had increased by this time, and one of the Wellingtons had its hydraulics shot away, but it made a successful belly-landing back at base. The second attack by another sixteen aircraft only found thin concentrations of motor transport, and there were no outstanding results. More vehicles and tents were found between the beach and the road some miles to the east of Buerat, and these were bombed and machine-gunned with good results. There were now few worthy ground targets in range of the few night bombers left in the Middle East, and they were switched to attacks on the airfields on Crete to hinder enemy operations in reinforcing their troops in Tunisia. Tymbaki and Heraklion were attacked on three nights towards the end of the month, with forty-four sorties despatched and generally good results claimed.

The Liberators of No. 160 Squadron, now based at Shandur on the Great Bitter Lakes, carried out two attacks on Naples on 11/12 and 14/15 December, despatching six aircraft on each occasion but with few results seen due to haze and low cloud. One of the Liberators on the first attack dropped its bombs *and* its bomb doors three miles north-east of the target! On 18/19 December the Liberators marked their first appearance in Tunisia by bombing Sousse, operating via LG 139 (Gambut) in Cyrenaica. Two more attacks on Sousse were carried out on 22/23 and 27/28 December, with six aircraft despatched in each case. The small numbers of aircraft were able to do little damage, but in the last attack many large fires were started near the Commercial Quay, and one huge fire just north of the quay with black smoke to 6,000 feet. One crew claimed four direct hits on a motor vessel, which was left blazing from end to end, and the fires were visible for seventy miles. Six Liberators then went to Sfax on 30/31 December, where bursts were seen on the quays, warehouses, and on a railway nearby.

*   *   *

The Allies, and particularly the Americans, had hoped that the battle for Tunisia would have finished before the end of 1942, so that their attentions could move to Europe and the possibility of opening a second front in France in the summer of 1943. However, they did not foresee that Hitler would pour troops into Tunisia at the end of 1942, and fight desperately to retain a foothold in North Africa. As we have seen, the early successes of *Torch* had floundered in the rain in December, and been held by the determination of the Germans to fight for every inch of ground. The Casablanca Conference (codenamed *Symbol*) was held at the Anfa Hotel in Casablanca, Morocco, from 14 to 24 January 1943, to plan the future strategy of the Allies. Given the situation in North Africa and the Far East it was clear that an early attack in Northern Europe was difficult, if not impossible, and the British were able to talk the Americans out of it. Thus, the key decision affecting operations in the Mediterranean was that Sicily should be invaded as soon as possible following the end of hostilities in Tunisia. The air forces in the Mediterranean area were also to be reorganized, and the first step was the setting up of the Mediterranean Air Command under the command of Air Chief Marshal Sir Arthur Tedder. The strategic bombers, including No. 205 Group, were placed under the Northwest African Strategic Air Force (NASAF), commanded by Major-General J.H. Doolittle.

The Casablanca conference also resulted in what became known as the 'Casablanca Directive', which was to act as a general guide to the operations of the British and American strategic air forces for the rest of the war. It stated that the primary object of the bombers would be the progressive destruction and dislocation of the German military, industrial and economic system, and the undermining of the morale of the German people to a point where their capacity for armed resistance was fatally weakened. Within that general concept, the primary objectives were to be, in the following order of priority: German submarine construction yards, the German aircraft industry, transportation, oil plants and other targets in the enemy war industry. This directive was supplemented in June 1943 by the *Pointblank* Directive, which accorded the highest priority to the destruction of the German fighter force and the industries that supplied it in order to counter the very high losses being experienced by RAF Bomber Command and the USAAF Eighth Air Force over Germany. Both of these directives were to play a part in determining the priorities of the Wellington squadrons in 1943, and of No. 205 Group and the USAAF Fifteenth Air Force in Italy to the end of the war.

The year opened with Eisenhower preparing for an attack on Sfax to cut communications between the Axis armies in Tunisia and Libya. He was forestalled, however, by a German counter-attack (*Eilbote*), which resulted in some early successes for the Axis forces, mainly against weak and poorly equipped French troops. The fighting died down on 24 January with the Germans having gained good positions from which to launch further attacks. Allied counter-attacks continued until the 28th without endangering the enemy's positions on the passes through the Eastern Dorsale. Meanwhile, advance units of the Eighth Army crossed the Tunisian frontier on 29 January, forcing Rommel ever backwards, but now allowing him to join his forces with those of von Arnim's 5th Panzer Army.

The Allies now occupied a very long and sprawling front line, stretching over 150 miles from the coast in the north to El Guettar in the south. By the beginning of February most of Rommel's troops had retreated into the Mareth Line, a very

143

strong defensive position, and he was in a position to release troops to co-operate with von Arnim. All was fairly quiet on the ground in Tunisia until the Germans launched a series of heavy attacks against the American 2nd Corps in the southern sector of the front. The German offensive opened on 14 February, when von Arnim attacked from Faid towards Sidi Bou Zid, and was followed on the 15th by an attack towards Gafsa by Rommel's forces. All the German attacks went well, and the inexperienced American troops were out-matched by Rommel's veterans. The attack on the key American position in the Kasserine Pass began on the night of 19/20 February, and the next day the Americans fell apart in the face of heavy attacks by two Panzer Divisions. However, the successes were short lived, as French, British and American troops were rushed into the area, and the defences eventually held. By the morning of 24 February the Pass was again in Allied hands, and Rommel was retreating back into the Mareth position. The Axis had won no ground, but had inflicted considerable losses in men and material on the Allies and won a great psychological victory. However, the Axis forces also had heavy losses, and would have much greater difficulty in replacing them. They attacked again in the north on 26 February (Operation *Ochsenkopf*), and sporadic fighting would continue in the northern sector throughout March.

The year started quite well for Nos 142 and 150 Squadrons operating from Algeria, and in January they flew 222 sorties on 20 nights. Three aircraft were lost in these operations, two running out of fuel while trying to find their base in bad weather and the third crash-landing at Blida after a fight with an enemy aircraft. Fourteen attacks were directed at Bizerte docks and town (169 sorties), and two on the docks at Ferryville near Bizerte. Two attacks were made on the airfield at Sidi Ahmed, and one on the airfield at Elmas on Sardinia. Although these figures are fairly impressive for units operating in very difficult circumstances, most of the bombs were dropped through thick cloud on the estimated position of the targets, and almost no results were observed. Things got a lot more difficult in February and March as the weather and serviceability problems got worse, with only 109 and 98 sorties despatched respectively. Bizerte continued to be the main target, although airfields on Sardinia and in Sicily started to receive increased attention in February and March. Overall, in the three months between January and March the bombers in Algeria flew 429 sorties, of which 322 (75 per cent) went to the ports, and 104 (24 per cent) to the airfields.

There were a few diversions from the attacks on ports and airfields. On 13 January it was decided that the two squadrons would provide a single Wellington every day to act as a 'strike' crew against enemy submarines, should any be located by Coastal Command. One of No. 142 Squadron stood by on the first day, but was not called upon. In fact, only one attack is recorded in the Squadrons' ORBs, on 18 January, when a 'strike' crew of No. 150 Squadron answered a call from Coastal Command. It attacked what was thought to be a submarine at periscope depth, but no hits were claimed. A second diversion took place on the night of 21/22 January, when two Wellingtons were detailed to drop food containers to a detachment of French troops encircled in the southern Tunisian battle front. One was forced to take evasive action, during which a petrol flap became undone, and it had to jettison its containers and return to base. The other flew to the indicated area, but no signals were displayed and the containers were dropped along the side of the road where the troops had been reported.

On 22/23 January eleven aircraft were despatched to attack the airfield at Medenine in southern Tunisia in support of operations by the Eighth Army. Although weather conditions were good, the target had no easily identifiable features and was difficult to locate. Nevertheless, all the crews reported having bombed the approximate position of the landing ground, and a successful attack was claimed. Tripoli fell to the Eighth Army on the next day. On the last night of the month thirteen aircraft, all carrying overload petrol tanks, attacked the port of Trapani in Sicily, which was an important Axis supply point. This was a new target for No. 330 Wing, and a successful attack was carried out by thirteen Wellingtons in the face of intensive searchlights and flak. Although the number of aircraft employed was insufficient to cause really serious damage, the moral effect must have been great as the town had not been raided for some time.

During the first two weeks in February, before the Germans opened their counter offensive in Tunisia, the two Wellington squadrons at Blida flew sixty-three sorties on six nights, three to airfields in Sardinia and Sicily and three to the docks at Bizerte. The aim of an attack on the airfield at Elmas on 1/2 February was to hamper the activities of enemy bombers to aid the passage of an Allied convoy bringing supplies and reinforcements to Tunisia. All nine aircraft attacked the target in good weather, and many bursts were recorded on hangars and on the landing ground. A similar operation was launched on 7/8 February in order to protect another convoy that was proceeding along the coast. The targets were the airfields at Villacidro, Elmas and Decimomannu, and sixteen aircraft took off. The weather en route was favourable, but cloud started to build up as the target area was approached, and many of the aircraft bombed on ETA.

On 9/10 February ten bombers again went to Trapani in Sicily, where good weather enabled all aircraft to locate the target area and all bombed successfully. However, the flak defences were considerably heavier than any previously encountered, and a number of aircraft were hit. One of No. 150 Squadron had a shell burst very near the rear turret, wounding the gunner (Sergeant J.D. Baird) very seriously. The machine attempted to put in at Bone, but couldn't make contact and landed at Maison Blanche instead. It transpired that a shell splinter had pierced Sergeant Baird's lung from the rear, and he died in hospital the following morning. Another Wellington from the same unit received a hit while the bomb doors were open; the overload tank was holed and a fire started. Quick work by the crew managed to put the fire out, and it was able to reach base. A belly-landing had to be made as the hydraulic system was unserviceable, and the aircraft was damaged beyond repair.

Conditions in the target area during the three attacks made on the docks at Bizerte (on 3/4, 4/5 and 13/14 February – a total of twenty-eight sorties) usually meant that poor results were obtained. The lack of a moon, extreme darkness and cloud made identification of the target area very difficult, and the bombing was scattered. A good example of the efforts being put in by the ground crews came on 4/5 February when one of the aircraft of No. 150 Squadron was still being serviced shortly before take-off was due, and the armourers managed to bomb it up in just twelve minutes. For the rest of the month the two Squadrons continued their attacks on Bizerte, despatching forty-seven sorties on four nights. Weather conditions in Algeria were still poor, but were good in the target area on 15/16 February and a concerted attack was made. After a few cancelled operations the weather forecast was again favourable on 22/23 February, and another concentrated and successful attack was made. One Wellington of No. 142 Squadron failed to return, and several crews reported having seen an aircraft crash into the sea north of the target. This was the first aircraft lost from the squadron in North Africa due to enemy action.

On 25/26 February the aircraft operated from Maison Blanche as Blida was unserviceable for loaded aircraft, taking off between 0155 and 0230 hours so that they would return at dawn. At the time the weather was not very promising, and many of the crews found 10/10 cloud at the target. Others reported 'sizeable breaks' in the clouds, and bombed through them. One Wellington returned early, but was not picked up by the radar at Maison Blanche. It crashed in cloud into a hillside near Rivet, south east of the airfield, at 0530 hours, and all were killed. The final attack was on 28 February/1 March, and although the moon was in its last quarter, clear conditions over Bizerte resulted in another successful attack. Operations against Bizerte and Tunis continued in March, but the Squadrons only managed thirty-three sorties in three operations on 1/2, 3/4 and 12/13 February. The weather was generally very bad throughout this period, and when operations were carried out the Wellingtons often found cloud or ground haze over the target area. On 20/21 the target was the docks at Ferryville, and for a change the weather was good en route and over the target. All the aircraft located and bombed the target area, carrying out a concentrated and successful attack.

As the battle at Mareth opened the two Squadrons operated in support of the Eighth Army once again, and were directed to attack the landing ground at El Maou (near Sfax) on 21/22 March. The target was difficult to find despite good visibility in the area, being merely a patch of flat ground surrounded by olive groves. No. 142 Squadron ORB states that 'in consequence of our attack it is feared that the Tunisian olive crop will suffer considerably'. Three aircraft claimed to have bombed in the near vicinity, but no definite results were observed. The results were no better on 22/23 March, when eleven bombers went back to El Maou in excellent weather and with a full moon being very helpful in pinpointing the target area. However, once again the landing ground was very difficult to identify, and the olive groves took another pasting! The weather then intervened again, and it was not until 30/31 March that the Wellingtons operated against Decimomannu in Sardinia. Fourteen bombers were despatched, but despite a good weather forecast, the weather en route was poor, with 10/10 low cloud. All crews obtained pinpoints on the coast, but on approaching the target area found it covered by a valley mist. The enemy (described in No. 142 Squadron ORB as 'Wops' or 'Jerries') did not disclose the location by opening fire, but some aircraft claimed to have bombed flak positions and three claimed to have bombed the landing ground itself. On the last night of the month it was back to Bizerte, where the weather was good as far as Bougie, but after that 10/10 cloud and intermittent rain was encountered. All crews were compelled to bomb through cloud, and most chose to bomb flak and searchlight positions.

*　　　*　　　*

On 1/2 January 1943 fourteen Wellingtons took off to attack the airfield at Heraklion on Crete in a continuation of the raids that had started in December 1942. As usual, weather conditions were poor, with the target obscured by cloud and haze, and six of the aircraft abandoned the operation. The others attacked the estimated position of the airfield, where bursts were seen and one small fire started, but otherwise no results were observed. As the aircraft were returning to base, they were warned that an intruder was operating in the area, and they were ordered to orbit away from the vicinity of Menastir until an 'all clear' was given. Unfortunately, the American 9th Bomber Group operating from nearby Gambut failed to douse their flare path or instruct their returning aircraft to extinguish navigation and landing lights until it was too late. The intruder therefore switched his attentions to Gambut, and bombed their runway and shot up a B-24 coming in to land. When the 'all clear' was given, No. 231 Wing reported that four of its aircraft were still outstanding, but it later transpired that these had landed at Mersa Matruh, where two crashed but both crews were unhurt.

In order to try to resolve some of the organizational problems at this time the Group was placed under the operational control of the Desert Air Force on 7 January 1943. Arrangements were made for all serviceable aircraft to proceed to Benina, together with No. 231 Wing Operations Room personnel. The Wing did not operate again until the night of 8/9 January, when a series of operations against targets in the Western Desert were ordered as part of the Desert Air Force's preparatory air operations for Montgomery's attack on the Buerat position. The first was by ten Wellingtons against enemy vehicles at Misurata Cross Roads, followed on 11/12 January by an attack by twenty-one aircraft on buildings and vehicles at Homs. Four more attacks were carried out between 13/14 and 18/19 January, with a total of seventy-five sorties flown against roads and traffic in the neighbourhood of Churgia, Tauorga and Gheddahia. The Albacores of the Fleet Air Arm were back in action with the bombers, and their illumination was as good as ever and enabled the Wellingtons to obtain good results despite the fact that the enemy vehicles were well dispersed. The airfield at Castel Benito was also attacked on 17/18 and 19/20 January, following reports that the bulk of the enemy air forces was now concentrated there. Intense and very accurate flak was reported in the Tripoli area, particularly from a flakship in the harbour. Early on 23 January British troops entered Tripoli unopposed, and at noon General Montgomery formally received the surrender of the city from the Italian Vice-Governor of Tripolitania.

Alexander Clifford was with the first troops into the town, and at first found it to be remarkably untouched by the war – 'like entering a provincial town in peace time' – but then he got to the harbour area:

> Here there were signs of war. Every street showed the familiar signs of bombing – heaps of rubble, blackened, hollow facades, pitted walls, twisted iron shutters, and dozens of signposts pointing to shelters. But no English manufacturing town would have called this damage bad. I began to wonder whether those endless British and American raids on Tripoli had really been any good at all.
>
> Then we swept into the Piazza Roma, and round to the right into the Piazza Castello, which has one side open to the sea, and we saw at once that our bombing had been superb. The famous Spanish Mole looked like a low stony ridge. It had lost almost all resemblance to masonry. Only the derelict warehouses and installations showed what it had been. The surface of the water bristled with the rigging and funnels of sunken ships. Half a wooden

schooner was moored in the Piazza Castello. The other half had been cut clean away. All round there was evidence of fine, accurate bombing.[6]

However, Solly Zuckerman's report on the effect of the air raids on Tripoli was 'pretty discouraging':

> In spite of the fact that the majority of the thousand or so RAF aircraft which had attacked Tripoli at night during the preceding two years had claimed to have reached their primary target, fewer than twenty per cent of their bombs had fallen within the city limits, which comprised an area of approximately five square miles. Less than ten per cent had fallen within some two miles of the point at which they were aimed...There was little relation between the claims made by the pilots in their sortie records, the effects as they were experienced by the citizens of Tripoli, and the damage that Sandy and I had seen...Morale in the town had nonetheless been poor, and...during the period of the attacks, more than half the population had either evacuated to live on its outskirts, or 'trekked' – sleeping on the periphery and returning to their homes in the mornings.[7]

There is no doubt here that Zuckerman was applying the standards of the area bombing offensive against Germany, where the acreage of destruction in the major cities was the benchmark. It could be argued that Italian morale in Libya was much more fragile than that of the citizens of Germany, and hence bombs which missed their targets by some distance could still be effective. Also, unlike Tobruk, Tripoli had never been absolutely vital to the Axis armies in the Western Desert, particularly during the battles at El Alamein and the subsequent retreat. Nevertheless, the bombing must have disrupted the off-loading of supplies during the night, and thus made the daylight attacks on the port more effective.

On 23 January the Group reverted to the control of Headquarters, Royal Air Force Middle East, and was slowly regaining its strength. As well as No. 231 Wing (Nos 37 and 70 Squadrons), it was now to control No. 462 (Halifax) Squadron. This had been re-organized and brought up to strength at LG 237, and was placed under the control of No. 236 Wing at Solluch. No. 231 Wing was based at the Magrun Landing Ground, and the Group HQ was in the adjoining village. The Group ORB comments that the 'change of camp site from desert to green fields provided a striking contrast and the drop in night temperature was also marked'. All the squadrons were warned to stand-by for operations against targets in Sicily from the night of 26/27 January, but bad weather intervened and operations were not possible until the 29th. By this time No. 40 Squadron, which had returned from Malta and had been resting at LG 237, was brought up to rejoin the Group and also placed under No. 236 Wing at Solluch. On 29/30 January six Halifaxes and fourteen Wellingtons were despatched to attack targets at Catania and Messina, where bursts were observed and fires and explosions reported. One Wellington of No. 40 Squadron failed to return. On 31 January/1 February eighteen Wellingtons and seven Halifaxes went back to Sicily, but the operation was hampered by bad weather and few results were observed. One of the Halifaxes landed at Malta on return due to engine trouble.

At the beginning of February it was becoming evident that No. 205 Group would soon have to move into Tripolitania to keep up with the advance of the Eighth Army, which had crossed the Tunisian border on 29 January. A reconnaissance of the Misurata area was carried out by the AOC to find suitable airfields, and these were later pinpointed and named as Gardabia Main, Gardabia East and Gardabia West (all approximately seventy-five miles south-east of Tripoli). The Squadrons suffered from bad weather early in the month, and concentrated their efforts on Sicily, attacking Palermo three times on 3/4, 5/6 and 8/9 February. In the first attack sixteen Wellingtons and seven Halifaxes took off, but weather conditions at the target were only fair. A combination of cloud and haze and what was believed to be a smokescreen prevented successful identification of shipping. Bursts were seen on the North Mole, at least two fires were started in the harbour area, and a big explosion took place as the aircraft were leaving. In the second attack seventeen Wellingtons and nine Halifaxes were despatched, but poor weather conditions again hampered the whole operation. Icing conditions were encountered soon after take-off, and the target was obscured by 9/10 cloud. One Wellington failed to return, and one Halifax crash-landed near Barce after running out of fuel. On 8/9 February twenty Wellingtons and six Halifaxes took off, but yet again weather conditions proved somewhat worse than anticipated and much cloud was found over Sicily. Only ten aircraft located Palermo, and bursts were seen in both the harbour and the town areas. One Halifax and one Wellington failed to return. They then stood down between 9 and 15 February to permit the moves of the Group and Wings and Squadrons to their new locations at Gardabia.

Nos 37 and 70 Squadrons moved to the Gardabia area around the middle of the month, and were joined there by Nos 40 and 104 Squadrons with their Wellingtons, and by No. 462 Squadron with its Halifaxes. No. 104 Squadron had been at LG 237 resting from its arduous period in Malta, and became operational again on 8/9 February, sending three aircraft to Palermo. Before this a single Wellington was despatched to Crete on a Special Operation on 4/5 February. Flying Office McRae and his crew:

> ...did a food drop to some Australian troops beleaguered in a mountainous area in Crete. They had signalled their plight and asked for assistance. This was a tricky and delicate night mission, not only because of the navigation over mountainous terrain to the drop area, but also because of the timing which was of the utmost importance so far as the security of the troops was concerned. The operation was carried out successfully and the troops signalled their thanks. Flying Officer McRae was later awarded a DFC.[8]

Moving into Tripolitania with heavy aircraft presented many problems of supply of petrol, oil and bombs, as stocks were strictly rationed in the Western Desert Command. The long journey for road convoys was very uneconomical, and the port of Tripoli had only recently been opened. The Group was expected to be operational again by 15 February, and large quantities of supplies would be needed by this date. The Western Desert Air Command protested the move, and asked that it be delayed 'until the supply situation in clarified'. However, on 9 February a signal was received from Headquarters, RAF Middle East that the operations of No. 205 Group were regarded as of greater importance than those of the Western Desert Force. Thus, all possible Army and Air Force transport facilities were put at the disposal of the Group in order that it might meet its deadline. After being the poor relation for two months, the Group was now back up to five squadrons and receiving some priority of supplies. The AOC Western Desert Air Force was not the only one affected by the change in priorities. The move forward of the strategic bomber force meant that the Eighth Army had their own intake of petrol and supplies reduced at a time when they were building up stocks for the assault on the Mareth Line. The AHB Narrative states that this 'led to some extremely frigid signals from Rear Eighth Army HQ which General Alexander had…to override'.[9]

The conditions at Magrun had been pretty good, and a detachment of No. 40 Squadron had been comfortably settled in there alongside No. 70 Squadron after its return from Malta. Gardabia was far less hospitable – 'real desert again: nothing but sand and rocks.' Many of the No. 40 Squadron aircrew were new boys recently arrived from OTU in England, and one (rear gunner George Henfrey) recorded his first impression:

> Beyond the scrub lined airstrip the scanty remains of a stone fort were visible, and, still further inland, a slight escarpment marked the limit of this coastal plain. Stunted camelthorn was dotted over the landscape and under thousands of stones scattered around lived armies of scorpions. Flies abounded, particularly in the precincts of those artificial flowers, the 'Desert Lilies' (latrines), which were dotted about in suitably convenient spots.[10]

Another new arrival (RAAF observer Jack Liley) stated that 'at first sight it was a bit of a shock':

> All we could see was bare stony desert with about 20 Wimpies dispersed here and there, and at one end a tent encampment consisting of two or three large tents…with smaller…army type tents and also scatterings of vehicles, mostly 3-tonne trucks, jeeps,etc., and including a van-like truck, used as a kind of control tower, beside which was a white arrow indicating the direction of the runway.[11]

Liley was surprised to find that the Middle East Command Wellingtons were still being flown with a crew of six, including two pilots. Bomber Command in the UK had abandoned this in May 1942, operating with five man crews and with one pilot.

Chappell also had a poor opinion of Gardabia. On 12 February he flew there from Solluch, over the old El Agheila positions, over the Marble Arch erected in honour of Mussolini, and through sandstorms and rainstorms with violent gusty winds. He describes it as 'merely a brown runway scraped clear of grass and scrub'. Hungry and cold, they struggled to put up tents in the wind and rain, and later walked a mile or so for a meal. Rain, strong winds and dust-storms meant that operations were cancelled until 20/21 February, when the squadron's Wellingtons went to Palermo again. Chappell also had a poor view of No. 462 Squadron's Halifaxes, commenting that it was a 'joke bringing Halifaxes to the Middle East with Merlin engines when our 104 Wellingtons with Merlins so often have trouble due to overheating'. It was generally agreed by all that the Hercules engine was much better in North African conditions.

The move to Gardabia involved a trek forward of 500 miles, but by 15 February all the main unit parties had arrived and the Group was again operational. However, bad weather over Sicily meant that it could not despatch any aircraft until the night of 20/21, when thirty-four Wellingtons and eight Halifaxes took off for Palermo. Visibility at the bases was not very good, and by 2300 hours there was a great risk that it would deteriorate further. It was also certain by this time that the target area would be covered by 7/10 to 9/10 cloud, and it was decided to recall the aircraft at once. However, ten Wellingtons and one Halifax failed to pick up the recall signal, and went on to Palermo. Attacks were made through gaps in the cloud, and six fires were started, but the Group ORB states that 'altogether it was an extremely disappointing conclusion to a most promising operation.' One Wellington of No. 37 Squadron failed to return, and one of No. 70 Squadron crash-landed west of Gardabia and another crash-landed at Gardabia Main with a burst tyre. The Squadron ORB commented that it was 'not a very happy introduction to Gardabia'.

On 22/23 February Nos 231 and 236 Wings put up a maximum effort of thirty-three Wellingtons and six Halifaxes against Palermo. Explosions and fires were caused in the town, and bombs were seen to burst across the naval jetties and in the dock area. A number of big fires were burning when the aircraft left the target area, and one was reported to be very large with much smoke. One Wellington of No. 104 Squadron landed back at Malta due to shortage of petrol and engine trouble, and one of No. 40 Squadron failed to return. Operations were again planned against Palermo on the next night, but the Group was informed that it was to revert to the operational control of Advanced Air Headquarters, Western Desert, as the Eighth Army prepared to renew its push at Mareth. The target was switched to the landing ground at Gabes West, a base for Stukas and fighters, and twenty-five Wellingtons and six Halifaxes operated. The aircraft took the enemy completely by surprise and the flare path was still on when the first aircraft arrived. However, it was quickly extinguished, and ground haze made it extremely difficult for the later aircraft to locate the airfield itself. Thus, bombs were dropped over a fairly wide area, and some of the aircraft bombed Gabes town instead. Moderate but very accurate heavy flak was experienced at both targets. One Wellington of No. 40 Squadron ditched on the return trip, and all crew took to the dinghy. After eighty-two hours they reached land, and with some help from Arabs eventually returned to base.

The bombers were scheduled to go back to Gabes West on the next night, but as the aircraft prepared to take off a Wellington of No. 70 Squadron burst a tyre and crashed. It caught fire and exploded, but all the crew escaped. Because of the risk of further tyre bursts, now increased due to the many bomb splinters scattered around, the remaining nine aircraft of No. 231 Wing were cancelled. The twenty-three aircraft that operated again found much difficulty in locating the primary target, and some attacked Gabes Town. Only one or two small aircraft were seen on the ground and a few small fires were started, but a 4,000-lb bomb dropped on Gabes Town produced a violent explosion felt at 10,000 feet. The aircraft of Nos 37 and 40 Squadrons, which shared Gardabia East with No. 70 Squadron, were diverted to Gardabia Main on return due to the earlier crash.

It was clear that Gardabia East was unsuitable for bomber operations, and the AOC ordered the move of No. 231 Wing to a new landing ground at Gardabia West. This was effected immediately, and the Wing operated again on 25/26 February against Gabes West Landing Ground and Gabes Town. Instead of spreading the attack over a period, as was done the previous night, the two Wings concentrated their effort into a single concentrated blitz and No. 37 Squadron provided an illuminator for each of the targets. One of them was to fire a Verey cartridge if there were any good targets on the landing ground, otherwise the town was to bear the full weight of the attack. However, the signal was late in coming, and some of the aircraft bombed the landing ground and some the town. Altogether, the results were rather better than on the previous night. Aircraft on the ground were hit and a couple of fires started, and a 4,000-lb bomb exploded in the area of the barracks in the town. Thirteen Wellingtons and five Halifaxes went to Gabes West Landing Ground and Gabes Town once more on 26/27 February in what again proved to be a very effective attack.

On the 27th the Group once more came under the operational control of Headquarters Royal Air Force Middle East, and until further notice its targets were to be shipping in Palermo Harbour and the Messina Train Ferry. Seven Wellingtons (including two illuminators) and nine Halifaxes took off to attack Palermo on 28 February/1 March, where weather conditions were good, but due to either a smokescreen or low thin cloud no shipping could be seen. Thirteen aircraft bombed the dock area, and a 4,000-lb bomb was seen to burst in the town close to jetties and other bursts were seen in the town and dry dock area.

At the end of February the policy for the Group was reviewed in the light of the demands of the bomber squadrons in India and the general availability of reinforcements of Wellington aircraft. It was decided that the supply of Wellingtons would only permit a total of eighty aircraft in the Group, and there would therefore continue to be four squadrons of twenty aircraft – Nos 37, 40, 70 and 104 Squadrons – as well as the Halifaxes of No. 462 Squadron. With the Eighth Army about to attack the Mareth Line it was likely that the Group's squadrons would have to move forward again into the Tripoli area, and the Group ORB comments that:

> The future so far as the Group is concerned is full of possibilities, and appears at present to be linked entirely with the fortunes of the Army and Air Forces pushing Westwards into Tunisia.

The Liberators of No. 160/178 Squadron (the unit was renumbered as No. 178 Squadron on 15 January) were still operating from Shandur, on the Great Bitter Lakes, and under the control of the USAAF 9th Bomber Command. They continued operations on a small scale throughout January. Six aircraft were detailed to attack Tunis on 5/6 January, but only two were able to pinpoint the target area due to low cloud, and the remaining four aircraft attacked Sousse instead. On seven nights between 8/9 and 15/16 January the Liberators were ordered to bomb road junctions at Tripoli, and a total of thirty-four sorties were launched against these targets. Some of the aircraft also dropped leaflets in the Homs-Misurata area. On 17/18 January the target was the Castel Benito airfield, where bursts were seen and a fire started on the Western side. By this time the Squadron had just about run out of serviceable aircraft, as no engines were available to complete engine changes, and it was ordered to stand-down from operations. On 1 February the Squadron ORB records that instructions were received from 9th Bomber Command that it was to move from Shandur to Ghemines/Hosc Raui (twenty miles south of Benghazi) at the end of the month.

The Squadron resumed operations on 10/11 February, when five aircraft were detailed to attack Heraklion, but severe weather conditions caused all the aircraft to abandon their task over or south of Crete. They tried again on 13/14 February, when one bombed Kastelli Pediada and three bombed Heraklion. Bursts were seen over the north end of the runway at Kastelli Pediada, and a large fire with much black smoke was reported south of the main runway at Heraklion. They carried out two more attacks on Heraklion on 16/17 and 20/21 February, and in the first all five aircraft located and bombed the target area, and bursts and two small fires were seen. The second attack was a failure, and only one of the five Liberators claimed to have bombed at Heraklion. Two were unable to locate the target and bombed the runway at Kastelli Pediada instead, and one bombed flak positions thought to be at Maleme. On 22 February the main road party of No. 178 Squadron set off for Ghemines/Hosc Raui, and arrived safely by the 27th.

*   *   *

At the beginning of March 1943 the Eighth Army was in front of the Mareth Line, and Montgomery, in his usual cautious manner, was preparing a typical set-piece assault. In the first operation in March from Libya twenty-two Wellingtons took off to attack Palermo on 1/2 March. The operation was handicapped because the two aircraft of No. 40 Squadron that were to provide illumination developed engine trouble on the way to the target, and both had to force-land at Malta. Also, considerable cloud and a smoke screen over the port made bombing and observation of results extremely difficult. Sixteen aircraft eventually located and attacked Palermo, starting a few fires in the target area. One Wellington of No. 70 Squadron was caught by searchlights and flak, and hit in the hydraulic tank. Forced by the condition of his aircraft to land against a red light, Sergeant Stockdale ran into an aircraft of another squadron that had previously landed on the flare path. The Squadron ORB comments that the 'collision did little good to either aircraft'!

During March the squadrons in Libya were heavily involved in operations in support of the Eighth Army on the Mareth Line. On 2 March the Group was again placed under the operational control of Advanced HQ Western Desert for three nights, and on 2/3 March the target was enemy troop and transport concentrations in the Mareth area. Twenty-three Wellingtons and five Halifaxes operated in clear weather, and had no difficulty in locating the target area. Illumination was provided by an aircraft of No. 40 Squadron, but hardly any good targets were found – one or two camps and a few vehicles. Some small fires and explosions were reported, and a stick of bombs was seen to burst on a searchlight and gun position. Another flare-dropper from No. 40 Squadron should have operated, but it got lost and missed the target area. The pilot turned north, and then went out to sea – and finally dropped his flares forty minutes late. On his return he landed at No. 70 Squadron by mistake, took off again, and this time landed at No. 104 Squadron. At this point he gave up the struggle, and went to the squadron intelligence tent for interrogation. Chappell knew the crew from his time in Malta, and there was much amusement and leg-pulling before the embarrassed crew went off for breakfast.

It seems that things were not going well for No. 40 Squadron at this time. Chappell records that at lunchtime on 4 March a fire and thick black smoke were seen coming from the direction of No. 40 Squadron's landing ground, and comments that they 'have had wretched luck and serviceability lately'. The Wing Commander of No, 104 Squadron suggested that 'it looked as if poor 40 Squadron had become thoroughly brassed off and were burning their planes'! It turned out that it was two trucks laden with petrol that had caught fire. Gunby also comments on the difficulties of No. 40 Squadron, so clearly all was not well with the unit.

Twenty-nine Wellingtons and five Halifaxes successfully attacked targets in the

Mareth area on the next night, including buildings in the village, camps and roads, and vehicles dispersed in Wadis around Mareth village. A 4,000-lb bomb from No. 104 Squadron burst close to the road junction amongst twelve vehicles, and one aircraft attacked gun positions and searchlights, scoring near misses. A Wellington of No. 40 Squadron failed to return. The Group remained under AHQ Western Desert until 8 March, but were not called upon to operate against ground targets. On 8/9 March thirty-four Wellingtons took off to attack shipping at Palermo harbour once again. Cloud obscured the results for most of the aircraft, but some bursts in the town south of the harbour were reported. One Wellington arrived too late for the 'blitz' period and bombed 'lights in Sicily', and the port throttle of another jammed and it bombed Licata before making for Malta with a petrol shortage. Another three aircraft also ran short of petrol and landed at Malta, and the misfortunes of No. 40 Squadron continued with two early returns and two crash-landings.

On 9 March there was a very strong wind in the Gardabia area, and then a sudden sandstorm blew up in the late afternoon. It got very hot and unpleasant, and Chappell tells how things were made worse by hundreds of flying insects 'invading the mess and all tents, dive bombing the occupants and all lights'. Not surprisingly, operations were cancelled due to the weather conditions, and the next day was an unpleasant grey windy day and operations were again cancelled. Then on 11/12 March thirty-seven Wellingtons and ten Halifaxes attacked the Palermo area, where visibility was bad at first and the illumination by three aircraft of No. 40 Squadron was ineffective due to the thick cloud. However, much of this cleared after a while, and the aircraft that waited for the emergency blitz found fair conditions. Most claimed to have bombed the target area, and several fires were seen. One was a large orange fire that was still going well when the last aircraft left the area. Some of the Wellingtons of No. 104 Squadron bombed an existing fire in the northern area of Palermo, and other aircraft bombed gun positions in the harbour area.

Chappell (page 146) gives a very good account of the organization of a typical bomber unit at this time, and it is worth quoting in full:

> In the Royal Air Force the squadron is the operational unit with the aircraft, pilots and other aircrew members who do the actual flying and the fighter or bomber missions against the enemy. The ground personnel of the squadron maintain and service the aircraft and provide for the needs of the flying men and themselves.
>
> The bomber squadron in wartime may number about 500 men to maintain and operate a normal establishment of 16 to 24 aircraft. Because of its compact size and its direct involvement in the actual fighting the squadron members usually develop a strong sense of comradeship and pride in their unit. A bomber squadron is divided into two flights each with a squadron leader in charge and the commanding officer of the squadron is a wing commander in rank.
>
> A wing is a small headquarters unit which exists to control or serve two or three squadrons. Many of the officers are General Duties (Flying) now engaged in specialist non-flying duties such as Operations, Intelligence, Armament, Navigation, Engineering, Transport, Administration, etc. The average age of the officers is usually greater than on a squadron and the

officers' mess environment is somewhat different. There are no aircraft – and flying and operations are a little further away.

A wing is commanded by a group captain who can exert a strong personal influence upon this relatively small unit and upon the two or three squadrons for which he is responsible.

No. 236 Wing at Gardabia served No. 104 Wellington Bomber Squadron and No. 462 Halifax Bomber Squadron. In its turn 236 Wing was responsible to the Group Headquarters of No. 205 Group RAF.

Nos 37 and 70 Squadrons were under the control of No. 231 Wing, and No. 40 Squadron was under the direct control of the Group H.Q until late May.

The Group again came under the control of Advanced Air Headquarters Western Desert on 14 March, but was not called upon to operate until the 17/18th. On this night No. 231 Wing was ordered to attack troop concentrations on the road between Mareth and Kettena village, and thirteen aircraft of No. 37 Squadron took off. Before the Wellingtons of No. 70 Squadron could follow the operation was cancelled due to bad weather over the target area, and a recall signal was sent out. Three of the aircraft failed to pick up the signal and went on to bomb the target, and saw their bombs fall across dispersed vehicles off the Mareth road. The tempo now started to increase as the attack at Mareth got underway on the night of 19/20 March. Thirty-six Wellingtons took off, but the operation was hampered by poor weather. The early aircraft reported up to 10/10 cloud at three thousand feet, but this improved later. A few vehicles were observed and bombed, and about a dozen fires started. One Wellington from No. 70 Squadron failed to return, and an aircraft was seen to hit the ground and explode in the target area. A couple of hours after take-off heavy rain made both base landing grounds unserviceable, and a diversion signal was broadcast to all returning aircraft instructing them to land at Castel Benito. Not all the aircraft picked this up, and those that didn't were eventually got down safely at Gardabia Main or East. Gardabia West was reported to be 'completely U/S for at least 24 hours'.

The official history comments that a remarkable feature of the air support given to the Eighth Army at this time was that of No. 205 Group from 17/18 March onwards under the operational control of AHQ Western Desert. It states that close on 500 sorties were flown in a tactical role by the Wellingtons and Halifaxes, supported by the FAA Albacores as 'pathfinders'. On 20/21 March AHQ Western Desert called for a maximum effort, and all serviceable Wellingtons from Nos 37, 40 and 70 Squadrons back at Gardarbia were flown forward to Castel Benito to take part in the night's operation. The Halifaxes of No. 462 and Wellington IIs of No. 104 Squadron were to operate from and return to base. Altogether, eleven Halifaxes and forty-five Wellingtons attacked enemy concentrations, transport and encampments between Mareth and Katena, supported by the Albacores of No. 821 Squadron FAA. Three large and numerous smaller fires and two violent explosions in the Mareth area were reported. Three of the aircraft also machine-gunned the beaches east of Katena, transport on the Mareth–Gabes road, and a searchlight position that was quickly extinguished. One Wellington of No. 104 Squadron force-landed in the sea, but the crew were picked up and reported back to base two days later. AOC Advanced Air Headquarters, Western Desert, signalled congratulations on a most successful operation, and called for maximum effort from the Group until further notice.

On 21/22 March sixty-five aircraft took off to attack troop and transport concentrations at Mareth, ten aircraft of No. 104 Squadron doing a double sortie from Castel Benito. The aircraft of No. 37 Squadron reported that the weather and visibility were good, and concentrations of vehicles on the coast road and roads at El Hana and Gabes were bombed. Bursts were seen and a fire started south-west of Gabes. Other squadrons reported that the weather was not so good and illumination was poor, and although a certain amount of motor transport was found and bombed, on the whole very few vehicles were seen and these were well dispersed. Only one medium and three small fires were reported. Two aircraft of No. 104 Squadron were lost, and another was damaged beyond repair when its undercarriage collapsed on landing at Castel Benito. One of the missing Wellingtons came down in the sea 150 yards north-west of Zarzis, with three crew members drowned and two of the others injured. The other crash-landed near the main road at Zamzur, with two crew members slightly injured.

On 22/23 March thirty-six Wellingtons and ten Halifaxes attacked concentrations of vehicles on the road between Mareth and Gabes, with those of No. 70 Squadron doing double sorties from Castel Benito. The aircraft of No. 40 Squadron were unable to take part due to heavy rainstorms during the day, which made the landing ground at Gardabia South unserviceable. Visibility was good, and several fires and violent explosions were reported. One Wellington of No. 70 Squadron failed to return, the pilot of which had only been commissioned on this day. On the next night twenty-six aircraft bombed enemy positions between Gabes and Mareth, where bursts were seen amongst concentrations of vehicles by the roadside and in wadis in the Katena area, and several fires and a particularly violent explosion were reported. On 24 March Chappell records that the 'Eighth Army has had setbacks at Mareth and south of El Hamma and need our continued bombing support in the battle area.'

The Eighth Army had opened its assault on the Mareth Line on 19 March (Operation *Pugilist*), but as Chappell notes, things did not go well. By the 23rd Montgomery realized that the main attack had failed, and he altered his plan. Earlier reconnaissance had shown that the Mareth Line could be outflanked to the south, and Montgomery had already sent the New Zealand Corps through the Matmata hills in such a flanking manoeuvre. By 23 March the New Zealanders were in contact with elements of the 21st Panzer Division near the western entrance to the Tebaga Gap, and Montgomery now decided to reinforce them with the 1st Armoured Division. The flanking move would become the main effort, while 30th Corps would try to contain as much of the enemy force as possible at Mareth. However, the Germans defended the Gap strongly, and a plan was devised by Air Vice-Marshal Broadhurst to concentrate a massive air strike in order to paralyse the enemy for long enough to permit the ground forces to break through (Operation *Supercharge*). The RAF's plan was that during the nights 24/25 and 25/26 March the bombers of No. 205 Group and the Desert Air Force were to attack targets in the battle area in order to destroy motor transport and telephone lines, and to deprive the enemy of sleep. The bombardment would continue until 1530 hours on the 26th, when three formations of day-bombers of the Desert Air Force were to attack from low level, dropping their bombs in a precise pattern so as to create disorganization in the enemy ranks. Then, as the artillery barrage opened and the ground troops rose from cover, formations of fighter bombers would arrive in relays every fifteen minutes and fly continuously over the enemy and ahead of the advancing troops.

On the night of 24/25 March seventy-three sorties were flown against the enemy's positions south of El Hamma in the Tebaga Gap, with No. 40 Squadron operating double sorties and sending out fourteen aircraft each time. Quite a fair amount of motor transport was seen scattered in wadis, and was bombed with good results. The attacks caused over ten fires and several violent explosions amongst dispersed MT and troop concentrations. One large fire was seen about fifteen miles south of El Hamma, and several direct hits were registered on roads. All the aircraft returned safely from what was 'a most successful operation', but some were caught by accurate batteries on the coast and badly holed. It was more of the same on the next night when sixty-eight sorties were flown against the El Hamma position. No. 37 Squadron flew double sorties of thirteen aircraft each time, landing at Castel Benito after the first sortie and returning to Gardabia West after the second. In the first phase it reported a very violent explosion and three small fires amongst dispersed transport. Several more fires were started by other aircraft later, and direct hits on vehicles were seen. Six fires were still burning when the last aircraft left the target, giving off volumes of thick black smoke. One Halifax of No. 462 Squadron force-landed at Zuara with engine trouble after jettisoning its bombs.

Following the RAF assaults planned by Broadhurst, the guns supporting the New Zealand Corps opened up at 1600 hours on the 26th, and as the New Zealanders attacked the sun shone in the faces of the enemy and a strong wind blew the dust clouds thrown up by the bombs and guns into his eyes. By dawn on the 27th the British were through the Gap and threatening El Hamma, but the Germans cobbled together yet another of their improvised defence lines and held them off. Meanwhile, the Axis forces had begun to abandon the whole Mareth position on the night of 25/26 March, and were slipping away to the North. There was little fighting during 28 March, but the battles at Mareth were over. The Eighth Army had won a great battle, but, once again, had proved to be poor finishers. The enemy had got away once more, and retreated to a line at Akarit, some forty miles to the north of Gabes and the last natural barrier against access to the coastal plain of Tunisia from the south.

As the battles at Mareth came to an end the attentions of the heavy bombers were directed at Gabes on 26/27 March, and fifty-two Wellingtons and seven Halifaxes attacked enemy concentrations in the area with mixed results. The aircraft of No. 37 Squadron found that illumination over the target was good, and the weather good but with a slight haze. Other aircraft reported that weather conditions were poor, with thick haze over the target and poor illumination, which made location of targets difficult. The illuminating aircraft from No. 70 Squadron located the target area, but was forced to return with serious engine trouble. Transport, roads, railway sidings, barracks and gun positions were attacked and several fires started, but some aircraft were forced to jettison after being unable to find any targets. One of the Wellingtons of No. 104 Squadron machine-gunned one of the fires on the ground without any results being observed. One Wellington of No. 37 Squadron failed to return.

As the Axis forces retreated towards their new defence line at Akarit, the bombers attacks were concentrated on enemy transport at cross roads at Oudref and Wadi Akarit. Fifty-two Wellingtons and four Halifaxes took off on 28/29 March and carried out a successful operation, with plenty of targets seen around the railway sidings at Oudref. Several good fires and a violent explosion were reported, and two of the aircraft machine-gunned ground targets in the area. A 4,000-lb bomb burst close to a very large fire, thought to be stores. Gunby comments that No. 40 Squadron 'operated the long-awaited Mk III Wellingtons for the first time'. The re-equipment of the Group squadrons with the Hercules-powered Mk IIIs and Xs had been under way for some months, but was a slow process. Nos 40 and 104 Squadrons were still 'struggling on with…worn-out Mk IIs', and they were not to be fully re-equipped with the much superior Mk IIIs and Xs for another three months. The age and condition of some of the Wellingtons still being operated in North Africa was a cause of concern to many, and conversion to the Hercules-engined aircraft was extremely slow. The condition of engines coming back from overhauls in Cairo was also giving concern, and it was found that locally made piston rings were unsatisfactory and wearing faster than they ought.

The Group ORB comments that it was announced on 30 March that the Eighth Army had advanced and occupied the Mareth defences, and the enemy once again appeared to be in retreat. The target for that night was given as the Sfax–El Maou Landing Ground, and Albacores illuminated the target for fifty-five Wellingtons. They caused many fires and violent explosions visible from eighty miles away, and it was believed that an ammunition dump had been hit. One Wellington of No. 104 Squadron ditched in the sea off Tunisia after an engine cut. Chappell comments that the operation 'was one of our most successful ever for spectacular results'. Although the target was the landing ground, 'we seem to have hit something else that burned and exploded with 25 fires counted'. No. 37 Squadron ORB reports an 'unfortunate accident' after one of its aircraft had landed. The rear gunner, Sergeant Alexander Spice, left his turret and walked into the propeller and was killed instantly.

The Liberators of No. 178 Squadron, still operating under the control of the USAAF 9th Bomber Command, were in the process of moving to their new location at Hosc Raui (Ghemines), south of Benghazi. The Squadron continued to be very short of serviceable aircraft, and only flew thirty-six sorties on six nights in March. The first, on 4/5 March, saw six aircraft despatched to Naples, and five located and bombed the target area. Two small fires were started, and one large explosion resulted in a short-lived fire. One of the Liberators failed to return. Seven Liberators went to Naples again on 13/14 March, detailed to attack the Vittoria Emanuele Mole, but 10/10 cloud obscured the target area and two brought their bombs back to base. One aircraft dropped its bombs in the vicinity of Messina, two on lights seen in the vicinity of Naples, and one in the approximate position of Siderno Marina. Another mission on 18/19 March was even less successful, and all seven aircraft were recalled by 9th Bomber Command due to bad weather. On 21/22 March five Liberators went to Naples. One returned early due to engine trouble, but the other four located and bombed the target area. Bursts were seen, but results were not observed. Then on 24/25 and 29/30 March six bombers were despatched to attack the ferry terminal at Messina on both nights. The first attack was reasonably successful, but on the second the aircraft were unable to locate their primary or secondary targets due to 10/10 cloud and brought their bombs back.

*　　　*　　　*

In the 142 days/nights between 10 November 1942 and 31 March 1943 the night bombers went out on 113 of them. The Wellingtons of No. 205 Group and the Liberators of No. 178 Squadron flew 2,982 sorties and lost 61 aircraft. Most operations were carried out by small numbers of aircraft, and it was not until the end of March and the operations in support of the attacks on the Mareth Line that substantial numbers of aircraft took to the air. Almost half the sorties (45 per cent) were directed at the ports and shipping in harbour, and another 32 per cent to military targets in the battle area. Most of the rest (22 per cent) went to airfields.

NOTES

1. Gunby, *Sweeping the Skies*, page 213.
2. Quoted in Gunby, *Sweeping the Skies*, page 212.
3. Alexander Clifford, *Three Against Rommel*, page 314.
4. Solly Zuckerman, *From Apes to Warlords*, page 178.
5. AHB Narrative, *The Middle East Campaigns*, Volume IV, pages 451–452.
6. Alexander Clifford, *Three Against Rommel*, pages 346–347.
7. Solly Zuckerman, *From Apes to Warlords*, pages 177–178.
8. Chappell, *Wellington Wings*, pages 134–135.
9. AHB Narrative, *The Middle East Campaigns*, Volume IV, page 486.
10. Gunby, *Sweeping the Skies*, page 221.
11. Gunby, *Sweeping the Skies*, page 222.

CHAPTER SEVEN

The End in Africa – April to July 1943

On the night of 10/11 May 1943 thirteen Wellingtons of No. 40 Squadron had the distinction of being the last unit of No. 205 Group to carry out a night-bombing attack in North Africa. They bombed the road between Hammamet and Menzel Temime, in good weather and with no opposition. On 12 May 1943 a signal was received from Headquarters, Northwest African Tactical Air Force: 'No further operations required in connection with this campaign.' All organized resistance in Tunisia had ceased, and this marked the end of No. 205 Group's long campaign throughout the battles for North Africa. The Group ORB states 'Leave and rest to commence in all units.' On the following day the Group reverted to the operational control of Headquarters, RAF Middle East, but did not operate again until 21 May.

Operations had been winding down in April, and the attention of the night bombers was already starting to move away from Tunisia, although some attacks continued on Bizerte and Tunis. The official history makes the point that the:

> ...operation of these aircraft, though directed to the common purpose, for the most part were carried on outside the fields of battle and were not necessarily linked closely in time with events on the ground.[1]

This was particularly true of the Liberators at Hosc Raui (Ghemines), operating under the control of the USAAF 9th Bomber Command. They only carried out ten operations during April, totalling fifty-eight sorties, and another three (eighteen sorties) during the final stages of the fighting in Tunisia in May. All were directed at targets in Italy or Sicily, reflecting the changing focus for the Allies. Palermo was attacked four times, Naples four times, Messina twice, and single attacks were carried out on Catania, Bari, and Reggio di Calabria. In the period covered by this chapter the Liberators would be joined by the Halifaxes of No. 462 Squadron, concentrating all the RAF heavy bombers in North Africa under a single command.

The two Wellington squadrons in Algeria (Nos 142 and 150) remained at Blida until 5 May, and then moved to Fontaine Chaude, sixty miles south of Bone, operating under the control of NASAF. During April there were sixteen nights when no operations were possible due to bad weather, and only 256 sorties were flown on the fourteen nights when the weather improved sufficiently to allow the bombers to take off. Even then, the operations took place in weather almost as bad, providing yet another hazard for the bombers. Also, apart from two attacks on enemy vehicles and troop concentrations at Enfidaville, the aircraft from Blida played little direct part in the final land battles in Tunisia. There were a few attacks on Bizerte and on the Tunis area, and a few more on airfields on Sardinia. The squadrons of No. 205 Group (Nos 37, 40, 70, 104 and 462) were still based in the Gardabia area throughout April and most of May 1943, operating under the control of Advanced Air Headquarters Western Desert, and generally more intimately concerned with the ground battle than those based in Algeria. By the beginning of June all of the Wellington squadrons were based at Kairouan in Tunisia, and were being given the same targets by NASAF. They all came under the operational control of No. 205 Group at the end of the month.

On the ground a limited offensive to regain the initiative on the First Army's front in the north was launched on 27 March, and although the country was not easy and the weather was wet, on the afternoon of the 30th the 46th Division entered Sedjenane. In the south the end of March saw the Axis forces established in their new positions sixty kilometres to the north-west of Mareth, at Wadi Akarit near Gabès. The Akarit position had great natural advantages, vouched for by Rommel who would have preferred to stand there rather than at Mareth. It would be extremely difficult to force by a frontal assault, despite the great superiority of the Allies on the ground and in the air. On 29 March the 1st Armoured and New Zealand Divisions began to probe the defences, and attacks were pressed forward against very stubborn opposition. Most of the Axis troops started to withdraw successfully at nightfall on 6 April, and once again the Eighth Army had won its battle but had failed to finish the enemy off. Although Kairouan was entered on the 11th, the enemy on the Eighth Army's front was to remain out of touch until Enfidaville.

The first week of April was fairly quiet, and General Alexander's forces on all fronts regrouped and prepared themselves for the final battle for Tunisia. There then began a period of fighting, the outcome of which was to break the enemy's back before the final blows were delivered in May. The US II Corps moved to the northern end of the Allied front, and would attack in the north towards Bizerte. The British First Army was to attack in the centre towards Tunis, and the Eighth Army from the south through Enfidaville. On 11 April, elements of the First and Eighth Armies met each other twenty miles south of Kairouan, and the Axis forces were now firmly locked up in the Tunis defences. On 19 April the Eighth Army attacked the Germans in the Enfidaville position, but the Germans held on. The final battles to reduce the Tunis bridgehead opened on 22 April, and against determined opposition ground relentlessly forwards. Allied victory was certain, but the fighting was hard and often bitter, and towards the end of April the general offensive was slowing down.

By 30 April it had become clear that the Eighth Army's attack from Enfidaville into well-held and difficult terrain would not succeed, and Alexander therefore transferred the 7th Armoured Division, the Indian 4th Infantry Division and the 201st Guards Brigade from the Eighth Army to the First Army. On 3 May US troops took Mateur, less than fifty miles north-west of Tunis, and on 5 May British forces broke through the defences of the 5th *Panzerarmee* to the south of Tunis. The German defence was cracking, and the enemy broke into groups that, in the final week, were cornered and hunted down into surrender. The final assault was launched on 6 May by the British 9th Corps, and on the afternoon of 7 May British troops entered Tunis and American troops captured Bizerte. On 9 May the 2nd US Corps cornered von Vaerst and what remained of Pz AOK 5, and demanded its unconditional surrender, with which von Vaerst complied at noon. On the same day the *Luftwaffe* withdrew to Sicily and Pantellaria, and by the 12th the Italians had followed suit. The British 6th Armoured Division took Hammamet on 10 May, but the remnants of the old Afrika Korps under General Messe were still dangerous and 'mainly preoccupied in ensuring that its long service in Africa be brought to an honourable conclusion'.[2] Von Arnim surrendered on 12 May and Messe on the 13th, thus ending hostilities in North Africa.

*   *   *

The two Wellington squadrons in Algeria were grounded by bad weather at the beginning of April, and then a successful attack was carried out by fifteen aircraft on the docks at Trapani (Sicily) on 4/5 April. Two attacks on Tunis followed, and the first attack by sixteen aircraft on 5/6 April was helped by excellent visibility en route to the target and the bombing was concentrated and very successful. One of the aircraft carried a French officer who was in command of an anti-aircraft battery near Blida, and it circled near the target to give him the opportunity of observing the enemy flak. Apparently, he was more impressed by the accuracy of the bombing than by that of the enemy AA fire. The eight crews of No. 150 Squadron were reported to be 'all new, this being the 1st trip for many'. On 6/7 April the targets were the marshalling yards at Tunis and Djebel Djelloud, and successful attacks were evenly divided between the two yards.

The weather then intervened again until the night of 9/10 April, when fourteen aircraft attacked enemy troop and MT concentrations on the roads around Enfidaville. The weather was cloudy en route, but with good visibility in the target area and a helpful moon. One aircraft of No. 150 Squadron 'stood off dropping flares by the light of which other crews saw motor transport on the roads'. One of the Wellingtons of No. 142 Squadron failed to return. On 10/11 April, the airfields at Elmas and Decimomannu were bombed, and another Wellington of No. 142 Squadron failed to return and was thought to have gone down in flames in the target area. On the next night it was back to the Enfidaville area, where the attack was mainly concentrated on an airfield south of St Marie du Zit and roads in the vicinity. One of the Wellingtons of No. 150 Squadron failed to return, and some crews reported seeing what might have been an aircraft going down in the target area. It later transpired that the aircraft was hit by flak and disabled. All of the crew baled out except the pilot (Sergeant Leekie), who had to stay with the aircraft because it was then too low. He made a crash-landing between the battle lines, and he and all the other crew members walked to our own lines by dawn.

On 12/13 April twenty-two aircraft attacked the landing ground at Megrine (Fochville) near Tunis, and on 14/15 April Decimomannu and Elmas were bombed again by twenty-four aircraft. The main attack concentrated on Decimomannu, where fires were started, and others bombed the Elmas and Villacidro landing grounds. The docks at Bizerte came under attack on 16/17 April, and on the next night the Wellingtons went to Tunis again. The attack was concentrated on the marshalling yards, causing a large explosion and fires. All the aircraft were directed to Maison Blanche on return due to strong cross winds at base. One aircraft of No. 142 Squadron crash-landed due to damaged hydraulics, and another failed to return. One aircraft of No. 150 Squadron was holed by flak, and the petrol tanks damaged. It carried on until the fuel ran out, and came down in the sea off Algiers. The crew were picked up by a destroyer thirty-six hours later and taken to Gibraltar suffering from exposure. The weather then closed in again, and the next operation was to the docks at Bizerte on 23/24 April. Cloud was encountered over the whole journey, with extreme darkness, haze, and medium cloud over the target. Most of the aircraft were unable to pinpoint the docks, and bombed fires seen burning near the goods station. Several aircraft were holed by moderate heavy flak and some crew members were wounded, but all the aircraft returned safely.

Twenty-four aircraft attacked Decimomannu on 24/25 April, and then brought their attacks closer to the battlefront by attacking the airfields at El Aouina and Sidi Ahmed on 28/29 and 29/30 April. In the first attack the aircraft carrying incendiaries placed them right on the target, and most of the following aircraft bombed the resulting fires. This attack was judged to be one of the most successful yet carried out on this type of target. The second attack was marred by an accident to one of the aircraft of No. 142 Squadron, which crashed on take-off and burst into flames. The remaining aircraft were unable to take off due to the obstruction caused by the crashed aircraft. The ones that did get off found 10/10 cloud and thundery showers, and all aircraft had to bomb the estimated position of the airfield. One of the Wellingtons of No. 150 Squadron crashed into hills near Sourna, Algeria, on the return journey, and all members of the crew were killed. On 27 April the advance party of No. 150 Squadron left for Fontaine Chaude, followed by a party from No. 142 Squadron on the next day.

The weather was bad again on the night of 30 April/1 May, and remained so for the next three nights. Then on 4/5 May there was another stand-down as the move to Fontaine Chaude was to start first thing on the next morning. The road convoys left early in the morning, followed by all the aircraft carrying the ground crews. On arrival they found that the camp had been laid out and all the tents erected by the American engineers attached to NASAF. Nos 142 and 150 Squadrons were now formed into 330 Wing, under the command of Group Captain J.A. Powell DSO, OBE. The first operation from Fontaine Chaude was against the docks at Trapani on 6/7 May, and the thirteen aircraft immediately flew into 10/10 cloud with violent electric storms and intense rain thirty miles from base. The bad weather conditions persisted for over 100 miles en route to the target, and the Wellingtons found 7/10 cloud, haze and intense darkness in the target area. Identification of ground detail was impossible, and bombs were dropped on lights and flak positions on the Sicilian coast. One aircraft of No. 150 Squadron landed back at Biskra on return, and another came down 'on a grassy plain' outside Guelma. One Wellington of No. 142 Squadron was heard asking for a homing signal, and was later found to have force-landed in Algeria. It came down on the beach near Cap Oum Achiche, and after two unsuccessful attempts to lift them off by landing craft they were taken by road to Philippeville.

On 8/9 May the targets were airfields in Sardinia, and twenty-five aircraft took off in two waves and bombed throughout the night. The weather was cloudless on the way out and back, but intense darkness and ground haze made target identification very difficult. The aircraft bombed on flares and on timed runs from actual pinpoints, attacking Villacidro, Monserrato, Elmas and Decimomannu. On the next night twenty-two bombers went to Palermo, flying through deteriorating weather, but it cleared over the target area and the port was easily identified in brilliant moonlight. On the return trip the weather again deteriorated over the sea, and eight aircraft landed at Bone and three at Biskra. One of the Wellingtons of No. 142 Squadron had an engine cut on the way back, and was abandoned near Montcalm. The rear gunner had difficulty getting out and landed with both legs broken, and the bomb aimer fractured some ribs. On 11/12 May twenty-two aircraft were despatched to attack the port of Marsala in Sicily, but in spite of perfect weather some bombed at Mazara di Val and Trapani instead. In the final attack from Algeria before hostilities ended on 13 May, twenty-one aircraft took off to bomb the docks and marshalling yards at Naples. The weather was excellent en route and over the target area, but after the first aircraft had bombed a smoke-screen gradually spread over the whole area. Most of the aircraft claimed to have bombed successfully, however, and several fires were started in the industrial area.

Following the surrender of the Axis forces in Tunisia, very few operations were carried out by the night bombers for the rest of the month, and most of these were flown by the Wellingtons of No. 330 Wing from Fontaine Chaude. On 13/14 May twenty-three aircraft of Nos 142 and 150 Squadrons were despatched to Cagliari on Sardinia, where the first aircraft to bomb caused a huge explosion in the Montixeddu fuel oil storage area and a large fire that was visible for eighty miles. On the next night the target for seventeen aircraft was Palermo, and on 15/16 May sixteen aircraft took off for Trapani. Although the weather began to deteriorate between the North African coast and Sicily, most bombed the target area. One Wellington of No. 142 Squadron and two of No. 150 Squadron failed to return, but one of the latter was later reported to have force-landed in Algeria.

On 16/17 May twenty-one aircraft took off for an 'exceptional target for tonight's operation', to bomb the seaplane base at Lido di Roma and to drop leaflets on the city. The base was bombed and machine-gunned, and was reported to be 'defended by a single machine gun'! On 17/18 May sixteen aircraft took off to bomb the port at Alghero, and Squadron Leader Mathewman of No. 142 Squadron was accompanied by a distinguished guest – General Doolittle, who 'went to observe results'. These were reported to be good, and included a large fire in the centre of the town. Some of the aircraft machine-gunned the fire and flak positions from as low as 200 feet, and Flight Lieutenant Allen of No. 142 Squadron went down so low that he had to lift a wing to clear a church steeple.

The weather then intervened on the night of 18/19 May, but had cleared by the next night to allow nineteen aircraft to take off to attack the airfields at Decimomannu and Villacidro. The first aircraft over Villacidro found the airfield lights still on, and attacked it from 400 feet, sustaining hits from light flak on the way. The lights stayed on for some twenty minutes, and the flare path at Decimomannu was also lit and lights showed on the perimeter. Crews confirmed three or four aircraft burning on the ground after the attack, and fires were started that were visible for forty minutes after the first aircraft had bombed. Then on 20/21 May nineteen Wellingtons went back to Decimomannu and Villacidro, and Cagliari was also attacked by aircraft carrying 4,000-lb bombs. The targets for seventeen aircraft on the night of 21/22 May were the airfields in Sicily, where one of the Wellingtons of No. 142 Squadron approaching Castel Ventrano saw a three-star cartridge fired into the air, and all the flare path was lit in answer. It promptly dived into the attack at 300–400 feet, laying a stick of bombs down the flare path, and coming out at fifty feet to avoid the defences. One of the aircraft of No. 150 Squadron failed to return.

After a stand-down for one night, twenty-three aircraft from No. 330 Wing opened the attack on the island of Pantellaria on 23/24 May. The weather en route was cloudless, but a slight haze and intense darkness in the target area made pinpointing very difficult. Consequently, bombing was done mainly on Dead Reckoning, and few results were observed. The Wing went back to Pantellaria on 29/30 May (twenty-two aircraft) and 31 May/1 June (twenty-one aircraft). As the attacks built up, the aircraft often flew double sorties, with new crews taking over as the Wellingtons landed, although a shortage of bombs at Kairouan sometimes hampered operations. We will cover the brief campaign against Pantellaria and Lampedusa in detail later in this chapter. In between, on 24/25 May, the bombers attacked the docks at Olbia on Sardinia, and six or seven good fires were noted. One aircraft hit an ammunition dump, and a very large explosion was caused, which was seen from forty miles away. A Wellington flying at 7,000 feet felt the effect of the blast, and smoke rose to 4,000 feet.

*   *   *

The squadrons of No. 205 Group were still based in the Gardabia area throughout April and most of May 1943, operating under the control of Advanced Air Headquarters Western Desert, and generally more intimately concerned with the ground battle than those based in Algeria. They were given no targets to attack until 4/5 April, when thirty-one Wellingtons and five Halifaxes bombed Sfax town. All the aircraft bombed the target area, but bursts only were seen except for one small fire in the railway yard. One 4,000-lb bomb fell in the factory area, and a second fell just west of the railway station. During the night of 6/7 April the bombers attacked concentrations of vehicles on the Mahares–Sfax Road and Sfax town. Thirty-eight Wellingtons from Nos 37 and 70 Squadrons operated in two waves, with good illumination provided by Albacores. They bombed and strafed small groups of vehicles, camps and buildings, but they just missing the main withdrawal of the enemy from the Akarit position and few results were claimed. Between the two attacks thirty-five Wellingtons from Nos 40 and 104 Squadrons went to Sfax town, where bursts were seen in the area of the railway sidings, phosphate quay and warehouses. Two 4,000-lb bombs burst near the railway station and to the south-west of the town, but results were not observed. One aircraft of No. 40 Squadron did not return, and another crashed on landing.

At this time Chappell tells of a trip he made to Tripoli 'to collect Welfare requirements'. He flew in a Halifax of No. 462 Squadron, which he describes as 'a very ropey kite…with severe clanking from the starboard inner engine'. After a slow climb away from Gardabia, they staggered on over plantations of small trees and sometimes palms, alternating with brown sandy patches. To the south were the rugged grey green Tarhuna Hills, with contour-like markings from the horizontal strata and deep gashes of winding wadis. To the north were glimpses of blue sea and white sandy beaches. The final run was made over green trees lining a straight stretch of road, and into 'a rectangular airfield with ruined hangars on one side – Castel Benito'. The Halifax followed a DC3 and a Hudson into land, and was followed by Beaufighters. A very large collection of wrecks and other aircraft were crowded around the perimeter, 'probably some of the wrecks resulting from 205 Group bombing'. The Americans were in possession of half of the airfield and the RAF occupied the other half.

Fifty-five Wellingtons and five Halifaxes operated against Sfax town and the Mahares–Sfax road on 7/8 April, as the enemy fell back from the Akarit position. The illumination was again provided by the Albacores, and small groups of

165

vehicles and some encampments were attacked. Bursts were seen and a few fires started, with one fairly large red fire among dispersed vehicles and two tented camps straddled with bombs. One Wellington of No. 37 Squadron dropped a 4,000-lb bomb on the town, observing a burst followed by a big explosion with much black smoke. Two aircraft came down low and machine-gunned vehicles, setting at least one lorry on fire. In Sfax town bombs were seen to burst among buildings just south-west of the Arab Quarter and on railway sidings, but thick haze prevented accurate observation of results. One of the Wellingtons of No. 104 Squadron, piloted by Wing Commander Mount, failed to gain height after take-off and crashed into some hills near Gardabia Main. Fortunately, the grassy undulating country around Gardabia was ideal for emergency landings, and none of the crew was seriously injured. The Merlin-engined Wellington struggled after take-off in the high temperature conditions, and was brought down gently onto a low hilltop without detonating the bombs or causing a fire.

On 8 April the Group ORB reported that the general situation in Tunisia continued to be favourable for the Allies, and progress was being made on all fronts. In the south Rommel's forces were retreating and Chekira, twenty-five miles south of Mahares, had been reached. That night fifty-three Wellingtons and six Halifaxes set off to attack road targets south of Sousse and in the area between the road and the coast. Unfortunately, the target area was too far in the enemy's rear, as their main formations had not yet reached Sfax. Cloud made the location of targets difficult, and it was found that the flares were dropping over a wide area. Some bombed the airfield at El Djem, thirty miles south of Sousse, and the town of Sousse itself, but many just bombed any targets of opportunity that presented themselves. Chappell tells the story of Squadron Leader Trumper and a new crew he was taking on their first operation. Seeing the flak and getting a glimpse of Sousse harbour through the cloud, the Squadron Leader shouted 'in we go'. The bomb aimer thought that he had said 'let them go', and promptly dropped all his bombs into the sea! Alan Moorhead went to Sousse just after the Eighth Army took the town, and gives a nice account of the state of the town and harbour:

> ...we entered the blasted town of Sousse. For months this place had been attacked by the RAF and the United States Air Force; and now driving in through the target area along the docks it was a frightening sight...It was not so much the general devastation, it was the violence with which everything had been done. A grand piano had been picked up from a basement and flung onto a housetop. The roof of one apartment building had been flung bodily onto the next building. The palm trees on the waterfront looked like those photographs one used to see after a hurricane had passed through Florida. The ships in the bay were set in a frame of blackened warehouses and they were in all stages of decomposition – the ships that had been merely hit and sunk, those that had been beached by a near miss and subsequently broken up by the waves, those that had been entirely disintegrated. Bits of cork, broken scraps of lifeboats and rope and spars were mingled with the tangled mess of the railway lines that ran down to the docks. The walled Arab section – the Kasbah – had been split open and the midday sun poured in over all its tawdry and shabby secrets; the labyrinthine brothels, the sweet-vendors' shops, the miserable foetid courtyards where the Moorish women wasted their obscure and furtive lives.[3]

Sfax fell on 9 April, and the attentions of the night bombers now turned to the airfields in an attempt to destroy the remaining enemy air forces in Tunisia. During the night thirty-eight Wellingtons were despatched to attack the landing ground at Menzel Temime, where illumination was good and several fires were started. Some of the aircraft were unable to locate the primary target, and bombed the town and roads at Temime and one dropped a 4,000-lb bomb on a crossroads at Enfidaville. On 11 April Rommel's forces were reported to be in full retreat across the coastal plain north of Sousse, and fifty-eight Wellingtons and two Halifaxes bombed buildings, blast shelters, and dispersed aircraft at Sainte Marie du Zit. The target was well illuminated, and runways, dispersals and buildings were bombed with good results. One good petrol fire was started, buildings were set alight, one of which exploded, and when the last aircraft left the scene around twenty fires were burning fiercely. One aircraft of No. 40 Squadron was seen to catch fire over the target, which quickly spread from nose to tail before it went down. Another of No. 104 Squadron was blown to pieces on landing when three hung-up bombs exploded. The rear gunner was severely injured, with a broken leg and burns, and all the rest of the crew was killed.

On 12/13 April sixty Wellingtons divided their attacks between the two landing grounds of Menzel Temime and Korba South. They started several fires on both targets, but few other results were observed due to cloud. One of the Wellingtons of No. 70 Squadron was hit by flak, the pilot (Sergeant Petrie) had his left foot almost severed by shrapnel, and other members of his crew were injured. The bomb aimer took over the pilot's seat and flew the aircraft back to base, where Sergeant Petrie took over again. Despite intense pain, and with his left foot strapped to the rudder bar, he brought the aircraft in to land. The undercarriage refused to respond, despite the use of the emergency oil pumps, and he crash-landed somewhere between LG 104 and base. The cabin had to be cut to allow for his removal, and his leg was amputated the following morning. One aircraft of No. 104 Squadron failed to return.

The attacks on the airfields near Tunis were kept up on the next seven nights, with attacks on the landing grounds at Korba, Sainte Marie du Zit, Borj Le Boeuf, Soliman, and Creteville. Some 179 sorties were flown between 13/14 and 19/20 April, and generally good results reported. The enemy flak was often intense and night fighters were operating over the area in a desperate effort to protect the airfields during these last days in Tunisia, and seven aircraft were lost. Many reports in the ORBs at this time attest to the ferocity of the flak, which was usually very heavy and accurate. On 13/14 April a Wellington of No. 70 Squadron failed to return, and another aircraft of the same unit reported having seen an explosion at about 2310 hours, followed by pyrotechnics in mid-air. On 15/16 April two aircraft were seen to go down in flames over the target, and on 16/17 April one aircraft from No. 104 Squadron did not return. On 19/20 April three aircraft were lost. One Wellington of No. 37 Squadron had engine trouble on the return trip, and eventually ditched north-east of Gabes with only two survivors. Two aircraft from No. 40 Squadron failed to return, and were believed to have been shot down over the target area. The weather then intervened, and the next operation was by twenty-five Wellingtons on 23/24 April against the Soliman landing grounds.

An interesting feature of these raids was the presence of a Wellington from No. 162 Squadron, the electronic surveillance and countermeasures unit. It was flown by Flight Lieutenant H.D. Van der Linden, carried a crew of eight, and was described in the No. 40 Squadron ORB as on 'Special Operations'. The No. 162 Squadron ORB shows that a Wellington (DV931) flew to Gardabia on 4 April 'on detachment to 40 Squadron for ops'. It carried out three missions that the ORB describes as 'Type 3 investigations', and also bombed targets on roads around Gabes–Sfax–El Djem and the airfield at Menzel Temime. It returned to Benina on 11 April, and three days later was followed by another Wellington (HD957), also captained by Flight Lieutenant H.D. Van der Linden. This aircraft carried out two Type 3 investigations and bombed the landing grounds at Korba South and St Marie du Zit. It seems likely that No. 162 Squadron was monitoring radio signals to enemy night fighters during the attacks on the landing grounds.

At 1120 hours on 20 April Chappell states that there was 'a hell of a bang', and when he looked out of his tent he saw a huge cloud of smoke and bits of flying debris. A Halifax of No. 462 Squadron had blown up at Gardabia Main, and black smoke and flames from the wreckage covered the area. What had previously been a busy scene, with armourers loading the bomb bays of the aircraft from several trolleys loaded with bombs, had been transformed into one of horrible carnage. A fire tender and an ambulance rushed over to the fire and got within a hundred yards or so, but it was obvious that nothing could be done. The ambulance people managed to pick up three survivors, despite the risk that further explosions might occur. While they were there, more bombs exploded with another ear-splitting crack, sending a plume of smoke over a thousand feet into the air and pieces of metal whizzing around more than half a mile from the scene. The explosions were heard fifteen miles away, and human remains found scattered all around the camp. Two NCOs and seven armourers were killed, three were missing (blown to pieces), and many injured – 'a ghastly business and a major disaster for the squadron'.

No. 462 Squadron was suffering from many problems at this time anyway, and its ORB reported that the 'operational efficiency of the Squadron during the month was greatly impaired by an unusually large number of engine failures'. There were no replacement Merlin engines available, and the Squadron was forced to switch engines from one aircraft to another to keep a few flying. Eventually, it was just not possible to do any more switching of engines, and 60 per cent of the Squadron's aircraft were transferred to No. 61 MSU to await new engines. A great deal of concern was being expressed about the short life of overhauled engines and of failures during the first forty-eight hours of running. At this time the Commanding Officer of the Squadron also asked for permission to remove the mid-upper and front gun turrets on the Halifaxes to decrease weight and reduce the load on engines, and this was granted later in the month. The CO also obtained the loan of five Wellingtons from No. 40 Squadron, but 'after two operations were carried out, these aircraft were recalled'. The Squadron did not operate again until 6/7 May, and the Wellington squadrons also stood down after the operation on 23/24 April and did not operate again until 4/5 May.

The reason for the stand-down was a signal from Advanced Air Headquarters Western Desert stating that the Group was to concentrate on building up serviceability in preparation for intensive operations during the anticipated enemy evacuation of Tunisia. Twenty aircraft were bombed up each day and kept on stand-by just in case attacks on 'specially important targets' were ordered, but none were called for. The Air Officer Commanding No. 205 Group visited Headquarters,

RAF Middle East on 27 April, and on his return proceeded immediately to the headquarters of NATAF to discuss the policy regarding the Group's role in future operations. A signal was then received on 28 April, stating that airfields were being prepared for the bombers in the El Djem area, thirty miles south of Sousse, and as soon as they were ready the bombers would be moved forwards to these new locations. Also at this time, arrangements were made for the Gardabia airfields to be used as forward landing grounds for the 9th USAAF Bomber Command, in preparation for attacks to prevent the evacuation of Tunisia.

Gunby reports one of the members of No. 40 Squadron as saying that everyday life at Gardabia 'was quite simply tedious'. Apart from the occasional film show, most of the time was spent gambling and drinking cheap gin! Another important pastime was catching sand spiders – *Solifugid arachnid* – which were large and extremely aggressive relatives of spiders. They were about the size of a man's hand, with tremendous double jaws, very fast, and ready to attack anything. The airmen caught the spiders and kept them in containers, and staged spider fights by putting two of the creatures together in a jar. One spider won so frequently that its owner was accused of drugging it! Other and more dangerous forms of recreation were the habit of throwing 'found' Italian hand grenades around, and letting off revolvers out of sheer boredom. Many became 'sand-happy', cultivating eccentricities that would have had them locked up in normal times.

On 2 May a signal was received from Headquarters NATAF that they would be taking over the operational control of the Group with effect from 0800 hours on the following day. The next operation came on 4/5 May, when forty aircraft attacked enemy concentrations in the Tebourba area of the Cap Bon Peninsula. Low cloud made identification of the target area very difficult, but bombs were dropped across roads, railways and buildings, and three fires were started in the Bir Meharia area. One of the Wellingtons of No. 40 Squadron was unable to locate its base due to the bad weather, and carried out a square search dropping flares to try to identify its position. Fast running out of fuel, the Captain finally ordered the crew to bale out and the Wellington crashed at Cussabat near Homs. Further attacks in the battle area around Tunis and Cap Bon took place on the next six nights, with 234 sorties flown and seven aircraft lost. On 5/6 May the Wellingtons attacked the area contained by the Tebourba–Djedeida, Furna–La Mornashia and Bir Meherga–Cheylus-La Mohammedia roads. The Army laid out lights to direct them to their targets, and the whole area was thoroughly bombed. The returning Wellingtons were diverted to Castel Benito due to fog, where one overshot the runway and was slightly damaged. One of the Wellingtons of No. 40 Squadron failed to return.

On 6/7 May fifty-eight Wellingtons and ten Halifaxes were despatched to attack enemy transport and troop concentrations moving back to Tunis from Massicault, Hammamet and Pont Du Fahs. Weather conditions were dangerous due to air currents and electric storms, but most of the aircraft scored direct hits along the Pont Du Fahs–Bir Meharga road. Many fires were seen to start, one of which was thought to be an ammunition dump, and another looked like an oil fire. Two aircraft failed to return. One Wellington of No. 40 Squadron was believed to have crashed in the target area, and a Halifax of No. 462 Squadron sent out an SOS at 0240 hours and came down in the sea. The crew spent ten days in their dinghy, and eventually came ashore near Homs on 18 May. They were all very weak, but recovered quickly. One of the Wellingtons of No. 104 Squadron had an engine cut on landing at Castel Benito. It undershot, hit an obstruction, and was damaged beyond repair. All the crew members were safe.

A maximum effort was called for on 7/8 May to harass and destroy enemy troops and vehicles that were attempting to reform in the south of the Cap Bon Peninsula following the breakthrough of the Allied armour on the approaches to Tunis and St Cyprien. However, due to a bad weather forecast only twenty-six Wellingtons operated, and most of these brought their bombs back, jettisoned, or bombed 'targets of opportunity'. The small number that bombed in the target area reported few positive results. One of the aircraft of No. 70 Squadron returned to base early with engine trouble, and crashed near the airfield and caught fire. The injured rear gunner was the only survivor. Another aircraft from the same Squadron did not return, and five bodies of this crew were subsequently found on the Nabaul–Grombalia road. On 8/9 twenty-four Wellingtons and five Halifaxes again attacked targets in the battle area, with good illumination provided by Albacores. A number of fires were started, with one large one at Hammamet. Bombs were seen to burst amongst buildings, and on roads and road junctions. One stick of bombs was dropped across a petrol dump, setting off a series of explosions and a huge fire with smoke rising to 6,000 feet. Two Wellingtons failed to return, but the crew of one from No. 40 Squadron walked into La Fauconnerie later in the day, having force-landed in a lake off the Sfax road.

On 9/10 the targets were roads and beaches on the west coast of Cape Bon, with the Albacores again providing illumination. Twenty-eight aircraft found targets in poor weather, but 6/10 to 10/10 cloud obscured vision in many areas. On the next night, in the final attack in the North African campaign, thirteen Wellingtons of No. 40 Squadron bombed the road between Nabaul and Menzel Temimi in good weather. On the following day the Group reverted to the operational control of Headquarters, RAF Middle East, and no further operations took place until 21 May. Congratulatory messages were received from NATAF, one of which read:

> Personal for Commanders from Air Marshal Coningham. Well done the Tactical Air Force. The capture of Tunis and Bizerte sets the seal upon your mastery and present dominance of the African air. But of deeper significance and more lasting value is the record of intimate collaboration with the land forces in their battle. You have been true comrades in arms. I join with you in expressing the warmest felicitations to our grand armies in their richly deserved success. For the future I am sure they may count even more upon you.

*   *   *

Decisions made at the Casablanca conference in January 1943 determined that the Allies would next attack Sicily (Operation *Husky*) and then the Italian mainland. The main targets assigned to the strategic bombers in the early stages of the Air Force Plan for the campaign were the airfields in Sardinia and Sicily from which the enemy might attack the invasion fleet. In May the majority of the Allied attacks on airfields were directed against those in Sardinia, mainly at Villacidro and Decimomannu. In June the strategic bombers began an intensive bombardment of the airfields in the west of Sicily. Castelventrano, Sciacca, Milo and Boccadifalco were hit repeatedly in a succession of raids that continued until 30 June. By far the greatest damage was sustained at Castelventrano following a series of attacks by Fortresses and Wellingtons. The ports of Naples, Messina and Palermo were also to be attacked in order to interfere with any build up of strength of the enemy forces in Sicily. However, many of the RAF and USAAF units required to be rested after the Tunisian campaign, and extensive airfields construction was in progress in northern Tunisia to provide cover for the Sicilian campaign.

Following the surrender of the Axis forces in Tunisia the Wellingtons of No. 205 Group at Gardabia did not operate again until the night of 21/22 May. Command arrangements at this time were causing quite a few problems. On 17 May a signal was received from Headquarters, RAF Middle East 'in lieu of one from North African Tactical Air Force', informing the Group that a maximum effort on Messina was required on 18/19 May. A force of sixty-two Wellingtons and thirteen Halifaxes was duly prepared, but an hour before take-off a telephone message was received stating 'Do not require 205 Group operations tonight.' The message was said to have come from NATAF, but had been routed via No. 211 Group and passed from No. 1 Fighter Sector Controller. The Group SASO instructed the Sector to find out the name of the person at NATAF who had originated the message, and stated that the cancellation must be confirmed before the Group called off operations. Take-off was postponed for one hour, and at 2250 hours Sector informed the Group that the message had come from a Colonel McGregor of Forward Bomber Control. No confirming signal came from NATAF, but the Group SASO reconsidered the situation and cancelled the operation.

Between 21 and 24 May the Group carried out three missions (120 sorties) to Messina in an attempt to hinder the build up of German forces in Sicily. On 21/22 May sixty Wellingtons attacked the marshalling yards south of the Ferry Terminal, and direct hits were seen on the terminal buildings, the central railway station, the quay, and on the railway near the power station. Opposition from heavy AA was intense but inaccurate, and all the aircraft returned safely. Four put down at Malta, where one of No. 37 Squadron crashed on landing and was destroyed by fire. The Group ORB comments that:

> This was the first occasion on which 'Blitz' methods had been concentrated into a simultaneous attack of one minute. The attack was, in fact, divided into two separate one minute 'blitzes', but the method adopted proved to be practical and was adopted for many subsequent operations.

On 23/24 May thirty-two Wellingtons were detailed again to attack the area south of the Ferry Terminal, where bombs were seen to burst in the area of the harbour, railway sidings and the power station. The third attack on Messina involved twenty-eight aircraft, and started a few fires in the harbour and near the railway station. Heavy AA was fairly accurate and three or four night fighters were seen, but all the aircraft returned safely – two landing at Malta.

Towards the end of May all the Wellington squadrons in Libya and Algeria moved to the Kairouan area in Tunisia, and would eventually operate together under the control of No. 205 Group and NASAF. On 24 May the two squadrons of No. 330 Wing commenced their move from Fontaine Chaude to Kairouan West (Allani), with some of the aircraft doing a double journey to transport the ground crews. On arrival, they were confronted with a serious shortage of tents and the complete absence of sanitary arrangements, but by sharing the existing facilities between the Wing HQ and the two squadrons they all managed to get by.

The Wellington squadrons of No. 205 Group also started their move from Gardabia to the Kairouan area, a distance of about 550 miles, during May, although there were concerns about the adequacy of bomb and petrol supplies at the new locations. The advance parties of Nos 40 and 104 Squadrons left on 5 May, but various other supply and maintenance parties were temporarily held up pending clarification of the supply situation at Kairouan. No. 40 Squadron had been transferred from the direct control of Group Headquarters to that of No. 236 Wing on 21 May, thus taking the place of No. 462 (Halifax) Squadron (see below). Nos 40 and 104 Squadrons were both settled at Alem East/Cheria by 28 May. The two squadrons of No. 231 Wing (Nos 37 and 70 Squadrons) moved to Kairouan North (Temmar) by 30 May. Liaison was immediately sought with the nearest fighter sector to facilitate safe movement of aircraft, and agreement was reached on the routeing of aircraft through recognized corridors. On the night of 1/2 June a grass fire about two miles from No. 236 Wing caused considerable concern, and threatened to engulf the camp and dispersed aircraft.

The move to Kairouan for No. 205 Group was not without controversy, and there appears to have been a lot of grit in the wheels of command in the North African theatre at this time. Orders and counter-orders flew about in all directions. At first, Headquarters, RAF Middle East, asked the Group to select landing grounds in the Gabes–Ben Gardane area, and then it was told that the Mediterranean Air Command was selecting landing grounds for it in the El Djem area. Air Headquarters Western Desert now joined in the debate, and said that revised plans had made it impossible for the bombers to use these landing grounds and that sites had now been chosen in the Kairouan area. Headquarters, RAF Middle East, now became concerned about getting supplies forward to bomber bases in Tunisia, and ordered the Group to stay where it was for the time being. Eventually, the powers-that-be managed to sort things out, and the moves to Kairouan were on.

Chappell travelled from Gardabia to Kairouan by road with the No. 236 Wing party, setting off on 26 May. He passed through palm tree oases, Italian colonization schemes, vineyards, small olive groves, and patches of desert. He stayed at the RAF hotel in Tripoli on the first night, but spent the second night sleeping in the staff car and shaved in cold water the following morning. As they approached the Tunisian frontier the road gradually got worse and the land drier, with salt marshes on the seaward side. The traffic became quite dense, mainly with military vehicles being towed back for repairs. Near the Mareth Line there were round stone huts with thatched roofs and black sheep in the fields. Minefields were everywhere with their black triangles and red and white signs. Small cemeteries and cairns of stones marked areas of severe fighting, and nearer Mareth there were anti-tank ditches and barbed wire – and more minefields. The Wadi Akarit area impressed Chappell, with all its bridges blown up, graves on each side of the road, and shell holes, dugouts, observation posts and mines everywhere. Sfax was 'the first European-like town since Tripoli', but the port area had been heavily damaged by the bombing. Kairouan 'showed up white ahead with mosques and buildings peering over the brown walls'. Around the walls were pools of smelly water, and the smells and filth were 'impressive'. The new landing ground at Cheria was 'scraped from black earth, looks most uninviting and the weather is hot and sticky'.

172

Gunby also has some interesting things to say about Kairouan. Pilfering by the locals was endemic, with thefts from tents at night leading at one point to an (unsuccessful) attempt to boobytrap a tent with hand grenades. However, the faults were not all on one side, as the airmen often cheated the local Arabs during barter deals, and there were numerous examples of thoughtlessness, such as low flying to panic a camel train. Gunby also states that at Kairouan No. 40 Squadron had better facilities than at any time since Kabrit in November 1942, including a visit by an Army Mobile Bath Unit! A swimming gharry (lorry) drove each day to the beach at Sousse, and attractive coastal resorts such as Hammamet became available as rest camps.

Their first operation from their new home for the squadrons of No. 330 Wing came on the night of 27/28 May, when thirteen aircraft were detailed for intruder operations against airfields in Sardinia. They took off in waves at intervals between 2020 and 0120 hours, with each aircraft spending about an hour in the target area. Haze and intense darkness made pinpointing very difficult, but Villacidro, Elmas and Decimomannu were all bombed. Sixteen aircraft went to the Sicilian airfields on another intruder operation on the next night, the main targets being Bo Rizzo, Castel Ventrano, and Milo, but, again, intense darkness and some haze prevented good pinpointing. The airfields at Bo Rizzo and Milo were caught by surprise by the first aircraft to attack, which found their lights still on. Few results were seen, but the main object of preventing enemy aircraft from using the landing grounds was achieved. An enemy aircraft attacked Kairouan West on this night, dropping three small bombs near the Sergeants' Mess, but it caused no damage or casualties.

No. 330 Wing also carried out small attacks on targets at Naples and southern Italy on 1/2 and 3/4 June respectively. Nine aircraft were detailed for the operation on the town and docks at Naples, but one of them hit a car while taking off, causing damage to the bomb doors. The aircraft immediately returned to base, and another also returned early due to engine trouble. The weather was good en route, and all the remaining crews reported being able to identify the target clearly. Many saw their bombs falling among port buildings and industrial facilities. The second operation was a combined bombing and nickelling mission over Southern Italy by five aircraft. Two went to Reggio di Calabria, two to Catanzaro, and the fifth ran into a cold front and returned to bomb Syracuse in Sicily. Syracuse was also the target for three aircraft on 5/6 June, and after bombing the port they went on to drop leaflets on Syracuse, Catania and Messina.

*   *   *

Almost as soon as the Tunisian campaign was ended the Allied Air Forces switched the main weight of their attacks to the two islands of Pantelleria and Lampedusa. These lay between North Africa and Sicily, and aircraft and submarines from them could have interfered with the invasion. Pantelleria is a small rocky island, measuring eight-and-a-half by five-and-a-half miles, lying in the channel between Tunisia and Sicily and about 140 miles north-west of Malta. It would provide excellent radar facilities for the Allies, and its possession would simplify the problem of protection of convoys to and from the assault beaches. Pantellaria had been variously described as an Italian Gibraltar or as an Italian Heligoland. The Allies seemingly faced a difficult task, with only one possible landing area near the town and harbour of Porto di Pantellaria at the north-west end of the island.

173

However, the harbour was small and shallow, the currents were tricky, and the surf ran high. The Italian military had designated Pantellaria as a 'forbidden zone' since 1926, and its defences were formidable, at least on paper. Underground hangars claimed to be impervious to bombs had been constructed, and the surface was dotted with powerful anti-aircraft defences. The garrison of some 12,000 men was established in well-entrenched positions, and was well provisioned.

The objects of the air operations against Pantellaria prior to D-Day were to reduce the morale of the garrison, to destroy any defences that might oppose or impede the Allied assault, and to prevent reinforcements reaching the garrison from Sicily. It was subjected to constant bombing attacks between the end of May and 11 June, rising to a crescendo for five days between 7 and 11 June. It has been estimated that over four thousand tons of bombs were dropped on the island, destroying the anti-aircraft gun emplacements, communications, ammunition stores, air-raid shelters, and all the elements of the artillery system. The Wellingtons of No. 330 Wing contributed sixty-six sorties in three attacks on Pantellaria at the end of May (see above) and another 152 sorties in seven attacks in June. On 3/4 June it was the turn of No. 205 Group to join in the assault, and it flew 147 sorties in five attacks on Pantellaria. In all, the Wellingtons dropped some 700 tons of bombs over the island. At this time a significant change in the organization of No. 205 Group occurred. On 2 June the Group ORB recorded that it was 'indicated that we should work in conjunction with 330 Wing at KAIROUAN ALLANI and from this time 330 Wing and 205 Group were given the same targets'. For the moment the Wing and Group were working together under the operational control of NASAF, and the Group would not take over full operational control of Nos 142 and 150 Squadrons until July (see next chapter).

On 1/2 June sixteen aircraft from No. 142 Squadron were despatched to Pantellaria, followed by nineteen from No. 150 Squadron on the next night. On 3/4 June it was the turn of No. 205 Group, when twenty-nine aircraft from Nos 40 and 70 Squadrons went to the island in their first operation from Kairouan. Several small fires were reported, and one large fire that was visible seventy miles away. Bursts were also seen across the Central Mole, and a violent explosion was reported in the town area. On 4/5 June an accident occurred as the aircraft of No. 330 Wing were taking off. Seven aircraft of No. 142 Squadron got away, but as one of No. 150 Squadron prepared for take-off, a flare ignited inside the aircraft and it caught fire. The crew hastily abandoned the aircraft, and it subsequently blew up. Two other Wellingtons waiting to take off also caught fire after being hit by debris, and were completely destroyed. After the fire had been brought under control five aircraft of No. 150 Squadron managed to take off, and two of these were able to make double sorties. The weather was good for the operation, and all fourteen aircraft were able to identify the target. Many bomb bursts were seen and good fires were started in the town.

Twenty-one aircraft of Nos 37 and 104 Squadrons operated on 5/6 June, carrying out continuous attacks over five hours, and bombs were seen to burst on the town, barracks, and in the harbour area. A 4,000-lb bomb started a big fire near some storage sheds, and minutes later a violent explosion took place. Seven or eight other fires were started in the area around the base of the Mole. On the same night a single Wellington of No. 150 Squadron dropped a 4,000-lb bomb on the docks but it failed to explode, and the aircraft also dropped leaflets over the island. The

Wellingtons of Nos 142 and 150 Squadrons flew in the region of twenty-eight sorties on 6/7 June, although the squadron ORBs are somewhat unclear and it is difficult to be sure how many sorties were actually completed. Visibility over the target was good, and flares were used to assist crews in pinpointing the target. The majority successfully bombed the town and docks, where many bursts were seen. General Vandenberg of the USAAF flew with one of the crews of No. 142 Squadron. On 7 June the two squadrons of No. 330 Wing spent the day at Kairouan West burning off the dry grasses and weeds that covered the landing ground, as a measure to reduce the fire risk during operations following the accident a few nights before. No. 142 Squadron ORB states that it was obvious 'in the light of experience that it would have been of great advantage to have completely cleared the ground by this method prior to the movement of the Squadron even if the arrival had thereby been delayed'.

On 7/8 June twenty-four Wellingtons attacked the island and started fires in the town and at the base of the Central Mole, and a ship in the harbour was also left burning. One aircraft of No. 104 Squadron failed to return, and a signal was later received that the captain had been picked up by the destroyer HMS *Lookout* and taken to Malta. The other crew members had died of exposure in the sea after the dinghy failed to release when they ditched.

On 8/9 and 9/10 June a total of sixty-one aircraft bombed the town and harbour, and then a final major attack on Pantellaria was ordered by NASAF on the following night. No. 330 Wing's aircraft operated alongside those of No. 205 Group for the first time, and a total of seventy-six sorties were despatched. The two squadrons of No. 330 Wing contributed a remarkable total of forty-five sorties, with some aircraft doing three trips. However, there were problems for the squadrons from No. 205 Group, which Chappell records as having 'a nightmare night' due to the weather. Rain during take-off rendered No. 231 Wing's airfield unserviceable, and only nine aircraft of No. 37 Squadron managed to get off. On return, they were diverted to No. 236 Wing, where they all landed safely before the Wing started its operations. There then followed a series of catastrophes. An aircraft of No. 104 Squadron swung when taking off and piled up on the runway, and the remaining six aircraft of that Squadron had to be cancelled while the runway was cleared. After this was done, No. 40 Squadron succeeded in getting thirteen aircraft off before one crashed on the runway and caught fire. It exploded, and destroyed three of the aircraft of No. 231 Wing that had previously landed there. Five of the crew of the crashed bomber were killed, and only the rear gunner survived. The airfield was now unserviceable, and the Wing's aircraft were diverted to No. 330 Wing.

As a result, only thirty-one Wellingtons from the Group were able to add to the forty-five sorties from No. 330 Wing. The weather was good and the results most successful, but two aircraft of No. 104 Squadron were shot down over the target, and it was suspected that night fighters were responsible. A few days later Flying Officer Edwards and two of his crew returned to No. 236 Wing, having baled out and landed safely on the island. They had watched the occupation of Pantellaria by Allied forces on the following morning. The other two members of Edwards' crew and all of the crew of the other aircraft were never found, the latter being on their last operation before completing their tour. Chappell reports that the following morning the landing ground was a shambles, with fears that unexploded bombs were about to go up. The tents were put out of bounds several times, but the bombs were still lying in the wreckage. The following night, as a briefing for an attack on Lampedusa was taking place, the bombs went off without warning, and everyone 'dived for the floor in wonderful style'.

On the morning of 11 June units of the 3 Infantry Brigade Group landed on Pantellaria under the cover of an air and naval bombardment, and almost immediately received the surrender of the garrison. Churchill was to record later in his memoirs that the only casualty was a man bitten by a mule! There is no doubt that the heavy bombardment had a severe effect on the morale of the largely Italian garrison, and contributed greatly to the decision to surrender without a fight. However, an unfortunate consequence of the success of the bombing attacks was the development of a belief that the dropping of a large number of bombs on strong points in advance of troop movements would 'make land movements a matter of flitting from one dazed body of enemy troops to another'. This was First World War thinking all over again, and it had been proved to be wrong time and time again in that conflict. The views of those who knew better were reflected in a memo Tedder later wrote: 'Pantellaria is becoming a perfect curse.' The curse would consign Cassino and Caen to their destructive fates later in the War.

After Pantellaria it was the turn of Lampedusa, a much smaller island only fourteen square miles in extent. On the night of 11/12 June heavy rain again prevented No. 231 Wing from operating, and only twenty Wellingtons from the Group attacked Lampedusa town. There was some cloud en route, but visibility was very good over the target and all the crews were able to identify the town by the light of the moon. As the first aircraft approached some of them saw flames in the town, and it was thought that these were caused by the guns of MTBs off the coast. Altogether, the small island received 268 tons of bombs and numerous shells from bombarding ships. On the morning of 12 June it also received an unscheduled visit from an Air/Sea Rescue Swordfish, which had got lost and ran out of fuel. Upon landing on the airfield, the pilot was surprised when the Italian commander arrived soon afterwards to offer the surrender of the island. This was accepted, and after filling up with enemy petrol, the Swordfish took off and landed near Sousse. That evening the captain of a British destroyer completed the formalities, and the still smaller islands of Linosa and Lampione surrendered a few hours later.

*   *   *

From 27 June the Wellingtons at Kairouan were joined by three squadrons of Wellingtons from Bomber Command (Nos 420, 424 and 425 Squadrons), ordered to North Africa in preparation for the invasion of Sicily. They were established at Telergma (near Constantine in Algeria) by 4 June, but moved to the Kairouan area (Zina and Pavillier) later in June and were formed into No. 331 Wing. The three squadrons were all Royal Canadian Air Force (RCAF) units, equipped with Wellington Xs, and operating with No. 6 Group Bomber Command when they were ordered to North Africa. No. 420 (Snowy Owl) Squadron had been based at Middleton St George when the order came, No. 424 (Tiger) Squadron was at Dalton, and No. 425 (Alouette) Squadron was at Dishforth. The last named was unique in RCAF history in being designated as a 'French-Canadian' unit. The sea parties for the three Squadrons left their respective bases on 15/16 May, travelling by train to Greenock and embarking on the SS *Samaria* and SS *Duchess of York* for the journey to Algiers.

The No. 420 Squadron ORB gives us the best account of the sea journey, telling how the *Samaria* sailed from the River Clyde on 19 May. For the first few days, life aboard ship was a lazy one, with small groups spending the time in sing-songs, playing cards, reading, writing, and sun bathing. The seas were comparatively calm, and it would have been an uneventful trip had not a few enemy aircraft bombed the convoy. The destroyer escort occasionally dropped depth charges, but no submarines were sighted and no torpedo attacks carried out. Towards the evening of the 25th the convoy 'passed down the channel with TANGIER on our right', and was passed by two hospital ships 'blazing with lights...an impressive sight.' The *Samaria* reached the port of Algiers at 1000 hours on the 27th, and disembarkation began at 1030 hours.

The sea party marched from Algiers to a transit camp four miles away, and then went on by rail to Boufarik to await further orders. Great concern was expressed about the arrival of the unit's baggage, as RCAF and Army kit bags had all been piled up together on the quay at Algiers. It took days to sort things out, and many personnel lost valuable kits. The unit was joined by the sea parties from Nos 424 and 425 Squadrons at Boufarik, and stayed there until 15 June, maintaining a high standard of discipline considering that it was billeted in a winery. After disembarking from the SS *Duchess of York* on 26 May, the personnel of No. 424 Squadron also proceeded to Boufarik, where the officers were forced to billet with the NCOs. This was 'not apparently too good for discipline', as the Squadron Leader in charge had to stand and wait for a seat at breakfast while the sergeants finished smoking their cigarettes! Most of the squadron left for Kairouan on the 14th, and arrived 'tired, dirty and most anxious for a good wash'. The Squadron Leader and Adjutant, who had been taken ill at Boufarik, travelled on later by car and it broke down in the mountains on the way.

Twenty aircraft from No. 420 Squadron departed from Middleton St George for Portreath at 0920 hours on 31 May, and left Portreath at 0615 hours on 1 June. They encountered enemy opposition passing over the Bay of Biscay, and two aircraft were reported missing. Eighteen arrived at Ras El Ma at 1500 hours on 1 June, and left for Blida at 1300 hours on 2 June. One overshot the runway on landing, causing damage to the tail wheel assembly, and had to stay at Blida while it was repaired. The others flew on to Kairouan via Telergma. The air party of No. 425 Squadron left Portreath on 4 June and arrived at Telergma on the same date. One crew had to abandon their aircraft over Portugal due to enemy action. Two members of the crew were wounded and all were interned in Portugal. Two of the Wellingtons became unserviceable at Telergma, and were left there for repair.

Several advance parties from the three squadrons set off for Kairouan early in June to start to set up camp. Tentage was scattered over a wide area, and oil and gas stoves had to be built from bits scavenged from dumps. The MO (Medical Officer) of No. 420 Squadron 'pinpointed where the desert lilies should be and the class of latrines to be used', and all personnel were consuming a fair amount of salt each day due to the heat and humidity. The No. 420 ORB states that rations were good – 'but oh for a juicy steak'! However, No. 424 Squadron ORB tells us that there were a number of complaints about the food, which the Canadians thought to be poor and in short supply. Their MO ordered a consignment of tomatoes to be destroyed as unfit for human consumption.

On 23 June it started to rain ('it came down in buckets'), and in a few minutes the camp was a sea of mud. Eight of the aircraft of No. 424 Squadron flew in from Telergma at this time, and all made a perfectly good landing. The rain continued all night, and as most of the tents had not been set the officers and airmen slept where they could. The recently arrived aircrew slept in their aircraft, and others slept in trucks, the hospital, and in the aircraft. The rain stopped at 1700 hours on the 24th, and the next day the sun shone and things gradually got back to normal. No. 424 Squadron ORB records that: 'After a long lay off the aircrew were beginning to feel soft, so morale reached a high level when we were asked for 5 sorties on the night of June 26/27.' They flew their first operation on 26 June to the Sciacca airfield in Sicily, and thereafter operated alongside No. 330 Wing and No. 205 Group.

*   *   *

The strategic air forces available for Operation *Husky* comprised elements from the Northwest African Strategic Air Force and the USAAF Ninth Air Force. The former consisted of the nine Wellington squadrons based at Kirouan and four Bombardment Groups of the 5th USAAF Bombardment Wing with B-17s in Algeria. The IX Bomber Command had five Bombardment Groups operating B-24s from Libya, and it also controlled the operations of the Halifaxes and Liberators of Nos 178 and 462 Squadrons at Hosc Raui. The Americans thus had about 350 four-engined heavy bombers and the RAF some 100 Wellingtons and 20 Halifaxes/Liberators potentially available for Operation *Husky*. Bomber Command in the UK would also play its part by attacking Italian industrial and communication targets.

After the island of Lampedusa fell the efforts of the Group and No. 330 Wing were again directed towards Sicily. On 13/14 June thirty-six aircraft from Nos 231, 236 and 330 Wings took off to attack railways and marshalling yards in the Ferry Terminal area at Messina. The weather was clear over the target, but a smokescreen was in operation near the ferry. Bomb bursts were seen near the railway station and the ferry terminals, and in the town. The next operation on 14/15 June was to four airfields in Sicily: Trapani Milo, Bocca di Falco, Sciacca, and Castel Ventrano, and for the first time the Wellingtons of No. 330 Wing are mentioned in the No. 205 Group ORB. The weather was good, and crews were clearly able to identify their targets in the light of the moon. The weather caused the cancellation of an attack on the docks and marshalling yards at Olbia on 15/16 June, and on the next night thirty-four Wellingtons from all three Wings took off to attack the port and marshalling yards at Naples. Cloud prevented accurate observation of results, but one large fire was seen near the railway station. After another cancellation eleven aircraft of No. 150 Squadron went to Syracuse on 18/19 June. The weather was good, with perfect visibility due to a full moon, and most crews were able to identify the town area. However, the Group squadrons again had their operations cancelled due to bad weather.

On 19/20 June the target was the Ferry Terminus and marshalling yards at Messina, and a 'blitz' attack by fifty-eight aircraft was called for. There was some cloud en route, but over the target it was clear, with excellent visibility. A number of fires were reported, one visible 100 miles away, and two 4,000-lb bombs were thought to have burst in the town and near the railway station. However, a smokescreen made accurate observation of results difficult. One aircraft of No. 37 Squadron failed to return after having sent an SOS from a position approximately seventeen miles north-east of Hergla, and a search by aircraft and launch only discovered an overturned dinghy. Nickels were also carried on this operation, and a signal from NASAF on this day emphasized the importance of distributing leaflets over all target areas in Sicily as an integral part of forthcoming invasion. On the next night Naples was the target, and thirty-one aircraft were detailed for the operation. Although the weather was excellent, results were difficult to observe due to a smokescreen covering the harbour and part of the marshalling yards. One of the Wellingtons of No. 142 Squadron came down in the sea off Cap Bon, but all the crew were subsequently rescued.

The pace of operations was kept up on 21/22 June when thirty Wellingtons went to the Salerno marshalling yards. Chappell went on this operation to see for himself how difficult the nickel dropping was, as crews had been complaining about the task. The weather en route was clear, but there was a slight haze over the target and results were difficult to assess. Bursts were seen across the town and marshalling yards, one large and many smaller fires were seen, and two 4,000-lb bombs were seen to explode in the marshalling yards themselves. The next night the Wellingtons attacked the town and docks at Olbia, with six aircraft of No. 231 Wing due to carry twelve mines to be laid just outside the harbour and the remainder of the aircraft bombing as a diversion. Only five minelayers operated due to a lack of 'vegetables' and/or fittings, and nine mines were successfully laid. The diversion was reported to be of great assistance, causing three good fires and explosions in the town.

On 23/24 June ten Wellingtons of No. 150 Squadron went to the marshalling yards and sulphur factories at Catania. The weather en route was good, and most of the crews had no trouble in identifying the target in the bright moonlight. Although the bombs fell in the target area, it was doubtful whether the sulphur works were hit. A heavy rain storm with thunder in the early afternoon of the 23rd made the Group's landing grounds unserviceable, and so none of their aircraft took part in this operation. On the following day the Group ORB tells how 'a posse...disposing considerable armament made a sally in the KAIROUAN area'. It seems that several booby traps had been found in the squadron camps during the last few weeks, and the posse set off to find the culprits. The search was unsuccessful, and only 'some old clothes and two "wogs" were apprehended'! The target for that night was Olbia port and marshalling yards, but No. 231 Wing was still suffering from the rain of the previous day and was forced to cancel operations. Nineteen Wellingtons took off, and bursts were seen between the seaplane base and railway station and on military installations south of the target.

On 25 June No. 236 Wing moved from Kairouan Cheria to Hani West, which Chappell says was to escape the mud and the floods. No one was sorry to leave the black soil of Cheria, but the insects and smells were just as bad at the new location. The target given for that night was the oil refinery at Bari, but there was considerable haze and extreme darkness over the target. Only seventeen Wellingtons of the thirty-one despatched claimed to have bombed the target area, where bursts were reported in the centre of the refinery and a fire with thick black smoke 'coming from the extension of the Oil Refinery'. Unfortunately, photographs later revealed that the flares had been dropped over a small village several miles away from the refinery. Most of the bombs fell on and around the village, and the attack was a complete failure.

The target on 26/27 June was the harbour and marshalling yards at Naples, with ten aircraft each from Nos 231, 236 and 330 Groups detailed. Twenty-five of the Wellingtons bombed Naples in good weather, and numerous small fires were started. One large orange fire was believed to be from a chemical works. One of the Wellingtons of No. 104 Squadron failed to return. On this night No. 331 Wing operated for the first time, when fourteen aircraft from Nos 420 and 425 Squadrons attacked the airfield at Sciacca in Sicily. The weather was good and the visibility clear, and a successful attack was claimed despite some accurate heavy flak over the target. One of the aircraft of No. 425 Squadron had an encounter with a Ju 88 and the wireless operator/air gunner was severely wounded in the leg. One Wellington from the same Squadron failed to return.

The build up to D-Day for the landings in Sicily started in earnest on 26 June, and a directive was received from NASAF warning that seventy-two aircraft would be required nightly from the combined force of No. 205 Group and Nos 330 and 331 Wings. This could be stepped up to 100 sorties at short notice. In fact, the nine Wellington squadrons operated on all twelve nights between 27 June and 8 July, and flew 711 sorties. On 27 June Headquarters, RAF Middle East agreed that Nos 330 and 331 Wings should come under No. 205 Group control while the Group was operating under the command of NASAF.

On 27/28 June the target was the Villa San Giovanni Ferry Terminal, and sixty-five Wellingtons were despatched. Visibility was excellent, the accurately dropped flares clearly illuminated the target, and a successful attack was carried out. Many bursts were seen in the marshalling yards and railway sidings, and it was believed that the ferry terminus was extensively damaged. One aircraft of No. 420 Squadron failed to return. No. 424 Squadron had all sorts of problems on this, its first, operation in the theatre. Twelve aircraft were detailed, but bombs had to be manhandled from the dumps, and despite a huge effort only eight aircraft could be bombed-up in time. The problems experienced by the armourers was further indicated when one of the aircraft lost its 4,000-lb bomb as it left the runway. The aircraft did not notice anything, and carried on to the target! Another had a puncture on the take-off run and crashed, dropping its 4,000-lb bomb in the process. Fortunately, neither of the big bombs went off, and two aircraft took off after the accident with the bombs still on the runway.

On 28/29 June sixty-nine aircraft were detailed to attack Messina, and most bombed the ferry terminus and marshalling yards. A 4,000-lb bomb burst near the Citadel area of the harbour, and three fires were seen in the marshalling yards. One aircraft each of Nos 104 and 70 Squadrons failed to return. The latter signalled that he was returning with engine trouble, but nothing further was heard. No. 331 Wing suffered badly on this night, with two aircraft of No. 424 Squadron missing and one of No. 425 Squadron ditched out of fuel. One of the crew drowned, but the others were all picked up. The bombers went back to Messina on 29/30 June, but intense darkness made the location of the target very difficult and not all the illumination fell over the target area. Most crews claimed to have put their bombs close to the ferry terminal and marshalling yards, and several small fires were seen. Six aircraft of No. 37 Squadron were diverted to Hani West and two crash-landed at base (one damaged beyond repair). One aircraft of No. 425 Squadron failed to return. On the last night in June the target was the barracks and railway station at Cagliari. Thick haze made identification of the target very difficult, and the illumination was poor as two of the three flare droppers returned early. Most crews reported bursts in the town, and a 4,000-lb bomb was seen to burst very near the main railway station. The aircraft reported one very large deep red fire in the vicinity of the station, visible for about thirty miles, and three or four smaller fires.

On 1 July a directive was received from NASAF, stating that from the night of 1/2 July onwards the operational effort would be divided between two main targets. If the weather prevented an attack on one of these targets then the whole effort would be switched to the other. The targets for this night were Palermo (thirty aircraft) and Cagliari (twenty aircraft). Twenty-nine got to Palermo in good weather, but it was very dark and a ground haze obscured the target area. Many of the aircraft 'had difficulty in pinpointing and could not say with certainty where their bombs fell' (No. 150 Squadron ORB), and No. 37 Squadron reported that 'Illumination for the target was again unsatisfactory.' However, Rome Radio reported that 'damage was widespread'. Nineteen aircraft of No. 331 Wing attacked at Cagliari in fair weather, seeing bomb bursts, but few definite results were observed.

On 2/3 July the two targets were Trapani (twenty sorties) and Olbia (thirty sorties). At Trapani, the aircraft attacked in good, clear weather and with the aid of excellent illumination by No. 104 Squadron. The bombing was well concentrated, and two 4,000-lb bombs were dropped in the target area, one between the barracks and the harbour. At Olbia, a great many bursts were seen in what was a limited target area. A large explosion followed by a great volume of black smoke came from a group of buildings in the south-west corner of the target, possibly huts containing stores and explosives. One report (No. 425 Squadron) suggested that an arsenal 'seemed to have been hit as many successive explosions were seen for several minutes', and fires could be seen from twenty miles away. One aircraft of No. 70 Squadron failed to return, and was thought to have gone down in flames over the target. One of No. 425 Squadron's aircraft got lost on the return journey and ran out of petrol, and it landed on the coast five miles north of Sfax in approximately three feet of water. Two crew members were seriously injured, but the rest got away with a few cuts and bruises.

The targets on the next night were Trapani (thirty-five sorties) and Cagliari (twenty-five sorties), but a forecast of bad weather conditions at Cagliari caused all the aircraft to be diverted to Trapani. Reports were contradictory, with some saying that the illumination was good and there was no cloud below 11,000 feet, and others reporting some cloud, slight ground haze, and intense darkness. Some crews claimed to have put their bombs in the marshalling yards and good results were claimed, including three large fires. Others said that pinpointing was difficult with 'many bombs...dropped indiscriminately'. On the same night three aircraft from No. 331 Wing were entrusted with a special operation to distribute a million nickels over Rome and to bomb the seaplane base at Lido di Roma.

On 4/5 July the targets were shipping in Catania harbour and the airfield at Villacidro, the latter attack designed to prevent aircraft taking off to attack an Allied convoy. Thirty-one aircraft took off for Catania, and most of them attacked what was believed to be the target through 7/10 cloud at 11,000 feet, some low cloud, and thick haze below that. Twenty-five aircraft attacked Villacidro in very dark and hazy conditions, and only nineteen aircraft claimed to have positively identified the target. One aircraft of No. 142 Squadron failed to return. A message had been received one hour after take-off that the aircraft was returning to base due to engine trouble, and sea searches were carried out throughout the following day. Traces of the missing aircraft and its crew were reported at 1100 hours, but no rescue was carried out. One of the Wellingtons of No. 70 Squadron also failed to return, and was later found to have crash-landed in Kelibia Salt Lake. All the crew were safe.

On 4 July a signal from NASAF notified the Group that an attack on several Sardinian airfields during the next few days would be part of a 'special operation', and particular attention should be paid to the times specified for the attacks. On 5/6 July sixty Wellingtons were detailed to attack the airfields in the Gerbini area, spread over four hours. However, the weather forecast for the target area predicted that it would be very dark and covered by a thick haze, and NASAF reduced the effort by 50 per cent. Twenty-eight aircraft eventually took off, but the hazy conditions made identification of the targets problematic and the amount of damage caused was difficult to assess. Only one aircraft claimed to have attacked the main airfield, and the remainder bombed 'flat country in the immediate vicinity on which were suspected satellites.' No. 420 Squadron ORB states that results were poor, and 'it is not known if targets were reached'. One aircraft of No. 40 Squadron failed to return, and was probably the Wellington seen to crash in flames north of the main landing ground at Gerbini.

On 6/7 July it was the turn of Palermo and Sicilian airfields, but an accident at No. 424 Squadron reduced the number of aircraft operating. At 2000 hours one of its aircraft 'suddenly caught fire' and blew up at Pavillier, and a number of airmen who had been sitting under the wing before the fire were struck by flying shrapnel. One was killed instantly, and another had his right arm blown off. Three were badly burned, and two of these died of their injuries during the night. Fragments from the bursts flew all over the camp, causing grass fires. A few seconds after the first explosion another aircraft nearby also caught fire and blew up, but there were no further casualties. By this time all available personnel were fighting fires that threatened the whole camp, and this included the Commanding Officer of No. 331 Wing (Group Captain Dunlap) who 'worked like any AC2'. Needless to say, operations were cancelled for the night. In the end, twenty-five aircraft attacked Palermo, but ground haze hindered the accuracy of the bombing and results were not observed in most cases. Two aircraft of No. 37 Squadron and one of No. 142 Squadron failed to return, and nothing was heard from them after take-off. Twenty-seven Wellingtons attacked five airfields in Sardinia, starting several fires and causing an explosion at Pabillonis. One of the aircraft of No. 70 Squadron was abandoned near the airfield on return, but all the crew were safe.

On 6 July the Group ORB reported that considerable trouble was being experienced with the Merlin-engined Wellington Mark IIs due to very high daytime temperatures – an average of 84 degrees at take-off for the last ten days. A signal was sent to NASAF stating that No. 104 Squadron was being temporarily withdrawn from operations due to the impossibility of keeping oil and glycol temperatures down to reasonable limits. The resultant strain on the other 236 Wing Squadron (No. 40 Squadron) was acknowledged. Also, a signal was received from NASAF ordering No. 205 Group to assume full operational responsibility for 330 and 331 Wings until further notice.

On the next night, the Wellingtons were detailed to attack three airfields in Sicily

– Gerbini, Catania and Comiso. Seventy-four were able to take-off, and twenty-six of them attacked at Gerbini, but results generally unobserved due to darkness and haze. Twenty-eight bombed Catania, where most crews identified the target visually with flares and were satisfied that the bombing was successful. Twenty-four attacked Comiso, where seven crews visually identified the runways and buildings and the remainder bombed with the aid of good pinpoints at Comiso and Vittoria towns. One Wellington of No. 70 Squadron failed to return, nothing being heard from it after take-off. On 18/19 July a repeat performance of the previous night's effort was ordered by NASAF, with thirty aircraft on each of Gerbini, Catania and Comiso airfields. A total of eighty-seven aircraft took off, a figure only previously exceeded on four occasions during the crisis in the desert and the battles at El Alamein. Haze again made identification of targets difficult, but twenty-one aircraft succeeded in finding and bombing Gerbini, twenty-five attacked Catania, and twenty-six attacked Comiso. Only the Comiso attack was regarded as fairly successful, with most of the aircraft on the other two targets bombing on estimated positions. Two aircraft of No. 40 Squadron failed to return.

*   *   *

No. 178 Squadron at Hosc Raui (twenty miles south of Benghazi) was having terrible problems keeping its few Liberators in the air, and only despatched twenty-four sorties on four nights between 14 May and the end of the month. The targets were Messina (twice) and Augusta (twice), and most claimed to have bombed the target areas. In the second attack on Messina on 20/21 May one returned early due to engine trouble, and another was hit by flak over Reggio di Calabria and jettisoned its bombs over the town. On 27/28 May five Liberators set off for Augusta, but one had considerable trouble locating the target area, and eventually gave up the search and bombed a beacon believed to be on the headland off Augusta. In order to get around the problem with the serviceability of the Liberators, the Squadron started to receive Halifaxes in May as a stop gap, and operated two of them to Augusta for the first time on the night of 31 May/1 June.

On 20 May No. 462 Squadron at Gardabia Main received instructions that it was to leave No. 205 Group and join No. 178 Squadron at Hosc Raui under the operational control of the USAAF and administrative control of Air Headquarters AF Eastern Mediterranean. The advance road party left on 22 May, followed later on the same day by the advance air party. On arrival at the new location, the advance party was given a warm welcome by No. 178 Squadron, which opened its canteen to them. The Americans also provided valuable help, laying on machinery for clearing dispersals and roads. The main road convoy arrived on 29 May, and the Squadron ORB recorded that the 'new location is proving to be very dusty and it is feared that it will have an adverse effect on serviceability'. In the attack on Augusta on 31 May/1 June the six Liberators and two Halifaxes from No. 178 Squadron were joined by seven Halifaxes of No. 462 Squadron, operating from Hosc Raui for the first time. Two of the Halifaxes returned early due to electrical failure and hydraulic trouble respectively, and one had all its bombs hang up and was forced to jettison them into the sea. Six Liberators and four Halifaxes claimed to have located and bombed the target area, one bombed on ETA, and another attacked an unidentified area on the east coast of Sicily. Two of the Liberators crashed on landing and one burnt out, but both crews were safe.

During June and the early part of July, as the build-up for the invasion of Sicily got underway, targets around the Straits of Messina and the Catania area became the main focus of the attacks of the heavy bombers. The purpose was to prevent the flow of supplies and reinforcements to the enemy on Sicily, although the number of aircraft involved was small and the impact unlikely to have been great. The harbour area, airfields and marshalling yards at Catania received fifty-three sorties (thirty-seven by the Halifaxes and sixteen by the Liberators) in six attacks between 4/5 June and 7/8 July. The attacks were often hampered by bad weather and poor visibility, with haze and darkness making the target very difficult to identify and few results observed. The ferry terminal and port area at Messina was attacked twice, on 7/8 and 25/26 June, by a total of seventeen Halifaxes and six Liberators. One Halifax returned early from the first operation, and one failed to release its bombs on the second. After trying for some time to get them to drop, it decided to abandon the mission, and jettisoned most of them manually into the sea on the return journey. The aircraft eventually landed safely with some bombs still on board. Thick ground haze and a smoke screen prevented accurate observation for the remainder of the aircraft in the second attack, but bursts were seen on the railway station and buildings nearby.

Three attacks were made by a total of twenty-four Halifaxes and seven Liberators on Reggio di Calabria on the Italian side of the straits of Messina, with the airfield and ferry terminal bombed. In the first operation on 10/11 June two Halifaxes returned early due to engine trouble, one crashed on landing, and four Liberators had to be diverted to Lete on return. Thirteen aircraft found and bombed the target in good visibility, and a direct hit was scored on a hangar, which quickly caught fire. An explosion followed, after which the fire burned with intense white flames. Other fires were seen on the airfield perimeter, and in stores and barracks. In the second attack on 20/21 June, six Halifaxes attacked the terminal and marshalling yards, and some half dozen fires were left burning. On the same night, five Liberators and three Halifaxes were despatched to attack the ferry terminal at Villa San Giovanni, but one of the Halifaxes returned early due to electrical failure. The other seven aircraft located and bombed the target area, where bursts were not seen due to haze but many small fires were observed. On 28/29 June one Halifax had to return immediately due to engine trouble, and the other seven Halifaxes and two Liberators only identified the Reggio di Calabria area with much difficulty after prolonged searching due to heavy ground haze. No results were seen.

On 17/18 and 22/23 June the heavy bombers attacked the airfield at Comiso, on the south-western end of the island. Ten Halifaxes and four Liberators took off in the first attack, but two returned early due to engine trouble. Bomb bursts were seen among buildings on both sides of the airfield, and one large red fire and four smaller ones were seen. One of the Halifaxes experienced engine trouble just before reaching the target, but carried on and bombed the airfield and landed at Luqa on Malta on three engines on return. In the second attack, nine Halifaxes and five Liberators were despatched, but one returned early due to engine trouble and another was unable to locate target after an extensive search and jettisoned its bombs in open country. The others found target identification very difficult due to ground haze and low cloud and some bombed the estimated position of the airfield and flak concentrations. Few bursts and no results were observed.

One of the Halifaxes of No. 178 Squadron was hit by flak in front of the rear turret just after releasing its bombs. The intercom system immediately went dead, two crew members were injured, and a fire developed near the oxygen supply above the entrance hatch. The fire was put out by the prompt action of the Flight Engineer (Sergeant H.E. Paxton), but during this time the port outer engine cut and could not be feathered. After putting out the fire, Sergeant Paxton attended to the two injured men, putting a tourniquet on Sergeant Houston's arm. The other injured man, wireless operator Sergeant Stimpson, kept trying to contact Malta but was not successful as the aerials had been shot away. The rear gunner could not release himself from his turret as the bulkhead doors were jammed, and Sergeant Paxton was busy again, forcing the doors open. The captain, Sergeant Tattersall, decided to try to reach Malta with the port inner engine intermittently on fire and the starboard rudder controls shot away. Although the hydraulics were unserviceable and the port undercarriage damaged, he eventually made a perfect landing with a flat tyre. On further inspection, approximately 500 holes were found in the aircraft, and the elevators had been partly shot away.

*   *   *

The Wellingtons of No. 205 Group and the four-engined bombers at Hosc Raui and Gardabia Main operated on 86 of the 100 nights between 1 April and 9 July 1943 (the night before the invasion of Sicily was launched), flew 3,437 sorties, and lost 69 aircraft. The pace of operations increased in this period, as the final battles for Tunisia were fought and during the preparations for the invasion. Just over half of the sorties (51 per cent) were directed at the ports and shipping in harbour, and another 30 per cent went to airfields.

NOTES

1. TMAME, Volume VI, page 391.
2. TMAME, Volume VI, page 454.
3. Alan Moorhead, *African Trilogy*, page 577.

CHAPTER EIGHT

Sicily and the Invasion of Italy – July to September 1943

The Allied invasion of Sicily (Operation *Husky*) began on the night of 9/10 July 1943, and ended with the withdrawal of all Axis forces from the island on 17 August 1943. The invasion brought about a crisis in the Italian government, leading to the arrest of Mussolini and the appointment of Marshal Badoglio as head of state. The American 82nd and the British 1st Airborne Divisions started the assault, but the operations did not go well. The weather was poor, and the aircraft towing the gliders and carrying the paratroopers were manned by inexperienced aircrew. They were not used to flying in the dark and through flak and searchlights. Many released their gliders too early; sixty-nine fell into the sea and fifty-six were scattered far from their objectives. Hundreds of paratroopers were dropped into the sea and drowned, and most of the others were again widely scattered. Nevertheless, the main landings went in on 10 July, and twelve divisions (some 160,000 men and 600 tanks) of the British Eighth and US Seventh Armies were brought successfully ashore on the south-east coast of Sicily.

The British met with little resistance, but US forces were held back for a time by strong counter-attacks from the German Hermann Göring and the Italian Livorno Divisions. The British advance went well at first, and by 13 July they had captured Augusta and Ragusa. The next stage in the plan was to make a bridgehead across the Simeto River at the Primosole bridge, seven miles south of Catania, and this led to a hard little battle between British and German paratroops. The 1st Parachute Brigade had 115 casualties out of a force of 292 men employed, and failed to hold the bridge. An attempt to retake the bridge by the paratroops on 15 July was repulsed, but it was eventually captured intact at dawn on 16 July. Elsewhere, Canadian forces took Caltagirone, forty miles inland from Syracuse, on 16 July, and the Americans took Agrigento, before beginning their drive northwards to Palermo. By 17 July the enemy's plan was clear – he would withdraw into the north-east corner of Sicily, and eventually withdraw altogether across the Strait of Messina. To do so he would have to pivot on Catania, and therefore would have to hold on to the city for as long as possible. While the Axis forces held Catania, they could continue to deny the Allies the greatest prize – the airfields on the plain to the south. Following the capture of the Primosole bridge, the Eighth Army advanced on Catania, but by the 20th was struggling against stubborn opposition.

By now, the Eighth Army was beginning to show definite signs of fatigue, and as the drive on Catania faltered, the 1st Canadian Division was pushed inland to try to get around the western side of Mount Etna and outflank the enemy positions. Meanwhile, the Italians were surrendering in droves to US forces in western Sicily. On 22 July, Patton's 2nd Armoured Division captured Palermo against light opposition, and trapped some 45,000 Italian troops in western Sicily. Increasingly,

Montgomery moved the main weight of his attack west of Mount Etna, pushing towards Adrano, which fell on 6/7 August after much hard fighting. Catania itself had been entered on 5 August, and the 2nd US Corps on the left flank took Troina on 6 August, and two days later had captured Cesaro, about forty miles from Messina. In the north, Patton was pushing along the north coast of the island, and on 4 August the 3rd US Division had reached a very strong enemy position at San Fratello on the Furiano River. Patton landed a battalion of infantry and some guns and tanks behind this position on 8 August, but this small force was soon fighting for its life. However, 3rd US Division pushed on, and eventually relieved the hard-pressed force. The 2nd US Corps had now secured the line of the Naso–Floresta–Randazzo road, and Messina was less than thirty miles away. The Italians had begun to evacuate Sicily on 3 August, and on the night of 11/12 August the Germans started to pull out across the Strait of Messina, using over a hundred small craft covered by some 500 AA guns. US troops entered Messina on 16 August, but the Axis evacuation of 100,000 troops had been completed by the next day with little real interference from the Allies.

*   *   *

During the fighting in Sicily the Wellingtons at Kairouan operated on thirty-five nights and flew 2,647 sorties against targets on the island and in Southern Italy. The key date for No. 205 Group during this period came on 15 July 1943, when it assumed full operational control of Nos 330 and 331 Wings. The force now comprised nine squadrons: No. 231 Wing (Nos 37 and 70 Squadrons) at Kairouan North/Temmar; No. 236 Wing (Nos 40 and 104 Squadrons) at Hani West; No. 330 Wing (Nos 142 and 150 Squadrons) at Kairouan West/Allani; and No. 331 Wing at Zina (Nos 420 and 425 Squadrons) and Pavillier (No. 424 Squadron).[1]

A significant proportion of the effort during the period (714 sorties – 27 per cent) was directed at railway targets in Italy in an attempt to disrupt the flow of supplies and reinforcements to the island. The vast fleet assembled for the invasion and now lying in easy range of the enemy air forces provided an excellent target, and the bomber airfields were another major target for the Wellingtons. The airfields on Sicily were attacked early in the campaign; attention then switched to the airfields across the straits of Messina and on the toe and heel of Italy, and finally airfields in and around Naples were bombed. In all, 582 sorties were despatched to the airfields, comprising 22 per cent of the total effort. However, the greatest proportion of the Wellington's sorties during the period came between 5/6 and 16/17 August, and were directed at beaches around Messina, from where it was believed that the enemy was embarking troops and equipment being evacuated from Sicily. A total of 857 sorties (32 per cent) were despatched to the beaches, but failed to halt the flow.

On the night of 9/10 July, as the airborne troops were on their way to Sicily, a big and complicated set of bombing operations was aimed at Catania and Syracuse, intended to cover the glider operations by the British 1st Airborne Division. Seventy-nine aircraft were to attack Syracuse, and, of these, six were to attack the seaplane base and six the marshalling yards. The remainder were to attack an area selected to create a diversion for the airborne troops while they formed up to prepare for the assault on the town. Another force of nineteen Wellingtons was to attack Catania marshalling yards and military installations, while Bostons dropped dummy paratroops in that area to mislead the enemy into thinking that Catania was the objective. Nineteen Wellingtons were given the task of preventing enemy reserves from resisting the invading forces at Canicatti, Caltanissetta, Caltagirone and Palazzolo. Lastly, twelve aircraft of No. 331 Wing were to carry out a *Mandrel* operation to swamp enemy radar off the south coast of Sicily to swamp enemy radar, and Rome and Naples were allotted one Wellington each for nickelling (leaflet dropping). Gunby records that the bombing at Syracuse 'had to be done without flares, to avoid illuminating the airborne operations, and at low level to achieve the necessary accuracy'. It also had to be carried out continuously over a period of three hours, and so dangerous did it seem that Group Captain MacNair of No. 236 Wing suggested that it was a case for volunteers – but 'there was no hesitation in response'.

In the end, the nickellers were cancelled due to the non-arrival of special leaflets, and the *Mandrel* operation was reduced to six aircraft on instructions from Tedder. A total of 117 aircraft took off on the various operations, and, of these, 55 Wellingtons attacked the Syracuse Isthmus in clear weather and good visibility. Nine Wellingtons attacked the seaplane base, with many direct hits reported. Nineteen Wellingtons attacked Catania, and bursts were seen across the town and docks but no results were seen. One aircraft of No. 37 Squadron failed to return from this operation. Fifteen aircraft attacked the four enemy concentration points, where good fires were started. No. 104 Squadron reported that a 4,000-lb bomb was seen to burst in the northern part of the town of Canicatti, and other bombs were seen bursting near the railway station and across the town. The Group ORB states that the general tone of reports was that of 'a hell of a party'. The *Mandrel* operation was carried out as directed, but one of the aircraft from No. 424 Squadron failed to return. It was later reported that it had ran out of fuel and force-landed near Medenine.

The Wings were informed that a further maximum effort would be called for on the following night, with the main operation (*Snowboots*) designed to confuse the enemy regarding various airborne operations. An attack on Augusta was intended to distract the enemy's attention from landings of airborne troops west of the town, and an attack on Catania was to lead them to think that an airborne landing was imminent at that place. However, *Snowboots* was cancelled, and only a few disjointed operations took place. One Wellington of No. 70 Squadron had already taken off on *Snowboots* and had to be recalled. The mission assigned to No. 331 Wing (an attack on the Gerbini airfields) went ahead, but only fifteen aircraft took off due to an accident on the runway. An aircraft blew up while taking off, and all the crew were killed. The wreckage was blown all over the runway, and further operations were cancelled. Fourteen of the Wellingtons claimed to have bombed the target area over a period of three to four hours, and found almost no opposition.

Operation *Snowboots* was again cancelled on 11/12 July, and the airfields at Trapani, Marsala, Mazzara del Vallo and Montecorvino Ravella were attacked instead. The attack on Trapani, Marsala and Mazzara del Vallo was to precede a naval bombardment at 0100 hours, and care had to be taken to be away from the target before this started. Seven aircraft attacked Trapani and most bombs were dropped in the town area, but searchlight dazzle prevented observation of results. Fifteen attacked Marsala, where a large fire was started, followed by explosions, and other fires in the town area and in the area between the railway station and the port. Ten aircraft attacked Mazzara del Vallo, which was located in good visibility and bombs were seen to burst across the town and on factories east of the town. One fire was started in the town area, which was visible from forty miles away. The naval bombardment was seen to commence as the aircraft left the area. Twenty-six Wellingtons bombed Montecorvino Ravella airfield, where bombs fell on the hangars and other buildings and aircraft on the ground were machine-gunned.

On the next night, thirty-one Wellingtons again successfully attacked the airfield at Montecorvino Ravella. Fires were started in buildings, a direct hit on a hangar was reported, and towards the end the whole area was covered in clouds of black smoke. Another forty-five aircraft were sent to attack enemy concentrations at Enna and Caltanissetta, and most of the crews claimed to have bombed their respective targets. After further confusion over Operation *Snowboots*, forty-five aircraft were eventually detailed to attack Messina on 13/14 July, and thirty-two aircraft to Palermo. Forty-two Wellingtons attacked at Messina with good results, bursts being seen across the marshalling yards and near the Custom House. Two large explosions were observed, culminating in a red glow and a pall of black smoke, and another fire visible eighty miles away was also started. Thirty aircraft attacked at Palermo, where many bursts were seen in and around the marshalling yards and the main railway station. No. 37 Squadron reported that a 'huge cloud of smoke was visible over the target after bombing'. One aircraft each of Nos 330 and 331 Wings failed to return.

The direction of the attacks by No. 205 Group was now changed to Italian targets – airfields, docks and rail communications. On 14/15 July fifteen aircraft attacked the airfield at Capodichino, near Naples, and many bursts and fires were seen on the landing ground and buildings. Seventeen attacked the airfield at Pomigliano, a few miles north-east of Naples, and had no difficulty in locating and bombing the landing ground. Many bursts were seen and fires started both in buildings and along a line of aircraft, followed by a series of explosions. Forty-four Wellingtons attacked the docks at Naples, which were partly obscured by a smokescreen. Good fires were seen burning, and bursts were seen at the landward end of the Vittoria Emmanuele Mole. One of the Wellingtons of No. 104 Squadron failed to return, and it was believed that it had engine trouble and was making for home when it went missing.

On the next night the docks and marshalling yards at Villa San Giovanni and Reggio di Calabria, on the Italian side of the Straits of Messina, were the targets. Twenty-six Wellingtons were detailed to attack Villa San Giovanni, and claimed good results. Another twenty-one aircraft carried out a successful attack at Reggio di Calabria, where the target was well lit by accurate flare droppers and the bombing appeared to be well concentrated. A 4,000-lb bomb was dropped at the junction of the railway track from the harbour and the main track through the town, and other bursts were observed across the quays and in the town. Thirty-two Wellingtons continued the attack on the airfields, detailed to attack Reggio, Vibo Valentia and Crotone. Many fires were started at all three targets and a large explosion at Vibo Valentia was thought to be an ammunition dump going up. On 16/17 July, thirty-two aircraft went to Naples marshalling yards and twenty-eight to the airfield at Capodichino. They left many fires burning at Naples from which a terrific explosion occurred, but later arrivals could only bomb on estimated positions due to the smokescreen. Bombs were seen to burst across the landing ground at Capodichino and a number of aircraft and buildings were set on fire. One Wellington of No. 142 Squadron failed to return. Another nine aircraft from the Group were entrusted with the task of distributing leaflets carrying a joint message from Churchill and Roosevelt over Rome, Naples, and the principal towns of Sicily.

On 17/18 July, thirty-four aircraft attacked the airfield at Montecorvino, where cloud and ground haze made identification difficult. Bursts were seen across the landing ground and buildings, and several fires started. The aircraft reported one big fire with pyrotechnics, and a large explosion, which may have been an ammunition dump. Another twenty-two aircraft bombed the airfield at Pomigliano, where, once again, identification was difficult. Six fires were started, one 'emitting green lights' and another giving off explosions. There were also two or three fires reported in the aircraft factory immediately south of the airfield. One of the aircraft of No. 424 Squadron crashed about forty-five miles north of Kairouan, and two of the crew were killed. The others had abandoned the aircraft just before the crash, and all landed safely but with some injuries. The ORB for No. 420 Squadron, which was stood down on this day, provides a nice snapshot of life at Kairouan:

> The 'Y' had a good movie, a very large number of men attended the showing. The padre reported very good attendance at the Church Service. A mobile Bath Unit is now visiting the Squadron every Thursday. The weather has been very hot, Sirocco wind blowing in from the desert. Our water supply has been curtailed due to trouble at the supply water hole. The water bowsers are now drawing water from Kairouan. Arrangements are now being made at Monastir to open a rest camp for aircrew. Two crews will go there for a 48 at same time and will be replaced by others every second day. The daily swimming parties for ground crew is still appreciated. The officers' mess has a radio installed there – we at least get the news now. Morale is quite high on the camp.

On the next night the Group was stood down except for four aircraft of No. 70 Squadron, which dropped leaflets ('Citizens of Rome') over Rome in the early hours of 19 July. The Squadron ORB reported that 'Serious discontent is rife in Italy; she is seething with revolts and the Fascist System now lies in a melting pot.'

Photographic reconnaissance reports had shown a considerable force of Ju 88s on the airfield at Aquino, and NASAF ordered an attack by 'all available aircraft' on the night of 19/20 July. However, the Group felt that 'this effort was unnecessarily large for one aerodrome', and asked for additional targets. In the end, sixty-four aircraft were detailed for Aquino and fifty-six for the airfield at Capodichino, with the attacks to be concentrated in two waves on each target. Reports from the attack on Aquino suggested a very successful raid, the aircraft bringing back stories of direct hits on buildings and hangars, which resulted in a mass of flames visible sixty miles away. Many aircraft were seen to be burning on the ground, and columns of black smoke rose to a height of 4,000 feet. Chappell recorded that the attack was 'one of the best we have ever done'. A thick haze at Capodichino prevented easy location of the airfield, and only two or three fires were reported.

On the following night the targets were the marshalling yards at Naples and the airfield at Crotone. Thirty-one Wellingtons bombed Naples, where bursts were seen in the yards and the dock area. Thirty-seven aircraft attacked Crotone, and all the photographs taken substantiated the claim that the target was 'well and truly pranged'. Bursts across the landing ground and hangars were reported, causing a 'terrific explosion' and a number of fires. Chappell records 'an extraordinary happening' when one of the Wellingtons of No. 104 Squadron came back from Naples minus the wireless operator. He had been at the flare chute preparing to release a photo-flash when the aircraft was caught in searchlights and the pilot took violent evasive action. On coming out of the dive, a bump was felt by the entire crew, and the rear gunner reported a black shape going past his turret on the starboard side. On going back to investigate, the navigator found that the astrodome was off and lying broken on the floor, and there was no sign of the wireless operator. Ground examination of the aircraft showed fabric torn on top of the fuselage and on the starboard tail elevator, and two dents on the elevator. Leaving an aircraft through the astrodome was extremely dangerous because of the danger of hitting the tail, but apparently the wireless operator had been the only survivor of a severe crash in England after his aircraft hit a church steeple. It seems that he had panicked when the aircraft dived sharply to avoid the searchlights.

On 21/22 July, thirty-nine aircraft set off to attack the railway junction at Salerno, with many of the Wellingtons carrying a proportion of delayed action bombs to disrupt rail communications for as long as possible. At this time No. 104 Squadron was being re-equipped with Wellington Marks III and X,[2] and these had now started to operate. Low cloud seriously interfered with the attack, but a number of bursts were claimed to be in the right place and debris from one building near the station was seen to be thrown into the air. On the same night an attack on the airfield at Capodichino was reduced when one Wellington of No. 331 Wing swung off the runway and dowsed some flares. Cloud also prevented accurate location and bombing at this target as well, and only two aircraft definitely claimed to have hit the target. Two of the Wellingtons failed to return, one each from Nos 142 and 420 Squadrons.

The bombers went back to the marshalling yards at Salerno on 22/23 July, and also attacked the airfield at Pratica di Mare. Salerno was well illuminated, and thirty-three aircraft bombed the tracks and a bridge in the vicinity of the railway yards. A large fire was seen near the locomotive shop. Thirty aircraft bombed at Pratica di Mare, where sticks of bombs straddled the landing ground and two fires were started. One aircraft of No. 104 Squadron failed to return. A faint but undecipherable message had been picked up, and flares were seen falling fifty miles south of the target area. The aircraft had been detailed to illuminate the target, and it may have had trouble and had to jettison its load. One aircraft of No. 37 Squadron made a belly-landing at Hergla due to engine trouble, but the crew were unhurt. One of No. 424 Squadron had engine trouble on the return trip, and force-landed at Cap Bon. The undercarriage did not lock and the Wellington ground-looped, but all the crew were safe and the aircraft was subsequently repaired. On the next night, thirty-three aircraft again attacked the railway junction at Salerno, with a high percentage of incendiaries being carried. The aim of the attack was 'to prevent the flow of war material from the industrial North to hard-pressed Sicily by destroying the Rail Junction'. Most of the aircraft were confident that their bombs fell in or very near the marshalling yards, where three major fires giving off dense clouds of black smoke were started. Another thirty-eight aircraft attacked the docks at San Giovanni in good visibility and good illumination, and most of the bombs were estimated to have fallen in the target area. One large fire giving off volumes of black smoke was seen.

An entry in No. 424 Squadron's ORB on 26 July gives us an insight into the relations between the Canadians and the British. Having announced the resignation of 'Benito' and a feeling that 'the war will not last long now', it goes on to say:

> The Squadron was notified that the bread ration will be cut from 12 ounces to 6 by the RAF Stores (DID). It will be hard on the Airmen. The Squadron will have to take steps to buy bread from the natives. Much cursing at the RAF and their system by the men. This does not help to better understanding between Canadians and the British. Letters are going from bad to worse and although censors are severe, conditions like these do not help feeling and letters for Canada are very bitter against the British. Numerous men have to be paraded before the Adjutant concerning this. They say, 'Well if we can't write about it now it does not mean we will forget. Some of us will live to get back home and then there will be talking.' Other Squadrons report the same attitude.

After two nights without operations due to bad weather at the airfields (Chappell reports 'a thunderstorm with rain and dust blowing everywhere'), the targets for 26/27 July were the airfields at Capodichino and Montecorvino Ravella. Thirty-one aircraft attacked Capodichino, where the weather was 'rather hazy.' Bursts were seen in and around the landing ground, and two hangars were claimed to have been hit and set on fire. Thirty-nine Wellingtons bombed at Montecorvino Ravella, where many sticks of bombs were seen to drop across the landing ground and two 4,000-pounders hit buildings on the north-west side of the airfield.

On 28/29 July, NASAF ordered thirty sorties on each of Capodichino and Montecorvino airfields, but the effort on Capodichino was reduced when a Wellington of No. 424 Squadron blew up while taking off. The aircraft was completely destroyed, and the wreckage blocked the runway and caused the cancellation of the last four aircraft. The crew only had two more trips to complete their first tour of operations and were 'very popular in the Squadron'. All were killed. Twenty-one attacked the airfield at Capodichino, but found 6/10 to 10/10 cloud down to 4,000 feet and only five saw the airfield. The others made dead reckoning runs from a pinpoint on Mount Vesuvius, and few if any results were observed. Similar conditions were found at Montecorvino, and twenty-two bombed estimated positions. Two Wellingtons of No. 104 Squadron failed to return, nothing being heard after take-off. Chappell records:

> I greatly admire the way in which my squadron friends stand up so quietly, cheerfully and bravely to the risks and terrors of the night operations. Some have signs of strain in premature greyness, a few have nervous twitches of some muscles particularly the eyes, some are tense at briefing, nearly all of us drink heavily and relax on 'Stand Down' nights, sometimes with boisterous activities of mess games to follow...We live an unnatural life away from our wives, lovers and families, yet we remain kind and considerate to each other.

A Bombay (L5857) of No. 216 Squadron flies over the Western Desert on its more familiar transport duties. The Bombay was a sturdy and competent aircraft, could carry eight 250lb bombs on external racks, and was armed with two hydraulically-operated single-gun turrets in the nose and tail. They carried out their first bombing operation to Tobruk on the night of 14/15th June 1940. This particular aircraft was destroyed in an air raid on Kufra on 25th September 1942. (IWM, CM 780)

Fires still burn at Tobruk after RAF bombing attacks in January 1941. The port fell to British and Australian troops on 22nd January, and 25,000 Italians were captured, along with 208 guns and 87 tanks. Combined British and Australian losses were about 450. (RAF 1939-1945, HMSO, Crown Copyright)

The menace of the desert – dust storms driven by hot or bitterly cold winds, giving hours of unabated, gritty misery. But in the winter there was sometimes too much water and lots of lovely mud.
(RAFME, HMSO)

A Wellington of No. 37 Squadron being prepared for a raid, probably at LG 09/Bir Koraiyim, in January 1941. Groundcrew are about to refuel T2508 which has just had its port mainwheel replaced after bursting a tyre on landing. (IWM, CM 368)

The nose art on T2508, seen in close up above reads "Defaecamus Luces Purpuras" and apparently involves a bodily function performed from a great height! (IWM, CM 407)

A Wellington IC of No. 38 Squadron Detachment taxying at Luqa. A number of aircraft from the squadron were detached to Malta between August and October 1941. (IWM, CM 1358)

Wellington Mark II (Z8524) of No. 104 Squadron at a desert ALG, about to be loaded with 500-lb GP bombs for a sortie. The front turret has been removed from this aircraft, which carries 52 operation symbols on its nose. (IWM, ME (RAF) 6297)

A convoy of No. 70 Squadron pause for a quick meal in the desert. Another move to yet another landing ground was always just around the corner, and often Rommel was not far away as well. (Peter Jackson collection)

Groundcrew servicing a Wellington IC of No. 38 Squadron at Shallufa in 1941. An engine mechanic on top of the port engine catches a box spanner thrown up by a colleague on the ground, while two other groundcrew clean the cockpit of sand with a vacuum cleaner and another cleans the Perspex on the front gun turret. (IWM, CM 795)

Boeing Fortress I (AN532) of No. 90 Squadron on the ground at Shallufa. Four aircraft were detached to the Middle East in November 1941, but only carried out a few operations with No. 205 Group. The detachment was renumbered as No. 220 Squadron on 1st December 1941 and transferred to the maritime reconnaissance role. (IWM, CM 1582)

The Liberators of No. 159/160 Squadron detachments and HALPRO B-24s attacked the Italian fleet in daylight in June 1942, operating in conjunction with RAF Beauforts. As the Liberators dropped their bombs from on high the Beauforts came in low to launch their weapons. (RAFME, HMSO)

Early in 1942 the Wellingtons of No. 38 Squadron started training in the torpedo-bombing role, and this still from a film shot by the RAF Film Production Unit shows a practice torpedo drop in the Gulf of Suez by AD597. (IWM, CM 5037)

The torpedo-carrying Wellingtons of No. 38 Squadron could carry their weapons over many hundreds of miles, attacking shipping at night from a few feet above the sea. (RAFME, HMSO)

The crew of Liberator AL511 of No. 108 Squadron walk from their aircraft at Fayid. Note the 'Dumbo' motif painted on the nose. This aircraft failed to return from a bombing sortie over Tripoli on 3rd May 1942. (IWM, CBM 1261)

In the photograph on the left Halifax Mark II W1176 of No. 462 Squadron awaits its load of 500-lb MC bombs, being prepared by armourers at Fayid, prior to an attack on Benghazi. The photograph below shows Halifax W1170 taxying out for a raid on Axis positions in front of El Alamein. Both were taken shortly after the formation of the Squadron when Nos 10/227 and 76/462 Detachments were merged on 7th September 1942. Although nominally an Australian unit, the Squadron was composed mainly of British personnel. (IWM, ME(RAF) 6045 and ME(RAF) 6086)

Ice cold in Alex? Four members of the crew of HF833 of No. 37 Squadron which crash-landed 48km from Tobruk on the night of 30th/31st July 1942. The crew walked for nine days, and then split into parties of two. One of the parties was captured by the Germans, but the others were picked up by an Eighth Army patrol after 22 days in the desert. The men are Sergeant A.E.O. Barras RAAF, Sergeant J. Shirra, Sergeant A.I. Jones, and Flight Sergeant C.R. Warwick. (RAFME, HMSO)

Another two airmen who walked home. Flight Sergeant R.L. Spence RCAF and Sergeant J.K. Wood RAAF, who baled out from DV504 of No. 40 Squadron on the return flight from Tobruk on 7/8th October 1942. Four of the crew had set out to walk back to Allied lines, but two had to abandon the attempt due to exhaustion and injury. The water bottles are German, Italian, and British, and the leaky two gallon can of water which sustained them on their journey is still with them after 24 days in the desert. (RAFME, HMSO)

Some didn't make it back. Sergeant James Milford Jones (third from the left, on leave in Cairo with friends from No. 70 Squadron) flew as a navigator with No. 148 Squadron. He was reported missing from a raid on Benghazi on the night of 13/14th November 1942, and his family received the dreaded telegram (below) a few days later. Sergeant Jones has no known grave, and he and the rest of his crew are commemorated on the Alamein Memorial. (Alun Jones)

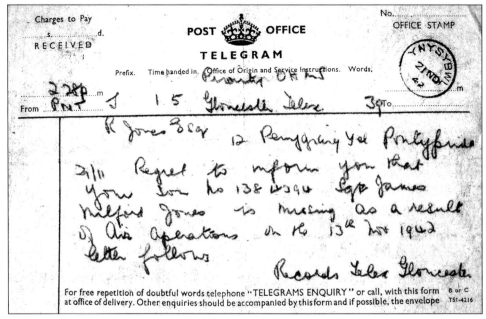

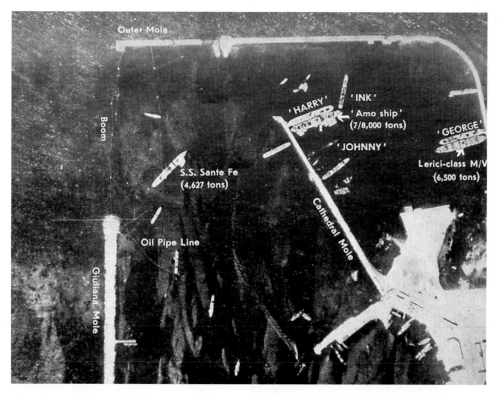

The above photograph shows Benghazi harbour on 14th September 1942, before the two outstanding raids on 16th and 22nd of the month. Two ships are off-loading on the converted wrecks 'George' and 'Harry'. In the photograph below the midday raid on 16th September by seven Liberators of No. 159 Squadron and seventeen B-24s of the USAAF 1st Provisional and 98th Groups has started. A direct hit is seen on the vessel which has moved away from 'George', a bomb has burst near 'Harry', and a stick is exploding around the pipeline from the Giuliana Mole. (RAFME, HMSO)

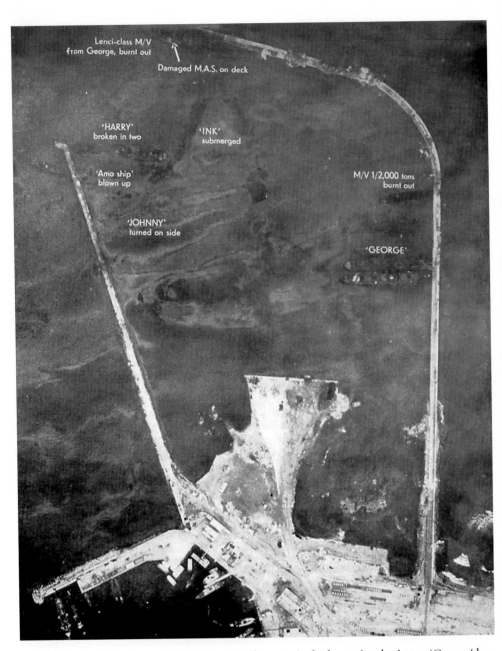

Lenci-class M/V
from George, burnt out

Damaged M.A.S. on deck

'HARRY'
broken in two

'INK'
submerged

'Amo ship'
blown up

M/V 1/2,000 tons
burnt out

'JOHNNY'
turned on side

'GEORGE'

In this photograph taken on 29th September the vessel which was berthed near 'George' has been towed to the Outer Mole and is burnt out, and an Italian MTB on her deck is damaged. The new vessel berthed at 'George' shows damage, and the ship alongside 'Harry', thought to be carrying ammunition of petrol, has exploded violently. Only the stern, pitched on to the Cathedral Mole, and tangled wreckage remain. 'Harry' has split in two and the stern half has sunk. The wrecked destroyer 'Johnny' has turned on port side, and only the starboard rail remains above water. 'Ink' has settled and is half submerged. A vessel of 1/2,000 tons which was berthed across the Mole from 'Harry' has been moved to the bend of the Outer Mole, and is burnt out. (RAFME, HMSO)

When the Eighth Army entered Benghazi on 20th November 1942 they found the harbour strewn with wreckage from the great bombing raids on the port. In the photograph above the stern of the ammunition ship hurled on to the Cathedral Mole can be seen, and behind it are the broken remains of 'Harry'. In the foreground is 'Johnny', awash. In the photograph below can be seen the spectacular damage east of 'Johnny'. The bow plates of the vessel have been curled right back over the shattered superstructure amidships. (TMAME, HMSO)

The men who kept the aircraft flying – R.A.F. Ground Crew in Tripolitania, January 1943.
(RAFME, Crown Copyright)

Wellington Mark IIIs of No. 150 Squadron at Blida, Algeria, are prepared for a raid on Bizerte in March 1943. Nos. 142 and 150 Squadrons were sent to North Africa at the end of 1942 to support Operation TORCH. In the foreground, armourers wheel a trolley-load of bombs towards an aircraft undergoing a final engine inspection. In the background, HF676 appears to be ready for action. (IWM, CNA 3970)

Wing Commander A. A. N. Malan, Commanding Officer of No. 150 Squadron RAF, briefs aircrew of his Squadron and those of No. 142 Squadron RAF at Kairouan West in July 1943. They will soon be taking off on a night bombing raid on a target in Sicily. (IWM, CNA 1088)

Armourers fuzing a 4,000-lb 'Cookie' at Kairouan West, Tunisia, before loading it into a Wellington Mark X prior to a raid on Salerno in support of the Allied landings in September 1943. Another airman carries winches aft of the bomb-bay in order to manoeuvre the bomb underneath the aircraft. (IWM, CNA 4071)

During the afternoon of 28th September the Kairouan area was hit by a violent thunderstorm, with torrential rain which lasted for over two hours. (Barbara Walker)

Wellingtons of No. 40 Squadron being prepared for a raid from Foggia Main in March 1944. (IWM, CNA 2704)

March 1944 – a member of No. 614 Squadron walks through a lake of floodwater in front of Halifax JN976 at dispersal following heavy rain at Celone. (IWM CNA 2685)

Ground crew of No. 178 Squadron enlist the help of a Coles Crane of No. 61 Repair and Salvage Unit to lift 1,500-lb sea mines ('cucumbers') at Celone in April 1944. The mines will be laid in the River Danube in a 'gardening' operation. (IWM, CNA 4211)

Wellingtons crews practise dinghy drill at Foggia Main after heavy rains in March 1944 created a flooded expanse on the airfield. One of the crews is launched onto the water in their J-Type rubber dinghy. (IWM, CNA 2723)

David Clark's crew at Amendola in the summer of 1944: Sergeants D.L. Clark, A.E.C. Lambert, H. John, E.J. Lane, and Flight Sergeant J.A. Challiner. They bombed the oil tanks at Giurgu in Romania on the night of 28/29th June 1944. A page from David Clark's logbook is shown below, and on the next page is a photograph taken by another No. 150 Squadron aircraft on the same raid. (David Clark)

Date	Hour	Aircraft Type and No.	Pilot	Duty	Remarks (including results of bombing, gunnery, exercises, etc.)	Day	Night
25·6·44	20·35	WELLINGTON F/SGT 'K'	CHALLINOR	REAR GUNNER	OPERATIONS: BUDAPEST (HUNGARY) TARGET OIL REFINARIES SIX 500lb. TWO 250lb BOMBS LIGHT & HEAVY FLAK SEARCHLIGHTS		7·00
28·6·44	20·15	LN3?3M F/SGT	CHALLINOR	REAR GUNNER	OPERATIONS: GIURGU (RUMANIA) TARGET OIL STORAGE TANKS HEAVY FLAK ME 109 SIGHTED SIX 500lb TWO 250lb BOMBS		8·00
		SUMMARY FOR JUNE UNIT 150 SQUADRON DATE 30TH JUNE TYPE WELLINGTON. SIGN 2? Gh?.			OPS FOR MONTH 49¼ TOTAL OPS HRS AT UNIT 43?5 TOTAL NON OP HRS AT UNIT 50 GRAND TOTAL AT UNIT 50 ?3?5		
		TOTAL N? OF SORTIES: 26			Dn C Bowm? QC 'A' FLIGHT.		

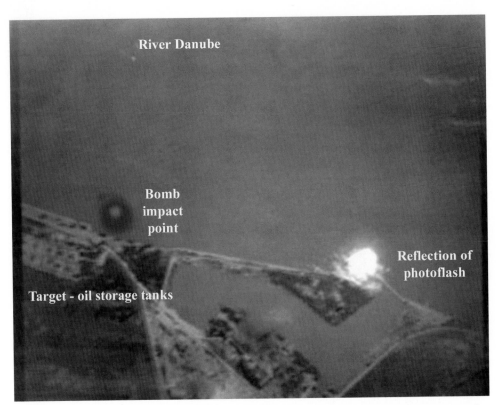

River Danube

Bomb
impact
point

Reflection of
photoflash

Target - oil storage tanks

The aircraft was moving from right to left along a horizontal line about halfway up the photograph. The bomb aimer would have released his bombs at a point in the middle of the photograph, and a very powerful magnesium flare was released at the same time. It descended on a parachute, and went off about 15 seconds after the bomb load had left the aircraft. During this time it was important for the pilot to hold the aircraft straight and level - a dangerous thing to do when the enemy was doing his best to kill you!

Liberator of 34 Squadron SAAF at Celone in the sumer of 1944. (Lawrence Isemonger)

Aircrews of No. 40 Squadron being briefed at Foggia Main in November 1944 before setting off on a raid on the marshalling yards at Sarajevo, Yugoslavia. (IWM, CNA 3265)

Ground crew of No. 31 Squadron S.A.A.F. relax in the sun at Celone in front of Liberator 'Q-for-Little Queenie II'. (Lawrence Isemonger)

Photograph taken during a daylight attack on German troop concentrations at Podgorica, Yugoslavia in November 1944. Smoke rises as the first sticks of bombs explode on the target. (IWM, C 4790)

A Liberator of No. 205 Group over the port of Monfalcone, Italy, in March 1945. Smoke from exploding bombs can be seen rising from the shipbuilding and repair yards. (IWM, C 5155)

A supply-dropping mission to Partisan forces in Yugoslavia in February 1945. A Liberator is seen approaching the dropping zone at Crnomelj. (IWM, C 5010)

Aircrew of No. 40 Squadron RAF don their flying kit before boarding their Wellingtons at Foggia Main for the last night bombing operation undertaken by the type. Six Wellingtons accompanied a force of Liberators making an attack on the marshalling yards at Treviso on the night of 13/14 March 1945. (IWM, CNA 3539)

This remarkable series of photographs shows Liberator KK320 of No. 37 Squadron which was hit by bombs dropped from another aircraft above it during a raid on Monfalcone in March 1945. The bombs are just about to hit the aircraft in the top photograph, and the second one shows the port engine streaming oil. The aircraft lost the propeller from the port inner engine, and suffered a large hole in the fuselage (see below). Its captain, Squadron Leader L. Saxby, managed to fly the aircraft home, where it was declared to be damaged beyond repair. (IWM, C 5162 and 5164)

These young pilots, navigators, bomb aimers, wireless operators and gunners are loyal to each other, and at Intelligence they are pleasant, friendly and courteous to deal with. The air war has not made them rough or cruel – rather the effect has been to make them more serious and thoughtful.

A nuisance raid on a battle area target at Adrano and Randazzo was ordered by NASAF on 31 July/1 August. The two towns were only ten miles from the British-Canadian–American bomb line, and the importance of positive target identification was stressed. The towns lay on the main rail and road communications to Catania, and the attacks were to be spread over the whole period from dusk to dawn. The railway ran around Mount Etna, which provided a good pinpoint – the summit was seen by many pilots – but much haze hampered the operation. Twelve aircraft claimed to have attacked Adrano, but of these only seven saw bursts in the town. Ten bombed at Randazzo under the same weather conditions, and no results were seen. A similar attack was launched on the next night, and once again the utmost importance of positive target identification was stressed. Twenty-four aircraft were detailed for Randazzo, but haze hampered visibility and the illumination was poor. Fourteen aircraft claimed to have bombed the town or the close neighbourhood, and five bombed the estimated position of Milazzo, the alternative target. One aircraft of No. 424 Squadron failed to return, and was thought to have gone down in flames ten miles south-west of Milazzo.

A large number of trucks containing supplies had been reported to be in the marshalling yards at Naples, and a two-wave attack was also carried out on 1/2 August. Fifty-one Wellingtons were detailed for the operation, carrying a maximum incendiary load and a number of long-delay bombs. Thick haze over the target area obscured ground detail, and the bombing was scattered. Only fourteen Wellingtons claimed to have seen and bombed the marshalling yards and a large area was covered with burning incendiaries. One of the aircraft of No. 40 Squadron was caught by searchlights and 'chased out to sea'. On return to base it was found to have holes in the wings and tail plane and a shell nose cap embedded in the bomb doors. This attack was repeated on 2/3 August, when seventy-one Wellingtons were detailed to carry out a 'blitz' attack at 2200 hours. For almost the first time on this target the conditions were good, with no cloud and little haze. Perfect illumination enabled all the crews to see and bomb the target area, and it was covered by burning incendiaries. The seaplane base was also reported to be ablaze, and a number of other buildings were on fire. Six or seven major fires were reported, including a very large one at the south end of the yards. A number of long delay bombs were also dropped to deter the enemy's efforts at clearing up afterwards. All the aircraft returned safely, but one of No. 425 Squadron crashed on the flare path after landing at Pavillier with a burst tyre. One aircraft from No. 150 Squadron caught fire while being refuelled after landing and was completely burnt out. The official history comments that:

> The Wellingtons flew 170 sorties against Naples, spread over three nights during the first week in August, and on the last occasion supplemented their bombs with 180,000 propaganda leaflets for the 'Mothers of Italy' and over a million for their sons in uniform. The producers of such propaganda make large claims for its effect but others regard the claims with scepticism, and the material with disgust.[3]

The Wellington squadrons were now being called upon to operate at a very high level, and on 3/4 August over a hundred aircraft attacked marshalling yards at Marina di Cantanzaro and Paola. Fifty-one aircraft were detailed for the first target, a yard on the eastern side of Italy now being used by the enemy to get supplies through to Sicily. They found the target area to be well illuminated, and many direct hits were claimed on the railway lines and repair shops. Three or four good fires were started in the yards, and much smoke was seen over the target area. Another fifty-seven aircraft took off for Paola, where, again, visibility was good and the illumination excellent. All the aircraft claimed to have bombed the station, locomotive sheds and marshalling yards, and one came down to 1,500 feet and strafed the marshalling yards. Photographic evidence suggested that both attacks were very successful.

Marshalling yards were again the targets for 4/5 August, when sixty aircraft were detailed to carry out a 'blitz' attack on Messina and forty-five at Battipaglia. The aircraft were warned to confine their bombing to the yards at Messina, as anything outside this area was regarded as 'friendly' due to the light naval craft that were harassing enemy shipping between the mainland and Sicily. Fifty-seven Wellingtons attacked the target, where numerous bursts and fires near the ferry terminal were reported. A 4,000-lb bomb was seen to burst in the yards, and another in the town. The majority of the aircraft claimed to have bombed the target area at Battipaglia, where a transformer station was hit and bursts were seen across the marshalling yards and engine sheds. One large fire was visible from twenty-five to thirty miles away.

As it became obvious that the enemy was withdrawing across the Strait of Messina, a series of attacks were made on the beaches to the north and south of Messina. Barges were being used to carry the troops away from Sicily in a 'Dunkirk'-style evacuation, although Messina itself was not to be bombed, as it was now regarded as 'friendly' territory. On the twelve nights between 5/6 and 16/17 August, attacks were made every night, and some 857 sorties despatched. Chappell records that the 'whole area of the Straits of Messina is now strongly defended by many flak batteries and night fighters', and twenty-five aircraft were lost.

Gunby provides us with some details on two of the losses from No. 40 Squadron. Flight Sergeant Harry Bartlett had been over the target for some time and had dropped half his bomb load. He then saw what he thought was 'one of the high level flares the Germans were supposed to be using'. He quickly realized that it was a Wellington 'going the other way and completely in flames – wings, fuselage, everything'. This must have been the aircraft piloted by Warrant Officer Henry Shepherd; no trace of the crew was ever found. Shortly afterwards, Bartlett's aircraft was hit by flak, and the starboard engine caught fire. He 'started the procedure to put out the fire – shut down engine, feather, press fire extinguisher button'. Unfortunately, the bomb aimer intervened and feathered the *port* engine, so the Wellington was now flying at 6,000 feet over hills, which were 4,000 feet high, with one engine stopped and the other throttled back and in flames. He was losing height quickly, and was then attacked by a night fighter. Running out of options, he gave the order to bale out, but was unable to reach his parachute and ditched the Wellington just off shore. Three of the crew were captured by German soldiers, and one was picked up by the Italians and later released. The fifth crew member either drowned or died when his chute failed to open.

Unfortunately, the heavy losses were not compensated for by a successful attempt to block the evacuation. The official history, commenting on all the air operations against Messina and its beaches, remarks that:

Interference with the evacuation from Sicily appears to have been inconsiderable, although the Germans record that thirteen craft were sank and three damaged. It is as easy to underestimate the effects of air operations such as these as it is to paint fanciful pictures based on claims which, though very probably true, cannot be proved. It is probably best, and nearest the truth, to form a mental picture of steady attrition which vexed the strong-willed and discouraged the irresolute among the enemy.[4]

And the official history of the RAF in the Second World War is even stronger on the ability of the Allies to complete the victory in Sicily 'by preventing the beaten Germans from leaving the island':

The answer was No. Hindered he was, but the losses he sustained were not great, despite the fact that the beaches and harbours, which he was using on both sides of the Strait, were subjected to continuous attack by fighter-bombers and by the Wellingtons of No. 205 Group, which bombed stretches of shore all along the toe of Italy.[5]

Despite all the efforts of the bombers, and despite the bombing of railways and roads in southern Italy, the Germans were able to withdraw the bulk of the forces that had fought in Sicily. They did this with great skill and resolution, and only at the very end did their departure become hurried – but even then it was never disorganized.

As well as the attacks on the beaches, the Wellingtons continued to bomb marshalling yards in Italy, at Naples, Lamezia, and Viterbo. On 6/7 August, fifty-two aircraft were despatched to attack the yards at Naples, where good illumination enabled the target to be positively identified. Bombs were seen to explode right on the yards, with three or four fires and one 'coloured explosion' particularly noticeable. One Wellington from No. 70 Squadron crashed ten miles north of Cape Maritimo, and one crew member was picked up by a mine-sweeper, alive and with only a broken arm. Another of No. 425 Squadron crashed just offshore near Cap Bon, killing all the crew. The body of the rear gunner was washed ashore the next day, but the remainder of the crew were trapped in the aircraft, which could not be salvaged due to the heavy seas. On 13/14 August, twenty-one aircraft attacked the marshalling yards at Lamezia, after American bombers had smashed bridges at each end, bottling up the contents. Illumination and visibility was excellent, and bombing was well concentrated. Eight large fires were started, and a huge explosion occurred in the centre of the yards. Twenty-three aircraft went back to Lamezia on 14/15 August, and fires were started there and in factory buildings south of the target.

On the next night forty-four aircraft attacked Viterbo, where the majority of flares fell wide of the aiming point and thin cloud made identification difficult for some of the Wellingtons. The bombing was hampered by the smoke from the flares hanging over the target, and seems to have been fairly well scattered according to some reports. However, many bursts were seen on and around the target area, and 4,000-pounders were dropped on the marshalling yards, the town, and on the barracks at the airfield. One aircraft of No. 420 Squadron got lost and jettisoned its bombs at an 'unknown location', and subsequently crash-landed near Kairouan after an engine cut. The last attack on marshalling yards, again at Viterbo, came on 16/17 August, but was spoiled by heavy mist and some cloud. Thirty-two aircraft claimed to have attacked the target area, many bombing on ETA or on flak positions. Results were unobserved except for two large fires, and it seems likely that the bombing was, again, widely scattered. One aircraft of No. 142 Squadron, captained by Wing Commander Augustus Gibbes, failed to return, and was believed to have been seen falling in flames near the target area. The crew of one Wellington of No. 104 Squadron baled out over Enfidaville due to a petrol stoppage, and although the aircraft was at around 600 feet when the captain left, there were no serious injuries. One aircraft of No. 150 Squadron crash-landed at Kelibia (south of El Haouaria) after an engine cut due to a petrol shortage.

As the campaign in Sicily came to an end, everyone in No. 205 Group was very tired after many nights of intensive operations. On 6 August Chappell records that he was feeling 'very washed out with so much night duty and insufficient sleep', and on 9 August that 'the only hope of rest is weather'. The Intelligence Officers from both No. 40 and No. 104 Squadrons were not functioning well, with one 'looking grey and tired and...short tempered' and the other was 'tired and briefed lethargically tonight'. A few days later one of the Intelligence Officers simply 'gave up', and caused 'an Intelligence crisis'!

On 12 August the Wing was entertained by Bob Hope, Frances Langford and Harry Pepper, performing on a hastily erected stage. A large audience watched the show, with the troops sitting on forms and on the ground or perched on trucks for grandstands. Bob Hope was 'very good indeed', and 'looked pale and tired but carried on gamely like a true comedian'. Frances Langford 'sang well and has a lovely figure so naturally she came over well'.

*   *   *

During the fighting in Sicily the Liberators and Halifaxes of Nos 178 and 462 Squadrons were still at Hosc Raui and under the control of USAAF 9 Bomber Command. They launched 186 sorties on sixteen nights from Libya, mainly against railway targets and airfields in Sicily and Southern Italy, although the numbers involved on each operation were always very small. On the night of the invasion eleven Halifaxes and two Liberators took off to carry out a diversionary attack on the Avila–Nata–San Paolo area of Sicily. Bombs were dropped at intervals and in small numbers all over the target area, and although no spectacular results were claimed, a number of small fires were seen in the area. A heavy air raid was observed to be in progress over Syracuse, which like other places on the east and south coasts of Sicily were brilliantly illuminated by flares. A large red pulsating fire was seen to the north in the direction of Catania, caused by their colleagues in the Wellington squadrons.

No operations were carried out on 10/11 July, and then on the next two nights the airfield at Reggio di Calabria was visited by fourteen and ten aircraft respectively. In the first attack, the airfield was straddled by bombs, and several small fires were seen around the perimeter and in hangars in the north-east corner. In the second attack, bursts were seen on the west and east sides of the airfield, and a small red fire started. The next operation was on 14/15 July, when ten Halifaxes and three Liberators took off to attack the railway station at Messina, which was already covered by glowing red fires from earlier attacks by B-17s. One of the Halifaxes of No. 462 Squadron was hit by flak and an order was given to bale out. Two of the crew later returned to the Squadron, reporting that they had come down in the sea off Cape Spartivento and were picked up by two different ships, but the others were lost without trace. On 15/16 July, seven aircraft attacked the airfield at Crotone, on the heel of Italy, and bursts were seen in the vicinity of the hangars and on the landing ground. A medium red fire was seen burning in the target area, and other fires covered the whole area of the airfield buildings.

On the 16th there were no operations carried out, but the ORB for No. 462 Squadron carried a reminder that death stalked the Middle East in many guises. LAC Samuel Lehrer – a 'Palestinian' and a maintenance assistant – died from typhus fever in the RAF Hospital at Benghazi. On 17/18 July, eight Halifaxes and one Liberator bombed railway facilities at Reggio di Calabria, where bursts were seen to the south of the target and one large blue-white fire and several small red fires started. One Halifax of No. 462 Squadron ditched after being hit by flak, and the crew were in their dinghy for eight days before being picked up by a destroyer. The target on 19/20 July was dispersed aircraft on Vibo Valentia airfield. Seven Halifaxes and two Liberators set off, but one Halifax of No. 178 Squadron returned early due to engine trouble. The other eight aircraft reached and bombed the target, where bursts were seen across the southern part of the landing ground, and several small fires were started. A large fire was observed burning among buildings north of the airfield, and other fires were seen in a hangar area inside the perimeter track.

The airfield at Reggio di Calabria was attacked on 23/24 and 26/27 July, with a total of twenty-two sorties launched. In the first attack a few bursts were seen at the southern end, and incendiaries seen burning along the eastern perimeter, but most of the bombs were believed to have fallen off target to the east and south. A large red fire started in the south was still visible twenty minutes after the aircraft left the target area. Seven Halifaxes and three Liberators took off on the second attack, but one Liberator jettisoned its bombs after experiencing engine failure. All the other aircraft located and bombed the target area, where three fires were started in the south-east corner of the airfield. One of the Halifaxes was attacked by an enemy fighter, which was seen to fall into the sea in flames, but due to the damage sustained during the attack the Halifax abandoned the operation and made for Malta. The marshalling yards at Reggio di Calabria were the target on 29/30 and 30/31 July, but in the first operation a dead calm settled over the airfield, and huge clouds of dust were raised by the first three aircraft that managed to take off. It became impossible for the others to operate, so the mission was cancelled and the three aircraft recalled. Nine Halifaxes and two Liberators took off in the second attack, and bursts were seen in the target area.

After a stand-down for two nights the bombers went back to Reggio di Calabria on 2/3 August, detailed to attack the marshalling yards and main railway station. All thirteen aircraft located and bombed the target area. Bursts were seen in many areas around the yards and in the town, and fires were started. One large fire just south of the marshalling yards gave off much black smoke, and a large red fire was also seen north of the town. The target was then switched to the marshalling yards and the harbour at San Giovanni between 5 and 14 August, with four attacks and sixty-two sorties flown. This represented a big effort by the four-engined bombers, but conditions over the target area were often poor and few positive results were recorded. Following the end of the fighting in Sicily there were no operations on 15/16 and 16/17 August, and an attack on the marshalling yards at Crotone on the toe of Italy on 17/18 August was cancelled. However, four attacks on the yards were launched between 18/19 and 27/28 August, with sixty-six sorties despatched and one Halifax of No. 462 Squadron lost on 18/19 August. The first two attacks were greatly hampered by haze, and many bombers failed to identify the yards clearly. The second two attacks fared much better, with clear visibility and good illumination, and analysis of the photographs obtained showed damage in the yards and adjacent chemical works. Extensive groups of fires were seen after the final attack on 27/28 August. The final operation in August was an attack on the airfield at Grottaglie on the heel of Italy by seventeen aircraft. However, weather and visibility was poor, and only four claimed to have identified and bombed the target area. One bombed a target of opportunity and the remainder abandoned the operation.

*   *   *

At 0635 hours on 17 August Captain Paul, commander of Engineer Battalion 771 in charge of the evacuation from Sicily, reported that the operation was complete. On the night of 17/18 August the Group was ordered to attack barges and railway lines and bridges between Briatico and Cape Suvero in an attempt to interfere with the withdrawal of Axis troops up the toe of Italy. Forty-seven aircraft claimed to have attacked various targets in the area with good visibility, and results were generally believed to have been very satisfactory. Small craft north of Pizzo and south-east of Suvero were found and attacked, railways and coastal towns were bombed, and fires were seen at Marina di Valentia, Pizzo and Lamezia. Two large explosions, believed to be fuel dumps, were seen near Pizzo, and direct hits were claimed on railway tracks and bridges three miles north of Pizzo. One aircraft of No. 420 Squadron failed to return.

There was now a lull on the ground as the Allied forces prepared for the invasion of the Italian mainland and negotiations were started between the new Italian government and the Allies. The shelling of the mainland from Messina began, with the battleships *Nelson* and *Rodney*, and later their sisters *Warspite* and *Valiant*, bombarding coastal-defence guns between Cape Pellaro and Melito at Calabria's southernmost point. Other warships made sweeps off Calabria's west coast and bombarded harbours, bridges, power stations and similar targets from Pellaro as far north as Scalea. On 3 September, Badoglio signed an armistice with the Allies in secret, and the Allies launched Operation *Baytown*, the invasion of mainland Italy. At 0345 hours on 3 September the Eighth Army's artillery opened fire on the Calabrian coast, and the assaulting troops crossed over without difficulties.

The bombers of No. 205 Group were mainly involved in attacking marshalling yards during this period, apart from a couple of attacks on coastal targets. The period literally began with a bang. An explosion occurred at Kairouan West at approximately 1500 hours on 18 August, while 'adjustments to the bombs for tonight's operations were being made'. The Wellington concerned was completely destroyed, and another aircraft standing nearby was also damaged by fire and written off. One aircraftsman was killed, and another was 'believed killed as no

198

identifiable remains of him could be found'. Another member of the ground crew was seriously injured and two slightly injured. Nevertheless, operations for the night, against a temporary bridge and its approaches on the River Angitola east of Pizzo, went ahead as planned. Forty Wellingtons took off, with the attack spread over one and a half hours. Mainly delayed action bombs were dropped, and thus no spectacular results were observed.

On 19/20 August, thirty-nine aircraft set off to bomb the coastal area at Pizzo, the majority selecting road and rail communications as their targets. A few bombed what was believed to be motor transport and barges on the beaches, and at least one bombed two small vessels seen offshore. One Wellington of No. 40 Squadron failed to return. During the early hours of the morning of 20 August, fog developed over the north-east Tunisian coast, and eventually covered all the Group's airfields. Nos 231 and 236 Wings landed the majority of their aircraft before the fog developed, but large-scale diversions were necessary for the aircraft of Nos 330 and 331 Wings. Altogether, forty-nine aircraft were successfully diverted, although there were four crash-landings by 331 Wing aircraft and one aircraft of No. 37 Squadron forced-landed. The need for additional emergency landing grounds was evident, and arrangements were made with the Americans for Enfidaville South and El Djem to be available at short notice when the Group was operating. Goubrines, Protville and El Aouina were also given diversion numbers.

From now on, the Group began a series of attacks on marshalling yards in order to disrupt traffic into Calabria by the west coast route and into Apulia by the east coast route. The railway targets included Foggia, Villa Literno, Battipaglia, Salerno, Bagnoli, Torre Annunziata, Taranto, Civitavecchia, and Aversa. Fourteen attacks were made between 19 August and 1 September and 947 sorties were flown, and the results were generally satisfactory. Nine aircraft were lost. In a major attack on the marshalling yards at Taranto on 25/26 August, eighty-two Wellingtons took off, and seventy-seven bombed the yards. Opposition was considerably less than had been expected, and a significant feature of the operation was that very little flak came from the inner and outer harbours, despite the presence there of units of the Italian Fleet. The bombers had attacked the yards at Torre Annunziata on 24/25 August, but subsequent photographs revealed that the bombing had been concentrated on the steelworks, leaving the marshalling yards comparatively undamaged. Eighty-three aircraft took off on 29/30 to try again, attacking in two waves. American medium bombers had attacked the same target during the day, and early arrivals reported dull red fires still burning in the target area. The whole district was visible by the light of well-placed flares, and the first wave started many small fires, some of which were still burning when the second attack developed.

The destruction of the Italian railway system continued with a particularly successful attack on Civitavecchia marshalling yards on 30/31 August. The city had a large and distinctive harbour area, and many important industrial plants and railway sidings to the north and south of the town. The first wave started fires that were visible eighty miles away, and these were still burning fiercely when the second wave started their attack. Many bursts were seen in the target area, and more fires were started, which were visible from the Sardinian coast. The whole area was described as 'one big fire', with fires seen in the chemical works, storage tanks, cement works and transformer station. The Wellingtons were ordered to fly over Rome on return in order to find out whether it was an open city. They were not fired on over the city, but some guns in the outer suburbs did open fire.

The Group's efforts during the month of August in support of the Allied ground operations in Sicily did not go without recognition from its masters. On 24 August, General Spaatz, Commanding General NAAF, visited Kairouan to present American decorations to officers of the Group and Nos 330 and 331 Wings, and the following day a message of commendation and congratulation was received from General Doolittle, General Commanding NASAF. On 28 August, warning was received that it would be necessary to move all the Wellington Wings from the Kairouan area to 'a new location outside African territory – this being in view of the approaching rains when it would be impossible to operate'. Preliminary preparations for the move were begun, but there were concerns about the Group's general state of mobility. Many of its motor vehicles were unserviceable, and urgent steps were taken to obtain the necessary replacement engines and other spares. The month of September opened with another warning signal to the effect that the Group was to be prepared to move to Malta. On 6 September, it was transferred completely from the Middle East Command to NASAF, but on the 13th it was confirmed that administrative control would lie with NAAF and operational control only with NASAF. Nevertheless, this was an historic change of command in that No. 205 Group now ceased to be a 'Middle East' formation, and its immediate future was 'now completely joined with that of the Allied Air Forces operating Northwards over Europe'. On 16 September the move to Malta was cancelled, and the Group was informed that it would stay in its present location until mid-November, when it would move to the Italian mainland.

The first target attacked in September was the marshalling yard at Aversa, a comparatively small yard north of Naples, and the Group ORB states that General Doolittle flew as second pilot in one of the aircraft of No. 331 Wing. The forty Wellingtons that took off found 8 to 9/10 cloud over the Italian coast and the target area, and both flares and bombing were somewhat scattered. Despite this, many crews claimed to have bombed the target, but others simply bombed 'somewhere in the area'. The invasion of the Italian mainland then meant that No. 205 Group would have to step up its efforts again, and airfields would return to the top of the target list.

*   *   *

On 3 September, the Eighth Army crossed the Strait of Messina unmolested, and by 5 September had captured San Stefano, ten miles inland. The German High Command had already decided that Calabria was expendable, and the few troops in the 'toe' and 'heel' of Italy gradually fell back as the Allies advanced. Meanwhile, the Italian government dithered, and in order to push them into action Eisenhower announced the Italian unconditional surrender on 8 September. Since the fall of Mussolini on 25 August, the Germans had been making preparations to ensure that all the functions formerly performed by the Italians would continue, even if Italy collapsed. It was also necessary to provide for the defence of southern Italy, and German troops had been assembled in the north for this purpose. Following Eisenhower's announcement, all Italian forces within the German-controlled areas of Italy, southern France, Yugoslavia, Albania and Greece were quickly disarmed and made prisoners of war.

German troops occupied Rome on 10 September, the day after the US Fifth Army landed at Salerno (Operation *Avalanche*), and Taranto was occupied by the British without resistance. At Salerno, the Allies met a hostile, strong and determined enemy, which disputed the landings with the utmost fury. For a few days the position was extremely serious, and the Allies briefly contemplated an evacuation. On the 17th, the Germans began a withdrawal from Salerno as the Eighth Army joined forces with the British and US troops in the beachhead. A few days later the Eighth Army had taken Bari, and by the end of September the Allies had reached Pompeii and were advancing on Naples. Marshal Badoglio and Eisenhower met aboard HMS *Nelson*, where a full armistice was signed.

The invasion of the Italian mainland meant that No. 205 Group would have to step up its efforts again, and airfields would return to the top of the target list. The landing grounds at Capodichino and Capua in the Naples area were the targets on 3/4 September, with fifty aircraft detailed for the former and thirty for the latter. Cloud, again, interfered with the operation, and the bombers had to search for pinpoints on the coast and in the target areas. The Capodichino attack was judged to have been only 'fairly successful', with a few scattered fires caused and some damage to hangars. The results at Capua were a bit better, and subsequent photographs revealed severe damage to buildings, cratering of dispersals, and eight aircraft damaged on the ground.

On 4/5 September the bombers went to the airfields at Grazzanise, north of Naples. The forty-three aircraft despatched to Grazzanise Main encountered cloudy conditions that made identification of the target difficult, and the results of the bombing were largely unobserved. Photographs later revealed that some of the aircraft bombed an area four miles ENE of the airfield, where an ammunition dump was destroyed. The thirty-seven aircraft sent to Grazzanise Satellite also met with cloud and electrical storms over the Italian coast, although the target area was clear. The actual target was difficult to find as there were no outstanding pinpoints, and no spectacular results were observed due to the large number of delayed action bombs carried. One of the Wellingtons of No. 37 Squadron caught fire over the target area, and was forced to jettison its bombs. The Captain remained in control of the aircraft while the crew fought the flames, which were eventually extinguished and the aircraft returned safely to base. One aircraft of No. 70 Squadron failed to return, and was reported to have caught fire and come down over the target area. Four parachutes were seen, and two of the crew who baled out were later released by the Italians.

On 5/6 September, fifty aircraft were detailed to attack the marshalling yards at Villa Literno, twenty miles north of Naples, but one aircraft of No. 142 Squadron crashed just after take off. Forty-eight Wellingtons bombed the target, and two 4,000-lb bombs fell in the centre and in the south end of the yards respectively. Incendiaries straddled the target, and two of the fires that were started were visible thirty miles away. A large orange explosion was also seen, and all indications were that the attack had been very successful. On the following night the marshalling yards at Battipaglia, fifteen miles south-east of Salerno, were attacked. A large accumulation of trucks had been reported in the yards, and forty-eight aircraft bombed the target in what again appeared to have been a highly successful raid. The yards were straddled with incendiaries, the repair depot and station were left burning, and one fire was visible fifty miles away. No. 424 Squadron ORB stated: 'A very concentrated effort, which must have given this target a very good pasting and put the Marshalling Yards out of joint for quite some time.' One of their aircraft failed to return, and was believed to have been shot down over the target.

On 7/8 September, fifty Wellingtons were detailed to attack the Viterbo Landing Ground, but the location of the target proved difficult due to haze and the main batch of flares was dropped over open country some five to ten miles west of the target. Consequently, the bombing was very scattered, and it was believed that most of the bombs fell in the open countryside. One Wellington of No. 104 Squadron burst a tyre on take-off, and it immediately burst into flames. All the crew were able to escape through the various escape hatches, and were uninjured except for cuts and minor burns. The Captain quickly ran to another aircraft that was parked nearby, and was able to taxi it to a dispersal area. All the bombs in the burning aircraft bar one exploded simultaneously, and the remaining one was disposed of the following day. Chappell records that 'Wing Commander Mount set the example by taking off over the still-burning debris and the other crews followed.' Chappell also tells a nice little story about the Australians in the Wellington squadrons:

> The Australians were a practical lot who readily became attuned to desert conditions. The weird and wonderful creatures that crawled and flew in the desert held few fears for them and horned vipers, scorpions, giant spiders and the ubiquitous dung beetles, became objects of fun and provided a means of playing practical jokes on the others, a form of humour not always enjoyed by the recipients.

On the night of 8/9 September, NASAF called for one hundred sorties on five targets near Salerno, the main object being to create a diversion to distract attention from the landings. As the aircraft were taking off, news came through that Italy had surrendered, but NASAF confirmed that the operations were to proceed. The main attacks were to be against Eboli and Battipaglia, while three diversionary attacks were also to be made against gun emplacements at Formia, the docks at Gaeta, and shipping in Forio harbour. Forty-one aircraft attacked the Eboli area in what was regarded as a well concentrated and successful operation. Some accurate heavy AA fire was encountered, and two aircraft of No. 70 Squadron were hit and one of these crash-landed on return. Thirty-seven bombed at Battipaglia, where the bombing was again well concentrated, with many sticks falling on the yards. The attacks on Formia, Gaeta, and Forio were also carried out successfully. No gun positions were seen at Formio, but the aircraft bombed roads and railways, and fires were observed in the town area. In all, a total of 104 sorties were despatched for the loss of the single aircraft of No. 70 Squadron.

On 9/10 September, the Wellingtons were detailed to attack the marshalling yards at Grosseto, on the main double track line between Rome and Livorno. Fifty-one aircraft attacked the target, which was well illuminated. Many bombs were seen to fall on the yards, and several fires were started. One aircraft of No. 142 Squadron failed to return after having sent an SOS, and it transpired that it had ditched in the sea between the target and Sicily. The crew were later picked up by a hospital ship. The task allotted on 10/11 September was the destruction of a road junction at Formia, north of Naples, and forty-nine aircraft attacked the target. The illumination was quite accurate and effective, and many bomb bursts were seen on the junction. One large and several small fires were left burning, and some bombs also fell on the nearby railway, setting off a number of explosions. The original orders for the next night called for a repeat of the attack on Formia, but the target was switched to the airfield at Frosinone, forty miles south of Rome, where over 100 aircraft had been reported. The attack was to be made in two waves, and the fifty-eight aircraft in the first wave attacked between 2100 and 2142 hours. Aircraft on the ground were left burning, large fires were seen in various buildings around the airfield, and a direct hit with a 4,000-pounder was scored on a hangar. Enemy aircraft took off during the attack, and one Wellington rear gunner 'had a brief but uneventful encounter with a Ju 88'. Forty Wellingtons took off on the second attack, bombing between 0059 and 0128 hours. Fires started during the first attack were still burning when the second wave reached the target. Their attack was rather scattered, but bursts were seen close to hangars and some new fires were started.

The Eighth Army occupied Brindisi on 11 September, and the following day Mussolini, held prisoner by the Badoglio government on the Gran Sasso, was rescued by German paratroopers who landed in gliders on top of the mountain. At Salerno, things were not going well. Although the beaches chosen for the landings were very suitable for an amphibious operation, the area was dominated by the hills and mountains that surrounded it on all sides but one. On 12 September, heavy German counter-attacks by six divisions forced the Fifth Army back to within five miles of beaches. The critical period was from 12 to 14 September, but the counter-attacks were halted and the beachhead held. Meanwhile, the Eighth Army encountered little resistance, and was moving in its usual ponderous manner up from the south and south-east of Italy. On the 17th the Germans began a withdrawal from Salerno, and on the 19th the Eighth Army joined forces with the British and US troops at Potenza. The enemy planned to hold a line south of Rome running from Gaeta through Isernia to Vasto, fighting a series of delaying actions as he retreated.

Road communications were the targets for the Group during the crisis at Salerno. On 12/13 September, it was called upon to bomb an important road junction near Castel Nuovo, and sixty-five aircraft attacked the target. The visibility was very good, the flares were very accurate, and all the Wellingtons found and bombed the junction without difficulty. Numerous bomb bursts were seen on the aiming point, and the last crews to leave were confident that the cross roads had been obliterated and 'should be out of use for some considerable time to come'. Photographs confirmed the accuracy of the bombing, with direct hits blocking the road leading west, and the other three roads were destroyed for lengths of about 250 yards. On 13/14 September, the targets given to the Group changed three times throughout the day, but, eventually, a road five miles east of Pompeii was selected. Ninety-two aircraft bombed the target in good weather and good illumination, and crews had no difficulty in locating the appropriate stretch of road. Many direct hits were claimed, and fires were started among stationary vehicles on the side of the road.

On 14/15 September, NASAF called for 'everything we could put into the air' for an attack on roads between Battipaglia and Eboli, and 128 Wellingtons took off (including one detailed for nickelling over Italy). The purpose of the raid was to render the road unserviceable for German Panzer Divisions operating against the Salerno beachhead from the East, and bombing had to be accurate as Allied troops were reported to be immediately west of Battipaglia. The bomb loads included seventeen 4,000-pounders, and more than a thousand 250-lb bombs were also dropped on the roads and towns. This was a record night for the Group, but was surpassed on the following night when the Group put 132 aircraft into the air (including three nickellers). Once again, the purpose was to continue to disrupt road communications in the Salerno area, the targets being roads between Torre Annunziata and Pompeii. Special attention was to be paid to a road junction immediately south-west of the Pompeii ruins, where the Herman Göring Division was reported to be concentrated. Another record tonnage of bombs was dropped, with all crews claiming to have identified the target in good visibility and excellent illumination, and the excellent results were later confirmed by daylight photographs.

By the night of 16/17 September, the German opposition at Salerno was weakening, and the Group's efforts were switched to airfields for three nights. The first attack was on the Cisterna Littoria airfield south of Rome, which had so far escaped attack by Allied bombers. The target was well covered with bombs, and up to fourteen burning aircraft were counted. Towards the end of the attack there was a violent explosion that threw smoke up to 1,000 feet, hampering the observation of results by the aircraft that attacked late in the raid. The last aircraft to leave reported that the whole area was blazing, and all indications were that the raid was an outstanding success. Photographic reconnaissance confirmed severe damage to the central and eastern hangars, and a direct hit on the western hangar. Runways and aprons were well cratered, and eleven aircraft were destroyed on the ground. The Rome–Naples railway line adjoining the landing ground also received a direct hit.

On 17 September a nice little story was reported in the No. 70 Squadron ORB. One of its Wellington IIIs (HF680) was declared to be 'tour-expired' and sent to the Repair Unit. The aircraft was one of a batch of 153 Wellington IIIs, Xs and XIs delivered between September 1942 and February 1943 by Vickers-Armstrongs, Squires Gate. It had arrived in the Middle East via No. 1446 Flight and No. 1 OADU, and had a very successful tour of operations consisting of forty-one successful trips with the Squadron. The ORB states that the 'old aircraft was given a hearty send off by the ground crews who have a high regard of its capabilities'. After its overhaul at the Repair Unit, the Wellington was passed on to No. 40 Squadron, and was eventually struck off charge on 25 January 1945. Another 'grand old aircraft to be sent away at this time' was DF689 with 317.33 hours to its credit and 44 successful operational trips. This aircraft, too, ended up with No. 40 Squadron, and was struck off charge on 25 January 1945.

On 17/18 September the target was Cerveteri, fifteen miles north-west of Rome, and seventy-three Wellingtons of all four Wings were despatched. Many aircraft had difficulty in pinpointing the target due to considerable haze and darkness, and the illumination was scattered. Photographs taken during the raid revealed that Furbara, two miles away, received the brunt of the attack, but despite this many fires were started at Cerveteri and aircraft on the ground were reported to be burning. Daylight photographs taken on the 19th confirmed the destruction of several buildings, damage to others, and craters on the landing ground. The western hangar had received a direct hit, and four Ju 52s and one other aircraft were burnt out. One of the Wellingtons of No. 40 Squadron failed to return, and other crews reported seeing an aircraft fall into the sea in flames off the target area. The aircraft was one of the illuminators, and one report suggested that the fire may have started from a hung-up flare. On the next night the target was Viterbo, and fifty-five aircraft attacked the target in two waves in the early hours of the morning. The aircraft of the first wave identified the target, illumination was good, and bombing was well concentrated over the airfield. One particularly large explosion sent smoke up to 5,000 feet, and hangars and aircraft on the ground were set on fire. The results of the second wave were not so spectacular, though several fires were started and bombs were seen to burst across the hangars and dispersal. One aircraft of No. 37 Squadron was missing, believed shot down over the target.

On 19/20 September, NASAF ordered an attack on a battle area target – the destruction of the River Calore road bridge at Benevento, fifty miles north of Salerno. Benevento was an important road and rail junction north-east of Naples in the valley of the Calore, and therefore an important focal point for routes to and from the battle area, which at the moment stretched across Italy east of Castellammare. Thirty-nine aircraft attacked the target, and one direct hit and several near misses were claimed. The approaches on either side of the river were covered by bombs, and the marshalling yards and railway station also received hits. A large explosion followed by a fire occurred north of the bridge, and a big fire was also observed at the south end. It was believed that considerable damage had been done to the bridge, and that it might be out of use for some time. On the next night, NASAF ordered a repetition of the previous night's attack, with special attention to the railway area to the north of Benevento. Of the fifty-one Wellingtons that took off, only thirty-eight were able to locate and bomb the target due to cloud. Bombs were seen to fall on the marshalling yards and roads, and the aircraft claimed to have straddled the bridge. Two 4,000-pounders fell in the town and on buildings north of the river. Some seven fires, one of them fairly large, were seen on the area between the bridge and the marshalling yards and one fire was burning in the centre of the town.

On 21/22 September, an attack was ordered on docks and shipping at Bastia (Corsica) to hamper the enemy retreat from the island. The weather en route to the target was not good, and one of the illuminators lost its way and dropped its flares twenty-five minutes late. Nevertheless, seventy-six Wellingtons attacked, and the raid appeared to be very successful. Ships, docks, warehouses, oil tanks and the mole all received direct hits. Reports indicated that up to three ships may have been hit, one burning with orange flames. Aircraft returning from the first wave reported that fires in the oil storage tanks were visible from twenty-five miles. By the time the last aircraft left the area, three main fires could be seen from seventy miles away. One of the Wellingtons of No. 104 Squadron force-landed in the sea off Marittimo after having sent an SOS at 0704 hours. An ASR (Air-Sea Rescue) operation was launched from Tunis, and the complete crew was picked up unhurt on the following day and taken to Borizzo.

As the Allies pushed towards Naples, the small town of Formia became a focal point for attempts to disrupt road and rail communications to the north of the city, and four attacks were made between 22 and 30 September and 200 sorties despatched. Forty-six aircraft attacked Formia on 22/23 September, but results were not spectacular. Hits were reported on both road and rail communications, and one 4,000-pounder fell between the roads at the junction east of the town. Two bombs were thought to have exploded on the factory south of the target, a 4,000-pounder burst 200 yards north of the factory, and a number of fires were left burning in the target area. In the attack on 25/26 September, the main objective was the main road to the east of the town, which connected Naples with the north. The road was very close to the coast on one side and to steep hills on the other, and, consequently, would be difficult to repair or bypass if heavily bombed. Forty-nine aircraft attacked in poor visibility, and the bombing was rather scattered and results difficult to observe. The attack appeared to be moderately successful, however, and hits on the cross roads and on other roads in the area were reported. One stick of bombs fell on the railway junction, and it was believed that a factory building near the road junction received a direct hit with a 4,000-pounder. During the return journey two aircraft collided over Ponza, but both returned safely to base with only slight damage and no injuries. One had its rudder rendered useless, and on landing it was found that it was at an angle of about forty degrees to the tail fin.

During the afternoon of 28 September the Kairouan area was hit by a violent thunderstorm, with torrential rain that lasted for over two hours. The airfield at Hani West (Nos 40 and 104 Squadrons) was completely flooded, and Nos 142 and 150 Squadrons at Kairouan West reported that their whole campsite was 'very muddy after a couple of hours' rain – the first for two months'. No. 424 Squadron at Hani East reported that a violent storm started at 1530 hours. The rain came down in buckets, and high winds blew up. The camp movie show had to be cancelled as the YMCA truck could not get through because of the road conditions. It was followed by the coldest night since the unit arrived in Africa. Hani East was a new landing ground being built by American engineers on high ground, and only one semi-permanent strip with a taxi track had been completed. There were hard standings for over a hundred aircraft marked out but not surfaced, and Group personnel were used to complete the approach roads to enable aircraft to be placed there. Other units moved their camp sites or parts of them to whatever high ground was in the vicinity. On 30 September No. 104 Squadron ORB reports that the MT section was moved out of a valley and up to higher ground to avoid flooding in the approaching rainy season. Orders were also issued by the commanding officer that anti-malarial precautions should commence. Issues of quinine tablets for aircrew and Mepacrine for ground staff were made by the MO, and mosquito nets were to be used and slacks and long-sleeved shirts to be worn after sunset. The Group ORB also remarks that the month of September was a notable one in that the camouflaging of all units was carried out 'with the aid of an American unit'. It goes on to say that the 'appearance of 205 Group changed from that of a purely desert formation to that of a force for use in types of country quite different to the deserts of Libya and Tripolitania'.

The next attack on Formia came on 29/30 September, after a stand-down for three nights due to the bad weather. Forty-four Wellingtons took off on the operation, and the crews all stated that illumination was good and the target was clearly identified. The bombing seems to have been well concentrated in the target area, although no fires were seen. The Wellingtons then went back to Formia on the last night of the month, when fifty-one aircraft were detailed. The weather forecast promised thunderstorms over the sea between the mainland and Sicily, and these were so severe that twelve aircraft found them impassable and abandoned operations. Five more aircraft returned early for other reasons, and one of No. 37

Squadron crashed near Menzel Temimi on the outward journey due to engine failure. The crew baled out safely, with the exception of the pilot, who jumped too low for his parachute to open and was killed. Thirty-seven aircraft reached the target area and found the weather to be good there, but the bombing was rather scattered. Many bursts were claimed on the road, and a fierce fire was reported among buildings east of the target. A brilliant green flash was also observed.

In between the first two and the last two attacks on Formia, the Group carried out major raids on Pisa and Livorno. On 23/24 September, thirty-nine aircraft bombed the marshalling yards at Pisa in a fifteen-minute blitz. Illumination was particularly good, and the yards stood out well. Bursts were seen all along the target, which were later covered by smoke and dust making observation of individual results difficult. Much rolling stock was seen and a number of fires were started, and two large explosions were reported. At the same time, forty-one Wellingtons bombed the San Giusto airfield at Pisa, where many aircraft were seen on the landing ground, and up to ten were claimed as destroyed. Bombs fell across the landing area, dispersals and hangars, causing many fires and explosions. Fires from Pisa were visible ninety miles away as the aircraft were leaving, and there was little doubt that a very good night's work was done. Daylight photographs later revealed that all through tracks in the marshalling yards were cut. One aircraft of No. 70 Squadron failed to return, and nothing was heard from it after take-off. One of No. 142 Squadron's aircraft ditched on the way out, but the entire crew were picked up by an infantry landing craft en route from North Africa to Syracuse.

The docks and shipping at Livorno were the targets on 24/25 September, and seventy-nine aircraft carried out a well concentrated attack. At the beginning of the raid, ships were seen to be steaming from the harbour to the open sea, and some crews reported near misses on these vessels. Illumination was good for the main attack, and the docks were well covered with bombs. One stick across a quay started a fire, suspected to be from oil storage tanks or a tanker, the glow from which was later visible from Elba. It was believed that the thermal power station was also hit. Twenty or more barges were observed in the target area, and direct hits were claimed on them, and one direct hit and several near misses on larger vessels were also reported. Daylight reconnaissance later confirmed five direct hits on the railway, damage to a chemical works and torpedo factory and hits in the dock area. One aircraft of No. 150 Squadron failed to return, and may have been the Wellington seen leaving the target with the port engine on fire. Another aircraft of No. 150 Squadron crash-landed and was burnt out, but the crew were all unhurt.

*   *   *

The two squadrons of four-engined bombers at Hosc Raui only managed 151 sorties in September, and twenty-one of these were abortive for various reasons. Four Liberators and sixteen Halifaxes were despatched to attack the airfield at Grottaglie, ten miles east of Taranto, on 3/4 September. The engine of one of the Halifaxes caught fire shortly after take-off, and it jettisoned its bombs and returned. Another was unable to identify the target, and was returning with its bombs when an engine failed while it was circling the base. It was forced to jettison the bombs into the sea, and made a successful landing. The illuminating aircraft from No. 462 Squadron also ran into problems. It dropped a flare on ETA, which failed to ignite, and then lost sight of the target. It failed to find it again, but dropped its flares anyway, hoping that this might enable the other flare droppers of No. 178 Squadron to pinpoint the target. However, most of the rest of the aircraft bombed on these flares, which were later believed to have been well off target. To end a bad night, one of the Halifaxes of of No. 178 Squadron failed to return, and all crews reported that they had seen an aircraft burst into flames over the target. It was seen to fall in a spin, and exploded on the ground, burning for a considerable time.

Their next operation, on 7/8 September, was to the airfield at Manduria, a few miles south of Grottaglie. Five Liberators and thirteen Halifaxes took off, but one Halifax returned early with engine trouble after jettisoning its bombs, and one of the Liberators was unable to locate the target and returned with its bombs. Once again, the illumination 'did not go according to plan'. One of the illuminators dropped its flares over the airfield at San Pancrazio, five miles from Manduria, and the other illuminated Manduria town. Most of the bombs fell on San Pancrazio, where bursts were seen but no results observed, and the rest on Manduria town. This was the last time that Halifaxes operated with No. 178 Squadron, as it was gradually receiving more Liberators and would once again become an all-Liberator squadron.

Between 10 and 16 September, the four-engined bombers made five attacks (forty-one sorties) on road communications at Potenza, in support of the Salerno landings. All the reports suggest that the bombers successfully located and bombed the target area in all five attacks, with good results. In the attack on 15/16 September, the aircraft were directed to bomb supply dumps at Potenza, but the illuminator from No. 462 Squadron dropped its flares three to five miles off target. However, most of the aircraft identified the target area, but no supply dumps were seen. Two of the Halifaxes and three Liberators bombed roads and railway communications around Potenza. One Liberator decided not to bomb due to confusion over some lights seen near the target, and jettisoned its bombs.

The bombers then switched their attention to the marshalling yards at Foggia, but the attack by only eight aircraft on 17/18 September can have done little damage. Bursts were seen across warehouses due north of the yards, and fires and explosions reported in the target area. The month ended with five attacks on airfields in Rhodes and Greece, at Maritza, Calato, Kalamaki, Larissa and Argos. Illumination was sometimes a problem once again, and failed completely in the attack by fifteen aircraft on Larissa on 27/28 September. One Halifax illuminator returned to base with engine trouble, and the other was hit by flak and went out of control after dropping some if its flares. None of the five Liberators were able to definitely identify the target, and three bombed what was believed to be the airfield and the other two jettisoned their bombs. Four Halifaxes bombed the target, but no results were observed. Three jettisoned their bombs, and one bombed flak concentrations believed to have been a few miles south-east of Lamia. One of the Halifaxes crashed on landing and burst into flames, but all the crew were safe.

On 26 September, Mediterranean Air Command signalled that No. 240 Wing HQ and No. 462 Squadron were to move from Hosc Raui to Malta, and that on arrival there they would come under the complete control of NAAF through No. 205 Group. The Liberators of No. 178 Squadron were to remain at Hosc Raui to complete its re-equipment, and then to rejoin No. 240 Wing. However, the move was later cancelled pending the move of all the bombers to Italy. Instead, the

Liberators and Halifaxes of No. 240 Wing moved just a couple of miles south to a new airfield at Terria, completing the move on 1 October.

*   *   *

The night bombers operated on 80 of the 84 nights between the invasion of Sicily and the end of September 1942, flew 5,863 sorties, and lost 81 aircraft. On twelve nights the Wellingtons and four-engined bombers launched more than 100 sorties, mainly in support of the landings in Sicily and Italy, and on another 26 nights they flew more than 80 sorties. For the first time, the emphasis was on railway targets (32 per cent), the main purpose of which was to prevent reinforcements from moving south through Italy, and airfields received 23 per cent of the sorties. Military targets in the battle area took up 18 per cent of the total effort, and another 987 sorties (17 per cent of the effort) were involved in the attacks on the beaches on the Straits of Sicily to try to hamper the evacuation of the island.

NOTES

1. The AHB Narrative *The Sicilian Campaign* states that No. 331 Wing also had the services of No. 2 Mobile Photographic Unit (detached from the 3rd Photographic Group). This was probably the 3rd Photographic Reconnaissance and Mapping Group, which operated under the control of NASAF. It flew Lockheed Lightning F-4s and F-5s and its airfields were located in the Kairouan area.
2. The Mark III featured the 1,375-hp Bristol Hercules III or XI engine and a four-gun tail turret, instead of two-gun. A total of 1,519 Mark IIIs were built and they had become the mainstays of Bomber Command through 1941. The Mark X was the most widely produced variant, of which 3,804 were built. It was similar to the Mark III except for the 1,675-hp Hercules VI or XVI power plant and a fuselage structure of light alloy instead of steel.
3. TMAME, Volume V, page 172.
4. TMAME, Volume V, page 171.
5. Richards and Saunders, *The Royal Air Force 1939–1945*, Vol 2, page 322.

CHAPTER NINE

The Group Moves to Foggia – October to December 1943

As September 1943 came to an end, two important objectives were achieved by the Allies in Italy. On 27 September, Foggia was occupied by the 4th Armoured Brigade, and on 1 October a squadron of the King's Dragoon Guards reached the centre of Naples. On 3 October the Special Service Brigade landed at Termoli, forty miles north of Foggia, and quickly linked up with troops moving north from Foggia. However, powerful German forces were on their way to the Termoli area, and the British had a tough fight to hold their position. Reinforcements were rushed in, and by the 6th the Germans had had enough and withdrew north-westwards. On 7 October the US Fifth Army was halted by German defences along the River Volturno, twenty miles North of Naples, and five days later began a major offensive to cross the river. Although bogged down by bad weather and skilful German defence, the Americans made gradual progress, and Kesselring eventually gave permission for a step-by-step withdrawal. This began on 14 October, and by 24 October the XIV Panzer Corps had retreated to the general line Raviscanina–Mondragone. By the end of the month both the US Fifth Army and the British Eighth Army had resumed the offensive, and made steady progress. The Fifth Army captured Isernia, fifty miles North of Naples, on 4 November, and linked up with Eighth Army moving north-west from Foggia.

On 2 October, the air forces received a message of congratulations from the Commanding General 15th Army Group (General Alexander) to the Commander of the Northwest African Air Force (General Spaatz), and it is quoted in full in the ORB of No. 104 Squadron:

> I have just returned from an extensive tour of the Fifth Army Front during which I talked with the Army and many subordinate commanders, their staffs and other ranks. General Clark has asked me to convey to you and to the Officers and men of the Northwest African Air Force whom you command, the sincere thanks and appreciation of the Fifth Army for the magnificent air support which has been given them. It has greatly heartened the ground forces and has contributed much to the success of their operations. All were most enthusiastic in their acclaim of the close and continuous support which has been given them by the Air Force.
>
> To the foregoing I would like to add my own appreciation and admiration of a task well done. Not only have your tremendous air attacks added greatly to the morale of the ground and naval forces but, in addition, they have inflicted on the enemy heavy losses in men and equipment. They have seriously interfered with his movements, interrupted his communications, and prevented his concentration of the necessary forces to launch large scale

attacks. You have contributed immeasurably to the success of our operations, and to the final victory which will inevitably follow.

Although No. 205 Group and the heavy bombers at Hosc Raui played only a small part in the air operations, their contribution to the round-the-clock bombing of roads, airfields and marshalling yards deserved recognition. The daylight attacks by the Tactical Air Forces and the USAAF heavy bombers were complemented by the activities of our small force of night bombers, and gave the enemy little respite from attack. The Wellingtons of No. 205 Group operated at a lower level during October 1943, launching only 916 sorties on nineteen nights. Of these, 33 per cent each went to railway targets and in support of the ground forces, and 30 per cent were directed at airfields.

*   *   *

In the first few days in October the Wellingtons continued their attacks on communications and airfields. On 1/2 October, forty sorties were ordered for an attack on pontoon bridges across the Volturno near Grazzanize, and another forty on road communications at Formia, fifty miles north of Naples. Eighty-three aircraft took off, but weather conditions again interfered with operations and thirteen returned early. The illumination for the attack on the bridges was poor, but visibility was good and most crews reported finding the target area with little difficulty. The northern pontoon bridge was swung back against the east bank of the river when the aircraft attacked, and the actual position was difficult to spot. Most dropped on the estimated position of the target, and the area was well covered with bombs, although no hits were claimed. Only one crew reported a direct hit on the town pontoon, and generally the bombing was scattered and inaccurate. The majority of aircraft claimed to have attacked the target at Formia, and photographs taken with the bombing confirmed that most of the bombs hit the target area.

Four aircraft were lost in these attacks. One Wellington of No. 37 Squadron was unable to locate base due to cloud and rain, and as its fuel was running short, the crew baled out near Korba – all landed safely. One of No. 40 Squadron's aircraft hit a pylon and was wrecked while attempting to land at Djedeidia, the crew escaping with minor injuries. Two aircraft of No. 424 Squadron failed to return, and nothing was heard from one of them after take-off. One of the aircraft signalled that it was returning to base with engine trouble, but gave no position and nothing further was heard. It transpired that the aircraft had ditched due to engine failure, and the crew carried out their dinghy drill with complete success. Other crews reported distress signals from the sea, and the complete crew was picked up by an American destroyer and landed at Oran.

Bad weather prevented operations on the next night, but on 3/4 fifty-two Wellingtons were despatched to attack the marshalling yards at Civitavecchia. The weather over the target was good, and the illumination was excellent. Many bursts were seen across the yards, direct hits were scored with two 4,000-lb bombs, and several fires were started. Oil storage tanks were also hit, and the area became enveloped in a pall of black smoke as the attack developed. One of the Wellingtons of No. 425 Squadron crash-landed at Oudna on return due to a failure of both engines, but the crew were uninjured. On the next night, and for the sixth time during the past fortnight, roads in the Formia area were the target for the

211

Wellingtons. The intention was to keep the important through road blocked to reinforcements moving south to the battlefront. The target was attacked by fifty aircraft, and the bombing was well concentrated. One 4,000-lb bomb was seen to burst a few yards north of the road, causing a huge cloud of dust and debris. Other direct hits were seen on the coastal road, and several fires started.

One aircraft of No. 104 Squadron failed to return, and some crews reported distress signals coming from the sea. The crew subsequently returned to their unit with a good tale to tell. They had bombed the target, but had been hit by light flak on the last run and both engines were damaged. The Wellington turned south, slowly losing height, and then turned east towards the coast. Despite having itsbomb doors wide open and the undercarriage down due to a failure of the hydraulic system, it ditched successfully two miles off the mouth of the Volturno. The captain, Flight Lieutenant McDermott, was injured but the rest of the crew escaped with minor cuts and bruises. The pilot's cabin was completely submerged, but the aircraft remained afloat for about three minutes and the crew took to the dinghy and paddled towards the shore. After two hours' paddling they landed and started to walk south along the shore through minefields and barbed-wire entanglements. At daybreak the crew met three Italians who were in search of pig food, and were entertained to breakfast. Eventually, they were taken to Naples, and then by ship to Bizerte.

On 5/6 October, the target was the airfield at Grosseto, a hundred miles north of Rome, and fifty-one aircraft bombed in good weather and good illumination. Many fires were reported, most of which were believed to be burning aircraft. One very large explosion was seen amongst the hangars, starting a big fire and causing the roof to collapse. An oil dump on the eastern side of the landing ground was also hit, and smoke from the fires and flares eventually obscured observation as the attack developed. The weather then prevented operations until the night of 8/9 October, when a road junction and bridges at Isernia, sixty miles north of Naples, was the target. Sixty aircraft were detailed for the operation, but cloud conditions made location of the target extremely difficult. Thirty-five aircraft claimed to have attacked the correct area, and direct hits on roads and buildings were claimed. However, photographs showed that the main weight of the attack fell in the Alfedena area, about twenty miles to the north, where there was a road junction that was very similar in appearance to that at Isernia. One of the Wellingtons of No. 40 Squadron returned with its hydraulic and electrical systems damaged, the bomb doors open, and only one wheel down. It was also suspected that a bomb had hung up, preventing a belly-landing. Chappell tells how they circled the airfield firing reds and calling on the radio, but their own receiver was useless. The decision was taken to abandon the aircraft, and it eventually dived straight down into the dispersal area and went up with a terrific 'woomph' of flame.[1]

Another adverse weather forecast prevented operations on the next night, and then the bombers went to Terracina. Fifty-four Wellingtons of all three Wings took off on the operation, but two crashed in Tunisia before reaching the coast due to engine failure. The remaining aircraft all identified the target area in good weather, assisted by excellent illumination. The bombing was well concentrated, and many bursts were seen to straddle the road. There was one direct hit with a 4,000-pounder, and the debris from the cliffs dislodged by the bombing was seen to have fallen across the coast road at one point. The attack on German communications in

Italy continued on 12/13 October, but with a change to a railway target – the track and bridges at Civitavecchia North. Fifty-one Wellingtons took off, but four returned early and one of them from No. 142 Squadron crash-landed at base. One of No. 150 Squadron had an engine catch fire outbound near Cap Bon, and it jettisoned its bombs and flares 'and landed on unused A/D on Enfidaville Road'. Weather along the route was bad, but the target was clear and crews had no difficulty in identifying it. Some of the bombing was rather scattered, but results appeared to be generally good. One of the Wellingtons claimed a direct hit on the northern bridges, and bursts were seen on the railway lines, the chemical works, and near the transformer station.

On 13 October heavy rain during the afternoon rendered the landing grounds of Nos 231 and 236 Wings unserviceable, but No. 330 Wing remained able to operate. During the night, seventeen Wellingtons from Nos 142 and 150 Squadrons attacked railway targets at Orbetello. Weather over the target was excellent, and several direct hits were claimed on the railway tracks and two fires were started. Over thirty aircraft were seen at the nearby seaplane base, and two aircraft machine-gunned them from 600 feet. The Group ORB states that despite 'the comparatively small scale, the whole operation appeared very successful'. The railway station and bridges at Talamone were the targets for the next operation, and once again the effort was limited by the continued unserviceability of the Kairouan Temmar landing ground (No. 231 Wing). Forty-seven aircraft of Nos 236 and 330 Wings were detailed, and attacked in good weather. Sticks were seen to fall in the close vicinity of the target, the rail tracks were straddled, a fire was started in the station buildings, and one aircraft claimed a direct hit on the canal bridge. Daylight photographs taken on 20 October showed that the canal railway bridge was severely damaged by direct hits, effectively blocking the line, and roads in the area were also blocked.

The attentions of the Wellingtons were now directed towards airfields in the Rome area. On 15/16 October, the Rome–Marcigliana airfield was the target, with the aim of destroying a large number of fighters reported to be dispersed around the perimeter. Kairouan Temmar was still unserviceable, but thirty-nine aircraft from Nos 236 and 330 Wings attacked and the raid appeared to be a great success. This was mainly due to a No. 40 Squadron Wellington piloted by Flying Officer R.L.W. Cheek, who machine-gunned the landing ground from 500 feet. Chappell tells how he seemed 'to have done more damage than the rest of [the] Group together'.[2] Flying Officer Cheek was also in one of the few aircraft to find Rome–Casale on the next night (see below), and he got an immediate DSO as a result of his efforts on these and subsequent nights. The runways, dispersals and hangars at Marcigliana were straddled with bombs, one of the airfield buildings was seen to blow up, and incendiaries started a very large fire. Two of the aircraft also machine-gunned seaplanes on Lake Bracciano.

The target for the next night was the Rome–Casale airfield, from which enemy fighters were operating. Nos 236 and 330 Wings again had to provide the entire effort, and thirty-nine Wellingtons took off. Bad weather along the route and over the target seriously interfered with the operation, and only six aircraft claimed to have identified Casale. Bombing by these few aircraft appeared to be effective, and a large explosion, followed by a fire and further explosions, was reported. One Wellington machine-gunned the dispersals from 500 feet, and another descended

213

to 200 feet to machine-gun trees, among which enemy fighters were believed to be dispersed. Two aircraft failed to return, and other crews reported seeing an aircraft come down in flames west of Rome. The weather again turned bad for the next three nights, but on 20/21 October thirty-nine aircraft of Nos 231 and 330 Wings attacked Furbara airfield. Up to eleven aircraft were left burning on the ground, and a large fire in the western corner of the landing ground was visible forty miles away. Hangars and buildings were also seen to be well ablaze, and daylight reconnaissance carried out on the following morning revealed an impressive amount of damage. A large three-bay hangar had been completely destroyed by fire, and other buildings severely damaged. The landing ground and dispersals were well cratered, two ammunition sheds were destroyed, and the Rome–Civitavecchia railway was cut. One aircraft of No. 142 Squadron failed to return, and was apparently shot down over the target.

On 21/22 October, road and rail bridges at Giulianova, on the east coast of Italy, were the targets, the aim being to delay enemy reinforcements moving south to the battle area. Chappell tells us that these bridges were important links in German communications along the eastern side of Italy between Pescara and Ancona, and that 'so far all bombing attempts to destroy the bridges have been unsuccessful'. The aircraft of No. 236 Wing were loaded with 'some suitable 500-lb bombs in sticks', and others carried 4,000-lb bombs with eleven-second delayed action fuses. The idea was that the delay would allow bombing from a low level, as these 'dangerous blast bombs' could give an aircraft 'a severe kick even at 8,000 feet'. Forty-eight aircraft attacked the primary target, and reports indicated an outstandingly successful operation. Direct hits were claimed on rail bridges with two 4,000-lb bombs, and roads and railways were well covered. Photographs taken during the attack confirmed damage to the railway bridge at two points and a direct hit on the road bridge. Chappell says that 'the raid seems to have been a brilliant success',[3] and it was probable that both road and rail bridges were severely damaged. Subsequent day cover showed the railway bridge to be completely severed by a direct hit in the centre, with further damage at both ends, and the coastal road was also cut.

On the next night the Group attacked what was described as 'another long distance target on the east coast of Italy' – the railway bridge at Portocivitanova. Fifty Wellingtons of Nos 231 and 330 Wings attacked in good illumination, and direct hits were claimed on the approaches to the road and railway bridges. Salvoes were also aimed at railway bridges at Porto Potenza Picena and Porto Sant Elpidio. Daylight reconnaissance showed that the railway to Ancona was cut by two direct hits at the southern end of the bridge, and one line was damaged by a direct hit at the northern end.

On 23/24 October, a major attack was launched on the airfield at Guidonia, described as 'in peacetime the "Farnborough" of the *Regia Aeronautica*', with special instructions to avoid damaging the buildings as far as possible. The objective was to destroy some fifty dispersed aircraft, and seventy-three Wellingtons carried out a very successful attack. At least one direct hit was claimed, and up to thirteen aircraft were reported as burning on the ground. Bursts were also seen among the runways, but smoke and dust prevented accurate observation of results. At about 0430 hours a violent explosion was seen near the special assembly shop, and as the Wellingtons left the target area eight large fires were visible forty miles away.

Daylight photographs confirmed that six aircraft were severely damaged or destroyed, the repair shop damaged by five direct hits, and the roof of another shed destroyed. There was considerable enemy fighter activity in the area, and two of the Wellingtons were seen to go down over the target.

Marshalling yards at Pistoia were the target for forty-six Wellingtons on the 24/25th, and bursts were observed amongst trucks and on the railway junction and buildings north of the yards. Several large fires developed as the raid progressed, and the whole area was obscured by smoke. Daylight reconnaissance revealed that the railway carriage shop had sustained severe damage to the roof, while a group of sheds east of the station had been gutted. There were direct hits on the sidings, but the through lines appeared to be unscathed. The starboard engine of an aircraft of No. 150 Squadron cut when over the sea midway between Corsica and the Italian coast, and the aircraft ditched sixty to seventy miles off Sicily. The ASR organization at Palermo was informed of the probable ditching position, and on 31 October news was received that the captain and two members of the crew had been picked up.

During the night of 25/26 October, Kairouan experienced the most violent thunderstorm since the Group's arrival. Uncharted rivers sprung up in the 231 and 330 Wings' camps, and by the morning the water level in the 330 Wing operations room had risen to four feet. No. 142 Squadron ORB states that 'a very violent tropical storm struck the camp site' during the evening. Many tents and living quarters were blown down and the whole site covered in thick mud. Flood water from the hills reached the camp site at about 0730 hours on the 26th, making the runways completely unserviceable and the roads impassable. Fortunately, the aircraft suffered no more than superficial damage, although they could not be moved. The next day was taken up in moving the airmen's site to dry ground nearer the centre of the unit. As far as equipment was concerned, the Squadron was operational again by the 29th, but the runways and dispersals were still unserviceable and remained so to the end of the month. No. 40 Squadron ORB (236 Wing) also reports heavy rain and high winds at Hani West, which caused the collapse of a number of tents, including the airmen's mess.

Chappell was out and about on the 25th, taking his new motorcycle into the mountains, but it died on him and he had to push it for three quarters of a mile and phone for transport. While he waited for it to arrive, heavy clouds were gathering overhead, and there were lighting flashes and rumbles of thunder. The storm broke as the truck arrived, and when he got back to camp a violent wind from the west threatened to blow the tents down. The rain came down in sheets, and the mess was inundated, but the Group Captain quickly rose to the occasion and organized large bowls of rum punch – using up all the emergency medical supplies of rum in the process! They soon 'began to take a lighter view of the storm and the flooded tents', although they were all standing in running water and mud inches deep.

On 29/30 October, NASAF called for a maximum effort from No. 236 Wing, the only Wellington unit operational at Kairouan, against Grosseto marshalling yards. Thirty-two Wellingtons from Nos 40 and 104 Squadrons set off in excellent weather, but one returned early with generator trouble. The others identified the target without difficulty, and the bombing was well concentrated and many incendiaries were seen burning in the yards. Photographs taken during the attack confirmed that the target was well covered, and daylight photographs showed the main line hit in several places and almost certainly blocked. On the next night the target was dispersed aircraft on Perugia airfield, and No. 236 Wing was again the only unit able to operate. Thirty-two Wellingtons took off, but one returned early due to mechanical trouble. The others attacked in good weather, and bombs fell across the dispersals and runways, resulting in one large and several small fires. Despite the small number of aircraft operating, the night was costly, with two aircraft of No. 104 Squadron believed to have been shot down by night fighters. Another aircraft was badly damaged by flak and the bomb aimer injured. A crash-landing back at base would have blocked the only serviceable runway in the Kairouan area, and so the aircraft was diverted to El Aouina, where Tunis offered better hospital facilities for the injured crew member. The landing was made without flaps or brakes, which resulted in the aircraft overshooting and a colliding with tents and a jeep, causing further damage. A fourth Wellington caught fire while taxying to dispersal, and was completely destroyed.

*   *   *

The Wellingtons of No. 331 Wing carried out their last operation with the Group on 3/4 October, and the three squadrons subsequently returned to the UK. The Group ORB states that the 'Canadian Wing' first operated from Kairouan on 28 June 1943, and during their period with the Group their Squadrons carried out 2,127 sorties. The three squadrons immediately began their preparations for their move back to the UK, and thus, an important component of No. 205 Group, prised with great difficulty from the grasp of Harris and Bomber Command, was to be lost to the theatre. At this time, Bomber Command had about 800 four-engined heavy bombers, and No. 205 Group fewer than 100 serviceable twin-engined Wellingtons – now to be considerably reduced. The three squadrons were actually taken off operations on 8 October, and notified that all their aircraft and equipment was to be transferred to other units. No. 424 Squadron ORB comments that the 'personnel of the Squadron appeared to be very pleased and happy about the movement', although they would be going back to the relatively more dangerous skies over northern Europe. The so called Battle of Berlin was about to start, and some 500 aircraft would be lost and 2,700 airmen would die.

The move involved all of No. 331 Wing, plus nine officers and 190 other ranks of No. 296 Squadron, an Albermarle squadron that had been flown to Algeria to take part in the airborne element of Operation *Husky*. Arrangements were made to make two separate moves, with the Wing headquarters, No. 420 Squadron, and No. 296 Squadron going first, followed by Nos 424 and 425 Squadrons. They were to go by road to the Tunis area, and then on by train to Algiers. No. 420 Squadron began their journey home on 17 October, and Nos 424 and 425 Squadrons left on the following day. No. 420 Squadron ORB reports that at 0300 hours on 17 October 'the camp was awake and breakfast served ... and all waste garbage collected and burned.' The Squadron formed up at 0500 hours in full marching order, and at 0555 hours the column moved away from Hani East and completed the first part of their journey to Le Bardo, a few miles west of Tunis, by 1300 hours. The train left at 2300 hours, with each wagon accommodating approximately twenty-five men and their kit. The ORB comments that the 'boys were tired and it was not long before many were asleep'.

Twenty-five miles out of Tunis, the engine on the train broke down, and by the time they got started again they were six hours behind schedule. The train made regular stops along the way so that the men could be fed, and the journey was generally uneventful and 'discipline and morale was at its best'. A wagon had been set aside as a hospital, and filled up very quickly as a lot of the men were suffering from jaundice. This had been affecting 'at least 25 per cent of the squadron' for a few days, and 'some were very sick'. At 2100 hours on 21 October the Squadron detrained at Maison Blanche, and were taken by road to Fort de l'Eau, which was four miles away. After the 'iron rations' received by the men en route, the meal served by No. 1 BPD on their arrival was greatly appreciated. The squadron then stayed at Fort de l'Eau for a few days, and many took the opportunity to visit Algiers. The camp had a beautiful setting within a cluster of trees close to the Mediterranean, with decent food and good quarters.

Nos 424 and 425 Squadrons arrived at Fort de l'Eau a little later, having left Hani East at 0600 hours on 18 October. The men had been warned that no one was to get off the train except at authorized stops, and no water was to be drunk other than that provided by the RTO. They arrived at Le Bardo sidings at 1300 hours, and the train left for Algiers at 2105 hours – 'one hour late'. The No. 424 ORB comments that the train had 'very dirty cars', and half of it was dropped off on the way and 'unfortunately our rations and tea were in the section of the train which was left behind'. The train moved at a snail's pace, but the 'country is beautiful and very picturesque', and it got bitterly cold at night as the train went through the mountains. The two squadrons arrived at Algiers at 2200 hours on 21 October, and detrained immediately. The hot meal and tea provided at Fort de l'Eau were most welcome, and the following morning 'all personnel appeared in good shape after a good night's rest'.

The final date for embarkation was set for the 26th, the squadrons sailing on the SS *Samaria*, and by 1100 hours all were aboard. On the 27th, the No. 420 Squadron ORB comments that:

> It is quite evident that the quality of the food served on board received many praises from all concerned. At least everyone was satisfied. Some of the remarks noted were, 'Ye Gods, what a meal', 'Hot rolls and real butter!', 'All you want to eat – no ruddy flies and sand!', etc. Practically all day troops were coming aboard and unwanted baggage was being loaded on. At 1545 hours the gang plank was rolled away and we drifted slowly away from the wharf to join a waiting convoy.

The No. 424 Squadron ORB comments that the *Samaria* 'seemed a fine ship and all personnel seemed to enjoy their meals'. The men quickly settled down to the ship's routine, and were detailed for various duties on board – guards, gunnery duties, blackouts etc. The weather was fair, the sea calm, and the large convoy was well protected by destroyers and flak ships. And so No. 331 Wing said goodbye to North Africa.

*   *   *

By the end of October, Kesselring had established his defence line on what became known as the 'Winter Line' and then the 'Gustav Line' – a series of positions defended in depth, based on the River Sangro in the East and the River Garigliano in the west, and with Monte Cassino at its heart. The Allies were able to nibble at this line, but it was not to be penetrated until May 1944, over six months later. The Fifth Army captured Isernia, fifty miles north of Naples, on 4 November, and linked up with elements of the Eighth Army moving north-west from Foggia. However, General Mark Clark told Alexander on 13 November that he had to call off his offensive in the Mignano Gap if his troops were not to become dangerously exhausted. The Eighth Army gained the heights on the Sangro, less than a hundred miles east of Rome, by the 8th of the month, and was across the river in strength by 23 November. On 1 December the British 10th Corps opened the US Fifth Army's offensive on the Garigliano, and we will look briefly at its course in the next chapter.

The first operation in November was an attack on the marshalling yards at Viareggio. The landing grounds of Nos 231 and 330 Wings were still unserviceable from the storm of 25 October, and the entire effort was produced by No. 236 Wing. No. 37 Squadron ORB reports that the onset of the wet conditions had been foreseen, and the 'domestic tentage for the most part had already been re-sited on higher ground where necessary'. It would not operate again until the night of 22/23 November. No. 70 Squadron also reports that it was unable to operate due to the condition of the runway at Kairouan Temmar. The severe storms at the end of October had damaged every mess and tent on the camp site 'due to the unprecedented fury of both the rain and wind'. On 4 November the Squadron played a rugby match against a Combined Group and 37 ASF – 'the only two unbeaten teams in the GROUP' – and beat them by eight points to nil. No. 142 Squadron reported that both their runways were still unserviceable due to thick mud.

Twenty-seven aircraft took off for Viareggio, but five returned early for various reasons and one was unable to locate the target and bombed the Pisa area instead. The remaining Wellingtons all attacked Viareggio, and found the target area brightly lit when they arrived. Direct hits on the canal bridge and on a building near the junction were claimed. Many aircraft reported bursts across the marshalling yards and branch line. Subsequent photographs showed hits on the marshalling yards and some tracks damaged, but the through lines were still serviceable. The repair shed was partially destroyed, and the secondary road to Torre del Lago was blocked by five craters. Two aircraft of No. 104 Squadron failed to return, and one appears to have crashed into the sea in flames off the Corsican coast on the outward journey.

On the next night, the target was the airfield at Fiano–Romano, a new landing ground recently brought into use by the Germans, and the object of the raid was to destroy some thirty single-engined fighters reported there. Thirty-six Wellingtons of Nos 236 and 330 Wings reached the target, and carried out an attack lasting over twenty minutes. Bombs were seen to explode on the landing ground and in the dispersal area, and at least three aircraft were reported to be on fire. Up to twenty dispersed aircraft were observed, and one aircraft of No. 236 Wing descended to 1,000 feet and machine-gunned them, setting one on fire. On the next night, bad weather was forecast en route to the proposed target, and operations were cancelled. Then, on 4/5 November forty-six aircraft of Nos 236 and 330 Wings took off to attack the marshalling yards at Orte, sixty miles north of Rome, and another of the many communication targets which had been attacked in the past months. The first flares fell north-west of the target (it was believed over Orte town), but the later illuminators rectified this mistake and the bulk of the bombing was accurate. Many bursts were seen in the marshalling yards and one large fire was burning when the Wellingtons left. Photographs later showed that an ammunition train had been blown up in the railway cutting to the north-west of the yards, demolishing a girder road bridge and cutting the rail tracks.

On 5 November, the 104 Squadron ORB reports that rain fell steadily for most of the morning and afternoon at Hani West, developing into a violent thunderstorm and gale at about 2300 hours. Parts of the camp were swamped and tents blown down, including the church, ration store, and gunnery tent. The storm eased off at about 0100 hours on the 6th, but rain continued to fall until dawn. Operations were cancelled until 8 November due to the weather and the state of the landing ground. No. 142 Squadron reports 'another violent tropical storm...worse than those of 26/10'. Once again, runways, dispersals and roads became completely unserviceable, but most of the tentage stood up to the flooding much better on their new site. The Squadron were involved in the 'customary routine of repairing flood damage, digging ditches and drying out soaked equipment'. The whole camp site was once more covered in deep mud. On the 8th a start was made in moving the aircraft from dispersals onto the EW runway, 'which looks as if it may become serviceable again', the NS runway having been abandoned once again. The movements continued on the next day, 'the aircraft being dragged down from dispersals...by four 3 ton lorries, leaving ruts in places 2' 6" deep.'

No. 236 Wing was able to despatch twelve aircraft to attack a railway bridge over the River Ombroni (south of Grosseto) on 8/9 November. Nineteen aircraft were originally detailed for this operation, but after twelve had taken off one became bogged down on the perimeter track, blocking it for the remainder. Five of the aircraft acted as flare-droppers, while six Wellingtons bombed the target. One 4,000-lb bomb was dropped from 600 feet, and a hit was claimed on the northern end of the bridge. On the next night twenty-five Wellingtons of No. 236 Wing took off to attack railway bridges at Pontassieve, but the weather conditions seriously hampered the operation. There was 10/10 cloud, rain, strong winds and icing conditions en route over the Italian mainland, and only ten aircraft claimed to have located the correct target. One hit on the bridge was reported, and several bursts across the railway tracks. One of the aircraft also machine-gunned trucks from 500 feet. Eleven aircraft bombed alternative targets in the Arno Valley and along the coast, while four jettisoned their bombs.

On 10/11 November, the target was the Recco railway viaduct, about eleven miles east of Genoa, and it represented the longest operation yet carried out by No. 205 Group from Kairouan. NASAF ordered that one 4,000-lb bomb should be carried, and this meant that arrangements had to be made for two aircraft (one acting as illuminator) to refuel at Decimomannu in Sardinia. Wing Commander Bagnall of No. 40 Squadron was carrying the 4,000-pounder, and when he arrived at Decimomannu it was deserted and 'looked in very poor shape'. He was met by an army officer who had no idea what he was doing there, but 'after much hard bargaining', managed to get some fuel but no flare path for take-off. Bagnall prevailed upon the army officer to park two jeeps with their headlights on at the end of the runway, which he did, but after a look at the huge bomb racked beneath the Wellington, he quickly scuttled off to safety. The take-off in the dark and over a very dodgy runway took ages, and Bagnall held his breath until he was well airborne.

The actual attack was equally heart-stopping, as the railway disappeared into a steep cliff immediately beyond the viaduct. Bagnall remembers that just as he reached the viaduct on a dummy run, with a few hundred yards to go to the cliff face, the flare above him went out and the aircraft was plunged into darkness. The bomb run itself was not so bad, but as the Wellington broke away after the bomb release, this time in the light of flares, the rear gunner could see the trees on the cliff flashing past his turret. In all, twenty-two Wellingtons of Nos 236 and 330 Wings attacked in bright moonlight, and the operation appeared to be entirely successful. The 4,000-lb bomb was dropped from 1,000 feet with an eleven-second delay, and scored a direct hit on the viaduct east of the river. The aircraft then machine-gunned a stationary train on the viaduct, west of the gap caused by the explosion. Six other crews claimed to have hit the viaduct, and one of the aircraft that arrived late in the operation reported considerable damage.

On the next night forty-one Wellingtons of Nos 236 and 330 Wings were despatched to attack the marshalling yards at Prato, a few miles north of Florence and another 'overload' target. They successfully located and bombed the yards, and delivered a well-concentrated attack. One violent explosion on the south-west edge of the marshalling yards and 'a fire with rocket like explosions' were reported, but considerable smoke obscured accurate observations. Chappell tells us that Flying Officer Cheek had another extraordinary bombing report after the attack on Prato. The crew bombed as detailed, and machine-gunned a light AA gun that was firing at them. They then went on to the airfield and marshalling yards at Pistoia, which they had bombed and strafed on 24/25 October. They shot up dispersed aircraft on the ground and dropped incendiaries on a train, which was set on fire. Then they saw a truck on the nearby *autostrada*, and strafed this as well. The attacks on the airfield were made at very low level, and the undercarriage was lowered to prevent damage to the propellers, the wheels touching the ground at one point. The aircraft fired 7,900 rounds and Chappell comments that 'this young man and his crew are setting a new style of night attack with their sheer audacity in going in at low levels to use the guns like a fighter bomber in daylight'.[4]

The next attack, on the Pontassieve marshalling yards and railway bridges on 12/13 November, was planned in two waves, with the aircraft of No. 236 Wing bombing at 2030 hours and No. 330 Wing bombing at midnight. Fourteen aircraft of No. 236 Wing claimed to have located the target, although No. 104 Squadron reported that there was 10/10 cloud over the target area and only five of its aircraft were able to find Pontassieve. Bursts were seen across the yards and buildings, causing blue-green flashes and explosions. Hits were also scored on the barracks south of the marshalling yards, where a fire was started and another fire was reported in the town, and one of the Wellingtons machine-gunned the yards and the barracks. One 4,000-lb bomb was aimed at the bridge, and the burst was seen close to the north-west corner. The eighteen aircraft of No. 330 Wing attacked through low cloud, which hampered observation of results. Despite this, the target area appeared to be well covered, and many incendiary fires were seen. Several large explosions were also reported, and the barracks were well ablaze. A good fire was also started near the River Arno five miles south of the target. A daylight reconnaissance made a fortnight later showed evidence of hits in the yards and on the bridge, but all damage had been repaired.

On the same night the bridge at Cecina was also attacked by one Wellington of No. 40 Squadron – piloted by Flying Officer Cheek again! The aircraft was armed with a 4,000-lb bomb set for an eleven-second delay, and the attack was made from a low level. The bomb was seen to hit the bridge, but it failed to explode.[5] However, five aircraft of No. 236 Wing that had failed to find Pontassieve then turned up to bomb the bridge as a secondary target, scoring hits at either end. Their bombs set off a violent explosion, which was believed to be the 4,000-lb bomb finally going off. Photographs taken after this attack showed a large portion of the bridge – two thirds of its width – missing near the centre on the seaward side.

On 13/14 November, twelve aircraft of No. 330 Wing set off to attack the Group's first targets in France. One 4,000-lb bomb was required on each target, and arrangements were made for these two aircraft to refuel at El Aouina. The first target for six of the aircraft was one that would become well known to the strategic bombers over the next few months – the railway viaduct at Antheor in the South of France. This viaduct was 540 feet long, 185 feet high, and contained 9 arches, each with a 29 foot span. It carried a double-tracked railway line across the mouth of a river a few miles east of St Raphael. Four located and attacked the viaduct, and although no hits were observed, the 4,000-pounder fell close to the foundations on the seaward side. Another six aircraft attacked the road and railway bridge at Nice–Californie, but, again, no hits were claimed and the 4,000-lb bomb did not explode. There was considerable AA opposition at both targets, and the attacks were hampered by the need to take evasive action.

The weather continued to be very wet and windy at Kairouan, but only occasionally prevented operations. The flat land around the camps had become very marshy, and parts of the main roads were often flooded and impassable. The enemy had demolished most of the bridges in the area during their retreat, and big detours often had to be made to get across the many wadis. In the middle of November it was decided to move the Wellington squadrons to Djedeida and Oudna, near Tunis, where all-weather airfields were available, and the Group Headquarters moved to Ariana. No. 231 Wing (Nos 37 and 70 Squadrons) moved to Djedeida No. 1 Landing Ground, No. 236 Wing (Nos 40 and 104 Squadrons) to Oudna No. 1 Landing Ground, and No. 330 Wing (Nos 142 and 150 Squadrons) to Djedeida No. 2 Landing Ground. All these landing grounds were much closer to Tunis, and much less likely to suffer from the flooding that afflicted the Kairouan area. Chappell reports that they were all excited at the prospect of leaving as the smell was as bad in winter as in the summer, and the mud and floods were hampering flying operations. Oudna was 'a more pleasing environment', surrounded by green farmland and with a river, Roman aqueduct, and a view of the mountains to help lift the spirits – and there was no smell! However, a gale hit the area on 23 November, ripping down tents.

Gunby recounts how the packing for the move to Oudna by No. 40 Squadron was memorable because of the presence of the local Arabs, who were all over the camp, and anything not closely guarded was likely to disappear very quickly. Every now and then, one or two Arabs would stray innocently over to a pile of gear left momentarily unguarded, and start rooting through the contents. Two of them went after the contents of the dismantled hospital tent, and were chased off by some of the airmen and a 'little Austin staff car':

> It was the CO and he was going full out. The Arabs immediately hicked up their sheets, as their nightshirt-like clothing was called, and went tearing away with the Austin right on their heels. The closer it got to them the faster they ran, and the higher they hoisted their sheets. Since they wore nothing under them, once they got to waist level the scene became a real comedy. Just when it seemed the Austin was going to win the race they jumped down into a wadi and escaped.[6]

No. 142 Squadron ORB gives a good account of the move to Oudna. The advance party of one hundred men and twenty lorries left early in the morning on 14 November, but bad roads and diversions delayed their arrival until 1630 hours, leaving just one hour of daylight. The men were quickly got under canvas and the lorries off-loaded and sent back to Kairouan. Work continued over the next few days to get the Squadron operational again:

> At 6 a.m. [on 15 November] work started, erecting the Maintenance marquees on the Technical Site down the runways, and continuing work on the Domestic Site. The Domestic Site is on sloping ground overlooking the runways but about 1½ miles distant from them. The camp is laid out in lines in a small area, very different from the widely dispersed camps we have had ever since leaving BLIDA in May. During the day the aircraft began to arrive and the CO and the Main party arrived by road at 1830 – after dark. After a hot meal tents were erected and everyone got under shelter.
>
> Work started again bright and early [on 16 November] off-loading the Main Party lorries, some of which had to go back again for the Rear Party. Although we could operate Group have been asked not to put us on tonight so that everyone may have a chance to get organized.

Although at least one Wing was available to operate on any night, no operations were carried out until the 22nd due to the weather conditions. On 22/23 November the target was the Rome–Ciampino airfield, from where enemy aircraft were reported to be harassing troops in the battle area. A smaller force was required to bomb the nearby marshalling yards. Twenty-seven Wellingtons attacked the airfield, where illumination was good and many aircraft were observed on the ground. Bombing was well concentrated, with bursts among the aircraft, but only a few fires were reported. Bursts were also seen among buildings on the airfield, and one of the three main hangars was seen to blow up. Thirteen aircraft bombed the railway junction, where it was believed that hits were scored on the tracks, but assessment of results was difficult due to haze. One of the Wellingtons of No. 70 Squadron failed to return. This aircraft gave an ETA in the normal way, and later received a QDM (magnetic heading back to base). When it failed to arrive a search over the sea was started, but met with no success.

For some time NASAF had been planning a night attack on the Villar Perosa ball bearing factory at Turin to complement a series of attacks carried out by the Fifteenth Air Force earlier in the month. This was a very long trip from Oudna, across the Mediterranean and over Sardinia and Corsica to the Ligurian Sea, and then over the mountain range to the plains of Piedmont and the Turin industrial area. On 24/25 November the meteorological branch at last forecast that weather conditions were favourable, and eighty-three aircraft were detailed to attack at 2100 hours. During the afternoon seven 423-type Wellingtons (i.e., those unable to carry overload tanks *and* 4,000-lb bombs) were despatched to Elmas on Sardinia, where refuelling facilities had been arranged. At the time of departure for the main force from Tunisia a strong cross wind was blowing at Djedeida, creating hazardous take-off conditions for the No. 231 Wing aircraft, and these thirty aircraft were accordingly briefed to leave later when the wind had dropped.

The operation, in addition to being completely ineffective, proved to be the most costly in the history of the Group, and seventeen aircraft (20 per cent) were lost. Gunby comments that the raid was a disaster comparable to the Nuremberg raid by Bomber Command in March 1944. Only nine aircraft reached the target area, and three of these did not bomb as the actual factory could not be distinguished. Six of the 4,000-lb bomb equipped aircraft sent to Elmas did not take off due to refuelling delays, but in the light of subsequent events this was, perhaps, fortunate. The heavy losses were primarily due to the weather conditions, which proved to be very different from those forecast. A severe front was encountered in the gulf of Genoa, with 8/10 to 10/10 low cloud north of Corsica. Navigation difficulties for the aircraft were further increased by a strong westerly wind. Chappell records that:

> I was roused by Operations at 0100 hours and told that the aircraft are in all sorts of trouble; some have landed in Sardinia, others have baled out or have not reported – and apparently the weather has made a shambles of the whole operation.[7]

Two of the missing aircraft were abandoned by their crews and all parachuted to safety. One ditched near Borgo (Corsica) and the crew was reported to be safe. One crashed at Monte Cane (Sicily), and only the rear gunner survived. Of the thirteen aircraft unaccounted for, three were in W/T communication with base during the night. One of No. 40 Squadron (the only 4,000-lb bomb-equipped aircraft to take off from Elmas) signalled that the crew were baling out over Sardinia. One of No. 70 Squadron received a QDM, and one of No. 142 Squadron signalled 'returning to base – bad weather'. Comprehensive searches were carried out from Bizerte and Corsica without success. ASR launches reported that sea conditions were such that there was little hope that dinghies could survive in the water.

The next target for the bombers was the Ombrone railway bridge (south of Grosseto) on 26/27 November, and the attack was planned in three waves. The fourteen aircraft of No. 236 Wing were to go in at 1900 to 1930 hours, No. 231 Wing (another fourteen aircraft) at 1945 to 2015 hours, and No. 330 Wing (twelve aircraft) at 2045 to 2115 hours. One aircraft from each Wing was to drop a 4,000-lb bomb from a low level and with an eleven-second delay. During the evening the weather forecast deteriorated, and the aircraft of No. 330 Wing were recalled shortly after take-off. All fourteen of No. 236 Wings aircraft located and bombed the target, and bursts were reported in the vicinity of the bridge and across the railway. Two aircraft claimed hits on the north end, but the structure appeared to be intact after the attack. The 4,000-pounder was dropped on the southern end, but failed to explode. Four aircraft of No. 231 Wing returned early, two due to the weather and two through mechanical failures. Three of the ten Wellingtons that reached the target claimed bursts within 200 yards of the bridge. The 4,000-pounder burst on the railway embankment twenty yards to the north, but no definite results were observed.

On 28/29 November fifty-six Wellingtons of all three Wings took off to attack the airfields at Ciampino, the intention being to destroy dispersed aircraft and crater the landing grounds. Accordingly, half of the aircraft were armed with 20-lb fragmentation bombs and half with 500-lb HE (high explosive) bombs. Thirty-nine aircraft claimed to have identified and attacked the airfields, some attacked a large factory building in the vicinity, and some are believed to have bombed Centocelle airfield by mistake. Of the two Ciampino airfields, the North one evidently proved the easier to locate, and hits on the hangars started a fire. There were near misses among dispersed aircraft on the ground, and two other fires were reported. No hits on buildings on the South field were claimed, and no fires were started. Bombs were seen to fall among dispersed aircraft, but no results were observed. The Group ORB comments that the 'operation as a whole appeared to have been indifferent'. One aircraft of No. 150 Squadron failed to return, and most crews reported seeing an aircraft coned by searchlights at approximately 2030 hours. It was seen to explode and fall in flames, and was either shot down by light flak or by a single-engined fighter reported over the target area.

At the end of November Chappell was invited to visit an American Fortress Group HQ, and when he got there their squadrons were forming up for a big effort on enemy airfields in the Rome area. He comments that the 'lengthy process of climbing and circling to get into battle formation for the massed flight to the target is an awe-inspiring spectacle'. He contrasts the day-bombing techniques of the Americans with those of No. 205 Group's night-bombing methods:

> I would think that the American daylight bombing produces more accurate attacks on a given target but that their losses must be extraordinarily high. How can they maintain morale in a squadron sometimes suffering ten per cent or greater losses on a single mission? The complementary nature of our two air forces in providing a 24-hour service for bombing tactical and strategic targets is something which must have a vital effect on the outcome of this war.[8]

*   *   *

As November drew to an end, news was received from NAAF Headquarters that the anticipated relocation to the Foggia area in Italy was now imminent. Shipping would be available to move the Group in the early part of December, and a Warning Order was eventually issued on 30 November, detailing all units to one of four shipping convoys that were to sail on 6, 9, 12 and 15 December respectively. Thus, November closed with preparations for the move to destinations in Italy not yet disclosed. In the first weeks of December all the Squadron ORBs record a confused and confusing movement of road/sea parties and aircraft from Tunisia to Italy. The Group ORB reported that 'the new aerodromes at Cerignola were not ready for night flying', despite assurances from US Fifteenth Air Force that both of the landing grounds would be ready for operations by 18 December. In addition, the weather was often atrocious, and settling in to their new location and getting operational again was clearly going to be difficult for the Group.

Only two operations were carried out from Tunisia in December, both directed at marshalling yards. On 1/2 December fifty-two Wellingtons took off to attack

Pontassieve marshalling yards, but three turned back before reaching the target – one due to icing and two with engine trouble. One of the returning aircraft collided with a Beaufighter on practice interception exercises about thirty miles off the coast, and both aircraft dived straight into the sea. The remaining aircraft found the target without difficulty; illumination was good and the bombing well concentrated. Many bursts, including two 4,000-pounders, were seen in the marshalling yards and on adjacent buildings, and at least one fire was started. After the attack the yards were obscured by dust and smoke. On return, an aircraft of No. 104 Squadron was set on fire by the accidental discharge of a Verey cartridge, and all the crew except the pilot baled out near Ferryville – the aircraft was never found. This was the last operation from Djedeida ('from African soil') for Nos 231 and 236 Wings prior to the move to Italy.

The final operation for No. 205 Group from North Africa was on 2/3 December, when sixteen Wellingtons of 330 Wing took off to bomb the marshalling yards at Arezzo. One returned early due to excessive petrol consumptions, and haze made identification of the target difficult for the remainder. Two were unable to locate the target area, and another bombed on estimated position. Several crews subsequently claimed to have seen bursts in the marshalling yards, but no conclusive results were reported. Then, on 4 December 1943 the Group suspended operations pending the completion of the move to Italy.

The main road/sea party of No. 37 Squadron 'prepared to move off in the morning' of 3 December, and all non-essential tentage and equipment was packed up. It eventually got off on 5 December, was loaded onto an LST at Bizerte on the 7th, and sailed on the following day. The party landed at Taranto on the 12th after an uneventful crossing, and on the next day moved off to Cerignola. Heavy rain that night left many vehicles bogged down by the following morning, but they reached Cerignola in the late afternoon of the 14th. The first air party of eighteen aircraft took off from Djedeida for Cerignola on 16 December, but was diverted to Foggia Main due to the state of the Cerignola airfields. They unloaded their equipment and personnel, and nine of the aircraft returned immediately to Tunisia. Vehicles from the main party eventually arrived to collect the kit and personnel, but only after a considerable delay due to poor communications. They all spent 'an uncomfortable night...owing to intense cold', and one of the Wellingtons that had remained at Foggia Main was written off when a USAAF P-47 Thunderbolt crashed into it. Another seven aircraft returned to Djedeida on the 17th, and a second air party then arrived at Cerignola on 20 December. However, operations from Cerignola were clearly going to be impossible for a while and so the Squadron personnel 'were able to concentrate on the inauguration of Christmas Festivities'. On 29 December an 'Operational Echelon' moved to Tortorella, with skeleton crews to operate ten aircraft.

The first road/sea party from the other squadron in No. 231 Wing, No. 70 Squadron, left Djedeida North on 2 December, and arrived at Cerignola on 15 December. The air parties left on 17 and 20 December, and had little to do except prepare for the Christmas celebrations. These included the Officers versus Airmen soccer match, won by the officers, and the traditional Christmas dinner with 'an abundance of Turkey and Pork, well done and greatly enjoyed by all.' On 29 December an advance party consisting of all aircrew and ground staff moved to Tortorella to prepare for operations.

Good accounts of the move to Italy are to be found in the ORBs of Nos 40 and 104 Squadrons (no. 236 Wing), and further details are given by Chappell and Gunby. The first part of the journey would take the road/sea parties to Bizerte, and Chappell made the journey in the Group Captain's Chevrolet staff car. They travelled around Tunis and 'along narrow roads through rolling open country to Ferryville and the Bizerta Lake.' Their long convoy of trucks parked near the docks, and for two days and nights they waited quietly for the navy to transport them to Italy. No. 40 Squadron's vehicles were parked in a marshalling area, with cooking facilities provided by the local military authorities. The Squadron ORB notes that 'a cinema, operated by Americans, provided welcome relief from the tedious business of awaiting embarkation orders'.

The main party of No. 40 Squadron embarked on an LST on 8 December, and were pleasantly surprised to find bunks, hot and cold water, and dining saloons. They had been expecting far more spartan quarters on a ship primarily intended for the transport of tanks and motor vehicles. Chappell tells us that their LST had an 'imposing ship's crest of Donald Duck wielding a tommy gun with a tank on his back and a shell passing between his legs'. The convoy set off at 0900 hours on 9 December, escorted by a couple of corvettes, and the next few days were spent 'quite uneventfully'. There was a pleasant cruise past Malta and Gozo, a journey that just over a year ago would have been fraught with danger as convoys were being fought through to Malta with great loss. The passengers had a perfect view of the 'glorious snow-capped peak of Mount Etna in Sicily rising majestically in a perfect cone to nearly 11,000 feet'. The coast of the toe of Italy looked green and attractive, with mountains behind a coast of fine beaches and beautiful villas. The journey ended in the 'magnificent harbour of Taranto on 12 December through the protective booms and...watching crowds into the inner harbour and disembarkation on a pebble beach'.

They were quickly ashore with their vehicles, and No. 40 Squadron ORB states that they were complimented on the behaviour of the men during the trip – 'the cleanest body of men I've yet transported' said the Captain. The journey to Foggia took them along narrow roads between olive groves, and at night they slept in their camp beds under tent tops slung between the trucks and olive trees. Chappell travelled on his motorcycle, 'along the edge of the Apennine plateau with olive groves, wide fields of green young corn and neat well-cultivated fields of vegetables'. He took turns with two others to marshal the convoy of vehicles at crossroads or turnings. On the evening of the 16th, they reached a pleasant olive grove that was to be the site of their camp, and started to put up their tents.

The official history of the RAF in the Second World War describes the area surrounding Foggia as 'a bleak plain', on the seaward side of which was 'the mountainous promontory of Monte Gargano, the spur on the heel of Italy.' In the middle of the plain was 'the dusty town of Foggia, of which the general appearance had not been improved by the frequent air attacks made upon it'. The town was surrounded by airfields constructed by the Germans, and they were 'of great extent and admirably suited for the operations of heavy bombers'. As we have seen, the airfields fell to the Allies in October 1943, and would soon enable the bombers of the American Fifteenth Air Force and the British No. 205 Group to strike deep into enemy territory. The flat area of grassland and olive groves became scarred with the runways and camp sites of the bomber units, and the Wellington wings and squadrons were able to appreciate for the first time the strength of American air power. They watched with interest and respect as the great daylight formations formed up and set off to attack distant targets.

Commenting on Cerignola No. 2 (quoted in Gunby), Wing Commander Bagnall stated that:

> The ground was flattened, muddy and there was obviously an awful lot of water retained in that area. They cleared a lot of olive groves away to lay this strip out and moved in a good deal of earth, from which the runway itself was raised. The first take off was a hairy experience. The excess water was actually forced up through this runway as you went over it. It squirted up in little water spouts which was really most frightening.[9]

The tented encampment at Cerignola No. 2 was equally wet, and after two days it was moved to a drier site in an olive orchard, where the men 'spent a couple of weeks…drinking the local wines and singing the Squadron songs in the mess'.

The Group HQ was to be located at Bari, and on 7 December the SASO (Group Captain McNair), SOSO (Wing Commander Mills) and a small advance party flew there to make contact with British and American elements of the USAAF Fifteenth Air Force. However, it quickly became apparent that the Operations Branch could not function effectively from Bari due to the very limited telephone communications with the Foggia area. Wing Commander Mills, therefore, set off to find suitable quarters near the Wings to serve as an Advanced Operational HQ. By 15 December, buildings in Cerignola had been requisitioned for offices and living quarters, and an Advance Signals and Operations party moved there from Bari. It was located in a school that provided adequate accommodation for Operations, Flying Control, Signals, and part of Intelligence, with rooms on the first floor for airmen's sleeping quarters. Considerable 'cleaning up' was necessary, including the 'polite but firm ejection' of a Balloon Headquarters and several members of the school staff. Officers' living accommodation also presented difficulties, as the half-built block of new flats requisitioned by the Fifteenth Air Force showed no prospects of being ready for occupation by 1 January. The best alternative available was 'a large house in the main street, opposite the Cathedral, owned by a notoriously pro-Fascist Baron'.

The Wellingtons were flown over from their old Tunisian bases between 13 and 21 December, but found that the Cerignola landing grounds were far from ready for night operations due to uncompleted runways and lack of suitable dispersals. The only practicable solution was for Nos 231 and 236 Wings to operate from Foggia No. 2 (Tortorella) and Foggia Main respectively, until their own airfields were ready. Foggia Main was a former *Regia Aeronautica* base, and had been repeatedly bombed by the Allies. Metal fragments tended to work their way to the surface of the unsealed runway, and wreak havoc with the treadless tyres of the Wellingtons. On 19 December Chappell visited the town of Foggia, and recorded that the country between Cerignola and Foggia was flat and fen-like, with mountains in the distance to the left (the Apennines) and to the right (Monte Gargano). The proximity of the mountains would cause many problems for the bombers over the next sixteen months or so. The town was badly damaged, and the marshalling yards were full of burned out wagons, twisted rails, and bomb craters – many no doubt caused by the bombers of No. 205 Group. Despite the primitive conditions at Cerignola, the Squadrons managed an excellent Christmas dinner, and had a good time in the messes afterwards.

The main party from No. 142 Squadron, consisting of 250 personnel and 51 vehicles, left Oudna at 0900 hours on 8 December, accompanied by a similar party from No. 150 Squadron and a smaller Wing party. All available tents and personal equipment was loaded onto the aircraft. The main party reached Naples at 1500 hours on 13 December, and proceeded to the dispersal area at Portici. Here, they found that the arrangements to receive their convoy were very inadequate – there was little food, less accommodation, and no information. They set off for the Foggia area on the following day through hilly country and over bad roads, and camped for the night at Pratola Serra after a journey of only about forty miles. The next day was worse, with only about thirty miles covered over very difficult roads and a fatal accident involving two of the Wing's vehicles. They were on the move again early on the 16th, and travelled through Foggia to Cerignola No. 3 Landing Ground some seven miles SSW of the town. By 1400 hours they were established in a farmhouse and orchard some one-and-a-half miles from the landing ground.

The first air party from No. 142 Squadron left Oudna by 0930 hours on 20 December, the eighteen Wellingtons each fully loaded with personal kit and four tents in the bomb bays, and with four ground crew passengers. At Cerignola, the incoming aircraft were quickly unloaded, and everything moved up to the domestic site and tents erected for the night. The aircraft then returned to base, and all got in except the last two, which had to land at Sidi-Ahmed as there was no flare path at Oudna. On the 21st all the remaining tents were struck early and loaded onto the aircraft, along with all the rest of the personal equipment, and over the next two days they all set off again for Cerignola. Two failed to arrive, one landing at Naples/Capodichino with pitch control trouble, and the other returning to Oudna with hydraulic problems. The Squadron was favourably impressed with Cerignola, the ORB commenting that the 'country here is very similar to the English countryside the resemblance being very striking after almost exactly 12 months in N. AFRICA'. No. 330 Wing remained at Cerignola No. 3, where there was some likelihood of being able to operate by the beginning of January.

The Group ORB ends its record of operations in December with a 'Farewell to Africa', which is worth quoting in full:

> On the 6 December, 1943, and at intervals of a few days, all the units of No. 205 Group began what was understood to be the last and certainly the biggest trek since they became mobile: the move from Africa to the mainland of Europe.
>
> The earlier Units travelled via Taranto and subsequent Units via Naples. It is probably typical of most, if a brief description of the move of the main party of Headquarters, No. 205 Group is given.
>
> On the 14th December, 1943, the convoy set out at 0600 hours for Bizerta. There had been rain that night, and there was a good fall during that day.
>
> On arrival at the docks the convoy was halted immediately opposite the yawning cavities of several LSTs. This yielded expressions of considerable delight as all our fore-runners had been kept waiting for 48 hours before embarkation. Excitement quickly died, however, when it was disclosed that the site was to provide our home for 48 hours.
>
> In spite of the reports of bomb damage at Bizerta during the period of

operations, there was not much visible until it was realized that the mass of twisted girders covering the site was all that remained of the buildings which had been the targets for operations. The litter had been added to by the dumping of every tin and bit of rubbish from miles around. This led to a 'wag's' dubbing us 'The Dead End Kids'.

The presence of mud inches deep did not materially worsen this lovely spectacle, which had the advantage of creating the feeling that there was no loss in leaving Sunny Africa.

Bully and biscuits were eaten at regular intervals during those 48 hours, off tables consisting of anything from a petrol can to the remains of a Heinkel.

Two days later we embarked, but not into those inviting cavities; they were much too close. Thanks to the MT drivers the operation was carried out without loss.

Next morning we set sail, leaving our last site in Africa, the 'rubbish dump of Bizerta'. The last visitor on board was an American complaining of the state in which our site had been left! A fatigue party was sent back to dispose of the six extra tins which had been passed unnoticed amongst the rest.

It was an uneventful voyage, apart from Acts of God, one of which was in the form of a very severe thunderstorm of tropical intensity. Unfortunately it coincided with the airmen's dinner period and there was many a soaked skin in consequence.

Dawn on the third day revealed a cloudless sky, the Isle of Capri, and the Bay of Naples – a sight worth travelling from the Middle East to see.

In the afternoon we were directed to our haven for the night – another rubbish dump only slightly better than that at Bizerta, with the added attraction of visitors from the Naples underworld clamouring for luscious Service biscuits.

The land journey took three days to complete. Through delightful mountain scenery the 3-tonners and their trailers trundled along, being literally squeezed through the narrow cobbled streets of villages perched on the tops of hills, in complete contrast to the village in the valley at home.

The rain and mud accompanied the convoy to the end, but all through the trek the spirit never weakened – 'the troops were in good heart'.

It is clear from other reports in the Group and Squadron ORBs that the move of the convoys was hampered by poor organization on the part of Headquarters, NAAF, with sailing dates altered and embarkation arrangements unsatisfactory. There were many delays at Bizerte, with some units waiting for up to four days before embarkation. The rear parties of all six squadrons in the Group had to wait for eight to ten days before being finally embarked on 26 and 28 December. There were also many faults with the loading organization, with vehicles being lined up in a certain order and then called forward for loading in a different order. All reports on the sea voyage are favourable, with everyone happy with the food and sleeping arrangements. On 10 December, Mediterranean Air Command became Mediterranean Allied Air Forces (MAAF), and into its headquarters was absorbed that of Northwest African Air Forces. The Northwest African Strategic Air Force was renamed Mediterranean Allied Strategic Air Force (MASAF), although its activities were unchanged.

*　　*　　*

On 27/28 December two Wellingtons of No. 150 Squadron were despatched on a new and 'highly secret mission' – the dropping of supplies to escaped prisoners of war in Northern Italy. They took off from Tortorella, and carried out the difficult operation successfully. The first bombing operation from Italy was also despatched from Tortorella, when twenty aircraft of No. 231 Wing were detailed to attack the Voghera marshalling yards, forty miles north of Genoa, on 29/30 December. One of the aircraft of No. 37 Squadron swung on take-off and hit another aircraft. The first Wellington was completely destroyed by fire, and its bombs exploded. All the crew were safe, although badly injured by the fire, and the second aircraft was also destroyed by fire. As a result of this accident, two more aircraft were unable to operate due to the debris on the runway, and only seven aircraft from No. 37 Squadron got off. There was much cloud over the route, and the target was also partially obscured by haze and cloud. Six (including the two illuminators) abandoned the operation for various reasons, and the remaining aircraft 'bombed what he believed to be the railway line south of Voghera rail junction'. Three aircraft of No. 70 Squadron also returned early, and only two definitely located and bombed the marshalling yards. Four bombed alternative targets. On return, all the aircraft landed at Foggia Main due to the crash of the No. 37 Squadron aircraft at Tortorella. Despite the lack of success, the No. 37 Squadron ORB reported that:

> This operation was carried out in spite of the great difficulties of servicing and bombing up aircraft without the background of a properly set up domestic and technical camp. A particularly fine effort was made by the armourers.

On the following night, nineteen aircraft of No. 231 Wing took off to attack the airfield at Treviso, but weather conditions again interfered with the operation. There was 10/10 cloud in two layers over the target area, and most aircraft pin-pointed themselves shortly before reaching the airfield and bombed the estimated position. One of the Wellingtons saw a lighted flare path through a break in the cloud, but this was immediately extinguished.

*　　*　　*

No. 240 Wing at Terria carried out nineteen operations in October, flying a total of 184 sorties, 57 by the Liberators of No. 178 Squadron and 127 by the Halifaxes of No. 462 Squadron. They lost two Halifaxes in the process – one crashed on take-off and the other was believed to have come down into the sea during an attack on Maritza. All of the operations were directed at airfields on Rhodes and Crete, except for one attack on the Antimachia landing ground on Kos by three Liberators and six Halifaxes on 18/19 October. Calato was bombed twice (seventeen sorties), Heraklion five times (fifty-three sorties), and Maritza eleven times (100 sorties). These operations were in support of an abortive attempt by the Allies to capture Rhodes and other islands in the Dodecanese. No. 178 Squadron was still operating at a low level, as it had very few serviceable Liberators on charge. Generally, the operations were reported to be fairly successful throughout the month, although their small scale can have resulted in very little damage.

In November the Liberators and Halifaxes only flew twelve operations, comprising 115 sorties. The Liberators could only manage forty-two of these sorties, and lost one aircraft. All bar one of the operations was against the airfields at Maritza (seven operations and sixty sorties), Heraklion (three operations and thirty-two sorties), and Calato (one operation and ten sorties). The weather was often indifferent, and few positive results were observed. The ORB for No. 462 Squadron records that on 17 November a cheque for fourteen pounds was received from the metal workers of Handley Page, 'to be used to buy amenities.' On 20 November it strikes a sadder note:

> A very tragic accident occurred during the afternoon whilst aircraft were being bombed up for the night's operation. At about 1500 hours a loud explosion was heard and volumes of black smoke was seen in the vicinity of the dispersals, and the fears that the Squadron had suffered a similar blow to that which happened at Gardabia Main on 20th April 1943 were soon confirmed. Aircraft BB443 had been destroyed while being bombed up, and the death roll was feared to be heavy.

All sections had an immediate roll call, and it was found that eleven personnel had lost their lives. Operations for that night were cancelled.

On 18/19 November, the two Squadrons had a change of target. The Liberators of No. 178 Squadron carried out their first ever mine-laying operation, covered by a diversion by the Halifaxes of No. 462 Squadron. Two Liberators were detailed to lay mines at the entrance to the harbour at Candia and two to lay mines across the straits of Khalkis. One of the minelayers on Candia failed to return, but the other three successfully planted their mines in the allotted areas. One was held by searchlights at Khalkis and engaged by intense AA from a ship during its first run across the channel. It abandoned the run, and, after successfully evading the opposition, came back and laid its mines. The pilot, Flight Lieutenant P.G. Brown, was awarded an immediate DFC, and his navigator/bomb-aimer, Flight Sergeant B.J. McGowan, was awarded an immediate DFM. Six Halifaxes were detailed for diversion bombing at Candia, and two at Khalkis. At Candia, one of the Halifaxes dropped flares east of the harbour mole, and then went on to bomb Heraklion airfield. Five bombed at Candia, where sticks of bombs were seen in the area of the warehouses south of the harbour. Explosions, followed by a very large yellow fire, were observed in the same area as the aircraft were leaving. At Khalkis, the target was the swing-bridge, and one of the aircraft identified and bombed the bridge, although visibility was poor. The other failed to locate the target after searching for an hour, and jettisoned its bombs before returning to base.

The final operation in November was carried out on the 21st/22nd, when four Liberators of No. 178 Squadron and nine Halifaxes of No. 462 Squadron were despatched to bomb the airfield at Heraklion. Two of the Halifaxes illuminated the target, but due to cloud cover and restricted visibility the full results of the bombing could not be observed. Several bursts were pinpointed in the target area, and what appeared to be an explosion occurred in the north-east part of the airfield. No. 240 Wing then temporarily suspended its operations, receiving instructions that it would not be called upon to operate (except in an emergency) until 2 December. This gave the Squadrons an opportunity to relax, and breakfast time was put back an hour – 'this met with unanimous approval!' Liberty runs into Benghazi were arranged, the messes were re-erected and re-organized, the domestic tents spring-cleaned, and the camp generally tidied up. A training programme was drawn up, with lectures on 'The Dinghy Radio', 'The Theory of Sighting', 'Harmonization' and 'Aircraft Recognition', and air-firing exercises were carried out. A bombing range was laid out at the old location at Hosc Raui, and bombing practice carried out daily. Attempts to introduce fighter affiliation exercises had to be abandoned because all the available fighters were needed elsewhere.

Entertainment for the month consisted of visits by two ENSA concert parties, 'A Smile and a Song' on 10 November and 'These Foolish Things' on 14 November, and a programme of music by the Sudanese Defence Corps band on 24 November. The shows were greatly appreciated and thoroughly enjoyed by all personnel, so much so that one party gave four performances instead of the scheduled two. The concert party of No. 462 Squadron was busily engaged rehearsing the Squadron pantomime 'Aladdin'. Sporting activities were also enthusiastically enjoyed by all. No. 462 Squadron fielded a very good rugby team, and was able to produce a 2nd XV due to the many rugby-playing recruits recently arrived on the Squadron. Six rugby matches were played during the month, and five soccer matches. Table tennis, darts and draughts were also popular, and many competitions were arranged.

The Liberators and Halifaxes of No. 240 Wing remained at Terria until the end of December, when they were moved to El Adem. During the month it was decided that No. 462 Squadron would no longer remain an 'Australian' unit. Its formation at Fayid on 6 September had merely been a fusion of crews and aircraft of Nos 10 and 76 Squadrons of Bomber Command, which had been temporarily loaned to Middle East Command. All its ground complement and all its aircrew except one were British, and it was less Australian in character than any other squadron in No. 205 Group. On 18 August 1943 Headquarters RAF Middle East admitted that only nineteen of the Squadron's aircrew members were Australian. It seems that Wellington crews suitable for local conversion to Halifaxes had been sent to the Middle East, and had been absorbed en route by No. 205 Group. Any Australian personnel left with the Squadron were to be transferred out, and replaced with RAF personnel. On the 28th the Squadrons commenced their move from Terria to El Adem, and the air parties left on the 29th and arrived on the same day. At the end of the month the advance parties had arrived at the new site, but the main road parties were still in transit.

The Wing only carried out eight operations in December, and flew a mere ninety-one sorties – thirty-three by the Liberators of No. 178 Squadron and fifty-eight by the Halifaxes of No. 462 Squadron. The Liberators were mainly involved in their new task of mine-laying, with the Halifaxes providing diversions. The 'gardening' plots were at Salonika, Salamis, Candia, Suda Bay, and Khalkis, and the mining operations were generally successful. There was also one attack on shipping in Suda Bay and one attack on harbour installations at Piraeus. The weather was often poor, and although the diversionary bombing seems to have helped the gardeners, few positive results were obtained. The Wing would remain in North Africa until March 1944 and we will pick up their story in the next chapter.

*   *   *

The night bombers operated on 60 of the 92 nights between October 1943 and the end of the year, and the move to Italy meant that the number of sorties despatched (1,920) was restricted during this period. However, losses were fairly heavy (47 aircraft lost), mainly due to the disastrous attack on the Villar Perosa ball bearing factory at Turin. Once again, the emphases were on railway targets (36 per cent) and airfields (36 per cent). Military targets in the battle area took up 16 per cent of the total effort.

NOTES

1. Chappell, *Wellington Wings*, page 205.
2. Ibid, page 206.
3. Ibid, page 207.
4. Ibid, page 210.
5. On 30 May 1944 Flying Officer R.L.W. Cheek was killed in a flying accident when the Wellington he was testing stalled and crashed. He had flown some forty-three operations, and was awarded the DSO for his daring and accurate bombing attacks.
6. Gunby, *Sweeping the Skies*, page 246.
7. Chappell, *Wellington Wings*, page 215.
8. Ibid, page 217.
9. Gunby, *Sweeping the Skies*, page 251.

CHAPTER TEN

Desolation and Mud – Early Operations from Foggia – January to April 1944

Now that the Wellingtons of No. 205 Group were more or less settled in their bases around Foggia, they could begin to play their part in the Combined Bombing Offensive against Germany. Attacks against marshalling yards and industrial targets would increase, and operations in support of the armies on the ground would decrease. The Allied medium and fighter-bomber tactical air forces had by now grown in size and expertise, and could easily handle the ground support operations. However, as the ground forces became stalled on the road to Rome, the heavy bombers would once again be called upon to help them break through. The road to Rome – Highway 6 – ran through the Liri valley, and to get to it the Allies needed to cross the Gustav Line and the Rapido/Garigliano River.[1] The Germans well understood that the Allies would have little choice other than to force the entrance to the valley by a frontal assault, and had placed their strongest defences in the valley and on the massive buttresses on its two sides. Thus, all operations on the ground at the start of 1944 would be dominated by the domineering heights of Monte Cassino. Operations began on 5 January 1943, when the 2nd US Army Corps began a new offensive to clear the approaches to the Rapido/Garigliano. After a week of heavy fighting, the Germans withdrew across the river to the main Gustav positions, and successfully repulsed British and American attempts to cross the river over the next few days.

The Allies did have another trick up their sleeves, however, and that was a plan (Operation *Shingle*) to land a strong force at Anzio, well behind the Gustav Line and only thirty-five miles from Rome. The objective of Operation *Shingle* was to get into the exposed rear of the German defences, and force them to retreat northwards past Rome. The landing by the 6th US Corps on 22 January took the Germans completely by surprise, and not a shot was fired at the Allied troops as they came ashore. As night fell, the enemy had still not appeared at Anzio, but Major General Lucas expected that the Germans would turn up soon and ordered everybody to dig in and wait. No deep reconnaissance was attempted, and all the efforts went into setting up a defensive perimeter and building up the force in the beachhead. As ever, Kesselring reacted with great speed, and strong forces were soon moving towards the beachhead. On the evening of the 23rd, the first attacks by the *Luftwaffe* on Allied shipping took place, and on the 25th tentative advances out of the bridgehead were checked by troops of the Herman Göring Panzer Division. In the end, the Anzio operation would cause more problems than it solved. Fierce fighting would continue in the beachhead for four months, until it was relieved by the troops that had finally broken through the Gustav Line. Thus, by the end of

January the US Fifth Army had failed to penetrate the Liri valley, and the 6th US Corps was penned in the Anzio bridgehead. The slugging match would continue for a long time yet.

The biggest enemy for the Air Forces in January 1944 was the weather. The Official History of the war in the Mediterranean and the Middle East comments that during January there were only six days of good flying weather west of the Apennines and three to the east of them. On the remaining days, the weather ranged from difficult through bad to impossible, and the effects of the bad weather were different for different types of aircraft on different days and nights. On the ground, the maintenance crews had to endure terrible conditions, and half-frozen aircraftsmen toiled in the open with numbed fingers to repair complicated and delicate machinery. At the end of the year there were severe storms in the Foggia area, with very heavy rain and high winds. The rain had started on the night of 30 December, and Chappell tells how a wet night was followed by 'an unforgettable day of constant heavy rain'. There was mud and water everywhere at Foggia Main, and most of the tents (only erected the day before) were 'now in poor shape'. A gale was also blowing, but it abated enough towards nightfall to allow 'an enormous and spontaneous celebration of the New Year by every serviceman who had access to a revolver, rifle or gun'. Machine-guns, 20-mm cannons, Bofors light AA guns and even heavy AA guns were fired into the damp skies, and shrapnel and shell splinters joined the falling rain to add to the misery. The men awoke to a gloomy day, wet and cold, and with a strong east wind. The large mess tent and kitchen tents had been flattened, but an issue of gumboots and a rum ration did something to improve matters.

On 1 January, operations against Wiener Neustadt were cancelled due to the weather. No. 37 Squadron reports that the New Year at Tortorella was ushered in by a wind and rain storm 'of great violence'. A considerable number of tents were found to be badly ripped with uprights and ridge poles broken. It became necessary to accommodate nearly fifty men in the Foggia transit camp, and an immediate search for billets was undertaken. For the next couple of days all personnel were involved in helping to get the tents up again. Struggling in thick mud and with a bitter wind howling, they succeeded in creating comparative order out of chaos. No. 40 Squadron reports that no operations were carried out in the first few days of the month, 'and time was mainly spent in "digging in" and preparing for the expected bad weather'.

Not only were living and working conditions terrible, but the drying of clothes and bedding presented a huge problem. This difficulty was only overcome with the help of the Mobile Field Hospitals and Army Field Hygiene Units in the area, which made their disinfectant plant available for the drying of clothing, and the US Army Air Force also supplied dry clothing. New billets were found for the 780 aircrew of the four squadrons in a former technical college in Foggia that had been badly damaged by the bombing. It was described as having no facilities, no windows, a cold water tap, and buckets for toilets, but after a few days' work the rooms were made windproof and fairly comfortable. The ground personnel remained on the airfields, and new tents were provided, together with more gumboots and raincoats. The ORB for No. 40 Squadron comments that intense cold and rain at the beginning of the month made it necessary to issue tots of rum to the ground crews.

All the landing grounds from which No. 205 Group had to operate were generally unsuitable, and accident rates tended to be high. For example, Torretto Landing Ground (Cerignola No. 3), at which Nos 142 and 150 Squadrons were based, had one runway, only thirty-five yards wide and with a pronounced camber. The numerous instances of aircraft swinging on take-off and landing could therefore be understood, particularly when many pilots lacked experience. Furthermore, these landing grounds were overcrowded, accommodating units of the USAAF as well as other squadrons of the RAF. It was also obvious that Cerignola No. 2 airfield was generally unsuitable, and was likely to remain so for some time. Therefore, it was decided to move No. 231 Wing to Tortorella, and the operational detachment of No. 37 Squadron moved forward on 6 January, with the administrative section following on 14 January. The whole of No. 70 Squadron moved on 14 January, and No. 231 Wing Headquarters on 29 January.

The Headquarters of No. 205 Group (Advanced Operations) at Cerignola was understaffed at first, but an Administrative Officer was attached from Group HQ and relieved the pressure on the Senior Operations Staff Officer and Signals Staff Officer. Personnel of the unit were housed in the house of Baron Manfreddi in the Via Ercole (the Officers' Mess), and in the 'Scola Media' (the lower floor as offices and the top floor as airmen's living quarters). A flat in the Via Roma was acquired for the use of the AOC, and part of the railway station yard and buildings became the airmen's cookhouse and the MT section. Further small buildings were taken over for the Sergeants' Mess and living quarters, sick quarters, and RAF Regiment Headquarters. Although many of the buildings were subsequently taken over by the Fifteenth Air Force, eventually a *modus vivendi* was arrived at. On 4 January officers of Nos 231 and 236 Wings travelled to Foggia to arrange the billeting of aircrew in the former technical college in the Via Alessandro Volta. Like most buildings in Foggia, it had been damaged by bombing, and was for the most part without doors or windows. The aircrew immediately began the task of improving elementary comforts, particularly seeking out heaters of various kinds as no supplies of stoves were available from RAF stores.

The spell of extremely bad weather continued into the New Year, with snow falling on 6 January, and this kept all three Wings grounded throughout the whole of the first week. The rear road/sea party from No. 37 Squadron arrived at Cerignola on 6 January, where the administrative unit was still in residence. They had had an unhappy experience at Naples, where disembarkation arrangements had been far from satisfactory. Vehicles had been assembled on the road without regard to units, and then moved off to an assembly area where personnel were expected to bivouac in the open although it was raining hard. After a considerable delay, the party was guided through Naples, but traffic control broke down. Some vehicles ended up at the American transit camp, and there was a further delay while the missing vehicles were located and re-directed to the correct camp.

*   *   *

The Group managed 650 sorties on 16 nights in January 1944, which was a creditable effort under the trying circumstances in which the Group found itself at the beginning of the month. Railway targets received 275 sorties (42 per cent of the total effort), industrial targets another 171 sorties (26 per cent), and airfields 125 sorties (19 per cent). On 7/8 January, a maximum effort was called for on the Reggio

Emilia aircraft factory, but No. 330 Wing's airfield (Cerignola No. 3) was unserviceable and repairs being carried out on the runway at Tortorella prevented No. 231 Wing from operating. Therefore, No. 236 Wing provided the whole effort from Foggia Main. Twenty-eight aircraft took off, but two returned early. The others attacked in clear weather and with good illumination, and carried out an accurate, well controlled attack. Photographs taken at the time revealed many direct hits in the target area, and smoke indicated a number of large fires. The damage was confirmed by subsequent photographs taken by the USAAF bombers that attacked the same target on the following day. The wireless operator of one of the aircraft of No. 40 Squadron baled out over Bologna, 'apparently under the misapprehension that the aircraft was out of control when it dived steeply to avoid flak'.

No. 330 Wing still could not operate on the next night when the target was the Villaorba Landing Ground, and forty-one aircraft of Nos 231 and 236 Wings took off. Conditions were favourable and the bombing appeared to be effective, but haze and smoke prevented accurate observation of results. Many photographs did not show the target airfield, and revealed no outstanding results. One aircraft of No. 37 Squadron developed engine trouble on the return journey and crashed on landing. The Squadron CO, Wing Commander McKenzie, was operating as second pilot and was seriously injured, fracturing his pelvis and dislocating his hip. Two other members of the crew also sustained injuries. Squadron Leader Beale assumed temporary command of the squadron.

On 10/11 January the Group attacked Sofia, following a daytime raid by the Fifteenth Air Force. The purpose was to 'strike at the morale of the Bulgarian people'. In other words, this was an area bombing raid, with the aiming point the city centre. Although the Group had often hit civilian areas in attacks on ports and railway targets, this was the first time that they had been directed expressly to bomb such a target, and it caused some consternation amongst the crews of No. 40 Squadron. This was quickly silenced by the CO, who said 'Those are orders and must be obeyed.' No. 330 Wing was still grounded, but forty-eight aircraft from the other two Wings took off. The weather was good, and the Wellingtons carried out a concentrated attack on the centre of the City. Several small fires were started, and one very large fire was visible for seventy-five miles on the return trip. One Wellington of No. 40 Squadron was unable to locate any airfield on which to land on return, and as it was running short of petrol the crew successfully abandoned the aircraft in the Foggia area. The Group ORB states that the raids appeared to have had a far greater effect on the morale of the Bulgarian people than could have been expected in relation to the amount of damage done. The 'reported disordered and wholesale evacuation of over 300,000 people undoubtedly led to considerable chaos in Sofia in particular and in Bulgaria in general, and has helped to weaken the already precarious position of the Bulgarian government'.

On the following night the target was Piraeus and shipping in the Halon basin. At the time, Piraeus was the most important Axis-held port in the eastern Mediterranean, maintaining a shuttle service with the Dodecanese and Crete. Nos 231 and 236 Wings despatched thirty-nine aircraft, but two collided shortly after take-off and had to return to base, where both landed safely. One of the aircraft of No. 40 Squadron had two blades break off its port propeller and the engine caught fire, but despite this the pilot made a successful landing with his bombs still on board. Two other aircraft returned early with mechanical failures, and thirteen abandoned the operation due to cloud and severe icing conditions. Twenty-four aircraft found a break in the clouds over the target and dropped their bombs, and although accurate observation of results was impossible due to intense flak and searchlight activity, photographs suggested that the target was correctly identified and fair results obtained. One aircraft of No. 104 Squadron failed to return. On 12/13 January, all three Wings operated against the airfield at Perugia, despatching forty-eight aircraft. Thick cloud over the target greatly hampered the operation, and those aircraft that got to the target area mostly bombed on ETA and many bombed targets of opportunity instead.

On 15/16 January, the Group was given two targets, the first being the railway line between Rimini and Ancona. Nine aircraft of No. 142 Squadron operated, but one returned early and two failed to locate the target and abandoned their task. Low cloud and extensive ground haze rendered the attack largely abortive, and only two hits on the line were claimed. In the second operation forty-nine aircraft from the three Wings were despatched to attack Salonika marshalling yards, but three returned early for various reasons and fourteen abandoned their task as they were unable to locate the target due to fog and low cloud. Twenty-nine aircraft claimed to have attacked the yards, most bombing on ETA, flares and flak. One of the Wellingtons, piloted by Group Captain Southwell, OC No. 330 Wing, force-landed at Gallipoli at first light, and he and his crew were interned at Istanbul.

On 16/17 January, thirty-nine aircraft were despatched on another attack on the Villaorba Landing Ground, but three returned early and four failed to locate the target and abandoned the mission. Thick haze prevented observation of results, and bombing was generally reported as scattered. However, the bomb load included a large number of 40-lb fragmentation bombs, and the attack appears to have been far more effective than first thought. The almost total lack of fighter opposition against a daylight raid on the same district the following morning was credited to the damage caused by the Wellingtons. On the next night twenty-four aircraft took off to attack Pisa marshalling yards, but one returned early after being unable to gain height due to severe icing conditions. Visibility was good except for some haze, and good illumination was provided by six of the aircraft, but bombing was only described as fair. Two 4,000-pounders were dropped slightly south of the yards, and other bursts were reported along the yards and across the adjacent aircraft factory.

On 18/19 January, the Wellingtons attacked another railway target when forty aircraft were despatched to Pontassieve marshalling yards. Thick haze made identification of the target difficult, the illumination was scattered, and the bombing consequently lacked concentration. Two aircraft carrying 4,000-pounders were detailed to attack the railway bridge at Pontassieve, but one of the bombs hung up and had to be released by jettison bar, and it fell in the town north of the yards. The other was aimed at the eastern end of the bridge, but was not seen to explode. One of the Wellingtons failed to locate the target and jettisoned its bombs, and one crashed on return and all the crew were killed. Another, lost and rapidly running out of petrol, was successfully abandoned near Naples. On the same night sixteen aircraft took off to attack the Rimini–Ancona railway line, but there was cloud down to 300 feet and in these dangerous conditions most aircraft jettisoned their bombs and returned to base. Two Wellingtons broke cloud and bombed roads between Varno and Ancona, and another bombed and machine-gunned a train at Porto d'Ascoli. One of the aircraft of No. 104 Squadron crashed in the hills south of the base, and Chappell tells us that the aircraft was 'found on top of the mountain ridge of the Gargano Promontory' and another from No. 40 Squadron 'had also been located in a similar position'. All crew members from both aircraft were killed.

Following a 'stand-down' due to the weather, forty-eight Wellingtons were despatched on 20/21 January to attack railway targets at Cecina, including a bridge and lines to the north and south of the town. Sixteen aircraft of No. 231 Wing made the first attack in cloudless but slightly hazy weather. The illumination was good, and two possible direct hits and various near misses on the bridge were claimed. Two Wellingtons collided over the target, but both returned with only minor damage. The weather had deteriorated somewhat when twenty-six aircraft of Nos 236 and 330 Wings arrived in the target area two hours later. Haze prevented accurate observation of results, and some aircraft jettisoned their bombs as they were unable to identify the target. The bomb loads included a large number of long delays (up to thirty-six hours), the object of the raid being to interrupt repairs to the bridge, which had been cut in the successful attack on the night of 12/13 November 1943. The latest information suggested that two spans of the bridge were still missing.

On 21/22 January forty-five Wellingtons took off to attack the torpedo factory at Fiume, carrying out a highly successful raid in clear weather and with good illumination. Large fires were started in and around the factory, visible for a hundred miles on the return journey, and photographs taken during the attack showed large volumes of smoke, some possibly coming from oil storage tanks. Later information confirmed the outstanding success of this raid. The torpedo factory, the oil refinery, the machining section of the ship yards, and a timber factory were set on fire. Two U-boats and one MTB were sunk, and about fifty houses destroyed. The weather intervened on the next night and operations were cancelled, but cleared sufficiently to allow an attack on the aircraft factory at Maribor on 23/24 January. Forty-nine aircraft from all three Wings took off, but the operation was almost entirely abortive due to extremely bad weather en route. Seven Wellingtons returned early, twenty-two were unable to locate the target, and two failed to return. Only eighteen crews claimed to have bombed somewhere in the vicinity of the target.

The weather again closed in for the next three nights, although a nickelling operation on Rome did manage to get off, and then on 27/28 January the three Wings despatched forty-one aircraft to attack the Arezzo marshalling yards. One aircraft of No. 70 Squadron caught fire soon after take-off and crashed, killing all the crew, and two returned early with mechanical defects. One of the Wellingtons of No. 37 Squadron failed to return. The attack was carried out in favourable weather with good illumination, and the bombing was reported to be accurate and concentrated. Numerous hits were recorded on and near the marshalling yards and railway lines, and the line was temporarily blocked. On the next night, marshalling yards at Foligno and Verona were the targets. Seventeen Wellingtons of No. 231 Wing took off for Foligno, but two returned early, one with engine trouble and the other after being hit by flak over Pescara. One Wellington of No. 37 Squadron failed to return. The others attacked in good visibility, with three 4,000-pounders dropped and good results claimed. Thirty-three aircraft of Nos 236 and 330 Wings left for

Verona, but three returned early for various reasons and one Wellington of No. 150 Squadron failed to return. Thick haze made identification very difficult, and most of the crews were far from enthusiastic about the results.

After two nights when the weather again prevented operations, fifty-five sorties were ordered for an operation on Trieste oil refinery on 31 January/1 February. However, those from No. 231 Wing had to be cancelled due to repair work on the Tortorella runway, and only thirty-five aircraft of Nos 236 and 330 Wings were despatched. One of these returned early with a damaged propeller, and a third was unable to locate the target and brought its bombs back to base. Visibility was poor and the illumination faulty, and the bombing was consequently scattered. Photographs taken by the bombers confirmed that they were over the target area, but subsequent reconnaissance photographs revealed that no important damage was caused to the refinery.

*   *   *

In February the Garrison Theatre at Foggia was visited by Lily Pons, the star coloratura soprano at the New York Metropolitan Opera. Miss Pons spent the morning of her visit with an American unit based at Foggia, and in the afternoon she came to the No. 37 Squadron camp at Tortorella. It was said that the Americans kept one of their aircraft circling the base at altitude so that Miss Pons could have some ice cream! Mears records that the officers and NCOs of No. 37 Squadron were not exactly overjoyed by the visit, especially as the Station Commander ordered the removal of a rather explicit mural from the mess wall. He also ordered that a special toilet should be prepared for the forty-six-year-old soprano in a nearby olive grove, and Toby Wing, an engineering officer with the Squadron, was put in charge of the job.

The toilet was built and a bucket placed therein as a receptacle – at the bottom of which Wing placed a small lump of calcium carbide. This substance, of course, is perfectly safe…until it gets wet, whereupon it produces flammable acetylene. All afternoon the singer was plied with the local vino, but her bladder held out until she was due to leave, when she set off to use the toilet. All eyes were fixed on the olive grove, waiting for the bang. The men were not disappointed, and were rewarded by sight of an international singing star sprinting across the olive grove with her skirt in her hands. As punishment, the Station Commander ordered that twenty members of the Squadron would have to attend that evening's concert.

On the ground the fighting at Cassino and Anzio continued unabated. At Cassino American troops reached the outskirts of the town and dug in, with the two sides sometimes separated by just a few yards. Positions changed hands repeatedly, and attack and counter-attack followed each other, as though driven by some devilish timetable. In describing the fighting, the Official History states that the American and German infantry 'were clinched, exchanging blow for blow with blind yet heroic pugnacity…the battle had lost all coherence except that which arose from the inflexible wills of the opponents'. To add misery to the trials of the troops on both sides, the weather began to worsen, with rain, sleet and snow. The US 2nd Corps tried one last attack on 11 February, but their brave efforts achieved little but high casualties and another bloody stalemate. They were relieved by the New Zealand Corps, and General Freyberg made his plans for yet another assault on Monastery Hill and Cassino town. These plans raised the question of the bombing of the Abbey itself, and although it had been agreed that the Abbey would be preserved if possible, its safety would 'not be allowed to interfere with military necessity'. On 13 February, leaflets were fired into the Abbey in special 'propaganda' shells to warn whoever might be inside that it would be bombed on 15 February. Between 0925 and 1005 hours on that day 135 B-17s dropped 257 tons of bombs and 59 tons of incendiaries on the target, and these were followed between 1035 and 1332 hours by forty-seven Mitchells and forty Marauders, which dropped another 126 tons. The Abbey was left as a roofless shell, but when the 7th Indian Brigade began its attack that night it had been occupied by paratroopers who had been presented with a superb defensive position in the ruins. The attackers made no progress and the attacks were called off a few days later.

Things went no better at Anzio, where on 3 February an attempt to breakout of the beachhead ended after an advance of just three miles in three days. Two days later the Germans began a full-scale counter-attack against the beachhead, and made good progress. By 11 February the Allies were pushed back to a final defence line at Anzio, and a few days later Kesselring launched seven divisions in a second major attack. The Germans made further gains over the next two days, but were repulsed by Allied artillery and warships. The fighting continued throughout the rest of the month, and on the 29th the Germans launched their third major offensive.

The bad weather that afflicted the ground battle also hampered the operations of No. 205 Group, and it was only able to operate on eighteen nights during February, launching 548 sorties and losing thirteen aircraft in the process. Even on those nights when operations did take place, they were more than once curtailed or ruined by bad weather. The Group ORB comments that 'About the middle of February, Army commitments in Italy demanded the use of the Night Bomber Force against tactical targets in close support operations within the battle area.' These operations gave rise to many difficulties due to 'the variable nature of tactical targets', with operations called at short notice and the Group unable to plan ahead. In all, some 357 sorties were despatched against targets just behind the battlefield in order to try to prevent reinforcements reaching the front. This represented 65 per cent of the total effort by the Group, with most of the remainder going to industrial and railway targets.

On the first night of February, the target was the aircraft factory at Maribor in Yugoslavia. The ongoing repairs to the runway at Tortorella prevented No. 231 Wing from operating, and the thirty aircraft were provided by Nos 236 and 330 Wings. The weather and the visibility were good, and early reports suggested that a concentrated attack had been carried out. However, the bombing photographs showed that the target attacked was not the Maribor factory but another some miles to the south-east. Considerable flak was experienced in the target area, and there appeared to be good co-operation between searchlights and night-fighters. One aircraft of No. 104 Squadron did not return, and was presumed to have been an aircraft seen to have been shot down over the target. After a stand-down for five nights due to the bad weather, forty-five aircraft were detailed to attack Padua railway yards on 7/8 February. Photographs confirmed that the correct target was attacked and many bursts were observed across the marshalling yards and in the built-up area nearby. One aircraft of No.37 Squadron, returning early with engine trouble and with its 4,000-lb bomb still on board, crashed on landing. The bomb exploded, killing all the crew and destroying the aircraft. One of No. 150 Squadron also brought back a 500-lb long-delay bomb, and it was 'lying under the a/c in dispersal and delaying work amongst the a/c somewhat'! It eventually went off at 1530 hours, destroying the aircraft but causing no other damage.

The poor state of the aircrew billets in Foggia was illustrated by an unfortunate accident on the morning of 6 February. Two NCO aircrew – Sergeant W.T. Dunn and Flight Sergeant E.W. Moody – were trying to collect firewood in a section of the building that had been severely damaged by bombing. The floors and walls collapsed, trapping them beneath tons of debris. Rescue squads immediately went to work, not knowing whether the two men were dead or alive. The work required considerable courage, given the difficult and dangerous conditions in the wrecked building, and further collapses were expected every minute. Two units were singled out for special mention for their work in the rescue – the 21st Aviation Engineer Regiment of the USAAF and a 'Palestinian' labour company of the RASC. Sergeant Dunn was got out after a few hours with injuries that were surprisingly slight, but Flight Sergeant Moody was not rescued until well after midnight. He was still alive and conscious and there seemed to be a good chance of him making a full recovery. Unfortunately, he died in hospital on 9 February, and was buried the following morning in the Bari War Cemetery. He was twenty-one years of age.

On 8 February No. 142 Squadron ORB reported that some of its Wellingtons were being fitted with the Mk XIV bombsight and the crews trained in its use. The bombsight had first entered service with Bomber Command in late 1942, and was a great improvement on the old equipment. Its main feature was that it was fitted with a gyro that could accommodate a 60-degree bank and 40-degree dive, and evasive action on the bombing run would not affect the sight's accuracy provided that at least ten seconds of the run were made in steady flight. A computer automatically conveyed adjustments to the sight, and the bomb aimer saw a graticule moving over the ground below him. If the aircraft was flying a correct course, the target appeared moving slowly down the graticule's longer axis while the bomb-aimer provided the pilot with the necessary corrections over the intercom. When the graticule's shorter axis bisected the target, the bombs were released.

On 8/9 February the marshalling yards at Rimini and Arezzo were the target. Fourteen aircraft of No. 236 Wing took off for Rimini, but there was 10/10 cloud down to 2,000 feet over the target and rain and icing conditions. All except three of the aircraft returned without attacking, either as a result of the weather conditions or in response to a recall signal. Thirteen aircraft of No. 330 Wing set off for Arezzo, but this operation was also completely ineffective due to the weather. Six of the Wellingtons jettisoned, six brought their bombs back, and one bombed an unidentified stretch of road and railway.

There followed another three nights when no operations were possible because of the weather. Then on 12/13 February attacks were ordered on road transport in the Campoleone and Cisterna area, north of the Anzio Battle Area. This was the start of a series of attacks on roads in an area north of the battlefield to try to prevent German reinforcements from reaching the beachhead. Seven attacks were launched between 12/13 and 18/19 February and a total of 357 sorties despatched against roads around and between Campoleone, Cisterna, Cecchina, Albano, Grottaferrata, Marino, Velletri and Genzano. The Squadrons often flew double sorties on these operations, the bombers returning to base to collect more bombs and setting off again. Although little was seen in the way of transport or troop concentrations, at least sleepless nights were ensured for the enemy columns moving through the area. Most of the crews usually reported fair results from these attacks, but haze often obscured the target areas and the weather was rarely good. Mears provides us with an account given by Ken Wallis of No. 37 Squadron of the aftermath of the attack on Albano town on 17/18 February:

> The bomb-load was 18 x 250lb NIR – bombs with a long rod extending from a nose fuse, to ensure detonation above ground to ensure maximum anti-personnel effect. They were deadly stores, becoming armed as they left the rack. Sometimes a 'stick' of bombs would jostle each other when dropped at short time intervals and they would detonate up to the bomber…After our second bombing of the target that night we returned to Tortorella in the first light of the morning.
>
> When preparing to land, I selected the wheels down, but we failed to get a green light for the tail wheel. We went round again and made many attempts to get the tail wheel down by lifting and lowering the undercarriage, without success. Finally I decided that the rear gunner should vacate his turret and that we would have to let the Wellington drag her tail on our metal strip runway. Then, at the last stages of the approach, the tail-wheel green light came on.
>
> We landed normally and taxied to the dispersal area. Just as I applied the brakes and was about to shut down the engines, one of the airmen ran towards us, moving his arms together indicating 'Close bomb doors.' Normally, of course, as soon as the engines were shut down the bomb doors would be opened, to relieve the hydraulics. I took note of his signals, leaving the bomb doors closed, and we descended the ladder. Then the reason for his signals was readily apparent. The nose of a 250lb bomb, with its rod about 18" long protruding from the nose fuse was sticking out through the gap in the bomb doors!
>
> If our tail-wheel had not come down at the last possible moment and if I had not been warned by that very observant and brave airman to keep the bomb doors closed we would certainly have been blown up. The bomb was made safe and removed. We all had a laugh and thanked the airman, who might well have made for the nearest hiding place and covered his ears when he saw what we were bringing back to dispersal. This is just one more instance of a brave deed that was deserving of proper recognition, but seemed 'all in the day's work' at the time.[2]

Three aircraft were lost in these operations. On 12/13 February one of the Wellingtons of No. 70 Squadron set course for base after bombing the target area, and then found that two bombs had hung up. The aircraft changed course in order to jettison the bombs in the Adriatic, and a landfall was made in the Bari area on returning to the coast. There was considerable cloud, and the navigator had much difficulty in pinpointing their exact position. He asked the Captain to descend to about 1,500 feet and almost immediately the aircraft crashed into a hillside fifteen miles south-west of Corato. The rear gunner was thrown clear, and, although suffering from shock, he succeeded in summoning help. The Captain was very seriously injured and taken to hospital in Andrea, and the other three crew members were killed. On 15/16 February one of No. 150 Squadron crash-landed at base after completing the operation and the pilot was killed and another member of the crew died in hospital. On 17/18 February an aircraft from No. 40 Squadron crashed immediately after take-off and exploded, killing five of the crew. Chappell tells us that it went in near the main road alongside Foggia, killing some civilians and a soldier, in addition to the crew members. The rear gunner was again a lucky man, and was blown clear still in his turret. On 18/19 February the crew of one aircraft of No. 40 Squadron that was temporarily out of control was ordered to bale out, after which the pilot regained control at 500 feet and landed safely.

While the Battle Area attacks were going on, information was received that shipping movements were taking place from the small port of Porto San Stefano, north of Rome near Orbetello. An attack was detailed for 16/17 February, and fourteen aircraft of No. 231 Wing operated first. A severe electrical storm with bad icing conditions was encountered north of Naples on the outward journey, and only ten Wellingtons reached the target area. No ships were seen in the harbour, and the aircraft bombed buildings and harbour installations instead. Only one of the seventeen aircraft from No. 236 Wing that followed on from this attack reported seeing some ships, but all bombed buildings in the harbour area as well. Two Wellingtons crashed on return. One of No. 40 Squadron came down ten miles south-west of Troia, and another of No. 104 Squadron crashed two miles west of the airfield. The crews of both aircraft were all killed. Chappell states that the No. 104 Squadron aircraft dived in while in the circuit, and buried itself in the ground. The pilot was talking to Flying Control seconds before the crash, and it was believed that the Wellington had iced up when coming down through the clouds. The other Wellington was later found crashed on a hillside with all crew members burned beyond recognition.

On the last night of the month the bombers attacked a 'Pointblank' target[3] for the first time, the Daimler-Puch aircraft factory at Steyr in Austria. The target was regarded as one of the most important factories in the German Fighter Industry complex, the destruction of which would affect the production of Bf 109 fuselages for at least six months. The Group's attack was planned to follow up a raid made by the Fifteenth Air Force on the previous day, but great difficulty was experienced in locating the target. Although the weather was fine over the target area, a covering of fresh snow made the identification of ground detail difficult and the night was particularly dark. Two aircraft of No. 236 Wing claimed to have located the target, and aimed their bombs at a large fire in factory buildings, and one of them was definitely plotted by photographs to be over Steyr. Most of the remainder were later plotted to be over Vöcklabruck town, thirty-five miles west of Steyr. Six of the bombers failed to return: one of No. 70 Squadron crashed five miles west of San Severo and all the crew were killed; one aircraft of No. 104 Squadron was successfully abandoned near Altamura; one of No. 142 Squadron crashed two miles from Castel Nuovo with three crew members killed and one later succumbed to his injuries; another aircraft of No. 142 Squadron was abandoned over Corsica and all the crew were safe; a third Wellington of No. 142 Squadron crashed six miles north of Ariano Irpino, with three members of the crew killed; finally, one of No. 37 Squadron was missing and may have been the aircraft reported apparently hit by flak over Trieste. Chappell records that the raid on Steyr 'was not very successful', and prints the story of the raid as told by Associated Radio Press on 26 February:

Two engined RAF Wellington bombers specialists in mopping up operations by night after American Flying Forts and Liberators have bashed a target by day have joined the Italy-based assault on Hitler's aircraft industry Thursday night with a blow at Steyr Austria already bathed in fires from two days of American pounding. Making their deepest foray yet against the enemy from Med. Bases the British Work Horses concentrated on the Daimler factory at Steyr pouring their bombs down accurately by light of leaping fires and scattered other explosives over built-up areas and railroads serving the Manufacturing Centre.

Chappell asks 'Why on earth should reporters write such utter tripe?' – a question much asked of today's tabloid journalists!

Towards the end of February a Wellington Mk X left Portreath in Cornwall bound for Rabat Sale in North Africa. Piloting the machine was a certain Sergeant Maurice Lihou, and he has provided us with an excellent account of his subsequent activities 'flying Wimpys around Italian skies'.[4] The route followed took them across the Bay of Biscay, nicknamed 'Junkers Alley' due to the long-range Junkers Ju 88Cs based in France that preyed on the aircraft being ferried across the bay to Gibraltar. However, the night was dark and cloudy, and they survived the difficult journey unmolested. A few days later they flew on to Foggia Main, landing in the pouring rain to a scene of 'desolation and mud...and a feeling of hopelessness came over the crew'. We will hear more about his first impressions of life at Foggia later in this chapter.

*   *   *

While the Wellington squadrons of No. 205 Group were starting their operations from Italy, the Liberators and Halifaxes of No. 240 Wing were getting used to their new location at El Adem, south of Tobruk. The four-engined bombers could only operate on ten nights (ninety-one sorties) during January, and only on five nights (thirty-seven sorties) in February. Most of these operations were either mining operations (thirty-two sorties) or diversionary attacks on the harbours in which the mines were being laid, and three operations (five sorties) were nickelling missions. The main party from No. 462 Squadron arrived at El Adem on New Year's Day, and 'only had one fine day before the rain and bad weather set in.' The weather greatly hampered the initial setting up of the Squadron, and things were made worse by an acute shortage of transport. All available vehicles had to make several trips to the old site at Terria, some two hundred miles away along the coast road around the bulge of Cyrenaica. It was not until the middle of January that all the equipment and aircraft were established at El Adem.

The Liberators of No. 178 Squadron did manage to get two aircraft off the ground on 2/3 January, detailed to lay mines in the Khalkis Straits in Greece. One laid six mines as briefed, but the other aircraft lost four mines, which fell out as bomb doors were being tested, and it returned to base with the other two. The Squadron sent another two aircraft to Khalkis on the next night, but this time both aircraft encountered 10/10 cloud up to 20,000 feet. They were unable to fly round it, and electrical storms made it impossible to fly through it. Both jettisoned two mines and brought the rest back to base. The bad weather prevented all operations on the next night, and then on 5/6 January three Halifaxes of No. 462 Squadron carried out a diversionary bombing attack on the harbour defences at Rhodes, while four Liberators of No. 178 Squadron successfully planted mines in the approaches to the harbour. The weather intervened again for the next three nights, but on 9/10 four Liberators of No. 178 Squadron and two Halifaxes of No. 462 Squadron were detailed to lay mines in the straits outside Salamis harbour, while four Liberators and five Halifaxes carried out a diversionary attack on flak and searchlight positions around the harbour. One of the Liberators lost three mines while selecting and arming them and abandoned the operation after jettisoning the rest, and one of the bombers was late on target and also abandoned the operation. The remainder of the minelayers and bombers successfully completed their task.

Two Liberators went to Khalkis again on 10/11 January, before the Wing began a mini-offensive on the harbour installations at Piraeus, once in conjunction with a No. 205 Group attack on the same target. Five operations (seventy-two sorties) were launched, but the continuing poor weather often hampered the attacks and few positive results were seen. On 11/12 January, sixteen aircraft attacked in good visibility, and good bombing runs were made despite very accurate and intensive flak, with bombs seen to fall on warehouses west of the Halon basin and near the dry dock. On 15/16 January another sixteen aircraft went to Piraeus, but most of them had to abandon mission due to 10/10 cloud and icing conditions. One of the Halifaxes crash-landed at base on return, and another that was diverted to Gambut swung off the runway on landing and its undercarriage collapsed. The next attack came on 22/23 January, but the thirteen aircraft found the target obscured by cloud and haze and few were able to visually identify the harbour area. Most bombed on flak and searchlight positions and few results were observed. The same conditions were found on 26/27 January, and although many bursts were seen in the target area, results were unobserved.

During January, HQ Fifteenth Air Force were advised by MAAF that the two RAF heavy bomber squadrons would arrive in Italy in mid-January for assignment to the Strategic Air Force, and for operations with No. 205 Group. The main road/sea parties of Nos 178 and 462 Squadrons and No. 240 Wing eventually left El Adem on 1 February, and had a fairly satisfactory journey to Cairo considering the condition of most of the transport provided. The journey through Cairo was enlivened by the cooking trailer falling apart in one of the city's main streets, much to the amusement of the local population. The few days spent in Cairo were greatly appreciated by everyone as many of the personnel had had no leave for some considerable time. The main party left Cairo at 0730 hours on 11 February, and the organization that had been reasonably efficient up until then now broke down. The train was due to arrive at Amyria at 1240 hours, but due to a leaky boiler it finally arrived at 1800 hours. After a very scrappy and unsatisfactory meal, transport arrived to move the Squadrons to the Transit Camp.

The problems continued when the party arrived at the camp when it became obvious that no arrangements had been made for their reception. They were eventually advised that all three units would have to be self supporting while at Amyria, which would have been fine had they known of this beforehand, but at the time it came as a bit of a shock. The three units eventually embarked at Alexandria on 15 February. The ship was Polish, and apart from a little overcrowding, was very pleasant, and the food for all ranks was excellent. After a slightly rough but otherwise uneventful voyage, the ship docked at Naples on 21 February and the passengers disembarked on the same day, only to find that most of their equipment had been unloaded at Taranto. After seven days in the Base Depot at Naples, during which time all personnel were able to visit places of interest around the city, the final stage of the journey was started on 28 February. This was the worse part of the entire move. Everyone was accommodated in cattle trucks reminiscent of the 1914–18 trench trains – 20 *hommes et* 40 *cheveaux* – and the weather across the Apennines was bitterly cold. The new site at Celone was eventually reached on the morning of 1 March, and everyone immediately set to work to prepare for operations. Everyone was were greatly pleased with the camp site, and found the grassy Foggia plain a great change after a very long spell of sand and dust in Libya.

Meanwhile, the air parties waited for their move to Celone. Life was not easy, with so many personnel already on their way to Italy with the road/sea parties, and the weather was terrible. El Adem was hit by a series of the worst wind and sandstorms that had ever been experienced in the desert. Tents were blown down, and wind breakers 'billowing like spinnakers' either split or broke away. Several roofs were lifted from the permanent buildings, the mess collapsed, and tins of food had to be handed out so that the men could prepare it for themselves in their own tents. There were not enough people left to bomb up and refuel the aircraft, but these old desert hands were used to such difficulties, and managed to carry out a restricted schedule of operations with the help of the station personnel at El Adem. Also during February, the crews of No. 462 Squadron were being asked to familiarize themselves with 'secret equipment…devices which have revolutionized the night actions of Bomber Command'. In November 1943, a number of crews had been sent back to the UK for training in the operation of H2S radar. This was in preparation for the Halifax squadron to assume a 'pathfinder' role when it moved to Italy, and they had brought a few of the sets back with them to start training the rest of the Squadron.

On 1/2 February, five Liberators laid mines in Suda Bay, while three Liberators and seven Halifaxes carried out a diversionary attack on defences. The next mining operation was on 9/10 February, when four Liberators successfully laid their mines in Candia harbour, with a diversionary raid provided by eight Halifaxes. One of the Halifaxes abandoned its task due to severe icing conditions, and while the remaining aircraft identified the target area, no results of the bombing were observed due to the poor weather. However, the diversion was successful in that none of the minelayers were troubled by flak. The other two mining operations, in the Khalkis Straits on 4/5 February and at Lemnos on 14/15 February, only involved five sorties altogether. The first was carried out successfully, but two of the aircraft were forced to abandon the Lemnos operation. The third aircraft successfully laid six mines in the port.

The air parties eventually discovered that they were to move to Celone at the end of the month, with the Liberators of No. 178 Squadron flying out on 28 and 29 February. They operated for the first time in Italy and for the first time under the operational control of No. 205 Group in an attack on Genoa on 11/12 March (see below). The Halifaxes of No. 462 Squadron left El Adem on 1 March, the airmen breakfasting long before it was light by the headlights of a three-ton truck, and the first aircraft taking off at 0700 hours. All bar two arrived safely at Celone – one returned with 'minor trouble' and the other landed at Cretone after developing a glycol leak. While the move was taking place, No. 462 became No. 614 Squadron,[5] and also operated with the Group for the first time on 11/12 March. The transformation had taken place on 3 March, and caused some problems as the Squadron settled down in its new location at Celone. When the AOC No. 205 Group visited the unit the Group did not seem to know what the new number would be, despite the fact that the official stamp for No. 614 Squadron was already in use in the orderly room.

There was also some confusion about the new role for No. 614 Squadron. Two new radar officers were now on the strength, and large quantities of H2S and Gee radio navigation equipment had been waiting for the Squadron when it arrived in Italy. While it seemed clear that the Squadron was to be a target marking ('pathfinder') unit, no one seemed to know for certain. Strong representations were made to the Group – 'and anyone else who appeared to be in the slightest way interested' – to clear up the situation! In the meantime, No. 614 Squadron were busy settling in and trying to deal with the seemingly never-ending stream of target-marking crews and H2S aircraft arriving daily from the UK. The Squadron ORB states that 'For once we were given time to become organized before being required to operate.' Although often operating with No. 205 Group, the Squadron would not actually come under its operational and administrative control until 10 May, following a move to Stornara.

*   *   *

The German attacks at Anzio ended on 3 March after heavy losses in men and tanks. The beachhead was now secure, and only came under periodic pressure from German long-range artillery and aircraft using guided bombs. Although these sometimes caused severe casualties in men, ships and equipment, they could do little to dislodge the Allied landings. However, the Allies also could do little to break out from the beachhead, and were forced to wait for rescue by the forces at Cassino. The fighting at Cassino in March followed the same bloody pattern as that in February, and with as little success. The pounding by the Allies and the stubborn and skilful defence by the Germans continued. The destruction of the monastery had failed, and so now the town became the target for the guns and the bombers. The Germans retreated into their bunkers in the ruins when the bombs and shells fell, and then came out again to cut down the attackers as they tried to advance through the rubble. A 'battle of Stalingrad model' developed, with every yard of ground laboriously cleared by snipers and troops with hand grenades, and then often lost again as the German paratroopers counter-attacked. On 22 March Alexander was forced to halt the frontal attacks and think again, and this ill-starred battle would go on for another two months yet.

On 19 March the Mediterranean Allied Air Forces launched Operation *Strangle*, a determined attempt to help the armies in Italy by interrupting and, if possible destroying, the enemy's lines of communication. The essence of the plan was for the bombers and fighter-bombers of the Tactical Air Force to attack railway targets, especially bridges, south of the line Pisa–Rimini. It was hoped that this would cause a build-up of rolling-stock carrying essential supplies in the various marshalling yards in northern Italy, where it could be destroyed by the strategic bombers of the USAAF Fifteenth Air Force and No. 205 Group RAF. Harbours and coastal shipping were also to be included in the programme, so that no means by which the enemy might supply and reinforce his troops would be left unmolested.

Operations by No. 205 Group were carried out on fifteen nights in March, and 833 sorties were despatched. This was a slight improvement over February, but the weather still interfered considerably with operations, especially during the second and third weeks of the month. No. 236 Wing's landing ground at Foggia Main was unserviceable for eight consecutive nights, and all the Wings suffered some disruption by the weather. The Group ORB states that four operations were worthy of special mention. The attack on Sofia marshalling yards on the night of 15/16 March was considered very successful. It was Maurice Lihou's third and final flight as second pilot, and he tells how they flew over Mount Cherni and found Sofia in the valley below 'lit up in all its glory'. There was no blackout, and the scene resembled a scene on a Christmas card or 'a giant birthday cake lit by a thousand candles'. Unfortunately, the returning crews ran into very bad weather when about halfway across the Adriatic. There was dense cloud down to zero feet in places, and icing conditions. Several aircraft were unable to locate their bases, and twelve of the total force of sixty-seven aircraft failed to return.

On 19/20 March, Monfalcone shipbuilding yards were attacked, and a good concentration achieved covering the submarine and electrical workshops, shipbuilding slips, and aircraft works. As part of Operation *Strangle*, eighty-one sorties were made on the night of 22/23 March against Padua West marshalling yards, where a large amount of rolling stock was reported and excellent results obtained. It was Maurice Lihou's first operation with his own crew, and all went well. Marshalling yards were again the target on 28/29 March, when Milan Lambrate was successfully attacked, the first operation against Milan from the Mediterranean theatre. In all, some 73 per cent of the sorties during March were directed at railway targets and another 14 per cent were 'area' attacks on industrial targets.

The ORB for No. 104 Squadron on 2 March gives an insight into off-duty activities at Foggia, mentioning that the 'Comrades Club' that was held at No. 236 Wing Headquarters every Thursday evening:

> …extend to personnel of this Squadron an invitation to attend the club for a cinema show, two performances are given and at each performance 20 seats are allocated to this Unit. The hospitality extended to us has been greatly appreciated, recent film shows have been of a high standard. 'The First of the Few' was screened quite recently and proved interesting as well as entertaining. Tonight's film was 'Girl Trouble' but quite a few men were also in trouble trying to find seats as the building was full to capacity.

On the camp at Foggia Main a canteen and recreation room had been opened by the Church Army, where tea and refreshments were on sale throughout the evening, and darts and other games available. The ORB comments that it appeared that 'a long felt want on the Squadron has at last been satisfied', as over 200 men visited the canteen on the first night and 'Favourable comments were heard regarding the quality of the tea served'! Life was a lot simpler in those far-off days and expectations lower, but conditions at Foggia were pretty terrible. Maurice Lihou tells us that when he and his crew arrived at Foggia at the end of February 1944:

They were taken to an old school building in the centre of town, where they received their second cultural shock. They were to be billeted on a second storey floor with dozens of other airmen. Each was given a palliasse (a mattress filled with straw) and they were to sleep on the floor with just about enough bed space to enable them to get out of bed. Some of the windows had been boarded up but others were without glass and were open to the elements...There was no furniture whatsoever in the long, narrow, high ceilinged room, neither were there any doors, which meant that the chill icy wind whistled around the room to add to the discomfort...The latrines...had chipped washhand basins with no plugs in them and the lavatories were without doors, openly displaying broken and chipped toilet basins with no seats...This and the smell of stale urine mixed with the overpowering smell of disinfectant was revolting.[6]

The mess was little better, filled with the smell of cooking and with insufficient room for everyone to sit down, and always there was the smell of powerful disinfectant. There were notices everywhere, warning about the dangers of VD, cholera, lice, and not to drink the water from the taps. And then it snowed! It came billowing into the room at night, and settled in a carpet on the floor and on the sleeping airmen.

For the bombers of No. 205 Group, the month began with further attacks in support of the troops fighting to hold on to the Anzio beachhead. The sixteen aircraft of No. 236 Wing that operated against the Velletri-Lanuvio area found thick cloud over the target area, and seven abandoned the mission and three attacked targets of opportunity. Sixteen aircraft of No. 330 Wing took off to attack the Cecchina-Lanuvio area, but two returned early and four abandoned their task after being unable to pinpoint due to cloud. One bombed the beaches at Circeo, one claimed to have bombed the road and river bank approximately ten miles south-west of Rome, and the others either bombed on a D/R run or through a gap in the cloud in the target area. No. 231 Wing did not operate, and second sorties for Nos 236 and 330 Wings were cancelled due to the bad weather.

On 2/3 March, sixteen aircraft of No. 231 Wing took off to attack the rail junction and marshalling yards at Orbetello, where bursts were observed in the yards and on railway lines and one direct hit scored in the factory area. Maurice Lihou had been posted to No. 37 Squadron, and this was his first operation, acting as second pilot. He tells us that the trip was uneventful and that 'the accommodation was far worse than Ops!' All the eighteen aircraft of No. 330 Wing sent to attack the rail junction also identified their target without difficulty, and claimed many direct hits on the tracks and two aircraft machine-gunned stationary railway stock and transport. A further seventeen aircraft of No. 236 Wing bombed the harbour and shipping at Porto San Stefano, and bursts were observed on the Mole and across the inner harbour. One aircraft aimed a stick of bombs at five or six small vessels in the bay to the east of the target and a small craft in the bay north of the main harbour was seen to be on fire. A special nickelling operation was also carried out over the Anzio and Cassino battlefields by a single Wellington of No. 70 Squadron, dropping 483,000 leaflets in German that included a message to Marshal Kesselring.

On 3/4 March, information was received that a German division was either in or moving through the small town of Bihac in Yugoslavia and heading for Italy.

However, the town could not be identified due to thick cloud from the Adriatic coast to the target, and most of the aircraft chose to attack the alternative target – the port of Zara – with good results. Bad weather then prevented operations for the next three nights before another attack was launched on harbour installations and shipping at Porto San Stefano. Eighteen aircraft from No. 330 and No. 236 Wings set off for the target, but haze and evasive action due to accurate flak prevented observation of the results. The weather then intervened again for three nights, and for the rest of the month, apart from the attack on Monfalcone mentioned above, all other operations were directed against railway targets – at Genoa, Sofia, Plovdiv, Padua, Vincenzo, and Milan–Lambrate.

Unfortunately, the attack on Genoa on 11/12 March was not a success as 10/10 cloud from Livorno to the target made identification impossible. Of the sixty-six aircraft despatched, only thirty-seven claimed to have attacked the target area, bombing on flares, flak and ETA. Four attacked alternative targets, three returned early for various reasons, and the remainder abandoned their task. Two attacks on Sofia followed (see also above), the second of which was hampered by cloud, but several aircraft bombed through gaps in the cloud or on ETA, searchlights and flak. The attack on the Plovdiv marshalling yards on 18/19 March was also spoiled by bad weather, and although some of the illuminators scattered their flares over the area in an effort to locate the yards, no aircraft was definitely able to identify the target. Following the attack on Padua on 22/23 March (see above), the bombers went back to the marshalling yards on the next night, and several crews reported fires still smouldering after the previous attack. Three new large fires were reported in the target area, and the explosions of three 4,000-pounders could be seen and felt. The whole of the target area was covered by smoke as the bombers left, and many incendiaries were burning fiercely. One of the Wellingtons of No. 104 Squadron failed to return.

The attack on Sofia on 24/25 March was ostensibly against the marshalling yards, but No. 70 Squadron ORB was clear that this operation was designed to continue the 'political war' – an area attack on the city itself to damage the morale of the civilian population. It mattered little what the intended object was, as 8/10 to 10/10 cloud was encountered over the target area and most aircraft bombed on ETA, flak and searchlights. Two Wellingtons failed to return: one from No. 40 Squadron was lost without trace, and another of the same Squadron ditched off Brindisi, the crew being picked up unharmed. Yet another crash-landed between Manfredonia and Foggia, with two crew members slightly injured. Maurice Lihou, in common with many others, got hopelessly lost on the way home, and eventually landed at Crotone, 'the last airstrip on the toe of Italy.' It was an emergency landing strip set up for just such a purpose, and the people there were delighted to have been of assistance and entertained their visitors royally. Crotone was nearly two hundred miles from Foggia, and they were extremely lucky to get there without running out of petrol. Had they missed it, they would have had to come down in the Mediterranean.

On 26/27 March, seventy-three Wellingtons and six Liberators took off to attack the marshalling yards at Vincenza, where the weather was somewhat hazy and the flare-droppers seem to have been slightly late in finding and illuminating the target. Bombing was rather scattered, although many sticks of bombs and incendiaries were seen in the marshalling yards and at least three 4,000-pounder bursts were observed in or very close to the yards. On the same night No. 142 Squadron ORB reported that 'Vesuvius is in eruption again with considerable violence', and drifting smoke and ash caused flying restrictions over the extreme south of Italy and the Naples area.[7]

Following the attack on the Milan–Lambrate yards on 28/29 March (see above), Sofia was the target again on the 29/30th. Illumination was on time, but the first flares seemed to have fallen slightly too far to the east, and the bombing was concentrated mainly on the south-east section of the city. Bursts were seen on and around the east end of the marshalling yards, in the vicinity of the freight yard and railway junction, and near the military school. Three 4,000-pounders appeared to have burst in the built-up area between the centre and east side of the city. Two large fires were reported to be still visible forty to fifty miles away. On the same night the rail bridges at Fano and Cesano were also attacked, but only one bomb was seen to fall near enough to have damaged the bridges and photographs failed to reveal any damage on either of them.

On 20 March it had been decided to stand-down No. 614 Squadron and concentrate on training the unit for its role as a target marking force. It was to consist of two operational flights each of eight H2S aircraft, along with a training flight. The Squadron would be brought up to establishment in equipment and ground personnel, and the training flight would supply replacement crews. These would be above-average crews drawn from the other squadrons in No. 205 Group with experience of night operations. They would be converted to Halifaxes and trained in Target Marking technique. At the time the Squadron ORB described itself as 'a motley crew' comprising: eighteen crews who had completed the PFF course at Newmarket but with little or no operational experience; two raw Halifax crews with no experience whatsoever; four ex-Wellington crews converting to Halifaxes but with little or no operational experience and no H2S or Gee or Mark XIV Bombsight experience; and eight crews with ops experience on the Squadron, but no H2S or Gee or Mark XIV Bomb sight experience. Training was slow to start off with, but by the end of the month the ORB reported that 'the programme is fast nearing completion'.

*　　　*　　　*

By the end of March 1944 the Allies' land forces in Italy had been forced to pause in their offensive against the German defensive positions, which spanned Italy from the mouth of the River Garigliano on the west coast to Pescara on the east coast. Alexander had decided not to launch large-scale operations up the Adriatic coast in order to reinforce the 5th Army on the western side of the Apennines. So far, all attempts to break the Gustav Line had failed in the face of determined opposition in the grim mountainous terrain. At Anzio, the 6th US Corps had been contained in its beachhead, safe from great harm but unable to break out. The offensive on the Gustav Line would not recommence until 11 May.

At the beginning of the month No. 205 Group comprised six squadrons of Wellingtons (Nos 37, 70, 40, 104, 142, and 150), and one of Liberators (No. 178). No. 231 Wing (Nos 37 and 70 Squadrons) was at Tortorella, No. 236 Wing (Nos 40 and 104 Squadron) was at Foggia Main, No. 330 Wing (Nos 142 and 150 Squadrons) was at Amendola, and No. 240 Wing (Nos 178 and 614 Squadrons) was at Celone. The Halifaxes of No. 614 Squadron were not yet formally part of No. 205 Group, but would become so in May. Meanwhile, they continued to work up in their new target-marking role, and often operated with the Group. On the night of 12/13 April the Squadron carried out a full-scale training exercise involving all available aircraft and crews. Taranto was the 'target', and arrangements were made for searchlight co-operation and Beaufighter night-fighter affiliation. On the whole the results were satisfactory, and the next stage of the training would involve crews being sent out on 'squadron private parties' over enemy territory to give them an idea of what sort of opposition they would be likely to encounter. Reinforcements were on their way for the heavy bomber units in the shape of two South African squadrons, Nos 31 and 34, both equipped with Liberators, but these would not become operational until May.

Maurice Lihou recalls how his crew were moved from the old school building to a new tented camp at Tortorella on 1 April. The tents were four and a half feet high, and so to get a decent headroom a hole about eighteen inches deep had to be dug inside. The floor was covered by a rubber ground sheet, and although this was an improvement of sorts, there were no beds or palliasses available. Everyone had to construct their own beds out of whatever materials they could scrounge, or sleep on the ground. The crews' kapok-lined flying suits usually acted as the mattress, and they slept under a couple of army blankets and their RAF greatcoats. Heating came from ingenious home-made oil-fired drip stoves, which were also used to boil the water for washing, shaving, making tea and cocoa, and for cooking. Apart from being an ever-present fire hazard, the stoves tended to attract large flying insects that burned with a terrible smell and made the tent uninhabitable. Lighting was usually by shaded candles or oil lamps, but these were rarely used because of the black out.

During the month the Group Headquarters moved to its new site in the Foggia area after almost four months spent at Bari, where 'the Headquarters Staff had been privileged to work side by side with Headquarters, Fifteenth Air Force'. The Group ORB comments that a fine spirit of co-operation had grown up between the Americans and the British, with the former always providing 'ready and cheerful assistance' when required. The period of working together had been most helpful in giving all departments of the Group the opportunity to study American methods of operation at first hand. The morning conference at Fifteenth Air Force Headquarters had been attended by RAF personnel, and details of No. 205 Group's operations outlined by Group Intelligence Officers. As the Senior Intelligence Officer for No. 236 Wing, Chappell made many visits to Bari to participate in the morning conferences, travelling with the Group Captain in the Fairchild Argus 'puddle jumper'. RAF officers also shared the 'decided amenities of the US Officers' Club and Coffee Bar', where many good friendships were made and Allied co-operation considerably strengthened. On 6 April Chappell travelled by truck to the new Group HQ at Foggia, and found it to be 'well laid out with new tents and a white-washed building for Intelligence'.

During April the Group operated on nineteen nights, flew 1,179 sorties, and lost twenty-four aircraft. The chief feature of the month's operations was the large number of attacks made on shipping and port installations in the western Italian ports of Genoa, Leghorn, Piombino, Spezia and San Stefano. In all, the Group made thirteen attacks and despatched 544 sorties (46 per cent of the total effort) to these targets and lost six aircraft. On the night of 10/11 April Flight Sergeant David Clark of No. 150 Squadron was the rear gunner in one of the Wellingtons despatched to Piombino. On the return trip they were attacked by a Ju 88, and the quietly understated combat report reveals nothing of the moments of sheer terror that must have gripped the aircrews at such times:

> At 23.42 when flying at 8,000 feet heading north at 41°25N 12°20E (NW of Anzio), the rear gunner observed a Ju.88 on a reciprocal heading about 1,000 feet below. The Ju.88 turned to port, climbed up and then came in to attack at about the same height as the Wellington and astern. When the range was about 600 yards, the rear gunner opened fire and believed hits were scored on the E. A/C [enemy aircraft]. At 500 yards, the Wellington corkscrewed and the gunner continued firing throughout the manoeuvre. About 1,000 feet was lost in height. The Ju.88 was next seen on the starboard quarter slightly below the Wellington at 600 yards. At 500 yards, the rear gunner opened fire and tracer was believed to have entered the E. A/C. It was last seen by the rear gunner and Wireless Operator when they noticed small bursts of fire coming from the cockpit and port engine. Shortly after, the Wellington entered cloud and Ju.88 was lost to sight. The Ju.88 was counted as a 'PROBABLE'. Rounds fired – 2,000.

Most of the attacks on the ports were harassing attacks carried out by waves of aircraft throughout the night in order to interfere with the enemy's attempts to load or unload supplies for the Italian front. Weather conditions were often difficult, and hazy conditions and extreme darkness made the target areas difficult to identify. On 20/21 and 21/22 April the weather deteriorated after the aircraft had taken off for the ports, and they were recalled. Of the 544 sorties despatched in total, seventy (13 per cent) were uncompleted for various reasons.

For the first time aircraft of No. 205 Group carried out three very successful mining operations in the River Danube on 8/9, 12/13 and 14/15 April, with a total of sixty-seven sorties launched. The Danube, which flows through Germany, Austria, Hungary, Yugoslavia, Romania and Bulgaria, could carry 10,000 tons daily and one barge could transport a load equivalent to that of a hundred railway wagons. The first mining operation was carried out by nineteen Wellingtons and three Liberators, and they successfully laid mines between Bazias and Belgrade. One of the Wellingtons ditched in the river after being hit by flak, but the pilot and bomb aimer later returned to their unit. The remaining members of the crew were thought to have been killed. The second operation by thirty-four aircraft was equally successful and 107 mines were laid. Several of the Wellingtons also strafed barges on the river, and a large vessel, possibly an oil tanker, was set on fire. This caused explosions that spread the fire to other ships. A column of thick black smoke rose to thousands of feet, and a large area of the river was well alight with burning oil when the aircraft left for home. These mining attacks took the Germans by surprise, and it was not until the middle of August that they were able to produce counter-measures (see Chapter 9). At first, the 'gardening' was always carried out in moon periods because the crews had to fly at no more than 200 feet, and heights of forty and fifty feet were often reported. Later, the use of Pathfinder aircraft and illumination by flares made it possible to operate over any part of the river during any period of the month.

On 8 April the Group carried out 'one of the most unusual operations of the

Group' – a special daylight operation by eleven Wellingtons against German troops reported to be surrounded by Tito's partisans in the small town of Niksic in Yugoslavia. All the aircraft carried one 4,000-lb bomb, and the formation was escorted by twelve Spitfires. The bombing was reported to have been well concentrated, and photographs showed that considerable damage was caused. Flying Officer Dunn of No. 40 Squadron took part in the attack:

> The aiming point was a long barracks. We were quite low and approaching just at the right angle and although no other aircraft were in sight I decided we would bomb straightaway as we were sure of the target and we had a good run in. We stayed low and the rear gunner reported that the bomb had gone off just in front of the building.[8]

Chappell comments that it was 'a hell of scramble to brief and get off in time using eleven Wellingtons carrying 4,000-lb bombs.' The target area 'had a clearly defined road pattern...and was therefore easy to identify'. He states that the bombing 'was well done', and some very good photographs were obtained.

The Group carried out two attacks on the Macchi aircraft factory at Varese during the month, on 1/2 and 11/12 April. On the first attack by six Liberators and sixty Wellingtons, the bombing was somewhat scattered, but bursts were observed in the target area. One good fire and one smaller fire were reported in the factory itself, and some fires were also seen in the town. Flying Officer V.L. Jackson of No. 150 Squadron had his starboard engine hit by falling incendiaries on the bombing run, and he returned to base on one motor. When he got back to base his other engine also cut out, but he made a successful belly-landing and was subsequently granted the immediate award of the DFC. On 6 April the following signal was received from Major General N.F. Twining, Commanding Officer Fifteenth Air Force:

> Operations of the Strategic Air Force from Italy during the past two days have resulted in terrific destruction of Hun aircraft and vital industrial establishments. This will go a long way towards bringing the war to an early end. The Hun Air Force cannot take the punishment as evidenced by his weak opposition to our attack on Budapest [on 3/4 April]. Pass to all Units my highest commendations on the results of these air battles. Our combination of night bombers, day bombers, and long range fighters represents a fighting force that cannot be beaten.

Although No. 205 Group was only playing a small part in the strategic air offensive, this message from General Twining is a good reflection of the doctrine underlying the offensive and the strong belief in its success. The second attack on the Macchi factory was a complete failure due to 10/10 cloud down to 4,000 feet over the target area. Fifty-four Wellingtons operated but only two definitely claimed to have attacked the target, and no results were observed.

On 3/4 April eight Liberators and seventy-nine Wellingtons were despatched to the Manfred Weiss armaments factory at Budapest. The target was easily identified by most of the aircraft, and incendiaries and bombs were reported to be well concentrated in the target area. One fire was visible sixty miles away. The attack followed an American raid on the marshalling yards at Budapest, and the combined effect led to an extensive evacuation of the civil population. Moderate heavy and intense light flak was encountered and there were many reports of night-fighters over the target area, and four Wellingtons failed to return. One ditched off Ternoli and the crew were rescued by an ASR Walrus and returned to Foggia. The captain of one of the lost aircraft was Squadron Leader H.H.B. Beale, DFC and Bar, one of No. 37 Squadron's outstanding figures. He had been with the unit since April 1943 and had commanded the Squadron from January 1944 to February 1944. Squadron Leader Beale had always distinguished himself by his outstanding courage and determination, unbounded energy, and his unfailing cheerfulness. One of the crew of this aircraft, Flight Sergeant Newman, later told the story to Kevin Mears:

> I remember for some reason that I was thoroughly enjoying the raid, everything seemed to be going great, the target was being plastered, fires everywhere and for a change I wasn't a bit frightened...We had just dropped our bombs when I had the feeling that the rear gunner was about to tell me something...When all of a sudden there were these explosions and flames. I looked aft and saw these tracers coming straight towards me and they seemed to part and go either side of me...and continued past me to the front of the aircraft. I was knocked down but pulled myself up and looked out on the starboard side and saw this ME110 parallel with the tail and so close that I felt I could reach out and touch it! I yelled out to the skipper that it was 110 and to dive to starboard. Already the flames had taken hold and we were burning like hell. The skipper shouted that the ailerons had been shot away and he couldn't control the aircraft and he said 'Bale out.' I had the terrible feeling of absolute terror come over me, I'll NEVER forget it as long as I live...All of a sudden I was no longer afraid [and] felt at peace with myself and was prepared for whatever was to happen, most peculiar...I turned back to the escape hatch again and there was Griff (Sergeant Griffiths, the rear gunner) just standing there, virtually a human torch...[9]

Flight Sergeant Newman struggled with the hatch until the slipstream caught him and pulled him clear. He and Flight Sergeant Jefferies were the only survivors and both were taken prisoner. Squadron Leader Beale got out, but died of his injuries five days later.

Two small attacks were also made on the shipyards at Monfalcone, by eleven aircraft on 11/12 April and six aircraft of the last night of the month. Good results were claimed on the first attack, when bursts were seen on a building at the western end of the pattern shop, at the end of the slips, and on the submarine workshops. The second attack encountered 10/10 cloud at 10,000 to 13,000 feet over the target area, but one Halifax went below the cloud and visually identified the target, seeing bombs bursting in the yards. The remaining aircraft bombed on Gee fixes, observing only bomb flashes and the glow of target markers below the cloud.

The other attacks during March were all directed at railway targets – the marshalling yards at Vincenza (55 aircraft), Budapest (two attacks by a total of 127 aircraft), Plovdiv (two attacks by a total of 52 aircraft), and two small attacks by Halifaxes on Mestre and Parma. The No. 70 Squadron ORB contains the following detailed account of the attack by six aircraft on Budapest on 12/13 April:

> Four of the aircraft carried one overload [fuel tank] each and approached via Lake Balaton and the 'long route', but the 2 x 4000lb aircraft...made a beeline

256

for the target, having no petrol to spare. After crossing the mountain in good weather, out aircraft approached the Budapest area, where the Danube was discernible though a thick haze hampered accurate pinpointing of the M/Yards, despite their length of one mile and breadth of ¼ mile. Illumination…was widespread, one batch well W. of the Danube and another too far South. Consequently IBs and HEs were also scattered, although some concentration of bombing was seen in the vicinity of the yards, where one or two small fires were visible. Several crews reported what seems to have been a good red fire, turning up dense clouds of black smoke from an area just south of the target. All our crews claimed to bomb in the target area although few results were seen owing to haze and smoke…In the Budapest area, one crew which was there on the previous raid, thought flak was less intense and less accurate. This may have been due to the throwing out of 'window' [small pieces of aluminium to confuse enemy radar]…which crews tried tonight for the first time. Its effects were most marked on the 15/20 S/Ls which were operating quite normally as crews approached, but waved ineffectively once 'window' was used and eventually doused whilst the attack was still in progress.

All the attacks on railway targets were fairly successful operations, but the attack on Turnul–Severin (the highest point on the Danube accessible to sea-going vessels) on 15/16 April stood out. Ninety-two Wellingtons operated and carried out an extremely well concentrated attack, with many bursts seen on the marshalling yards and across the railway workshops. One 4,000-lb bomb burst on the east side of the yards, causing a huge explosion followed by a fire and a column of black smoke, and another hit the grain silo and started a good red fire. The target was a mass of flames when the aircraft left, and the whole conflagration was visible for some 100–150 miles on the return journey. One of the Wellingtons of No. 40 Squadron failed to return, and two of No. 104 Squadron collided in the circuit over base on return and both were destroyed.

While taking off for the attack on Plovdiv on 17/18 April, one of the aircraft of No. 40 Squadron burst a tyre at Foggia Main, crashed and caught fire. All of the crew bar the rear gunner were injured, and the bomb aimer subsequently died. The incident was probably due to metal fragments left on the runway by the Allied bombing from the previous year, and despite the strenuous efforts to cope with the problem, tyre bursts were not infrequent. The tyres were carefully inspected prior to the take-off run, and the Group Engineering Officer had designed a powerful magnet to be towed behind a truck to clear the runway, but fragments were constantly working their way through. Tyre damage caused a very high wastage rate, and two more from No. 104 Squadron crashed due to burst tyres on 21 April. The Group ORB for April draws attention to a shortage of Wellington tyres, and a request that only heavy-treaded tyres be supplied for the Group. The problem was not solved until the Wellingtons were replaced by Liberators in 1945.

Chappell was in Foggia when the accident occurred, watching an ENSA show with Florence Desmond and the comedian Johnny Lockwood – Lockwood had joined the RAF in 1942 but was discharged in 1944. While Desmond was signing 'Sally' in the Gracie Fields style there was an almighty 'woomph' that shook the whole theatre. The RAF men knew that it was take-off time in the airfields and that a bomb must have gone off. The singer flinched and ran to the back of the stage, but came back on 'like a good trouper and finished her act'. Going out into the street afterwards Chappell could see a red glow and a huge plume of smoke rising over the houses, and there was another explosion. As he returned to Foggia Main he was stopped by MPs, who said that a 4,000-lb bomb was expected to go up at any minute, but managed to persuade the police that his presence was urgently required. The aircraft of No. 40 Squadron had swung off the runway and two other Wellingtons waiting to take off had also been involved, one of which was completely destroyed. It was remarkable that there had only been one death.

*   *   *

At the end of 1943 the decision was made to form two heavy night bomber squadrons in South Africa for service with No. 205 Group in Italy, both to be equipped with Liberators.[10] The first to be established was No. 31 Squadron, with Lieutenant Colonel J. A. Williams in command. Williams was a thirty-five-year-old from Johannesburg, whose family firm of construction engineers was well known throughout the country. He had enlisted in the SAAF in 1939, and had served with distinction with No. 24 (SAAF) in the Middle East, first as an ordinary lieutenant and eventually as Commanding Officer. Flying Marylands and then Bostons, the Squadron had been operational in the North Africa from 1940 right through to the final battles in Tunisia, and had then taken part in the invasions of Sicily and Italy. In December 1943, Williams was replaced as CO of No. 24 Squadron, and after a period of leave in South Africa, was given the task of forming the first heavy bomber squadron in the SAAF. He was the ideal man for the job, a born leader and an officer of great organizing ability, whose courage was an inspiration to all who served with him.

On 30 January 1940 the ground staff and personnel of No. 31 Squadron left Swartkop Air Station for Durban by train, and there boarded the troopship SS *Orbita* bound for Suez. The *Orbita* was a passenger-cargo ship of 15,495 tons built by Harland and Wolff at Belfast, and launched in 1914. Formerly owned by the Pacific Navigation Company, she served as a troopship from 1941 to the end of the war, and was eventually broken up in 1950 at Newport, Monmouthshire. As the ship left Durban the strains of 'Land of Hope and Glory' rang out in a rich soprano voice. It belonged to a smiling, matronly woman, dressed in white and with a red wide-brimmed hat, singing through a megaphone. This was Perla Siedle Gibson, the famous 'Lady in White' who sang her way into the hearts of many Allied servicemen entering and leaving Durban during the war. As the troopship edged away from the quay the tune changed to 'Wish Me Luck as You Wave Me Goodbye', and soon the *Orbita* had headed past the Bluff to begin the voyage up the east coast. At sea the wind was strong, the waves choppy, and the ship soon picked up the zig-zag trail of the grey corvette that would escort it on the first part of its journey.

Lawrence Isemonger tells us that, unfortunately, the *Orbita* lacked the amenities of larger troopships, and the journey to the Middle East was hardly a pleasure cruise. The sleeping and eating quarters were part of the cargo hold deep in the bowels of the ship, 'an inch or so above the bilges'. There were no portholes and the only ventilation was provided by large air ducts, which seldom seemed to produce any air. At night the stale smell of body odour and cigarette smoke was everywhere as the men tried to get to sleep on hard benches, tables, and the deck. The routine on board was monotonous, with 'rise-and-shine' at 6 am, followed by breakfast two hours later. After a general clean-up, the personnel assembled on deck for life boat drill and the daily inspection. The rest of the day was spent at leisure, reading or playing cards. The ship was so over-crowded that there was always a scramble for a bit of deck space to relax in, and many had to stand for hours or walk about stepping over reclining bodies. Fresh water for washing was only available between 6 and 8 am, after which there were only salt water showers. The food was terrible! The meat was a peculiar greyish colour, with an even more peculiar smell. There was no sugar, and the food was invariably cooked without salt. However, 'we did enjoy the delicious, freshly-baked bread'.

Land was sighted on 9 February, and the *Orbita* dropped anchor off Mombassa. The next morning it was off again, with a different corvette leading the way. Once past the Equator the blackout precautions started earlier, and there was the odd submarine scare as the ship made its way northwards towards Aden. Here, there was another halt to take on supplies and fuel, and then it was through the narrow Bab el Mandeb straits and into the Red Sea. On 19 February, nineteen days after leaving Durban, the low lying mountains fringing the town of Suez came into view. The *Orbita* anchored in the roadstead, and the passengers went ashore by tug. After a lunch of two thick dry cheese sandwiches and a Jaffa orange, they clambered aboard a train bound for Heliopolis. From there they were taken to the SAAF Base Depot at Almaza, cold and tired. After drawing another two blankets, they settled down in tents for their first night in Egypt. When the aircrew of No. 31 Squadron arrived at Almaza they were sent on to No. 1675 Conversion Unit at Lydda in Palestine (now the Israeli airport of Lod) to familiarize themselves with the Liberator bomber. Some of the aircrew had been recruited from coastal squadrons patrolling South African waters, while others were seasoned campaigners from squadrons that had served in East Africa, the Western Desert, and North Africa.

Meanwhile, time for the ground staff at Almaza passed very slowly, with little to do except for occasional trips to savour the fleshpots of Cairo. Eventually, after languishing in relative idleness for eight weeks, an advance party set off on 19 April to establish a base camp in the Egyptian desert. The site allotted was a short distance off the road leading from Cairo to Alexandria, forty kilometres from the capital at Gebel Hamzi, and thus known as 'Kilo 40' (LG 237). Four days after their arrival at Kilo 40 the rest of the ground staff moved in from Almaza, and on 27 April the first eight Liberators landed to be welcomed by violent wind and dust storms. The next day the newly promoted Colonel Williams was appointed as Commander of No. 2 SAAF Wing, the controlling body of the two South African heavy bomber squadrons. The other component, No. 34 Squadron, was still in the process of being formed. Lieutenant Colonel D.U. Nel, DFC, succeeded Williams as CO of No. 31 Squadron.

The version of the Liberator delivered to No. 31 Squadron was the B-24J, known to the RAF as the Liberator Mk VI. It required a crew of eight – two pilots, a navigator, a bomb aimer, three air gunners, and a wireless operator/gunner. More Liberators and their crews arrived at Kilo 40, and by 3 May the Squadron had its full allotment of sixteen aircraft. All maintenance work at Kilo 40 was carried out in the open in the scorching heat of the desert, and the Khamsin, which blew almost every day, filled the air with fine sand that penetrated everywhere. It got into the eyes, into the mouth, into the food, and into the machinery. It was impossible to work during the afternoon, and so everyone 'adjourned to their tent for a siesta until four o'clock', sweltering and sheltering from the sandflies under their mosquito nets. Water was scarce and had to be brought in from Cairo, and there was not enough to spare for washing dishes and cooking utensils – these had to be cleaned with a mixture of desert sand and cold water.

The difficult conditions proved too much for the 'new boys' of No. 31 Squadron, who had not been through the rigours of desert operations. Relations between the ground crews and the aircrew became strained, and matters came to a head when it became known that the officers were going to hold a dance to which South African nurses at Helwan had been invited. These were flown into Kilo 40 in a couple of Liberators, but when the dance was in full swing 'an unruly mob of other ranks' invaded the officers' mess and proceeded to ruin the proceedings. Someone loosened the guy ropes on the mess tent, the lights fused, and the CO was called upon to calm things down. The next morning a small bomb was found in the CO's tent, but it was generally believed that it had been meant for the adjutant against whom most of the complaints were directed. It all blew over following a lecture from the CO, and thereafter there was a noticeable improvement in the relationship between aircrews and ground staff.

No. 34 Squadron came into existence officially on 14 April 1944, but the bulk of the ground crews had left South Africa aboard HMT *Salween* at the beginning of March, voyaging from Durban to Tewfik. We have little information on the early days of the unit, as its ORB does not start until 4 June 1944, when the Squadron arrived at Ras-el-Boud (see next chapter). Commenting on events in April, the ORB states that 'A great deal of groundwork was done at SAAF Base Depot, Almaza...and the Squadron was really started at Base Depot long before it moved out to Kilo 40' to join No. 2 Wing SAAF as a 'shadow' squadron on 3 May. From the start the Squadron was faced with a grave shortage of personnel, especially fitter armourers and cooks. The MT drivers posted to the Squadron were 'very much below standard and...caused the Transport Officer tremendous difficulties'. We will pick up the stories of both the South African squadrons in the next chapter.

*   *   *

The weather took a heavy toll of operation during this period, and the night bombers were only able to go out on 70 of the 121 nights between January and April 1944. However, they managed to fly 3,352 sorties, and lost 74 aircraft in the process. Three operations involved more than 90 aircraft despatched, and another 12 more than 70 aircraft. Yet again, the main emphasis was on railway targets (39 per cent), and another 17 per cent went to industrial targets as the strategic bombing offensive from Italy intensified. Ports and shipping took up 22 per cent of the total effort.

NOTES

1. The Rapido flows across part of the entrance to the Liri valley, where it is joined by the Liri and then becomes the Garigliano, which flows south and then south-west to the sea.
2. Kevin Mears, *Wise Without Eyes*, pages 225–226

3. The 'Pointblank' directive was issued in June 1943, and ordered the strategic bomber forces to attack aircraft factories and associated industrial targets in order to restrict the activities of the German day and night fighter force.
4. See Maurice G. Lihou, *It's Dicey Flying Wimpys Around Italian Skies*.
5. No. 462 Squadron reformed on 12 August 1944 at Driffield. Still equipped with the Halifax, albeit the Mk III variant, it was now part of No 4 Group, operating as part of Bomber Command's Main Force until December 1944. On the 22nd, it stood down and by the end of the month had joined No 100 Group in the Bomber Support role.
6. Lihou, *It's Dicey Flying Wimpys Around Italian Skies*, page 33.
7. This was the last major eruption, and it destroyed the villages of San Sebastiano al Vesuvio, Massa di Somma, Ottaviano, and part of San Giorgio a Cremano. The USAAF 340th Bombardment Group was based at Pompeii Airfield, just a few kilometres from the eastern base of the mountain. Many of its B-25s were covered by the tephra and hot ash, which caused considerable damage to the fabric control surfaces, the engines, and the Plexiglass windows and gun turrets.
8. Gunby, *Sweeping the Skies*, page 260.
9. Kevin Mears, *Wise Without Eyes*, page 228.
10. Much of this account is taken from *The Men Who Went to Warsaw* by Lawrence Isemonger, supplemented by the Squadron ORBs.

CHAPTER ELEVEN

The Attack on Railways and Oil Targets – May to September 1944

The period covered by this chapter saw impressive victories gained by the Allied forces on the ground in the Mediterranean theatre. Rome fell, and the enemy were pushed back a hundred miles to the Gothic Line, north of Florence. A successful invasion of the South of France was also launched. The Group played a relatively small part in the fighting on the ground for much of the five months from May to September, and only about fifteen per cent of its 7,116 sorties were directed at targets in the battle areas. However, it often provided indirect support for the troops by attacking airfields (9 per cent of its total effort), ports and shipping (9 per cent), and railways and marshalling yards (33 per cent). The emphasis on railway targets reflected a debate that was going on in the planning for *Overlord* in the UK, and a difference of opinion between the RAF planners and the Americans. Tedder, guided by his advisor Solly Zuckerman, argued that the best way of interfering with the enemy's response to the invasion of Northern Europe was to disrupt railway communications by bombing the nodal points that controlled the railway system between Germany and France – the so-called Transportation Plan. The Americans preferred an all-out onslaught on the oil industry as the best way of disrupting German operations on land and in the air.

Thus, although the RAF night bombers in Italy were becoming more of a 'strategic' air force, they would continue to prioritize transportation rather than oil targets. The major *Pointblank* target of the enemy aircraft industry and the attack on oil facilities would be left to the much bigger USAAF Fifteenth Air Force at Foggia. Of the 14,533 sorties despatched in 1944, only 1,608 (11 per cent) were directed at oil targets, whereas 4,685 (32 per cent) went to railway targets. The difference in emphasis was even more striking in 1945, with a mere 100 sorties (2 per cent) going to oil targets and 2,580 (56 per cent) to railway targets. Between May and September, only 8 per cent of the Group's effort went to industrial targets, and another 15 per cent to oil targets. Before we cover these operations in detail, it is worth having a quick look at the ground battles that formed the ever-present background to the Group's activities.

At 2300 hours on 11 May the massed artillery of the Eighth and Fifth Armies opened fire on the Gustav Line. Some 1,700 pieces fired up to 420 rounds per gun over the next twelve hours, easily surpassing the bombardment that had begun the battle of El Alamein. Attacks by the French Expeditionary Corps in the Aurunci Mountains south of the Liri River and the crossing of the Gari/Rapido by the British 4th Infantry Division and 8th Indian Divisions meant that the door to Rome, if not fully open, was at least ajar. In the mountains above Cassino, Polish troops gradually began to work their way around to the north of the Abbey, and at 1020 hours on the 18th a patrol of the 12th Podolski Reconnaissance Regiment entered the Abbey and accepted the surrender of the last few defenders left inside. That afternoon the Poles linked up with the British 78th Division in the Liri valley, two miles west of Cassino town. The Germans had already begun a withdrawal to the Senger Line, some thirty miles south of Rome, and the Allies advanced quickly up the Liri Valley and along the coast. However, the Eighth Army needed time to re-organize, as getting 20,000 vehicles and 2,000 tanks through the Gustav Line was a major job taking several days. The assault on the German defences commenced on 23 May, and the line collapsed two days later, clearing the way for the advance northwards to Rome and beyond.

On the 23rd the US 6th Corps began its offensive from the Anzio bridgehead and the first contact between the US Fifth Army and the troops from the beachhead occurred on 25 May, but the breakout led to one of the most hotly debated decisions in the Italian campaign. The original plan was for the 6th Corps to advance towards Valmontone on Highway 6 to cut off the Tenth Army's retreat, and on 25 May it was driving north-eastwards to achieve this object. By the next day it would have been astride the line of retreat, but at this point General Mark Clark ordered Truscott to change his main line of attack to a north-westerly one towards Rome. The Germans were, therefore, allowed to retreat more or less unmolested, and were able to link up with the Fourteenth Army and make a fighting withdrawal to the formidable Gothic Line north of Florence. Clark's eagerness to grab the prize of Rome meant that an opportunity to inflict a major defeat on the enemy had been lost.

Kesselring had already authorized the Fourteenth Army to withdraw across the Tiber on the night of 3/4 June, and on the late afternoon of 4 June American advanced guards nosed their way into the city. General Mark Clark entered the city on the morning of 5 June, guided to the Capitoline Hill by an American priest and a boy on a bicycle. After the fall of Rome, the main Allied forces pushed on, as the German armies withdrew to defensive lines north of Rome. By the evening of 5 June the Fifth Army had reached or crossed the Tiber along most of its length from Rome to the sea. On its right, the Eighth Army progressed more slowly, through minefields, around blown bridges, and over blocked mountain roads. By 9 June the Fifth Army was fifty miles north-west of Rome, and a week later the Eighth Army was approaching Perugia. However, the momentum of the chase began to flag in the face of stiffening resistance as Kesselring rallied his troops for the defence of a coherent front. The Pisa–Rimini ('Gothic') Line, running along that last barrier of mountain before the country opened out into the wide plains of the Po Valley, was still far from complete and he was doing all he could to hold Alexander in the area to the south of it.

During the month of July the forces on the ground continued their steady advance while Kesselring gradually withdrew his forces to his new line of defence. The German forces were now well balanced and Kesselring's method was simple – to withdraw slowly to the Arno, turning to fight a series of rearguard actions – and there was little that the Allies could do to disrupt this programme. Despite some hard-fought and hard-won successes, the Allied line was still on average some twenty miles south of the Gothic Line. The possibility of a rapid advance to the north of Italy and into the Balkans diminished daily as stiffer and stiffer resistance was encountered along the whole front. Also, the Allied forces were being progressively reduced in preparation for the invasion of Southern France. Already, the French Corps had begun their withdrawal, and other forces would soon follow. On 4 August elements of the Fifth Army entered Florence, and a firm base now existed for the main attack on the Gothic Line, but on 14/15 August Operation *Dragoon* was launched, and the focus on the ground turned for the moment to the South of France.

The invasion of the Riviera postponed any operations in front of the Gothic Line. The withdrawal of seven divisions for Operation *Dragoon*, and the reinforcement of Kesselring by eight, removed all prospects of further rapid victories in Italy. North of Florence the Appenines turn north-west to form a barrier across any line of advance up the west coastal plain of Italy, and now Alexander moved his main effort to the east, which offered the only level approach to the Po Valley. The Eighth Army's attack was launched an hour before midnight on 25 August, and achieved complete surprise. Elements of V Corps and the Canadians quickly crossed the River Foglia and captured forward positions in the Gothic Line. Further advances followed on 31 August and 1 September, and on the early morning of 13 September Alexander launched the second half of his two-fold attack. There began a week of the heaviest fighting that either army had experienced, and on the 19th and 20th the remnants of the Germans withdrew from the heavily defended Fortunata Ridge. The Allies entered Rimini on 21 September, and by the end of the month the Line had been overrun except for a few places in the western sector. Then the rains began early and for the next six months mud ruled the Italian front.

*   *   *

During May 1944 the aircraft of No. 205 Group operated on twenty-seven nights and launched 1,571 sorties, a considerable improvement on previous efforts from Foggia. Railway targets took up 454 sorties (29 per cent of the total effort), and military targets in the battle area received another 432 sorties (27 per cent of the effort). The ports of Livorno (Leghorn), Piombino, Porto San Stefano and Portoferraio, on the east coast and north of Rome, also came under attack during the month (333 sorties – 21 per cent). The most important strategic target to be attacked was Bucharest, with a total of 204 sorties despatched in three attacks on the city and eleven aircraft lost. In two of the attacks the loss rates were 5 per cent and 9.7 per cent, the same sort of loss rates as those experienced by Bomber Command over Germany. These European strategic targets were defended by experienced and efficient flak defences, and by the night fighters of the *Luftwaffe*. It was inevitable that the ageing Wellingtons of No. 205 Group would suffer greater losses in these operations than in those over North Africa and Southern Italy.

Bucharest was visited by aircraft of the Group for the first time on the night of 3/4 May. The marshalling yards at Bucharest were the largest and most active in the Balkans, and with the Russians threatening Romania they were a critical link in the German supply chain. A strong cross wind at Foggia Main prevented sixteen Wellingtons from No. 236 Wing from taking off, and only the essential flare-droppers got away. A total of fifty Wellingtons, five Liberators and seven Halifaxes were despatched, but the operation was not a success. The target area was covered by cloud and haze, and the first flares were dropped by the Halifaxes by means of their special equipment. The Wellington illuminators were also hampered by the haze, and the illumination in general was scattered over a wide area of the city.

Although the yards received some bombing, the greater proportion of the bombs fell in the town area.

Two further attacks followed, on 6/7 and 7/8 May. In the second attack sixty-five Wellingtons, eight Liberators, and seven Halifaxes operated. The bombing was concentrated on the industrial area, with direct hits on factories and on the marshalling yards. At least four fires were started, including two big ones. Three Wellingtons and one Liberator failed to return. Gunby tells us that one Wellington of No. 40 Squadron was hit by flak over the Yugoslav coast, and both engines failed. After the rest of the crew had baled out the pilot recalled that:

> I made my way to the hatch and then remembered that I had not destroyed the IFF [identification, friend or foe – a device that enables radar to identify friendly aircraft] and so went back to the cockpit and did so and finally jumped. I have no recollection of the descent. My next memory is some 45 minutes later when I found myself walking along with my parachute trailing behind me. I had no idea where I was or where I had come from, but knew that I had to hide my parachute.[1]

The crew were captured by the Bulgarians and spent four months in wretched conditions. Another No. 40 Squadron Wellington was shot down by a night fighter, and the rear gunner was killed in the attack. The others baled out and ended up in an only marginally better Romanian camp. In the third attack six Halifaxes, three Liberators, and fifty-two Wellingtons operated. Once again, some of the crews had difficulty distinguishing the target area due to haze, and their task was made even more difficult by the smoke from fires started by the USAAF in a daylight raid. However, the bombing was well concentrated on the industrial area and the southern end of the marshalling yards. Fighter opposition was much greater than during previous attacks, and four Wellingtons, one Halifax and one Liberator failed to return.

As stated above, the main effort of the Group during May was directed at railway targets, the general object of which was to prevent the enemy bringing supplies southwards from France and Germany. The marshalling yards at Allessandria, Piacenza, Budapest/Rakos, Campina, Arezzo, Orvieto, and Milan/Lambrate all received attention, and results were generally reported to be good. The biggest raid was on Budapest/Rakos on 4/5 May, with six Halifaxes and sixty-four Wellingtons despatched. Although there was considerable haze over the target, several direct hits were claimed on tracks, including one 4,000-pounder at the northern end of the yards, and sticks of incendiaries fell across the north and south ends of the yards. One Wellington failed to return. Fifty-three aircraft went back to the Rakos yards six nights later, which they found covered by 10/10 cloud. The illumination was scattered all over Budapest, and only eight aircraft were able to identify the target visually through breaks in the cloud. The rest bombed on flares, flak, and ETA.

On 5/6 May the target was the marshalling yards at Campina, a fairly compact target situated in the centre of the Steaua-Romana oil refinery, twenty miles north-west of Ploesti. Seven Halifaxes and forty-one Wellingtons operated, and the raid was carried out in good weather and no cloud. Blind markers dropped their target indicators with great success, and all aircraft were able to attack in excellent illumination. Many direct hits were scored on the marshalling yards, the oil storage tanks north and south of the yards, and the adjacent oil refinery buildings. The bombing was reasonably well concentrated, and at the end of the attack the whole area was covered by smoke. One of the aircraft reported an oil fire with flames 200 feet high and smoke up to 2,000 feet. Three good fires among storage tanks to the north of the yard were still visible sixty miles away. One Wellington was forced to ditch on the return journey, with the wireless operator missing, believed drowned. Another two Wellingtons failed to return, and may have been shot down over the target.

As well as the raids on marshalling yards, the bombers also attacked railway bridges – small targets that were generally unsuitable for night attacks. On 6/7 May two Wellingtons were detailed to attack a railway bridge at Pitesti, Romania, but it seems that the wrong bridge was bombed (Chappell describes it as 'another unimportant bridge') as a road bridge was seen close beside it. One 4,000-pounder burst twenty-five yards west of the bridge, but no damage was observed. The other Wellington made four dummy runs before bombing, noting that the north end of the bridge was apparently already damaged. The 4,000-lb bomb was dropped from 150 feet, and seen to skid under the bridge near the centre. A big explosion followed, and a pall of dust and smoke hung over the bridge, but no definite results were observed despite two more runs being made over the target.

On the same night three Wellingtons were detailed to attack a railway bridge west of Filiasi, Romania, and all three identified the target. Two dropped their 4,000-pounders from low level, claiming direct hits on the bridge, but unfortunately neither of the bombs went off. The third aircraft bombed from 6,000 feet, but again the bomb failed to explode. One of the Wellingtons from No. 236 Wing that attacked here was flown by Wing Commander Harold Turner, and Chappell describes how he spent an hour at 600 to 1,000 feet searching for the bridge. When he eventually found it he made a number of careful dummy runs and placed his 4,000-pounder dead on the bridge, but it failed to explode. On the next night, two Wellingtons had another go at the bridge, with Wing Commander Turner again piloting one of them. He got his bomb to burst near the bridge, but without causing any apparent damage.[2]

The captain of the other Wellington, Warrant Officer Tom Bradshaw, had devised a method of aiming for this difficult target. The guns in the nose turret were trained at a certain angle of depression, and when the aiming point passed the muzzles of the guns the bomb was released. On the run the Wellington was hit by light flak, and the bomb aimer called out that he was wounded but could still aim the bomb. As the wireless operator went forward to help him, the bomb aimer called out 'bomb gone', but he was dead by the time that the wireless operator got to him. Meanwhile, the aircraft was in serious trouble, and the crew baled out. The four survivors met up with Chetnik partisans, and returned to Foggia fourteen weeks later. This was the second time that the crew had taken to their parachutes, as their aircraft had iced up over Foggia in February and they had had to bale out before the pilot managed to bring the aircraft down safely on his own.

On 13/14 May, the target for six aircraft was a bridge at Fornova Di Taro, near Parma, where two north-south railway lines joined before continuing southwards. The first illuminator found the target without difficulty, and dropped flares half a mile to the north. These showed up the bridge clearly, and one of the bombers claimed a direct hit, followed by sparks and splashes in the water. On 14/15 May fifty-one aircraft attacked railway bridges at Latisana, Tagliamento–Casarsa, and Avisio. Bad weather spoiled the attack at Avisio, but the other two targets were bombed successfully. However, the amount of damage caused was probably minimal, and one of the Wellingtons failed to return from the attack on Avisio. On 28/29 May four Wellingtons were detailed to attack the railway at Colle Isarco, on the Brenner Pass, where the intention was to cause an avalanche that would block the line where it ran under the mountains. One illuminator returned early and another was unable to locate the U-bend in the railway, but the two bombers considered that they were in the right position and dropped their 4,000-lb bombs on the mountain slopes. The bursts were seen, but no results observed due to the darkness. On 31 May/1 June twenty-five Wellingtons, two Liberators, and eleven Halifaxes were detailed to attack sheds, locomotives and railway tracks in the area of the Iron Gates Gorge on the Danube. The bombing seems to have been well concentrated, with the main concentration across the embankment near the engine shed.

A major part of the effort in May was directed against vulnerable points on roads in the Valmontone, Frosinone, Ferentino and Viterbo areas. These mainly lay in towns and villages, where the debris of shattered buildings could block narrow streets and create traffic jams that could be attacked by the Tactical Air Force in daylight. While the Germans stood on the Senger Line, the object of the attacks was to prevent reinforcements moving forwards. After the Germans had been forced out of the Line and from the Anzio beachhead, the objective was to interfere with their withdrawal. Both armies had to retreat northwards, and the lie of the roads behind them obviously governed the pattern of their withdrawals. The first attack came on 17/18, May, when fourteen Wellingtons were despatched to bomb a road at Frosinone. One of the Wellingtons was uncertain of the primary target, and attacked a road at Terracina instead. The remainder bombed the correct target, where sticks of bombs were seen to straddle the main road through the village. On the next night forty-five Wellingtons and six Liberators were detailed to attack roads in the vicinity of Frosinone, Terracina, and Valmontone, and many direct hits and near misses were claimed.

On 22/23, 23/24 and 24/25 May, roads at Valmontone and Ferentino were attacked by a total of 176 aircraft to prevent the German Tenth Army from getting away from Cassino. As we have seen, the US 6th Corps was advancing towards Valmontone at this time and with the same objective, until Clark diverted most of it towards Rome. Target identification was often difficult due to cloud, and illumination varied from 'scattered' to 'excellent'. Two Wellingtons of No. 70 Squadron failed to return on 23/24 May, and are believed to have collided over the target. Many crews saw what they thought was a collision, followed by an explosion and two burning masses falling to the ground. On the same night a Wellington of No. 330 Wing reported that they had encountered a Ju 88 over Ponza and shot it down. However, a later report was received that a Beaufighter was missing from a patrol in the same area, and must have been shot down in mistake by the Wellington. On 24/25 May, extremely bad weather en route to and over the target made the operation a failure, and of the sixty-five aircraft that operated, only thirty-seven reached the target area. One of the Wellingtons of No. 40 Squadron failed to return.

On 25/26, 26/27 and 27/28 May, the tactical targets were at Viterbo, some forty miles north of Rome, and 157 sorties were despatched over the three nights. The objective, once again, was to prevent reinforcements moving to the Rome area, although there were few still available. The German defence south of Rome was now down to a few battalions, and Kesselring knew that the end was near. In the first attack at Viterbo, fifty-six aircraft identified the target in excellent illumination, and bombs were seen to fall across roads and railway junctions at the north, south and east ends of the town. Many vehicles were seen entering Viterbo and on the roads to the south and south-west, particularly between Vetralla and Tarquinia. The next attack was carried out by forty-eight Wellingtons and six Liberators and was again successful, as was the third attack by seven Liberators and thirty-seven Wellingtons. Bombing was well concentrated on the road junctions to the north and south of the town, and two columns of vehicles a quarter of a mile long were seen on roads in the vicinity heading south. The last attack on tactical targets during the battle for Rome came on 30/31 May, when roads in the village of Subiaco were attacked. The village lay in a narrow valley, and was being used by some elements of the Tenth Army that were trying to get away from Cassino. The target was difficult to identify due to its small size and the illumination was scattered along the valley, but subsequent photographs confirmed that the bombing had been reasonably concentrated.

Mining in the Danube was again carried out successfully on four nights in May, and 104 sorties were despatched. The aircraft also machine-gunned barges and shipping on the river and gun positions along the banks. The biggest attack came on 31 May/1 June, when forty-two Wellingtons and ten Liberators successfully laid 129 mines in the River between Slankamen and Stari Banovic. One of the Wellingtons of No. 104 Squadron (piloted by 'one of the boys from "down under"') 'is reported to have gone in so low that a sardine was found in the pitot head'! One Liberator crashed on landing and burnt out, all the crew being killed. Coal traffic on the river was virtually suspended at this time. Ports were becoming overcrowded, storage facilities strained, and barges were piling up at Regensburg awaiting a tow to Budapest. On 1 June, listeners in London and Foggia were gratified to hear the Hungarian wireless warn all shipping between Goenuye and Piszke to remain where it was until further notice. Barges loaded at Svishtov at the end of April were still there on 10 June. Photographic evidence showed the Begej canal between Titel and Jecka to be full of inactive barges, while more than a hundred were dispersed along the banks of the Danube and the Sava. A local report stated that:

> The enemy has mined the Danube systematically and has achieved his object of upsetting the traffic in the Balkans...I am under the impression that the entire length of the river was only free for ship traffic for very few days. The enemy sets mines which are very difficult to sweep and are not to be swept by a few mine-detecting aircraft...The crews of the Danube vessels are creating difficulty. Frequently they desert, but it is intended to out-manoeuvre this by militarizing them. Finally it must be stated that the enemy by the mining of the Danube harms us very considerably and that at present we are unable to cope with the situation.[3]

As part of the attempts to interfere with the flow of supplies to the south, the ports at Genoa, Spezia, Leghorn (Livorno), Porto San Stefano, Piombino and Portoferraio were all attacked throughout the month. The Germans did not depend upon the seaways as a lines of communication nearly as much as the Allies, but were forced to move increasing quantities by sea as the traffic on railways and roads was continually interrupted by the Allied air forces. The attacks by the night bombers were really 'area' raids, and bombs fell indiscriminately on ships, harbour installations, railways, and on the towns themselves. Railway installations and the station were considerably damaged at Leghorn, rolling stock was destroyed, and all rail traffic temporarily suspended following the raids. At Piombino, a rolling mill and foundries were completely destroyed and 30 per cent of the town demolished.

Three other attacks were carried out in May. On 9/10 May a special operation was launched that was designed to breach the wall of a glider-bomb factory at Portes-les-Valences in Southern France. The intention was to breach a wall surrounding the factory so that partisans could enter the premises and make off with secret equipment and generally sabotage the works. The Wellingtons were operating at extreme range, and refuelled at Ajaccio (Chisonaccia) in Corsica. It seems that arrangements at the advanced base were 'practically nil', and crews had to carry out armament servicing themselves and also had to refuel their aircraft. At Portes-les-Valences, four crews were to come down over the factory at 500 feet and drop 4,000-lb medium case bombs against the factory wall. A diversionary attack was also to be carried out in order to cause confusion and help the partisans. Twenty-four Wellingtons were despatched, and the success of the operation depended on pinpoint bombing, which in turn depended on clear visibility.

Unfortunately, the operation was ruined by extremely bad weather, and all the crews reported thick cloud and icing conditions. Only three aircraft located the target, two carrying out the diversionary attack as planned, and all observed their bombs to fall in the correct area. Two bombs were believed to have hit the north-east corner of the factory, but the remaining crews jettisoned their bombs and returned to base. The ORB for No. 104 Squadron states that 'great secrecy surrounded the operation, in fact it was so secret that even the aircrews were unable to find it'! Chappell states that Squadron Leader Richards of No. 104 Squadron had static electricity build up and explode in his aircraft, causing minor damage to the astrodome and burning the fabric off the wing tips. One Wellington of No. 40 Squadron (captained by Flying Officer Johnny Huggler – 'a grand chap and on his last operation of this tour') failed to return. A fire was seen among the mountains, and it seemed likely that he crashed while trying to get below the clouds.[4]

On 14/15 May, eight Liberators set off to bomb the oil refinery at Porto Marghera in Italy, but only five aircraft located the target in very poor visibility. However, the illumination was good and bursts were seen in the target area, causing one small fire on a quay. A direct hit was also seen among storage tanks, causing an explosion and flames. On 29/30 May, thirty-eight Wellingtons, including six illuminators, took off to attack the airfield at Feuersbrunn in Austria. Thirty-five of the aircraft attacked the target in good illumination, and bombing was concentrated, with many sticks seen to burst across the airfield. One large fire was started in buildings at the north-east end of the airfield, and there were two other fires in the target area. Two big explosions were seen, one of which gave out vivid green sparks up to a height of 1,000 feet. One Wellington failed to return, and was believed to have crashed south of the target.

Notification was received during the month that No. 614 Squadron was to move to a new location at Stornara (Cerignola No. 4). This was to be the first step in making the Squadron operationally and administratively controlled directly by Headquarters No. 205 Group. The new domestic site was probably the most pleasant the Squadron had ever had, situated well away from the airfield in orchards. A movement order was issued on 4 May, with the Squadron ordered to continue operations from Celone until 8/9 May and to be operational at its new site on 10/11 May. In fact, the Squadron last operated from Celone on 7/8 May (against Bucharest), and lost a Halifax in the process. Its first operation from the new site was on 13/14 May, when eight Halifaxes attacked the marshalling yards at Milan–Lambrate. The move was carried out very efficiently, assisted by the American Bomber Group on the airfield, but great difficulties were soon experienced from dust at Stornara. The dispersals and perimeter tracks had not been finished when the aircraft arrived, and the oil and water treatment had not worn into the surface. The Squadron had previously operated from many landing grounds in the Western Desert, but it had never experienced anything like this. Operations had to be postponed for a considerable period while the engineers worked on the airfield, but there was still a considerable amount of dust at the end of May.

*   *   *

The beginning of May 1944 found No. 31 Squadron SAAF still in Egypt and 'getting organized and filling up deficiencies in equipment' at Kilo 40. The advance party of No. 34 Squadron had also been at Kilo 40 for a few days, and the rest of the Squadron arrived there on 3 May. The aircrews carried out circuits and landings to familiarize themselves with their Liberators, and looked forward to being able to carry out their first 'nursery' operation on 21 May. News was received on 8 May that No. 31 Squadron would move to Italy in June, but No. 34 Squadron would remain in Egypt for a little while longer. No. 31 Squadron ORB records that on the 12th the CO left in the morning for Lydda, 'and arranged his return so as to make a night-landing in order to test the flare path, the final equipment for which has just arrived'. The chance light was still not available, but one was borrowed for the occasion. Fortunately, everything went according to plan and the CO landed safely. By 17 May thirteen crews were complete and awaiting flying clothing, and further testing of the flare-path equipment and R/T procedures was carried out.

On 24 May six Liberators of No. 31 Squadron took off to participate in the Empire Day flypast at Gezira, and everything went well. The next morning was spent planning for the first operation, and crews were briefed and last-minute preparations made. Unfortunately, a final met report was received towards the end of the briefing forecasting 10/10 cloud at 4,000 feet over the target area, and the operation was cancelled. Thus, the first operation by the Liberators of No. 31 Squadron SAAF eventually took place on 27/28 May, after two postponements. Its first target was the airfield at Kastelli Pediada on Crete, and twelve Liberators, each carrying twelve 500-lb bombs, took off. Unfortunately, things did not go well. The bombers found the target area to be covered by dense cloud, and ten jettisoned their bombs into the sea. One bombed what was believed to be a group of

270

searchlights in the Suda Bay area, and the twelfth aircraft was forced to make an early return because of engine trouble. While trying to locate the emergency landing ground at Gianaclis, the navigator lost his bearings and flew over Alexandria. The crew received the shock of their lives when the air defences of the city opened up on them, and they narrowly escaped being shot down by 'friendly fire'! Those on duty in the operations tent at Kilo 40 heard the pilot's furious cursing when they picked up his call for help.

Ten Liberators of No. 31 (SAAF) Squadron again went to Kastelli Pediada on 31 May/1 June, this time with more success. One had to return early as the top of its turret cupola had blown off, but the other nine dropped their bombs within the target area, and all returned safely to base. The aim of the operation was to disrupt the air cover protecting a convoy of enemy ships carrying supplies and reinforcements to the German garrison on Crete. This convoy of three motor vessels, escorted by a destroyer, a light cruiser and several flak ships, was moving at night and taking cover by day under the cliffs of various Aegean Islands. During the early part of June the Liberators carried on operations against Crete and the Greek island of Paros as part of their 'working-up' process. Three attacks were made on shipping in the harbour at Heraklion, and one on the airfield at Marmara on Paros. In the attack on Heraklion on 3/4 June a 'mysterious civilian' took part in this attack, introduced to the crew as 'Major Koekemoer'. It was, in fact, Gert Nel, vice consul at the South African consulate in Cairo, and a relative of the OC of No. 31 Squadron, Dirk Nel.

On 16 June sixteen aircraft of No. 31 Squadron were scheduled to take off in batches of eight at one-hour intervals from 0400 hours and fly direct to Celone. Eleven successfully completed the journey, but the remainder either failed to take off or turned back due to some defect. The facilities at Celone were described as 'very inadequate', but the aircrews were fed by No. 240 Wing. On the following day the remaining five aircraft took off from Kilo 40, and four landed at Celone on the same day. The fifth aircraft had to land at Gambut with engine trouble. Their first operation with No. 205 Group would take place on 25/26 June against the Shell Koolaz oil refinery at Budapest (see below).

No. 34 Squadron had arrived at Kilo 40 expecting to be there for some time, and showers were laid on, cement floors were laid in some of the tents, and deep pit latrines were dug. However, laundry difficulties were experienced, 'and it was decided to try out a Gippo (Arab) Laundry together with a shoemaker, barber and watch repairer'. It was a dismal failure, as they 'ignored the latrine specially built for them and evacuated anywhere'. The barber's tools were in such a filthy state that his tent had to be put out of bounds until the MO was satisfied. They only lasted a week. Then bad news arrived – the Squadron had to move again to Rasin-el-Boud in Syria, twenty miles from Aleppo and near the Turkish border, to take part in a plan code-named 'Turpitude'. The ground crews, together with the headquarters staff of No. 2 Wing SAAF, left Kilo 40 at 0600 hours on 30 May and arrived at the new location at 1830 hours on 4 June. They had crossed the Sinai Desert in a ninety-seven-vehicle convoy and made their way through Palestine into Syria.

The aircrews of No. 34 Squadron flew over to Syria on 8 June, after completing their conversion course in Palestine. Their arrival at Rasin-el-Boud coincided with a fierce tornado that flattened most of the camp, but all were quickly occupied in a training regime that involved daily practice take-offs and landings. What they didn't know was that these were all part of the 'Turpitude' plan, the object of which was to intimidate neutral Turkey into joining the Allies. A force of infantry, tanks, and anti-aircraft units, along with two squadrons of Spitfires and the Liberators of No. 34 Squadron, had been moved up to the Turkish border to stage a sham demonstration of military might. The game of bluff continued until 27 June, when the ground staff of the Squadron was ordered back to Egypt. Their aircrews, together with about a hundred fitters, flew over to Kilo 40 on the next day, and the Liberators of No. 34 Squadron began to move to Celone on 5 July. On the following day the Advance Echelon of No. 2 Wing SAAF arrived in Italy, and No. 31 Squadron operated under the control of the Wing for the first time on 19/20 July in the attack on Fiume (see below). No. 34 Squadron flew its first operation to Pardubice oil refinery on 21/22 July (see also below).

*   *   *

During the month of June No. 205 Group operated on twenty-two nights and flew 1,356 sorties, with the weather preventing operations on five nights and stand-downs ordered on three nights. At the beginning of the month much of the effort was still against road communications in the Battle Area, with six operations being carried out against these targets between 3/4 June and 9/10 June. The most successful operation was the attack on road bridges across the Tiber between Rome and Ostia on 3/4 June in order to block the roads by which the enemy would probably attempt to retreat. Forty-four Wellingtons and six Liberators operated and carried out a very concentrated attack, with many bursts seen on and near both ends of the bridges and on the approach roads on either side. Later photographic reconnaissance showed that one of the bridges was surrounded by about 155 craters, and was itself damaged by five direct hits. Chappell records that:

> We received a message of congratulations from General Twining, the Commander of the 15th Air Force on a fine piece of work – also a message from the General Commanding Tactical Air Force – and a message from our own Air Officer Commanding 205 Group. It really was a splendid effort by all concerned. Our crews love something exciting and different and this Tiber Bridge provided such a target.[5]

Further attacks were carried out on roads at Terni, Viterbo, and Orvieto as the Germans retreated beyond Rome. However, the bulk of the effort in June (565 sorties – 42 per cent of the total) was directed at oil refineries and storage facilities, and good results were achieved at Giurgiu, Brod Bosanski, Almasfuzito and Trieste. This was the first time that No. 205 Group had devoted a major part of its effort to oil targets, and it would only do so for three months in the summer of 1944 (June, July and August).

On 2/3 June thirty-four Wellingtons, six Liberators, and four Halifaxes were detailed to attack quays and storage tanks on the north bank of the River Danube at Giurgiu. The illumination was good and the bombing was well concentrated, with bursts seen to cover the oil depot and loading area. Direct hits were claimed on the storage tanks, and a very large fire was started, which burned with a deep red colour and gave off black smoke to a height of several thousand feet. One of the Wellingtons of No. 40 Squadron failed to return. Forty Wellingtons, five Liberators, and eight Halifaxes went to Brod Bosanski on 10/11 June, and the bombing was again reported to be well concentrated in the refinery area. Direct hits were claimed across its centre and northern end, and a large explosion was followed by a big fire with orange-red flames. A photo reconnaissance revealed that direct hits and a fire destroyed several buildings and severely damaged many others, and at least six oil storage tanks were either destroyed or damaged.

On 12/13 June thirty-nine Wellingtons, ten Liberators, and eight Halifaxes attacked Almasfuzito, where direct hits were reported on storage tanks, causing large explosions, followed by sheets of flame and clouds of smoke. Photographs taken during the bombing showed a 4,000-lb bomb burst in the centre of the plant, and others showed three very large fires and the whole plant enveloped in thick black smoke typical of oil fires. On 26/27 June fifty-six Wellingtons, sixteen Liberators and ten Halifaxes went to the Aquila refinery at Trieste. The illumination was good and all the aircraft bombed on and around the target markers dropped by the Halifaxes at the centre and east end of the target area. Many sticks of bombs were seen to straddle the refinery, including a direct hit on the distillation plant, and a very large explosion was followed by a big fire that gave off smoke to the height of 3,000 feet. A large storage tank was believed to have been hit at the western end of the refinery, but the results of the bombing were obscured by much smoke towards the end of the attack.

Other attacks on oil targets were carried out during the month, but with mixed results. At Trieste on 9/10 June an attack by sixty aircraft was spoiled by scattered and inaccurate target marking by No. 614 Squadron, and one by sixty-one aircraft at Vado Ligure–Zinola on 22/23 June was hampered by cloud and poor illumination. In the major operation by 104 aircraft to the Shell Koolaz refinery on Czepel Island at Budapest on 25/26 June, six Liberators of No. 31 SAAF Squadron operated with the Group for the first time. Unfortunately, the illumination was well north of the target, and the majority of the aircraft bombed on its estimated position in relation to the River Danube, the north tip of Czepel Island and the docks. Another big raid by another 104 aircraft on the oil storage facilities at Giurgiu was carried out on 28/29 June, but cloud and electrical storms en route meant that the illuminators arrived late and the marking was scattered because of haze and extreme darkness. Some aircraft identified the target, but the majority bombed on its estimated position and the bombing was scattered over a wide area. Night fighters were reported over the target and on the inward and return journeys, and three Liberators, one Halifax and one Wellington failed to return. There were numerous reports of aircraft crashing in flames in and near the target area, and some crews thought that two aircraft collided over the target. On 13 September news was received that four members of one of the South African Liberator crews had been evacuated from a Bulgarian POW camp and would soon be returned to the Middle East.

Six attacks were also made on railway targets at Solznok, Nis (two attacks), Munich, Timosoara, and Ventimiglia, involving 350 sorties and the loss of nine aircraft. Forty Wellingtons, five Halifaxes and five Liberators were despatched to Szolnok (Hungary) on the first night of the month, but thick haze covered the yards and a railway bridge and the illumination was scattered. Few of the aircraft identified the yards, and the main concentration of bombing was plotted around the Puspok-Ladany marshalling yards forty-seven miles from Szolnok. The first attack by thirty-six Wellingtons, ten Liberators and eight Halifaxes on Nis (Yugoslavia) on 8/9 June was a success. The illumination was good, markers were well placed, and bombs were seen to fall directly across the marshalling yards and on buildings in the area. All the aircraft returned safely, but as Chappell was getting ready to interrogate the returning crews 'in the pale pre dawn light', a Wellington of No. 104 Squadron came in to make a good landing – then suddenly blew up 'with a tremendous crack and bang followed immediately by leaping fire and…horrible crackling noises'. A bomb had burst under the rear turret, and blown this and the rear gunner to pieces. The navigator had a leg blown off and later died in hospital, and the wireless operator was very seriously injured. The second attack on Nis on 14/15 June was less successful, although several sticks of bombs were seen to straddle the target area and one 4,000-lb bomb was dropped in the centre of the yards.

The biggest raid on a railway target was on Munich railway station on 13/14 June, when sixty-six Wellingtons, thirteen Liberators, and nine Halifaxes operated. Identification was difficult due to cloud over the target, and only a few crews were able to see the city. Most bombed on searchlights and flares and very few results were observed. Four aircraft failed to return, including one from No. 40 Squadron, which was coned near Munich. The wireless operator later recounted that the aircraft did a complete slow roll with the help of flak bursting under one wing before it gave up the ghost, and the crew were lucky to get out before it exploded. A very successful attack was carried out by thirty-two Wellingtons and nine Halifaxes on the Timosoara marshalling yards on 16/17 June, with the target area well covered with incendiary bombs. The marshalling yards were described as a mass of flames and explosions, and the ruins were still smouldering at 1500 hours the following day. Another successful attack was carried out by fifty-six Wellingtons, eight Halifaxes and three Liberators on the yards at Ventimiglia on 21/22 June. Bursts were seen across the centre of the target area, and a stick of bombs near the main railway station was followed by an explosion giving off considerable sparks of varying colours, and it was thought that an ammunition train had been hit. At the end of the attack the target was largely obscured by smoke, with at least two good fires visible.

One attack each was made on the airfields at Karlovo (Bulgaria) and Feuersbrunn (Austria). Forty Wellingtons, four Liberators and six Halifaxes were despatched to Karlovo on 11/12 June, the object being to destroy enemy fighters thought to be used to intercept the American daylight attacks on Ploesti and Bucharest. The bombing was well concentrated on hangars and dispersals, three hangars were set on fire, and dispersed aircraft at both ends of the airfield were also left in flames. Fifty-eight Wellingtons, twelve Liberators and eight Halifaxes were sent to Feuersbrunn on 29/30 June with the same object. They were to destroy aircraft on the ground and render the landing ground unserviceable, so that the enemy fighters would be prevented from attacking the USAAF bombers expected to be operating in the area the following day. Illumination was rather scattered, but most crews claimed to have identified the target visually and there was a good concentration of bombing on the northern dispersal area. A direct hit was claimed on a hangar at the north-east corner of the airfield, and several small fires seen around the airfield were thought to be aircraft burning.

*   *   *

The operational effort of No. 205 Group was considerably curtailed during July, with operations only taking place on 17 nights and 1,333 sorties despatched. Bad weather caused operations to be cancelled on three occasions, and there was a Group stand-down on eleven nights. The main weight of the Group's effort continued to be directed against oil refineries, with nine operations directed at six plants – one in Northern Italy (Fiume-ROMSA at Turin) and five in Romania: Bucharest–Prahova (three attacks), Brod Bosanski (two attacks), Smederevo, Pardubice-Fanto, and Ploesti–Romana Americana. A total of 760 sorties were launched against these targets and much damage was caused, although defences were always strong and fifteen aircraft were lost. With the decrease in Axis refined oil supplies from 14,000,000 tons to 4,700,000 tons annually as a result of Allied bombing attacks, the large Bucharest–Prahova oil refinery had become a target of the highest priority. A total of 218 sorties were launched against this target alone (the three attacks taking place on 2/3, 23/24 and 27/28 July), and good results were claimed from the first attack. The illumination was good, and the target indicators were placed very close to the aiming point. Alhough haze made observation of results difficult, three 4,000-lb bomb bursts were seen in the target area, and two sticks of bombs were seen to fall right across the refinery. At the end of the attack three fires were burning and large columns of smoke were observed at the north end of the target. The second and third attacks were marred by cloud, and the bombing was scattered with few positive results claimed.

Moderate flak and numerous enemy fighters were reported in the first attack, several encounters took place and one Liberator of No. 31 Squadron and two Wellingtons of No. 40 Squadron failed to return. The bomb aimer of one of the Wellingtons later returned to his squadron and reported that the aircraft had sustained very severe damage after three attacks by a Ju 88 and the crew baled out. He landed safely and contacted the partisans, and was evacuated by air after forty days. A report in the No. 31 Squadron ORB on 23 August stated that the pilot of their aircraft, Captain R.B. Bird, was interned in Romania, and on 4 September it further recorded that he and his navigator Lieutenant Nicholson had been repatriated with American forces from Bucharest. His aircraft had been attacked from below by a night fighter, and both port and starboard tanks set alight. Captain Bird ordered the crew to bale out, but two did not get out and their bodies were found later in the wreckage. Bird woke up three hours later in a ploughed field with a stiff neck and a sore back. He was captured and taken to the police station in the small town of Vida, thirty miles south-west of Bucharest. Here he made contact with the navigator, Ralph Nicholson, but they were subsequently separated – Nicholson going to hospital with an injured leg and Bird to a POW camp in Bucharest. After a few days in hospital Nicholson joined Bird in the camp, and both were released when the Russians entered the town at the end of August.

Another Liberator of No. 31 Squadron was attacked by a night fighter about twenty minutes before the target, and damaged in the port rudder and elevator. While taking evasive action two 500-lb bombs were thrown onto the bomb doors, but the pilot carried on to the target. On approach the bomb doors on the port side were manually raised and the other six bombs released by the second pilot (Lieutenant Cairns). He had barely returned to the cockpit when the aircraft was coned by searchlights, and Lieutenant Cairns assisted in righting the aircraft after evasive action. He then returned to the bomb bay where, without parachute or harness, he chopped away the runners on the port doors and cleared the remainder of the bombs.

The Brod Bosanski (Yugoslavia) oil refinery had been attacked previously on 10 June, but the boiler houses and distillation plant were still undamaged and oil storage tanks intact. Further attacks were carried out on 8/9 and 14/15 July and subsequent photo reconnaissance revealed severe damage to the whole plant, including storage tanks, administrative buildings and railway sidings. The Smederevo (Yugoslavia) oil refinery, although damaged in previous attacks by the Fifteenth Air Force, was still operating, and another attack was launched on this important target on 16/17 July. Photo reconnaissance showed that the boiler house (the primary objective) was almost completely destroyed by a direct hit, and much other damage was shown among the installations and storage tanks.

Another successful attack was carried out at Fiume on 19/20 July. Chappell did the briefing for No. 236 Wing. He then received some new information at the last minute and went around the aircraft on his motorcycle to explain the changes to the crews. He stood there watching the take-off as the Wellingtons taxied in line along the paths leading to the Chance Light to wait for the green light from control. Things went normally until 'a sudden terrific flash lit up the sky to the north followed by Very lights, and firework effects amidst a huge cloud of smoke mushrooming upwards'. One of the aircraft of No. 104 Squadron had crashed after sparks had been seen coming from one engine at take-off. It had immediately ploughed in and blew up, and all the crew were killed.[6] Shortly afterwards, Chappell left Italy and the 'Wellington Wings' for a new posting to Headquarters, RAF Middle East in Cairo, and we lose his interesting and invaluable comments on the operations of the night bombers. At Fiume the markers were late and the early bombing was scattered, but the illumination was eventually on target and the later crews obtained a good concentration. Photo reconnaissance confirmed that much damage was done, including some storage tanks destroyed.

The attack on the Fano oil refinery at Pardubice by sixty-three Wellingtons, twenty-five Liberators and six Halifaxes on 21/22 July was the Group's first visit to Czechoslovakia. The illumination was poor, haze and smoke covered the target area, and the bombing was generally scattered. A large explosion and some scattered fires were reported, but the conditions prevented any clear observation of results. Five Wellingtons and one Liberator failed to return. This was the first operation by No. 34 Squadron, and the ORB records that the unit was only asked to provide aircraft for this mission at 0930 hours and it was not until 1230 hours that the full briefing came through. The main ground party was still at Bari, and this meant that a tremendous amount of work had to be carried out by the few personnel at Celone to get four aircraft fully operational. Their efforts were in vain, as two of the bombers returned early with electrical and mechanical defects, one accidentally jettisoned its bombs fifteen minutes before reaching the target, and one of them didn't come back.

The final attack on an oil target was on the Romana–Americana refinery at Ploesti on 26/27 July. Fifty-three Wellingtons, twenty Liberators and eight Halifaxes operated, but an effective smoke screen meant that the attack could not be pressed home. Four of the Halifax 'pathfinders' dropped flares and target markers using their special equipment, but they were quickly obscured by the smoke screen. Bombing was generally scattered, but a few small fires and one large explosion were observed. One Liberator of No. 31 Squadron SAAF failed to return, and four bodies were washed ashore at Brindisi on 5 August. The condition of the bodies and the circumstances surrounding their recovery suggested that the aircraft had attempted a ditching on return from the target. Another Liberator from No. 31 Squadron was attacked by a night fighter on the return trip, and one engine was put out of action. The aircraft went into a screaming power-dive, and the pilot alerted the crew to prepare to bale out. However, he managed to regain control of the badly damaged aircraft, and made for home. It was then discovered that the navigator had disappeared, and was presumed to have baled out. While in the circuit over the airfield at Foggia and preparing to land, the control tower informed the pilot that there was something hanging beneath the aircraft. It transpired that the navigator's parachute had caught on the nosewheel door, and he was suspended by the strand lines below the aircraft. All efforts to retrieve the body were fruitless, and it had to be cut free south of the airfield. It was recovered the next morning from a cornfield.

Four attacks were made on the marshalling yards at Milan–Lambrate (two attacks), Verona and Brescia, involving 295 sorties and with seven aircraft lost. The attack on Verona on 5/6 July was carried out by seventy Wellingtons, twelve Liberators and eight Halifaxes. The illumination was good and on time, and the bombing was well concentrated on the yards. Two violent explosions were reported, one followed by an orange and red fire, and another oil fire with smoke up to 5,000 feet was also reported. The fires were still visible sixty miles from the target. Sixty-seven Wellingtons, nine Liberators and seven Halifaxes operated in the first attack on Milan-Lambrate on 10/11 July, and highly satisfactory results were obtained. The illumination and marking were excellent, many sticks were seen straddling the target, and a 4,000-lb bomb obtained a direct hit on the centre of the yards. The whole target area was covered by small fires with intermittent explosions. Two big explosions occurred, and at the end of the attack the target was well ablaze, with fires increasing and dense smoke rising. One Wellington of No. 40 Squadron failed to return.

The attack on Brescia by eighteen Wellingtons, six Liberators and seven Halifaxes on 12/13 July was also successful. Illumination was good, the target indicators were on target, and the bombing was well concentrated. Sticks fell across the yards and on the bottleneck leading to the sidings, and one 4,000-lb bomb burst produced grey smoke up to 2,000 feet. Then, on the next night another attack was launched on the Milan-Lambrate yards to complete the destruction of rolling stock trapped in the yards due to the cutting of the tracks at both ends. Seventy-four Wellingtons, seven Liberators and eight Halifaxes operated, and the illumination and marking were good. Many sticks and at least three 4,000-pounders were seen to burst in the target area, and a direct hit on the large locomotive shed resulted in a violent explosion. One dark red fire, believed to be oil, and several other fires were observed, with intermittent explosions that produced much smoke. Subsequent photographs confirmed that much damage was caused, with lines cut and the roof of a very large warehouse completely removed. Six of the aircraft failed to return.

Attacks were also made on the airfields at Feuersbrunn on 6/7 July and Valence/La Trasorerie on 24/25 July, the latter in co-operation with French Resistance forces. The attack on Feuersbrunn was particularly expensive, with thirteen aircraft lost from the sixty-one despatched. The illumination was late, with the result that some aircraft bombed visually, but there was a fair concentration on the airfield. Enemy fighters were very active, and many aircraft were seen going down in flames. However, over nineteen enemy fighters were claimed to have been destroyed on the ground, and as a direct result of the attack fifty enemy fighters were grounded and prevented from intercepting a subsequent USAAF daylight mission. The navigator of a Wellington of No. 70 Squadron later returned to his unit, and reported that his aircraft was hit by tracer, caught fire and went into a spin. Though not conscious of baling out, he came to in a field with a badly cut head and knees, and struggled some distance from the position of the crash before dawn. He contacted partisans on the same day, and after resting and letting his wounds heal, trekked under their care to Hum. He was then taken by lorry to a British mission, and was evacuated by air on 6 August.

The attack at Valence/La Trasorerie was intended to act as a diversion for French partisans. The bombers would crater the landing ground and trap aircraft at their dispersals so that the partisans could move in and destroy them. A most successful operation was carried out by twenty-two Liberators and seven Halifaxes, the latter providing good illumination and placing target markers right across the landing ground. Bombs fell on the airfield, on a hangar to the west of the airfield, and on buildings at the north-west dispersals. Explosions and fires were seen from the dispersal areas, and it was subsequently reported that some thirty enemy aircraft were destroyed. A fuel dump was also set on fire, and many casualties inflicted.

As well as the bombing operations, mines were successfully laid in the Danube on three nights in July. The biggest operation was carried out on 1/2 of the month, when fifty-seven Wellingtons, sixteen Liberators and three Halifaxes operated. In all, 192 mines were dropped in beds between Nyergsujafalu (30 miles east of Komarom) and Bazias (40 miles east of Belgrade). Mining was generally accurate, with crews seeing parachutes opening and splashes in the correct positions. Much accurate light flak was encountered, and several aircraft were hit and sustained casualties. Two Wellingtons of No. 40 Squadron and two from No. 104 Squadron failed to return. One of the former was hit by flak in the vicinity of Belgrade, the port engine put out of action, the hydraulic system damaged, and the wireless operator slightly wounded. As the aircraft was unable to gain height, the crew baled out. All landed safely, and they were evacuated by air after spending over seven weeks in the care of Chetniks. On the following night ten Liberators dropped sixty mines in eight beds between Vukovar and Giurgiu. The third mining operation was on 30/31 July, when thirty-four Wellingtons and eighteen Liberators dropped 175 mines in thirteen beds and strafed barges and light flak positions.

During the month the Group began a new sort of operation, dropping supplies to Italian partisan units in the Po Valley.[7] The Wellingtons from Nos 142 and 150 Squadrons were loaned to the Balkan Air Force and operated under its control, six Wellingtons each carrying out three such operations on successive nights between 24 and 27 July. The Balkan Air Force was formed in June 1944 to support partisan activity in the Balkans, which by that time had grown into a formidable opposition to the Germans. Churchill had informed the House of Commons in February 1944 that fourteen German divisions and six Bulgarian divisions were being contained by partisan forces in Yugoslavia. They could not have achieved this feat without the aid of the British and American Air Forces, and this had begun in May 1942 when four Liberators of No. 108 Squadron started supply-dropping operations (see Chapter 9). In March 1943 the 'special operations' force was increased when fourteen Halifaxes became available, and were operated by a re-formed No. 148 Squadron (see Chapter 5).

*　　　*　　　*

During August No. 205 Group operated on twenty nights, with the weather causing operations to be cancelled on seven nights, and three stand-downs ordered. A total of 1,362 sorties were despatched, and fifty aircraft lost. On 3 August Brigadier J.T. Durrant, SAAF, took over command of the Group from Air Commodore J.H.T. Simpson. Operation *Dragoon* was launched on 14/15 August, but the Group only made a small contribution to the landings. As well as the attack on Valence/La Trasorerie airfield at the end of July (see above), the bombers went to the marshalling yards at Portes-Les-Valences on 3/4 August. The lines north and south of the marshalling yards had been cut by the Fifteenth Air Force, trapping several hundred mixed rolling stock in the yards. Fifty-five Wellingtons, twenty-two Liberators and eight Halifaxes carried out the attack, and the illumination was good. However, the target indicators fell in two clusters, the main one to the south and another smaller cluster some miles to the north. Most of the aircraft dropped their bombs on the southern cluster, which turned out to be five miles from the yards, and the only damage was the temporary cutting of the main line to Avignon. A few aircraft bombed on the other cluster, and photographs subsequently revealed that this concentration was on target, but only scattered damage was caused to the yards.

On the night of Operation *Dragoon* forty-nine Wellingtons and seven Halifaxes carried out a well concentrated attack on the docks at Marseilles. Illumination was good, and sticks were seen to fall across the Basin Lazaret and on the moles and docksides. One large explosion was reported, and this started a big fire that was followed by several other explosions and fires. No. 37 Squadron ORB recorded that 'Part of the invasion fleet was seen by crews out last night on the way to the target – the invasion started at 0800 hours the following morning (15th August 1944).' Other Squadron ORBs also mentioned having seen the invasion fleet. No. 150 Squadron ORB stated that a 'large convoy of our shipping was seen in the straits between Corsica and Sardinia but were given a wide berth'. The most direct involvement by aircraft of the Group was by eight specially equipped Liberators of No. 34 SAAF Squadron, which carried out a special *Mandrel* operation aimed at jamming the enemy's Freya-type radar, and preventing his early warning of the invasion forces. This was the first full operation by the Squadron, lasting almost twelve hours per aircraft.

Forty-four Wellingtons and seven Halifaxes of No. 614 Squadron went back to Valence/La Trasorerie on 15/16 August, but the operation was a failure due to thick haze over the target. Illumination was very scattered, and although two of the three visual markers claimed to have identified the target, photographs showed that the main concentration of bombing was about ten miles to the north of the target. For the second night in succession an attack had been planned against the glider-bomb aircraft on the airfield at Blagnac–Toulouse, but this was again cancelled and the force diverted to Valence/La Trasorerie.

The first contributions of No. 205 Group to the battle in Italy in August were

279

attacks on the marshalling yards at Bologna and the yards and canal terminus at Ravenna, important rear links in the enemy's communications with what was to be the main battlefield. Thereafter, at the request of HQ Desert Air Force, the Group's effort was to be mainly directed against tactical targets for the rest of the month. The attack on Bologna on 24/25 August was carried out by fifty-four Wellingtons, sixteen Liberators and five Halifaxes. Illumination was good, and most of the bombing was on red target indicators at the north side of the yards. Several large and small explosions and at least three large fires were observed. One series of explosions gave off much red and green tracer, and appeared to be an ammunition train going up. On the next night fifty-one Wellingtons, sixteen Liberators and five Halifaxes went to Ravenna. The illumination was excellent, and the target indicators were well placed at the junction of the canal and the marshalling yards. A violent explosion resulted in a large fire visible up to seventy miles away, and the target was obscured by smoke at the end of the attack. Photographic reconnaissance revealed that all the through lines were cut, the station buildings hit, and heavy damage caused to industrial plants east of the yards.

The efforts of the night bombers were now directed against troops, equipment and supplies in the Pesaro area. Three attacks were carried out on 26/27, 27/28 and 28/29 August, with a total of 177 sorties despatched. The area – about eight miles behind the front line – was being used as a concentration area by the enemy, and a parachute division was known to be occupying it. In the first raid the bombers delivered harassing attacks over a period of eight hours, with good results. On the second night a 'blitz' attack was delivered with green target indicators used to mark the north and south boundaries of the target area, and red indicators to mark the town of Pesaro. Few results were observed due to the nature of the target, but bombing covered the area, and several explosions and small fires were started. On the third night another good concentration of bombing was obtained over the whole of the target area, and several small fires were started. When the Eighth Army moved into Pesaro much equipment was found destroyed and damaged, and it was reported that many casualties had been inflicted by the attacks.

The final attack in the battle area was on the marshalling yards at Ferrara on 31 August/1 September, when forty-nine Wellingtons, nineteen Liberators and six Halifaxes operated. Strong adverse winds resulted in many aircraft, including the illuminators, arriving late. However, the illumination was good, and the target indicators fell at the centre and east-centre of the marshalling yards. An excellent concentration was obtained, and although smoke and haze made the observation of results difficult, a large explosion and two fires were reported. A pall of smoke covered the whole of the target area after the attack. There was some accurate heavy flak, and two aircraft were holed. Two Wellingtons collided over the target, but only sustained minor damage and both returned safely to base.

Three attacks were carried out on oil targets, with 240 sorties despatched and eighteen aircraft lost – twelve of them in the attack on Ploesti on 9/10 August. By now, many of the oil plants had been destroyed or badly damaged, and the Romana Americana refinery at Ploesti, which was still in full production, had become a most important target. As a result, the defences had been greatly strengthened, and were estimated to comprise around a hundred searchlights and sixty heavy guns. Fifty Wellingtons, twenty-three Liberators and eight Halifaxes operated, and the ground defences concentrated on the illuminating Halifaxes. One had to take evasive action over Bucharest and arrived late, and one could not open its bomb doors due to flak hits. Two were unable to make bombing runs due to having to take constant evasive action, and two failed to return. Green target indicators were dropped on special equipment, but their position was very uncertain due to a very effective smokescreen. No results could be observed, but one fairly large fire was seen glowing through the smoke.

Many enemy fighters were active on the way to the target, with persistent attacks made with tracer and rockets. Two aircraft were coned and shot down by flak, and three others were badly damaged. Of these, the most seriously damaged was a Halifax of No. 614 Squadron hit by heavy flak just south of the Danube on the return journey. The nose was entirely wrecked, and a target marker bomb ignited in the bomb bay, setting the aircraft on fire. After an order to put on parachutes, the intercom system failed and in the resulting confusion four of the crew baled out. The bomb aimer, though badly wounded, managed to extinguish the fire, and the pilot brought the aircraft safely back to base. One of the aircraft of No. 70 Squadron, although damaged by flak, managed to reach Turkey and all its crew were returned safely through the Middle East. Another aircraft of the same squadron was abandoned over Yugoslavia, and all were returned safely by the partisans. Twenty-one members of other crews were taken prisoner, and evacuated from Bucharest after the entry of the Russians.

One Wellington of No. 37 Squadron was approaching Ploesti in bright moonlight when 'a blue searchlight flickered and caught us'. More searchlights found the aircraft, and then came the flak – 'all kinds of pink, blue and green lights flashing around us'. The Wellington shuddered as the bursts came closer, and small points of light appeared along the fuselage. A moment later the rear gunner was wounded, the port engine smashed, and the aircraft (by now 'certainly a pepper pot') began to plunge earthwards. The bombs were jettisoned, and as a duel was fought between the wounded gunner and a Ju 88, the Wellington laboriously climbed to 4,000 feet on one engine. After three attacks the night fighter broke away, the wireless operator dragged the gunner from the turret, and the pilot set course for Turkey, it being impossible to return over the Alps. On reaching the vicinity of Istanbul they came under fire again from Turkish batteries, and the other engine was knocked out. The crew took to their parachutes, and were picked up by shepherds who took them in an ox-cart to Istanbul. Here they were entertained – and made 'gloriously inebriated' – before being sent back to Foggia. In ten days they were again flying against the enemy.

The Germans had started to repair the Romanian oil refineries by 'cannibalizing' damaged installations, and it was therefore important to try to destroy any undamaged equipment in the refineries. On 17/18 August, sixty-five Wellingtons, nine Liberators, and six Halifaxes went to the Xenia refinery at Ploesti. Once again, the Ploesti defences were very active, and the smoke screen was especially effective. None of the aircraft were able to pinpoint the target, but target indicators were dropped on special equipment, and most bombed on these. No results were observed, and photo reconnaissance showed no fresh damage to the refinery. Three Wellingtons failed to return. One of them was attacked by fighters near Slatina, and sustained damage to the starboard engine. A course was set for Turkey, and the Bosphorus was reached, flying mainly on one engine. Here, in spite of navigation lights and SOS and other identifying signals being flashed, the Wellington was

281

greeted by intense and very accurate flak. After some time lights appeared on the Yesilkov airfield, but shipping continued to fire at the crippled aeroplane. On landing it caught fire and burnt out, but the crew were uninjured. After interrogation, the crew were moved to Ankara and eventually evacuated to the Middle East.

The third attack was on the Szony refinery on 21/22 August, and fifty-five Wellingtons, nineteen Liberators, and seven Halifaxes were despatched. The plant had been damaged in previous attacks, but was still estimated to be capable of producing 5,000 tons of distilled oil per month. Illumination was good, and all crews reported three clusters of red target indicators in the target area. Several sticks and two 4,000-lb bombs were seen to burst in the refinery, resulting in a large explosion and several small fires among the installations. Photographs showed that although a good concentration was obtained on that target and many new craters visible, little fresh damage was caused to the main plant. Three aircraft failed to return.

Two attacks were made on marshalling yards, at Kraljevo (Yugoslavia) on 10/11 and on Miskolc (Hungary) on 22/23 August. The raid on Kraljevo was the first attack by the Group on this marshalling yard, where there were important wagon building and repair shops, and which was reported to contain large amounts of rolling stock. Forty-three Wellingtons, six Liberators, and seven Halifaxes operated, the illumination was good, and a successful attack was carried out against negligible opposition. Sticks burst across the target area, and hits were claimed on the loco sheds and what was believed to be an ammunition truck. One large explosion produced flames up to 1,500 feet and much black smoke, and other explosions followed, leaving the target obscured by smoke. Photo reconnaissance showed substantial damage to railway installations and rolling stock, and all through lines cut. In the second attack forty-one Wellingtons, eighteen Liberators, and five Halifaxes went to Miskolc. Illumination for this operation was also good and target indicators were accurately placed, but the early bombing was scattered. Later aircraft obtained a good concentration on the markers, and sticks were seen to straddle the yards. Flak opposition was slight, but many fighters were active and three aircraft failed to return.

On 7/8 August forty-seven Wellingtons, nineteen Liberators, and eight Halifaxes were despatched to attack the airfield at Szombathely. All the aircraft identified the target without difficulty in excellent illumination, and numerous sticks of bombs were seen to cover the landing ground. Direct hits followed by fires were claimed on a hangar, and other fires were started in the north-eastern dispersal area and on the landing ground. Photo reconnaissance confirmed these claims, showing the landing ground completely unserviceable due to cratering, and damaged hangars. Four aircraft failed to return. Another airfield attack was made on 12/13 August when thirty-nine Wellingtons, fifteen Liberators, and seven Halifaxes were sent to Hadju Boszormeny. A large concentration of aircraft had been reported on this landing ground, but the operation was unsuccessful due to thick haze. Most of the aircraft bombed on two clusters of target indicators, which were believed to have fallen on the south-east corner of the landing ground, but the only results observed were two small fires near the markers and a larger one in the town. Subsequent photo reconnaissance showed that the main concentration of the attack was about two miles south-east of the airfield.

Only one attack was carried out on a port during August, by fifty Wellingtons, two Liberators and seven Halifaxes on Genoa on the 13/14th. All the crews identified the target in excellent illumination, and claimed to have carried out a well concentrated attack. Many sticks were seen to straddle quays and wharves, causing one large and several small fires, and explosions were visible in the target area for seventy miles as the aircraft returned. However, photo reconnaissance showed scattered and mainly light damage. One of the Wellingtons had a complete hang-up over the target, and later ran out of petrol on the return journey. The crew baled out successfully before it crashed near Rome. There was also only one attack on an industrial target when sixty-seven Wellingtons, twenty Liberators, and six Halifaxes were sent to bomb the St Valentin–Hermann Göring Nibelungen Werke on 20/21 August. This was a factory involved in the assembly of armoured vehicles, and it had not been attacked previously. It lay in woods south-east of Linz, and most of the aircraft seem to have bombed similarly shaped woods two miles to the north of the target. Subsequent photo reconnaissance showed only slight damage to the works itself. Two Liberators and four Wellingtons failed to return. One of the Wellingtons was later reported to have crashed near Plesso, and three bodies were found near the wreck. Another Wellington landed away at Naples, and when it took off again to return to base it crashed into a hill and all the crew were killed.

Five mining operations in the Danube were carried out during the month, with a total of thirty-nine sorties despatched. Most were completely successful, but thick haze occasionally hampered operations, and a few mines ended up on the river bank. Much light flak was encountered along the river, and some enemy fighters were sighted. The Germans were at last taking some steps to counter the minelaying operations, and in the middle of August they set up a de-magnetized station at Ruschuk and a squadron of minesweeping Ju 52s fitted with mine-detonating rings began to operate. Also, a Serbian tug-boat was taken over and modified as a minesweeper, but did not succeed in detonating a single mine. This was, perhaps, not surprising, as the captain directed operations from the safety of the river bank, and the crew of seven naval ratings were terrified by their new and dangerous task. Two Liberators were lost, and one of them, an aircraft of No. 34 Squadron SAAF, was seen to fall in flames and explode on the ground near Mohacs on 28/29 August.

*   *   *

Lawrence Isemonger[8] tells how on Sunday morning on 13 August the aircrews of No. 31 Squadron SAAF were relaxing after a difficult mission to bomb the airfield near Debrecen in Hungary. Above the barn of the farmhouse that served as the Operations Room at Celone a ragged white flag fluttered in the morning breeze, signifying that no operations were planned for that day. Then, just before midday, a klaxon horn sounded, calling the men to an urgent briefing. A sullen line of grumbling airmen wandered to the Operations Room, where they found that they were detailed to fly down to Brindisi. No further information was given to them, and the ten Liberators duly took off at 1300 hours. At about the same time ten more Liberators of No. 178 Squadron left Amendola, bound for the same destination.

When they got to Brindisi they were ushered into another briefing room, to be greeted by a Polish squadron commander. On the wall behind him was a shrouded map, and when he uncovered it the crew saw a thin red ribbon stretching across most of south-eastern Europe, from Brindidi to Warsaw. On 1 August the Polish Home Army had risen against their German oppressors as part of a nationwide rebellion, Operation *Tempest*. The Poles' chief objectives were to drive the German occupiers from the city and help with the larger fight against Germany and the Axis powers, but there were also important political objectives. If the Poles could liberate Warsaw before the arrival of the Soviet Army, it would help to underscore Polish sovereignty and to undo the division of Central Europe into spheres of influence by the Allied powers. The insurgents aimed to reinstate Polish authorities before the Soviet Polish Committee of National Liberation could assume control.

The uprising was intended to last for only a few days, until the Soviet Army reached the city, but the Russians encountered strong resistance and decided to bypass Warsaw instead of making a direct attack on the City. The Soviets did not advance beyond the city's borders until mid-September, and the Poles were forced to fight on alone for sixty-three days. By 16 September, Soviet forces had reached a point across the Vistula River, a few hundred metres from the Polish positions, but they made no further headway. This led to allegations that Stalin had wanted the insurrection to fail so that the Soviet occupation of Poland would be uncontested. Initially, the Poles seized substantial areas of the city, but they were exposed to heavy German counter attacks, and became desperately short of arms and ammunition. The RAF in the Mediterranean theatre was called upon to drop supplies to the Poles, but with Transport Command fully committed to the landings in the South of France, there were few long-range aircraft available. At first, the supply-dropping missions were carried out by the Halifaxes and Liberators of No. 1586 Polish Special Duties Flight and No. 148 (Special Duties) Squadron. However, the Liberators of Nos 178 and 31 and 34 SAAF Squadrons, No. 205 Group, were soon called upon to help them. They flew a total of sixty-eight sorties, of which some thirty-two were successfully completed, and fourteen aircraft were lost (21 per cent of those that took off).

No. 31 Squadron ORB tells how the briefing at Brindisi was 'somewhat sketchy due to the number of extra crews detailed from 240 and 2 (SA) Wings'. It goes on to say that Churchill was 'directly responsible for the detailing of 20 bomber aircraft…to supplement the Special Operations Squadrons mixed force of 10 Liberators and Halifaxes'. Take-off was to be at 1930 hours, so that the aircraft would cross the Yugoslav coast just after dark, but little was known of the conditions that might be expected over Warsaw. The Liberators would each carry twelve metal containers, eight foot long and weighing 350 lb. They were all packed with arms, ammunition and medical supplies for the Polish Home Army. The plan was to fly at about 15,000 feet over Yugoslavia, Hungary and Czechoslovakia, eventually crossing the Carpathian Mountains to a position north-east of Krakow. Here they would descend to 8,000 feet to try to find the Vistula River, their guide to Warsaw. Nearer to the capital they would descend again to follow the river through the city, and then look for the drop zone, which would be marked by a cluster of white lights with red flashes. By now the aircraft were expected to be flying at about 500 feet, and close to their stalling speed of 120 mph – and could be expected to be fired at by every enemy gun on the ground! If they got back then they would have covered 1,800 miles, mostly over enemy territory, and spent about eleven hours in the air.

Thus, on 13/14 August the twenty Liberators of Nos 31 SAAF and 178 Squadrons took off for the city, accompanied by another eight aircraft from No. 1586 Polish Special Duties Flight and No. 148 (Special Duties) Squadron. The weather was very bad en route, with thick cloud and electrical storms, and only twelve aircraft reached the target just before midnight. They found that the whole city was burning, and the smoke from burning buildings mushroomed upwards in sulphurous yellow clouds, making it difficult to see ahead. Warsaw 'presented an awe inspiring spectacle as the aircraft approached; the blazing buildings, light flak, searchlights and heavy machine gun fire making the dropping of the containers...an extremely hazardous operation'. Two were unable to locate their dropping points, while a third accidentally jettisoned its containers in the wrong place. Eight definitely identified the target and dropped ninety-six containers in the face of the intense light flak and machine-gun fire from all over the city. Some of it was reported to be coming from the Russian side of the Vistula. Three Liberators returned with significant damage, and three failed to return.

One of these from No. 31 SAAF Squadron was the first aircraft over Warsaw that night – and the first to be shot down! Liberator 'G' captained by school teacher Lieutenant Robert Klette made a second run over the city with one engine already ablaze. Minutes later, with all four engines out of action, he crash-landed on what the pilot took to be an open field on the outskirts of Warsaw. Unfortunately, it turned out to be an enemy landing ground, and the crew were all quickly captured. Another from the same squadron was shadowed by fighters before reaching the target, and the pilot had jettisoned its load south of the city and started climbing eastwards. The Liberator had one engine knocked out by flak, and was then coned by searchlights and hit again by light flak. Shortly afterwards, the pilot lost control of the aircraft and baled out, but the second pilot regained control and decided to head for Russia. Following further encounters with searchlights and flak, and further damage to the aircraft, he carried out a successful crash-landing at what Isemonger calls 'some outlandish place in Russia' and is otherwise variously reported as near Kiev and near the village of Emilchino.

On 14/15 August fifteen Liberators went back to Warsaw. Weather conditions were much better than on the previous night, but there was a great deal of intense and very accurate light flak and machine-gun fire. The enemy was clearly on the alert this time, and much stiffer opposition was encountered, especially north of the Carpathians. Six aircraft successfully dropped their containers on target, one dropped them near the target area, and one dropped its load on the wrong side of the river. Six of the Liberators failed to return, and the No. 31 Squadron ORB describes the operation as 'a vain suicidal effort to assist the Warsaw Poles, who, it was felt, could so easily be assisted by the Russian forces reported on the Eastern outskirts of the city.' One Liberator from No. 31 Squadron crashed into a Warsaw street, and Isemonger reports an eye-witness account given by a member of the Polish Home Army:

> The approach of aircraft was heard and a moment later artillery opened up all over burning Warsaw, filling the sky with dazzling flashes and weaving searchlights. We saw Allied aircraft cruising above and containers of supplies being thrown out. Then suddenly, one of the aircraft came down lower and lower. It flew down Midowa Street in the direction of the square, seeming to disregard the fury of the guns. We watched it breathlessly, amazed at the courage and heroism of the airmen. They were going to certain death and,

sure enough, as the aircraft reached the square, one of its wings struck a rooftop and crashed into the street below.[9]

The bodies of the crew were buried in the street where they had crashed, and were later re-buried in the snow-covered Krakow war cemetery in February 1947. Each coffin of the six South African airmen was formally decorated with the bronze 'Medal for Warsaw'.

Another Liberator from No. 31 SAAF Squadron was hit by flak over the target and three engines were set on fire, and it was eventually abandoned fifteen miles west of Warsaw. The pilot and four of the crew landed successfully and reached the British Mission in Moscow, but three crew members were killed. One body was found 200 yards from the crashed aircraft with parachute open, and presumably he pulled the ripcord too late. Two bodies were in the crashed aircraft, and they must have been killed or very badly hurt before the crash. A third aircraft of No. 31 SAAF Squadron was hit over the target area, and the pilot, Captain W.E. Senn, severely wounded in the thigh. He ordered the crew to prepare to abandon the aircraft, but regained control and managed to climb away from the target area. At no stage did the pilot intimate to the rest of the crew that he was injured, and successfully brought the badly damaged aircraft back to base without the aid of maps and with great difficulty in controlling the aircraft. Captain Senn had spent eleven hours and forty-five minutes at the controls of his aircraft, and was given the immediate award of the DFC.

On 15/16 August the target area was some ten miles west of Warsaw, and three aircraft of No. 31 Squadron SAAF were ordered to stand-by for the operations. This brought protests from the No. 2 Wing and No. 31 Squadron commanders, who maintained that they could not personally order any South African airman to take part in what was a suicide mission. Feelings among the men were divided, but in the end a call for volunteers was made. This proved to be unnecessary, as three aircraft of No. 178 Squadron did the run instead. One was forced to return early with engine trouble, but the other two successfully dropped their containers in the briefed area in the face of much machine gun and small arms fire. Neither aircraft was hit. The fourth and final operation to Poland in August took place on 16/17 August, when, in view of the very heavy losses incurred on the previous missions, it was decided to drop supplies to a reserve division of partisans located in the forests in the Lodz area. Nine Liberators operated, and four successfully dropped their supplies in the briefed areas. Four failed to return. Several enemy fighters were seen, and accurate flak was encountered at Krakow, where one aircraft of No. 31 SAAF Squadron was coned by searchlights and shot down. Another from the squadron crashed in the same area, and all the crew were killed. No. 31 Squadron's loss of eight aircraft in three operations, involving the loss of sixty airmen, reduced the unit to only eight crews, and left the remaining personnel completely stunned.

Supply dropping operations at Warsaw also continued on 10/11, 18/19 and 21/22 September, with twenty-one sorties despatched and only one aircraft lost. These operations were carried out at a much higher level than the suicidal missions in August, and away from the Warsaw area itself. The aircraft sent out on 18/19 September were recalled at 1800 hours when about to cross the Yugoslav coast, and they tried again on 21/22 September to drop supplies to Polish forces in the woods west of Warsaw. Three of the Liberators identified ground marker lights without difficulty and dropped thirty-three containers. The other two aircraft identified the correct area, but many lights were visible and they were unable to pick out the correct ground markers. These operations concluded the hazardous supply dropping missions to the Warsaw area. A total of 186 sorties had been despatched from Italy by the Polish, South African and British units of the Mediterranean Air Force, of which ninety-two were successful. Sixty-three aircraft failed to reach Warsaw, but returned safely to their bases. Thirty-one aircraft (17 per cent) were lost. Messages of congratulations were received from Air Vice-Marshal Elliot, Air Officer Commanding Balkan Air Force, and Headquarters, Warsaw. The latter radioed:

> The exertions of your Air Force have enabled us to continue fighting. Warsaw in arms send the gallant airmen their words of thanks and appreciation. We bow our heads to those who have fallen.

*   *   *

During the month of September the Group launched 1,496 sorties and lost eighteen aircraft. With the success of the landings in the South of France, the Germans were denied the use of rail routes through this area into Italy, and were forced on to only four routes into the country: the Brenner line into northern Italy, and the Tarvisio, Piedicolle and Postumia lines into the north-east. Thus, 843 sorties (56.4 per cent of the effort) were directed at railway targets, with marshalling yards at Bologna, Ferrara, Ravenna, Milan-Lambrate and Brescia in Italy receiving the greatest attention. Two yards in Hungary (Szekesfehervar and Hegyeshalom) were also attacked, and a railway viaduct at Borovnica in Yugoslavia.

The attack on Ferrara on 5/6 September by thirty-four Wellingtons, twenty-two Liberators, and six Halifaxes, was intended to cut the canal bridge at the west end of the yards to disrupt traffic to Bologna, Poggio Risco and Ravenna. Illumination was good, and the main cluster of target indicators fell at the north end of the bridge. Bombing was fairly well concentrated on these, and one large fire was started. However, photo reconnaissance showed that the main weight of the attack fell around the sugar refinery and stores depot to the west and east of the marshalling yards. Fresh hits were also scored on the sidings, and on the western approach to the canal bridge. The attack on the Bologna East marshalling yards on 12/13 September was the Group's first attack on these yards, and photo reconnaissance revealed that many had been tracks cut. Some accurate heavy and light flak was encountered and several enemy aircraft were sighted, and two Wellingtons of No. 70 Squadron failed to return. The viaduct at Borovnica carried the main Vienna-Trieste railway line, and it was attacked by sixty-five Wellingtons, fourteen Liberators and seven Halifaxes on 26/27 September. Although several rear gunners reported damage to the viaduct, photo reconnaissance suggested that no damage was done to the bridge structure. This was the last operation carried out by the two squadrons of No. 330 Wing (Nos 142 and 150 Squadrons) in the Mediterranean Theatre.

By now, many of the permanent bridges over the River Po had been destroyed, and the enemy had been driven to use pontoon bridges to maintain his vital communications across the river. These bridges were only used at night, and were drawn into the bank by day. The Group attacked one of these bridges at San Benedetto on 22/23 and 30 September/1 October. Forty-nine Wellingtons, thirteen Liberators, and seven Halifaxes carried out the first attack, but 10/10 cloud drifting across the target area hampered the operation. Flares were scattered and illumination poor, and the night photographs placed most of the aircraft some distance from the north-west end of the bridge. Thirty-two Wellingtons, ten Liberators, and eight Halifaxes operated in the second attack. This time the illumination was good, and clusters of target indicators were pinpointed close to the south end of the bridge. A good concentration was obtained on them, and one 4,000-pounder was claimed to have burst fifty yards west of the bridge. One of the Liberators of No. 31 Squadron crashed at San Severo. An investigation of the crash scene showed that parts of the aircraft were scattered over half a mile apart, and it must have broken up in the air. The aircraft had flown through heavy cumulonimbus cloud, with much turbulence, and might have been struck by lightning.

On 18/19 September the Group was called upon to help the ground forces at Rimini. The enemy was fiercely resisting the Eighth Army's attack, and had concentrated troops and equipment in an area WNW of the town. Sixty-nine Wellingtons, twenty-four Liberators, and seven Halifaxes operated, illumination was good and visual markers successfully marked the northern and southern boundaries of the target area with lines of target indicators. Bombing was well spread over the area, and subsequent reports revealed that the attack had been successful.

Two attacks were carried out on port facilities, at Ravenna on 9/10 September and at Salonika on 21/22 September. Fifty-three Wellingtons, nineteen Liberators and seven Halifaxes operated at Ravenna, and delivered a well concentrated attack. Photo reconnaissance confirmed many hits on marshalling yards, with through lines cut repeatedly, and the road overpass approach badly damaged. Industrial plants on both sides of the Darsena were virtually destroyed. No attempt was made to repair the damage, and the yards remained unserviceable until 4 October. The attack on Salonika was ordered because the enemy was known to be withdrawing troops from the Aegean Islands, and at least two divisions had been landed at the port. Much equipment had accumulated in the port area due to the sabotage of the rail system and the shortage of transport aircraft (see also below). Fifty-three Wellingtons, thirteen Liberators, and seven Halifaxes operated, and bombing was well concentrated on the target indicators. One very large explosion and one large and several small fires were seen in the target area, and were visible for 100 miles on the return trip. Flak was moderate but ineffective, and some enemy fighter activity was reported. One of the Wellingtons of No. 104 Squadron failed to return. It was later learned that the port engine was shot off over the target, and the aircraft crashed on the shore of Salonika Bay after all the crew had baled out successfully.

Mining in the Danube continued on 5/6, 6/7 and 10/11 September, with sixty sorties launched and all the operations carried out successfully. On 10/11 September a Halifax of No. 614 Squadron marked the route and illuminated the target, and this was the first time that target marking had been used on a mining operation. The crews reported that it was most useful, and all the 'gardeners' mined successfully.

The withdrawal of troops from Greece and the Aegean Islands was being hampered by the widespread cutting of rail communications by partisan groups, and was mainly being carried out at night and by air. On 13/14 September an operation was carried out to render the three landing grounds in the Athens area unserviceable, and to facilitate the interception of the enemy transports by intruder Beaufighters of the Balkan Air Force. Unfortunately, bad weather prevented the Beaufighters from operating. A total of sixty-five Wellingtons, twenty-five Liberators, and nine Halifaxes were sent to Eleusis, Tatoi and Kalamaki, but visibility was generally poor and few results were observed. A second operation was ordered on the following night, and sixty-two Wellingtons, twenty-two Liberators, and six Halifaxes were despatched to the three airfields and somewhat better results obtained. One Wellington of No. 70 Squadron failed to return, and many crews reported seeing an aircraft crash into the hills north of Naupaktos.

Nos 142 and 150 Squadrons carried out their last operations on the night of 26/27 September, and during the early days of October both squadrons and No. 330 Wing Headquarters were disbanded. The aircraft, equipment, and the majority of the personnel were absorbed by other units of the Group. The Wing had first come under the operational control of No. 205 Group in early July 1943, and during fifteen months of operations with the Group it flew over 4,700 sorties and dropped over 8,000 tons of bombs and mines. On 25 October No. 142 Squadron was reformed at Gransden Lodge in the UK as a Mosquito unit in No. 8 Group's Light Night Striking Force. No. 150 Squadron was also soon revived when 'C' Flight of No. 550 Squadron at Fiskerton was renumbered. In November the Squadron moved to its final wartime base at Hemswell, operating Lancasters from there until the end of the war.

On 23 August 1944 the pro-German Romanian Government fell, and Allied Armistice terms were accepted. There was at this time between 1,100 and 1,200 Allied prisoners of war in the Bucharest area, and arrangements were made to evacuate them by air. Operation *Reunion* was successfully carried out in three phases on 31 August, 1 September and 3 September, with a total of 1,166 personnel being flown out in 55 B-17s of the USAAF. This total included thirty-six members of No. 205 Group. During the month news was also received of a further twenty missing aircrew personnel, eighteen being evacuated from Bulgaria via Cairo and two reported safe in friendly hands in Northern Italy.

No. 104 Squadron ORB reported at the end of September that 'no aircraft have had to return to base with mechanical failure for two months thus keeping up the high standard of serviceability for the Squadron'.

*   *   *

As the weather improved during the summer months the night bombers were able to go out on 106 of the 153 nights between May and September 1944. They flew 7,116 sorties and lost 181 aircraft (2.5 per cent). Five operations involved more than 100 aircraft despatched, and another thirty-one more than eighty aircraft. The main emphasis was on railway targets (33 per cent), and for the first time oil targets figured strongly (1,573 sorties, 22 per cent). Military targets in the battle area involved 1,053 sorties (15 per cent of the total effort).

NOTES

1. Gunby, *Sweeping the Skies*, page 263.
2. Chappell, *Wellington Wings*, page 245.
3. Hilary St George Saunders, *The Royal Air Force 1939–1945*, Volume 3, page 227.
4. Chappell, *Wellington Wings*, page 246.
5. Ibid, page 249.
6. Ibid, page 252.
7. Note, the Group ORB records that the operations were 'over the Balkans', but the ORBs for Nos 142 and 150 Squadrons clearly state that they were carried out over northern Italy.
8. Once again, we are grateful to Lawrence Isemonger and his book *The Men Who Went to Warsaw* for some of the details given here.
9. Lawrence Isemonger, *The Men Who Went to Warsaw*, page 72.

CHAPTER TWELVE

Towards the End of the Road – October 1944 to April 1945

When we left Italy in September the rain was falling, the Allied armies were bogged in the mud, and the airfields were being transformed into lakes. Throughout the next six months small gains continued to be made on the ground, enemy counter-attacks were repulsed, and weary battalions regrouped and rested. The Allies made small gains – five miles in the west, twenty miles in the centre, and thirty to forty miles on the eastern flank – but it was hard going. Bologna still lay just beyond Alexander's grasp at the end of March 1945, but Faenza had fallen and the River Lamone formed the eastern boundary of the defence. April saw the commencement of the final battle for the destruction of the German forces in northern Italy. The last Allied offensive opened in the afternoon of 9 April 1945, and just under three weeks later the cease-fire was signed at Alexander's headquarters in the royal palace at Caserta, to take effect on 2 May.

During this time the Mediterranean Allied Strategic Air Force played a role that was by no means bounded by Italy or the Italian front. Its main component, of course, was the USAAF Fifteenth Air Force, which by the end of 1944 comprised twenty-one Heavy Bombardment Groups (six with B-17s and fifteen with B-24s) and could put more than 600 aircraft in the air on a regular basis. The American bombers often struck at railway communications in south-eastern Europe to aid Russian military operations against Hungary and Romania. Traffic from Germany to the Romanian front had to pass through Budapest, and from there move to the frontier along three routes, via Oradea, Arad and Turnu Severin. Austrian aircraft production centres at Wiener Neustadt were also attacked, and assaults made on enemy oil production and storage facilities. The refineries at Ploesti were bombed, and attacks also carried out on Budapest, Komarom, Gyor and Petfurdo in Hungary, on Belgrade, Sisak, Osijek and Brod in Yugoslavia, and on Trieste in Italy.

By comparison with the American effort, that of the RAF night bombers was considerably smaller. At the end of 1944 No. 205 Group had eight squadrons, and in its biggest operation between October 1944 and April 1945 it despatched ninety-four Liberators in support of the Eighth Army's attack on the Senio Line in northern Italy. At the beginning of October 1944 the two Liberator squadrons of No. 2 SAAF Wing (Nos 31 and 34) were at Celone, the two Wellingtons squadrons of No. 231 Wing (Nos 37 and 70) at Tortorella, the two Wellingtons squadrons of No. 236 Wing (Nos 40 and 104) at Foggia Main, and the Liberators of No. 178 Squadron and Halifaxes and Liberators of No. 614 Squadron at Amendola. They would remain at these bases until the end of the war, although No. 2 SAAF Wing temporarily operated from Foggia Main when Celone became unusable due to rain in January 1945. All the Wellington squadrons would convert to Liberators during this time, with No. 37 becoming operational with their new aircraft in December 1944. They were followed by No. 70 Squadron in February 1945, and Nos 40 and 104 Squadrons in March 1945.

Despite its relatively small size, the Group's contribution in the final months of the war was far from insignificant. It operated on 123 of the 212 days/nights between October 1944 and the end of April 1945, and flew 8,659 sorties. The main effort was directed at railway targets – marshalling yards and bridges. This was an extension of the Transportation Plan implemented prior to the invasion of Northern Europe, where the intention was to disrupt railway communications between Germany and France in order to interfere with the enemy's response to the invasion. Now the intention was to disrupt railway communications between Germany and Italy to aid the Allies' desperate attempts to complete the Italian campaign, and between Germany and the Balkans to aid the Russian advance. The main targets were in northern Italy, Yugoslavia (modern Slovenia and Croatia) and Austria, with two attacks on yards in Hungary. Just over two fifths of the total effort in these months (3,596 sorties, 41.5 per cent) went to railway targets, and in March 1945 over 80 per cent of the total effort was directed at marshalling yards and railway bridges.

The second major activity for the Group during this period involved supply dropping to partisan groups. The enemy had begun to withdraw his forces from the Balkans, and during October the Allied landings in Greece and the Russian advances in the east increased the tempo of his retreat. The only routes open to him were poor inland roads in Yugoslavia, all of which were threatened by partisans. In addition, partisan groups in the northern foothills of the Maritime Alps were attacking the supply routes for the German forces in Italy. Most of the supply drops went to the groups in Yugoslavia, but some went to northern Italy, and one to Poland. The target areas in northern Yugoslavia (modern day Bosnia and Herzegovina) were codenamed CRAYON (46°08'N, 14°00'E), GEISHA (45°30'N, 17°30'E), HARANGUE (45°18'N, 14°52'E), FLOTSAM (45°35'N, 15°12'E), TOFFEE (44°31'N, 18°43'E), BALLINCLAY (44°45'N, 18°40'E), and ICARUS (44°44'N, 16°40'E).[1] The major effort came in November 1944, when 787 sorties were despatched (46.8 per cent of the total for that month). In all, the supply drops comprised almost a third of all operations between October 1944 and March 1945.

Support for operations on the ground was a significant feature of the Group's effort, especially in November 1944 and April 1945. In the first case the attacks were directed against the German forces retreating northwards through Yugoslavia, with 521 sorties despatched against communications, MT and troop concentrations. The last Allied offensive in Italy opened in the afternoon of 9 April 1945, and the Group launched 629 sorties (50.3 per cent of the total effort for the month) in support of the ground forces. A different form of 'ground support' came in December 1944, when the political crisis in Greece created a need for reinforcement of the British troops in Athens. On 10 December arrangements were made for No. 205 Group to transport some 2,000 troops, equipment and ammunition into the Athens/Hassani airfield, using Manduria and Grottaglie as advanced bases.

*   *   *

Long spells of bad weather at the beginning and end of the month resulted in October being the poorest operational month since March 1944, when only 833 sorties had been launched. Stand-downs or cancellations due to the weather occurred on sixteen nights, and a total of 1,034 sorties were despatched on the other fifteen nights and twenty-six aircraft lost. Eight of the targets attacked (involving 567 sorties – 55 per cent of the effort) were marshalling yards: at Verona (two attacks), Bronzolo, and Trieste-Opicina in Italy; Zagreb, Maribor, and Vinkovci in Yugoslavia; and Szekesfehervar in Hungary; and some very effective operations were carried out. The supply dropping operations involved another 238 sorties (23 per cent of the total effort), and airfields (97 sorties, 9 per cent of the effort) and military targets in the battle area (89 sorties, 9 per cent) took up most of the rest. Various nickelling operations also took place throughout the month.

The campaign against the railway targets opened with attacks on the yards at Verona on 10/11 and 11/12 October. The two yards were key points on the Brenner Pass railway link, along which the enemy was rushing material to build a new defence line in North Italy. The first attack was by forty-two aircraft on the eastern yards, and the bombing was reported to be somewhat scattered and only a few small fires started. One Wellington of No. 104 Squadron and one Liberator of No. 178 Squadron failed to return. On the following night sixty-seven bombers went to the Verona West yards, where bursts were observed across the yards and two fires were started. The flak was intense and accurate, and around thirty searchlights were in operation. Several aircraft were coned and hit, and three Wellingtons failed to return. On 12/13 October the target for seventy aircraft was the small yard at Bronzolo, forty miles north of Verona, and again on the Brenner Pass line. The target was surrounded by high hills, and the Pathfinders had some difficulty in locating it. Consequently, the illumination was late, and the bombing was generally scattered. One Liberator of No. 178 Squadron was hit by flak en route, and had its bomb doors and six bombs blown away, but it continued to the target.

The fourth attack on a railway target in Italy in October was on the yards at Trieste–Opicina by sixty-four aircraft on 15/16 October. The bombing was well concentrated around the target indicators, three 4,000-lb bombs burst in the target area, and a violent explosion resulted in smoke mushrooming to 7,000 feet. Subsequent photo reconnaissance revealed widespread damage, with rolling stock derailed and the switching station and other buildings damaged.

The attacks on marshalling yards in October were not confined to those in Italy. Successful attacks were also carried out by seventy-seven aircraft on the Zagreb East marshalling yards on 16/17 October, and by eighty-two aircraft on the yards at Vinkovci on the 17/18th. A third attack in Yugoslavia, on Maribor on 21/22 October, was a failure. Eighty-three aircraft were despatched, but the operation was ruined by 10/10 cloud at 4,000 feet, which completely obscured the target. Two aircraft returned early, nine jettisoned, and one brought its bombs back after being unable to find the target. A few aircraft bombed visually from below the cloud, but the majority bombed on DR or the glow of flares. One Wellington of No. 37 Squadron became almost uncontrollable over the target area due to icing, and the captain ordered the crew to don their parachutes. The bomb aimer apparently mistook the order and jumped. One Liberator of No. 31 Squadron was returning early due to unserviceable turrets and jettisoned its bombs, but one bomb hung up and jammed the elevators, throwing the aircraft out of control. The crew were ordered to bale out, but only the beam gunner jumped before the pilot managed to regain control. Despite an intensive air-sea rescue search the next day, his body was never found.

Four other Wellingtons failed to return. One attack was made on the marshalling yards at Szekesfehervar in Hungary, the only route from Budapest to Vienna. The yards were known to be crowded, and eighty-two bombers attacked on 13/14 October. Photo reconnaissance showed extensive damage, with all through lines cut.

The supply dropping operations began on 4/5 October, when eighteen Liberators of No. 2 SAAF Wing successfully dropped 216 containers over five areas of Yugoslavia. Another crew received no answers to their recognition signals, and brought their load back. On 11/12 October another eighteen Liberators dropped 218 containers on two areas of Yugoslavia. One was unable to locate the target and brought its load back, and another dropped part of its load in the wrong area and brought the rest back.

Tragedy struck on 12/13 October when twenty Liberators from the two South African squadrons were despatched to drop supplies in northern Italy, at Bra, Vigone, and south-west of Lake Maggiore. An intimation of impending trouble was supplied by two crews who returned early and reported that the weather was very bad, with 10/10 cloud down to 5,000 feet. Only three aircraft succeeded in locating their targets by taking advantage of cloud breaks, and dropped thirty-six containers on ground signals. Eleven brought their loads back to base, and six failed to return. Five of them crashed into the mountains around the drop zone, and forty crew members all perished. One simply disappeared without trace. The No. 31 Squadron ORB states that these losses were 'an inexplicable and stunning blow'. The only explanation could be that the pilots were determined to drop their supplies successfully, and had crashed when they lost height in order to break through the cloud.

On 15/16 October seven Liberators dropped sixty containers in two areas of Yugoslavia, and an eighth failed to see any marker lights and dropped on a Gee fix. Then, on the next night six Liberators from No. 34 SAAF Squadron went back to the Warsaw area for the last time. Only one located the ground marker lights, and dropped twelve containers in response to the signals. Three crews were unable to find the markers and returned with their loads, and two failed to return. One was attacked by a night fighter about twenty miles north-east of Krakow, and caught fire. Lieutenant G.C. Dicks, the wireless operator, baled out on instructions from the captain, and later met the navigator (Lieutenant E. Colbert). The latter was last seen on 31 October near the village of Carna in the Krakow district, and he successfully evaded capture. The bomb aimer and two waist gunners were found in the crashed aircraft by Polish partisans. Another body, identified as the pilot Lieutenant J.A. Lithgow, was found with both legs broken and bullet wounds, and with his parachute open. Dicks also saw Germans escorting a South African prisoner shortly after the crash, presumed to be the tail gunner (Lieutenant S. Fourie). Lieutenant Dicks was subsequently handed over by the Russians in February 1945. The eight crew members of the other aircraft, also shot down by a night fighter, are buried in the Krakow Rakowicki Cemetery.

On 21/22 October three Liberators from No. 178 Squadron successfully dropped thirty-six containers on ground marker lights near Tuzla in Yugoslavia. Another three could not locate any lights in their drop area near Sanski Most, and brought their loads back. The Liberators of Nos 240 and 2 SAAF Wings carried out a daylight mission for the first time on 25 October. One aircraft returned early, but the remaining twenty-five dropped 290 containers in four areas. Most dropped visually on ground markers, but six dropped on Gee fixes. The Group's first large-scale daylight supply dropping operations were carried out on 29 and 31 October. In the first operation fifty-nine Wellingtons and fifteen Liberators successfully located their pinpoints, and dropped 354 containers. Most of the aircraft dropped visually and a few on Gee fixes, and results were good. The field reported that almost all the containers were collected successfully. In the second operation on 31 October fifty-eight Wellingtons and two Halifaxes were despatched, and field reports stated that although some of the 332 containers fell rather wide, general results were excellent.

The first of the two attacks on airfields during the month was directed at the three airfields in the Athens area (Tatoi, Kalamaki and Eleusis). Although they had been heavily bombed, they were still serviceable for limited numbers of aircraft, and twenty-two Wellingtons of No. 236 Wing were detailed to carry out harassing attacks on 9/10 October. These were the only aircraft from the Group able to operate, as all the rest were unable to take off from waterlogged runways. Bursts were observed across the landing grounds at Athens, but few results were seen. The other attack on an airfield was on Szombathely in Hungary on 20/21 October, and heavy damage was inflicted by seventy-five aircraft. The landing ground was rendered unserviceable, and six aircraft destroyed.

The enemy was still using the pontoon bridge over the River Po at San Benedetto (see previous chapter) and three harassing attacks were carried out on 4/5, 15/16 and 20/21 October, but with little or no success. The first attack was made by thirty-nine Wellingtons, seven Liberators and eight Halifaxes, but thick cloud completely obscured the target. Many of the attackers made several runs, but bombing was very scattered and no results were observed. Two returned early and four jettisoned after being unable to find the target. One Liberator of No. 178 Squadron failed to return. The second and third attacks, each by fifteen aircraft, were spread over a number of hours, and were purely harassing attacks intended to disrupt the movement of traffic.

The final 'gardening' operation in the River Danube took place on 4/5 October, when four Liberators and eighteen Wellingtons laid a total of fifty-eight mines. The mining operations had lasted for a little over six months, and during this time some 1,382 mines had been dropped in eighteen attacks by the bombers of No. 205 Group. There can be no doubt as to the outstanding success of these operations. The broad result was that the volume of traffic on the Danube was reduced by some 60 to 70 per cent. The enemy was forced to deploy very great quantities of anti-aircraft defences along a considerable length of the river, and many thousands of trained personnel to man them. Skilled minesweeping crews were diverted to the Danube at a time when their services were needed in home waters. Finally, considerable aid was given to the Russians in their westwards drive, as supplies and reinforcements for the Eastern Front suffered long delays.

Two small mining operations were also carried out in the Euripos Channel near Khalkis. With the increased pressure on the Balkan communications, these coastal waters had become vital to the enemy in his evacuation of the Aegean area. In both cases two Liberators from No. 240 Wing successfully dropped twelve mines in the channel.

In a daylight operation on 31 October five aircraft were despatched to Podgorica town, which the enemy was known to be using as an assembly point in his retirement to the north. One of them abandoned the operation due to cloud, but the remaining aircraft spent up to ninety minutes trying to break cloud, and eventually dropped four 4,000-lb bombs on Gee fixes. No results were observed.

*   *   *

November saw a considerable increase in the Group's activities, despite twelve days/nights being lost due to bad weather. A total of 1,680 sorties were despatched on eighteen days and nights, and twenty-one aircraft lost. A large proportion of the operations (sixteen bombing and six supply dropping) were carried out in daylight, with only eight bombing and six supply dropping operations taking place at night. Double sorties were flown on several occasions. During the month a report was received from the British Mission, Allied Control Commission, Romania, giving the location of the graves of forty-seven aircrew who had previously been reported missing from Group operations.

The supply dropping operations continued to form a major part of the Group's operations in November, with 787 sorties despatched (47 per cent of the total effort). The most notable supply dropping feat was the two operations on the 4th and 5th. The main force flew double sorties, despatched a total of 355 aircraft, and dropped over 350 tons of supplies. It was calculated that each of the four operations carried out on these two days put 4,000 fully equipped men into the field. Successful operations were also carried out on 1 November (seventy-two sorties), 24 November (seventy-five sorties), and 25 November (seventy-one sorties). The serious business of supply dropping had its lighter moments. A story went the rounds that shortly after a consignment of powdered eggs had been dropped the partisans radioed back: 'New explosives received. Please send directions for use.' The forces newspaper *The Union Jack* also reported that on one occasion a load of fish plates (metal bars that are bolted to the ends of two rails to join them together) was dropped in error in an area where no railways existed. The partisans signalled: 'Thanks for the fish plates. When are you going to drop the rest of the railway?'

As well as the operations to aid Yugoslav partisans, conferences were held at HQ Balkan Air Force on 3 November and at HQ Mediterranean Allied Air Forces on 8 November to consider the best methods of delivering supplies to partisans in northern Italy. Subsequently, five supply dropping operations were carried out between 10 and 16 November, with 214 sorties despatched. Very bad weather conditions prevailed for the night operation by forty-eight aircraft on 10/11, and as a result four Liberators and five Wellingtons returned early and six Wellingtons failed to locate the target and brought their loads back. Four Wellingtons failed to return, and all were subsequently accounted for. One had sent out a ditching signal, and two bodies were later washed ashore. The other three all crashed into hills on the return trip, and all the crews were killed. A daylight operation followed on the 11th and two on the 12th (a total of seventy-nine sorties), but the continuing bad weather hampered all three drops. A big night-time drop then took place on 16/17 November, when eighty-seven aircraft successfully dropped supplies to partisans in the northern foothills of the Maritime Alps.

Another big effort throughout the month of November was against the German forces retreating northwards through Yugoslavia, with 521 sorties (31 per cent of the total effort) despatched against communications, MT and troop concentrations.

On 8 November a daylight attack was carried out by forty aircraft on roads in the town of Novi Pazar, but the operation was hampered by cloud and sixteen brought their bombs back. Only ten of the bombers actually saw the target, and the others bombed on DR and/or Gee fixes. During the night thirty-eight aircraft were despatched to attack roads at Sjenica, and although 10/10 cloud obscured the target, fairly good results were claimed. The attacks reached their peak in the period 17 to 20 November, when well over 1,000 tons were dropped on roads, bridges and MT concentrations on the routes leading north-west from Novi Pazar. The enemy had no reserves of transport, and when a vehicle was knocked out its crew could only start to walk north, abandoning weapons and supplies that they could not carry. On the 17th, thirty-seven Wellingtons took off for attacks on the roads between Novi Pazar, Sjenica and Priboj, but were recalled after one hour and twenty-one returned to base. A more successful attack by thirty-six aircraft took place on the next day, bombing numerous small groups of MT that were parked along the road. One larger concentration of twenty to thirty vehicles was located and many were claimed to have been destroyed or damaged. The attacks continued on the 19th and 20th, with good results reported.

On 8 November the Group sent three Liberators and seven Halifaxes to attack the road bridge at Visegrad, but the attack was a failure due to 10/10 cloud over the target area. However, one crew reported it to be already broken, and this report was confirmed by an excellent photograph that showed one span to be completely missing. Subsequent photographic reconnaissance suggested that the enemy were making attempts to repair it, and the Group sent forty-three aircraft in another daylight attack on 19 November. They reported a good concentration around the bridge and claimed at least one direct hit. During the attack some of the crews saw a pontoon bridge across the river approximately half a mile south-west of the main bridge, and the Group sent twenty-seven bombers to attack it on the next day. When the attack was carried out the bridge was not in position, but an excellent concentration was obtained on the approaches, particularly at the west end of the bridge, where a direct hit was claimed on the approach jetty.

Successful raids were also carried out on troop concentrations in the towns of Rogatica, Uzice and Podgorica. The last named town was believed to be the assembly area for around 15,000 German troops, and the first attack on 6 November was the first time that the main bomber force had carried out a daylight raid since 8 April 1944. The seventy-two aircraft carried out a highly effective attack, and photo reconnaissance showed extensive damage in both the old and new towns. The partisans subsequently reported that 700 Germans had been killed and 150 motor vehicles destroyed. Seventy-one bombers went back to Podgorica on the night of 19/20 November, with the main weight of the attack falling on the east approach of the bridge and the adjoining town area. Rogatica and Uzice were both attacked successfully on 23 November by forty and thirty-three aircraft respectively.

As we have seen, the enemy had been driven to rely almost entirely on pontoon bridges for transport across the River Po, and on 16/17 November three Halifaxes and ten Wellingtons were despatched to destroy the one at Ficarolo. The bridge was not in position, but target indicators dropped in excellent illuminations straddled the northern approach. Bombing was very accurate, and several 4,000-lb bombs burst on and around the northern approach and two 4,000-lb bombs across the southern approach.

Only 17 per cent of the total effort in November (289 sorties) was directed at railway targets. Four attacks were carried out on the marshalling yards at Sarajevo between the 4th and 19th, with a total of 166 sorties despatched. In the first attack by nineteen aircraft on 4/5 November the bombers had strict instructions not to hit the town area. Due to a bank of low cloud or thick haze over the target area, only one aircraft dropped a 4,000-lb bomb after making several runs, but this failed to explode. The remaining aircraft jettisoned their bombs and brought the target markers back. On the next day seventeen aircraft went back to the yards at dusk, but two aircraft jettisoned and one returned early. The remainder obtained an excellent concentration around the target markers, which fell near the workshops. Approaching dusk made observation of results difficult, but one 4,000-lb bomb landed in the western end of the yards, and other sticks were seen to straddle the target. Photo reconnaissance showed very heavy damage to the western end of the yards, with all tracks cut and much rolling stock destroyed or damaged.

The biggest attack took place on 7 November, when fifty-two Wellingtons and thirty-six Liberators operated. The aircraft obtained a fair concentration on the target area, and at the end of the attack the yard was obscured by smoke and dust. One of the Wellingtons of No. 37 Squadron failed to return after being seen near the target with one engine smoking. Three of the crew returned to Italy at the end of the month, and reported that the aircraft had been abandoned after being hit by flak. All the crew landed safely and contacted partisans, and were evacuated via a British Mission. At first it was thought that the pilot and rear gunner had been captured by Chetniks, but both are buried in the Belgrade War Cemetery. Another Wellington from the same squadron exploded on touching down at base, with two crew members dead and three injured. The yards were hit again by forty-two aircraft on 18/19 November, bombing on the target indicators that were well placed immediately north-east of the workshops. Subsequent photo reconnaissance showed hits on the yards and the lines from the west and south west, probably cutting all through tracks.

The final attack on marshalling yards during November was that by seventy-nine aircraft on Szombathely in Hungary on 22/23. This big rail centre was of great importance to the enemy in his evacuation of the Balkans, but the attack failed due to a blanket of ground mist covering the target area. The illumination was scattered and up to eight miles off target, and the thick ground haze prevented the visual markers from identifying the target. No target indicators were dropped, and the bombing was very scattered. A few aircraft identified the town and river, and eight claimed to have located and bombed the target, but the majority aimed at flares and the glow of incendiaries. Three of the aircraft returned early, fourteen jettisoned, and two returned with their bombs. The combination of moon and thick ground haze created ideal conditions for fighters, and many enemy aircraft were active in the area between Zabreb and the target. In the vicinity of the target many sightings of enemy aircraft were reported, and six of the bombers failed to return. Major damage was also sustained by two of the aircraft. A Halifax was subjected to repeated attacks, the intercom system disabled, and the rear of the aircraft set on fire. A Liberator had one engine disabled in a single attack by a Ju 88. The bombers fought back, and a Wellington of No. 40 Squadron claimed a Ju 88 that was seen to burst into flames and crash. Another Wellington of No. 37 Squadron was also attacked by a Ju 88, which was engaged by the rear gunner and claimed as damaged. Other enemy aircraft were possibly damaged, and two single-engined aircraft were seen to crash in the target area.

As well as the attacks on the marshalling yards, a number of operations were directed at bridges in Italy, the first of a series of attacks on bridges that formed vulnerable points in the enemy's rail network in north-eastern Italy. The main targets were the bridges over the Tagliamento at Latisana and near Casarsa, but, as ever, these were difficult targets to hit and no important damage was caused. Another rail bridge, at Ljes in Albania (about fifty miles north of Tirana), was attacked by four Halifaxes on 7 November, but there was 9/10 cloud cover in the area and, again, no damage was done.

There was only one attack on airfields during the month. Increasing fighter opposition had been met by the American daylight missions over northern Italy, and many of these fighters were known to be using the Udine–Campoformida and Vincenza airfields. The Group was detailed to crater the landing grounds during the night, and so enable the Americans to deliver strafing and fragmentation bomb attacks on the grounded fighters during the day. The Udine–Campoformida airfield was attacked by twenty-three Wellingtons, thirteen Liberators and three Halifaxes, and target indicators were well placed just west of the centre of the runway. All aircraft bombed on the TIs (target indicators) or visually, and at least five direct hits were recorded on the runway and a substantial fire was started in the eastern block of buildings. Two Wellingtons of No. 70 Squadron failed to return, and it was later learned that both crashed in the Ancona area. The rear gunner of one of the aircraft baled out, but the rest of the crew were killed in the crash.

Twenty-two Wellingtons, thirteen Liberators and three Halifaxes attacked Vincenza, obtaining an excellent concentration on the target indicators, which fell just east of the runway. The landing ground was covered by bursts, and photographs showed that several fell on the runway. One Wellington of No. 40 Squadron collided with another from No. 104 Squadron on landing, with both aircraft damaged but the crews were safe. On the following morning the Fifteenth Air Force carried out their bombing and strafing attacks, and as a result the airfield was rendered completely unserviceable, with many aircraft on the ground destroyed and damaged.

*   *   *

Bad weather resulted in stand-downs on four days in December, and the cancellation of operations on seven other occasions. In addition, Celone was rendered unserviceable during the latter half of the month, with the result that No. 2 Wing SAAF was only able to operate a limited number of aircraft from Foggia Main. During the remaining twenty days, however, the Group was able to launch 1,352 sorties, and only lost three aircraft. The supply dropping missions continued by day and night throughout the month, with 520 sorties despatched (38.5 per cent of the Group effort). Attacks on military targets on the ground took up 28.5 per cent of the effort (385 sorties), and those on railway targets comprised 12 per cent (160 sorties).

During the month the decision was taken to eliminate high level and Gee-fix supply drops over Yugoslavia, except when supplies were very urgently needed.

Aircraft descended to 1,000 feet and dropped their loads visually, returning their containers to base if low cloud obscured the ground markers. On 2/3 December the cloud blanket that had prevented operations for several days still persisted over large areas of the Balkans, and as crews had strict orders only to drop visually, a large number of the sorties were unsuccessful. At the FLOTSAM area cloud was 10/10 at 3,500 feet, and only four of the fifty-three Wellingtons that operated were able to break cloud and locate the ground markers. Similar conditions existed at ICARUS, but seven Liberators succeeded in descending to 1,800 feet and dropped their loads. Two aircraft returned early, fifty brought back their loads, and two failed to return. One of the missing Wellingtons was found to have crashed into the hills north of San Marco (near Manfredonia), and all the crew were killed. For the first time the Liberators of No. 37 Squadron operated, the Squadron having started re-equipping with the aircraft in October. On 3/4 December supplies were urgently needed by the Yugoslav National Army of Liberation surrounding the Podgorica pocket, and dropping on Gee fixes was authorized if the area was covered by cloud. This was indeed the case, and reports from the field indicated that the dropping was scattered.

A very successful drop was carried out by fifty-six aircraft on 4 December, and another good operation was completed on the 6th by forty-three Wellingtons and thirty-eight Liberators. Weather conditions were good at the TOFFEE area, and a successful drop was achieved. All aircraft dropped on the ground markers, and photographs showed an excellent concentration of parachutes falling around it. At the BALLINCLAY area two sets of ground markers were seen a mile apart, and snow-covered ground made it difficult to distinguish them. Dropping was consequently somewhat scattered. Ground reports stated that results were not too good, and the containers were very scattered. A large number of parachute failures were observed, mostly among the Liberator drops. On 9/10 December thirteen Liberators were despatched to the CRAYON area, but were recalled due to deteriorating weather conditions. Another successful operation by forty-five aircraft in the TOFFEE area on 11/12 was the last supply dropping mission until 22 December, when forty-seven aircraft were sent to the FLOTSAM area. The operation was marred by thick cloud over the target, and thirty-five were unable to break through the 10/10 cloud and returned with their loads. The remaining eleven aircraft dropped ninety containers, and reports from the field showed that ten of the loads were recovered. Great admiration was expressed at the skill shown by the crews in dropping accurately under such conditions.

Thirty-one Wellingtons and nineteen Liberators went to Yugoslavia again on Christmas Day, and dropped 391 containers. Photographs showed a good concentration around the ground markers, and reports from troops on the ground showed that the drop was excellent, the average distance from the markers being only 200 yards. Four more operations were conducted between 26 and 29 December, with 134 sorties despatched and a good success rate obtained. On the 28th thirty-two aircraft went to a new dropping zone, codenamed HARANGUE, and another thirty-three went back there on the following day. Supply dropping operations were carried out on four days and four nights in January, with a total of 382 sorties despatched and three aircraft lost. However, cloud conditions caused many aircraft to return with their loads on several occasions, and 128 sorties (34 per cent) were abortive for various reasons. Those aircraft that dropped their loads maintained their high standard of accuracy, and although snow hampered the collection of the supplies in several cases, field reports suggested that the recovery percentage was very high.

Bombing was on a reduced scale throughout the month, and the main target was the German 21st Mountain Corps retreating north-eastwards from Podgorica. On 3 December reports were received that the enemy surrounded in the Podgorica pocket was making a thrust to escape through Klopot, and attacks were delivered against the bridges at Bioce, and roads and MT between Podgorica and Klopot. Eighteen Liberators and two Halifaxes were despatched to Bioce in the day, but 10/10 cloud considerably hampered the operation. Six aircraft broke cloud and bombed, observing bursts on both sides of the main bridge, but the remainder failed to get through the cloud and jettisoned their loads or brought their bombs back. That night roads and MT in the vicinity of the Podgorica pocket were the target for the Group, and fifty-one Wellingtons and two Liberators operated. Cloud was again 9 to 10/10 at 5,000 feet, but thirty-one aircraft attacked, observing hits and near misses on the road and on vehicles. A direct hit was claimed on a bridge south of Bioce (a different bridge to that attacked during the day). Three Wellingtons each carrying 4,000-lb bombs were briefed to attack a hairpin bend south of Klopot, but it seems that they bombed the wrong stretch of road.

On the seven days between 15 and 21 December the Group joined in the concerted air attack on the 21st Mountain Corps, and 316 sorties were despatched in eight attacks on targets at Klopot, Jablan, Matesevo, Kolasin, Bioce, Mojkovac, and Bifelo Polje. They claimed many vehicles destroyed and damaged, and when the Yugoslav National Army occupied Kolasin on the 31st they reported that some 800 vehicles had been destroyed or abandoned between Podgorica and Kolasin as a result of air attacks. The most successful attack by No. 205 Group took place on 18 December by twenty-five Liberators, thirty-eight Wellingtons four Halifaxes. In the words of the No. 70 Squadron ORB, they 'created havoc'. Large numbers of MT were located on the road, especially in the Bioce–Klopot stretch, where vehicles were massed nose to tail. Many hits were scored, resulting in numerous fires that were thickest on the bends near Vilac but visible all along the target stretch. One of these fires produced black smoke up to 3,000 feet and was thought to be an oil tanker ablaze, and another fire resulted in much exploding ammunition. Many of the aircraft strafed the roads, resulting in more fires and many damaged vehicles. At the conclusion of the attack the valley was filled with smoke rising to 7,000 feet and twenty to thirty fires were burning, mostly vehicles, but buildings were also set ablaze.

In December attacks were carried out on the marshalling yards at Sarajevo, and railway bridges at Verona–Parona, Casarsa (two attacks), and over the Piave near Susegana. The attack by thirty-six aircraft at Sarajevo on 19/20 December was a failure due to cloud completely obscuring the yards. The first attack on the bridge near Casarsa on Boxing Day achieved especially good results. One cluster of red target indicators fell at the west end of the bridge, and another near the centre. The bombing by twenty Wellingtons and fourteen Liberators was well concentrated, mainly towards the west end of the target. Three direct hits were claimed on the bridge, and one on the approach immediately west of it. One crew reported that the bridge appeared to be broken when the attack finished, and subsequent photo reconnaissance showed that the bridge was impassable due to several hits on the western approach. One of the hits had blown away the embankment, leaving the line suspended. Fresh damage was visible to the centre section of the bridge, and several near misses had probably caused structural weakening. The railway bypass had been cut, but repairs were already nearing completion.

*   *   *

During the first days of December a political crisis arose in Greece over the disbanding of the various guerrilla formations that had been fighting the Germans for some time. On 3 December a general strike commenced throughout the country, and gunfire was exchanged between the demonstrators and the police during a demonstration in Athens. Subsequently, the E.A.M. (the left-wing National Liberation Front) and its military arm ELAS (the Greek People's Liberation Army) attempted a *coup d'etat* in the capital, and British troops were asked by the Greek government to assist in suppressing the rebellion. ELAS had become the strongest of all the armed resistance organizations, controlling three-fifths of the country and having in its ranks more than 800 officers of the former National Army. Reinforcement of the British troops in Athens became necessary, and on 10 December arrangements were made with HQ Balkan Air Force for No. 205 Group to transport some 2,000 troops, equipment and ammunition into the Athens/Hassani airfield, using Manduria and Grottaglie as advanced bases. Fifty Liberators were flown into the advanced airfields on the afternoon of the 11th, and on the following morning 983 soldiers and their equipment were loaded onto them and flown to Athens without incident. One of the aircraft of No. 31 (SAAF) Squadron had to remain at Hassani after a taxying accident, but the remainder returned safely to base.

On the following day fifty-two Wellingtons and thirty-one Liberators were despatched to repeat the previous day's operation. The Wellingtons were stripped of bomb sights and other equipment, and proceeded to Grottaglie to be loaded with men and equipment. They delivered 879 Army personnel and their equipment and over 24 tons of ammunition to Athens/Hassani airfield. When the aircraft were due to return, however, weather conditions were poor, and only three Wellingtons and 24 Liberators succeeded in reaching base. Three Wellingtons landed away at Grottaglie and Manduria, and the remainder stayed at Hassani. On the following day the weather was still bad, and only thirty aircraft succeeded in returning to base. Ten had to abandon the flight, landing away at Araxos and Iesi airfields, and eight remained at Hassani. One Wellington of No. 70 Squadron overshot on landing at Araxos and sustained damage to both propellers. On the 15th and 16th all the remaining aircraft returned to base except two that were forced to stay behind at Araxos. Another Wellington of No. 70 Squadron was forced to land at Araxos due to bad weather and high petrol consumption. All three aircraft had to be abandoned when Greek guerrilla forces occupied the airfield on 15 August, and were looted and vandalized beyond repair. One of the crews got away by air, and the others were evacuated by sea, reaching Taranto a few days later. This was the last operation for the Wellingtons of No. 37 Squadron.

Although these two operations were successfully carried out, it was clear that operating from advanced bases resulted in some difficulties regarding the loading of the aircraft. Five subsequent operations involving 147 sorties were performed from Group airfields, and the difficulties were successfully eliminated, but not

302

without some friction with the Army. The No. 31 (SAAF) Squadron ORB reports that four aircraft were originally detailed for one operation, but a fifth was needed as the Signals Section needed to take with them a huge amount of 'miscellaneous equipment, personnel, motor cycles and sacks of maps'. It also states that the Army's lack of 'Air Sense' was clearly illustrated when the Squadron was asked to transport a few Jeeps! In all, a total of 2,043 Army personnel and 400 tons of supplies were delivered without incident.

*   *   *

The New Year opened with no changes for the Wings in terms of their home bases. No. 231 Wing was at Tortorella, with No. 37 Squadron fully operational on Liberators and No. 70 Squadron re-equipping with the four-engined aircraft. It would continue to operate its Wellingtons throughout most of January, and would also carry out its first operations with the new Liberators. No. 236 Wing (Nos 40 and 104 Squadrons) was at Foggia Main, with both its squadrons still flying Wellingtons. No. 240 Wing (Nos 178 and 614 Squadrons) was at Amendola, with No. 614 Squadron still using Halifaxes in addition to its Liberators. No. 2 SAAF Wing (Nos 31 and 34 Squadrons SAAF) was at Celone, but the appalling weather conditions meant that the landing ground was unusable and their aircraft had to operate from Foggia Main.

The weather was the main limiting factor when it came to operations in the New Year. The first fall of snow that winter came on New Year's Day, and during the month there were several fairly heavy falls. Rain fell almost incessantly for the whole of the month, and the resultant mud, coupled with the cold weather, made life thoroughly miserable for all. Thirteen degrees of frost were registered in the area on one morning, and the all pervading mud was frozen solid. At least conditions on the ground at Foggia Main were reasonable. No. 104 Squadron ORB records that the camp site there was based around six small farmhouses stretching for two miles along a narrow road, and it 'survived the weather conditions creditably'. Drainage was good and snow dispersed rapidly, but the vehicles carrying water and rations to the cookhouse churned up the ground and created very muddy conditions. However, the fierce snowstorms tested the Wing's shanty town accommodation to its limits, and an Australian pilot with No. 40 Squadron remembers going to bed in full flying kit, including his flying boots!

No. 37 Squadron ORB reports that 'rain, mud and cold influenced every sphere of the Squadron's activity'. The runway at Tortorella:

> ...although surfaced with pierced steel strip appeared more as a dirt road covered throughout by inches of liquid mud. It is over 2,200 yards long and yet was not sufficient for a fully loaded take-off. The retarding effect of mud on wheels, flaps and fuselage was such that the bomb load had to be reduced from 10,000 lbs to 9,000 lbs, that aircraft might safely clear the far 'hedge'.
>
> The same mud splattered into the runners of the bomb doors blocking, or at times freezing up, the free movement of the rollers upon which the doors shift. Many doors were damaged and failure of the bombing gear in the target area was frequent.

The Liberators were still fairly new to the ground crews, and their task was made more difficult by the rain, snow and cold. They worked in the open, and couldn't use gloves or other protective clothing without being handicapped in their work. Serviceability was never high, and was made worse by a change from Squadron to central Wing Maintenance. This meant that all periodic inspections, and all repairs beyond the capacity of squadrons to effect within twenty-four hours, were to be carried out in Wing Maintenance Units. However, the No. 231 Wing Maintenance Unit was fully employed with acceptance checks for newly arriving aircraft for No. 70 Squadron, and couldn't handle the extra work. No. 178 Squadron ORB comments that it was 'too early to estimate what the effect this change will have on the squadron operational effort and efficiency'. As well as all these difficulties, the continued operations from Foggia Main for No. 2 SAAF Wing also added considerably to the hardships of their ground staff, who had to spend much of their day 'commuting' from Celone.

The South African Wing had other problems that were not experienced by the RAF units. Lawrence Isemonger tells a story that casts light on the uneasy relations between the white servicemen in the South African forces and the members of the black Native Military Corps. The bad weather in January made it more convenient for No. 31 Squadron SAAF to acquire its own stores truck instead of having to rely on the Transport Section to provide a different truck and a different driver each day. The permanent driver assigned to the Squadron was Sergeant Joseph Mgwatyu, who was a good driver but somewhat erratic. Trips with him could be a nerve-wracking experience, and the truck often got bogged down in the mud or ended up in a ditch. Joseph was 'quite intelligent' and 'forever complaining about the lack of further advancement' for black servicemen. He became 'fractious and difficult to manage', and 'prone to disappear after lunch'. Longing to return to what he referred as 'ceeveelian' life, and under the influence of American comic books, he wanted to become a travelling salesman when he got back home. Unfortunately, he did not wait until he got back to South Africa before putting his get-rich-quick schemes into practice, and was caught trying to sell a fur-lined flying jacket. A few days later, he got into more serious trouble over a local farm girl, and at a subsequent court martial was sentenced to be reduced in rank and transferred out of the Squadron.

Isemonger tells us that many members of the Native Military Corps attached to SAAF squadrons proved 'an unfortunate source of serious trouble'. Used as truck drivers, fire-fighters, batmen, and for domestic chores in camp kitchens, the Africans 'could not cope with the over-night transition from raw tribal life to a sophisticated wartime existence among foreigners'. Not only did disciplinary problems arise, but they became 'completely uncontrollable under the influence of strong liquor which was freely available and relatively cheap'. At least one African was found guilty of murder and faced a firing squad. Their contact with the 'far more sophisticated Negro servicemen' of the USAAF did not help to improve matters, 'although the latter did not mix freely with our Africans'.

The War Diary of No. 31 Squadron SAAF reports that a clay pigeon range was under construction 'chiefly for the use of Air Gunners', who were to be 'encouraged to avail themselves of the opportunity of improving their marksmanship!' Further training for the gunners was provided by means of a 0.5 machine gun fitted to the Gunnery Leader's truck, which they were permitted to fire on 'stand-down' days, using ammunition that was unserviceable for operations. The use of defective ammunition led to a lot of gun stoppages, but this provided valuable experience for the gunners and tended to minimize problems whilst in the air. Food was a problem for the Squadron, with a lack of fresh meat and no coffee. There was little variety in fresh vegetables and fruit, and no tinned fruit had been issued since Christmas. Nevertheless, the canteen was running smoothly, and a new kitchen had been built. The living quarters were 'excellent', given the prevailing weather conditions, and although the camp was muddy, all the tents were perfectly dry and habitable. The Squadron sick bay was finally completed in January, and the 'interior décor was a pleasing symphony of green and white'.

Other squadrons were also trying to make things easier for their men. No. 178 Squadron had requisitioned a farm building and was building a bath house with which it hoped to provide hot baths for everyone by the end of the month. It had also decided to build fireplaces in the airmen's canteen and the briefing room. However, there was a serious breakdown in the water supply at Celone during January, due to both the extremely difficult conditions imposed by the mud and the unserviceability of many water bowsers. In consequence, facilities for bathing were very limited and a number of parasitic skin infections broke out. There had also been an increase in the incidence of VD during November and December, but this had declined following a talk to the other ranks by the Medical Officer! However, the ORB suggested that the decline may have had more to do with the fact that wine was 'being sold nightly and beer once a week' on the camp, and so the 'urge to "go to town" is removed'. An outbreak of smallpox in Foggia had caused the closure of the NAAFI Club to all personnel, although it was re-opened in January. Foggia town was placed 'out of bounds' to all personnel not vaccinated within the last two years.

*   *   *

The poor flying weather in January meant that the squadrons needed to make full use of the various radio aids to navigation available at the time. The most useful was Gee, with assistance from the base HF/DF stations, the VHF homer, and the radio range at Biferno. Most targets for the Group were well within Gee range, although flying low over mountainous country caused a deterioration in signal strength. During January Loran equipment (an American development of the radio navigation system) was also becoming available, and one was installed as a trial in a Liberator of No. 31 Squadron. Crews were encouraged to gain the maximum practice in all radio aids when returning from operations.

The night bombers in Italy were also catching up on other techniques that had been used by Bomber Command for some time. The month of January saw the first use of wind speed and direction plotting by a leading pathfinder aircraft of No. 614 Squadron. The pathfinders were fitted with a new Air Pressure Indicator, which allowed a more accurate wind to be calculated. It would send out tuning instructions about ten minutes before bombing was to commence, giving the wavelength on which it would transmit the information about the winds over the target area. The wind speed and direction was then broadcast for five minutes on the run up to the target, and the method resulted in a greater concentration of bombing. It seems that many bomb aimers had been relying on wind speeds and directions found by their navigators some distance from the target, which could be very different from those at the target itself.

The extremely bad weather that persisted throughout January meant that operations were greatly curtailed. One short spell of good conditions between the 3th and the 5th was used to advantage, but this was followed by twelve days during which only two operations were attempted. The weather then improved slightly during the next four days, but then closed down again, allowing only one operation during the last ten days. A total of twenty-two days were unfit for operations, and only 625 sorties were despatched throughout the month. However, the bare operational statistics do not tell the whole story. Although few operations were actually carried out, they were laid on almost every day and the aircraft were loaded up and the crews briefed. On several occasions the cancellations did not come through until the aircraft were just about to take off. When early operations were arranged the aircrews were woken up at 0500 hours, only to find out at the Met briefing at 0600 hours that the weather conditions were unfavourable and the operation scrubbed. The ground crews had an even harder time, loading and unloading supplies and bombs in intense cold during the early hours. No. 31 (SAAF) Squadron ORB records the difficulties experienced in simply getting bombs to the aircraft, as bomb trolleys were useless due to the mud. Also, the hardships endured by maintenance personnel in carrying out daily inspections were considerable.

Supply dropping operations were carried out on four days and four nights, with a total of 382 sorties despatched (61 per cent of the total effort for the month) and three aircraft lost. However, cloud conditions caused many aircraft to return with their loads on several occasions, and 128 sorties (34 per cent) were abortive for various reasons. Those aircraft that dropped their loads maintained their high standard of accuracy, and although snow hampered the collection of the supplies in several cases, field reports suggested that the recovery percentage was very high. On 15 January the weather improved enough for a supply dropping operation to the CRAYON area to be attempted, although a lot of the aircraft were bombed up for an attack on the Brescia marshalling yards and loads had to be changed in difficult conditions. No. 31 (SAAF) Squadron ORB reports that bombs had to be stacked in the dispersal areas between the aircraft, which was not a very satisfactory situation. Forty-seven Liberators and forty Wellingtons operated, but on arriving in the target area crews found that cloud was still 9/10ths. Only ten located the marker fires and dropped, while five others dropped on a glow seen through the cloud. Reports from the field stated that dropping was very scattered, but a fair number of containers were eventually brought in. It was believed that enemy troops in the vicinity lit fires to confuse the aircraft, and they also fired Verey lights and flashed torches.

On 18 January 1945 the long spell of bad weather at last broke, and two successful supply operations were carried out during the day. Thirty-one Wellingtons and forty-two Liberators were despatched to CRAYON, where the conditions were completely clear. Sixty-eight aircraft dropped 725 containers, and photographs showed an excellent concentration of chutes around the ground markers. In case enemy fighters from Udine airfield tried to intercept, the mission cover was provided by P 51s of the USAAF, but no encounters took place. Six Halifaxes and seven Liberators carried out an accurate drop of 142 containers at HARANGUE, and all bar one was successfully collected by ground forces. However, many parachutes were reported to have 'Roman Candled' (failed to open) with consequent damage to contents. No. 31 Squadron reported that this daylight operation, carried out in clear weather, brought home to the crews the 'hazards of searching such an area by night at low altitudes'. The exacting requirements of dropping the supplies on target, together with the mountainous nature of the terrain 'forcibly disclosed that though drops were generally unopposed, hazardous flying conditions amply balanced the lack of enemy opposition'.

All the bombing operations in January (243 sorties) were directed at railway targets. The first target for the bombers in the New Year was the famous Salcano Bridge over the River Isonzo.[2] It carried the single track railway line from Villach to Gorizia, and was now of increased importance due to the cutting of the Postumia route out of north-east Italy. The bridge boasted the largest stone arch in the world, an 85-metre span, and was built by Austrian engineers before the First World War. The Austrians then destroyed it during that war, and it was rebuilt by the Italians between the wars. Illumination was reported to be adequate in the attack by fifty-six aircraft on 3/4 January, and the main cluster of target indicators fell at the south end of the bridge. Although the bombing was well concentrated in the target area, smoke and valley mist made it difficult for the aircraft to see the results of the attack. Subsequent photographic reconnaissance showed that the bridge was undamaged, though there were some hits on the southern approach.

The second railway bridge to be attacked was at Latisana, already the subject of a number of attacks at the end of 1944. It had become more important after day bombers had broken the railway bridge at Casarsa on the Udine to Mestre line (see previous chapter), and its destruction would complete the disruption of all rail traffic into Italy from the east. It had been attacked recently and damaged by P-38 fighter-bombers of the Fifteenth Air Force, but reports had been received that it was open again for single line traffic. Fifty-three bombers went there on the night of 4/5 January, and complete success was achieved. Bomb strike photographs showed an apparent direct hit on the centre of the bridge, and photographic reconnaissance showed that one of the two supports carrying the new single track had been destroyed. The two short spans on either side of it had consequently collapsed into the river. After the success at Latisana, another rail bridge became the target for the Group when a daylight attack was carried out on 5 January at Doboj in Yugoslavia.[3] This was on a major supply route for the German forces in that country, and was attacked by forty aircraft. Two direct hits were claimed, but photographic reconnaissance showed no damage to the bridge itself. However, the line was made temporarily impassable by the heavy cratering of both approaches.

Only one more attack on a railway target was carried out in January, a night attack on the 20th/21st on the Udine marshalling yards by ninety-three aircraft. This was an important junction in north-east Italy, and had been attacked frequently by the RAF and the Fifteenth Air Force. Photographic reconnaissance confirmed that a good concentration of bombing had been achieved on the triple junction area, resulting in heavy damage to the locomotive depot and sidings. At least fifty wagons were destroyed, and through lines cut. Heavy damage was also caused to 'industrial installations' around the yards.

*   *   *

By the latter half of February No. 2 Wing SAAF was back at Celone, and the work of the armourers and ground crews was made a lot easier, aided by the great improvement in the weather and an issue of 'durable leather gloves'. However, there were still many difficulties to overcome at Celone. Revetments were at a premium and taxy strips narrow, with the result that aircraft frequently became bogged. Nevertheless, all ranks were delighted that they no longer had to spend half their day travelling to and from Foggia Main, where the uncertainty of everything played on their nerves and where they were exposed to the elements all day. No. 34 Squadron also reports that there was a 'remarkable change in the weather' towards the end of the month, and gum boots were exchanged for leather boots. All the squadron ORBs report that the improving weather greatly eased the strain on the maintenance crews, and on life in camp in general. They took the opportunity to finish off many of the outstanding jobs on their camps, including concreting the floors in messes, getting bath houses ready, and completing work on the camp roads. No. 104 Squadron also mentions the gramophone recitals – 'every taste is catered for, from "jive" to classical' – that were very popular during the month. Recordings of stage shows were also very much appreciated. No. 240 Wing praised the entertainment offered by the camp cinema at Amendola, and also the two ENSA Concert Parties that performed during the month.

Following the disappointing start to the year, an excellent recovery was made in February, and the Group largely returned to its 'proper role' of night bombing. A total of 1,316 sorties were despatched, and eight aircraft lost. The bomb tonnage dropped, 2,611 tons, was a record for a winter month and helped by the increasing number of four-engined heavy bombers with the squadrons. Operations were prevented by the weather on eight occasions, but during the remainder of the month bombing attacks were made on eight nights and one day, and supply dropping operations on five days and one night. The eight night bombing attacks (557 sorties, 42.3 per cent of the total effort) were directed against marshalling yards – Verona West (four attacks and 290 sorties), Graz, Udine, Padua North-East, and Brescia. Supply dropping was also a major feature of operations in February, with 384 sorties despatched (29.2 per cent of the total effort). Ports (303 sorties, 23 per cent of the effort) and oil targets (72 sorties, 5.5 per cent of the effort) were also attacked during the month.

Wing Commander D.B. Harris of No. 37 Squadron, who had taken over the unit in the middle of January, commented on the 'surprising example of the flexibility of a Heavy Night Bomber Squadron'. In February the Squadron dropped bombs by day and by night, did the same with supplies. The daylight sorties soon showed that fighter opposition was negligible, and that the 'blitz' method of bombing – a stream of aircraft at different heights on the same heading and over the target almost simultaneously – nullified the effects of flak to a large extent. The night sorties showed that fighter opposition was on the increase over the Po valley, but flak was very little in evidence. Crews tended to prefer the 'daylights', and they were certainly more effective. Navigation was easier, and ground detail gave a check on ETA for the 'blitz' technique. The daylight attacks also brought home to the crews the skill that was needed to accomplish a successful night operation.

No. 236 Wing (Nos 40 and 104 Squadrons) was converting to Liberators in February, although both continued operating with Wellingtons throughout the month. The good weather helped the intensive training programme, although No.

40 Squadron only put up one Liberator sortie during February and No. 104 managed four sorties. The latter's ORB commented that:

> Due to the efficiency and good serviceability of the automatic pilot in Liberators, a drill for bombing on George [automatic pilot] has been worked out and proved to be most satisfactory in the several Liberator operations that were carried out before the end of the month.

No. 178 Squadron ORB notes that the accuracy of night bombing steadily increased throughout the month, as the sustained effort in good weather allowed the crews to work up to a high standard. It was also noticeable that the flak at the marshalling yards was greatly reduced from previous months. At Verona, which was supposed to be defended by over two hundred heavy and light guns, the opposition was in no way serious. On the other hand, enemy night-fighter activity in northern Italy appeared to be on the increase. The change over to the Wing Maintenance system, whereby all inspections of fifty hours or more and all repairs that would take more than twenty-four hours were handled by the Wing Maintenance unit, was still causing problems in relation to serviceability. No. 178 Squadron records that for the best part of the month the Squadron could only put an average of eight aircraft per day in the air. The operational effort for the Squadron was further restricted by having to convert seven Wellington crews to Liberators.

The important yards at Verona were attacked four times during the month, but two of the attacks, on 8/9 February by seventy-eight aircraft and 12/13 February by seventy-three aircraft, were largely neutralized by thick ground haze. Photographic reconnaissance showed only slight damage to the yards after the first attack, and all through lines were still open. Some industrial and residential damage was visible north of the target. Flak was less than anticipated, and the maximum use of 'Window' resulted in it being very inaccurate for height. In the second attack very thick haze made identification of ground detail almost impossible. Only two of the visual markers dropped target indicators, claiming them to be at the extreme eastern end of the yards. However, photographs showed them to be in open country some two miles south-west of the target, and most of the bombing was concentrated on these.

However, the other two attacks, on 23/24 February by fifty-eight aircraft and on 27/28 February by eighty-one aircraft, were very effective. All the through lines were cut after the attack on 23/24 February, much rolling stock was destroyed, and considerable damage reported in the target area. The Fifteenth Air Force had also bombed the yards at this time, and some of the damage must have been attributable to the American bombers. The importance that the enemy attached to the junction at Verona West can be judged by the fact that all through lines were again operational by 1400 hours on the 26th. The success was, however, short lived as the attack on 27/28 February, again, effectively cut the through tracks at the eastern choke point. Illumination was good and red target indicators were placed in the centre of the target area. Crews reported the bombing to be well concentrated, and bomb strike photographs showed many bursts in the eastern half of the yards. Two good fires were started, and smoke and dust covered the target at the end of the attack. Photographic reconnaissance showed some eighty hits had been scored in the eastern portion of the yard, cutting several through lines at many points and damaging rolling stock and buildings.

Graz was bombed by seventy-three aircraft on 13/14, and was also attacked by the Fifteenth Air Force on 13 and 14 February, resulting in considerable damage. The yard was an important link in the German rail system behind the south Russian front, and this attack was the first deep penetration by the Group since 22/23 November. Illumination was good, and the target indicators fell at the south end of the yards. Photographs revealed the bombing to have been somewhat scattered, with the main concentration just south of the marshalling yards. A violent explosion and two large fires, one of which was thought to be oil, were observed. The attacks by the Fifteenth Air Force made it impossible to attribute particular items of damage to particular attacks. Photo reconnaissance showed many craters in the south locomotive depot and repair shops, and new damage to railway buildings. Some thirty wagons had been destroyed and residential damage was visible around the target area.

Good results were also achieved by seventy-seven aircraft at Udine on 20/21 February. Illumination was excellent and the main cluster of target indicators fell close to the aiming point at the triple junction. Bombing was well concentrated, and one stick of incendiaries fell across the aiming point and others immediately north of it. These started several fires, and two large explosions were observed in the target area. Photographic reconnaissance showed that the object of the attack was fully achieved, with the through lines cut and rolling stock destroyed. Heavy damage was also caused in the adjacent timber yard and stores, where fires were still burning sixteen hours later. Other industrial damage was visible north of the target area. Sixty-nine aircraft went to Padua on 22/23 February, after an interval of almost twelve months, and an effective attack was carried out. The main cluster of target indicators fell immediately north of the centre and west end of the marshalling yards, and most crews bombed on these. Considerable smoke and haze obscured the observation of results, but bomb strike photographs showed concentrations across the east and west ends of the target area. Subsequent photographic reconnaissance revealed over thirty craters in the marshalling yards, cutting all through lines. Around twenty wagons were destroyed and direct hits on station buildings.

Supply dropping was another major feature of operations in February. The Group sent seventy-four aircraft to the FLOTSAM area on 2 February and seventy-three to the same area on the next day, and both drops were very successful. Then on 4 February forty-eight Liberators, nineteen Wellingtons and two Halifaxes were despatched to the FLOTSAM and CRAYON areas, but the weather was very bad and one of the Wellingtons crashed soon after take-off, hitting the ground near Apricena. Only two aircraft were able to get below the cloud and drop their containers at FLOTSAM, and all the others brought their loads back to base. The weather had closed in at Foggia when they came back, and three Wellingtons crashed in the Gargano mountains and another crash-landed at Lesina. Successful operations were then carried out by forty-four aircraft at FLOTSAM on 7 February and by sixty-four aircraft at TOFFEE and BALLINCLAY on the 14th. The last drop in February was on 25/26 February in the ICARUS area, when sixty-three aircraft all found the target area and carried out an excellent drop. The majority of the supplies were delivered to hard-pressed Yugoslav Army troops in Slovenia, and the following message was received from their Headquarters:

Slovenia Headquarters wishes to express deepest gratitude of Army and civilians for recent drops of military stores.

The highlight of the month for the Group was the daylight attack on the Naval Armaments Depot at Pola.[4] Reports had been received that supplies of torpedoes and ammunition stored at Pola were being used to launch attacks on Allied shipping carrying supplies to the Yugoslav mainland. The first operation was launched on the 1st, but 10/10ths cloud at the target prevented the attack being delivered. All the aircraft except one Liberator jettisoned or brought their bombs back to base. The Group tried again on 21 February, when seventy-three aircraft operated, this time with complete success. Subsequent photographic reconnaissance revealed extensive damage throughout the depot, with at least eight buildings completely obliterated, and severe damage caused to the quay in the west area. Another very effective daylight attack was made by seventy aircraft on the naval base at Fiume on 16 February, where the primary target was an armed merchantman in the fitting out basin. Photographic reconnaissance confirmed a most successful attack. The boiler shop was completely gutted, and the floating dock severely damaged and left submerged. On the next day sixty-eight bombers went to the naval dockyard at Trieste, but the bombing was very scattered and due to prior and subsequent raids by the Fifteenth Air Force it was impossible to judge the effects of the Group's efforts.

The Group went to Fiume again on the 15th, but this time the ROMSA oil refinery was the target for seventy-two aircraft. Unfortunately, the bombing was rather scattered, and covered some one-and-a-half miles of the waterfront. Photographic reconnaissance showed more than twenty craters cutting tracks in the marshalling yards, the complete destruction of a large building by the oil harbour, and damage to factories on the east of the refinery.

An interesting development was mentioned in the Group ORB in February. At the end of January, permission had been received from HQ Mediterranean Allied Air Force to proceed with the formation of a Mosquito marking flight in No. 614 Squadron. Mosquito training commenced on the 4th at Foggia Main, but due to the non-availability of aircraft and the tardiness of the ferrying services, training was at a standstill by 10 February. However, five pilots went solo in four days, and the navigators managed to achieve a good standard in radio navigation. The only mention of Mosquitos in the Squadron ORB states that on 30 April three Mosquitos left for temporary duty at Malta. Late in the afternoon, news was received that one had crashed at Capodichino, and the pilot (Flying Officer W.C. Robinson) and navigator (Flight Sergeant D.I. Mutton) were both killed. Another development mentioned at this time was that the Group was starting to plan for its post-war role in transport operations, and details of freight and personnel transport modifications to the Liberators were being designed by the Group.

*   *   *

Improved weather conditions throughout the month enabled the Group to operate on twenty nights and two days. A total of 1,402 sorties were despatched, 3,621 tons of bombs dropped, and ten aircraft lost. Operations were prevented by unfavourable weather conditions on ten occasions, with five consecutive days at the end of the month spoiling what was hoped to have been a record month for sorties and tonnage dropped. Seventeen operations (1,151 sorties, 82 per cent of the total effort) were carried out against marshalling yards, with Villach North, Graz and Verona East each receiving two visits. Only one supply dropping operation was carried out in March, on 15/16th, when excellent drops were made by the sixty aircraft involved.

Sixty-seven Liberators, eight Wellingtons and two Halifaxes were despatched to the Verona East (Porto Vescovo) marshalling yards on 2/3 March. Illumination was scattered, and the main cluster of target indicators fell at the extreme west end of the yards. A 'Master Bomber' technique was employed for the first time, and he issued instructions to undershoot the markers. Although a good concentration on the west of the yards was reported, the bomb strike photographs showed that the majority of aircraft were north of the target. Photographic reconnaissance showed that only slight damage had been caused to the yards and only a few tracks were cut. On 9/10 March sixty-two Liberators went to the Verona area again, this time to bomb the railway bridge at Parona di Valpolicella. Some flares were dropped four miles south-east of the target, illuminating a bridge in Verona itself, and this was marked by a red target indicator. The Master Bomber ordered crews to ignore this, but about a third of the force did not hear the instructions. The main illumination was accurate and target indicators fell some 200 yards south-east of the bridge. Bombing was fairly well concentrated, with many sticks covering the approaches and two or three straddling the bridge itself. One possible direct hit was claimed on the north end of the target, but although bomb strike photographs showed the bridge enveloped in smoke, photo reconnaissance showed that the structure was intact. Enemy aircraft were active during the operation, and a number of significant encounters took place.

The third visit to Verona, by sixty-four Liberators and eight Wellingtons, came on 11/12 March, and resulted in a most successful attack. Two clusters of target indicators fell on the yards and another was 400 yards to the south. The Master Bomber directed crews on to the northernmost clusters and a good concentration was reported. Several small fires and explosions occurred in the target area, and one large explosion was confirmed by bomb strike photographs to have been in the State Railway Factory. One stick of incendiaries fell along the yards and others to the east. Photo reconnaissance showed an excellent concentration of hits running north to south across the yards, temporarily cutting all through lines and most sidings. Approximately thirty-five wagons had been destroyed, and severe damage was visible to station buildings and to factories and warehouses to the north and east of the yards.

The small marshalling yard on the Italy/Yugoslavia route at Casarsa was reported to be handling a large volume of traffic at night, and to hold around 300 rolling stock. Forty-four Liberators and seven Wellingtons were sent to bomb the yards on 4/5 March, and in good illumination the target indicators were placed immediately north of the target. The Master Bomber's instructions to this effect were generally well received and the bombing was reported to be concentrated on the target. A stick of incendiaries covered the whole length of the yards, and a series of explosions was thought to be an ammunition train going up. Subsequent reconnaissance photographs were of poor quality and the serviceability of through lines could not be determined, but heavy damage had been inflicted on the locomotive sheds, repair shops and station buildings. Some thirty units of rolling stock were knocked out, and a goods train west of the marshalling yards had been derailed.

The first attack on the yards at Graz came on the night of 5/6 March. Sixty-two Liberators and one Wellington set off, but the attack was a complete failure due to 9/10 cloud at the target. The single Wellington and one Liberator returned early, and two Liberators jettisoned and five returned with their bombs after being unable to locate the target. The flares only illuminated cloud, and the only visual marker dropped on his fifth run on the estimated position of the target. Bombing was very scattered, and no results were observed. Two Liberators failed to return. One of these was seen coned and shot down by flak over Trieste, and crashed in Yugoslavia. The other is thought to have been the victim of a night fighter over the target. The second attack on Graz came on the last night of the month, after the five days of unfavourable weather had grounded all aircraft. The target was illuminated by eight aircraft of No. 614 Squadron, which dropped target indicators in a cluster mainly on the south-east corner of the yards. The bombing by seventy-one aircraft of all four Wings was reported to be fairly well concentrated. Fires were started that were visible for fifty miles, although cloud and smoke hampered observation of detailed results. One Liberator did not return, but news was later received that four crew members were safe. Photographic reconnaissance showed scattered damage, largely by fire, to industrial and residential buildings.

A supply dropping operation to Yugoslavia was originally planned for 7/8 March, but it was cancelled and a double attack on marshalling yards at Gemona and Udine was substituted. Twenty-nine Liberators and eight Wellingtons were despatched to Gemona, but the weather en route was extremely bad. One Liberator and five Wellingtons abandoned the operation, and nine other aircraft failed to locate the target. The weather over the target area was somewhat better than during the previous operations, but cloud considerably hampered the attack. The remaining aircraft bombed on the Master Bomber's instructions, undershooting red target indicators by 300 yards, and reporting a fair concentration with two fires in the target area. Photo reconnaissance showed slight damage to rolling stock and buildings, but the through lines were unscathed.

Thirty-eight Liberators went to Udine in the other operation, but bad weather en route forced two aircraft to return early and three failed to locate the target and returned with their bombs. Another developed engine trouble, and also had to turn back. This aircraft encountered severe conditions on the way home, and was thrown violently about the sky. The rudders became very heavy, the aircraft spun to port and starboard, and it nearly went over onto its back. Two of the crew baled out under instructions from the captain, but the pilot eventually regained control and landed safely on three engines. The attack itself was a comparative failure. The target indicators were placed some 350 yards north of the aiming point, and although the Master Bomber broadcast corrections, cloud prevented most crews from getting good runs and the bombing was reported to be very scattered. Photographic reconnaissance showed some damage in the town, including factories, the power station and road overpass, and some heavy areas of fire damage. Railway damage was confined to a large warehouse, which was severely hit, and slight damage to tracks. One Liberator of No. 31 Squadron, the crew of which were 'all comparative newcomers to the Squadron', failed to return.

The north-eastern marshalling yards at Padua were the next railway target for the Group, and the attacking force on 12/13 March comprised fifty-four Liberators and seven Wellingtons. Five blind illuminators and three visual markers of No. 614 Squadron provided adequate illumination and marking. Four clusters of target indicators fell along the yards, and two slightly to the south of them. The Master Bomber ordered bombing to be aimed at the western clusters, and most crews reported the main concentration to be well placed around them. A large explosion occurred at 1951 hours, and a good fire was burning in the target area when the aircraft left. Photo reconnaissance showed hits along the whole of the marshalling yards. All through lines were cut, and some forty wagons destroyed. The station and goods depot had received further damage, and there was heavy damage in residential and industrial areas north of the yards.

On 13/14 March six Wellingtons and sixty-three Liberators went to the north-eastern marshalling yards at Treviso. The illuminators and markers of No. 614 Squadron did a good job, but some of the aircraft bombed before the target indicators fell, causing dust, which hampered the markers. Only two crews failed to hear the Master Bomber, and all reported good bombing. Incendiaries were seen burning south and west of the yards, and large explosions and fires seen in the target area. The glow from the fires was visible for sixty-five miles on the return journey. Photo reconnaissance showed two through lines cut at the south end of the yards, with over 200 wagons trapped inside. The yards at Vincenza were attacked by sixty-five Liberators on 18/19 March, and the illuminators and markers accurately marked the centre of the yards. A good concentration of bombs was reported by crews, although incendiaries seemed to be somewhat scattered. The target indicators were not accurately pinpointed due to intense smoke in the target area, but two large explosions were reported and several fires were seen in the yards. Photographic reconnaissance showed scattered damage throughout the yards. Sheds and buildings were hit, a turntable was put out of action, and about fifteen rolling stock were destroyed or damaged.

The yards at Bruck in Austria were the next railway target to receive attention. On 19/20 March seventy-eight Liberators were despatched to the target, but ground haze prevented accurate observation and illumination was reported to be scattered and inadequate. Target indicators fell in several widely scattered groups, and bombs were dropped over a wide area. No results were observed other than a few fires, but these were thought to be forest fires. One of the Liberators of No. 31 Squadron failed to return, and the navigator (Lieutenant V.G. Felton) later told Lawrence Isemonger[5] that the No. 3 engine had caught fire on the way to the target. The pilot ordered the crew to abandon the aircraft north-east of Trieste, and all baled out safely. Felton landed in a tree in the dark, and not knowing how high it was he spent the night there 'nesting'. When day dawned he found that he was no more than five feet from the ground! He made his way to nearby Ljubljana and gave himself up to the local German garrison. Seven of the crew became prisoners of war, but the second pilot (Flying Officer Baird), evaded capture. He surprised everyone by arriving back at Foggia, having hitched hundreds of miles.

On 20/21 March it was the turn of the Pragersko marshalling yards in Slovenia, which were accurately illuminated by eight Liberators of No. 614 Squadron and attacked by sixty-five Liberators. An excellent concentration of bombing was reported, and a violent explosion took place at 2101 hours. Flames leapt to over 100 feet, giving the appearance of an ammunition truck exploding. Numerous smaller fires were reported, and the target area was covered by smoke. Photographic reconnaissance showed excellent results, with large quantities of rolling stock, the repair shop and many other installations completely destroyed. Several lines were either cut or blocked. On 21/22 March seventy-eight Liberators went to the marshalling yards at Novska. The markers were dropped in good visibility, and the first reds landed on the aiming points and were bombed immediately. The greens fell about 200 yards to the north-east of the yards, and the Master Bomber's instructions first to bomb the reds and then the greens were clearly heard. An exceptionally good concentration of bombs and incendiaries were reported, and large fires and explosions were seen, one fire being visible for fifty miles. The whole target area was left covered in smoke, with many explosions still taking place as the aircraft left the area. Photographic reconnaissance showed many of the sidings obstructed by craters, and much wrecked rolling stock.

The first attack on the yards at Villach north took place on 22/23 March, and seventy-five Liberators were despatched on this occasion, with eight aircraft of No. 614 Squadron illuminating and marking the target. Individual results were not seen due to the target being covered in smoke, but several good explosions were seen, and a red glow from a large fire was seen by returning aircraft. Photographic reconnaissance showed a concentration of hits to the north, extensively damaging a residential area, but little new damage to the yards themselves. One Liberator of No. 178 Squadron failed to return, and was seen to go down in flames over the target area. The second attack came on 25/26 March, when good illumination enabled thirty-eight aircraft to attack with much better effect than the earlier operation. The target indicators fell close to the centre of the yards, the instructions of the Master Bomber were carried out, and bombing was well concentrated. The target area was quickly covered in smoke, but many large explosions were reported, and the glow from the fires was visible up to eighty miles away. Photographic reconnaissance showed the goods depot and trans-shipment sheds almost completely destroyed. Approximately fifty wagons were burnt out, and much damage was caused to residential buildings and sheds in the area. One Liberator of No. 34 Squadron failed to return, having received a direct hit over the target. It immediately burst into flames, and was seen to turn onto its back and crash in the target area.

Two more attacks on marshalling yards took place in March. On 23/24 March fifty-one aircraft went to St Veit East, where the illumination was adequate. The target indicators fell in two clusters on the western end of the yards and about 300 yards east of the southern end. Good concentrations of bombs were dropped, causing the whole area to be quickly obscured by smoke and almost obliterating the markers. Two sticks of incendiaries fell along the yards, and three or four fires and several explosions were observed by returning aircraft. Photographic reconnaissance showed approximately twenty items of rolling stock and a large warehouse destroyed, and several buildings gutted. Through lines at the southern choke point had been cut, and residential buildings near the northern choke point severely damaged.

On 24/25 March fifty-one aircraft were despatched to the Dobova marshalling yards. The visibility in the target area was good, and excellent illumination and accurate marking ensured a very successful attack. Two target indicators were dropped in the yards and two just to the north, and crews bombed under the direction of the Master Bomber. The target area was soon obstructed by smoke and dust, but several large explosions were observed. Two big fires were visible for fifty miles as the aircraft made their way home. Some of them reported a convoy of over 200 vehicles moving north on the Karlovac–Zagreb road, some of which were on fire. Photographic reconnaissance showed heavy damage to the marshalling yards, with all tracks cut and around 100 trucks destroyed or damaged. A direct hit was scored on the overpass 200 yards to the north-west of the yards.

The rest of the month was taken up with a series of attacks on many different kinds of targets. The first was a daylight attack on the coal wharves in the Arsa Channel, on the east coast of the Istrian Peninsula in modern Croatia, which handled the entire movement of coal from the Albona coalfields. The wharves were attacked by fifty-one aircraft on the first night of the month, but they found the target completely obscured by 10/10 cloud. One bombed through a small gap and three on Gee fixes, but the remainder jettisoned or returned to base with their bombs. The bombers would go back to the wharves with greater success in April.

On 3/4 March the Group carried out a 'quadruple operation', with two forces laying mines off Venice and Pola, while diversionary bombing attacks were carried out against Porto Marguera oil storage depot and Pola naval dockyard. The Group ORB states that the 'desired secrecy was not completely achieved, both mining forces being sighted and engaged by light flak'. In the Venice area eight Liberators laid forty-eight mines from low level in two beds immediately outside the main harbour entrance and in the entrance itself. Another four Liberators mined the Fasana Channel from low level, while a fifth aircraft dropped five mines from high level into Pola harbour. While the 'gardening' was going on six aircraft illuminated and marked the Porto Marguera oil storage depot, and twenty-one Liberators bombed the target. Two of the Liberators jettisoned after hang-ups, and one had to take avoiding action on its bombing run to avoid a twin-engined aircraft on a reciprocal course. It found that the target indicators had gone out on its second run, and returned with its bombs. The crews that bombed the target reported a fair concentration, with sticks falling across markers in the north-west of the target area and in the storage tank area. Photographic reconnaissance showed fresh craters around the depot, but the only noteworthy damage was a direct hit on one large tank. Enemy aircraft were active in the area, and at least twelve sightings occurred, including that of a possible jet aircraft. However, a Halifax had been on fire for a short period over the target and a Liberator had exhaust damper trouble, and these reports were treated with caution. Crews were certain that some sort of jet aircraft had been present, having been especially impressed by its great speed.

Four Liberators of No. 614 Squadron carried out extremely accurate marking of the Pola Naval Ordnance Depot. Two of the aircraft provided good illumination for the two visual markers to place their target indicators dead on target – a small island in the harbour. Twenty-six Liberators and seven Wellingtons attacked the depot, and although some bombing was very wide and several sticks fell in the harbour, a fair concentration was achieved. Crews reported three explosions in the target area, and a stick of bombs straddled the swing bridge that connected the island to the mainland. Photographic reconnaissance showed some damage to shops and administrative buildings, and a possible hit on a submarine secured to a jetty.

Finally, a very successful daylight attack was made by sixty-one Liberators against the shipyards at Monfalcone on 16 March. They bombed visually in good weather, and heavy damage was done to floating docks and harbour installations. A large explosion was observed in the central target area, which subsequently proved to be a small oil lighter moored alongside the quay. Strikes were recorded on the mole, across the shipbuilding yards, in the Cant aircraft works, and on other installations in the harbour area. Photographic reconnaissance confirmed the very extensive destruction to the aircraft works, to buildings in and near the electrical and railway workshops, and to shipping and harbour facilities.

In the attack on Monfalcone on 16 March, a Liberator of No. 37 Squadron (KK320) was hit by two bombs dropped from above. The aircraft, captained by Squadron Leader L.C. Saxby, was hit on the port inner engine, and the propeller and the front part of the No. 2 engine were torn away. A huge hole was also made in the fuselage on the port side, the top turret was destroyed, and the bombardier and wireless operator were slightly injured. Despite this extensive damage, Squadron Leader Saxby brought the aircraft successfully back to Tortorella. A remarkable photograph taken from above during the raid shows five bombs falling on or very near the aircraft, and another taken afterwards shows the pilot standing in the hole in the side of the bomber. The Liberator was judged to be beyond economic repair, and was struck off charge on 26 April 1945.

*   *   *

April was a memorable month for the Group in that it saw the commencement of the final battle for the destruction of the German forces in northern Italy. The last Allied offensive in Italy opened in the afternoon of 9 April 1945, and just under three weeks later the cease-fire was signed at Alexander's headquarters in the royal palace at Caserta, to take effect on 2 May. The Group launched 1,251 sorties, half of which (629 sorties, 50.3 per cent of the total effort) were in support of the ground forces. Marshalling yards again figured prominently in the list of targets again this month, with 513 sorties launched (41 per cent of the effort). The railway attacks were on Trento (two operations), Novska, Brescia, Innsbruck, Villach North, and Freilassing.

The Eighth Army launched its attack on the Senio Line in northern Italy on the evening of 9 April, the objective being to push the enemy back to their strongly fortified positions on the Santerno River. That night ninety-five aircraft from the Group were despatched to attack two positions along the Santerno ('Pig' and 'Whistle'), the object being to destroy the defences and so make possible the crossing of the river the next day. Due to the proximity of friendly forces a plan was devised whereby the Army would mark the centre of each area by firing red marker shells, and these would be further marked by the usual target indicators. This proved to be very successful on the more northerly target ('Pig'), where a tremendous concentration of bombing was achieved. Not one single bomb fell outside the area laid down, and 'utter devastation' was caused along the river defences, which enabled the ground forces to establish their first bridgehead the next day with very little opposition. Due to the extreme accuracy required, no second runs were to be allowed, and fifteen aircraft either jettisoned or returned with their bombs. Subsequent reports from the ground bore out the claims made by the crews, and photographs showed excellent concentrations on the target area.

317

This and later bombing attacks brought the following signal from General McCreary:

> Am most grateful for the heavy and continuous support you are giving to the 8th Army. Your accurate and devastating attacks are causing great disruption to the enemy. Your bombing of the Santerno defences played a most important part in forcing of this river obstacle. I should be grateful if you would convey the thanks of all ranks of the 8th Army to all officers and men under your command.

The forward troops who had a grandstand view of the bombing were reported to be 'very enthusiastic'. The southern area ('Whistle') was not marked in time by the Army, and so was not attacked.

Another operation in support of the Eighth Army was launched on 11/12 April, namely an attack on the concentration of enemy troops, defences and dumps in the Bastia area, where Highway 16 crosses the River Reno. It thus lay a little ahead of the forward troops, and on a main supply route to the enemy front. The target was not marked by the Army, but once again a terrific concentration of bombing was achieved, despite the fact that forward troops were no more than 2,000 to 3,000 yards away. Seventy-six aircraft bombed the area, and excellent results were reported, with many explosions and fires being observed. The objectives of the raid were achieved in that the enemy was denied the use of essential roads for moving supplies. The disruption meant that the enemy had to abandon this route, and redirect his retreat over the Reno to Traghetto, about ten miles north-west of Bastia.

The town of Argenta was the next target in support of ground operations, and this was bombed on the night of 12/13 April. Forty-two aircraft bombed the specified area, which was illuminated and marked by eight aircraft of No. 614 Squadron. Once again, the concentration was exceptional, and reports from the ground forces stated that the destruction was very great. Roads were cratered and blocked with rubble, and fires were seen for forty-five miles on the return journey. Photographs showed the whole area covered with smoke, and photographic reconnaissance confirmed that considerable damage was done to the town and surrounding villages.

Portomaggiore was attacked on the next night, another key point dominating the vital Argenta Gap. This attack and another on 17/18 April were both highly concentrated, and the area was eliminated as a communications centre. In the first attack eight aircraft of No. 614 Squadron illuminated the target, and fifty-seven aircraft bombed. One large explosion and many fires were seen by the crews, and the only part of the target area to escape with relatively light damage was the extreme south-eastern part. Otherwise, roads were entirely covered with rubble and craters, bridges were destroyed, and rail communications severed. Photographs showed severe damage to the area, with through lines blocked, a road and footbridge demolished, severely cratered roads, and such extensive damage to the town itself that all road traffic would be forced to make a detour to move from east to west. In the second attack eight aircraft of No. 614 Squadron illuminated and marked the target to be bombed by thirty-nine aircraft of all Wings. Bombing was again reported to be well concentrated and photographic reconnaissance showed that with the exception of the south-eastern area, the remainder of the town was devastated. All through routes were cut, and little or no activity was visible.

On April 14 the Fifth Army opened their attack with the objectives of by-passing Bologna, and on the night of 16/17 April the Group was given the task of destroying the bridge over the River Reno and the communications centre of Casalecchio. Seventy-nine aircraft reached the target, which was illuminated and marked by eight Liberators of No. 614 Squadron. Unfortunately, the target indicators were extinguished by an excellent concentration of bombs, which resulted in the Master Bomber abandoning the operation. However, fifty-eight aircraft successfully attacked the target, and the remainder returned with their bombs as instructed. Subsequent reconnaissance showed very heavy damage to the town, with all approach tracks cut, railway lines cratered, and many buildings gutted and destroyed. The bridge over the river was hit and destroyed, and sufficient damage was created in Casalecchio to disrupt enemy communications.

The last close support operation for the Group was at the small town and communications centre at Malalbergo. In this attack seven PFF aircraft illuminated and marked the target for sixty-two Liberators of all four Wings, and all crews reported good concentrations on the town. Subsequent photographic reconnaissance showed heavy damage to roads, canal banks and railway lines. From this time onwards the front was moving so rapidly that the air support provided by the tactical air forces was sufficient.

The first of the two attacks on the marshalling yards at Trento took place on 2/3 April, when eighty-three aircraft were despatched to the target. Low cloud at the target prevented observation of ground detail, and only sixty-six aircraft were successful in dropping bombs. No results were observed beyond a number of explosions and one large fire, and photographic reconnaissance showed only scattered damage to station buildings and goods sheds. The second attack on 8/9 April took place in good visibility, and the eight illuminators and markers of No. 614 Squadron did a good job. Forty-five bombers attacked the target area, and bombs were dropped on the target indicators to the north and south of the yards. Two explosions and several small fires were seen. Photographic reconnaissance revealed only scattered damage, with five or six hits cutting tracks and damaging some half-dozen wagons. A near miss derailed three trucks near the southern choke point, but little damage was seen in the northern yards.

The bombers went to the Novska marshalling yards on 3/4 April, and better weather enabled the aircraft to carry out a successful operation. Seven Liberators of No. 614 Squadron accurately illuminated and marked the target, and fifty-two bombers dropped their bombs in a good concentration. Two large explosions were reported, which soon developed into good fires. Subsequent photo reconnaissance showed heavy damage to the yards and surrounding buildings, sheds and parked stores. All through lines were cut, and tracks at the eastern choke point were severely damaged. The same treatment was delivered to the Brescia West yards on 4/5 April by sixty-nine Liberators and eight pathfinder aircraft. Excellent illumination and good visibility enabled the aircraft to carry out a good attack, with several fires and explosions observed. Photographic reconnaissance showed that through lines were blocked, and many buildings fairly severely damaged, including those of the Breda arms factory. Two Liberators collided in mid-air prior to landing and all crew members in both aircraft were killed.

On 10/11 April the target was the railway station and marshalling yards at Innsbruck. Six Liberators of No. 614 Squadron illuminated and marked the target, and forty-four aircraft bombed in good weather. Photographs showed a good weight to have fallen to the north end of the yards, and many craters around the station buildings and goods depot. Through lines were cut and about fifteen wagons seen to be destroyed. The Villach North yards were due to be attacked on 15/16 April, but the aircraft were recalled due to 10/10 cloud in the target area. Two aircraft did not hear the cancellation order, and went on to the target. One Liberator failed to return, and was believed to have been shot down over the target area.

The Verona/Parona rail and road bridge was again visited by fifty-seven aircraft on 20/21 April. Eight aircraft illuminated and marked the target, which was quickly obscured by smoke. Three hits were claimed on the bridge, and all crews reported good concentrations in the area. One of the Liberators was repeatedly attacked by enemy aircraft, and received several hits, particularly in the empennage. The tail gunner was wounded in the leg and thrown from the turret into the aircraft, which was by then on fire. The beam gunner was also wounded, and in the confusion baled out. He successfully evaded capture and later returned to the Squadron. The second pilot extinguished the fire, rendered first aid to the wounded, and assisted the pilot in a very difficult landing. He also manned the beam gun and obtained probable strikes on a Ju 88 fighter. Both the pilot and the second pilot received the immediate award of the DFC. A further visit to this increasingly important escape route was made on 23/24 April, when forty-six Liberators bombed the target. The bombing was concentrated on and around the target indicators, with one or two sticks seen to straddle the bridge. The line was definitely cut, and the masonry of the bridge damaged.

Apart from the attacks in support of the ground forces and those on railway targets, the Group carried out two raids on other targets. The month had opened with another daylight attack on the coaling wharves in the Arsa Channel. Fifty-six Liberators reached the port and bombed visually in good weather. The target area was very small, consisting only of a conveyor belt and a few cranes, but well concentrated sticks were reported bursting across the jetty and wharf. Two large explosions were seen with orange flames just east of the target, visible for eighty miles on the return. The whole area was left obscured by a thick pall of smoke and coal dust. Photographic reconnaissance showed good concentrations in the target area, with the quayside well cratered and tracks cut and destroyed. Fairly accurate heavy flak was experienced in the target area, and thirteen aircraft sustained minor damage.

One other attack was carried out on a port in daylight, when Monfalcone was visited for the second time on 5 April. Two floating docks had been sunk in the attack on 15 March, but a third dock had been overlooked. Thus another daylight attack was ordered to destroy the remaining dock, and to sink 'E' and 'F' boats in the vicinity. Forty-seven aircraft of all four Wings bombed in good visibility, and many crews reported direct hits on specified targets. Reconnaissance showed the small floating dock sunk, one 'F' boat sunk and one damaged, and severe damage to the CANT aircraft works. Much rolling stock and works and buildings were destroyed or damaged in the area, and cranes and other heavy equipment were also damaged.

On 25/26 April the Group was directed to attack marshalling yards at Freilassing, a small town about two miles north-west of Salzburg and just over the Germany/Austria border. It was situated close to a major Wehrmacht depot, and was supposed to be very intimately connected with the much publicized 'Nazi Redoubt' in the Alpine areas of Germany and Austria. The Allies believed that vast stores and strong fortifications were being built up there in preparation for a last stand. The yards at Freilassing were very full when the attack by ninety-two Liberators went in on the night of 25/26 April, and photographs confirmed the aircrews' reports of a good concentration of bombing. Many fires and explosions were seen in the yards, and about 300 pieces of rolling stock were destroyed. The goods depot was totally destroyed, and the station damaged. Subsequent photographic reconnaissance showed very severe damage to the area, with many direct hits on the tracks causing complete blockages to lines. This attack, followed by further raids by the Fifteenth Air Force, almost completely destroyed the town of Freilassing. However, when the Allied armies penetrated Bavaria and western Austria at the end of April, they met little serious resistance, and the National Redoubt was shown to have been a myth.

Although the bomber crews of No. 205 Group did not know it at the time, the attack on Freilassing was the last time that they would drop their bombs on the enemy. Their long war was all but over.

*   *   *

Due to the bad weather the bombers only operated on 122 of the 212 days/nights from October 1944 to April 1945, but managed to fly 8,686 sorties and lost 80 aircraft. On 4/5 November the Group despatched 199 sorties in two supply dropping and one bombing operation, a record for the Group, and almost matched it on the following day when it despatched 192 sorties. A major part of the total effort was the supply dropping operations (2,377 sorties, 27 per cent), but railway targets continued to provide the lion's share of the total (3,615 sorties, 42 per cent). Seventeen per cent of the sorties went to military targets in the battle area, mainly during the final days of the Italian campaign.

NOTES

1. If the reader looks at these map co-ordinates in Google Earth then the mountainous nature of the terrain will become obvious, as will the dangers of flying over it at a low level and often in the dark.
2. Now in Slovenia, and known as the Solkan Bridge over the River Soča.
3. Now in Bosnia and Herzegovina.
4. Now Pula in Croatia.
5. Lawrence Isemonger, *The Men Who Went to Warsaw*, page 165.

CHAPTER THIRTEEN

Epilogue

The final operations by the aircraft of No. 205 Group were something of an anti-climax. After four days of unfavourable weather conditions, an attack was planned on Figo Bay at Pola on 30 April, but it was subsequently cancelled. Thus, the last operation in April was carried out by a Liberator of No. 31 Squadron SAAF, which dropped leaflets over Karlovac, Zagreb, Sisak, Brezice, and Pola in Yugoslavia. It was obvious that the end was very near. The weather was bad, and during the confused period in the first week of May it was difficult to see what use could be made of the strategic bombing forces at Foggia. The Fifteenth Air Force carried out its last operation on Tuesday, 1 May, when twenty-seven B-17s bombed the main station and marshalling yards at Salzburg. On 4 May the Group was ordered to prepare for attacks on two targets, including the marshalling yards at Bruck, but these were later cancelled. On the 5th it was ordered to stand-by for a demonstration flight over the Gorizia–Trieste–Fiume area by all available aircraft, but this, too, was cancelled. There was then a stand-down until 7 May, when two Liberators of No. 614 Squadron flew a special nickelling mission over Austria. They took off from Amendola at 1905 hours and returned at 0040 hours on the 8th, having successfully dropped their leaflets.

On 8 May 1945 the Allies formally accepted the unconditional surrender of the armed forces of Nazi Germany and brought to an end Adolf Hitler's Third Reich. This was a time for congratulatory messages all round, and the Operational Record Books are full of them. On 15 May the following message was received from the King:

> To you and all those under your command I send my heartfelt congratulations on the overwhelming victory by which you are bringing to so triumphant an end your long and arduous campaign in Italy.

The following messages were also received:

> On my own behalf and on behalf of the Chief of the Air Staff and the rest of the Air Council, I send you and all ranks under your command warmest congratulations on the magnificent part played by the RAF and the air forces of the Dominions and Allies in the long and arduous campaigns in Italy culminating in the total surrender of the enemy's forces in that theatre. Side by side with their comrades in the United States Army Air Forces they fought hard and worked hard in the air and on the ground to achieve and maintain mastery of the Mediterranean sky and then by disrupting the enemy communications and by direct support of the Allied armies they contributed decisively to the resounding victory now won. Our heartfelt thanks to you all for this massive accomplishment.

> Archibald Sinclair (Secretary of State for Air[1])

In this hour of triumph we wish to convey our personal thanks to all Signal Personnel in the American and British Air Services for their vital contribution in bringing the war in our theatre to a victorious conclusion. Our brotherhood is sealed and the cherished memories of our perfect co-operation will remain with us for all time.

> Air Vice Marshal R.S. Aitken (Chief Signals Officer, HQ Mediterranean Allied Air Forces) and Brigadier General A.W. Marriner (Communications Officer, Army Air Forces in the Mediterranean Theatre of Operations)

On handing over No. 205 Group to Air Commodore McKee, I would like to take this opportunity of thanking all officers, NCOs and airmen for the loyal support they have given. Also to congratulate you all for the great part you have each individually played in bringing about the final victory in Europe. Good luck to you all and let me assure you that your future welfare is in very good hands.

> J. Durrant, Brigadier, SAAF

Congratulatory messages were also received from the Prime Minister, the Air Council, Mr Henry L. Stimson (the American Secretary for War), and from the Deputy Supreme Commander (Tedder). A message of appreciation from the Commanding Officer of No. 37 Squadron to his men nicely sums up the feelings of all the squadron COs at the time:

I wish to thank every single man of No. 37 Squadron for the great individual sacrifice and personal effort he has made towards victory in Europe. The long separation from home and five years of war work that the majority of you have endured is recognized and greatly appreciated. I sincerely hope with you all, that an early victory over Japan will soon leave us free to return home to where we belong – the United Kingdom.

The Group then assumed a new role, transporting supplies to the Udine area in Northern Italy. Although the fighting against the Germans had come to an end, arguments with a former ally now flared up. For a few weeks it looked as though the Allies now might have to fight the Yugoslav National Army. Yugoslav forces had advanced rapidly into the area around Trieste and also into Austria, and refused to return to agreed demarcation lines. They held full control of Trieste until 12 June, a period known in the Italian historiography as the 'forty days of Trieste', and during this period hundreds of locals were arrested and some of them disappeared. It seemed for a while that the elements of the Fifth and Eighth Armies in the forward areas might have to fight to persuade the Yugoslav forces to retreat. These elements were at the end of long and inadequate lines of communication, and the Group was called upon to transport supplies of essential materials to forward supply dumps until the docks at Trieste and other facilities could be brought into operation. During the period 7 to 25 May, 1,225 sorties were flown, and over 4,000 tons of supplies transported.

The first of these missions came on VE Day itself, when the Squadron was ordered to fly food and fuel to Rivolto airfield, near Udine, and thirteen aircraft delivered 395 boxes of 'Compo' rations and 1,008 tins of petrol. Many of the

Squadron ORBs comment that there was some disappointment when 'the two days' holiday declared with the cessation of hostilities' was denied them. The squadrons were usually asked to make two separate deliveries, each entailing the employment of an average of eight to ten aircraft, and the demands on flying crews and ground staff were great. The first flight usually took off at 0730 hours and the second at 1500 hours, and this often meant that aircraft that had operated in the morning had to be serviced and loaded again in readiness for the afternoon's delivery. On the 21st the No. 104 Squadron ORB reported that 'the most varied cargo so far was carried today when supplies ferried to Aviano airfield included petrol, crates of cheese, [and] cases of dehydrated potatoes'.

The supply missions to Northern Italy meant that pilots had to land the Liberators and take off again from grass airfields. The first airfield to be used was Rivolto, where the runway quickly gave way under the strain of the heavily loaded bombers. It was only used for two days, and was followed by Lavariano. This field finally gave way under the strain, the surface becoming rutted and soft in patches, so Aviano was used during the latter part of the month. Many difficulties were experienced in take-off from Lavariano, and one aircraft of No. 178 Squadron crashed, killing the pilot. The problems were attributed to inexperienced pilots failing to raise the nose sufficiently on the take-off run, but the fault soon disappeared. No difficulty was experienced in flying conditions over Italy throughout the month, with the exception of one day when low cloud was encountered in the Udine area. Although they missed the VE-day holidays, the aircrews were usually happy to make these supply trips by daylight. They were able to fly low over old target areas, and the pleasures included landing in a field for a picnic lunch from broken Compo ration boxes.

From the middle of the month the supply-carrying missions gradually gave way to the transport of personnel. Large numbers of Allied prisoners of war were arriving in Italy, and had to be repatriated to the UK. The authorities wanted to get the men home as quickly as possible, but shipping was limited and the job was given to No. 205 Group. The crews needed to familiarize themselves with the route and procedure, however, and the work started in a small way. Only crews who had completed 100 hours on Liberators and a total of 500 hours flying were employed on these trips, and they needed a personal recommendation from their CO. The aircraft also required modification. All armour-plating, recoil mechanisms of guns, ammunition, bomb sights and other unnecessary ancillary equipment were taken out. Passenger carrying racks were fitted in the bomb bays. New tyres were fitted whenever possible, and only thoroughly reliable machines were used on these flights. The first missions were completed on 15 May and increased in momentum towards the end of the month. Between 15 and 31 May forty-eight successful trips were completed and 1,203 Allied prisoners of war conveyed to the UK.

The crews consisted of pilot, engineer, navigator, wireless operator, and one extra crew member to act as air host. All control and briefing for the flights were undertaken by RAF Transport Command, and before carrying passengers each crew had to carry out a training flight to the UK and back in order to familiarize themselves with the route and conditions. The briefing and emplaning of twenty-five PoWs per aircraft was done initially at Pomigliano, but the runway there was barely sufficient for take-off and the flights were switched to Bari. The PoWs were landed at Westcott (ten miles north-east of Oxford) or its satellite at Oakley in the

UK, and the aircraft then flew to Holmsley South (near Bournemouth) for servicing and briefing of crews for the return flight. Each aircraft carried three 'J' type dinghies or twenty-five 'K' type dinghies and sufficient Mae Wests for all passengers. The crews soon learnt that trooping called for more individual responsibilities than did 'blitz operating'. It required a much deeper knowledge of the aircraft capabilities, of the weather en route, of aircraft loading, and of long distance routes. The weather was often pretty bad, and a number of fronts over Central and Southern France gave pilots experience in flying in weather conditions they had not hitherto met on operations or training in South Africa and the Middle East. However, these trips were in very high favour, as a forty-eight-hour pass in England was often obtained, and the opportunity for compassionate forty-eights in England for ground personnel was not missed.

Towards the end of the month No. 2 SAAF Wing commenced the transport of personnel of the South African Army and Air Force to Cairo. As a result of the new assignment the Wing Commanding Officer (Colonel J.A. Williams) was transferred from the Group to set up a base in the Middle East to receive the South Africans in transit. The former Paratrooper Brigade camp at San Severo was taken over as a transit camp, and on 26 May a draft of 150 6th Division personnel emplaned at Foggia bound for Cairo. By the end of the month, thirty-three of these missions were completed and 822 personnel conveyed.

The Liberators were also involved in the transport of American troops from Rosignano to Bari, and from Pisa to Naples. On 29 May they took thirty German PoWs and their guards from Forli to Gicia. June started with the transport of French PoWs to Istres, and transport flights to Cairo began later in the month. The Group also sent four aircraft to transport Army personnel going on leave to Ford airfield in the UK, and further flights to take South Africans to Cairo followed on 27 and 30 June. The Cairo run was welcome for the employment and relaxation it gave aircrew, but added little to their experience in airmanship – the weather was invariably good, and the navigation aids and the aerodromes excellent. The endeavour was to use these 'milk runs' as training exercises in advanced cross country techniques: the difference between Rhumb Lines and Great Circle Tracks; the use of Track rather than Air Miles per gallon; the choice of height for the route; the use of American Cruising Curves, and so on.

The activities of May indicated that the maintenance of peace was likely to prove as strenuous as its achievement. The ground crews had to work night and day to 'maintain this extraordinary effort', and often 'the opinion was voiced that the peace entailed a greater effort than the war'. The end of the war in Europe did not bring the relaxation and inactivity that was expected, and there was little celebration on VE-day:

> …indeed most people seemed too tired, or reflective, to take part in demonstrations. The only 'incident' was the conflagration of a haystack near the airmen's canteen, which was assumed to be a happy coincidence of spontaneous combustion.

The bulk of the strain was felt mainly by the armourers and ground maintenance personnel who carried out the hard work of loading supplies. One squadron did finally get its VE-day break on 27 and 28 May when a forty-eight-hour stand-down was ordered, but the celebrations were confined to late breakfasts and the running of the maximum number of liberty gharries to the beach. During the month of July the weather at Foggia became very hot. The temperature hovered between 97 and 105 degrees, and a high wind brought with it thick clouds of dust. Work at the airfields started as early as 0530 hours, and effectively ended at lunchtime.

Many squadron ORBs mention various entertainments going on at this time, such as a whist drive in the Sergeants' Mess or 'a dance in the Airmens' Mess with the 231 Wing band present'. No. 37 Squadron ORB mentions 'the grand opening of the "Beer Garden and Airmens' Canteen" by the CO, followed by a concert by the Squadron "talent" aided by the 231 Wing band'. Two Italian companies gave concerts during the month, in conjunction with ENSA, and film shows were a popular diversion. Football was still very popular, despite the warm weather, with most of the games being played in the evening after the heat of the day. However, cricket was 'gradually coming into its own', and preparations were being made for the opening of a district league. No. 178 Squadron built a new Airmen's Mess, a great improvement on the old one as it was located in a permanent building, and the floor in the Sergeants' Mess ration store was concreted and a meat safe built. It was also decided to enlarge and remodel the stage in the Squadron concert hall, as it had proved too small to allow ENSA shows to be staged.

On 22 May a party of officers and airmen set out on a tour to Florence under the EVT scheme[2] to seek out 'places of educational interest which should be visited'. On 10 June the first of a weekly series of EVT tours to Rome left the Wing with six members of No. 37 Squadron setting off on the seven-day trip. Naples and Venice were also hoped to be included in the same scheme. A census was taken of personnel who might wish to have vocational or resettlement training 'in addition to the compulsory 1-hour per week on the latter subject'. Demobilization and a return to civilian life was very much in the minds of all military personnel, and among the older men there was some apprehension as to the operation of the release scheme. On 23 May a lecture on the Release and Resettlement Scheme was given by a Ministry of Labour official. On 8 June it was announced that two officers had been appointed as the Squadron Postal Voting Officers for the forthcoming election. On 11 June the Squadron started discussion groups with the exciting topic of 'The Pre-Fabricated House in Post-War Planning'!

*   *   *

The aircrews who flew with No. 205 Group were mostly extremely young men, some straight from school, and drawn from all walks of life and all social classes. They grew up very quickly, and those who completed their first tour of operations developed an unusual maturity, one that perhaps no other form of experience in life could have produced. The isolated tented camps inhabited by the Group (and conditions at Foggia were almost as primitive as those in the desert) made for a homogeneous way of life, and a good deal of fraternization took place amongst all ranks. In particular, goodwill and breezy camaraderie existed between the aircrews and the maintenance crews. Armourers, refuellers, riggers, radio technicians and the general maintenance teams were constantly on the go and sometimes involved in dangerous tasks – defusing unexploded bombs, fire-fighting blazing Wellingtons, and repairing airstrips in between enemy bombing attacks. The aircrews did much to try to make the lives of the airmen more interesting, taking them up on air tests, and giving them lifts when going on leave.

Aircrews spoke in a language of their own – of erks, flighties, wingcos, groupies, ground loops, goons, gongs, prangs, dicey dos, shaky dos, sprogs, vegetables, gardening, heavies, cookies, roddies, fans, flaps, kites, jinking, belt ups, beat ups, and shoot ups, of 'going for a Burton', 'getting the chop' and 'buying it', of 'binding bastards' and 'gabardine swine', and of the ubiquitous gremlins, the mysterious, mischievous spirits born in 'Fremlin' beer bottles. These poltergeists of the RAF were blamed for suddenly making guns, turrets, radio equipment and every form of aircraft paraphernalia unserviceable for no apparent reason.

Graphic descriptions of experiences over heavily defended targets were told with an air of nonchalance, and without dramatics. Their chances of survival and occasionally their thoughts and expectations about their return to 'civvy street', were frequent topics. Some wag would always intervene if things got too serious: 'Belt up, you blokes! What did you join up for?' The rejoinder would be an ironic 'to hurl back the Hun, of course!' and 'to strike a blow for liberty!' The aircrews were not in general an over-pessimistic lot. All had hopes of eventually returning to civilian life, but to have a chance every member of the crew had to be efficient and vigilant. Training manuals and posters often featured 'Pilot Officer Prune', a beginner pilot who made all the silly mistakes, and the inference was that 'Prunes' deserved their fate but efficient pilots and crews would escape. In fact, it was clear that even the best crews were sometimes lost through no fault of their own, and an element of luck was essential. There was no discrimination so far as a well directed burst of flak was concerned – *that* was a matter of luck! The law of averages did not apply in this kind of business.

Some aircrews were superstitious – one was meticulously careful about making up his bed before he took off and others wore good luck symbols. Some of the more fatalistic would argue that if a bullet had your name on it you had had your chips anyway, but the more logical ones would counter this by saying that there was no point in taking evasive action if such were the case. The belief sometimes grew up that some aircraft letters were unlucky, and Chappell noted that aircraft with letters A, B, F, R and V each recorded either seven or eight losses, and aircraft with letters J, K, O, Q, X and Y recorded only one loss. He once took note of what happened to twenty-five crews of No. 104 Squadron in their operational tour of some thirty to forty operations. Eighteen crews survived to be rested, while seven crews were lost in a period of some three to four months. However, this period was one of relatively low operational losses, and Chappell felt that it was more likely that between one-third and one-half of Wellington crews in No. 205 Group were killed or went missing during their first tour.[3]

While it was not the place of the aircrews to question the target they were ordered to attack, sometimes the targets did not appear worthwhile. Well-defended and/or distant targets could bring greater losses to the squadrons than the material damage that might be inflicted on the enemy. Crews preferred 'interesting' targets such as a bridge, an aircraft factory, an oil refinery that would produce large fires, or a marshalling yard with photographic evidence of likely ammunition trains and other war supplies. They liked to attack targets in the battle area, where they knew that their bombs would affect the enemy directly as they tried to shelter near their parked vehicles, guns and tanks. The bomber crews were not so keen on a heavily defended harbour targets like Benghazi or Tobruk or Sousse, where many bombs fell into the water, and ships were hard to see and hit. It was the job of the squadron commander and the intelligence officer at briefing to show that every target was worthwhile, and that the attack was a valuable contribution to the war effort.

Sometimes a problem arose among the members of a bombing crew if they were not happy about the captain's method of attack. Dare-devil young pilots often liked to dive down low to machine gun the target area after an attack, and while this activity might bring some crews into interrogation laughing from the fun of delivering such an attack, not all crew members would welcome the extra risks. Some crew members would voice their unhappiness in being forced to take part in what they believed to be unnecessarily risky and crazy activities. Attacks on bridges were often performed at low altitude to make sure of accuracy, but these were planned attacks authorized by the CO, and not therefore the cause of any crew disagreement.

The Empire Air Training Scheme brought together some of the best, carefully selected, intelligent young men from each of the Allied nations and from a variety of home backgrounds – and they learned to like and respect each other. Mixed crews were usually happy crews, and no one would think of letting down his crew or his own nation by showing cowardice over a target. What would an 'Aussie' say if a 'Pommy' showed he was frightened or vice versa? Could the ex-public school boy show his frailty to the miner's son or vice versa? Or could the new crew on their first 'op' with their wing commander as captain of the aircraft do anything but perform according to training and the textbook? Did anyone break down under the strain? Some of the incidents of crew members baling out of aircraft in difficulties were clearly cases of nerves strained to breaking point. Very occasionally, a crew jettisoned their bombs for no good reason and returned to base instead of attacking a target, or bombed outside the flak at Tobruk rather than go over the target. It was not possible immediately to identify such a crew unless a crew member talked out at interrogation or in private to intelligence officers or their flight commander. However, if such off-target attacks were continued it was likely to be detected or suspected because of the lack of photographs of the target normally taken with bombing.

The RAF referred to such rare cases as 'lacking in moral fibre' (LMF), and when they could be identified, most COs were anxious to help them. They might send them on extra leave to recover, or take them off operations before their tour had been completed and post them to administrative posts, or send them for retraining into some duty other than flying. Periods of intense operations, often involving double and even triple sorties on battle area targets during Army crises, occurred in 1942 and 1943 in North Africa and in Italy in 1944. At times like these aircrews were working close to the limits of human endurance and physical signs appeared of the very severe nervous strains and tensions. The characteristic signs were twitches of the facial and eye muscles and occasionally jerky movements of an arm or shoulder, inability to sleep, overindulgence in alcohol or smoking, greying or whitening of the hair, attachment to mascots and other eccentricities of behaviour. Severe cases were said to be 'bomb happy' or 'op tired', and most commanding officers were essentially humane and considerate when dealing with such cases of overstrain.

*　　*　　*

When the war came to an end the squadrons of No. 205 Group were all based around Foggia: No. 2 SAAF Wing (Nos 31 and 34 Squadrons) were at Celone, No. 231 Wing (Nos 37 and 70 Squadrons) at Tortorella, No. 236 Wing (Nos 40 and 104 Squadrons) at Foggia Main, and No. 240 Wing (Nos 178 and 614 Squadrons) at Amendola. All were now fully equipped with Liberators. The first of these units to disappear from the theatre was No. 614 (County of Glamorgan) Squadron, which was disbanded in Italy in July 1945 and renumbered as No. 214 Squadron. It was reformed as a fighter squadron at Llandow in South Wales in May 1946, and finally disbanded in March 1957. The next to go was No. 178 Squadron, which left Italy in August 1945, moving to Ein Shemer (between Haifa and Tel Aviv) and then to Fayid. It was re-equipped with Lancasters and eventually was renumbered as No. 70 Squadron. Its numberplate was not to be used again.

The South Africans were given a stormy farewell from Italy early in September. The main party of No. 2 SAAF Wing was due to leave Foggia on 7 September, but the weather changed suddenly on the evening before and rain bucketed down for over an hour. Tents were blown down by gale force gusts of wind, and thunder and lightening added to the noise and confusion of the hectic farewell parties as the Wing personnel got ready to leave Celone. The rain continued on the next day, and by lunchtime the entire camp was flooded. The main party eventually got away by train at 0400 hours on the 8th, and travelled to Brindisi for the sea journey to Egypt aboard the *Caernarvon Castle*. It had been planned that an advance party would fly to Shallufa on 8 September to prepare for the arrival of the sea party, but the atrocious weather forced many postponements. It eventually left on the 13th, but the eleven people in the party carried so much excess baggage that the tailskid of the Liberator bumped over the tarmac as it taxied to the end of the runway. Everybody had to move forward in the aeroplane to get the tail up, and the overloaded aircraft eventually took over eight hours to cover the 1,500 miles to Shallufa. The main party arrived three days later.

The Wing carried on operations from Shallufa until December, although an official statement on repatriation had been issued in October and during the month some personnel left for the base depot at Almaza on the first stage of their journey home. Armistice Day was commemorated on 11 November, and the Commanding Officer (Colonel G.T. Moll) broke down as he read the names of the 269 men who had lost their lives on active service with the Wing. Meanwhile, the RAF had taken on the task of flying aircraft back to the UK on expiry of their permissible life, and one of the first planes to leave under this arrangement crashed on the island of Crete, killing all on board. The last operation by the Wing was a flight to Foggia on 2 December by ten Liberators, and the final parade took place on 7 December.

The departure of the South Africans in September left just the four veteran squadrons in Italy. No. 70 Squadron had carried out its first operation way back on 17 September 1940, No. 37 Squadron began operating in the Middle East on 13 November 1940, No. 104 Squadron had arrived in Malta in October 1941 and first operated against Tripoli on the 19th, and they had been joined at Luqa by No. 40 Squadron later in the month. All four units left Italy in October 1945, thus effectively ending the life of No. 205 (Heavy) Bomber Group. No. 37 Squadron moved to Aqir in Palestine. Although disbanded at Shallufa in March 1946, it was soon reformed as a heavy bomber squadron by the renumbering of No. 214 Squadron, equipped with Lancasters. It would remain in the Mediterranean area, first as a bomber unit and then as a maritime reconnaissance unit (reformed from a nucleus of No. 38 Squadron), equipped with Lancasters and Shackletons, until finally disbanded in September 1967. No. 70 Squadron also moved to Aqir, and was disbanded at Shallufa in March 1946. Like No. 37 Squadron, it was reformed as a heavy bomber squadron by the renumbering of No. 178 Squadron (see above), equipped with Lancasters, but was again disbanded in April 1947. Reformed as a transport squadron in May 1948, equipped with a variety of aircraft, it remained in the Mediterranean area until June 1975. It is still in existence as a transport squadron.

No. 40 Squadron moved to Abu Suier in Egypt, where it was re-equipped with Lancasters and operated as a heavy bomber squadron until disbanded at Shallufa in April 1947. It saw further incarnations as a transport squadron, equipped with Avro Yorks, and as a bomber squadron, equipped with Canberras, until finally disbanded in February 1957. No. 104 Squadron also moved to Abu Suier, where it was re-equipped with Lancasters until disbanded at Shallufa in April 1947. It saw further incarnations as a bomber squadron equipped with Canberras and a guided missile unit equipped with Thor missiles until finally disbanded in May 1963.

*   *   *

No. 205 Group and its associated units flew 49,148 sorties between June 1940 and May 1945, lost 938 aircraft (1.9 per cent), and suffered 3,185 aircrew killed or missing, 239 wounded and 403 captured. It was the only force of heavy night-bombers in the Mediterranean theatre in the Second World War, and it was forced to use the venerable Vickers Wellington long after this aircraft had been relegated to the training role in the United Kingdom. The Group's aircraft were often 'hand-me-downs', passed from units in the UK to the Middle East and then from one squadron to another until their useful life was ended. But the Wimpey was a tough old bird, and served the Group well right up to the last year of the war. The conditions in which the air and ground crews operated were usually primitive, with landing grounds scraped out of the bare desert or surrounded by a sea of mud. There were no pubs, often no beer, and the only contact with their families were the letters from home. In the Western Desert they lived nomadically, and in an emergency the whole camp could be bundled into trucks and be on the road within an hour or so. In the summer it was extremely hot by day, with millions of flies. In winter the nights were bitterly cold, and torrential rains often turned landing grounds into swamps. Things did not improve much when the squadrons got to Italy. The area surrounding Foggia was described in the official history as a bleak plain, in the middle of which was 'the dusty town of Foggia, of which the general appearance had not been improved by the frequent air attacks made upon it'. The rain came down by the bucketful, and in the winter the snow fell and the mud froze. Despite all this, the Group battled on to the end. It is hoped that this book is some small recognition of the debt that we all owe to those who flew through the darkness and into the light.

NOTES

1. He remained a minister until May 1945, when the coalition ended. In the 1945 general election on 5 July he narrowly lost his seat. His margin of defeat is one of the tightest on record – he came third, even though the victor had only fifty-nine votes more than him. In 1952 he accepted elevation to the House of Lords as Viscount Thurso.

2. With the end of the war in Europe and everyone thinking about demobilization, realization dawned that hundreds of thousands of men had joined up and would be returning to civvy street with no experience of working life and with no trade or profession to fall back on. Such people were going to need help and so the EVT, or Educational and Vocational Training Scheme, came into being and was operated throughout all the armed forces.

3. Overall operational losses for No. 204 Group were around 940 aircraft from 49,000 sorties, or around 1.9 per cent. This would suggest that a squadron of fifteen aircraft might expect to lose one every four operations, and a tour of thirty operations would see about seven crews lost – about the number that Chappell first calculated.

APPENDIX I

205 Group Battle Honours

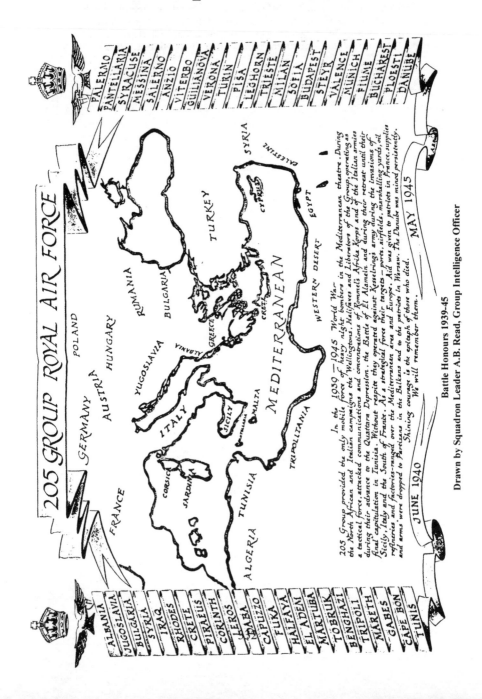

In the 1939 – 1945 World War, 205 Group provided the only mobile force of heavy night bombers in the Mediterranean theatre. During the North African and Italian campaigns the Wellingtons, Halifaxes and Liberators of the Group, operating as a tactical force, attacked communications and concentrations of Rommel's Afrika Korps and of the Italian armies during their advance to the Quattara Depression, the Battle of El Alamein and during their retreat until their final capitulation in Tunisia. Without respite they operated against Kesselring's army during the invasions of Sicily, Italy and the South of France. As a strategical force their targets – ports, airfields, marshalling yards, oil refineries and factories – ranged over the Mediterranean area and Europe. Aid was given to patriots in France, supplies and arms were dropped to Partisans in the Balkans and to the patriots in Warsaw. The Danube was mined persistently.

Shining courage is the epitaph of those who died.
We will remember them.

Battle Honours 1939-45

Drawn by Squadron Leader A.B. Read, Group Intelligence Officer

APPENDIX II

Orders of Battle

In June 1940 No. 216 Squadron was the only night bomber squadron operating in the Middle East, based at Heliopolis and equipped with Bristol Bombays and Vickers Valentias. In September it was joined in the order of battle by No. 70 Squadron at Kabrit, which had been re-equipped with Wellingtons. In November two squadrons of Bomber Command (Nos 37 and 38) were ordered to the Middle East. A small number of aircraft of No. 37 Squadron joined others that were operating from Malta as the 'Luqa Wellington Detachment' and carried out a number of sorties from the island. In December the Wellingtons on Malta were formed into No. 148 Squadron, and in the Middle East an important administrative change occurred for the heavy bombers on 20 December when No. 257 (Heavy Bomber) Wing was formed at Shallufa. Thus, at the end of December 1940 the order of battle for the Wing was:

No. 37 Squadron at Shallufa (Wellington ICs)

No. 38 Squadron at Fayid (Wellington ICs)

No. 70 Squadron at Kabrit (Wellington ICs)

No. 216 Squadron at Heliopolis (Bombays and Valentias)

No. 148 Squadron at Luqa with its Wellington ICs was under the control of Air HQ Malta. No. 216 Squadron carried out its last bombing operations in January 1941, and reverted to its transport role. No. 148 Squadron was forced out of Malta in March, and moved to Kabrit in Egypt. The bomber force in the Middle East was expanded in August when No. 108 Squadron was re-formed at Kabrit, equipped with Wellingtons. On 23 October 1941 No. 205 (Heavy Bomber) Group was formed at Shallufa, and took command of the following squadrons:

No. 37 Squadron at Shallufa (Wellington ICs)

No. 38 Squadron at Shallufa (Wellington ICs and Wellington IIs)

No. 70 Squadron at Kabrit (Wellington ICs)

No. 108 Squadron at Fayid (Wellington ICs)

No. 148 Squadron at Fayid (Wellington ICs)

Further reinforcements for the Wellington squadrons arrived in October 1941, when two more (Nos 40 and 104) were detached from Bomber Command to operate from Luqa under the control of Air HQ Malta. In November No. 108 Squadron received a few Liberators for long-range operations over the Balkans, but did not operate the new aircraft until 11 January 1942. In January No. 104 Squadron started to move from Luqa to Kabrit, and at the end of the month RAF Station Kabrit was reformed as No. 236 Medium Bomber Wing. In February No. 40

Squadron at Luqa was temporarily disbanded, and was re-formed at Abu Suier on 1 May 1942. At the end of May the order of battle was:

No. 37 Squadron at LG 09 (Wellington ICs)

No. 38 Squadron at Shallufa (Wellington ICs)

No. 40 Squadron at Abu Suier (Wellington ICs)

No. 70 Squadron at LG 104 (Wellington ICs)

No. 104 Squadron at LG 106 with detachment at Luqa (Wellington IIs)

No. 108 Squadron at LG 105 and Fayid (Wellington ICs and Liberator IIs)

No. 148 Squadron at LG 106 (Wellington ICs)

In June elements of Nos 159 and 160 Squadrons arrived in the Middle East en route to the Far East with their Liberator IIs, but stayed in Egypt due to the crisis in the desert. No. 160 Squadron was effectively absorbed into No. 159 Squadron at this time. In July the crisis brought further reinforcements in the shape of detachments of Nos 10 and 76 Squadrons with their Halifaxes. These two units operated with the support of ground crews from Nos 227 and 454 Squadrons respectively, and the detachment from No. 76 was later supported by No. 462 Squadron. On 7 September the composite units 10/227 and 76/462 were absorbed into a re-formed No. 462 Squadron. In the same month the composite 159/160 Squadron was restyled as No. 160 Squadron. When the Battle of El Alamein opened in October 1942, the Wellingtons of No. 205 Group and the heavy bomber units in Egypt were organized thus:

No. 231 Wing (Nos 37 and 70 Squadrons) at Abu Suier (Wellington ICs)

No. 236 Wing (Nos 108 and 148 Squadrons) at LG 237 (Wellington ICs)

No. 238 Wing (Nos 40 and 104 Squadrons) at Kabrit(Wellington ICs and Wellington IIs)

No. 242 Wing (No. 160 Squadron) at Aqir (Liberator IIs)

No. 245 Wing (No. 462 Squadron) at Fayid (Halifax IIs)

In December the bombing force in North Africa was reinforced by another two squadrons from the UK (Nos 142 and 150 Squadrons with Wellington IIIs) to support operations in Tunisia. No. 330 Wing was formed in North Africa on 9 December to take control of the two squadrons. At the end of 1943 two of the squadrons in the Middle East (Nos 108 and 148) were disbanded. The Liberators of No. 108 Squadron had already been re-designated as the 'Special Liberator Flight', involved in supply dropping operations to partisans in the Balkans, and was later re-numbered as No. 148 Squadron. In January 1943 No. 160 Squadron was absorbed by the re-formed No. 178 Squadron. By the end of February the order of battle for the Group was:

No. 40 Squadron at Gardabia East, under the direct control of Group HQ (Wellington ICs)

No. 231 Wing (Nos 37 and 70 Squadrons) at Gardabia East
(Wellington ICs and Wellington IIIs respectively)

No. 236 Wing (Nos 104 and 462 R.AAF. Squadrons) at Gardabia Main
(Wellington IIs and Halifax IIs respectively)

No. 178 Squadron was at Shandur with its Liberator IIs, under the direct control of RAF Middle East Command. No. 330 Wing (Nos 142 and 150 with Wellington IIIs) was at Blida, now under the control of the Northwest African Strategic Air Forces. In May, with the invasion of Sicily pending, three more squadrons (Nos 420, 424 and 425 RCAF) were moved from the UK to North Africa on a temporary basis. By this time No. 178 Squadron was operating a few Halifaxes due to a shortage of serviceable Liberators. By July 1943 the nine Wellington squadrons were all gathered together in the Kairouan area in Tunisia, under the control of No. 205 Group:

No. 231 Wing (Nos 37 and 70 Squadrons) at Temmar
(Wellington IIIs and Xs)

No. 236 Wing (Nos 40 and 104 Squadrons) at Hani West
(Wellington IIs, IIIs and Xs)

No. 330 Wing (Nos 142 and 150 Squadrons) at Kairouan West
(Wellington IIIs and Xs)

No. 331 Wing (Nos 420, 424 and 425 Squadrons, RCAF) at Zina and
Pavillier (Wellington Xs)

The four-engined bombers of Nos 178 and 462 Squadrons were at Hosc Raui, under the control of USAAF IX Bomber Command, and later moved to Terria and El Adem. In October the three squadrons of No. 331 Wing returned to the UK. At the end of 1943 the six Wellington squadrons moved from North Africa to Italy. The four-engined bombers would remain at El Adem for a while longer, still under the control of IX Bomber Command. At the end of January 1944 the order of battle was:

No. 231 Wing (Nos 37 and 70 Squadrons) at Tortorella (Wellington Xs)

No. 236 Wing (Nos 40 and 104 Squadrons) at Foggia Main
(Wellington IIIs and Xs)

No. 330 Wing (Nos 142 and 150 Squadrons) at Cerignola No. 3
(Wellington Xs)

Nos 178 and 462 Squadrons at El Adem (Liberator IIIs and IVs and
Halifax IIs)

In February No. 31 Squadron SAAF arrived in Palestine, without aircraft, and would eventually join No. 205 Group in Italy. No. 462 Squadron, en route to Italy, was re-numbered as No. 614 Squadron. In April No. 34 Squadron SAAF arrived in Palestine, also without aircraft, and No. 178 Squadron had now moved to Italy. By the end of July all the bomber squadrons were in Italy, and the two SAAF squadrons were operational. This order of battle would pertain until the end of the war, although there were occasional changes of airfields, sometimes due to the weather:

No. 2 SAAF Wing (Nos 31 and 34 Squadrons SAAF) at Celone
(Liberator IVs)

No. 231 Wing (Nos 37 and 70 Squadrons) at Tortorella (Wellington Xs)

No. 236 Wing (Nos 40 and 104 Squadrons) at Foggia Main
(Wellington IIIs and Xs)

No. 240 Wing (Nos 178 and 614 Squadrons) at Amendola
(Liberator IIIs and IVs and Halifax IIs respectively)

No. 330 Wing (Nos 142 and 150 Squadrons) at Regina (Wellington Xs)

In October 1944 No. 37 Squadron began to re-equip with Liberators, signalling the beginning of the end of Wellington operations with the Group. October also marked the end of the service of Nos 142 and 150 Squadrons in the Mediterranean theatre, and both were temporarily disbanded. All the Group's squadrons were gradually converted to Liberators, and by the end of April 1945 the final order of battle was:

No. 2 SAAF Wing (Nos 31 and 34 Squadrons SAAF) at Celone
(Liberator VIs)

No. 231 Wing (Nos 37 and 70 Squadrons) at Tortorella (Liberator VIs)

No. 236 Wing (Nos 40 and 104 Squadrons) at Foggia Main (Liberator VIs)

No. 240 Wing (Nos 178 and 614 Squadrons) at Amendola
(Liberator IVs and VIIs respectively)

APPENDIX III

The Squadrons

THE FIRST IN ACTION – *No. 216 Squadron*

Badge: An eagle, wings elevated, holding in the claws a bomb.

Motto: *CCXVI dona ferens* (216 bearing gifts)

Authority: King Edward VIII, May 1936

The squadron registered this badge and motto, which had been in use previously for a number of years.

In April 1931 the Squadron was designated as a 'bomber-transport' unit, and at the outbreak of war was based at Heliopolis in Egypt equipped with Vickers Valentias and Bristol Bombays. It carried out a number of bombing operations between June 1940 and January 1941, most of which were directed at Sidi Barrani, at the ports of Tobruk and Derna, and the airfields at El Gubbi, El Adem and Benina. Although Heliopolis remained as the Squadron's base throughout its brief period of operations, it operated via Mersa Matruh, Maaten Bagush, and Fuka/Fuka Satellite, due to the distances involved for its Bombays. The venerable Valentias were not excused from operations, carrying out a few anti-submarine patrols in December. The last recorded bombing operation by the Squadron was on 2 January 1941, when two Bombays attacked Bardia. Since the night of 14/15 June it had flown 123 sorties (119 by Bombays and four by Valentias) in forty-nine operations, with four Bombays lost and one crashed. Eighteen men had died and two were badly injured on operations.[1]

THE WELLINGTON SQUADRONS – *No. 37 Squadron*

Badge: A hawk hooded, belled and fessed, wings elevated and addorsed. This badge is indicative of the duties of blind flying.

Motto: Wise without eyes

Authority: King George VI, April 1943

At the outbreak of war the Squadron was at Feltwell, equipped with Vickers Wellingtons. Seven hours after the outbreak of war it took part in the first bombing operation from the UK when six Wellingtons were despatched to attack German warships in the vicinity of Heligoland. It was also involved in the infamous operation to the same area on 18 December 1939 when a force of twenty-two Wellingtons, including six from No. 37 Squadron, were pounced upon by enemy fighters. No. 37 Squadron lost five of its aircraft, and a direct outcome of the battle was the decision to fit Wellingtons with armour plate and self-sealing fuel tanks. It also played a major part in the decision to end daylight bombing attacks.

In November 1940, by which time it had flown many more bombing operations in Northern Europe, No. 37 moved to the Middle East. The first Wellington ICs left Feltwell on the 8th, and arrived at Malta on the following day. Some operated from Luqa for a while, but most were in Egypt by the end of the month, initially at Kabrit, but all serviceable aircraft were at Fayid by 30 November. Its first operation was on the night of 8/9 December, when seven aircraft were despatched to attack the airfields at Benina. During the month the squadron operating via LG 60 and LG 09 as ALGs, and moved its permanent base to Shallufa on 17 December.

The Squadron spent the whole of 1941 at Shallufa, still equipped with its trusty Wellington ICs. It operated via Fuka Satellite, LG 09 and LG 104 for desert targets, and LG 21, Maaten Bagush Satellite and LG 60 were sometimes used for refuelling on return trips. Detachments were at Menidi (Greece) between 12 and 22 February, between 7 and 23 March, and between 4 and 19 April, and these aircraft sometimes operated via Paramythia. During the crisis in Iraq it was at Shaibah between 1 and 12 May, with a small detachment still at Shallufa.

Following the success of the *Crusader* offensive the Squadron started to move forwards to Benina, near Benghazi, on 19 January 1942, but the move was cancelled when Rommel counter-attacked and the Squadron eventually settled at LG 76. It left there on 1 February, and moved back to Shallufa, operating via LG 09 as ALG. A large detachment was at Malta from 21 February to the last week of March, and the Squadron moved to LG 09 on 27 April to better support operations on the Gazala Line. Rommel intervened once again, winning the battle at Gazala and forcing the Squadron back to LG 224 (near Cairo) on 26 June, and then to the Suez Canal area, where it settled at Abu Suier on 29 June 1942. This remained the Squadron's home until November 1942, when Operation *Supercharge*, the breakout at El Alamein, got underway. On 6 November it moved forwards to LG 224, and on the 13th it moved forwards again to LG 106. On the 29th it moved to LG 140, where it remained until January 1943.

During January the Squadron operated detachments from Benina before moving completely to Benina on 20 January, and then it went on to El Magrun on 28 January. It moved into Tripolitania in February (Gardabia East on the 14th and Gardabia West on the 25th) to better support the Eighth Army's operations in southern Tunisia. While it was at Gardabia West it started to lose its Wellington ICs, re-equipping with **Wellington IIIs** and **Wellington X**s in March 1943. The Mark IIIs did not stay with the Squadron for long (less than a month in fact), but the Mark Xs stayed until October 1944. The next move for the Squadron came on 30 May 1943, when it moved into Tunisia (Kairouan North/Temmar) in preparation for operations against Sicily and Italy. It remained in the Kairouan area until 16 November, when it moved nearer to Tunis, to Djedeida No. 1. This was its final base in North Africa, as the proposed move to Italy came about in mid-December. By 16 December the Squadron was at Cerignola No. 2 (San Giovanni) in the Foggia area.

On 13 January 1944 the Squadron moved to Tortorella, which was to be its home until the end of the war. In October 1944 the Squadron began to be re-equipped with **Liberator VIs**, and carried out its last Wellington sorties on 13 December 1944 when ten aircraft were despatched to carry troops and supplies to Athens. The first Liberator operation was on 2/3 December, with two aircraft being despatched to drop supplies to partisans in Yugoslavia. The final operation by the Squadron came on 25/26 April when twelve Liberators went to the Freilassing marshalling yards and another completed a successful nickelling mission to Verona and Padua.

SUMMARY OF OPERATIONS:

Year	Aircraft	Sorties	Eff.	Alt.	DNCO	Lost
1940	Wellingtons	58	54	1	3	1
1941	Wellingtons	892	710	71	111	31
1942	Wellingtons	1,812	1,526	108	178	34
1943	Wellingtons	1,576	1,387	77	112	26
1944	Wellingtons	1,842	1,635	55	152	41
	Liberators	53	34	0	19	0
Totals		1,895	1,669	55	171	41
1945	Liberators	633	545	0	88	5
Totals		6,866	5,891	312	663	138

Eff: Effective sorties; **Alt:** Alternative targets bombed; **DNCO:** Did Not Complete Operation

The Squadron suffered 337 men killed in action, 79 injured, and 52 made prisoners of war.

No. 38 Squadron

Badge: A heron volant

Motto: *Ante lucem* (Before the dawn)

Authority: King George VI, February 1937

The heron was chosen because it is found in great abundance in East Anglia, where the unit was formed. A further reason was that herons rarely miss their mark, become active as twilight descends, and are formidable fighters when attacked.

The Squadron had a low-key introduction in the Second World War, and did not fly its first operation until 17 November, when six Wellingtons carried out an armed reconnaissance over the North Sea. Its first bombing operation was on 3 December 1939, when three of its Wellingtons carried out a daylight raid against German warships in the Heligoland area. Bombing operations did not begin in earnest until the German march into the Low Countries in May 1940, but after operations in Northern Europe, including attacks on the invasion ports and Berlin, the Squadron moved to the Middle East in November 1940. The sea party left Marham on 12

November, and the first **Wellington ICs** left on 22 November, arriving at Ismailia and Heliopolis on the 24th and 25th. The Squadron was established at Fayid by 7 December, and carried out its first operation on 8/9 December when six Wellingtons went to the Benina airfields.

No. 38 Squadron moved to Shallufa on 18 December, and remained there during most of its period with the night bomber formations, although it often had large detachments operating elsewhere. While at Shallufa, the Squadron used LG 60, Fuka Satellite, and LG 09 as ALGs when operating against desert targets. Following the success of Wavell's *Compass* operation, the Squadron moved a detachment to Gambut on 8 March 1941, using Benina as an ALG, and was fully established at Gambut from 31 April. However, it was not to stay there for long, and had to retreat quickly through Sidi Azeiz, Sollum, and Fuka Satellite, arriving back at Shallufa by 9 April. A detachment was at Eleusis in Greece between 11 and 15 April.

Early in August 1941 the Squadron's aircraft were moved progressively to Luqa on Malta. By the 5th most of its Wellingtons were operating from the island, and during September and most of October all of its aircraft were at Luqa. At this time the Squadron started to receive some **Wellington IIs**, but they were not a success and were all gone by the end of October. The Squadron left Malta towards the end of October, and all of its aircraft were back at Shallufa by the 29th. They were still there in January 1942, using LG 09, LG 60 and El Adem as ALGs, but were now starting to embark on a new career.

During January the Squadron started training for torpedo-dropping operations, and although still based at Shallufa, the two sections gradually began to separate operationally. The bombers operated via LG 09, Gambut and Bu-Amud (LG 147), and the torpedo aircraft operated via LG 05 (LG 'X'). This division continued into June 1942, with the bombers now operating via LG 104, LG 106, LG 117 and LG 224, and the torpedo aircraft continuing to operate via LG 05 before moving to Malta. In the following month the Squadron disappeared from No. 205 Group ORB, and was eventually transferred to the operational and administrative control No. 201 (Naval Cooperation) Group with effect from 28 July. From now on they would operate almost solely on mining and torpedo bombing operations.

SUMMARY OF OPERATIONS:

Year	Aircraft	Sorties	Eff.	Alt.	DNCO	Lost
1940	Wellingtons	68	65	0	3	0
1941	Wellingtons	1,074	919	66	89	20
1942	Wellingtons	515	323	23	169	9
Totals		1,657	1,307	89	261	29

The Squadron suffered 75 men killed in action, 10 injured, and 27 made prisoners of war.

No. 40 Squadron

Badge: A broom.

Motto: *Hostem acoe lo expellere* (To drive the enemy from the sky)

Authority: King George VI, February 1937

The broom was chosen to immortalize the frequent exhortation of Major 'Mick' Mannock, the famous World War I pilot who served with the squadron, to 'sweep the — Huns from the air!'

The Squadron's unofficial name in the Second World War was 'Abingdon's "own" squadron'. It started the war flying Fairey Battles with the Advanced Air Striking Force in France, but was fortunate to return to the UK in December 1939, before the decimation of the AASF in the Battle of France. However, the Squadron then converted to Bristol Blenheims, and suffered with the rest of the day bombers of No. 2 Group Bomber Command in the summer and autumn of 1940. It converted to Wellingtons with No. 3 Group in November 1940, and operated by night from Alconbury against targets in France and Germany. In October 1941 it was decided that No. 40 Squadron 'should be posted abroad for temporary duty in the Middle East'. It flew out in two flights of eight aircraft, the first of which left Alconbury on the night of 23/24 October but one failed to arrive at Malta.

The next flight was routed via Gibraltar, taking off from Hampstead Norris – a small OTU field on the night of 25/26 October. The first two aircraft got off, but both the heavily laden Wellingtons were damaged by hitting the hedgerows and small trees at the end of the take-off run. The third crashed after taking off, and all ten occupants were killed. The departure of the remaining aircraft was cancelled, and they eventually left via Portreath. The home echelon continued to operate from Alconbury for a while, but on 14 February 1942 was re-numbered No. 156 Squadron. Six of the nine **Wellington IC**s that had arrived in Malta operated on the night of 28/29 October against the marshalling yards at Tripoli.

The detachment continued to operate from Luqa under very difficult conditions until February 1942, but was formally disbanded on the 14th. However, the last recorded operation from Luqa was on 16 February, after which the Air Echelon left for India via the Middle East, leaving a small Ground Echelon behind. The Squadron was then reformed at Abu Suier on 1 May 1942 from the remains of the Middle East echelon and elements that returned from India. Its first recorded operation was against the Landing Grounds at Tmimi on 22/23 June, and it moved to Shallufa on the following day. On 19 August it joined No. 238 Wing at Kabrit, and remained there up to and during the El Alamein battle.

In November 1942, following the successful conclusion of the battle, the Squadron began a series of moves forwards. On 8 November it moved to LG 222A, on the 13th to LG 104, and on the 26th to LG 237. A large detachment operated from Luqa between 8 and 23 November in order to attack targets in Tunisia, and all its operations were from the island in December and up to 21 January 1943. The ground echelon that was still at LG 237 briefly moved to Heliopolis to help with major overhaul and maintenance work, but on 20 January 1943 it moved back to LG

237, ready to receive the Wellingtons returning from Malta, and was placed under the control of No. 231 Wing.

On 4 February the Squadron began the move into Tripolitania, first to El Magrun, and then to Gardabia East by the 14th. At this time it came under the direct operational and administrative control of Group HQ, and was moved again on 13 March to a new landing ground at Gardabia South. Also in March it began to receive **Wellington IIIs**, and would operate these aircraft until April 1944. Another move to the Kairouan area (Alem East) followed at the end of May, and during the month the first **Wellington Xs** were taken on strength. The faithful ICs finally did their last work with the Squadron in June.

The Squadron would remain under Group control until 25 June, when it joined No. 104 Squadron at Hani West as part of No. 236 Wing. It stayed in the Kairouan area until November, before moving to Oudna No. 1 on the 18th prior to the impending move to Italy. This came about in December, and by the 16th it was established at Cerignola No. 2. However, conditions there were not good, and it moved on to Foggia Main by the end of the month. This would be its home until the end of the war, and in February 1945 it converted to **Liberator IVs**.

SUMMARY OF OPERATIONS:

Year	Aircraft	Sorties	Eff.	Alt.	DNCO	Lost
1941	Wellingtons	274	261	3	10	5
1942	Wellingtons	1,490	1,311	60	119	29
1943	Wellingtons	1,640	1,504	25	111	35
1944	Wellingtons	1,941	1,695	51	195	42
1945	Wellingtons	340	268	0	72	3
	Liberators	189	158	0	31	1
Totals		**529**	**426**	**0**	**103**	**4**
Grand Totals		**5,874**	**5,197**	**139**	**538**	**115**

The Squadron suffered 296 men killed in action, 61 injured, and 104 made prisoners of war.

No. 70 Squadron

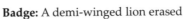

Badge: A demi-winged lion erased

Motto: *Usquam* (Anywhere)

Authority: King Edward VIII, October 1936

The lion was used as a badge by No. 70 Squadron for many years prior to 1936 and is, in fact, thought to date from the time when the unit flew aircraft powered by Napier Lion engines.

At the outbreak of the Second World War No. 70 Squadron was a bomber-transport unit, based in Egypt, and flying Vickers Valentias. On the day that Italy declared war, No.70 Squadron moved from its base at Helwan to Heliopolis, but operated purely in its transport role for the next few months. In September 1940 it became the first unit in the Middle East to be designated for conversion to Wellingtons, and the first **Wellington ICs** reached the unit on 1 September, via Malta. The Squadron moved to Kabrit on 9 September, and became operational on the night of 18/19 September when five aircraft attacked targets in the Dodecanese Islands.

The Squadron remained at Kabrit until January 1942, mainly operating via Fuka and Fuka Satellite when attacking desert targets. Detachments moved to Greece in November 1940 (at Eleusis from the 5th and at Tatoi from the 12th), and in December 1940 and January 1941 at Menidi. From 3 February the Squadron had a large detachment at El Adem, using Benina as an ALG. The detachment stayed there until Rommel attacked, and between 6 and 15 April it was forced to retreat through Sidi Azeiz, Capuzzo and Fuka, back to Kabrit. It now settled down to attacking the usual round of desert targets, usually operating via Fuka, LG 60, LG 104 and LG 253 as ALGs.

Following the *Crusader* battles the Squadron moved forwards to LG 75 in January 1942, but Rommel's counter-offensive saw it going quickly backwards again. It was at LG 104 on 5 February, and after the Axis success in the Gazala battles in June it was withdrawn to LG 224 (near Cairo) on 26 June. The Squadron then settled at Abu Suier in the Canal Zone on 29 June, and stayed there until after the Battle of El Alamein. Operations were sometimes conducted via LG 86 and LG 224, and in November 1942 it was on the move forwards again. Its first stop was at LG 224 again (6 November), then to LG 106 (11 November), and finally it crossed the border into Libya to LG 140 (30 November).

The Squadron remained at LG 140 throughout December, and then moved to Benina on 19 January 1943 and to El Magrun four days later. At this time **Wellington IIIs** began to arrive, and the old ICs saw their last action. The move into Tripolitania came in February (Gardabia East on the 19th and Gardabia West on the 25th), following on the heels of the Eighth Army as it advanced towards Tunisia. During April 1943 Wellington Xs joined the Squadron, working alongside the Mark IIIs until November. The Squadron itself moved into Tunisia on 25 May, to the Kairouan area (Temmar), from where it would operate against targets in Sicily and Italy until 15 November.

A brief stay at Djedeida No. 1, near Tunis, preceded the move to Italy in December, first to Cerignola No. 2 (20 December) and then Tortorella (29 December), its base until the end of the war. In January 1945 the Wellingtons were gradually replaced by Liberator VIs for the Squadron's final operations against the enemy.

SUMMARY OF OPERATIONS:

Year	Aircraft	Sorties	Eff.	Alt.	DNCO	Lost
1940	Wellingtons	110	97	1	12	3
1941	Wellingtons	849	756	34	59	9
1942	Wellingtons	1,800	1,573	83	144	45
1943	Wellingtons	1,517	1,352	58	107	24
1944	Wellingtons	1,998	1,754	57	187	54
1945	Liberators	505	461	0	44	3
	Wellingtons	86	60	0	26	2
Totals		591	521	0	70	5
Grand Totals		6,865	6,053	233	579	140

The Squadron suffered 341 men killed in action, 56 injured, and 99 made prisoners of war.

No. 104 Squadron

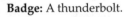

Badge: A thunderbolt.

Motto: Strike hard

Authority: King George VI, December 1936

The device in conjunction with the motto implies the unit's formidable intentions and power.

At the outbreak of the Second World War, the Squadron was a No. 6 Group training unit, and was later absorbed into No. 13 OTU. In April 1941 the Squadron was re-formed at Driffield as a Wellington unit, and began to take part in the night-bombing offensive against Germany. In mid-October 1941 it was ordered to send aircraft and some ground crew to Malta, and on 14 October the advance party left Driffield and flew to Stanton Harcourt under the command of the redoubtable Squadron Leader H. M. 'Dinghy' Young.

On the following day another twelve aircraft moved to Stanton Harcourt and three to Portreath. They should have left for Malta on the 16th, but adverse weather reports delayed their departure. Eventually, six left on the following night and arrived safely at Malta at around 0500 hours, and a seventh aircraft arrived from Portreath. These were all **Wellington IIs**, capable of carrying 4,000-lb 'blockbuster' bombs, and all flew direct to Malta without needing to break the journey at Gibraltar. They didn't have long to settle in, and six operated on the 19th against Tripoli. The home echelon continued to operate from Driffield for a while and then on 14 February 1942 it was re-numbered as No. 158 Squadron.

No. 104 Squadron remained at Luqa until January, and then started to move to Kabrit very early in the month. On 30 January RAF Station 1942 Kabrit was reformed as No. 236 Medium Bomber Wing, and assumed control of Nos 104 and 148 Squadrons. The Squadron continued to be based at Kabrit until May, operating from LG 09, LG 104 and LG 106 against desert targets. It moved to LG 106 on 13 May, and sent a detachment to Malta on the 24th. After Rommel attacked at Gazala, the Squadron moved back to Kabrit on 26 June, and remained there until after the Battle of El Alamein. With effect from 19 August 1942 the Squadron was controlled by No. 238 Wing.

November 1942 was a busy month for the Squadron, involving a series of moves in the desert and then a major 'detachment' to Malta. The first move was to LG 224 (7 November), and the first detachment to Luqa was between 7 and 13 November. The next moves in the desert were to LG 104 (12 November) and LG 237 (27 November), but by now all the Squadron's aircraft were operating from Malta and would continue to do so until 21 January 1943. The Ground Echelon remained at LG 237 until the Wellingtons returned from Malta, and then moved to Solluch on 6 February. It became operational in 205 Group again on 8/9 February, and was now under the administrative and operational control of No. 236 Wing, along with No. 40 Squadron. It moved to Gardabia Main in Tripolitania on the 14th.

The next move came in May, when the Group moved its base to the Kairouan area in Tunisia. No. 104 Squadron was to be based at Cheria (Alem East), and arrived there on 26 May 1943. A month later, on 24 June, it moved a few miles to Hani West. In July, the Squadron began to be re-equipped with **Wellington Xs**, and would operate the type until February 1945. All the Group squadrons moved nearer to Tunis in November, prior to leaving Africa for Italy, and No. 104 was briefly based at the landing ground at Oudna No. 1 from the 18th.

Its stay there lasted just over three weeks, and then it was off to Europe – first to Cerignola No. 3 (13 December) and then to Foggia Main (30 December). This was to be its home until the end of the war, and in February 1945 it converted to **Liberator VIs**. It used its new aircraft for the first time in a supply dropping operation on 14 February, but teething troubles meant that its Wellingtons carried on operating until the end of the month. The Squadron flew its last operation on 25 April 1945, when twelve Liberators went to the marshalling yards at Freilassing.

SUMMARY OF OPERATIONS:

Year	Aircraft	Sorties	Eff.	Alt.	DNCO	Lost
1941	Wellingtons	290	259	13	18	5
1942	Wellingtons	1,299	1,097	45	157	44
1943	Wellingtons	1,367	1,169	65	133	38
1944	Wellingtons	1,955	1,719	70	166	30
1945	Liberators	241	223	1	17	1
	Wellingtons	253	207	0	46	2
Totals		**494**	**430**	**1**	**63**	**3**
Grand Totals		**5,405**	**4,674**	**194**	**537**	**120**

The Squadron suffered 350 men killed in action, 45 injured, and 52 made prisoners of war.

No. 108 Squadron

Badge: An oak leaf

Motto: *Viribus contractis* (With gathered strength)

Authority: King George VI, July 1938

The unit was originally formed at Stonehenge and it adopted an oak leaf as a badge being symbolic of strength and age.

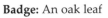

The Squadron was re-formed at Kabrit in Egypt on 1 August 1941 as a bomber squadron equipped with **Wellington ICs**, and first operated on 27/28 August when one Wellington was despatched to Benghazi. It moved to Fayid on 12 September, using LG 253, LG 104, LG 60, LG 09 and LG 105 as ALGs for desert targets. In November the Squadron began to be re-equipped with **Liberator IIs**, the first aircraft arriving on the 29th. However, the second one did not arrive until 9 December, and the first operation did not take place until 11 January 1942 when a single Liberator went to Tripoli.

By March 1942 all the Squadron's Wellingtons were at LG 09, only returning to Fayid when major inspections were due. The few Liberators continued to operate from base. On 20 May the Wellingtons moved to LG 105, but the Liberators continued to operate from Fayid and in June were 'attached' to No. 159 Squadron and designated as the 'Special Liberator Flight'. The Wellingtons then moved to Kabrit on 26 June, sometimes operating via LG 86 and LG 224, and when the front stabilized at El Alamein it moved forwards again to LG 237 ('Kilo 40') near Cairo on 19 August. At this time the now all-Wellington Squadron joined No. 236 Wing alongside No. 148 Squadron.

Following the Battle of El Alamein, the Squadron made the usual move forwards to support the advancing Eighth Army. It went to LG 09 on 13 November, but then was halted in its tracks. The last operation by its Wellingtons was on 25 November, when five aircraft attacked the landing grounds at Marble Arch. On the following day all aircrews were split up between Nos 37, 70 and 148 Squadrons, and the rest of the Squadron personnel were moved back to LG 237 to take over the Special Liberator Flight. It was formally disbanded on 25 December 1942.

SUMMARY OF OPERATIONS:

Year	Aircraft	Sorties	Eff.	Alt.	DNCO	Lost
1941	Wellingtons	281	261	9	11	1
1942	Liberators	66	46	0	20	2
	Wellingtons	1,475	1,312	45	118	24
Totals		**1,541**	**1,358**	**45**	**138**	**26**
Grand Totals		**1,822**	**1,619**	**54**	**149**	**27**

The Squadron suffered 75 men killed in action, 25 injured, and 43 made prisoners of war.

No. 142 Squadron

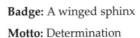

Badge: A winged sphinx

Motto: Determination

Authority: King George VI, June 1937

The badge commemorates the Squadron's early association with Egypt.

In the early months of the Second World War the Squadron served with the Advanced Air Striking Force in France, flying Fairey Battles. On 10 May 1940 it gained the distinction of being the first AASF unit to bomb the advancing German forces as they swept into the Low Countries. Later that month it was one of the Battle squadrons that attacked the Meuse bridges in an attempt to slow the German advance. It was withdrawn to the UK in June 1940, and converted to Wellingtons prior to joining the strategic bombing offensive against Germany.

In December 1942 it was ordered to move to Algeria, along with No. 150 Squadron, to support the Allied landings in north-west Africa. It was established at Blida by the 19th with its **Wellington IIIs**, the two squadrons being organized into No. 330 Wing. Its first operation came on 28 December, when a single aircraft set off to bomb the docks at Bizerte. It was not an auspicious start, as the 4,000-pounder hung-up and had to be released manually. It was reported to have fallen near barracks in the west of Bizerte town.

The Squadron remained at Blida until May 1943, when it moved eastwards to Fontaine Chaude, but this was only a temporary move. On 26 May it was off again to Kairouan West (Allani), to join the other Wellington squadrons in North Africa. In June it started to re-equip with **Wellington Xs**, and also came under the effective operational control of No. 205 Group for the first time. However, this was not formally confirmed until July.

In November the Wellington squadrons moved nearer to Tunis prior to their transfer to Italy, and No. 142 found itself at Oudna No. 2 for about five weeks. By 21 December 1943 it was at Cerignola No. 3 (Toretta), and moved to Amendola on 15 March 1944. Following another move to Regina on 4 July, it was disbanded on 5 October and its aircraft and crews distributed to the other Wellington squadrons in Italy. However, this was not the end of its war, and the Squadron was reformed at Gransden Lodge in the UK as a Mosquito squadron with No. 8 (PFF) Group's Light Night Striking Force.

SUMMARY OF OPERATIONS:

Year	Aircraft	Sorties	Eff.	Alt.	DNCO	Lost
1942	Wellingtons	5	2	1	2	0
1943	Wellingtons	1,652	1,506	30	116	36
1944	Wellingtons	1,338	1,156	41	141	29
Totals		2,995	2,664	72	259	65

The Squadron suffered 166 men killed in action, 33 injured, and 22 made prisoners of war.

No. 148 Squadron

Badge: Two battle axes in saltire

Motto: Trusty

Authority: King George VI, February 1938

The battle axes were selected as being well-tried and formidable weapons.

A few days after the outbreak of the war the Squadron moved to Harwell and became a training unit with No. 6 Group, and was later absorbed into No. 15 OTU. It was re-formed in Malta in December 1940 to take control of the *ad hoc* formation of Wellington bombers then operating from the island. Equipped with **Wellington ICs**, the new Squadron remained at Luqa until March 1941, always operating under very difficult conditions. It was eventually forced out of Malta and withdrawn to the Middle East, its aircraft starting to leave on 2 March. The sea party left on 23 March, and by the 26th all were more or less established at Kabrit.

Kabrit was to remain its home for the next year or so, with the Squadron operating via Fuka, Fuka Satellite, LG 09 and LG 60 for attacks on desert targets. However, detachments from the Squadron were back at Luqa for two weeks between 12 and 27 April 1941, and again between 25 June and 22 July. Meanwhile, operations continued against desert targets, sometimes using El Adem, LG 75, LG 'Z' and LG 104 as ALGs. In October the first **Wellington IIs** arrived on the Squadron, and the 'final' operations with the old ICs took place. However, the Merlin-engined aircraft were not a success in the desert, and the Squadron was relieved to get ICs back in April 1942.

In March and April 1942 the Squadron operated from LG 106, ten miles east of El Alamein, and a detachment was on Malta between 21 and 26 April. On 15 May all personnel moved from Kabrit to LG 106, but were back at Kabrit by 26 June as the Eighth Army retreated into the El Alamein positions. As the front stabilized and preparations for a major battle were underway, No. 148 Squadron moved forwards again to LG 237, ten miles west of Cairo. Here it remained until the general advance after the successful conclusion of the El Alamein battle took it back to LG 106 on 12 November 1942, and then on to LG 09 on the following day.

On 1 December No. 148 Squadron moved to LG 167 (Bir el Beheira No. 2) near Gambut, and on the 8th a detachment of twelve Wellingtons was sent to Malta. A week later the Squadron was disbanded, and its crews and aircraft absorbed by the other Wellington units on the island and in Libya. It would soon rise again. On 14 March 1943, it reformed at Gambut in the 'Special Duties' role, equipped with Halifaxes and Liberators, responsible for supplying Partisan groups throughout the Balkans and as far afield as Poland. At the end of the war the Squadron re-equipped with standard bomber Liberators, moving back to Egypt in November 1945, where it was again disbanded on 15 January 1946.

SUMMARY OF OPERATIONS:[2]

Year	Aircraft	Sorties	Eff.	Alt.	DNCO	Lost
1940	Wellingtons	103	81	14	8	4
1941	Wellingtons	938	816	39	83	23
1942	Wellingtons	1,767	1,561	33	173	42
Totals		2,808	2,458	86	264	69

The Squadron suffered 167 men killed in action, 25 injured, and 47 made prisoners of war.

No. 150 Squadron

Badge: In front of a cross voided, two arrows in saltire, the points uppermost

Motto: Always ahead'

Authority: King George VI, March 1939

The cross is adopted in reference to the arms of Greece, where the unit formed. The arrows symbolize service as a fighter squadron.

In the early months of the Second World War the Squadron served with the Advanced Air Striking Force in France, equipped with Fairey Battles, and was one of the units that attacked the Meuse bridges in an attempt to stem the German advance. Withdrawn to the UK in June 1940, it was re-equipped with Wellingtons and took part in the strategic air offensive against Germany. In December 1942, after having flown 1,717 sorties from the UK with Battles and Wellingtons, it was ordered to move to Algeria to support the Allied landings in north-west Africa.

It was established at Blida by the 19th with its **Wellington IIIs**, and along with No. 142 Squadron was organized into No. 330 Wing. Its first operation came on 28 December, when six aircraft set off to bomb the docks at Bizerte. The Squadron remained at Blida until May 1943, when it moved eastwards to Fontaine Chaude, but this was only a temporary move. On 26 May it was off again to Kairouan West (Allani), to join the other Wellington squadrons in North Africa. In June it started to re-equip with **Wellington Xs**, and also came under the effective operational control of No. 205 Group for the first time. However, this was not formally confirmed until July.

In November the Wellington squadrons moved nearer to Tunis prior to their transfer to Italy, and No. 142 found itself at Oudna No. 2 for about five weeks. By 21 December 1943 it was at Cerignola No. 3 (Toretta), and moved to Amendola on 15 February 1944. Following another move to Regina on 4 July, it was disbanded on 5 October and its aircraft and crews distributed to the other Wellington squadrons in Italy. However, this was not the end of its war, and the Squadron was reformed on 1 November at Fiskerton from 'C' Flight of No. 550 Squadron, equipped with Lancasters. Between 11 November 1944 and 25 April 1945 it flew 827 operational sorties, and dropped more than 3,827 tons of bombs on enemy targets.

SUMMARY OF OPERATIONS:

Year	Aircraft	Sorties	Eff.	Alt.	DNCO	Lost
1942	Wellingtons	16	11	0	5	0
1943	Wellingtons	1,719	1,563	51	105	22
1944	Wellingtons	1,433	1,251	49	133	30
Totals		3,168	2,825	100	243	52

The Squadron suffered 162 men killed in action, 10 injured, and 20 made prisoners of war.

THE FIRST LIBERATOR UNITS – *NOS 159 AND 160 SQUADRONS*

Badge: In front of logs enflamed, a peacock's head erased, in the beak a woodman's axe.

Motto: *Quo non, quando non* (Whither not? When not?)

Authority: King George VI, November 1946

The badge was awarded after the end of the war, and after the Squadron's service in India and over Burma. The peacock's head commemorates its association with Burma, the axe its pathfinder activities in blazing the trail, and the flames of fire suggest the destruction caused by its bombing.

Badge: A Sinhalese lion rampant holding a Sinhalese sword

Motto: *Api soya paragasamu* (We seek and strike)

Authority: King George VI, January 1945

The design is indicative of the unit's operations from Ceylon.

Both these units had a brief (and partial) involvement in the Middle East, but did form the basis of No. 178 Squadron, which had a long and illustrious history in the theatre. No. 159 Squadron was formed at Molesworth, Huntingdonshire, on 2 January 1942, as a Liberator heavy-bomber unit for eventual transfer to the Far East. Records of its early history are incomplete, but we do know that the air echelon arrived in the Middle East some time in late-May or early-June 1942, and were detained there by Tedder.

No. 160 Squadron was formed at Thurleigh, Bedfordshire, on 16 January 1942, also as a Liberator unit bound eventually for the Far East. Its air echelon arrived in the Suez Canal Zone in en route to India in June, and five of its aircraft were used to provide air cover for a west-bound convoy to Malta. It, too, was detained in the Middle East. We know that No. 159 Squadron was based at Fayid by 7 June, and was joined there No. 160 Squadron on 11 June. Both echelons were serviced by elements of Nos 147, 454 and 458 Squadrons. The first recorded operation by the joint unit was on 11 June 1942 when a single Liberator bombed the dockyards and shipping at Taranto.

While operating from Egypt the two units were known as Nos 159 and 160 Squadrons (Middle East Detachments). They moved to St Jean in Palestine on 2 July, and then to Aqir on 12 August. On 16 September 1942 the joint squadron was restyled as No. 160 Squadron, and the surviving Liberators of No. 159 Squadron were sent on to India Squadron between September and November 1942. No. 160 Squadron moved to Shandur on the Great Bitter Lake on 8 November, and was absorbed by No. 178 Squadron on 15 January 1943.

Although it is difficult to be sure about the operations of the two units, it seems that they flew in the region of 262 sorties as Nos 159 and 160 Squadrons (Middle East Detachments) and No. 160 Squadron. During this time they lost seven aircraft, with thirty-two men killed in action, one injured and five captured.

No. 178 Squadron

Badge: A demi-lion erased, holding a flash of lightning

Motto: *Irae emissarii* (Emissaries of wrath)

Authority: King George VI, May 1945

The Squadron operated in or over North Africa, Sicily and Southern Europe. The lion is symbolic of Africa and the offensive spirit of the unit, and the flash of lightning its striking power.

The Squadron was formed at Shandur, in the Suez Canal Zone of Egypt, on 15 January 1943 from officers and aircrew of No. 160 Squadron, and equipped with **Liberator IIs**. It inherited some of the ground staff of Nos 159 and 160 Squadrons (Middle East Detachments), and also personnel of No. 147 Squadron (a servicing unit attached to No. 160 Squadron). Its first operation was on 16/17 January 1943 when two Liberators bombed the primary target of Tarhuna Gate, Tripoli, and another bombed Benito Gate, Tripoli, as an alternative.

The Squadron moved to Hosc Raui, twenty miles south of Benghazi, on 4 March, and remained there until October. Due to supply and serviceability problems with the Liberators it took on board some **Halifax IIs** in May, and continued to operate both types until September. At this time the Liberators and Halifaxes of Nos 178 and 462 Squadrons (No. 240 Wing) were operating under the control of USAAF 9th Bomber Command. Also in September, the Squadron started to receive some **Liberator IIIs**, and the Halifaxes were gradually phased out. In October 1943 No. 178 Squadron moved the short distance to the neighbouring airfield at Terria, its home until the end of the year. It was still operating at a low level, as it had very few serviceable Liberators on charge, but in November the Squadron carried out their first ever mine-laying operation.

The New Year brought another move, to El Adem, near Tobruk, and also the arrival of **Liberator IVsv**. The main occupation of the Squadron at this time was still mine-laying, and would remain so until the move to Italy. This came about in March 1944, when No. 178 Squadron moved to Celone and came under the administrative and operational control of No. 205 Group. On 4 July it moved again to Amendola, its home until the end of the war. Its final operations came on 25 April 1945, when twelve aircraft went to the marshalling yards at Freilassing and another two carried out a special nickelling mission to Fiume, Trieste, Udine, Pola, Ljubljana, Maribor, Zagreb, and Karlovac.

SUMMARY OF OPERATIONS:

Year	Aircraft	Sorties	Eff.	Alt.	DNCO	Lost
1943	Halifaxes	137	117	3	17	1
	Liberators	464	355	35	74	5
Totals		**601**	**472**	**38**	**91**	**6**
1944	Liberators	1,555	1,346	6	203	27
1945	Liberators	682	583	1	98	4
Grand Totals		**2,838**	**2,401**	**45**	**392**	**37**

The Squadron suffered 200 men killed in action, 9 injured, and 24 made prisoners of war.

THE CANADIANS – *NOS 420, 424 AND 425 SQUADRONS, RCAF*

Badge: A snowy owl

Motto: *Pugnamus finitum* (We fight to the finish)

Authority: King George VI, March 1943

351

Badge: An heraldic tiger's head erased

Motto: *Castingandos castigamus* (We chastise those who deserve to be chastised)

Authority: King George VI, June 1945

Badge: A lark Volant

Motto: *Jet e plumerai* (I shall pluck you)

Authority: King George VI, January 1945

In May 1943, with the invasion of Sicily pending, it was decided to reinforce the night bomber squadrons then based in Tunisia, and three squadrons were moved from the UK to North Africa. They were Nos 420, 424 and 425 Squadrons, RCAF, part of No. 6 (RCAF) Group, Bomber Command, and based respectively at Middleton St George, Dalton and Dishforth with their **Wellington Xs**. By 4 June they were all established briefly at Telergma in Algeria, but moved to Zina (Nos 420 and 425 Squadrons) and Pavillier (No. 424 Squadron) in Tunisia later in the month.

The three squadrons came under the effective control of No. 205 Group in late June, but this was not formally confirmed until July. The first operation for Nos 420 and 425 Squadrons was against Sciacca airfield in Sicily on 26 June, and that of No. 424 Squadron was against the port of San Giovanni on the following night. All three squadrons moved the short distance to Hani East late in September 1943, but by 17 October they were on their way back to the UK.

SUMMARY OF OPERATIONS:

Squadron	Sorties	Eff.	Alt.	DNCO	Lost
420	728	695	3	30	10
424	667	631	2	34	14
425	731	683	9	28	9
Totals	2,126	2,009	14	92	33

The three Squadrons had 108 men killed in action and another eight injured.

THE HALIFAX UNITS – *NOS 10/227 AND 76/454/462 SQUADRON DETACHMENTS*

Badge: A winged arrow

Motto: *Rem acu tangere* (To hit the mark)

Authority: King George VI, September 1937

The winged arrow is to indicate great speed and is also a reminder that the air bomb is the successor of the arrow of medieval times.

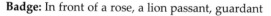

Badge: In front of a rose, a lion passant, guardant

Motto: Resolute

Authority: King George VI, March 1938

A white rose is introduced in the badge to commemorate the Squadron's association with Yorkshire where it was formed. The lion in its guardant attitude is indicative of readiness to attack or defend at all times.

The Handley Page Halifax was a mainstay of Bomber Command for much of the Second World War, but played only a small part in bomber operations in the Middle East and Mediterranean. It began in June/July 1942 when sixteen **Halifax IIs** and crews each of Nos 10 and 76 Squadrons were detached from their bases at Leeming and Linton-on-Ouse, Yorkshire, to the Middle East. Both detachments were based at Aqir, Palestine from 5 July, where No. 10 Squadron was serviced by elements of No. 227 Squadron and No. 76 Squadron by elements of No. 454 Squadron, two squadrons that were non-operational and without aircraft. The support for No. 76 Squadron Detachment was later provided by No. 462 Squadron (RAAF).

The units were first shown in No. 205 Group ORB as 'Halifaxes of 249 Wing', and their first recorded operation was on 11 July when a single Halifax went to Tobruk. They remained at Aqir until September, by which time they had launched 280 sorties and lost seven aircraft. On 7 September the two detachments were amalgamated into...

No. 462 Squadron, RAAF

(No badge authorized)

The Squadron was formed at Fayid in the Suez Canal Zone of Egypt on 7 September 1942 by the amalgamation of Nos 10/227 and 76/462 Squadron detachments. Although nominally an 'Australian' unit, due to the manner of its formation it contained very few Australians. Its first operation was on 8/9 September when five Halifaxes bombed shipping and jetties at Tobruk. Following the Battle of El Alamein, it moved first to LG 237 (Kilo 40) on 13 November, and then into Libya to LG 167 (Bir el Beheira No. 2) on 29 November. Serviceability was always a problem for the four-engined bombers, and only fifty-seven sorties were flown in October and seventy-three in November. By the middle of December the Halifaxes were back at LG 237, and only eight sorties were despatched during the month.

At the beginning of January 1943 the original aircrews from Nos 10 and 76 Squadrons began their journey back to the UK, and on the 18th the rest of the Squadron moved back again to LG 167 'where a 2nd tour of operations would begin'. The road convoy had no sooner arrived at the new location than they were told that they had to move on to Solluch, south of Benghazi, and here its main role became attacks on harbours and shipping in Sicily. It moved again in February to Gardabia Main in Tunisia to operate in support of the ground campaign there, returning to Cyrenaica when these operations drew to a close in late May.

At this time the Liberators and Halifaxes of Nos 178 and 462 Squadrons (No. 240

Wing) were operating under the control of USAAF 9th Bomber Command. They operated from a succession of airfields in Cyrenaica: Hosc Raui (22 May – 1 October 1943), Terria (1 October 1943 – 1 January 1944), and El Adem (from 1 January 1944). On 1 February 1944 the Squadron departed from Libya for Celone in Italy, but was disbanded en route and renumbered as No. 614 Squadron.

SUMMARY OF OPERATIONS:

Year	Aircraft	Sorties	Eff.	Alt.	DNCO	Lost
1942	Halifaxes	234	202	8	24	5
1943	Halifaxes	734	599	25	110	11
1944	Halifaxes	65	47	0	18	1
Total		1,033	848	33	152	17

The Squadron suffered twenty-four men killed in action, four injured, and three made prisoners of war.

No. 614 (County of Glamorgan) Squadron

Badge: On a demi-terrestrial globe, a dragon passant

Motto: *Codaf i geislo* (I rise to search)

Authority: King George VI, December 1938

The red dragon shows the connection with Wales.

The Squadron was originally formed in Cardiff on 1 June 1937 as an Auxiliary Air Force army co-operation unit, and by the outbreak of war had a collection of Hinds, Audaxes and Lysanders on strength. It began to re-equip as a bomber squadron at Odiham, Hampshire, in August 1942, equipped with Bristol Blenheims. The Squadron was transferred to North Africa in November 1942 in support of the *Torch* landings, and was eventually disbanded in Sicily in February 1944.

On 3 March 1944 it was revived as a bomber squadron when No. 462 (RAAF) Squadron was re-numbered en route from El Adem to Celone in Italy. Its first operation was on 11 March 1944 when seven Halifaxes went to the marshalling yards at Genoa. On 10 May 1944 it moved to Stornara, and on 15 July 1944 it moved again to Amendola. In August 1944 it began to convert to **Liberator VIIIs**, although the Halifaxes remained on strength until March 1945. The Squadron's final operation was on 25 April 1945, when eight Liberators went to the marshalling yards at Freilassing. It was disbanded at Amendola in July 1945, and renumbered as No. 214 Squadron. It was reformed as a fighter squadron at Llandow in South Wales in May 1946, and finally disbanded in March 1957.

SUMMARY OF OPERATIONS:

Year	Aircraft	Sorties	Eff.	Alt.	DNCO	Lost
1944	Halifaxes	815	710	3	102	15
	Liberators	101	83	0	18	0
Totals		916	793	3	120	15
1945	Halifaxes	71	61	0	10	0
	Liberators	395	350	0	45	1
Totals		466	411	0	55	1
Grand Totals		1,382	1,204	3	175	16

The Squadron lost seventy-four men killed in action, four injured, and twenty made prisoners of war.

No. 2 SAAF Wing

At the end of 1943 the decision was made to form two heavy night bomber squadrons in South Africa for service with No. 205 Group, both to be equipped with Liberators. The first to be established was No. 31 Squadron, closely followed by No. 34 Squadron, and both eventually came under the control of No. 2 Wing SAAF. The Administrative Instruction (External) No. 655 announcing the formation of the Wing was dated 14 April 1944, and the Wing HQ was established at Kilo 40 early in May 1942, under the command of Colonel J.A. Williams DSO, DFC.

No. 31 Squadron SAAF

On 30 January 1944 the ground staff and personnel of No. 31 Squadron left Swartkop Air Station and boarded the troopship SS *Orbita* bound for Suez. It arrived there on 19 February and the passengers boarded a train bound for Heliopolis. From there they were taken to the SAAF Base Depot at Almaza, where the aircrew were sent on to 1675 HCU Unit at Lydda in Palestine to familiarize themselves with the Liberator bomber.

On 19 April an Advance party of the ground staff left Almaza for LG 237 (Kilo 40), and on 27 April the first eight **Liberator MkVIs** landed. By 3 May the Squadron had its full allotment of sixteen aircraft. Its first operation took place on 27 May 1940, to Kastelli Pediada airfield in Crete. The move to Italy followed in June, the Squadron arriving at Celone on the 16th. On 19/20 July the Squadron operated for the first time under the control of No. 2 Wing SAAF, having previously operated under No. 240 Wing. Operations continued from their new base until January 1945, when atrocious weather made the airfield unserviceable and the aircraft had to operate from Foggia Main for a few weeks. The final operation was on 30 April 1945, when a single aircraft carried out a nickelling mission to Karlovac, Zagreb, Sisak, Brezice and Pola.

SUMMARY OF OPERATIONS:

Year	Aircraft	Sorties	Eff.	Alt.	DNCO	Lost
1944	Liberators	797	695	1	101	25
1945	Liberators	624	542	0	82	2
Grand Totals		**1,421**	**1,237**	**1**	**183**	**27**

No. 34 Squadron SAAF

34 SQUADRON

The bulk of the Squadron's ground crews left South Africa aboard HMT *Salween* at the beginning of March 1944, and the Squadron came into existence officially at Almaza on 14 April 1944. It moved out to Kilo 40 as a 'shadow' squadron on 3 May. We have little information on the early days of the unit, as its ORB does not start until 4 June 1944, when the Squadron arrived at Rasin-al-Boud (near Aleppo in Syria).

They arrived at their new location on 4 June, but were only there for just over three weeks before the ground personnel were on the move again to the Delta, leaving the Aleppo area on 27 June. All the aircraft and aircrews, along with around eighty ground crew, left for Kilo 40 on the next day. The Liberators started flying to Celone on 5 July, carrying most of the flying personnel and 150 ground staff. The boat party arrived at Taranto in the SS *Empire Pride* on 17 July, and began the long road journey to the Foggia area, eventually arriving at Celone on 26 July.

Its first operation was on the night of 21 July 1944, when four aircraft set off for the Pardubice (Fanto) oil refinery in Czechoslovakia. Operations continued from Celone until January 1945, when bad weather made the airfield unserviceable, and the aircraft had to operate from Foggia Main for a few weeks. The final operation was on the night of 25 April 1945, when twelve aircraft were despatched to the marshalling yards at Freilassing.

SUMMARY OF OPERATIONS:

Year	Aircraft	Sorties	Eff.	Alt.	DNCO	Lost
1944	Liberators	640	568	0	72	11
1945	Liberators	602	514	1	87	6
Grand Totals		**1,242**	**1,082**	**1**	**159**	**17**

The two Squadrons suffered 214 men killed in action, 32 made prisoners of war, and 49 missing. In 1992, 67 ex-members of 31 and 34 Squadrons were awarded the Polish Warsaw Cross for the role in the relief operations.

NOTES

1. All the statistics are derived from the author's own research into the Operational Record Books of the squadrons involved, and are all subject to the reservations mentioned in the Preface.
2. Includes the activities of the Luqa Wellington Atachment prior to the formation of the Squadron.

APPENDIX IV

Maps

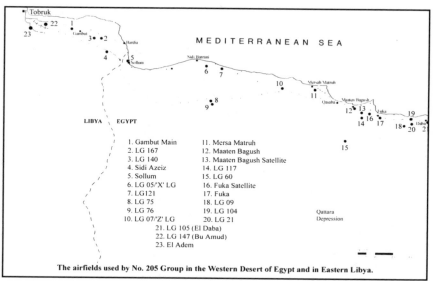

1. Gambut Main
2. LG 167
3. LG 140
4. Sidi Azeiz
5. Sollum
6. LG 05/'X' LG
7. LG121
8. LG 75
9. LG 76
10. LG 07/'Z' LG
11. Mersa Matruh
12. Maaten Bagush
13. Maaten Bagush Satellite
14. LG 117
15. LG 60
16. Fuka Satellite
17. Fuka
18. LG 09
19. LG 104
20. LG 21
21. LG 105 (El Daba)
22. LG 147 (Bu Amud)
23. El Adem

The airfields used by No. 205 Group in the Western Desert of Egypt and in Eastern Libya.

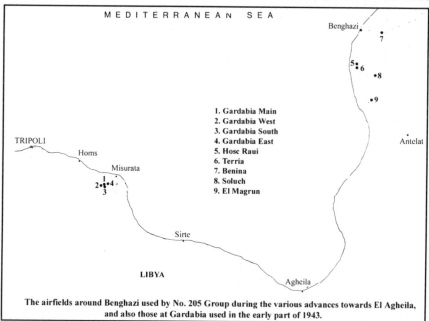

1. Gardabia Main
2. Gardabia West
3. Gardabia South
4. Gardabia East
5. Hosc Raui
6. Terria
7. Benina
8. Soluch
9. El Magrun

The airfields around Benghazi used by No. 205 Group during the various advances towards El Agheila, and also those at Gardabia used in the early part of 1943.

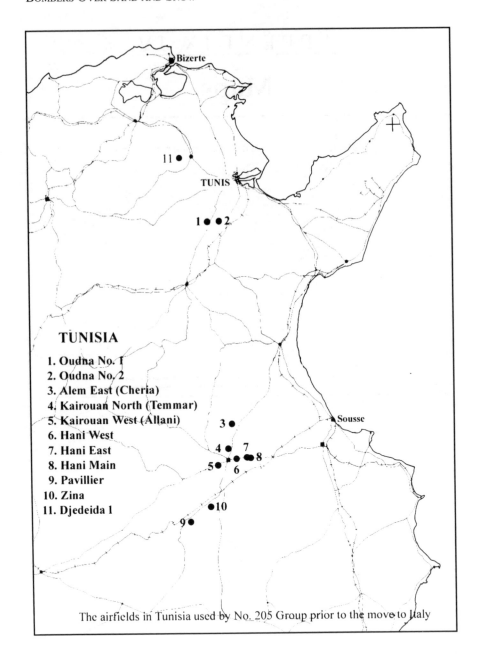

TUNISIA

1. Oudna No. 1
2. Oudna No. 2
3. Alem East (Cheria)
4. Kairouan North (Temmar)
5. Kairouan West (Allani)
6. Hani West
7. Hani East
8. Hani Main
9. Pavillier
10. Zina
11. Djedeida 1

The airfields in Tunisia used by No. 205 Group prior to the move to Italy

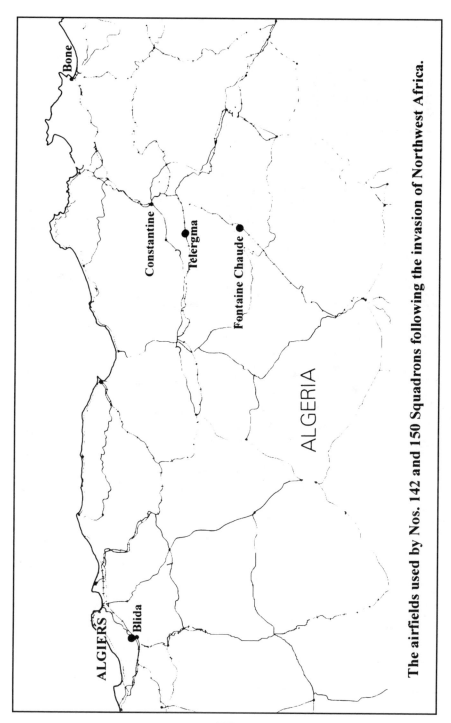

The airfields used by Nos. 142 and 150 Squadrons following the invasion of Northwest Africa.

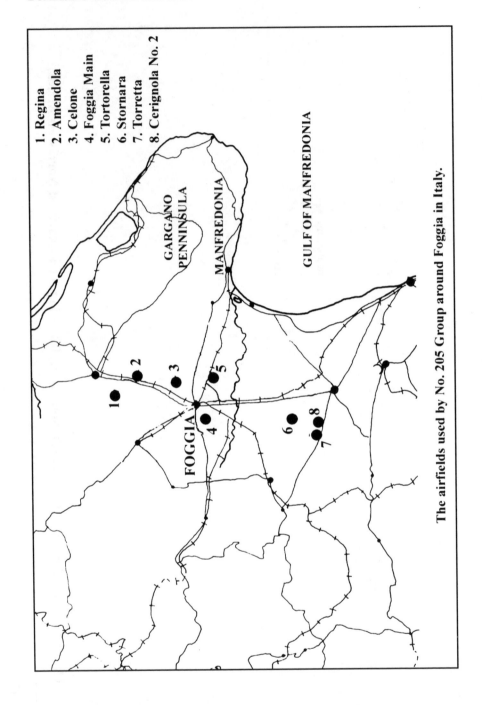

1. Regina
2. Amendola
3. Celone
4. Foggia Main
5. Tortorella
6. Stornara
7. Torretta
8. Cerignola No. 2

GARGANO PENNINSULA

MANFREDONIA

GULF OF MANFREDONIA

FOGGIA

The airfields used by No. 205 Group around Foggia in Italy.

Bibliography

African Trilogy, the Desert War 1940–1943. Alan Moorhead, Cassell.

Air War Europa. Eric Hammel, Pacifica Press.

Another Dawn Another Dusk. Kenneth Ballantyne, Laundry Cottage Books.

Beam Bombers, the Secret War of No. 109 Squadron. Michael Cumming, Sutton.

Bomber Losses in the Middle East and Mediterranean. David Gunby and Pelham Temple, Midland Publishing.

Bomber Squadrons of the RAF and their Aircraft. Philip Moyes, MacDonald and Janes.

Climbing Turns. Patrick Foss, Linden Hall.

Dust in the Lion's Paw. Freya Stark, Arrow Books.

First Victory. Robert Lyman, Constable.

From Apes to Warlords. Solly Zuckerman, Harper Collins.

Halifax at War. Brian J. Rapier, Ian Allan.

It's Dicey Flying Wimpys Around Italian Skies. Maurice G. Lihou, Air Research.

Lie in the Dark and Listen. Ken Rees, Grub Street.

Malta: The Hurricane Years. Christopher Shores, Brian Cull and Nicola Malizia, Grub Street.

Malta: The Spitfire Year. Christopher Shores, Brian Cull and Nicola Malizia, Grub Street.

Middle East 1940–1942, a Study in Air Power. Philip Guedalla, Hodder and Stoughton.

R.A.F. Middle East, the Official Story of Air Operations, February 1942–January 1943. HMSO.

R.A.F. Squadrons, C. G. Jefford, Airlife.

Royal Air Force 1939–1945. Denis Richards and Hilary St George Saunders, HMSO.

Sweeping the Skies, a History of 40 Squadron Royal Flying Corps and Royal Air Force. David Gunby, The Pentland Press.

The Army Air Forces in World War II, Vols 2 and 3. Wesley Frank Craven and James Lea Cate, The University of Chicago Press.

The British Bomber Since 1914. Francis K. Mason, Putnam.

The Liberandos. James W. Walker, 376th Heavy Bombardment Group Veterans Association.

The Liberator in Royal Air Force and Commonwealth Service. James D. Oughton, Air Britain.

The Mediterranean and Middle East (seven volumes) . I.S.O. Playfair and C.J.C. Molony, HMSO.

The Men Who Went to Warsaw. Lawrence Isemonger, Freeworld Publications.

The Middle East Campaigns (Operations in Libya and the Western Desert) Vols. I–III. Air Historical Branch, RAF Narratives, printed under MoD licence by MLRS Books; Crown Copyright Reserved.

The Middle East Campaigns (Operations in Libya, the Western Desert, and Tunisia) Vol. IV. Air Historical Branch, RAF Narratives, printed under MoD licence by MLRS Books; Crown Copyright Reserved.

The Middle East Campaigns, Vol. XI, Malta. Air Historical Branch, RAF Narratives, printed under MoD licence by MLRS Books; Crown Copyright Reserved.

The Sicilian Campaign. Air Historical Branch, RAF Narratives, printed under MoD licence by MLRS Books; Crown Copyright Reserved.

Three Against Rommel. Alexander Clifford, George G. Harrap & Co.

Through Darkness to Light. Patrick Macdonald, Images Publishing (Malvern).

Vickers-Armstrongs Wellington. Ken Delve, The Crowood Press.

Vickers-Armstrongs Wellington. Michal Ovcacik and Karel Susa, Mark I Publications.

Voice From the Stars – A Pathfinder's Story. Tom Scotland.

Wellington Wings, an RAF Intelligence Officer in the Western Desert. F.R. Chappell, William Kimber & Co.

Wise Without Eyes. Kevin Mears, Hooded Falcon Publications.

FILES HELD AT THE NATIONAL ARCHIVES:

No. 257 Wing	AIR 26/359–361
No. 205 Group	AIR 25/816–834
No. 37 Squadron	AIR 27/388–396
No. 38 Squadron	AIR 27/397–405
No. 40 Squadron	AIR 27/412–416
No. 70 Squadron	AIR 27/613–622
No. 104 Squadron	AIR 27/821–824
No. 108 Squadron	AIR 27/849–851
No. 142 Squadron	AIR 27/972–977
No. 148 Squadron	AIR 27/994–999
No. 150 Squadron	AIR 27/1008–1017
No. 178 Squadron	AIR 27/1119–1125
No. 216 Squadron	AIR 27/1332–1337
No. 420 Squadron	AIR 27/1825–1826
No. 424 Squadron	AIR 27/1834–1836
No. 425 Squadron	AIR 27/1837–1840
No. 462 Squadron	AIR 27/1916–1917
No. 614 Squadron	AIR 27/2121–2122
No. 31 Squadron SAAF	AIR 27/357–359
No. 34 Squadron SAAF	AIR 27/377–378

Index

Ships are in their alphabetical order in *italics*. Groups, Wings, Squadrons and other RAF units are under 'Royal Air Force', and units of the RAAF, RCAF, and SAAF are under 'Royal Australian Air Force', 'Royal Canadian Air Force', and 'South African Air Force'. All army units are listed under 'Army', followed by the nation (e.g. 'Army, British'). Operations are listed alphabetically under 'Operations'.

3rd Division: 187
82nd Airborne Division: 186
Arnim, Generaloberst Hans-Jurgen von: 143-144, 162
Arno: 220-219, 263
Arsa Channel, coal wharves: 316, 320
Astell, Flying Officer W.: 99
Athens/Hassani airfield: 50, 292, 302
Auchinleck, General Sir Claude: 48, 74, 90, 94, 98, 101, 109, 111
Audax, Hawker: 51
Augusta: 32, 108, 183, 186, 188
Aversa: 199, 200
Avisio, railway bridge: 266-267

B

B-17, see Flying Fortress
B-24, see Liberator
B-25, See Mitchell
B-26, see Marauder
Ba.65, Breda: 23
Badoglio, Marshal Pietro: 186, 198, 201
Baghdad: 51-55
Bagnall, Wing Commander: 219-220, 227
Baird, Flight Lieutenant: 76
Baird, Flying Officer: 314
Baird, Sergeant J.D.: 145
Balkan Air Force: 278, 289, 296, 302
BALLINCLAY, supply dropping area: 300, 310, 292
Bamford, Wing Commander T.W.: 133
Barce: 59, 87, 149
Bardia: 18, 22, 36, 39, 44, 48, 50, 59, 71, 73-74, 82, 112-113, 132
Bari: 24, 31-32, 39, 160, 179, 201, 227, 242, 243, 253, 276, 325
Bartlett, Flight Sergeant Harry: 194
Basra: 50, 51
Bastia: 205, 318
Battipaglia: 194, 199, 201-204

Bayerlein, Colonel Fritz: 115-116
Bazias: 254, 278
Beale, Squadron Leader H.H.B.: 237, 256
Beare, Wing Commander: 72
Beaufighter, Bristol: 61, 165, 225, 253, 267, 289
Bebbington, Sergeant Dennis: 119
Beda Fomm, battle of: 38
Belgrade: 32, 254, 278, 291, 298
Belhamed, Crusader, fighting at: 74
Benghazi: 12-13, 22,-24, 27, 36, 38-39, 41, 43, 48, 50, 56-60, 63, 66, 69-75, 79, 84, 87-88, 91, 98-101, 104, 106, 111-113, 120, 123, 130, 139-140, 183, 197, 232
Benina: 22, 27-28, 35-36, 38, 43, 48, 50, 56, 59, 70, 74-75, 79, 87, 91-92, 131-132, 168
Berbera: 20-21
Berka: 36, 50, 56, 59, 70, 74, 80, 88, 91, 92
Berwick, HMS: 26
Bevan, Sergeant K.W.: 91
Bf 109, Messerschmitt: 80, 83, 92, 122, 244
Bir el Beheira No. 2 landing ground: 131
Bir Hacheim: 87, 89, 97-99, 101
Bir Koraiyim, see LG 09
Bird, Captain R.B.: 275
Bismarck, Major General Georg von: 115
Bizerte: 130, 133-136, 144-146, 160-163, 170, 212, 223, 225-226, 229
Blenheim, Bristol: 12, 15, 17-18, 36, 38, 60, 88, 109-110
Blida: 133, 144-146, 160, 162, 177, 222
Bocca di Falco: 171, 178
Bologna: 237, 280, 287, 291, 319
Bombay, Bristol: 9, 12, 17-18, 20-22, 24, 35-36, 39-40, 55, 99
Bonaventure, HMS: 35
Bone: 145, 160, 163

Booth, Squadron Leader: 114
Boston, Douglas: 187, 258
Bottomley, Air Chief Marshal Sir
    Norman: 30
Bowyer,Sergeant Trevor: 119
Bradshaw, Warrant Officer Tom: 266
Breconshire, HMS: 93
Brenner Pass: 267, 287, 293
Brereton, Major General Lewis H.:
    106, 130
Brescia: 277, 287, 306, 308, 317, 319
Brew, Sergeant Stan: 114
Brindisi: 29, 31, 39, 72, 74, 83, 203,
    251, 277, 283-284, 329
British Chiefs of Staff: 22, 60, 90, 94,
    97
Broadhurst, Air Vice-Marshal Harry:
    156, 157
Brod Bosanski oil refinery: 272, 275-
    276, 291
Brookes, Sergeant J.: 103
Brown, Flight Lietenant P.G.: 231
Bruck: 314, 322
Bu-Amud, see LG 147
Bucharest: 9, 264, 270, 274, 275, 281,
    289
Budapest: 255-257, 265, 268, 271, 273,
    291, 294
Buerat el Hsun: 87-88, 141-142, 147
Buq Buq: 44, 128

C

Caernarvon Castle, SS: 329
Cagliari: 108, 134, 164, 181
Cairns, Lieutenant: 275
Cairo: 10, 13, 17, 81, 109, 121, 246,
    259-260, 276, 325
Calabria: 198-200
Calatos-Lindos airfield: 22, 40, 41,
    47, 49-50, 92, 208, 230-231
Caltagirone: 186, 188
Campbell, Brigadier General J.C.
    'Jock': 73
Campbell, Sergeant D.G.: 54-55

Canal Zone, Egypt: 81, 103, 109, 112
Candia: 231-232, 247
Cap Bon: 28, 169-170, 179, 191, 195,
    213
Cape Spartivento: 26, 197
Capodichino: 189-190, 192, 201, 228
Capuzzo: 22, 44, 46-48, 50, 78, 81,
    128, 138
Casablanca: 143, 170
Casarsa: 299, 301, 307, 312
Caserta, royal palace: 291, 317
Casino: 176, 217, 234, 240, 248, 250,
    262-263, 267-268
Castel Benito: 32, 33, 72-74, 76, 80,
    142, 147, 152, 155-157, 165, 169-170
Castel Nuovo: 203, 244
Castelvetrano, airfield: 83-84, 164,
    171, 173, 178
Catania: 32, 62, 84, 89, 93, 107-108,
    135-136, 148, 160, 173, 179, 181,
    183-184, 186-188, 193, 196
'Cauldron, the' (Gazala battle): 98-99
Cecchina: 242, 250
Cecina: 221, 239
Celone: 247-248, 253, 270-272, 276,
    283, 299, 303-305, 308, 329
Cerignola No. 3 Landing Ground,
    see Toretto
Cerignola: 224, 225, 227, 228, 236
Chaplin, Wing Commander J.H.: 91
Chappell, F.R.: 98-100, 103, 124, 135-
    138, 150, 153-154, 156, 158, 165-
    166, 168, 172, 175, 179, 190-192,
    194, 196, 202, 212-215, 220-221,
    223-224, 226-227, 235, 239, 244-245,
    253, 255, 257-258, 266, 269, 272,
    274, 276, 327
Cheek, Flying Officer R.L.W.: 213,
    220, 233
Cheria: 172-173, 179
Chetniks: 266, 278, 298
Chief of the Air Staff: 60, 106-107,
    111, 121

Gazala: 36, 46, 48, 50, 59, 70, 74-75, 78, 87, 89, 90, 97-98, 101, 107,129, 138, 139

Gebel Hamzi, see LG 237

Gee navigation aid: 248, 252, 256, 305

GEISHA, supply dropping target area: 292

Genoa: 219, 230, 247, 251, 254, 268, 283

Gerbini: 89, 135-136, 182-183, 188

Ghazal: 110-111, 126-127

Ghemines, see Hosc Raui

Gibbes, Wing Commander Augustus: 196

Gibraltar: 14, 26, 61, 130, 133, 245

Gibson, Perla Siedle ('Lady in White'): 258

Giurgiu: 272-273. 278

Gladiator, Gloster: 15, 40, 51-53

Godwin-Austen, Major General A.R.: 20

Gorizia: 307, 322

Gothic Line: 262-264

Gravell, Sergeant R.G.: 108

Graz, marshalling yards: 308, 310, 312-313

Grazzanise: 201, 211

Great Bitter Lakes: 104, 114, 132, 142, 152

Griffiths, Sergeant: 256

Grosseto: 202, 212, 215, 219, 223

Grottaglie: 198, 207-208, 302

Gunby, David: 114, 154, 158, 173, 188, 194, 221, 223, 226-227, 265

Gustav Line: 217, 234, 252, 262-263

H

H2S radar: 247, 248, 252

Habbaniyah: 50-53, 55, 86, 105

Haifa: 11, 23, 329

Halifax, Handley Page: 106, 112-113, 120-121, 123-124, 126-129, 132-133, 138-141, 148-158, 160, 165-171, 178, 183-185, 196-197, 207-209, 230-232, 245-247, 252-253, 256-257, 264-265, 270, 272-274, 276-280, 281-284, 287-289, 295, 297-299, 301, 303, 306, 310, 312, 316

Halfaya Pass: 35, 44, 48, 81-82, 101, 128, 130, 138

Halverson, Colonel Harry A.: 104-105, 112

Hammamet: 160, 162, 169-170

Hammett, Sergeant E.E.: 91

Hani East: 206, 216-217

Hani West: 179, 180, 187, 206, 215, 219

HARANGUE, supply dropping area: 292, 300, 306

Harris, Air Chief Marshal Sir Arthur: 94, 106-107, 133, 216

Harris, Wing Commander D.B.: 308

Hayter, Flight Lieutenant A.R.H.: 94

He III, Heinkel: 53, 123

Heliopolis: 11, 17-18, 21, 25, 55, 259

Helwan: 11, 20-21, 260

Henfrey, Sergeant George: 150

Heraklion: 65, 81, 92, 100, 122, 140, 142, 146, 153, 230-231, 271

Hercules, Bristol, aero engines: 150, 158, 209

Hinaidi (El Raschid) airfield: 52-54

Hitler, Adolf: 127, 322

Holloway, Bruce: 75

Homs: 147, 152, 169, 170

Hope, Bob: 196

Hosc Raui: 153, 158, 160, 178, 183, 185, 196, 207, 208, 211, 232

Houston, Sergeant: 185

Howard, Sergeant J.E.: 54

Hudson, Lockheed: 15, 165

Huggler, Flying Officer Johnny: 269

Hurricane, Hawker: 15, 93, 103

Nicholson, Lieutenant Ralph, SAAF: 275
Nile Delta: 105, 109, 118
Nis: 273-274
Northwest African Air Force (NAAF): 200, 208, 210, 224, 229
Northwest African Coastal Air Force (NACAF): 144
Northwest African Strategic Air Force (NASAF): 143, 161, 163, 171, 174-175, 178-183, 190, 192-193, 200, 202-203, 205, 215, 219, 222, 229
Northwest African Tactical Air Force (NATAF): 160, 169, 170-171
Novska, marshalling yards: 315, 317, 319

O

Oboe blind bombing equipment: 77
O'Connor, General Richard: 35, 36, 44
Ohio, SS: 113
Olbia: 165, 178, 179, 181
Operations:
Agreement: 119, 120
Avalanche: 201
Barbarossa: 55
Battleaxe: 48, 56
Baytown: 198
Bigamy: 120
Brevity: 48
Compass: 35, 44
Crusader: 10, 48, 56, 66, 69-71, 73-74, 76, 78, 81, 85, 95
Dragoon: 264, 279
Eilbote (German): 136, 143
Harpoon: 107-108
Hercules (German): 107, 111
Husky: 170, 178, 186, 216
Jostle: 77, 78
Lightfoot: 125-126
Ochsenkopf (German): 144
Overlord: 262
Pedestal (Malta convoy): 108, 113

Pointblank: 143, 244, 261-262
Portcullis (Malta convoy): 123, 136
Shingle: 234
Snowboots: 188-189
Stoneage (Malta convoy): 123, 136
Strangle: 248-249
Supercharge: 125-126, 156
Tempest (Poland): 284
Torch: 130, 134, 143
Turpitude: 271
Vigorous (Malta convoy): 100, 105, 107-108
Oran: 130, 134
Orbetello: 213, 244, 250
Orbita, SS: 258-259
Orion, HMS: 40
Orvieto: 265, 272
Oudna: 211, 221-222, 228
Oxford, Airspeed: 51

P

P-38, Lightning, Lockheed: 307
P-51, Mustang, North American: 306
Padua, marshalling yards: 241, 249, 251, 308, 310, 313
Palermo: 33, 61-63, 72, 93, 149-154, 160, 163-164, 171, 181-182, 186, 189
Palmer, Sergeant D.: 31
Pantellaria: 25, 28, 161, 164-165, 173-176
Panuco, SS (tanker): 122
Paramythia: 40, 41
Pardubice-Fanto oil refinery: 272, 275-276
Park, Air Chief Marshal Sir Keith: 138
Patton, General George: 187
Pavillier: 176, 182, 187
Paxton, Sergeant H.E.: 185
Pegasus, Bristol, aero engine: 17, 21
Penelope, HMS: 88
Pepper, Harry, entertainer: 196
Perugia: 238, 263, 280
Pescara: 214, 252

Luqa Wellington Detachment: 25, 28, 31, 33-34
Commands:
  Bomber Command: 9, 10, 15-16, 21, 24-25, 28, 57, 77, 104, 106, 133, 143, 150, 176, 178, 209, 216, 232, 242, 247, 261, 264, 305
  Fighter Command: 24
  Middle East Command: 10, 25, 27, 46, 200
  Transport Command: 284, 324
  Western Desert Air Command: 149
Flights:
  No. 1586 Polish Special Duties Flight: 284-285
  No. 1446 Flight: 204
  Special Duty Flight: 63, 72
  Special Operations Flight: 120, 131
Groups:
  No. 1 Group: 133
  No. 2 Group: 60
  No. 3 Group: 21, 30, 42, 68
  No. 6 Group: 176
  No. 8 Group, Light Night
Striking
Force: 289
  No. 100 Group: 261
  No. 201 (Naval Cooperation) Group: 107, 118
  No. 202 Group: 17, 36
  No. 204 Group: 59
  No. 205 Group: 9-10, 16, 68-69, 78-82, 84, 87, 94, 97, 101-102, 104-105, 107, 113, 118-121, 123, 125, 128-134, 134, 136, 141, 143, 148, 149, 155, 157, 159-161, 165, 169, 171-172, 174-175, 178, 180, 183, 185, 187, 189, 195-196, 198, 200-201, 206, 208, 211, 216, 219, 224-226, 228, 232, 234, 236, 241, 245-250, 252-255, 258, 264, 270-272, 274, 279, 284, 289, 291,

295, 301-302, 320, 322-324, 326-329
  No. 211 Group: 171
Headquarters:
  Advanced Air Headquarters, Western Desert: 75, 82, 132, 140, 151, 153-156, 161, 165, 168
  Air Headquarters Eastern Mediterranean: 183
  Air Headquarters Western
Desert: 80, 172
  Headquarters Desert Air Force: 280
  Headquarters Malta: 9
  Headquarters Mediterranean: 35
  Mediterranean Allied Air Force: 296, 323
  Headquarters Middle East: 9, 20, 35-36, 60, 66, 76, 79, 82, 132, 141, 148-149, 152, 160, 169-172, 180, 232, 276
Squadrons:
  Signals Squadron: 78
  No. 10 Squadron: 106, 112, 120, 232
  No. 14 Squadron: 109
  No. 37 Squadron: 16, 24-27, 31-32, 35-36, 39-40, 43, 49, 52-53, 58-59, 64-65, 68, 81-82, 86, 90, 93, 95, 97-98, 101-104, 110, 112, 115-117, 120-121, 124, 131-133, 140-142, 148-149, 151-152, 155-158, 160, 166-167, 171-172, 174-175, 178, 180-182, 187-189, 191, 199, 201, 205-206, 211, 221, 225, 230, 235-237, 239-241, 244, 252-253, 256, 279, 281, 291, 293, 298-300, 302-303, 308, 317, 323, 326, 329-330
  No. 38 Squadron: 24-27, 35-36, 41, 43-44, 47, 49, 57-59, 61, 63-64, 66, 68, 70-73, 88, 90-92, 95, 97-101, 107, 112, 118, 330
  No. 39 Squadron: 89

No. 40 Squadron: 57, 64, 68, 72, 75-76, 80, 83, 87, 89, 93, 95, 97, 101-102, 110, 114, 116-118, 120-121, 125, 131, 133-138, 148, 149, 150-158, 160, 165, 167-170, 172-175, 182-183, 187, 193-194, 196, 199, 204, 206, 211-213, 215, 221, 223, 226, 235, 237, 239, 244, 251-253, 257-258, 265, 267, 269, 272, 274-275, 277-278, 291-292, 298-299, 303, 308-309, 329-330

No. 55 Squadron: 44

No. 69 Squadron: 122

No. 70 Squadron: 12, 21, 23-24, 27-28, 36, 39, 41, 43, 46-48, 51-53, 55, 58-59, 65, 68, 79, 90, 92, 95, 97-98, 102-104, 112, 115-121, 123-125, 127-129, 131-133, 141-142, 148-153, 155-157, 160, 167, 170, 172, 174, 180-183, 187-188, 190, 195, 201-202, 204, 207, 218, 221-223, 225, 230, 236, 239, 243-244, 250-253, 257, 267, 278, 281, 287, 289, 291-292, 299, 301-304, 329-330

No. 73 (Fighter) Squadron: 27

No. 76 Squadron: 106, 112, 232

No. 84 Squadron: 86

No. 89 Squadron: 131

No. 90 Squadron: 71, 95

No. 104 Squadron: 68-69, 72-73, 83-84, 90, 95, 97-98, 100-101, 103-104, 107-108, 110, 112, 115-117, 120-121, 124-125, 128, 131, 133-139, 149-156, 158, 160, 165-167, 169, 172, 174-175, 180-182, 187-189, 191-192, 196, 202, 205-206, 210, 212, 215-216, 218-221, 225-226, 238-239, 241, 244, 249, 251-253, 257, 269, 274, 276, 278, 288-289, 291-293, 299, 303, 308-309, 324, 327, 329-330

No. 108 Squadron: 59-60, 66, 68, 85-87, 90, 95, 97-98, 101, 103-104, 108, 112, 116-117, 120-121, 123-124, 127, 131, 140, 279

No. 109 Squadron, Detachment, Middle East: 76-78, 95

No. 113 (Blenheim) Squadron: 27

No. 115 Squadron: 28

No. 138 Squadron: 83, 137

No. 142 Squadron: 133, 144, 146, 160, 162-164, 174-175, 179, 182, 187, 190-191, 196, 201-202, 206-207, 213-215, 218-219, 221-223, 228, 236, 238, 242, 244, 252-253, 278, 287, 289

No. 147 Squadron: 132

No. 148 (Special Duties) Squadron: 284-285

No. 148 Squadron: 28, 32-35, 39, 43, 46-47, 55, 59-61, 65-66, 68, 70-71, 76, 79, 90, 94-95, 97-104, 108, 112, 115-118, 120-121, 124-127, 131-132, 134, 139-141, 279

No. 150 Squadron: 133, 144-145, 160, 162-164, 174-175, 178-179, 181, 187, 193, 196, 206-207, 213, 215, 221, 224, 228, 230, 236, 240, 242, 244, 252-253, 278-279, 287, 289

No. 159 Squadron: 104-106, 108, 112, 120

No. 160 Squadron: 104-106, 121-122, 125-126, 132-133, 140, 142, 152

No. 162 Squadron: 77-78, 95, 97, 112, 120, 122-125, 127, 129, 168

No. 178 Squadron: 132-133, 152-153, 159, 178, 183, 185, 196-197, 208, 230-232, 245-247, 252-253, 283-284, 286, 291, 293-295, 303-305, 309, 315, 324, 326, 329-330

No. 208 Squadron: 71, 115

No. 211 Squadron: 18

Stalag Luft III: 64
Stalin, Joseph: 284
Stark, Dame Freya: 52
Steel, Squadron Leader: 89
Steyr, Daimler-Puch aircraft factory: 244-245
Stimpson, Sergeant R.W.: 185
Stimson, Henry L. (US Secretary of State for War): 323
Stirling, Short: 60
Stockdale, Sergeant: 153
Storey, Flight Lieutenant S.: 76
Stornara: 248, 270
Strait of Messina: 184, 186-187, 189, 194, 200
Stumme, General Georg: 122
Suda Bay: 50, 81, 112-113, 122, 126, 232, 247, 270
Suez: 11, 81, 121, 259
Sunderland, Short: 25
Swordfish, Fairey: 15, 60-61, 63, 88, 120, 176
Syracuse: 173, 178, 186-188, 196, 207
Szekesfehervar marshalling yards: 287, 293-294
Szombathely: 282, 295, 298

T
Tafaraoui airfield: 130
Taranto: 25, 29, 31-33, 104, 107-108, 122, 199, 201, 207, 225-226, 228, 247, 253, 302
Tatoi: 24, 39, 289, 295
Tattersall, Sergeant H.G.: 185
Tebaga Gap: 156-157
Tedder, Air Chief Marshal Sir Arthur: 12, 14, 16, 70, 92, 104-107, 111, 119-121, 143, 176, 188, 262, 323
Tel el Aqqaqir: 126, 127
Telecommunications Research Establishment: 77
Telergma: 176-178
Temmar: 172, 187, 213, 218, 210
Terracina: 212, 267

Terria: 209, 230, 232, 245
Thoma, General Wilhelm Ritter von: 118, 127-128
Thunderbolt, Republic (P-47): 225
Tiber, River: 263, 272
Timberlake, Brigadier General Patrick: 130
Timosoara: 273, 274
Tipton, Pilot Officer John: 80, 83
Tirana: 39, 41
Tmimi: 36, 59, 70, 98-99, 101
Tobruk: 12, 17-18, 20-24, 36-39, 41, 46-48, 57-58, 73-75, 100-101, 104, 106-107, 111-115, 118-119, 121-122, 130, 138-139, 148
TOFFEE, supply dropping area: 292, 300, 310
Toretto Landing Ground (Cerignola No. 3): 228, 236-237
Torre Annunziata: 199, 204
Tortorella: 225, 227, 230, 235-236, 240-241, 243, 253, 291, 303, 317, 329
Totland, HMS: 133
Transportation Plan: 262, 292
Trapani: 72, 135, 145, 162-164, 178, 181, 188
Trenchard, Sir Hugh: 10, 15
Treviso: 230, 314, 319
Trieste: 240, 244, 272-273, 291, 293, 311, 313-314, 322-323
Tripoli, Libya: 12-13, 38-39, 44, 46-48, 57, 60-63, 66, 68-73, 76, 80-91, 93, 106, 111-113, 132, 137, 140, 145, 147-149, 152, 172, 329
Tripoli, Syria: 11
Tripolitania: 16, 43, 60, 72, 80, 89, 147-149
Trumpeter, Squadron Leader: 166
Truscott, General Lucien: 263
Tug Argan Pass: 20
Tunis: 134-137, 146, 160-162, 167, 169-170, 205, 216, 221, 226
Turin: 223, 275

Villach, marshalling yards: 307, 312, 315, 317, 320
Villacidro: 145, 162-164, 170, 173, 181-182
Villar Perosa ball bearing factory: 222, 233
Vincenza: 251-252, 256, 299, 314
Vistula, River: 284-285
Viterbo airfield: 202, 205
Viterbo: 195-196, 267-268, 272
Vitoria Veneto (Italian battleship): 105, 108
Volturno, River: 210-212

W

Wadi Akarit: 158, 161, 172
Wadi Natrun: 110, 127
Wallis, Ken: 243
Walrus, Supermarine: 15, 256
Warsaw: 284-286, 294, 297
Warspite, HMS: 198
Wasp, USS: 94
Watts, Flight Lieutenant J.: 139
Wavell, Field Marshal Sir Archibald Percival: 23, 35, 38-39, 41, 43, 48, 51, 60, 104
Wellesley, Vickers: 12
Wellington IC, Vickers: 21, 59, 69, 121, 136,
Wellington II, Vickers: 60, 62, 68, 70, 83, 121, 155, 158, 182

Wellington III, Vickers: 133, 136, 158, 191, 204
Wellington Type 423, Vickers: 223
Wellington X, Vickers: 158, 176, 191, 245
Wells, Squadron Leader R.J.: 21, 60, 85
Welshman, HMS: 122
Western Desert Force: 35, 149
Westphal, Colonel: 86
White, Sergeant R.A.: 91
Wiener Neustadt: 235, 291
Wilhelmshaven, Germany: 15, 16
Williams, Lieutenant Colonel J.A. (SAAF): 258, 259, 325
Wing, Toby: 240
'Winston's Wellingtons', see No. 109/162 Squadron
Woods, Major H. (KRRC): 117
Yates, Flying Officer: 27
York, Avro: 330
Young, Squadron Leader H.M. 'Dinghy': 68, 95
Yugoslav National Army of Liberation: 300-301, 323

Z

Z 506B, Cant: 23
Zagreb: 293, 298, 316, 322
Zina: 176, 187
Zuckerman, Solly: 139, 148, 262